MOTOCOURSE™

THE WORLD'S LEADING GRAND PRIX & SUPERBIKE ANNUAL

CMG
PUBLISHING

CONTENTS

MOTOCOURSE 2008-2009

is published by:
Crash Media Group Ltd
Number One
The Innovation Centre
Silverstone Circuit
Silverstone
Northants NN12 8GX
United Kingdom
Tel: +44 (0)870 3505044
Fax: +44 (0)870 3505088
Email: info@crash.net
Website:
www.crashmediagroup.com

Printed in Italy by
ALSABA industrie grafiche,
Z.I. Belvedere S. Antonio
53034 Colle Val d'Elsa (SI)
Tel: +39 (0)577 905311
Website: www.alsaba.it

ISBN: 978-1905334-32-2

DISTRIBUTORS

Gardners Books
1 Whittle Drive, Eastbourne,
East Sussex, BN23 6QH
Tel: +44 (0)1323 521555
email: sales@gardners.com

Menoshire Ltd
Unit 13
21 Wadsworth Road
Perivale
Middlesex UB6 7LQ
Telephone: +44 (0)20 8566 7344
Fax: +44 (0)20 8991 2439

NORTH AMERICA
Motorbooks International
PO Box 1
729 Prospect Avenue
Osceola
Wisconsin 54020, USA
Telephone: 1 715 294 3345
Fax: 1 715 294 4448

Dust jacket: Valentino Rossi took his
sixth premier-class title in 2008. He has
now featured on the jacket of
MOTOCOURSE on more occasions than
any other rider.

Title page: Going out at the top. Troy
Bayliss marked his farewell season with
another hard-earned World Superbike
Championship title.

FOREWORD by Valentino Rossi		5
EDITOR'S INTRODUCTION		6
THE TOP TEN RIDERS OF 2008 Ranked by the editor		8
THE STATE OF RACING by Michael Scott		14
UNHOLY TRINITY		20
MotoGP technical review by Neil Spalding		
LEGACY...		30
Kevin Cameron examines the two-stroke engine's enormous contribution to technological advances in motorcycle racing.		
GORGEOUS GEORGE		34
Jorge Lorenzo – rider profile by Michael Scott		
MOTOGP RIDERS AND TEAMS		37
Team-by-team guide by Matthew Birt		
250cc RIDERS AND TEAMS by Michael Scott		56
125cc RIDERS AND TEAMS by Michael Scott		58
2008 GRANDS PRIX		61
WORLD CHAMPIONSHIP RIDER'S POINTS TABLES compiled by Kay Edge		206
SUPERBIKE WORLD CHAMPIONSHIP REVIEW by Gordon Ritchie		209
ISLE OF MAN TT REVIEW by Mark Forsyth		246
BRITISH SUPERBIKE REVIEW by Ollie Barstow		252
SUPERSPORT WORLD CHAMPIONSHIP REVIEW by Gordon Ritchie		258
SIDECAR WORLD CHAMPIONSHIP REVIEW by John McKenzie		260
US RACING REVIEW by Paul Carruthers		262
MAJOR WORLDWIDE RESULTS compiled by Kay Edge		268

editor
MICHAEL SCOTT

publisher
BRYN WILLIAMS

text editor
IAN PENBERTHY

art editor
STEVE SMALL

design and production
ROSANNE MARRIOTT

results and statistics
KAY EDGE

sales promotion
SIMON SANDERSON

office manager
WENDY SALISBURY

chief photographers
GOLD & GOOSE
David Goldman
Gareth Harford
Mirco Lazzari
Patrik Lundin
Telephone +44 (0)20 8444 2448

MotoGP bike illustrations
ADRIAN DEAN
f1artwork@blueyonder.co.uk

Editor's Acknowledgements

The Editor and staff of MOTOCOURSE wish to thank the following for their assistance in compiling the 2008–2009 edition: Henny Ray Abrams, Katie Baines, Jerry Burgess, Paul Butler, Peter Clifford, Maria Garcia, Henk Keulemans, Isabelle Lariviere, Iain Mackay, Michele Morisetti, Elisa Pavan, David Pato, Marc Petrier (FIM), Julian Ryder, Roberta Vallorosi, Debbie van Zon, Ian Wheeler and Günther Wiesinger, as well as the riders and technicians quoted in this book, Alpinestars, Marlboro and Repsol hospitality staff, and numerous colleagues and friends.

Photographs published in MOTOCOURSE 2008–2009 have been contributed by:

Chief photographers: Gold & Goose.
Contributing photographers: Gavan Caldwell; Clive Challinor, Dave Collister; Martin Heath; Tom Hnatiw/Flick of The Wrist Photography; Neil Spalding; Mark Walters; Andrew Wheeler/automotophoto

www.motocourse.com

FÉDÉRATION INTERNATIONALE DE MOTOCYCLISME

Speed   Fair-Play   Passion
Hi-tech   Excellence   Respect   Courage

We care about
Motorcycling !

HEADQUARTERS / SIÈGE

11, ROUTE DE SUISSE
CH - 1295 MIES
SWITZERLAND / SUISSE

TEL + 41 22 950 95 00
FAX + 41 22 950 95 01
info@fim.ch - www.fim.ch

FOUNDED 1904

FOREWORD by VALENTINO ROSSI

IT'S been my year again, but it didn't come easily. I had some very tough rivals, tough conditions, tough battles. I've won a lot of good championships, like the first with Yamaha in 2004, but I think this is the one that I put in the most effort. I worked every weekend at the races, but also away from the track to stay concentrated. And I've really enjoyed all of it. That is why, even after winning the title, I still try to win more races. That is my pleasure, my pride and my duty.

Looking back on the year, apart from the mistake I made at Assen, I think I can be proud. We had to adapt the bike to different tyres, and that took a lot of work. But there was something else, something new for me. I feel I was different in some important ways from the person who took four championships in a row.

At the end of 2005, I had won all the important targets of my career, in 125, 250, 500 and MotoGP. It was like I was unbeatable. In 2006, when I didn't win early in the year, I thought we had time to fix it. This was a mistake.

The next year was even harder. I could look at mechanical and other problems in 2006, but in 2007 it was mainly Stoner and his very fast Ducati.

It was very important for me to learn how to lose. In 2008, the level of concentration and effort was the highest ever. I knew that it wasn't my right to win. I had to work for it.

And I'm not finished yet. I am still enjoying racing as much as ever – maybe more. That is why I signed to stay with Yamaha for two more years. I had some chances to go to other teams, but I have already changed once, and proved to myself I can still win.

What is more important is to have a good atmosphere in the team. At Yamaha, that is fantastic, from Jerry Burgess and the other guys in my garage to the top Japanese management. I am very happy there. Their part in my success is vital.

I am proud to have been on the front cover of *MOTOCOURSE* as champion more than any other rider.

GOOD RACERS MAKE GOOD RACING

I'T'S too soon to understand how the 2008 season will be perceived in the future, but from the perspective of a couple of months, it was the year of acquiescence. Of acceptance of fate. And a year, with the single-tyre rule, of yet more fundamental changes. Although this is not so much a change of regulations as a change in racing principles.

Technical restrictions are not the way to secure close racing. MOTOCOURSE agrees with this view, expressed by Yamaha engineering supremo Masao Furusawa. Grand prix racing's current urge for change by regulation seems to indicate a degree of panic by rights-holder Dorna.

With World Superbikes gaining factory support from BMW and Aprilia in 2009, and KTM likely to follow; with MotoGP having alienated the last two by killing off the 250s; with hoped-for sponsorship still not having arrived at the start of the year; and with a world recession threatening to make things much, much worse, perhaps panic is an appropriate reaction.

After all, Dorna's interest is entirely commercial. The sporting side only comes into the equation inasmuch as it spins the money. Which leaves nobody to take the broad view, to take care of the sport as a whole.

The FIM largely abandoned sporting control when it elected to share in the profits instead. There were signs in 2008 that its new president, Vito Ippolito, wished to regain some of that power. This will not happen quickly, if at all.

Racing has been through bigger changes in its history than those forced through with unseemly haste in 2008. There is another force that has helped it to survive.

It is driven by riders, and by talent. That was the biggest encouragement of 2008.

Rossi's return to reclaim his crown was a great achievement, because the competition was fiercer than any he had faced in his career. Pedrosa's pressure faded, but Stoner's was constant and fierce. And likely to become more so.

There were talented rookies as well, two in particular. Double 250 champion Jorge Lorenzo made a blazing start to his MotoGP career; his old sparring partner, Andrea Dovizioso, also made an impact. Both, along with raw rookie James Toseland, gave some of the old hands some good lessons in overtaking.

The depth of talent is reminiscent of the Golden Age of the late 1980s and early 1990s, spanning such greats as Lawson, Spencer, Gardner, Rainey, Schwantz and Doohan.

It's got nothing to do with whatever new F1-style rule changes – control electronics, control engine design, even treaded tyres – that the worried ringmasters might dream up.

It is good racers who make good racing. We are in a period rich in good racers.

MICHAEL SCOTT
Wimbledon, London
December, 2008

Above: Serial winners– Rossi outstripped both Angel Nieto (left) and Giacomo Agostini in 2008.

Top left: Hard and fast. Casey Stoner on the night-for-day grid at Qatar.

Left: More fresh talent. Dovizioso tests the Repsol Honda he will ride next year.

All photographs: Gold & Goose

1 VALENTINO ROSSI

ROSSI said it himself: it had been the hardest work and the most concentration he'd ever had to put into winning the World Championship. This being number eight, his was the voice of experience.

The numbers had already put him among the greats, and he passed several more milestones in 2008, including exceeding Agostini's old record total of 68 wins in the premier class – Rossi ended the year with 71.

But he really did have to work for it. The fortunes of his rivals ebbed and flowed, but Rossi stood against the tide, and turned it his way.

That happened at Laguna Seca, with a performance under pressure that proved the undoing of what, until then, had been a potentially devastating charge by Stoner, who had just racked up three wins in a row.

Valentino came into the year on the back of two title losses and on brand-new Bridgestone tyres. It wasn't until race four that he resumed his winning habit, with three in a row. Then an uncharacteristically headstrong first-lap mistake at Assen lost him many points, and it wasn't until round ten that he took the overall lead from Pedrosa.

By then, Stoner was coming on strong and a serious threat. Rossi told his crew chief, Burgess, 'I don't want to lose this title', something he'd never said before. Now he really showed the strength of his ability and the depth of his commitment. Looking increasingly jaunty, he forced the pace, and Stoner started to fall off.

Thirty in 2009, Rossi has committed to two more years with Yamaha. He starts this valedictory period as still the best of the best.

LUCK did not especially run the defending champion's way in the early part of 2008. Although he won in the dark at Qatar, it took another six races before the Ducati and its rider were settled and fettled enough for another win.

Now came a surge of strength reminiscent of his domination in 2007: four poles and three wins were the focal point of a spell when the Australian was almost always fastest, almost every time the track was open.

Perfectly in tune with the latest electronic aids, and able to make the absolute most of them, Stoner is of the breed of rider who likes to get away up front. But he is not afraid of hand-to-hand combat if necessary and has had some memorable battles with Rossi over the last two years.

Granted, Rossi did take him to pieces eventually at the American GP and thereafter, when three crashes in a row – twice out of the lead – reminded everyone of the 'Rolling Stoner' tag from 2006. But it had taken an almost superhuman effort from the veteran, and Stoner bounced back for two more wins, his equilibrium barely disturbed and his commitment as strong as ever, in spite of an increasingly debilitating wrist problem.

And he was still just 22. Inevitably, his racecraft will continue to improve with experience and surely he will be formidable for the foreseeable future.

Stoner often seems to need to be angry, but he is also very articulate, when he's in the mood, about the sensations and art of racing a motorcycle. He was the reason Rossi had to work so hard in 2008, and is likely to remain so in 2009.

2 CASEY STONER

3 JORGE LORENZO

LORENZO'S two 250 titles were high-class affairs, so it was a fair inference that he would impress in his first MotoGP year. Nobody could have anticipated his impact, however, when he set pole position in his first three races. On the rostrum for the first two, he won the third.

At the next race, in China, he started to make impact of a different kind, starting a series of spectacular crashes. This revealed another aspect: his courage and competitive instincts – unable to walk, he was fourth in that race, and back on the rostrum after another tumble in France at the next round.

Heavy crashes at the following two rounds left him not only bruised, but also a bit subdued for the middle of the season; he suffered another big tumble at Laguna – more pain for the summer break.

But he still visited the rostrum twice more, and was one of a handful of riders who regularly made a nonsense of the dictum that overtaking is difficult on an 800.

Schooled since boyhood to be a world champion by an apparently obsessive father, Lorenzo approaches his task very earnestly. Although his crashes made him look like a hot-head and he likes to play the jester to the crowd after a win, he's a considered rider, who generally gets faster through the course of a race.

As he has gained maturity, he's also managed to cast off his youthful aggressive streak. He has cast off his father-manager too, and in 2008 his replacement manager and long-term guiding hand, ex-rider Dani Amatriain.

Lorenzo was loyal to Michelin to the end, and it will be interesting to see how he gets on with the switch to Bridgestone in 2009, when he will be on equal equipment to Rossi. Nobody could rule out a few more 'Lorenzo's Land' victory flags next year.

ROOKIES are not supposed to be this fast; MotoGP machines shouldn't be this easy to ride. Like his 250 sparring partner, Lorenzo, Dovizioso disproved the rules comprehensively from the start of the season to the end.

He did it in his own way: unobtrusively, but very effectively. He failed to score just once – only Nakano equalled this, only Rossi bettered it – and although he stood on the rostrum but once, he was nine times in the top five.

The Italian didn't have a lot going for him during his rookie season. He was on a satellite Honda in a poor year for the breed, and on the less-favoured Michelin tyres. He might well have stayed in the background while he adapted to his first four-stroke experience.

Adapt he did, but so effectively that he was a thorn in the side of Hayden on the supposedly superior factory Honda from the very start, beating him more often than not in the races – nine times to six – and also in the championship.

Dovizioso, like Lorenzo a London-based tax exile, has a lean and scruffy look, and he doesn't indulge in the 'star' antics of other riders of his generation. In the same self-effacing way, he has been thoroughly loyal to Honda throughout his career, even when – as almost always so far – this has been a drawback in title terms.

The reward seemed almost pre-ordained: it was certainly no surprise when he was promoted to the factory team in place of Hayden for his second year in the big class. He is likely to prove a troublesome team-mate for Pedrosa.

4 ANDREA DOVISIOSO

5 MARCO SIMONCELLI

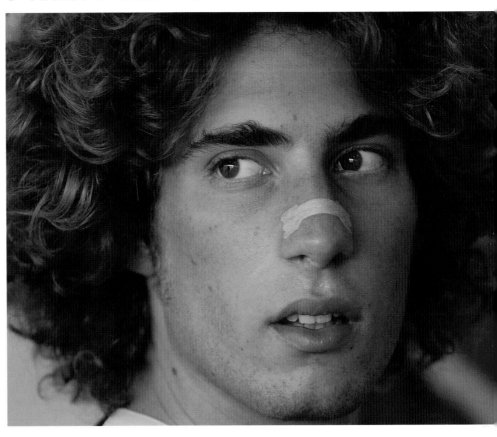

INASMUCH as this is a list of the lion-hearted, Simoncelli has earned his place on it with just such a performance on his way to winning the 250 World Championship, his first. As well as the heart, he also has a mane like a lion and more than a touch of star quality. As well as a roaring, laughing voice.

From the same area of Italy as a crop of talent, including Rossi, Melandri and Dovizioso, the rangy and charismatic Gilera rider was an impressive presence in the 125 class, but took a couple of years to find his feet in 250s. As a result, he wasn't among the pre-season favourites. Nor did he have one of the latest heavily redesigned factory bikes.

All the same, after nine rounds, he was leading the championship, having equalled the favoured Bautista's two wins and claimed more rostrum finishes. He'd done so in a string of hard-fought races, during which he'd demonstrated conspicuous toughness and determination, in addition to obvious speed.

Only then was he rewarded with the latest Aprilia – rebadged Gilera – and he became even stronger, taking four more wins for an assured championship.

Now 21, Simoncelli has plans for one more 250 year before moving up to the big class. Time for him to tame a wild streak. He was involved in a number of controversial incidents, clashes and crashes during 2008, although each time he escaped with nothing more than a stern warning.

It all goes to make him a fearsome and feared competitor. 'I don't give presents to the other riders,' he smiles. A friend of Rossi – they train together, riding motocross in winter – he surely has a big future.

THERE'S a certain grudging nature about any award or special recognition for Pedrosa. The gloomy youngster won few new friends in 2008, with his petulance about tyres and the sulky manner in which he forced Honda into an embarrassing mid-season switch from Michelin to Bridgestone. But he also won two races and led the title chase until the tenth round – on a bike and tyres that were generally a little off the pace. That proves he's a leading player. And it was a crash in Germany, rather than any failure of will, that brought his title challenge to a premature conclusion.

There was even some backlash by season's end, when his austere manager/mentor, Alberto Puig, found himself in the firing line for most of the criticism. Pedrosa was increasingly viewed as an innocent if serially misled party.

Pedrosa qualified on the front row nine times. His light weight meant that frequently he led into the first corner. His preferred strategy is to build on that early advantage and run away. When caught, however, he has not shown himself willing or able to engage in hand-to-hand combat. With a new generation of fierce fighters moving up to join the established tough guys, this is a definite weakness.

Much was expected of Dani when he moved to the big class in 2006, but he hasn't really delivered. The 2009 season will be crucial. If he cannot show himself capable of anything other than winning from the front, he is likely to be swept aside by the tide of talent, both old and new.

After all, Spain has another brighter and certainly more charismatic prospect in Lorenzo.

6 DANI PEDROSA

7 NICKY HAYDEN

ALL told, the 2006 champion had a dismal season. Most felt that he deserved better. With the factory Repsol team's attention seemingly fixed on teammate Pedrosa, Honda's last champion has had much to deal with over the last three years. Niggles that were compounded in 2008 by an engine lacking the sharp power character that better suits his gung-ho riding style.

Actually, that's an over-simplification. Hayden does have dirt-track roots and prefers to ride with the bike unfashionably loose, but he's also a hard worker who has achieved pre-eminence by application as much as talent. In this way, with many hours of practice, he has become a consummate wet-weather rider, when smoothness and control are everything.

By the mid-point of the year, he had managed to persuade HRC to let him race the rortier pneumatic-valve-spring engine. At first, it played him false, but as reliability and performance improved so too did his results. In the last five races, he made the rostrum twice – his first for over a year – and was never out of the top five.

At the same time, Nicky was overtaken more often in 2008 than he overtook anybody. The excuses were valid enough, but he needed to keep making them.

Dropped by Honda, he was picked up directly by Ducati, willing to take a chance that his combination of a full-on riding style and a capacity for seriously hard work will gel on the Desmosedici, which could hardly be more different from the Honda in the way it relates to its rider.

Popular to the last, Nicky Hayden had the good wishes of all in his brave move.

BAUTISTA disappointed his legion of supporters in 2008 with a costly lack of consistency. In the first six races, he fell or ran off the track four times. The loss of points was irrecoverable, the errors ill-affordable and, given his status, also unforgivable.

To his eternal credit, he remained exuberantly cheerful, at least outwardly. Except for a spat after the British GP, where Simoncelli had cost him his chance of a win with an over-ambitious attack that had pushed the Spaniard almost off the track.

The bad start took the gloss off what otherwise was an impressive season for a rider brimming with natural talent and clever racecraft. He took four wins and a string of rostrum finishes, all distinguished by some really fine, close and hard racing, most especially with Simoncelli. And to be fair, one of those crashes – at Jerez, which also brought down Simoncelli – was the result of a seized engine.

For some reason, Bautista struggled frequently in the first couple of laps, with a full tank of fuel. Only when the load had lightened slightly would he be able to move forward. This he would do with an impressive sense of purpose. He's a more polished rider than Simoncelli, but also a willing fighter when the occasion demands.

Bautista had been earmarked for a move straight to MotoGP in 2008, but that had presupposed success in his second 250 season, and in the end he preferred to stay on for another crack at the quarter-litre title. At 23 in 2009, he should not linger too much longer.

8 ALVARO BAUTISTA

9 LORIS CAPIROSSI

LORIS turned 35 in April, but showed few signs of growing old or even growing up. Throughout a very difficult season, he continued to prove that anyone who thought his latest factory contract was simply a comfortable option for the end of his career was mistaken.

There were days when his performance was below par, but in general these were because of either injury or machine weakness. Loris's level of effort and commitment were shining examples, however. And the injuries proved it.

He was an innocent victim – of de Angelis – in Catalunya, suffering bad injuries to his throttle hand that ruled him out for two races. He returned, possibly a bit prematurely, at Assen, only to be punished disproportionately for a tumble at the fast Ramshoek corner in practice, when his own footrest gouged a chunk out of his already injured right forearm.

By now even many younger riders might have throttled back or taken a month off to recuperate. Capirossi fought on, and when he was back to full strength after the summer break, he scored his only rostrum finish of the year at Brno, in a fine ride.

Loris's results may have been disappointing, but he was only ten points behind stalwart team-mate Chris Vermeulen, in spite of four zero-points scores, including two non-starts. And both were riding an ill-favoured machine, forever playing catch-up with the pace-setters up front.

There's plenty of life in the old dog yet.

THERE may be an element of nationalism in putting the ex-double Superbike champion in this select company. Some might think other riders more deserving: team-mate Colin Edwards had some of his best ever races, Chris Vermeulen was solid, Toni Elias was patchily excellent and also on the rostrum twice. Occasionally Alex de Angelis was absolutely inspired, while Randy de Puniet was always very, very fast – although both spent too much time in the gravel trap.

But James did bring something extra to the grid. He may be a mild-mannered pianist off the bike, but he's a really hard fighter when he's on it.

This was evident from the first race at Qatar, where a front-row start and strong battles with the leaders yielded an impressive sixth. He repeated that position at the next race, and four more times during the season. He was only three times out of the top ten, and in Australia proved a real obstacle to Rossi.

Toseland suffered somewhat during the solid grind of the European season. He was learning new tracks as well as a new bike and tyres, and for a while it meant that he faded into the background. His home GP was an unmitigated and humiliating disaster.

But he made a big impression on the other riders, who found him hard to pass and eager to attack. When Vermeulen and more than once Dovizioso criticised his forceful style, there was a tang of sour grapes.

Toseland proved himself worthy of his support, and he will be stronger in 2009.

THE AGE OF CHANGE

Sweeping changes and new rules took GP racing by the scruff of the neck in 2008. But will they be changes for the better? MICHAEL SCOTT investigates...

THERE was much to be pleased about during 2008: booming crowd figures, soaring TV audiences and the cult of Rossi growing ever stronger. There was also much about which to be concerned.

Last impressions linger, and those left by the final GP of the year at Valencia, and its immediate aftermath, were rather bleak. A triumph of technology, but not much fun for the fans.

Sunday's racing saw the usual 125 thriller, and classic last-lap drama for the doomed 250s. But the MotoGP race was a dreary series of laps where each rider circulated at his optimum speed, the gaps between

990s, and when Elias had beaten Rossi by two-thousandths of a second, it had cost him the title.

A few weeks before Valencia, the most fundamental technical rule change since the switch to four-strokes in 2002 had been made. Ostensibly, it was for different reasons – safety was the Holy Grail – but it also promised possible relief from processional racing. This was of course the one-tyre rule, rushed through in a couple of weeks, after dangling threateningly for the previous year or more.

Dani Pedrosa, third at that race, expressed the hope that tyres with less grip might hand more chances to the

tion change: the replacement of the 250 class. And it had ridden roughshod over long-established racing principles. A prototype, in the new definition, is still a prototype, even if it has a production-bike engine. Dorna chief executive Carmelo Ezpeleta said so.

At least he was doing something. In the absence of visible success for other recent initiatives, this was important. 'Something' is what chief executives are supposed to do.

One frivolous past initiative was the introduction of the VIP MotoGP paddock within the paddock, which in its second year remained too often an all-but deserted

come, along with stalwart Repsol and relative newcomer Fiat. But other teams were hanging on by their fingernails, while Team Roberts had gone, although there was still a hope that the promise of backing from Las Vegas would not turn out to be a never-land phantom.

By the year's end, the gloom of the general economic turn-down made the likelihood of finding new backing even more slender. Even Jorge 'Aspar' Martinez, principal of the two biggest teams in 250 and 125, had to abandon plans to run a MotoGP Kawasaki when he could not find the right backing. At the same time, 125 and 250 sponsor Polaris World, a Spanish property development company, pulled out for 2009. By contrast, however, another new Spanish team was created: the Onde 2000 squad will run Sete Gibernau on a Ducati in 2009.

A lack of financial backing is only one concern. Another is factory support. The four Japanese manufacturers have remained loyal and not only have paid lip service to Dorna's move to elevate MotoGP at the expense of the other classes, but also have voted with their feet. Japanese factory presence in 250 and 125 is negligible; the move to production-based 600 four-strokes as a 250 replacement is just what they'd been pressing for. But from

Europe, only Ducati is fully committed.

In 2008, there were two blows to hopes of adding variety to the MotoGP grid. The first considerably strengthened the rival production-bike series, World Superbikes.

The news that BMW intended entering World Superbikes in 2008 finally and firmly dashed any admittedly slender hopes that it might join MotoGP instead. The car company has been a stalwart supporter of MotoGP, as official provider of cars, so this was something of a slap in the face. BMW would join Aprilia on the Superbike grids; KTM is expected also in the future.

The second blow was KTM's sudden announcement at the penultimate round that it would be quitting the doomed 250 class forthwith. With Honda and Yamaha already gone, this effectively makes the 2009 series a one-make Aprilia benefit, for as long as it remains a two-stroke 250 class. At the time of writing, there had been 27 applications for entry, so there should be at least enough to fill the grid. But it is also likely to hasten the introduction of the proposed 600cc replacement class. This may begin in 2010 instead of 2011.

The age of change has developed an impetus of its own; only time will show whether or not the changes were of benefit.

ONE TYRE FITS ALL

Improved technology has led to the impasse of processional racing: grippier tyres, vaulting progress in traction control and the demand for fuel efficiency by the 21-litre tank rule. But there is a strong feeling that it has been hastened by a series of misguided rule changes in recent years – and the new tyre rule, along with the proposed 250 replacement, might prove to be more of the same.

In the opinion of Masao Furusawa, Yamaha's overall engineering chief, 'too much regulation is not the way to improve competition.' He was talking about the need for possible future electronic limitations, another looming spectre. But the principle remained valid.

A single-tyre rule brings MotoGP into line with most other major motorsports, including F1 and World Rally, as well as several lesser two-wheel series, world and national Superbike series included. It remains to be seen whether the actual production Bridgestones will perform better or worse than the company's top tyres of 2008; it also remains to be seen whether they will lead to safer or closer racing. What is obvious is that while discussions had been going on for more than a year, the rule was adopted with unseemly haste, and in spite of the fact that both tyre companies at least said that they did not want it.

Above: Lone Star- Hayden goes to work on a Ducati at his first test.

Above right: Stoner leads, the others follow – procession at Valencia.

Above centre right: The MotoGP-only paddock was often a ghost town.

Right: People power – Valencia crowd was another record-breaker.

Photographs: Gold & Goose

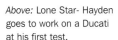

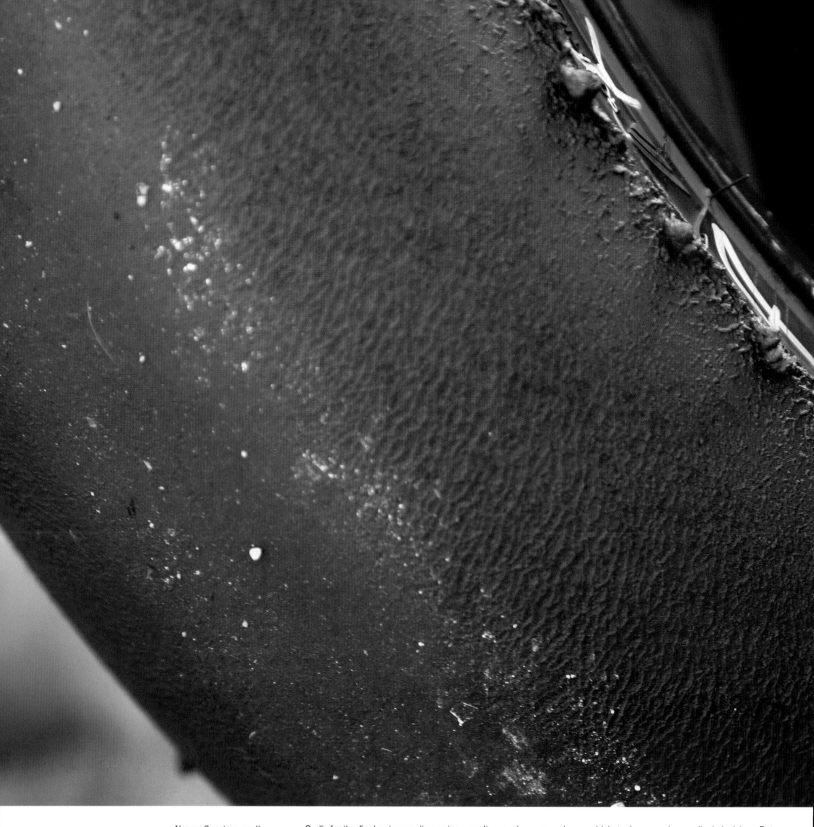

Sadly for the final outcome, lip service wasn't enough,
but neither loser Michelin nor winner Bridgestone did
anything positive to stop it.

The tyre controversy had been building for years and
has been well documented in these pages. In 2007, the
first radical change was the restriction in number – to 31
(14 front, 17 rear), to be pre-selected on the eve of first
practice. This did for Michelin, denied the home advantage of special tyres for the European events, and
helped Bridgestone's final climb to ascendancy. All the
more so when Rossi, tired of being beaten by Stoner,
demanded that he move also to Bridgestone for 2008.

At Michelin's encouragement, and against the will of
Bridgestone, which had become the biggest supplier on
the grid, tyre numbers were increased in 2008 to 40
(18 front, 22 rear). But that wasn't enough to save
Michelin from the tide of history. After a stronger start,
the French company stumbled at three races in a row:
the Sachsenring, Laguna Seca and Brno.

After a continuous motorcycle grand prix history going
back to the 1970s, three bad races may seem a small

sample on which to base such a radical decision. But
the problems had been accumulating, and this was
enough to trigger a series of events that rapidly led to
cataclysm.

One key was the action of Dani Pedrosa's manager
and crew chief, Alberto Puig, at Brno: the former racer
tried right up until the start of the race to call a strike by
Michelin users. He was roundly criticised, but soon it
transpired that he had the backing of tough HRC chief
Masumi Hamane. A year before, newly appointed
Hamane had blocked a request by Pedrosa and Hayden
to follow Rossi's move to Bridgestone, and had expressed Honda's unswerving loyalty to Michelin. Now his
patience had worn out.

Things moved fast after that. Hamane demanded that
Pedrosa (although not the outgoing Hayden) switch to
Bridgestone as soon as possible. But when the GP circus convened again two weeks later, at Misano, matters
were accelerated through the influence of an impressively powerful Spanish bloc, Dorna and sponsor Repsol.
The precipitate move was announced after the race.

Both Michelin and Bridgestone told *MOTOCOURSE* that they had agreed to this unexpected haste in an attempt to take the heat out of the situation, and thereby 'to try to avoid the single-tyre rule'. But by now the mere mention of this possibility had the alarming ring of a self-fulfilling prophecy. Or, in the eyes of some, a conspiracy, something already inevitable.

There had been other key developments at Brno. Single tyres had been discussed increasingly over the previous 18 months or so. Among the riders and teams, some were ardent supporters, while others were just as adamant in opposing the idea.

Now another dimension gained importance. The supposed increase in corner speeds had also been under discussion, and the two could be linked. Control tyres offering less grip would slow speeds. This, in turn, would solve another growing problem for circuit owners. With several crashes having taken riders to the safety barriers, there had been a stream of requests to move the barriers back here, install gravel traps there…

At Brno after the summer break, the matter was back on top of the agenda. And it stayed there on Saturday night, when Ezpeleta called a special meeting of all MotoGP riders to discuss corner speeds and related safety problems.

Control tyres were among several possibilities discussed. Later, Ezpeleta would talk as though the whole thing was being done at the request of the riders, but there was doubt over the strength of support. According to Chris Vermeulen, only about five had been for the restriction, 'all Michelin guys … and they hadn't been saying that earlier in the year when Bridgestone was having problems.' Rossi couldn't recall numbers, but thought 'more were in favour than against. The only thing we all agreed was to go back to 990cc.'

Never mind the wisdom of consulting riders on matters of policy when their interest is properly concentrated on the race the next day, and those following over sub-

sequent weeks. Ezpeleta had what he wanted – sanction from the riders for the oxymoronic concept that worse tyres make for greater safety.

The next round of meetings took place at Motegi, and Dorna tabled a proposal for a single-tyre rule. Both IRTA and the MSMA (manufacturers) voted in favour, in advance of the all-important GP Commission meeting at lunchtime on Saturday. Then came a hiccup. The commission stayed its hand to give the tyre companies the chance to avoid the inevitability of this change. If Michelin could find eight riders, the rule would not be imposed. But it had little over 12 hours in which to do this.

Behind closed doors, the lobbying was intense. There were rumours, denied at the time, that Stoner was in favour of Ducati switching to Michelin, on the same 'benefit by difference' grounds that had taken the Italian company on to Bridgestones in the first place. That would account for five riders; Michelin needed to find only three more. The Kawasaki team entertained a similar idea, until it was quashed that night by a decision from above, from factory level. There were similar discussions at Suzuki, although they didn't get quite as far. It was a long shot at best, but especially when it had to be decided by 9am the following morning. Unsurprisingly, the rescue bid failed, and news came from the GP Commission of the final decision in favour of a single tyre supplier.

Ezpeleta dressed the announcement with honeyed words of safety, saying that it was at the riders' request, as a safety measure. Asked by *MOTOCOURSE* how tyres with less grip could be safer, his reply was avuncular: 'Don't play with that.'

The process was in overdrive. Tyre companies had to swallow their objections and were given less than a week to tender to supply. Bridgestone, according to motorcycle racing chief Hiroshi Yamada, held intensive meetings over the next three days before deciding to tender. Dunlop expressed no interest. And, by the fol-

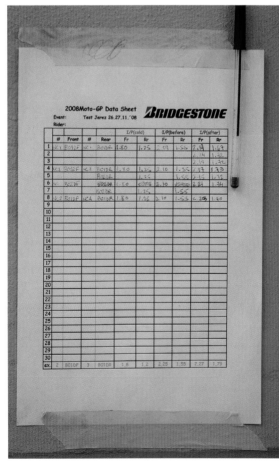

lowing race in Australia, Michelin did likewise.

Somewhat ashen-faced, Jean-Philippe Weber, the man who had presided over the debacle for Michelin, explained that the company was firm in the belief that, at the top level, motorsport should have free competition. Michelin might be prepared to support a single-tyre rule in a lesser series, but not at grand prix level. Hardly less shocked, Yamada justified Bridgestone's change of policy. The Japanese company wanted to be in MotoGP under any condition.

Later Yamada would enlarge on what to expect from the new generation of tyre. Some grip would be sacrificed necessarily, he said, for greater all-round performance, giving an overlap between the two compounds that would be available at each race. Bridgestone intended to halve the number of tyres supplied, to 20 per rider for the weekend, and was confident that every rider would be able to find something suitable for his motorcycle and riding style, every weekend. On one point he did not agree – that lower corner speeds would mean more safety. Corner speeds are slower in wet conditions, he pointed out, and yet you have more accidents.

There remained one last act, played out on Monday and Tuesday after the Valencia race. This was the first test of the proposed new tyres. Bridgestone had enough for all, and only Tech 3 was absent as the supposed longer-lasting, lower-grip compromise tyres made an impressive debut. Far from lacking grip and lowering corner speeds, the tyres allowed each of the top three in the race (Stoner, Rossi, Pedrosa) to improve on the previous day's time by an average of a tenth of a second. That, according to Rossi's crew chief, Jerry Burgess, was because of slightly better track conditions. Tyre-wise? 'We really couldn't notice much difference.'

The trial run was cut short by another potential problem – day two was damp. Not damp enough for wet tyres, but too damp for slicks. Intermediates were required, but there was no provision for intermediates in the Bridgestone proposal. And none at the track. Only when it really started raining could wet tyres be deployed. By then, most of the big names had left.

Much remained to be seen. Nobody had endurance-tested the tyres over race distance. Doubtless, the specifications of the tyres will also change. Something will have to be done to solve the problem of intermediate conditions.

But in many cases, riders who had been keen on the change were less sure once the axe had fallen. There were concerns that a lack of tyres would mean long down-times in the pits during practice, and that the new tyres would suit the current top Bridgestone men, Rossi and Stoner, at the expense of those teams whose riders and/or machines have always preferred something different. This would make the racing less competitive rather than more so. There was also the sad realisation that the era of qualifying tyres had come to an end: no more of those killer laps in the last five minutes of the session. And there were fears that a lack of competition-driven tyre development would eventually have an impact on street riders, whose benefits from racing to date include both radial and mixed-compound tyres.

Above all, there was a deep sense that the switch had downgraded the exclusivity of the premier series for mainly short-term interests, and that an important precedent had been set. All the more so because of the ultimate haste, which suggested panic.

What next? Control ECUs? Standardised engine architecture?

WHEN IS A PROTOTYPE NOT A PROTOTYPE?

Change is never comfortable. When it involves the destruction of a long-standing corner-stone of traditional motorcycle grand prix racing, it is even somewhat fright-

ening. But opponents of the forthcoming 600cc class, which will take the place of the 250s, might take heart from the example of MotoGP, at least in its 990cc iteration. After three years, few missed the old 500s any more.

In all probability, the 250s will soon slip to the back of the mind in the same way. No matter how pure, light, sophisticated and elegant today's quarter-litre machines may be, no matter how much they represent the perfect training ground for a MotoGP prototype, once they are consigned to history, they will stay there.

The death of the class is part of a larger drive against the two-stroke engine, with Honda in the van. The Japanese industry in general has supported this, but elsewhere there are strong pockets of resistance, both at industrial level and from individual engineers. Many still believe that the simple, efficient and increasingly clean-burning two-stroke has much to offer.

The pollution question is as hazy as an old-fashioned two-stroke's exhaust. At the manufacturing stage, a two-stroke has a very clear advantage over an infinitely more complex four-stroke, with its hundreds of cast, forged and machined valve-train components. Ease of maintenance is another two-stroke plus, as is performance per cubic capacity.

In racing terms, two-stroke engines are also very amenable to hands-on technicians – and extremely cheap to run. A worn-out two-stroke usually requires only a new piston and cylinder barrel, which can be fitted in a matter of minutes. Four-stroke MotoGP engines arrive in sealed boxes; those needing service are flown back to the factory for exacting rebuilds. This two-stroke advantage is particularly powerful at grass-roots level, where a switch to four-strokes has seen a huge rise in costs for a rider just starting racing.

At the same time, advances in fuel injection, synthetic oils and new materials have led to significant progress in cutting the two-stroke's biggest drawback – visible exhaust pollution. Racing has been an important aid in developing these technologies.

These are some of the technical facts that impinge on the wisdom of the decision to drop 250 two-strokes in favour of 600 four-strokes. There are other questions. One concerns the nature of the machines. Current 250s are proper racing bikes in every sense, fully adjustable suspension and gearing being the major characteristics. They provide the best possible training for MotoGP, according to the words and results of such graduates as Rossi, Stoner, Pedrosa, Lorenzo and Dovizioso.

In the words of two-stroke defender and guru Harald Bartol of KTM, a bike with a huge, heavy and complex, 600cc, four-stroke engine is 'a donkey compared with a racehorse'.

None of these arguments can change the fact that after 2010, and perhaps even sooner, the 250 class will be replaced by a new category of machine. The chassis can be as you like, within the regulations; the engines will be production-based and only lightly modified 600cc, four-cylinder four-strokes.

Regulations have to be finalised, but the proposal from the MSMA at Motegi laid down guidelines that allow little deviation. One aspect will be a rev limit of 16,000rpm, which is less than the more hectic 600s manage on the street; another proposal is for a 20,000-euro claiming rule for engines. A control ECU is another strong possibility.

The Japanese factories all have ready candidates as engine donors, and doubtless more to come, but have pledged that there will be no actual factory teams (we shall see about that). It is also something of a new dawn for independent chassis manufacturers. And, donkeys or not, it could also mean some very close racing – if the 600 World Supersport class is anything to go by.

Right: Two KTMs lead two Gileras and an Aprilia, with a Honda at the back. Next year, Aprilia will be alone.

Below: Bridgestone kept the details under wraps.

Bottom: The smaller classes are effectively a single-tyre class: Marco Simoncelli claimed Dunlop's 200th consecutive win at Motegi.

Photographs: Gold & Goose

This close similarity to the established junior brother to World Superbikes is one surprise of the new class. Questions were asked as to how motorcycling could justify two world championships that are so very alike. And as to whether the new owners of the officially production-based series will be kicking up a rumpus in the near future.

In fact, Ezpeleta had tried to avoid – or at least sidestep – this clash: Dorna's original proposal earlier in the year had suggested 625cc four-strokes. Just 25cc would make the difference, in the same way that 990 prototypes were different from 1000cc street bikes. This was rapidly quashed by the manufacturers' association on grounds of cost, among other things: they make 600s, and that's what they want to race.

One major impetus, according to Ezpeleta, had been to reduce costs for the participants. The pro-two-stroke lobby scoffed at this, citing sky-high maintenance for top-level racing four-stroke engines. It remains to be seen whether this can be kept under control by strict engine limitations. But Dorna had a point, and the last two bastions of 250 racing had conspired against themselves in this respect.

In spite of repeated requests from Dorna to keep costs under control, Aprilia had continued technical development apace. The Italian factory had in its gift the machinery necessary for any serious championship contender. Gift, however, is the wrong word. The cost of leasing a top-level factory machine, especially the all-new RSA, ran to six million euros or beyond – not that

far short of a MotoGP Honda. There was little relief in view from KTM, still establishing itself as a force in the class and with just one bike available for lease, also at a high cost.

The RSA Aprilia, the best-ever racing 250, was a step too far – and the last straw that triggered Dorna's drastic action.

By 2011, the 125s will be the last two-strokes going grand prix racing – and the last of the original World Championship classes to have survived with the capacity unchanged. By then, it will be clearer whether they are living on borrowed time, or whether the pro-two-stroke faction will have achieved enough headway to make a difference.

This is not impossible, depending on the progress of a new motorcycle announced during 2008 and ready to race in 2009. The Maxtra follows F1 practice, marrying specialist racing technology from around Europe. The engine comes from Dutch engineer Jan Witteveen, architect until three years ago of Aprilia's success and now working independently. The chassis is from Harris Performance in England, with GP roots that reach back to Barry Sheene, as well as being supplier of official works replica 500 Yamahas in the 1990s. The project is headed by former Suzuki team chief Garry Taylor and has an actively involved patron in John Surtees. But it is a Chinese machine, in that it is entirely paid for and backed by the Haojue factory. Chinese engineers will be directly involved, and the long-term aim is not only for greater involvement in GP racing, including possibly Mo-

toGP, but also the manufacture of production-racing 125s based on the 2009 prototype.

The GP paddock took this enterprise much more seriously when it learned of the scale of the Chinese motorcycle manufacturing empire behind the project. Haojue made almost three million motorcycles in 2007 and was set to double that figure by 2010. Almost 10,000 people work in its ultra-modern factory complex. In racing terms, it is a sleeping giant.

Haojue is just one Chinese factory; much will depend on the machine's impact on GP racing. Success could see other Chinese manufacturers follow. And the two-stroke engine is a staple for many of the nation's small utilitarian motorcycles. With the weight of the Chinese industry behind them, the two-stroke disciples might find a new lease of life.

The cause is lost for the 250 class, however, and with that loss comes another: to the status of the second-level World Championship. The replacement motorcycles will have much more in common with production racing than GP competition.

Can they still be called prototypes? Certainly so, insisted Ezpeleta, in an animated Press briefing at Catalunya. Spluttering with impatience, he grew more and more explosive as he attempted to justify how a one-off chassis married to a production engine was enough to make the whole bike a prototype.

By any dictionary definition, he was as wrong as he could be. By the definition of the series' rules, it mattered not a jot.

UNHOLY TRINITY

Neil Spalding examines the three factors that are blamed for

THIS was the year of the naysayers, critics of the way MotoGP is developing and the technologies that have made the last seven years one of the golden ages of racing motorcycle development. The technologies under fire have had a massive effect on the racing, its quality and the way bikes will develop.

Supposedly in the face of demands for increased safety as well as reduced costs, rule changes have been made that will affect MotoGP for ever. The single-tyre rule sounds innocuous, but given the massive effect tyre design has on the development of a bike, it isn't. The winners over the next few years will be those whose current design fits the available tyres the best. And subsequent technical development will depend on who controls the direction of tyre development. Assuming there is any.

Three technologies in particular define the current face of our sport: electronics, tyres and fuel.

ELECTRONICS

The fuel limits are critical, and electronics ensure that the best possible use is made of the fuel available. Let's take it as given that now all the engines are engineered with optimal combustion chambers, porting, valve design and valve actuation, and have the lowest imaginable levels of internal friction. After you've exhausted all of those avenues, you have to depend on the throttle strategy to eke out the fuel.

From some scary and injurious beginnings, ride-by-wire has become the norm and today is a very refined science. Ducati's system clearly requires some faith from the rider, but the major manufacturers are aiming to beat the Italians with more conventional-feeling throttle response.

Consider Stoner's corner exit. As the bike approaches the apex, he piles on throttle – not full throttle, but certainly more than the bike could handle at that point if it had a conventional wire throttle. In that situation, the rider is, as Jerry Burgess puts it, 'ahead of the traction control', and the control system is doing the work. Unlike some of the bikes on the grid, the Ducati electronics are quick enough and accurate enough, once they have been carefully programmed during practice, to let the bike accelerate as quickly as it can from full lean purely on the basis of information received from the on-board gyroscopes, wheel-speed and location sensors.

As the bike becomes more upright, and without any additional throttle, a different strategy is brought into play. Slightly more power than can be used is gener-

ated and a deliberate misfire created to control it. As soon as the bike is in this zone, Stoner can be seen to dial on even more throttle, and as soon as the grip and angles of lean improve, the misfire stops. This corner-exit strategy gets the engine operating at its peak and deliberately destroys just enough power to obtain the desired level of wheelspin. Unfortunately, it also uses more fuel, although overall the Ducati is very fuel efficient. Some of the fuel burned on those hard corner exits is probably saved while rolling through the apex, since the mixture need not be enriched to give the rider a good throttle connection – the electronics take care of that.

Yamaha approached things slightly differently. The company values agility and rider control through the twists above all else. The strategy is never to generate more torque than can be used by the tyre at any time. This means that it uses a little less fuel in the transition to upright, where the Ducati would be misfiring, and this probably allows a little more fuel to improve rider feel mid-corner.

There is no doubt that the electronic throttle played a big part in the Yamaha's improvement in 2008, not only for corner exits, but also in corner entries and fuel management. It's no coincidence that the Yamaha could perform extremely well with four different riders – all four on the front row at one time or another – whereas only Stoner and very occasionally Elias managed to get the best out of the Ducati.

It's equally clear that there is a big disparity between the 'flying-on-the-ground' systems employed by Ducati and Yamaha and those further down the pit lane. Honda has caught up somewhat, but only on the works bikes, while Suzuki and Kawasaki appear still to be in the previous generation of controls. These separate the functions of traction control and throttle control. Both will have to improve if they wish to compete.

The top crew chiefs all support this 'electronics war'. The general consensus is that while chassis and engines are still developing, the basic philosophies are under control. But now we have an electronics competition – a battle between the throttle-control specialists at the back of the garage, kept busy all weekend refining the traction and corner-entry/exit controls and fuel maps for each bike. We have rapid evolution of complex systems, but these in turn will develop into simpler broad-brush systems that ultimately will be used on the road. This affirms the whole point of prototype MotoGP development.

TYRES

Michelin and Bridgestone continued their ferocious fight, but after Michelin had found the constraints of the 2007 tyre rule too difficult, and following some fairly brutal negotiations, the rule was revised to allow 40 tyres per weekend. Early results were promising. Qatar was a proper fight between a resurgent Michelin, with a new and competitive cold-conditions tyre, and Bridgestone, which had Rossi joining Stoner in the line-up. Bridgestone won the first race, Michelin the next two. By round four, however, Rossi had got his Yamaha dialled in and started to win. Thereafter, he and Stoner dominated; Michelin took only one more win – Pedrosa at Catalunya.

When Rossi had followed Stoner in 2007, he had understood what he was seeing: a particularly stable rear tyre married to a front tyre that would still grip when most of the weight had been shifted to the rear under acceleration. This was one part of the reason for the Ducati's hugely competitive drive out of corners. When Rossi successfully politicked himself on to Bridgestones for 2008, he didn't just want any old Bridgestones, he wanted ones just like Stoner's.

The first race was a disappointment for Rossi. In spite of pre-season testing, the machine changes required to get the best out of the Bridgestones hadn't been fully understood. After the first race, Yamaha shortened the back of the motorcycle and extended the front. This enabled Rossi to load weight on to the rear wheel on acceleration and made the front tyre really work for its living.

The changes put Rossi back in the title hunt. By then, the Michelin runners understood his strategy and also began shifting weight rearward to improve drive off the corners. The softer Michelin carcass couldn't take this, and it didn't take long for Lorenzo in particular, after several high-sides, to decide not to proceed in this direction.

Mid-season, Michelin dropped the ball, and the reasons were not all technical. At the Sachsenring in pouring rain, the French company had two types of wet tyre, but insisted that all the riders should use the harder of the two compounds – it was not confident that the soft tyre would last the distance. Pedrosa and then also Edwards and Lorenzo crashed.

At the next race at Laguna Seca, operating far from home, Michelin got it completely wrong. Tyres brought for a searing hot California summer simply didn't work in the unseasonally cool winds. Dani Pedrosa, still walking wounded from his big Sachsenring crash, went home,

Left to right: Tyres, fuel and electronics set the pace in 2008.

Below: Stoner uses the electronics to the limit on the Ducati. Only he was capable of doing so.

Photographs: Gold & Goose

processional racing, and analyses the bikes of 2008

Above: The Michelins might have got hot enough to steam in Brno, but they simply didn't grip.

Bottom left: Dovizioso gets a new Michelin.

Below right: Honda has only once used chilled fuel.

All photographs: Gold & Goose

while Hayden was reduced to trying intermediates in practice.

Then at Brno, in spite of testing there some two months previously, Michelin's tyres were a complete disaster. The fronts simply could not generate the grip required, and most of the Michelin riders were on the back of the grid. Dorna was clearly upset, but not as much as HRC President Hamane, who held three meetings with Michelin before deciding that it had no idea of how to sort out its problems.

Three mistakes in a row meant that within two weeks, Dani Pedrosa had switched to Bridgestone, and within four weeks of that, the GP Commission had voted to move to a single tyre supplier for 2009. In another three weeks, it was confirmed that Bridgestone would be the supplier.

It seems that riders will be confined to 20 slick tyres for the full weekend. What matters is the construction and development applied to those tyres.

The best-performing Bridgestones particularly suit the Ducati design. The Desmosedici's combination of weight distribution and suspension favours a particularly stiff rear tyre and a front tyre capable of generating grip with almost no weight on it. If this design is to be frozen, then all MotoGP bikes will start to resemble the Ducati, in weight-distribution terms at least. Another aspect of design experiment will have been curtailed.

FUEL

The rules say that each bike can only carry 21 litres of fuel. Ducati has pushed the boundaries from the beginning. With a very efficient motor and a world-leading engine control arrangement that prioritises fuel economy, the Ducati system got in front in 2007 and is still one of the best. It works by dividing the circuit into sectors. The fuel map is tailored to provide the most effective fuelling in each sector – lean running while on traction control in the corners, and full fuel while blitzing down the straights. The throttle system employs two gyroscopes to monitor lean and pitch, and can measure wheelspin sufficiently accurately for the rider to trust it on all corner exits – that's different from the rider being able to persuade himself to trust it. Used as it was designed to be used, the throttle system gets the bike around the whole track using the least possible fuel.

Ducati has another nice trick: chilling the fuel. In the days of the early 990s, there was a 24-litre limit, but no temperature restriction. There are numerous reports that 'cool fuel' can increase the power by lowering the temperature of the charge in the inlet port and making it more dense, but some at Honda don't seem to believe this. It is also possible that although the fuel chemistry is very well defined and controlled, Ducati's Shell fuel might react particularly well to lower temperatures.

The density increase is beyond doubt. Volume decreases by approximately 0.125 per cent for every 1°C rise, so if you start the warm-up lap with the fuel in the tank 15 degrees below ambient, you effectively get an additional 390cc. With the fuel injection system, this means that when the bike gets to the starting grid after sighting and warm-up laps, it still has 21 litres available for the race.

The rules specify that fuel must be no cooler than 15 degrees below ambient, but there is no specific test procedure. The current practice is for the outside of the fuel tank to be checked with an infra-red temperature detector immediately prior to the bikes leaving their garages. What a good lawyer would make of this practice is a moot point.

Ducati has always cooled the fuel; Honda has not. Some innate conservatism stopped them from joining the rest in the pit lane. However, when Hayden ran out of fuel at Assen, after effectively foxing the integral fuel saving strategy, Honda finally relented. At the next meeting at the Sachsenring, one of the circuits where the bikes use the least amount of fuel, the fuel was chilled. One wonders how much this belated move has cost Honda over the last four or five years.

The most important thing about a fuel limit is that you simply cannot afford wheelspin – it is a waste of fuel. For the last few years, the strategy has been to build power while rationing fuel. Unless the fuel limit is raised, we are not going to see much wheelspin again. In a carbon-conscious world, it is hard to think of an argument to favour such a change.

DUCATI

Below: The Ducati uses the engine as a stressed member, the chassis bolted directly to the cylinder heads.

Bottom left: Melandri's bike was exactly the same as Stoner's.

Bottom right: Note carbon fibre mount for instruments and electronics. Fuel catch tank is below.

Photographs: Gold & Goose

DUCATI finished 2007 as undisputed master. At Jerez, just before the Christmas break, the Italian company tried new technology that improved performance even further. We believe it to be a variable-length inlet system, partner to the very sophisticated and accurate ride-by-wire throttle. Testing revealed more mid-range power and the opportunity to use lower rpm in certain circumstances, saving fuel to make more power on the straights.

Either the system was not co-ordinated perfectly with the throttle or not calibrated correctly, since it introduced some sort of pumping sensation into the output that upset the bike in corners. Ducati won the first race, but then Stoner suffered, losing places through his attempts to make up for a bike that wouldn't quite do what he wanted.

Ducati soon reverted to the 2007 throttle system. By round seven, however, the new system was back and sorted, and Stoner started to win again.

Ducati's 2008 D16 Desmosedici GP8 was almost identical to the GP7. There were software changes, and Ducati talked about a few changes to help the mechanics, but in truth there was nothing much wrong with the '07 bike that could be easily improved. Development focused on making it more usable by other riders. Even then, new team rider Melandri simply could not deal with a system that required him to delegate to the computer the subtle throttle control of his connection with the tyre. Elias had different problems, solved by changing the rear suspension link.

The 800cc motor is the second generation of Ducati V4, most of the problems of the 990 having been sorted by re-arranging the engine into a shorter package, with a better centre of gravity and particularly efficient engine internals.

Ducati's basic strategy remained unchanged: to make as much power as possible and then work out how to get it to the finish.

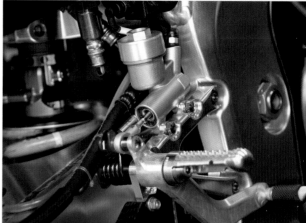

Above: Hayden's Sachsenring bike had pneumatic valve springs. Compressed-air top up bottles (at 200 Bar) are on top of the airbox.

Right: The customer Hondas looked identical to last year's machine.
Photographs: Neil Spalding

Far right: Honda brake detail – some parts looked as if machined by a watchmaker.
Photograph: Gold & Goose

HONDA

IT was ironic that Honda was among the casualties of the move to 800cc, since the company had pushed hardest for it. The 2007 design massively underestimated what was required. The 2008 customer versions of the bike were uprated, with more efficient motors and Mk2 chassis, and populated the middle and back of the field.

The new works bike was debuted at Valencia immediately after the end of the 2007 season, using a remodelled engine for a lower centre of gravity and reduced pitch. Importantly for Hayden, however, the new chassis looked significantly roomier and far simpler to build than the almost art-deco 2007 version.

The new bike had pneumatic valve springs and power characteristics clearly intended to take the fight to Ducati. But the riders didn't like it. The power was abrupt, lacked mid-range and did not have a friendly character mid-corner. After two tests, the engine was retrofitted with steel-valve-spring cylinder heads from the previous year. This became the main racing project.

Honda's misery became worse. At Qatar tests one week before the race, neither Pedrosa nor Hayden could make the new chassis work in the long corners. During the following week, Honda built four production bikes from spares and flew them to Qatar. Pedrosa was quickly back on the new bike; Hayden raced the replacement.

The same basic theme continued for the first half of the season: Nicky clearly unsettled and unhappy with the way the bike felt, but Dani fairly happy as long as his tyres gripped. By mid-season, however, the much talked about pneumatic-valve-spring project was back, this time with a completely new engine. Although it fitted the same chassis, it appeared to have a different Vee angle; certainly the cylinder heads looked bigger.

Different bore and stroke dimensions were rumoured, and riders spoke of completely changed engine character. Hayden liked it, and at his first race at Assen he was heading for a podium before the other side of the bike's character asserted itself – he ran out of fuel just 50 metres before the finish. From that point on, however, he was able to ride more as he wished on a bike with better horsepower.

Michelin's mid-season *faux pas* led Honda to a controversial change to Bridgestone tyres for Pedrosa. He was given the pneumatic valve springs at the same time. His next outing was at the test after the Misano GP. That was successful, but it took him a few races to become used to the different riding style necessary to get the best out of the tyres.

Honda's customers didn't get much in the way of updates, although Dovizioso's stellar performances in the last few GPs made one suspect that he had access to better engine components. From Brno onwards, Nakano tested the prototype 2009 customer bike, using a steel-valve-spring engine in a new chassis, similar to that campaigned by the Repsol riders during the first half of the year.

YAMAHA

Below left: Toseland's number two bike has new brakes. Note 'flexy' top triple clamp.

Below centre: By Le Mans Rossi had a short swing-arm, axle at the front of its adjustment.

Below far right: Lorenzo's Yamaha: note the two gyroscopes on top of the air intake.

Photographs: Neil Spalding

Bottom left: Rossi's M1. Chassis side bracing improves braking stability.

Photograph: Gold & Goose

Bottom right: A tangle of cables, a jumble of sensors and processors. This is Edwards's machine.

Photograph: Neil Spalding

YAMAHA'S racing history seems to have been punctuated by periods of brilliance followed by lethargy. The 2007 800 was quite a good effort, but was aimed too much towards easily finishing races on 21 litres of fuel.

By the end of 2007, with the championship gone, Yamaha had begun testing new technologies, particularly a pneumatic-valve-spring cylinder head. This led to a couple of embarrassing failures, but it was well prepared for the start of 2008. There were two teams: the factory Fiat Yamaha squad and Tech 3, somewhat upgraded from satellite to semi-works status, and receiving the pneumatic heads and other upgrades later.

Rossi had also switched to Bridgestones, which he believed necessary to take the fight to Stoner and Ducati. He arrived at the first race at Qatar confident. As well as the tyres, he had a pneumatic-valve-spring engine and Yamaha's new, very sophisticated engine control system. As a measure of the new Yamaha's friendly nature, ahead of him on the grid in his first MotoGP race was rookie Toseland on the steel-spring version of the engine. The Englishman had a good race, capped by sixth place. But Rossi was a disappointed fourth, off the podium and beaten by a Michelin-shod Yamaha ridden by rookie team-mate Jorge Lorenzo.

Rossi had suffered wheelspin in the later laps. From then on, he and crew chief Jerry Burgess were on a mission: to make the Yamaha chassis work for a full MotoGP race distance with the design of Bridgestone tyres initially developed for Ducati.

Most of the bikes in the pit lane are close to the minimum weight of 148kg. When the rider with his leathers, helmet and safety equipment, and 21 litres of fuel are added, the total weight on the tyres is somewhere around 250kg. How this weight is distributed front to rear makes a lot of difference to the way the tyres work.

The Ducati chassis seems to load up the rear far more than the new 2008 M1 Yamaha. Now Rossi and Burgess had to find out just how much weight they could move towards the rear without disturbing the rest of the design of the bike. At Jerez, the axle was moved forwards; by Estoril, the front forks also had been moved to the limit. By China, there was a new, shorter swing-arm, and shortly after that the option of a modified chassis to move the front wheel even further forward.

Rossi started to win regularly with the original chassis at the limit of adjustment, with the short swing-arm. Much more weight was now on the rear tyre, helping to develop heat and grip, while Bridgestone's amazing front kept holding on.

The other three M1s ran on Michelins, and while officially no data was transferred from the Bridgestone side to the other, it was obvious that they were trying to match the corner drive that Rossi's new set-up had achieved. By contract, Lorenzo had access to the same parts as Rossi, and he certainly tried the short swing-arm on several occasions. It soon became clear, however, that the Michelins had difficulty in accepting this sort of weight shift. Lorenzo's bike ended the year with the weight shifted only slightly rearwards compared with Rossi's.

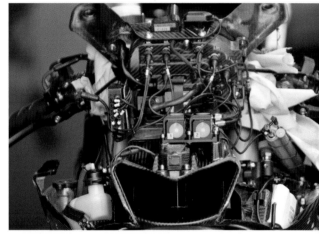

KAWASAKI

KAWASAKI started the 800 era strongly, with an initial aim of having the fastest accelerating bike. Improved corner entry was the next goal. There would be no new 2008 bike. Instead Kawasaki aimed to convert a bike designed for corner-exit stability to be stable also on entry – and then to make a new bike based on that information.

Initial testing concentrated on trying to improve slipper clutch settings. This development appeared to stop once more effort had gone into finding the right throttle settings to match the clutch. At the same time, the swing-arm was extended, giving the bike an even longer wheelbase.

At the factory, a new 'screamer' engine was under development, reverting to the 180-degree crankshaft design Kawasaki had used when it first came to MotoGP. It wasn't because the irregular-fire 90-degree crankshaft wasn't thought to be good. The technicians wanted to see if the regular pulses of the 'screamer' would give enough extra power on the straights to make up for the reduced corner grip. The company seemed to have neglected the development of the main race engine, and by the third round it was clear that this was woefully down on power.

On a bike that was too slow and wouldn't hold its corner line, Hopkins was injured trying to stay competitive. This set back the project further. In the meantime, Anthony West had been struggling to make the bike respond. Clearly more sensitive to chassis settings than Hopkins, he was simply not prepared to take risks to try to make up for the machine's deficiencies. New swing-arms were fitted to Hopkins's bike in an attempt to allow him to use the Ducati/Rossi Bridgestones, but to no avail. By mid-season, Kawasaki had given up with the 2008 version of its machine. A new bike was under development back in Japan.

Kawasaki has tried resolutely to stick with the across-the-frame four, its trademark on the street, but it also wanted to be different from Yamaha. It is quite possible there is only one right arrangement for a given motor layout, so if Kawasaki turns up in 2009 with a bike that is shorter, with a higher centre of gravity and with other similarities to the M1, it won't be copying the Yamaha. The reason will be because that's the only way to make an across-the-frame four competitive.

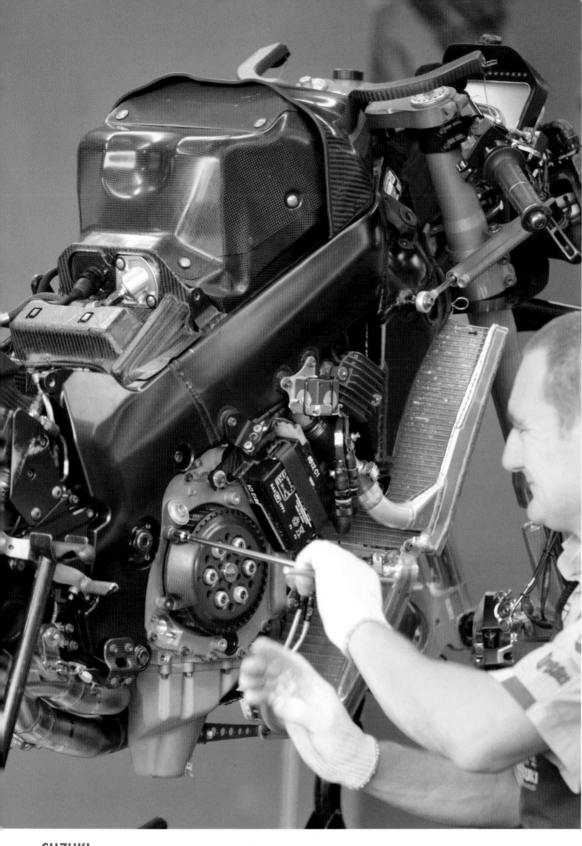

Left: Suzuki reverted to the 2007 chassis for the first half of the season. Here a mechanic is stripping the clutch after a practice start.

Photograph: Neil Spalding

SUZUKI

SUZUKI prepared for the 800 class by building a 990 version the year before, only to discover that it too had also completely underestimated the needs. The 2008 bike had a new chassis, better packaging with lots of small items relocated and better aerodynamics. By the time of the last two pre-season tests, however, it was clear that something wasn't right. At both Phillip Island and Qatar, Suzuki couldn't get near the rest of the field, and rather than persevere with something that clearly had major problems – we believe it was chatter – it went back to what it knew.

The 2008 machine was raced by Chris Vermeulen in Qatar, but he pulled in with tyre problems. From then on, the 2007 chassis and bodywork were used all the way through to the Brno test.

Experimentation didn't stop, and for much of the year Vermeulen tried longer front forks in an attempt to improve turn-in. Suzuki was still having difficulty using the RJ Bridgestones, the Rossi/Stoner tyres. The Brno chassis raised the front of the engine by between 15 and 20mm. This might have impinged upon the airbox above the engine, and therefore required fuel to be moved back and underneath the seat. The net result of these changes was to move a significant part of the weight rearward, and Suzuki was able to use Bridgestone's finest from that point on.

The Suzuki motor is capable of staying with the best, but the team's exclusive use of Mitsubishi Electronics appears to count against it, because Yamaha and Ducati have raised the game to such an extent. At several races, Suzuki riders were able to compete without any traction control – almost unthinkable when you consider how the Ducatis and Yamahas work.

The new direction in electronics is for total throttle management at all points on the circuit, from engine braking to slide and wheelspin control. Good racing doesn't require all the sophistication, but if your opponents have it and you don't, you are at a disadvantage.

250cc: AN ENGINE TOO FAR

Below left: The new RSA 250 was shorter. The vertically stacked gearbox and the high setting of the upper carburettor are visible.

Below top right: Honda shows its gearbox.

Below centre right: KTM's 'old' chassis has air intakes through the frame.

Bottom right: Bottom end of KTM shows ignition pickup for 90 degree crank.

All photographs: Neil Spalding

HONDA made its last 250s in 2007, and for a few years now Yamaha has only produced very small batches of the ubiquitous TZ250. For Aprilia and KTM, though, it has been full speed ahead in the year when the fate of 250 two-strokes was finally sealed.

KTM introduced the 250 in June 2005. Technically speaking, it was a very simple design – a doubled-up version of the manufacturer's 125 reed-valve single. Slightly under-square with a 54.5x54mm bore and stroke, the motor had a claimed power output of 110hp at 13,000rpm. As a parallel twin, and with transfer ports on the cylinder sides, it was slightly wider than a single-crank V-twin.

KTM race director and two-stroke specialist Harald Bartol took the opportunity to experiment with irregular firing intervals, and current crankshaft settings at 90 degrees give the best traction. This requires a balance shaft, but means that the bike has very centralised weight while maintaining some of the benefits that make a Vee-format engine effective.

KTM tried a new chassis half-way through the year in an attempt to boost Kallio's assault on the championship. This was narrower and held the engine in a different position, but it didn't deliver the expected benefits, and Kallio went back to the old chassis for the balance of the year.

It became apparent, however, that while Bartol's choice of reed valves allowed him to build inexpensive and useful motors, it also denied him the final edge when competing with Aprilia's latest and extremely effective disc-valve motors.

Reed-valve engines can be easily upset by differences in atmospheric pressure. The disc-valve Aprilias seem less critical on jetting, making it easier to obtain the best mixture for power.

Aprilia debuted a new V-twin, designed to address a historic weakness: the length of its twin-crank V-twin. With the old engine, one crank was in front of the other, and the gearbox shafts were disposed in the same way behind them. The consequence was a short swing-arm. This makes chain-pull more difficult to control.

The new engine changed the arrangement. Where before drive had been taken off the rear crank, now it came off the front, the cylinder pointing downwards more acutely, while the rear crankshaft was moved forwards and upwards. In addition, the gearbox shafts were vertically stacked rather than horizontal. This comprehensive redesign gave a saving of almost 40mm.

When this was first contemplated, it would have been an effective counterstrike against Honda, which was particularly good in this regard. It seems, however, that this was a step too far. Without Honda competition, eventual champion Simoncelli managed to run the first half-year on the old engine. It did force KTM to push its reed-valve technology to the limit and ultimately to withdraw at year's end.

Aprilia's RSA 250 is both the finest 250 engine ever built, and also the motor that drove the final nails into the coffin. KTM's withdrawal made it likely that the four-stroke 600s will take over a year earlier than originally planned.

Above: KTM 125: electric water pump is in the foreground.

Top right: Aprilia RSA motor. Disc valve intake is on the far side of the cylinder.

Right: And this is how it fits in the chassis.

Below: Smith's Aprilia was a full works RSA, seen here at Donington.

Photographs: Neil Spalding

125cc: **THE DISC-REED DIVIDE**

THE half-size, single-cylinder two-strokes reflected a similar battle between disc and reed valves, with KTM employing reeds and Aprilia its signature discs. As with the 250s, the fuelling settings were easier to get right for the Aprilia.

The Italian motor is well developed, and the latest RSA version, introduced two years ago, uses an idea that is not new, but that has always been difficult to make reliable.

Historically, disc valves are located on the crankshaft ends, on the side of the engine. This restricts the size and shape of the airbox, although it frees up exhaust design, allowing pipes to run straight back under the seat rather than looping under the engine. Reed-valve engines like the KTM have the carburettor behind and at the base of the cylinder. This makes for a more direct intake path, as well as cooling and oiling the big-end directly with fresh mixture. This placement also allows a much more effective airbox, beneath the fuel tank.

Aprilia's latest motor has these advantages while retaining the disc valve. This is operated by a short shaft, leading from a 90-degree bevel drive on the crankshaft.

Initially there were problems, a harmonic resonance destroying the disc drive shaft. For 2008, the motor had a harmonic damper that appears to have solved the problem.

Another development that gave trouble was a lighter con-rod. Aprilia denied that it was titanium, but whatever material was used, it was not reliable in the unforgiving environment of a GP engine – there were several con-rod failures at the start of the year.

The old engine proved still competitive, with several riders – most notably Britain's Scott Redding – being able to use it effectively on tighter courses such as Donington and Indianapolis. This may be due to the power characteristics or weight distribution. The engine makes a little less horsepower, but probably a little more torque in the mid-range, while the straight-back exhaust run allows more freedom in engine location within the chassis.

LEGACY...

The two-stroke engine changed every aspect of motorcycle racing and forced technological advances in all areas. Now it is to be ruled out of the 250 class.
KEVIN CAMERON looks at what we gained, and what we will lose…

IF current Dorna initiatives succeed, the 250 GP class will soon be replaced by some kind of limited 600 four-stroke formula. What have we gained from the years of two-stroke grand prix domination, and what will we lose? After 1974, no four-stroke engine ever won a grand prix championship in any class until the rules were changed in 2002, giving MotoGP four-strokes 990cc compared to the 500cc displacement of existing two-strokes.

The greatest gifts of the two-stroke era were the flood of cost-effective and available production racing machines that enlarged the sport bottom to top, and steeply rising two-stroke engine power, which forced a long-overdue revolution in tyres, chassis and suspension. When raceable four-strokes emerged in quantity during the mid-1980s, that revolution was ready to carry them.

In our era of mass-produced, raceable and affordable sport bikes, it's easy to forget that it wasn't always so. Nothing of that kind existed through the 1950s and '60s, so grand prix privateers rode the classic British racing singles – Norton and AJS/Matchless. Two-stroke production racers would take over from the classic singles, whose manufacture ended around 1962–63, and

which faded in the later 1960s. Yamaha's first durable 250 production racer was the TD1-C of 1967, and by 1970 its updated successors had become good enough to win world championships – 250 two-strokes had become the established path to professionalism. In 1973, using technology proven in the production racers, Yamaha entered the 500 class with a factory machine. By 1975, the class was dominated by two-strokes.

Before that, the 500 class had been won 17 years in a row by MV-Agusta. That, plus a lack of participating factories and riders in the class, had elicited proposals for its abolition in the 1960s. Two-stroke dominance had two immediate effects, however: it restored the competition that had left the class with Gilera in 1957, and it introduced the newly powerful Japanese manufacturers and a wide stream of new riding talent.

In the late 1930s, when the diesel cylinder scavenging scheme of Adolph Schnuerle was applied to a production bike by DKW, the result was a 5hp 125 single, the RT125. Currently, using a highly refined version of Schnuerle scavenging, a 125cc GP engine makes 60hp – a 12-to-1 gain in 70 years. Four-stroke power made a 3-to-1 gain over the same period. Why the difference?

In a four-stroke, each of the four functions – com-

pression, power, exhaust and intake – has its own piston stroke. In a two-stroke, some functions must occur simultaneously to fit all into just two piston strokes. The gas-exchange process must occur very quickly, but the piston cannot provide the push this requires. That function is provided by the resonant-duct exhaust pipe, powered by the engine's exhaust pulses. It generates rapidly alternating sound waves – suction and pressure – at the cylinder's exhaust port. The suction wave rapidly pulls fresh mixture through the cylinder from the crankcase, and just as the cylinder fills and the charge begins to be lost through the open exhaust port, the pressure wave arrives to push it back into the cylinder as the exhaust port closes. As pointed out by the late L.J.K. Setright, the resonant-duct exhaust idea was applied to the pulse-jet engine of the wartime German flying bomb, which employed the bouncing duct wave to power the four familiar functions. Both Walter Kaaden of MZ and Erich Wolf of DKW coupled such a resonant duct to a two-stroke cylinder in the 1950s, doubling and then tripling its power. It is interesting that the flying bombs had reed intake valves, just like many modern two-strokes.

Most of the gain in the specific power of four-strokes

Left: The 2008 250s represent the last evolution of a machine that revolutionised racing.
Photograph: Gold & Goose

Bottom: The simplicity of a two-stroke: cylinder-top view of KTM's parallel-twin 250. What you see is what you get.
Photograph: Neil Spalding

has come from increasing rpm, as engineers quickly mastered the process of filling the cylinder. The 6,500rpm of a Manx Norton of 1939, multiplied by three, becomes 19,500 – a fair estimate of the rpm reached by today's 800cc MotoGP four-strokes. Two-strokes have seen a similar rpm increase of about 3-to-1 – from 4,500 in 1939 to 13,500 or more today – but at the same time their net, stroke-averaged combustion pressure has grown by about 4-to-1. This has resulted mainly from incremental improvements to resonant duct shape, and to the details of cylinder port aiming and sizing.

At present, the best four-strokes are able to fill their cylinders to about 25 per cent above atmospheric pressure by a combination of intake, exhaust and airbox resonance effects. It appears that the best two-strokes fill their cylinders to a similar 30 per cent above atmospheric pressure through resonance effects. Two-stroke rpm is limited by the time required for cylinder gas exchange, such that a 125cc single may peak at 13,500–14,000rpm. A similarly developed, notional GP four-stroke 125 single might peak at 21,000rpm, making 40hp to the two-stroke's 60. The modern two-stroke has done what was long considered impossible – achieved or even exceeded four-stroke cylinder filling and net, stroke-averaged combustion pressures. Furthermore, it does this for every revolution.

There is a cost in such dependence upon resonance effects. If the engine and its resonant duct become too far out of step, torque and power fall because the pumping effect is lost. This is the cause of the two-stroke's relatively narrow power band.

By 1970, the simple 'thought experiment' of combining two existing 250 two-stroke twins to make a 500-four suggested competitive power. When Yamaha challenged MV in 1973–75, the latter's four-stroke was generally faster and clearly more powerful, but the two-stroke offered superior braking and handling. MV left the scene in 1976, when its bike was making just over 100hp to Yamaha's 90–95hp. However, it had a new, Ferrari-inspired flat-four four-stroke under development, offering the promise of 110hp. Had MV's engineers enjoyed the further benefit of today's four-stroke technology, their 500 might have made over 160hp – a power way beyond the reach of the two-strokes of the time.

Yet had that power been conferred upon MV by an angel of future technology, the engineers would have

been even less able to translate it into GP success than they were with their own 100hp effort. As MV riders of the early 1970s closed the throttle and began braking, engine braking caused rear tyre hop, which became slides as the machines leaned into turns. Traditional short-travel suspensions had to be stiff enough not to bottom, so the bikes hopped and skipped over irregular surfaces, abusing the tyres with extra heat. The grip of early slicks twisted tubular-steel chassis, causing such chatter that treaded tires had to be used at the front, even at some sacrifice of grip. Conventional suspension dampers – then just sophisticated door closers – were overfaced by 500 racing's new intensity. Their damping fluid and internal air mixed to form a bouncy 'whipped cream' that encouraged violent weave at high speeds.

We humans cling to traditional solutions until the pain of their failure becomes unbearable. That's what happened in chassis, tyres and suspension in the 1970s, and the result was a flood of new technologies that were forced into being by horsepower climbing rapidly past 100. The first wheat to fall before evolution's ruthless cutter-bar was the narrow, treaded, hard rubber tyre, which was replaced first by Dunlop's wide, almost featureless Daytona tyre of 1974, then by Goodyear's true slick and ultimately by a general rush to slick designs for all dry racing. Wheels rapidly grew wider to properly support rear tyres that were eight inches wide.

Next was conventional suspension, which had long prospered under the rubric of 'That which moves least, handles best'. In its place there was much softer, long-travel suspension, able to soak up the greater suspension forces of the new machines, which spent so much time on only one wheel. With it came dampers pressurised by sealed gas cells, which delivered better control of damping, since they eliminated 'whipped cream'.

Steeply rising tyre grip made steel 'broom-handle' tube chassis derisory. In the 1980s, nearly all makers switched to large-section, twin aluminium beam chassis, with larger, stiffer forks and swing-arms.

As engine power rose through 150hp, traditional bias-construction tyres began running too hot to last more than seven laps. In 1984, Michelin led the switch to semi-radial construction and the cooler running it offered.

When, at last, raceable four-stroke production motorcycles began to reach the market in the mid-1980s, all of the aforementioned technologies were ready for application to them. Up to that time, powerful four-stroke production bikes, like the Kawasaki 'Z', Suzuki GS and Honda CBs, had really been oversized examples of 1960s technology. The combination of lighter, more capable liquid-cooled four-strokes in two-stroke-inspired chassis created a new future.

A central two-stroke problem – whether we consider engines for submarines, heavy trucks or racing motorcycles – is high piston temperature. In four-strokes, combustion occurs every other time the piston reaches TDC, allowing plenty of time for the piston to transmit its heat to the cooler cylinder wall. In two-strokes, it takes place twice as often. If that extra heat is not extracted from the piston, it may become too hot to be lubricated and will seize. In addition, by overheating the fresh mixture, a hot piston provokes combustion knock. For this reason, cylinder liners made of iron, a poor heat conductor, were abandoned in early 1960s two-strokes in favour of thin hard coatings plated directly on to the aluminium cylinder, which promoted rapid heat transfer. When four-stroke development created its own piston temperature problems, this technology was also employed, saving some three kilos of weight in the process.

During the 1970s, urban air pollution required social legislation to improve the control of combustion in all its

engine was planned to peak at 22,000rpm, a speed for which Honda already had good combustion research. Unfortunately, it required pistons that were able to survive peak reversal accelerations of 11,000 g – only now being attained in F1. That is a higher rate of acceleration than that of a shell fired from an eight-inch artillery piece – and the forged-steel shell (the gun's 'piston') survives it only once. In the end, the NR reached 136hp at 19,000rpm, but the two-strokes – lighter, more powerful and more reliable – had moved out of reach.

Today, we think of traction control as being a very modern concept, but in fact it was the special problems of the 500 GP two-stroke that forced engineers to improve engine smoothness. Smooth power allows the rider to match it accurately to available traction, but power with steep peaks and dips compels the rider to deal with sudden traction loss. In 1989, 500s were coming off corners in a hectic series of alternating slide-outs and hard hook-ups, each threatening to be the Big One. In 1990, corner exits became suddenly smoother and much more secure, thanks to torque smoothing from altered ignition advance curves for the first three gears. This same technique of passive smoothing would be applied to the Honda RC211V in 2002–03 by Jeremy Burgess. Beginning in 1978, Yamaha and then the other makers broadened and smoothed two-stroke power with variable exhaust-port height systems. In the 1990s, Honda injected water into the pipes of its NSR500s, cooling the exhaust gas by evaporation, lowering the speed of sound within and making the pipes resonate from as low as 6,000rpm. When 990cc four-stroke power pushed MotoGP bikes out of shape in the 21st century, engineers already had plenty of experience with the kinds of technologies required to deal with it.

Two-strokes were relatively cheap to develop because the major tools were manual ones: the die-grinder for porting changes; the hacksaw and welding torch for exhaust pipe shape and length; and the lathe for cylinder head shape. For years, paddocks resounded into the night with the whine of die-grinders and the 'pop' of acetylene torches being lit. Today, the only trackside engine work is performed on laptop computers – no one fettles engines at race tracks because the task has become too specialised. We have lost the opportunity for many to work with primary variables easily and relatively cheaply. Yamaha's 1965 250 production racer sold for £740 rising to about £1,160 for 1973's more complex version and £2,600 in 1980. Greater complexity pushed the last TZ250s over £16,000, and many times that sum is now rumoured for a full 250 programme from Aprilia. What had been an attractive proposition for many had evolved into a costly speciality for a very few. Somewhere on this curve of rising cost and complexity, it became cheaper for the privateer to bypass the 250s and begin racing on a £4,500 600 Supersport bike with £1,600-worth of basic modifications

In leaving behind the two-stroke era, we are losing an innocence – a time of technical mysteries initially as likely to be solved by individuals as by factories. Years of R & D put that behind us – at the top level, privateers no longer exist. Today, engineers know so much about every smallest detail of racing that the question is no longer what to do, but rather which of many possible research directions will yield the greatest effect for the money spent. This process has created enormous machine sophistication and, for those in the know, understanding. Here is the pay-off. Racing and production bikes are closely related. That allows factories to recoup some of the costs of racing by applying its technologies to next year's production machines. Let us hope it stays that way.

Above: Changing carburettor jets and settings on Kallio's 250 KTM.

Above left: Last of a long line – the rider's view of the Yamaha TZ.

Top: Harald Bartol, two-stroke believer.

Right: Aprilia's terminal 250 engine, a staggered-crank V-twin with clearly visible rotary-valve inlets.

Photographs: Neil Spalding

forms. Simple two-strokes, wasting 30 per cent of their fuel from transfer to exhaust during scavenging, needed a new technology. Because that technology did not appear soon enough, two-stroke road bikes were all but eliminated.

The needed technology is direct fuel injection (DFI). If, instead of scavenging the cylinder with the fuel/air mixture, we scavenge it with pure air, then add fuel only when the exhaust port has closed, we eliminate the two-stroke engine's major emissions problem. Then it becomes a very attractive, low-friction, low-emissions engine capable of delivering excellent fuel economy. Today such DFI two-strokes are to be found in some outboards, personal watercraft and snowmobiles.

The big problem with DFI in two-strokes is forming an evaporated, ignitable mixture in the cylinder in just a fifth of a crank revolution – much less time than is available in a four-stroke. That required the development of a new and unusual kind of injector that was capable of delivering the fuel charge very quickly and breaking the fuel into fast evaporating, much smaller-than-normal droplets, preferably no larger than ten microns.

Such injectors were developed, but they came too late to prevent the phasing out of two-strokes from the road-going fleet by 1985. Today, the rapid, fine-particle-size injection technology has found a new application in direct-injection four-stroke engines, such as Cadillac's highly-efficient and powerful CTI V6.

An infrequently discussed aspect of the two-stroke era in GP racing was that two-stroke development was less resource intensive and therefore accessible to even quite small organisations. Because two-strokes did not require the development of high-speed valve mechanisms, individuals such as Erv Kanemoto, Kel Carruthers and Jan Witteveen could build winning engines without requiring major R & D budgets. A cadre of experienced two-stroke experimenters came into being, and their work rapidly increased two-stroke capability.

In the late 1970s, Honda attempted to stem the tide of two-stroke dominance with its V4 NR500 oval-piston, eight-valve four-stroke, but success required piston alloys and design practices that had not yet evolved. The

GORGEOUS GEORGE

Not since Rossi has a premier-class rookie made the same sort of impact as Jorge Lorenzo. No surprise to the Spaniard, however. Thanks to visualisation techniques, he'd seen it (and a whole lot more) before. MICHAEL SCOTT charts the rise of the self-assured Yamaha rider.

RACERS have always talked about 'the combination'. It means having everything right: the bike, tyres, mentality, talent, confidence...

And, after Rossi, if you want to be a really successful modern racer, also the showmanship. It's no good just winning, and then grinning broadly and waving. To make the most of your business of racing, you need to put on a show.

Jorge Lorenzo has understood this. His 'Lorenzo's Land' flag is a studied response. Not for him the Disneyesque caricatures beloved of Rossi. Being Spanish, Lorenzo is both more earnest and more grandiose. More theatrical: when he wore a Roman costume on the rostrum to celebrate his second 250 title, it was the genuine article from the film *Gladiator*. And more enigmatic, as when he turned up with an identically dressed and helmeted doppelganger at Le Mans in 2007.

It is all exactly as befits a young man whose hobby is acting and who attends a drama class in English when he's at home at his flat in Chelsea, London.

More proof, if any were needed, that Jorge is not just a bloke who discovered he was pretty handy at riding a motorcycle, went racing and achieved success. Far from it. Lorenzo's world championship career has been planned and plotted ever since his early childhood.

His father, José Manuel (popularly known as 'Chicho'), began grooming him for the role soon after he could walk. 'When I was three years old, my father built me a bike – because he was a mechanic and didn't have money to buy one. I started to compete in minicross. When I was seven, I dedicated myself completely to motorbikes.'

The training, at home on the island of Majorca, was deadly serious, including rehearsals of how to behave on the rostrum and mock Press interviews. 'We used to play a lot of games, me and my father, to do with racing. Sometimes we would do an interview, something like that. But it was only a game, for when I wasn't riding,' Jorge affirms.

Later Chicho revealed his obsessive streak to the world with a book describing his methods, entitled *Asi Se Prepara Un Futuro Campion* (*Thus a Future Champion is Prepared*), published by Hispano Europa. But early in his GP career, as he switched from 125s to 250s, Jorge made a career step of his own, abandoning the family mentorship. 'When I was a child, until 17, my model, my inspiration to become a man was my father. And my dad was ... so introverted. And I was like him. And when I became free, I was more open to the people round me.'

Jorge joined the small stable of compatriot and ex-racer Dani Amatriain, then making a name as a riders' manager. The pair went on to take two 250 titles and move to MotoGP, but by the end of 2008, Amatriain had run into personal difficulties, and Lorenzo was the first of his riders to abandon ship, signing up with a new manager for the future. He also abandoned the racing number 48, which he had used during his time with Amatriain, and held a lottery among his fans to decide on a replacement for 2009.

Jorge was a pioneer of the new breed of 15-year-old GP racers. The minimoto, 50cc and 125cc junior champion could hardly wait. He became the youngest

Left: 'Look into my eyes. Not around my eyes …'

Below: Lorenzo's first GP, at Jerez, 2002.

Below left: The stunt is theatrical, the *Gladiator* gear genuine. San Marino, 2007.

Bottom right: Le Mans, 2008, and Lorenzo (second), Rossi (first) and Edwards (third) celebrate a Yamaha clean sweep.

Photographs: Gold & Goose

ever rider to take part in a World Championship in 2002, at Jerez. He had to miss the Friday qualifying because he didn't turn 15 until the Saturday. A Caja Madrid Derbi was warmed up and waiting: he qualified 33rd and finished 22nd.

He won his first GP in 2003, three more the next year, finishing fourth overall. Then he moved up to 250s. Others making the same move were Dovizioso (who had won the 125 title), Stoner and Barbera. Lorenzo, riding a Fortuna Honda, narrowly failed in his quest to become the youngest-ever race winner in the class at 18. It was not for want of trying. So hard, in fact, that twice he clashed physically with de Angelis, the second occasion (at Motegi) earning him a one-race suspension and the rebuke of having 'ridden in an irresponsible manner causing danger to other riders'. There had been, officials explained, 'cumulative infringements'.

This enhanced his reputation as – well, being rather feisty. In his 125 days, more than once he'd taken a swing at his mechanics, hurled his helmet around the pit or stormed off in a huff. I asked him about it, back at the start of 2006. He explained manfully, 'When things are bad, I [he makes the sound of an explosion]. But I am better now. I try to improve all the time, not only as a pilot, to go faster and faster. I like to im-

prove my person with other people – how I speak with them, and mechanics…'

True to his word, three years later, Jorge had earned a pit-lane reputation for being not only egotistical, but also a very dedicated professional. Behind the pits also, the charm offensive had been sustained. Lorenzo makes time for his fans and the Press, gives thoughtful interviews and plays the game thoroughly. In this, he has improved upon the example of his racing hero and role model, Max Biaggi, whose serial success in the 250 class he had watched on TV as a child. 'He was the first person I was watching. I really like him, you know, and I want to become like him.'

He didn't match Max's run of four 250 titles, however. But he did dominate 250s for two years before moving on. He won eight races in 2006 and nine in 2007, chased all the way by Dovizioso. By then, he'd already been snapped up by Yamaha, and he joined the premier class right in the cat-bird seat, as Rossi's team-mate.

After three years of the amenable – and, importantly, slower – Edwards alongside him, Rossi was less than impressed. When I asked him, he was typically impish. 'I think it is too soon for him to be in this class,' he replied seriously, before bursting into laughter. You can draw your own conclusions.

Jorge's start in the class was stunning. He was on pole for the first three races, on the rostrum at the first two, and the winner of the third. This drew comparison with a similar debut by Jarno Saarinen, with similar statistics, in 1973. In fact, genius Finnish racer Saarinen won two of the first three races, but was killed at Monza during the fourth round, one of the greatest tragedies of grand prix racing. A cruel, but in fact much kinder fate awaited the precocious Lorenzo.

Things turned nasty after that win. He had hasty surgery to his right forearm to cure arm-pump, then suffered a massive high-side crash in China that fractured one ankle and tore ligaments in the other. In a wheelchair, but undeterred, he was back the very next day. He qualified on the second row and finished a strong fourth. At the next round, in France, he crashed twice again in practice, but raced through from 11th to second, back on the rostrum. Condition notwithstanding, he gave sea-

soned MotoGP riders a brutal refresher course in overtaking techniques – in his fifth race.

At the time, he told me that he preferred pain to not racing: 'I keep pushing mentally. I have the passion to conquer this moment. I am a rider and I love the bikes, so it is difficult for me to watch a race, to watch on TV and not to participate, not to be there and to try to be in front.' And when he is out there? 'It is always a fight of two minds. One says, "Only finish"; the other says, "You can try and stay with them."'

Lorenzo relies on a mental approach, having learned visualisation techniques at his father's knee. 'You just have to be clear, and you can be there. If you think you can do it, maybe you do it. If you don't think this, it is for sure that you are not going to do it,' he explains. 'I have always imagined my success for the future. Anyway, 50 per cent of the time, I don't get it. I imagined I could win in my first year. The difference is to produce this imagination to reality, to a real race.'

So he also relies on his talent, of which – with some justification – he speaks highly. The new-generation MotoGP 800s are not too easy to ride, he says, as Rossi and some others have suggested. This is not the reason for his early success, and similar for fellow rookie Dovizioso. At the first tests, he had been two seconds off the pace, he said. But by the first race, he was able to set pole.

'I respect Rossi's opinion,' he said. 'But I think if a rider is fast, he is fast on all bikes. If you look at Max Biaggi, in his first 500 race – pole position and he won.

'For me, it was quite easy at the beginning. I had good tyres and a good bike, and other riders had some difficulties. I had the tools to win or to get on to the podium. Then, as the other riders advanced, they had the tools more than me. In the middle of the championship, the situation changed and it was the opposite. We had problems and others were fast.'

The problems were the series of crashes – two more spectacular and injurious ones at Catalunya and Laguna Seca, another at Mugello. They did slow him down a bit, he admits; he settled himself before coming on stronger again by the end of the year. 'I don't know if I am riding better now,' he told me at the end of the year. 'But for sure more safe, and more fast.'

And for sure more famous. Fame is natural enough, given his speed and his results, but Jorge has managed to take it further than that. He is savvy to the media, and knows there is room only for one Spanish rider at the peak of Spanish popularity. Because of this, he did not shrink from a public spat with Dani Pedrosa at the start of the year. It had to do with the fact that Pedrosa had ignored him on the rostrum at Qatar. 'I should have thought I deserved some acknowledgement,' Lorenzo told Spanish reporters. By the time they got to Jerez for the next round, it took the intervention of the King of Spain to make the pair give each other grudging congratulations.

'I am tired of speaking about our relationship,' Jorge told me later. 'I would like to have a good relationship with him, and with everybody, but it is not always possible.' Then he added cannily, 'For me, it's a good thing, to be fighting with Pedrosa for example, because this fight will become something in Spain. Our fight makes racing even more popular in Spain.'

Lorenzo is part of the Hispanicisation of racing, an inevitable consequence of the Dorna take-over, which has gone hand in hand with the national passion of the people. Spain is hardly new to bike GP racing. Like Pedrosa and Elias, Jorge is one of a number of riders whose careers have been favoured and nurtured on the GP ladder, always with the best machinery and the best sponsorship. The lollipop he sucks every time he stands on the rostrum, for instance, represents years of backing by the manufacturer of the Chupa Chups sweet. And the accumulation of a tidy sum of money.

But Lorenzo is more than merely Spanish and talented. It's difficult to believe that he would not have got to the same place, even without special favour. After all, he was working on it long before Dorna became involved with racing, with a degree of professionalism inculcated by his equally dedicated father. Racing isn't just a sport: racing is everything. And racing success is achieved both on and off the motorcycle.

'I am not only interested in races. In win and win, like … other riders. Some riders only want to ride and to win. I think in this sport, you need to be good in relationships with the Press and the fans, and not only riding the bike – to be professional, and also to be a good person. If you only want to win, and you are selfish and you don't want to demonstrate your emotions for the people, you don't grow up professionally.'

Above: Three poles in a row … and a first MotoGP win to follow. Portugal, 2008.

Top: Lorenzo turned 15 during the Spanish GP of 2002, so he had to miss the first day of practice.

Left: The number 48 will go, but not the lollipop helmet.

Photographs: Gold & Goose

TEAM-BY-TEAM

MOTOGP REVIEW

2008 Teams and Riders

MATTHEW BIRT

Illustrations

ADRIAN DEAN

FIAT YAMAHA TEAM

TEAM STAFF

Lin JARVIS: Managing Director,
Yamaha Motor Racing

Masao FURUSAWA: Executive Officer,
Yamaha Engineering Operations

Masahiko NAKAJIMA: Team Director

VALENTINO ROSSI PIT CREW

Davide BRIVIO: Team Manager

Jeremy BURGESS: Crew Chief

Mechanics:
Bernard ANSIAU
Alex BRIGGS
Brent STEPHENS
Gary COLEMAN (assistant/logistics)
Hiroyami ATSUMI: Yamaha Engineer
Matteo FLAMIGNI: Telemetry

JORGE LORENZO PIT CREW

Daniele ROMAGNOLI: Team Manager

Ramone FORCADA: Crew Chief

Mechanics:
Walter CRIPPA
Javier ULLATE
Valentino NEGRI
Juan Llansa HERNANDEZ (assistant/logistics)
Takashi MORIYAMA: Yamaha Engineer
Carlo LUZZI: Telemetry

VALENTINO ROSSI
Born: 16 February, 1979 – Urbino, Italy
GP Starts: 210 (150 MotoGP/500cc, 30 250cc, 30 125cc)
GP Wins: 97 (71 MotoGP/500cc, 14 250cc, 12 125cc)
World Championships: 8 (5 MotoGP, 1 500cc, 1 250cc, 1 125cc)

JORGE LORENZO
Born: 4 May, 1987 – Palma de Mallorca, Spain
GP Starts: 111 (17 MotoGP, 48 250cc, 46 125cc)
GP Wins: 22 (1 MotoGP, 17 250cc, 4 125cc)
World Championships: 2 (250cc)

THE word 'team' should be used loosely to describe Yamaha's official factory effort in 2008. While both Valentino Rossi and Spanish sensation Jorge Lorenzo ran in the colours of Fiat Yamaha, the team effectively operated as two completely separate entities.

Rossi's success in personally engineering a switch to Bridgestone tyres – while Lorenzo would remain on Michelin for his rookie campaign – necessitated the introduction of a dividing wall within the garage to separate the two sides. The barrier was enforced to prevent any leak of intellectual property between the rival tyre factories, and thus forced Yamaha into a major team re-structure to accommodate the situation.

Masao Furusawa remained the figure-head and close confidant of Rossi in his role as executive officer of Yamaha Engineering Operations. Masahiko Nakajima was moved to the newly-created position of team director, overseeing both Rossi and Lorenzo, while also being charged again with project leader duties for the YZR-M1. That freed previous incumbent Kouichi Tsuji to return to Japan as senior engineer, allowing him to focus on technical developments to avoid a repeat of the humiliation Yamaha and Rossi had suffered in 2007. Shigeto Kitigawa remained as general manager of the Technical Development Division.

The reshuffle saw former team director Davide Brivio work exclusively with Rossi, being responsible for the Italian's side only, which included Rossi's all-conquering technical crew, headed by legendary Australian crew chief Jerry Burgess.

Colin Edwards's former crew chief, Daniele Romagnoli, was

YAMAHA M-1

SPONSORS & TECHNICAL SUPPLIERS: Wudy • Acer • KerSelf • Michelin • Bridgestone • Blauer • Fastweb • Alpinestars • DID • NGK • Magneti Marelli • Beta • Brembo • 2D
Öhlins • Marchesini • Flex • KeraKoll

ENGINE

Type: 800cc, across-the-frame, in-line 4; irregular firing intervals, DOHC, 4 valves per cylinder, pneumatic valve return system. • Power: Around 225bhp at 1,8250rpm

Ancillaries: Magneti Marelli electronics, NGK sparking plugs, full electronic ride-by-wire • Lubrication: Yamalube

Transmission: Gear primary drive, multi-plate dry slipper clutch, six-speed constant-mesh cassette-type gearbox, DID chain

CHASSIS

Type: Fabricated aluminium twin-beam (Rossi short swing-arm version to suit Bridgestones) • Weight: 148kg • Dimensions: Length, 2,050mm; wheelbase, 1,440mm; height, 1,140mm; width, 645mm • Fuel: 21 litres

Suspension: Öhlins TTxTR25 48mm forks front; TTxTR44 shock with linkage rear • Wheels: Marchesini 16in front (16.5in for Bridgestone); 16/16.5in rear • Tyres: Michelin/Bridgestone

Brakes: Brembo carbon-carbon 320mm front; Yamaha steel rear

installed as Lorenzo's team manager, while Ramon Forcada was recruited from LCR Honda to help mould the double world 250 champion's copious potential.

Overseeing both was Lin Jarvis in his unchanged role as managing director of Yamaha Motor Racing.

Stung by a woeful maiden 800cc campaign, Yamaha had worked tirelessly over the winter to meet Rossi's demands for a much-improved YZR-M1 machine. His threat at the end of 2007 had been unequivocal – build a better bike or he would quit at the end of 2008.

Under the glare of the Qatar floodlights and the media spotlight, Rossi was conspicuous by his absence from the podium on his much-hyped Bridgestone debut. He was winless going into the fourth race in Shanghai, and the knives were being sharpened just at the point when he embarked on another record-breaking spree. He romped to a sixth MotoGP title, while becoming the most successful premier-class rider in history for good measure.

Free from the distraction of the tax scandal that had deflected much of his attention from the track at the back end of 2007 – he had settled at 35 million euros in February – Rossi claimed the first of nine wins in China. At ease with running his own affairs, having split from his long-serving management company, Great White London, run by the aloof Gibo Badioli, he negotiated a new two-year Yamaha contract himself, which was announced at Laguna Seca.

Laguna kicked off a run of five successive wins, during which he surpassed Giacomo Agostini's all-time 500/MotoGP wins record of 68. Win number 69 came in a storm-hit Indianapolis race, and he finished with a record points tally of 373, 16 podiums in 18 races; the only blot on his copybook was a first-lap crash in Assen – he remounted and finished 11th.

The dividing wall actually might have worked in favour of Lorenzo, who, cocooned in his own half of the garage, could focus solely on his own riding and solving his own problems. The start of his rookie campaign affirmed why Rossi had appeared so reluctant to have the Spaniard join him at Yamaha. Three successive poles and then a maiden victory in only his third race, in Estoril, emphasised why Yamaha had signed him as far back as 2006.

The bubble burst quickly next time out in China, however, when Lorenzo was the victim of a sickening high-side, which left him unable to walk unaided for several weeks. He had caught the eye with swashbuckling and cavalier displays, but when he tumbled heavily again at Le Mans, he fought back to produce a memorable display of overtaking to finish second. He would suffer further painful crashes in Catalunya and Laguna Seca, enduring severe concussion in Spain that ruled him out of the race.

Having swept to the triple crown in 2008, winning the rider, team and constructor titles, Yamaha also had reason to celebrate post-season. Fiat had been intent on renewing its title sponsorship for another two years as negotiations were concluded in September, but as the global credit crunch began to hit the automotive industry hard, the Italian giant suddenly reassessed its marketing strategy. A withdrawal seemed inevitable, but Malaysian fuel and oil giant Petronas was waiting in the wings. Then, in early November, Fiat finally signed for 2009 and 2010.

REPSOL HONDA TEAM

TEAM STAFF

Masumi HAMANE: HRC President
Kosuke YASUTAKE: Managing Director
Kazuhiko YAMANO: Team Manager
Roger VAN DER BORGHT: Co-ordinator

NICKY HAYDEN PIT CREW

Pete BENSON: Chief Mechanic

Mechanics:
Mark LLOYD
Craig BURTON
Koji KAMINAKABEPPU
David GUITTEREZ
Yuji KIKUCHI: Tyres
Ramon AURÍN: Telemetry
Hiroki AZAWA: Showa
Hirohito YOSHIKI: HRC Engineer

DANI PEDROSA PIT CREW

Mike LEITNER: Chief Mechanic

Alberto PUIG: Crew Chief

Mechanics:
Jordi PRADES
Mark BARNETT
Christophe LEONCE
Masashi OGO
John EYRE: Tyres
Jose Manuel ALLENDE: Telemetry
Manuel OLIVENCIA: Showa
Masato NAKATA: HRC Engineer

NICKY HAYDEN
Born: 30 July, 1981 – Owensboro, USA
GP Starts: 99 (MotoGP)
GP Wins: 3 (MotoGP)
World Championships: 1 (MotoGP)

DANI PEDROSA
Born: 29 September, 1985 – Sabadell, Spain
GP Starts: 130 (52 MotoGP, 32 250cc, 46 125cc)
GP Wins: 29 (6 MotoGP, 15 250cc, 8 125cc)

ONCE the most feared and revered team in MotoGP racing, the Repsol Honda team found itself creating headlines for all the wrong reasons for the majority of 2008.

Honda's official factory squad had undergone a major management reshuffle at the end of 2007 as HRC sought new direction and leadership following a disastrous first attempt at the 800cc era. Respected HRC managing director Satoru Horiike had been relieved of his duties before the end of 2007, his replacement, Kosuke Yasutake, being a much more subdued figure. Kazuhira Yamano, a former mechanic to Mick Doohan, who had served under Jerry Burgess, was given the thankless task of being team manager; while HRC President Masumi Hamane was in his first full year in the position.

Hamane was a much more frequent paddock visitor than predecessor Suguru Kanazawa. Having presided over some of the most turbulent times to affect Honda's once-dominant squad, Hamane announced his intention to step down in 2009; Tetsuo Suzuki will assume the hot seat.

The year could not have started in worse fashion. Number-one rider Dani Pedrosa broke his right hand on the opening day of testing in Sepang, and it was immediately apparent that a new pneumatic-valve-spring V4 motor, built under the guidance of RC212V project leader Shinichi Kokubu, was woefully lacking in performance. Kokubu was relieved, while replacement Takanori Okuma barely lasted a year in the job.

The new motor wasn't ready until June, when veteran test

HONDA RC212V

SPONSORS & TECHNICAL SUPPLIERS: Michelin • Bridgestone • Brembo • NGK • RK • Showa • Showa • Denko • Snap-On • MIVV

ENGINE
Type: 800cc, 77-degree V4; 360-degree crank, DOHC, 4 valves per cylinder, pneumatic valve return system (Hayden from British GP; Pedrosa from Indianapolis) • Power: Over 225ps
Ancillaries: HRC electronics and ride-by-wire throttle and fuel injection system, NGK sparking plugs • Lubrication: Repsol
Transmission: Gear primary drive, multi-plate dry slipper clutch, six-speed constant-mesh cassette-type gearbox, RK chain

CHASSIS
Type: Fabricated aluminium twin-tube • Weight: 148kg • Dimensions: Length, 2,050mm; wheelbase, 1,440mm; height, 1,130mm; width, 645mm • Fuel: 21 litres, Repsol
Suspension: Showa 47mm forks front; gas shock with linkage rear • Wheels: Enkei 16in front (16.5in for Bridgestone); 16/16.5in rear

Tyres: Michelin/Bridgestone

Brakes: Brembo carbon-carbon 314/320mm front; HRC steel 218mm (Hayden 255mm) rear

© ADRIAN DEAN

TADAYUKI OKADA

Born: **13** February, 1967 – Ibaragui, Japan
GP Starts: **115** (71 MotoGP/500cc, 44 250cc)
GP Wins: **6** (4 500cc, 2 250cc)

rider Tadayuki Okada raced it to a respectable 14th in Mugello to obtain reliability and performance data, most notably on fuel consumption.

By that time, with five podiums in the first six races, including a trademark runaway win in Jerez, Pedrosa was leading the World Championship. Another victory in Barcelona, followed by further podiums at Donington and Assen, kept him ahead of Valentino Rossi.

With half the season completed and Pedrosa leading the standings, HRC began to harbour genuine hopes of a sustained title challenge. Those hopes were quickly extinguished in a rain-lashed Sachsenring race, however, when the Spaniard crashed out while holding a commanding lead of nearly seven seconds. His injuries forced him to withdraw early at Laguna Seca, less than a week later, and his title challenge wilted from that moment.

What followed tested Honda's patience to breaking point, but also highlighted the extent to which the Japanese management had surrendered control to Pedrosa and his maverick mentor and manager, Alberto Puig.

As Michelin's tyres struggled badly in Brno, Hamane himself endorsed Pedrosa's planned – but not implemented – face boycott. The Spaniard, who was working in tandem with crew chief Mike Leitner again, then demanded a switch to Bridgestone tyres, amid rumours that he had threatened to go AWOL unless his wishes were granted.

Honda and Bridgestone, with much behind-the-scenes collusion by Repsol and Dorna, agreed to strike a hasty deal that saw the factory team become the second to be split by a dividing wall.

Pedrosa ran Bridgestones for the last five races, but failed to win any. And he was the subject of more unwanted attention in the final throes of the season, when Puig launched a needless and bitter verbal attack on Nicky Hayden. He was reprimanded by Honda and warned sternly about his future conduct.

Hayden had long known that 2008 was to be his swansong at Honda. Working again with crew chief Peter Benson, the 2006 world champion had been told at the British GP that he was surplus to requirements, Andrea Dovizioso having been signed to take his seat. It was at the same race that Hayden finally had persuaded Honda to give him the pneumatic-valve-spring motor to race after weeks of fruitless pleading.

The controversy surrounding Pedrosa's switch to Bridgestone galvanised Hayden, who had been left out of the deal. He didn't finish outside of the top five in the last five races, in a confidence-restoring run that included two podiums and three front-row starts. His podium at home in Indianapolis was his first for 15 months, but he was due for pastures new in 2009.

Having been notified of his release in late June at Donington Park, Hayden immediately began pursuit of the Ducati ride alongside Casey Stoner. It might seem a poisoned chalice to some, but Hayden was undaunted by Marco Melandri and Toni Elias's struggles. His move to the Bologna factory was confirmed immediately after the Indianapolis race, and he went straight into Ducati duties, making a guest appearance at a dealer conference.

Above: Full factory strength – the Repsol Honda team.

Top: Pedrosa out alone, as he liked it best.

Centre: HRC President Masumi Hamane (*left*) and MD Kosuke Yasutake.

Bottom left: Pedrosa and chief mechanic Mike Leitner.
Photographs: Gold & Goose

DUCATI MARLBORO TEAM

TEAM STAFF

Claudio DOMENICALI: Managing Director

Livio SUPPO: Project Manager

Francesco RAPISARDA:
Communications Director

Amadeo COSTA: Team Co-ordinator

Davide BARALDINI:
Warehouse & Components

CASEY STONER PIT CREW

Cristian GABARRINI: Race Engineer

Bruno LEONI: Chief Mechanic

Mechanics:
Roberto CLERICI
Andrea BRUNETTI
Giorgio CASTURA
Lorenzo GAGNI

Gabriele CONTI: Electronics Engineer

MARCO MELANDRI PIT CREW

Christhian PUPULIN: Race Engineer

Davide MANFREDI: Chief Mechanic

Mechanics:
Massimo MIRANO
Michele PERUGINI
Mark EDLER
Luciano BERTAGNA

Marco FRIGERIO: Telemetry

CASEY STONER

Born: 16 October, 1985 – Southport, Australia

GP Starts: 113 (52 MotoGP, 31 250cc, 30 125cc)

GP Wins: 23 (16 MotoGP, 5 250cc, 2 125cc)

MARCO MELANDRI

Born: 7 August, 1982 – Ravenna, Italy

GP Starts: 173 (97 MotoGP, 47 250cc, 29 125cc)

GP Wins: 22 (5 MotoGP, 10 250cc, 7 125cc)

World Championships: 1 (250cc)

DOMINATING as it had done in the inaugural 800cc campaign, Ducati's factory squad was always going to find it difficult to replicate the incredible accomplishment of winning the triple crown in 2007. And so it proved, Casey Stoner being beaten resoundingly to the individual honour by a resurgent Valentino Rossi, and Ducati surpassed by Yamaha's transformed YZR-M1.

A phenomenal 2007, in which the Bologna factory had embarrassed its Japanese rivals for the first time, saw Ducati sticking to the winning formula for 2008. Senior management and the backbone of the team remained unchanged, with Filippo Preziosi remaining an essential element of Ducati's assault in

his role as technical director. Further up the power chain, Claudio Domenicali remained and ran Ducati Corse, while Gabriele Del Torchio was in his second year as Ducati's president. The most visible of Ducati's management structure was project manager Livio Suppo, who filled a multitude of roles, which included consultant on rider selection for the satellite squad.

Inevitably, Stoner's crew remained identical to 2007, when he'd salvaged his reputation as a prolific crasher to win ten races in a cruise to his maiden world title. Again, Stoner worked closely with long-time crew chief Cristian Gabarrini, whom he trusted and respected implicitly, while electronics engineer Gabriele Conti and chief mechanic Bruno Leoni were almost

DUCATI DESMOSEDICI GP8

SPONSORS & TECHNICAL SUPPLIERS: Alice • Shell Advance • Bridgestone • Sandisk • Enel • Riello • ups • Alfa Romeo • AMD • Bosch • Breil • Magneti Marelli • NGK • Regina Chains • SKF • Termignoni • USAG

ENGINE

Type: 800cc, 90-degree V4; 360-degree crank, DOHC, 4 valves per cylinder, desmodromic valve gear, variable-length inlet tracts • Power: Around 225bhp, revs to 19,500rpm

Ancillaries: Magneti Marelli electronics, NGK sparking plugs, full electronic ride-by-wire • Lubrication: Shell Advance

Transmission: Gear primary drive, multi-plate dry slipper clutch, six-speed constant-mesh cassette-type gearbox, Regina chain

CHASSIS

Type: Multi-tube adjustable steel trellis, aluminium swing-arm • Weight: 148kg • Dimensions: N/a • Fuel: 21 litres, Shell

Suspension: Öhlins TTx20 42mm forks front; TTx36 shock with linkage rear • Wheels: Marchesini 16.5in front; 16/16.5in rear

Tyres: Bridgestone • Brakes: Brembo carbon-carbon 320mm front; steel 200mm rear

constant companions during the pit-box technical debriefs.

In the fiery Aussie, Ducati had a devastatingly quick rider, and a more rounded individual after his 2007 domination. Yet again, he was the only rider capable of posing a serious threat to Rossi, and his final tally of 280 points is a record for a runner-up.

Stoner started in ominous fashion with victory in Qatar, but then a series of nightmares had virtually dropped him out of title contention by the British GP. His early-season slump had been hardly of his own doing. A broken Dorna camera transponder had hindered him severely in Estoril, and he had suffered his first Ducati no-score at Le Mans with an engine failure.

He forced his way back into contention with rampant wins at Donington, Assen and the Sachsenring, but a demoralising defeat by Rossi in Laguna Seca was followed by successive crashes in Brno and Misano. Both came while he was leading and coming under attack from Rossi, and the spills delivered a mortal blow to his hopes of mounting a successful title defence. He did bounce back to win two of the last three races while contending with the aggravating pain of a left wrist injury that had been caused in 2003 and that had flared up again in Misano.

Stoner was even more of a one-man band than he'd been in 2007, with Marco Melandri finding the task of taming the Ducati completely unfathomable. Having inherited the crew that had failed to help Loris Capirossi conquer the GP7, Melandri struggled even more; crew chief and technical co-ordinator Christhian Pupulin failed to make any significant progress in easing his discomfort.

Rumblings that Melandri's two-year contract would be torn up early emerged after only three races, and when John Hopkins was injured in Assen, the Italian volunteered to split with Ducati to take the vacant Kawasaki until the American was fully fit again.

It was confirmed in Germany that Melandri and Ducati had reached an amicable agreement to terminate their contract after just one season, but Suppo pledged to persevere with the dumbfounded Italian for the remainder of the season. After the summer break, he was part of a three-way reshuffle that almost came off.

In the wake of leaks that Melandri had secretly tested the ZX-RR at the Autopolis facility during the summer break, Kawasaki agreed to axe Anthony West in favour of him. This would have given Ducati the chance to bring in veteran Spaniard Sete Gibernau, who was hankering for a return after retiring at the end of 2006. The deal collapsed only in the final stages of negotiation. Melandri ended the season with just one top-six finish, and on six occasions, he scored no points.

Ducati again proved in 2008 that it was constantly driven by innovation. The season hadn't even reached the half-way stage when Preziosi rolled out a prototype version of the GP9, resplendent with carbon-fibre chassis. Alan Jenkins had a heavy influence on the concept in his role as aerodynamicist, while Ferrari Formula One expertise was also employed.

In Japan, the bosses also exhibited their penchant for adopting unconventional strategies, when Ducati seriously flirted with the idea of a dramatic switch to Michelin tyres for 2009 in a bid to head off the implementation of the controversial single-tyre rule.

Above: Melandri skims the kerb.

Top: The 'red army' at full strength.

Top right: Project manager Suppo.

Left: Stoner's men – chief mechanic Bruno Leone, and (far left) race engineer Cristian Gabarrini.

Below left: Melandri in conference with Pupulin and Suppo.

Photographs: Gold & Goose

TECH 3 YAMAHA

TEAM STAFF

Hervé PONCHARAL: Team Manager

Gérard VALLEE: Team Co-ordinator

Eric REBMANN: Parts Manager

Olivier BOUTRON: Fuel/Tyres

COLIN EDWARDS PIT CREW

Gary REYNDERS: Crew Chief

Mechanics:
Jerôme PONCHARAL
Josian RUSTIQUE
Lauren DUCLOYER
Andrew GRIFFITH: Telemetry

JAMES TOSELAND PIT CREW

Guy COULON: Crew Chief

Mechanics:
Benoît BRUNEAU
Alexandre DUPONT
Julien LAJUNIE
Nicolas GOYON: Telemetry

COLIN EDWARDS
Born: 27 February, 1974 – Houston, Texas
GP Starts: 102 (MotoGP)
World Championships: 2 (World Superbike)

JAMES TOSELAND
Born: 5 October, 1980 – Sheffield, UK
GP Starts: 18 (MotoGP)
World Championships: 2 (World Superbike)

Photographs: Gold & Goose

A MICHELIN tyre deal, closer links to Yamaha and the arrival of two world champions in the form of Colin Edwards and James Toseland injected fresh impetus into the Tech 3 Yamaha team as it embarked on its eighth MotoGP campaign. Based in France, the squad had seen its fortunes flounder in recent years, having spent 2006 and 2007 struggling to remain competitive on Dunlop tyres.

Without the technical equipment needed to run consistently close to the front, team boss Hervé Poncharal had found it increasingly more challenging to attract investment, and again the team operated without a title sponsor. Smaller investment came from the likes of Wudy and KerSelf in cross-over deals

from the official factory team.

Poncharal had also found the task of hiring top-calibre riders difficult, but double World Superbike champions Edwards and Toseland were arguably the team's strongest line-up since Olivier Jacque and Shinya Nakano had ridden together in 2003.

Edwards was still contracted directly with Yamaha in Japan, and his experience proved invaluable to the factory and Michelin during winter testing. With Toseland and factory rider Jorge Lorenzo being rookies, much of the tyre testing legwork fell to Edwards. He was also an unsung hero for Yamaha, providing vital feedback and information in late 2008 while Valentino Rossi recovered from a wrist injury.

TECH 3 YAMAHA M-1

SPONSORS & TECHNICAL SUPPLIERS: Motul • Michelin • NEC • Pollini • Wudy • KerSelf

ENGINE

Type: Type: 800cc, across-the-frame, inline 4; irregular firing intervals, DOHC, 4 valves per cylinder, initially steel valve springs, then pneumatic valve return system

Power: Around 225bhp at 1,850rpm • Ancillaries: Magneti Marelli electronics, NGK sparking plugs, full electronic ride-by-wire • Lubrication: Yamalube

Transmission: Gear primary drive, multi-plate dry slipper clutch, six-speed constant-mesh cassette-type gearbox, DID chain

CHASSIS

Type: Fabricated aluminium twin-beam • Weight: 148kg • Dimensions: Length, 2,050mm; wheelbase, 1,440mm; height, 1,140mm; width, 645mm • Fuel: 21 litres

Suspension: Öhlins TTxTR25 48mm forks front; TTxTR44 shock with linkage rear • Wheels: Marchesini 16/16.5in front; 16/16.5in rear • Tyres: Michelin

Brakes: Brembo carbon-carbon 320mm front; Yamaha steel rear

Striking an instantly successful relationship with crew chief
Gary Reynders, Edwards revelled in the best GP form ever in the
first half of the season. Without the pressure to deliver results
prevalent in the factory team, he was rejuvenated and only off
the front row once in the opening five races, which included
pole position in front of China's sparsely populated grandstands.
A third in a Yamaha podium clean sweep at Le Mans was
matched by the same result in fortuitous circumstances in
Assen, where he benefited from Nicky Hayden's cruel luck in the
dying seconds.

Such an impressive start earned Edwards a new deal with
Tech 3 after he'd quickly dismissed previous thoughts that 2008
would be his last season in MotoGP. He had talked briefly with
Kawasaki, and had been Troy Bayliss's recommendation as his
replacement in Ducati's World Superbike squad. Edwards
agreed fresh terms in Germany, however, and the deal was
made official at his home race in Laguna Seca.

The announcement, though, coincided with a sudden and
alarming slump in form. Edwards could only manage a best of
tenth in the next four races. By the time the circus arrived in
Japan, Yamaha bosses were not happy and communicated their
displeasure directly to him in a frank meeting. The Texan was
told he might be switched with Ben Spies, who had just signed
with Yamaha's WSB squad. After this, Edwards recovered his
form and ended with sixth in Valencia.

Toseland had arrived as Britain's best hope for MotoGP success in years, and he started in stunning fashion. He claimed a
debut front row in Qatar and finished within inches of Valentino
Rossi, in sixth. When he raced through a debilitating bout of
bronchitis to sixth in Jerez, Tech 3 and Yamaha moved quickly
to exercise a September-deadline option on the Englishman. He
was signed for 2009 at the third race in Portugal, although for
the remainder of his rookie year his fortunes fluctuated.

He scored six top-six finishes, one from an inspired ride at
Phillip Island, where he diced for a time with Valentino Rossi
and Jorge Lorenzo. The undisputable low point was a disastrous
British GP, where he had been given star billing in front of a
record crowd. A first-corner crash saw him finish 17th with only
one footrest. Toseland was often impressive, but he earned a
reputation for being over-aggressive at times. Andrea Dovizioso
questioned his tactics in Jerez, Le Mans and Phillip Island, while
others passed comment on his robust style.

Toseland's 11th in Valencia secured fourth place for Tech 3
in the coveted Team World Championship table, ahead of
Suzuki's factory squad by a single point, and the distinction of
being top independent team.

Having previously raced together for Castrol Honda, Toseland
and Edwards gelled instantly, and Tech 3 arguably had the most
harmonious garage in the pit lane. That was until the final round
in Valencia at least. The atmosphere in the team was soured
when it emerged that a change of crew chiefs had been reluctantly sanctioned by Poncharal. Toseland had been growing increasingly concerned about communication with the hugely
experienced Guy Coulon. As the season wore on, his confidence
in the relationship grew more fragile and he instigated a switch
in Sepang. Reynders supported the transfer too, so for 2009
Coulon will work with Edwards, who was incensed.

RIZLA SUZUKI

TEAM STAFF

Fumihiro OOHNISHI: Group Leader
Paul DENNING: Team Manager
Howard PLUMPTON: Operations Manager
Shinichi SAHARA: Technical Manager
Keiichiro FUKUZAWA: Engine Development
Tetsuya SASAKI: Chassis Development
Davide MARELLI: ECU Control Assistance
Tex GEISSLER: Data Analysis
Richard FRANCIS: Sub-assemblies
Russell JORDAN: Parts and Logistics
Tim WALPOLE: Press Officer

CHRIS VERMEULEN PIT CREW

Tom O'KANE: Chief Mechanic

Simon WESTWOOD: Crew Leader

Mechanics:
Tsutomo MATSUGANO
Ray HUGHES
Mark FLEMING (assistant)
Renato PENNACCHIO: Telemetry

LORIS CAPIROSSI PIT CREW

Stuart SHENTON: Chief Mechanic

Ian GILPIN: Crew Leader

Mechanics:
George DZIEDZIC   Jeffrey OH
Jez WILSON (assistant)
Gary McLAREN: Telemetry

LORIS CAPIROSSI
Born: 4 April, 1973 – Bologna, Italy
GP Starts: **282** (171 MotoGP/500cc, 84 250cc, 27 125cc)
GP Wins: **29** (9 MotoGP/500cc, 12 250cc, 8 125cc)
World Championships: **3** (1 250cc, 2 125cc)

CHRIS VERMEULEN
Born: 19 June, 1982 – Brisbane, Australia
GP Starts: **54** (MotoGP)
GP Wins: **1** (MotoGP)
World Championships: **1** (World Supersport)

HAVING enjoyed its best MotoGP campaign for seven years in 2007, Suzuki saw little reason to tamper with its successful and tight-knit factory team. The single and obvious change came in the arrival of lion-hearted Italian veteran Loris Capirossi, who ended his Ducati misery to replace the departing John Hopkins.

Again, the team was under the stewardship of Briton Paul Denning, who had become a well-established paddock figure, having cut his management teeth in the British Superbike arena prior to 2005. Senior Japanese management also remained the same for 2008, with Fumihiro Oohnishi fulfilling the role of group leader once more, while Shinichi Sahara was technical manager.

Rizla filled the role of title sponsor for a third season, although by the end of the year, the global credit crunch had cast doubt over an extended deal. It was deep into November before a decision was expected, and Rizla already had ceased its backing for Suzuki's British Superbike team after a long and successful partnership.

Capirossi slotted straight into the squad that had run Hopkins, with Suzuki stalwart Stuart Shenton heading the triple world champion's crew. Shenton had guided Schwantz to

SUZUKI GSV-R

SPONSORS & TECHNICAL SUPPLIERS: Brembo • Bridgestone • 2D • Öhlins • Lumberjack • Motul • Mitsubishi • Yoshimura • Kokusan • Denki • Toyo Radiator • MAG Tools • RK Chain
DID • NGK • AFAM • Puig Racing Screens • DAF • Dread

ENGINE

Type: 800cc, 75-degree V4; 360-degree crank, pneumatic valve return system • Power: Around Around 210bhp
Ancillaries: Mitsubishi electronics, NGK sparking plugs, electronic ride-by-wire • Lubrication: Motul
Transmission: Gear primary drive, multi-plate dry slipper clutch, six-speed constant-mesh cassette-type gearbox, RK chain

CHASSIS

Type: Fabricated aluminium twin-beam • Weight: 148kg • Dimensions: Length, 2,600mm; wheelbase, 1,450mm; height, 1,150mm; width, 660mm • Fuel: 21 litres, Elf
Suspension: Öhlins TTx20 42mm forks front; TTxTR44 shock with linkage rear • Wheels: JB Magtan 16.5in front; 16/16.5in rear • Tyres: Bridgestone
Brakes: Brembo carbon 305 or 314mm front; steel rear

BEN SPIES
Born: 11 July, 1984 – Memphis, USA
GP Starts: 3 (MotoGP)

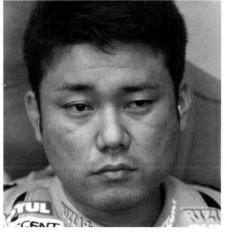

KOUSUKE AKIYOSHI
Born: 12 January, 1975 – Kurume, Japan
GP Starts: 3 (MotoGP)

NOBUATSU AOKI
Born: 31 August, 1971 – Sumaga, Japan
GP Starts: 168 (111 MotoGP/500cc, 57 250cc)
GP Wins: 1 (250cc)

Suzuki's last title in 1993.

Chris Vermeulen's side was also unchanged, with Tom O'Kane serving as crew chief for the Aussie, who remains the only Suzuki victor in the modern four-stroke era.

Hopes that stability and continuity would yield more success never fully materialised, however, the 2008 GSV-R scoring only three podium finishes.

Vermeulen was the team's most successful rider again, although his two podiums came hardly out of the blue. He claimed third in the Sachsenring race in Germany in the rain-soaked conditions in which he usually flourishes. He equalled that result at Laguna Seca, a favourite circuit for him and the GSV-R V4.

In a year when Suzuki's machine development stagnated somewhat, Vermeulen's future became a hot topic around mid-season. Andrea Dovizioso was constantly being linked with Suzuki, but protracted talks led to Vermeulen agreeing to a one-year contract extension in Misano.

Capirossi claimed one rostrum, in Brno, as he took full advantage of Michelin's embarrassing failure to supply competitive tyres, yet his future was never really in serious doubt. With wily manager Carlo Pernat pulling the strings, the Italian was believed to have had a new deal in place as early as June, but the renewal of his contract wasn't announced until Vermeulen's, in a joint statement issued between Misano and Indianapolis.

Capirossi's year was severely interrupted by an injury-hit mid-season. He was taken out in Catalunya, and a broken right hand forced him to withdraw from the British GP. His misfortune opened the door for American Superbike champion Ben Spies to make his MotoGP debut earlier than anticipated at Donington Park. He qualified in a superb eighth in the wet and finished in a respectable 14th.

Capirossi returned in Assen, only to suffer a grotesque puncture wound in his right arm when a footpeg pierced his leathers and skin during a vicious high-side suffered in practice. Spies was already in Holland, but incredibly declined the chance to step in at the 11th hour. His refusal was met with howls of derision in the paddock and some bewilderment at Suzuki, although the American redeemed himself somewhat with impressive top-eight finishes in wild-card appearances at Laguna Seca and Indianapolis.

His performances, though, were not enough to seal the permanent berth with Suzuki he so desperately craved. The manufacturer had crushed hopes of Jorge Martinez leasing a third GSV-R when Japanese management informed Dorna boss Carmelo Ezpeleta in Le Mans that it wouldn't be extending its participation to three bikes in 2009.

Spies eventually had to move to World Superbikes with Yamaha to fulfil his aspirations away from America.

Suzuki employed more riders in competition than any other squad, although test rider Kousuke Akiyoshi's experience was a short-lived affair, his wild-card appearance in Japan lasting just three corners before he high-sided out. Veteran tester Nobuatsu Aoki also wild-carded in Sepang, testing prototype parts for the 2009 GSV-R. He finished 17th.

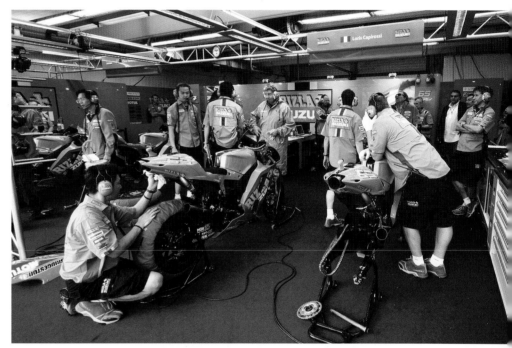

Above, from left: Stuart Shenton, Tom O'Kane, Paul Denning.

Above centre: Above centre: Blue, but not rhapsodic – the Suzuki garage.

Left: Left: Aoki's year-end bike had a silenced exhaust.

Photographs: Gold & Goose

SAN CARLO GRESINI HONDA

TEAM STAFF

Fausto GRESINI: Chairman &
Managing Director

Carlo MERLINI: Commercial &
Marketing Director

Fabrizio CECCHINI: Technical Director

SHINYA NAKANO PIT CREW

Antonio JIMENEZ: Chief Mechanic

Mechanics:
Andrea BONASSOLI
Ryoichi MORI
Alberto PRESUTTI
Jonny DONELLI (assistant)
Diego GUBELLINI: Telemetry

ALEX DE ANGELIS PIT CREW

Fabrizio CECCHINI: Chief Mechanic

Mechanics:
Simone ALESSANDRINI
Ivan BRANDI
Marco GASTALDO
Renzo PINI (assistant)
Francesco FAVA: Telemetry

SHINYA NAKANO
Born: 10 October, 1977 – Chiba, Japan
GP Starts: 167 (133 MotoGP/500cc, 34 250cc)
GP Wins: 6 (250cc)

ALEX DE ANGELIS
Born: 2 February, 1984 – Rimini, Italy
GP Starts: 148 (18 MotoGP, 65 250cc, 65 125cc)
GP Wins: 1 (250cc)

FAUSTO Gresini's satellite Honda squad had seen its fortunes plummet in recent years, and 2008 was to mark an all-time low in the history of the Rimini-based squad. For the first time in nine attempts in MotoGP, Gresini's team failed to notch a podium finish, and its once unrivalled status as the leading satellite squad diminished further.

Running in the new colours of San Carlo – an Italian snack-food manufacturer that was the team's fourth major backer in as many years – Gresini opted for a blend of youth and experience in 2008.

The eager, but occasionally over-exuberant Alex de Angelis was signed for his rookie campaign, and while he showed

flashes of inspiration, his season was punctuated with mistakes, which even drew criticism from Gresini himself. Working under the guidance of technical director Fabrizio Cecchini, the San Marino rider had two inspirational races, on both occasions progressing from tenth on the grid to fourth. The first, in Mugello, would have preserved Gresini's podium record had it not been for a woeful start, while the second was equally impressive as he surged through at a soaked Sachsenring.

There were only three other races, though, in which de Angelis managed top-ten finishes. Otherwise, his was a campaign littered with errors. One indiscretion forced Loris Capirossi to miss the British GP after a tangle at Catalunya,

GRESINI HONDA RC212V

SPONSORS & TECHNICAL SUPPLIERS: Castrol • Bridgestone • Agos • Morellato • Manpower • Domino •Berner • Leo Vince • Milwaukee

ENGINE

Type: 800cc, 75-degree V4; 360-degree crank, steel valve springs

Power: Over 210ps • Ancillaries: HRC electronics and ride-by-wire throttle and fuel injection system, NGK sparking plugs • Lubrication: Castrol

Transmission: Gear primary drive, multi-plate dry slipper clutch, six-speed constant-mesh cassette-type gearbox, RK chain

CHASSIS

Type: Fabricated aluminium twin-tube • Weight: 148kg • Dimensions: Length, 2,050mm; wheelbase, 1,440mm; height, 1,130mm; width, 645mm • Fuel: 21 litres

Suspension: Showa 47mm forks front; gas shock with linkage rear • Wheels: Enkei 16.5in front; 16/16.5in rear • Tyres: Bridgestone

Brakes: Brembo carbon-carbon 314mm front; HRC steel 218mm rear steel rear

while another crash narrowly avoided taking out Valentino Rossi at Phillip Island.

Many saw de Angelis as an unpolished diamond, however, and he had been linked with the Alice Ducati team before he extended his Gresini deal shortly before the inaugural Indianapolis GP.

Seasoned Japanese campaigner Shinya Nakano provided the experience as he worked under crew chief Antonio Jiminez. Gresini had been reluctant to hire the former Kawasaki rider, although he relented at the behest of HRC management, who insisted on the Japanese rider remaining within its stable.

Nakano was a model of consistency and had the proud record of finishing all 18 races. Only once did he fail to score points too, and he ended with a best of fourth place in Brno.

One thing that remained steadfast in 2008 was Gresini's close and rock-solid relationship with Honda. Despite floundering results, the team is still held in high regard by the Japanese manufacturer, and further proof was provided in Brno, where Nakano started the first of seven races aboard a full-factory-spec RC212V machine. His results hadn't warranted such an elevation in equipment, and there were frayed tempers elsewhere, most notably from Andrea Dovizioso, who considered himself a much more worthy recipient.

Nakano's best results were on the factory V4, and while he and Gresini refuted the suggestion, it was thought that Nakano had been given the bike to assess its performance on Bridgestone rubber for Dani Pedrosa.

There was further evidence of Honda's close link to Gresini in the latter stages of the season. As previously with Sete Gibernau and Marco Melandri, Honda agreed to supply a factory RC212V for 2009, a move that lured Toni Elias away from a third Kawasaki ride with Jorge Martinez.

Elias's return to Gresini after a year with the Alice Ducati squad left Nakano frozen out. He was in the frame for that same Kawasaki ride, but Martinez's Spanish investors had little interest in investing in Nakano, and the deal collapsed.

Nakano eventually signed a deal to join Max Biaggi in Aprilia's factory Superbike team.

Above: Undivided pit garage combined youth and experience.

Top right: Team principal Fausto Gresini.

Top left: De Angelis had moments of sheer inspiration.

Centre left: Crew chiefs Cecchini (*left*) and Jimenez.

Left: Nakano lit up on the grid at Qatar.
Photographs: Gold & Goose

KAWASAKI RACING TEAM

TEAM STAFF

Ichiro YODA: Racing Director
Michael BARTHOLEMY: Competition Manager
Naoya KANEKO: Technical Manager
Danilo CASONATO: EFI Engineer
Andrea DOSOLI: EFI Technician
Marcel DUINKER: Suspension Engineer
Tim DE BOT: Suspension Technician
Rob ROSTON: Parts and Logistics
Eddie HENRY: Engine Technician
Ian WHEELER: Marketing & Communications

JOHN HOPKINS PIT CREW

Fiorenzo FANALI: Chief Mechanic

Mechanics:
Benoit LEFEBVRE
Florian FERRACCI
Jason CORNEY
Robert KLEINHERENBRINK
Gerold BUCHER: Telemetry

ANTHONY WEST PIT CREW

Juan MARTINEZ: Chief Mechanic

Mechanics:
Emanuel BUCHNER
Jerome GALLAND
Pedro CALVET Alex DUINKER
Emmanuel ROLIN: Telemetry
Francesco FAVA: Telemetry

JOHN HOPKINS
Born: 22 May, 1983 – Ramona, USA
GP Starts: 111 (MotoGP/500cc)

ANTHONY WEST
Born: 17 July, 1981 – Maryborough, Australia
GP Starts: 136 (43 MotoGP/500cc, 92 250cc, 1 125cc)
GP Wins: 1 (125cc)

Photographs: Gold & Goose

K AWASAKI'S factory team was to have made its major MotoGP breakthrough in 2008. The first 800cc ZX-RR had been a surprise performer in 2007, and with the big-money signing of John Hopkins and the promise of significant technical developments, expectancy had been heightened ahead of the first race. By year's end, however, Kawasaki had been humiliated both on and off the track, Hopkins and Anthony West scoring 62 fewer points between them than Andrea Dovizioso had done on his own at JiR Scot Honda.

Competitions manager Michael Bartholemy and technical director Ichiro Yoda were forced to contend with the regular sight of a ZX-RR at or close to the back of the field in most races. Yoda, ZX-RR project leader Yoshimoto Matsuda and technical manager Naoya Kaneko were unable to extract any major per-

formance gains from the in-line four, and an ambitious attempt to roll out a Screamer in-line four-cylinder motor also backfired. Its exhaust note resonated like a Formula One car off the grandstands when it broke cover in testing at Sepang, but it was a futile exercise that was quickly abandoned when it became clear that the motor didn't yield any performance improvements.

Working under crew chief Fiorenzo Fanali, who would retire at the end of the season, Hopkins had a morale deflating and injury-hit campaign that seriously hindered development. On the other side of the garage, Australian Anthony West couldn't grasp his golden opportunity with a factory-team, after years of toil on uncompetitive machinery.

Hopkins's reputation had flourished in 2007 during his last year at Suzuki, but his hopes of repeating that form at Kawasaki

KAWASAKI ZX-RR

© ADRIAN DEAN

SPONSORS & TECHNICAL SUPPLIERS: Monster • Elf • Bridgestone • Akrapovic • FCC • Touch 4 • Magneti Marelli • AXIO • AFAM • DC • EK Chains • NGK • Nichirin • 2D • Beta • Flex • 3M

ENGINE

Type: 800cc, across-the-frame, in-line 4; irregular firing intervals, DOHC, 4 valves per cylinder, pneumatic valve return system
Power: 215bhp • Ancillaries: Magneti Marelli electronics, NGK sparking plugs, electronic ride-by-wire • Lubrication: Elf
Transmission: Gear primary drive, multi-plate dry slipper clutch, six-speed constant-mesh cassette-type gearbox, EK chain

CHASSIS

Type: Fabricated aluminium twin-beam • Weight: 148kg • Dimensions: Length, height and width n/a; wheelbase 1,420mm (adjustable) • Fuel: 21 litres, Elf
Suspension: Öhlins TTx20 42mm forks front; TTx36 shock with linkage rear • Wheels: JB Magtan 16.5in front; 16/16.5in rear • Tyres: Bridgestone
Brakes: Brembo carbon-carbon 320mm front; steel rear

JAMIE HACKING

Born: 30 June, 1971 – Oswaldtwistle, UK

GP Starts: 1 (MotoGP)

were derailed. He suffered a massive crash in the rain during testing at Phillip Island, and would find out weeks later that the accident actually had broken his hip. Then he received cracked vertebrae in another big crash at Catalunya, and after that was lucky to escape far more serious injuries at Assen, where he lost control of his ZX-RR at 175mph at the fifth-gear Ramshoek left-hander. Mercifully he careered into a wooden Cinzano advertising hoarding feet first. He broke his left ankle and bones in his right leg, but was thankful to have got off relatively lightly considering the nature of the high-speed tumble.

A best of fifth at Estoril was one of only four top-ten finishes, although Hopkins did claim a front-row start at Brno, only to plummet to 11th in the race. He was also embroiled in one of the stories of the season when he failed to ride on the opening day at Misano. A lingering rib injury was the 'official' reason, but the paddock was awash with speculation amid allegations that he had gone on a late-night drinking binge as a result of personal problems.

West, who had earned his slot at Kawasaki after impressing in the second half of 2007, when he had stepped in to replace the retiring Olivier Jacque, also had a nightmare campaign. He worked with Spanish crew chief Juan Martinez, who previously had masterminded nine premier-class victories for Sete Gibernau, but the only result of any note was an impressive fifth at Brno, just as he was learning that his contract for 2009 would not be renewed.

Hopkins's injury misfortune did open the door for British-born American Superbike stalwart Jamie Hacking to make a shock MotoGP debut at Laguna Seca at the age of 37. Chaz Davies and Roger Lee Hayden had been considered, but Kawasaki America wanted veteran Hacking, and he certainly didn't disgrace himself. He qualified 17th and came through to a respectable 11th.

Kawasaki's bid to quickly erase 2008 and plot a 2009 revival took many forms throughout the year and was, to say the least, a drawn-out and complicated process. Andrea Dovizioso and Alvaro Bautista had been prominent candidates, but as in 2007, Kawasaki had maintained close tabs on Marco Melandri, and the Italian was duly signed at Indianapolis.

Promising talent Bautista remained a contender through his connection with Jorge Martinez, who had run the Spaniard in the 250cc World Championship. For most of the season, Kawasaki flirted with the idea of running a third factory bike for 2009, if only to accelerate development. Bartholemy campaigned and lobbied tirelessly to bring the project to fruition, and with Martinez having Spanish investors; the prospects seemed favourable, despite the gloomy economic climate.

But Bautista refused to leave 250s, while Toni Elias rejected the offer. With the plan on the brink of collapse, Kawasaki said it would lease the bike, but with the stipulation that the rider had to be previous Kawasaki incumbent Shinya Nakano. The directive came all the way from the top in the powerful form of President Shinichi Tamba, who held lengthy meetings with Bartholemy at the Japanese GP.

The nomination of Nakano cooled the interest of the Spanish investors, however, and the plan had collapsed by the end of the season.

Kawasaki shuffled personnel at the end of the season too, Fanali departing. Kaneko moved to become Hopkins's crew chief, while former Team Roberts chief engineer Tom Jojic was signed to make a full-time return to the paddock. Jojic had worked with test and development rider Olivier Jacque throughout 2007, and his new role is to act as a link between the crews and Japanese engineers as Kawasaki seeks to improve communication between its on-track team and factory staff developing new parts in Japan.

Above: West's crew chief, Juan Martinez.

Top right: West shone occasionally in the wet.

Centre left: Michael Bartholemy (*above*) and Ichiro Yoda faced many puzzles.

Centre right: A troubled first Kawasaki year for Hopkins.

Photographs: Gold & Goose

ALICE DUCATI

TEAM STAFF

Felix RODRIGUEZ: Logistic Co-ordinator

Fabiano STERLACCHINI: Technical Director

Manuel CESSEAUX: Ducati Electronics Engineer

Liam SHUBERT: Warehouse & Components

TONY ELIAS PIT CREW

Fabiano STERLACCHINI: Race Engineer

Marco BALEIRON: Chief Mechanic

Mechanics:

Paul RUIZ

Thomas LANTES

Pedro RIVERA

Jose CONTRERAS: Electronics Engineer

SYLVAIN GUINTOLI PIT CREW

Sergio VERBENA: Race Engineer

Martin ZABALA: Chief Mechanic

Mechanics:

Michele ANDREINI

David LOPEZ CACHEDA

Francesco GALINDO

Andrea OLEARI: Telemetry

TONY ELIAS

Born: 26 March, 1983 – Manresa, Spain

GP Starts: 145 (62 MotoGP, 48 250cc, 35 125cc)

GP Wins: 10 (1 MotoGP, 7 250cc, 2 125cc)

SYLVAIN GUINTOLI

Born: 24 June, 1982 – Montelimar, France

GP Starts: 117 (37 MotoGP/500cc, 80 250cc)

A SEASON that promised so much ultimately delivered so little for Ducati's satellite team. There was a struggle for results on track that was cast against a backdrop of controversy and upheaval behind the scenes.

The Madrid-based Pramac d'Antin effort was in its fifth year of association with Ducati, and the arrival of Toni Elias and Sylvain Guintoli, coupled with Alice running as title sponsor, hinted at a bright future.

Again, team management duties fell to Spaniard Luis d'Antin, who had formed his squad in 1997, while ownership was shared with Pramac CEO Paolo Campinoti, who ultimately would become a much more prominent figure as events unfolded during the year.

Elias was the team's number-one rider, and he was assigned to technical director Fabiano Sterlacchini, while Guintoli arrived looking to build on a series of impressive performances aboard the Dunlop-shod Tech 3 Yamaha in 2007. The Frenchman worked under the guidance of Sergio Verbena, who had served previously as a data technician to veteran Brazilian Alex Barros.

Once more, Ducati placed extra emphasis on its desire to forge closer links to the satellite squad, and Manuel Cessaux was an electronics engineer who worked directly for the Bologna factory, but exclusively with the Alice-backed squad.

Elias and Guintoli, though, did little to dispel the myth that the GP8 was a bike that only Casey Stoner could master. Be-

ALICE DUCATI DESMOSEDICI GP7

SPONSORS & TECHNICAL SUPPLIERS: Telecom Italia • Pramac • Corvera • Bridgestone

ENGINE

Type: 90-degree V4; 360-degree crank, DOHC, 4 valves per cylinder, desmodromic valve gear • Power: Around 225bhp, revs to 19,500rpm with variable-length inlet system (from Sachsenring on) • Ancillaries: Magneti Marelli electronics, NGK sparking plugs, electronic ride-by-wire • Lubrication: Shell

Transmission: Gear primary drive, multi-plate dry slipper clutch, six-speed constant-mesh cassette-type gearbox, Regina chain

CHASSIS

Type: Multi-tube adjustable steel trellis, aluminium swing-arm • Weight: 148kg • Dimensions: : Length, height and width n/a • Fuel: 21 litres, Shell

Suspension: Öhlins TTx20 42mm forks front; TTx36 shock with linkage rear • Wheels: Marchesini 16.5in front; 16/16.5in rear • Tyres: Bridgestone

Brakes: : Brembo carbon-carbon 320mm front; steel 200mm rear

tween them, they only claimed five top-ten qualifying results, and Elias only five top-ten finishes. He was largely an anonymous figure until he enjoyed a minor revival with successive podium finishes in Brno and Misano. And had he not been black flagged for failing to observe a ride-through penalty for jumping the start in Catalunya, he would have made the chequered flag in every race.

Despite a lacklustre campaign, Elias was still a wanted man, and Jorge Martinez was stunned when in Indianapolis he rejected the chance to ride a third factory Kawasaki ZX-RR. His brief resurgence after the summer break had also prompted Ducati to express an interest in retaining his services, but the temptation of a factory Honda back in Fausto Gresini's satellite squad proved too much and he rejoined the Italian's team on the eve of the Australian GP at Phillip Island.

Guintoli showed his adeptness in wet weather once again. He was seventh in a storm-lashed MotoGP debut at the iconic Indianapolis circuit, but his best result of sixth came in the Sachsenring deluge.

The dark clouds that had loomed large over the German GP summed up a turbulent weekend for the squad. Rumours of d'Antin's shock departure had been confirmed in a short statement at the start of the weekend. A flurry of speculation circulated the paddock – of financial irregularities, unpaid bills and unpaid team personnel. The storm seemed to threaten the existence of the team, but Campinoti stood resolute and vowed that the show would go on.

Logistic co-ordinator Félix Rodríguez was thrust into the limelight as new team manager, and he oversaw the day-to-day running of the team for the remainder of the season, while d'Antin was neither seen nor heard from again.

For 2009, Campinoti's squad will field the most inexperienced riders in MotoGP. The team had eyed the likes of Ben Spies, Sete Gibernau and 250cc World Champion Marco Simoncelli, but two names remained constant on the rumour mill. Finn Mika Kallio was signed from KTM's 250 squad, while Niccolò Canepa's reward for impressive performances as Ducati's test rider earned him a full-time slot.

Both were confirmed officially at the Malaysian GP.

Above: Guintoli on the paint.

Top row, from left: Luis d'Antin, Elias over the line, Fabiano Sterlacchini.

Centre left: Ex-125 racer Stevie Jenkner of Bridgestone.

Left: Elias made the rostrum twice.
Photographs: Gold & Goose

JiR SCOT HONDA

ANDREA DOVIZIOSO

Born: 23 March, 1986 – Forli, Italy

GP Starts: 116
(18 MotoGP, 49 250cc, 49 125cc)

GP Wins: 9 (5 250cc, 4 125cc)

World Championships: 1 (125cc)

TEAM STAFF

Gianluca MONTIRON: Team Director
Cirano MULARONI: Team Manager
Michele MORISETTI: Communications

ANDREA DOVISISO PIT CREW

Gianni BERTI: Technical Co-ordinator
Pietro CAPRARA: Crew Chief
Mechanics:
Emanuele VENTURA Lorenzo CANESTRARI
Fabio GAROIA Filippo BRUNETTI
Bernard MARTIGNAC: Data Recording
Elena GALLINA: Spare Parts

THE only 'new' addition to the 2008 MotoGP grid, JiR Scot Honda actually had been born out of a merger between two existing teams.

Gianluca Montiron had been the leading light behind the formation of JiR for the 2005 campaign, an ambitious project to use Japanese investment and Japanese riding talent to challenge the world. The bold move faltered following the dismal performances of Makoto Tamada and Shinya Nakano, and the loss of Konica Minolta at the end of 2007 forced Montiron into a major re-think.

Scot team boss Cirano Mularoni had stated his intention to move to MotoGP mid-way through 2007, but he had been unable to secure the lease of an RC212V and had had to ponder other options. The solution was a merger that gave Montiron's JiR outfit a stay of execution, while Scot got to realise its MotoGP ambitions.

In truth, Montiron was effectively leasing his infrastructure and place on the grid as he took up the role of team director, with Scot providing the bulk of the investment. Mularoni, in his role as team manager, also promoted the majority of his 250 team into the premier class. Long-term Montiron technical director Giulio Bernadelle departed, and his place went to Gianni Berti, while Pietro Caprara was installed as crew chief.

At least the amalgamation restored the on-track fortunes of JiR, the deal also including the promotion of highly-rated young Italian Andrea Dovizioso, who had won the 2004 125cc World Championship with the Scot outfit and who had been under contract already with Mularoni for 2008.

Dovizioso certainly lived up to the hype, although he gained only one podium, in Sepang. He immediately proved himself an adept racer at the highest level, how-

ever, only once failing to improve his qualifying position in a race. Too often, though, he was unable to overcome the restrictions of racing a satellite Honda. His only blemish was a tumble out of the top five in Estoril.

The London resident ended with ten top-six finishes, and although he flirted with the prospect of moving to Kawasaki and Suzuki factory teams, the likelihood of him of leaving Honda's stable for the first time in his world championship career always seemed remote.

Even before the first race, it was rumoured that Dovizioso had been earmarked for the official Repsol Honda team, and this was confirmed finally at the Japanese GP.

While Dovizioso's future had been sorted out with the minimum of fuss, determining the future of what he'd left behind was far less harmonious.

In Laguna Seca in late July, Scot announced that it was to sever all links with Montiron's JiR operation to pursue plans to run its own effort in 2009. The split effectively left the two factions pursuing the lease of one bike, with Honda insistent that it would not increase the allocation of RC212V machinery beyond the six bikes it had fielded in 2007.

Montiron believed he had an agreement with Honda for 2009, and began talks with interested sponsors and riders. Among the star-studded list were Nicky Hayden, Sete Gibernau and Ben Spies. But Mularoni had an ace up his sleeve and struck the decisive blow by revealing his intention to promote Japanese rider Yuki Takahashi from his 250 team. Honda's insatiable desire to have one of its own in its ranks swung the deal in Mularoni's favour, and it was announced at the Twin Ring Motegi, minutes after Dovizioso's departure to Repsol Honda had been confirmed.

HONDA RC212V

SPONSORS & TECHNICAL SUPPLIERS: HRC •Michelin • Gioco Sicuro • Kopron • Dixell • DID • Beta • Flex

ENGINE

Type: 800cc, 75-degree V4; 360-degree crank, steel valve springs • Power: Over 210ps • Ancillaries: HRC electronics and ride-by-wire throttle and fuel injection system, NGK sparking plugs • Lubrication: Repsol

Transmission: Gear primary drive, multi-plate dry slipper clutch, six-speed constant-mesh cassette-type gearbox, DID chain

CHASSIS

Type: Fabricated aluminium twin-tube • Weight: 148kg • Dimensions: Length, 2,050mm; wheelbase, 1,440mm; height, 1,130mm; width, 645mm • Fuel: 21 litres

Suspension: Showa 47mm forks front; gas shock with linkage rear • Wheels: Enkei 16in front; 16.5in rear

Tyres: Michelin

Brakes: Brembo carbon-carbon 314mm front; HRC steel 218mm rear

LCR HONDA

RANDY DE PUNIET

Born: 14 February, 1981
– Maisons Laffitte, France

GP Starts: 166
(53 MotoGP, 80 250cc, 33 125cc)

GP Wins: 5 (250cc)

TEAM STAFF

Lucio CECCHINELLO: Team Manager
Oscar HARO: PR
Elisa PAVAN: Press Relations

RANDY DE PUNIET PIT CREW

Christophe BOURGIGNON: Chief Engineer

Mechanics:
Joan CASAS Casanovas XAVIER
Chris RICHARDSON
Manolo ZAFFERANI: Telemetry
Atsushi SHIMUZU: HRC Engineer
Hamish JAMIESON: Chassis/Suspension

THE LCR Honda squad's third season in MotoGP and its 13th in the grand prix arena had a sense of 'Friends Reunited'. Highly regarded team owner Lucio Cecchinello had signed Randy de Puniet, who had raced for the Monaco-based outfit on an Aprilia 250 in 2003 and 2004, winning four races. The Frenchman arrived from Kawasaki's factory team with crew chief Christophe Bourgignon, signed to replace the departing Ramon Forcada, who had left to spearhead Jorge Lorenzo's rookie campaign at Fiat Yamaha. Bourgignon was boosted by the arrival of former factory Suzuki and Kawasaki crew chief Hamish Jamieson. Crucially, the pair had in-depth knowledge of bike set-up and, importantly, intimate knowledge of each other's approach, having worked together at the Red Bull WCM squad.

Jamieson had been recruited primarily as an independent suspension technician, following a deal to ditch Showa for Öhlins that had been concluded too late for LCR to have a full-time Öhlins technician at its disposal. Cecchinello actually had bought the Öhlins equipment from the ill-fated Ilmor team.

The season started brightly, with de Puniet qualifying on the first two rows in Qatar and Jerez. On Michelin's impressive qualifying tyres, he performed admirably, claiming a total of nine second-row starts. Optimism that he would build on the promise exhibited in 2007, however, was largely misplaced. On six occasions, he started inside the top ten, but finished outside of that group. Twice he didn't even finish the first lap, although in his defence, his Assen tumble had been caused by an overeager Valentino Rossi. His best result was sixth on a torrid weekend for Michelin at Laguna Seca.

By the end of the year, de Puniet had the unenviable distinction of being MotoGP's most prolific crasher for the third successive season! His final tally was 22, which only took into account the 18 races. He'd almost matched that tally in winter testing alone, and the falls placed extra financial strain on Cecchinello's squad, which again operated without a title sponsor. The Italian had adopted a revenue generating policy that had served well in previous years, having a number of smaller investors, although online betting firm Eurobet was one of the leading backers once more.

A two-year contract meant that de Puniet would return for the 2009 season.

Photographs: Gold & Goose

HONDA RC212V

SPONSORS & TECHNICAL SUPPLIERS: Eurobet • Michelin • Givi • TS Vision • Electronics Discount • Dinamica • Fomindistrie • Deca

ENGINE

Type: 800cc, 75-degree V4; 360-degree crank, steel valve springs • Power: Over 210ps • Ancillaries: HRC electronics and ride-by-wire throttle and fuel injection system, Denso sparking plugs

Transmission: Gear primary drive, multi-plate dry slipper clutch, six-speed constant-meshcassette-type gearbox, RK chain

CHASSIS

Type: Fabricated aluminium twin-tube • Weight: 148kg • Dimensions: Length, 2,050mm; wheelbase, 1,440mm; height, 1,130mm; width, 645mm • Fuel: 21 litres

Suspension: Öhlins TTx20 42mm forks front; TTx36 shock with linkage rear • Wheels: Enkei 16in front; 16/16.5in rear

Tyres: Michelin

Brakes: Brembo carbon-carbon 314mm front; HRC steel 218mm rear

MIKA KALLIO

ALVARO BAUTISTA

MARCO SIMONCELLI

HIROSHI AOYAMA

HECTOR FAUBEL

ALEX DEBON

HECTOR BARBERA

250cc: DOWN, NOT OUT

ENTRIES for the doomed 250 class were down by one compared with 2007, shrinking the grid still further to 24. Even so, it comprised a wide range of machinery and riders, although without the two main players of the year before – both Dovizioso and Lorenzo had gone to MotoGP. Happily, there was still plenty of high-end talent to make for a good year.

The 2007 crop of bright 125 rookies – Luthi, Bautista and Kallio – were joined by three more: Pasini, Faubel and Pesek.

Machine demographics had leant yet further in favour of the Aprilia V-twin at the start of the year – and even more so at the end, when KTM announced its withdrawal. By then, the long-deferred replacement for the 250s had been decided – production-based, so-called 'prototypes', which might even arrive in 2010, a year earlier than planned, as a result of KTM's departure.

In total, and including four Gilera-badged variants, 17 of the bikes on the grid were Aprilias. The balance was made up by three KTMs, one more than 2007, plus three of the all-but-extinct Japanese 250s, two Hondas and one Yamaha. The extra KTM was in Repsol colours, the important sponsor having bowed to the inevitable when Honda, with whom it had had a long-term relationship, declined to supply

factory-level machines.

As always, the Aprilias covered a wide range of quality and performance.

There was an all-new and substantially redesigned factory Aprilia, the RSA, alongside the LE model in all its many variations, ranging from seasoned private bikes that were two or more years old to kitted machines that were the equivalent of the previous year's factory bikes. At the start of the year, the new bikes went to a select group: Bautista, Barbera, Pasini, Luthi and Debon. By mid-season, Simoncelli, who had been beating them all on a top-level LE with a Gilera badge, also had been given an RSA to complete the season.

APRILIA/GILERA

Once again, the highest level of backing, support and expectation went to Jorge 'Aspar' Martinez and his Mapfre-sponsored Aprilia team – part of the Spanish former multi-champion's empire, which extends into the 125 class, although plans to move into MotoGP in 2009 appeared to have stalled.

It was headed by pre-season favourite, Alvaro Bautista from Spain, who carried the hopes of a nation with him. In spite of four wins, however, he was beaten

overall. His team-mate was another Spaniard, who had followed in his footsteps from the same team in the 125 class. Hector Faubel had been narrowly defeated for the title by Talmacsi. His best was a single sixth place.

Lorenzo's old Lotus Aprilia team had brought in veteran campaigner Alex Debon, who had produced several strong wild-card rides for the team in 2007. On one of the five RSAs, he was set for a year of high achievement. He was joined by Aleix Espargaro, in his third year and from Granolliers, right by the Catalunya GP track. His best would be a fifth.

Also favoured with an RSA was the Hungarian Team Toth, which fielded the eponymous principal's son, Imre, in a second 250 year after a long and undistinguished period in 125s, and struggling to make the points. The team retained another fancied Spaniard, Hector Barbera, who was given the factory bike. He faced an adventurous, but winless and ultimately painful season.

The other two-rider team was Blusens Aprilia, a much lower-level affair. Neither of the original riders saw out the full season. Ulsterman Eugene Laverty soldiered on with an uncompetitive bike until he broke bones in his foot in a crash in practice at Indianapolis, after which he gratefully took up an offer in World Supersport, where he

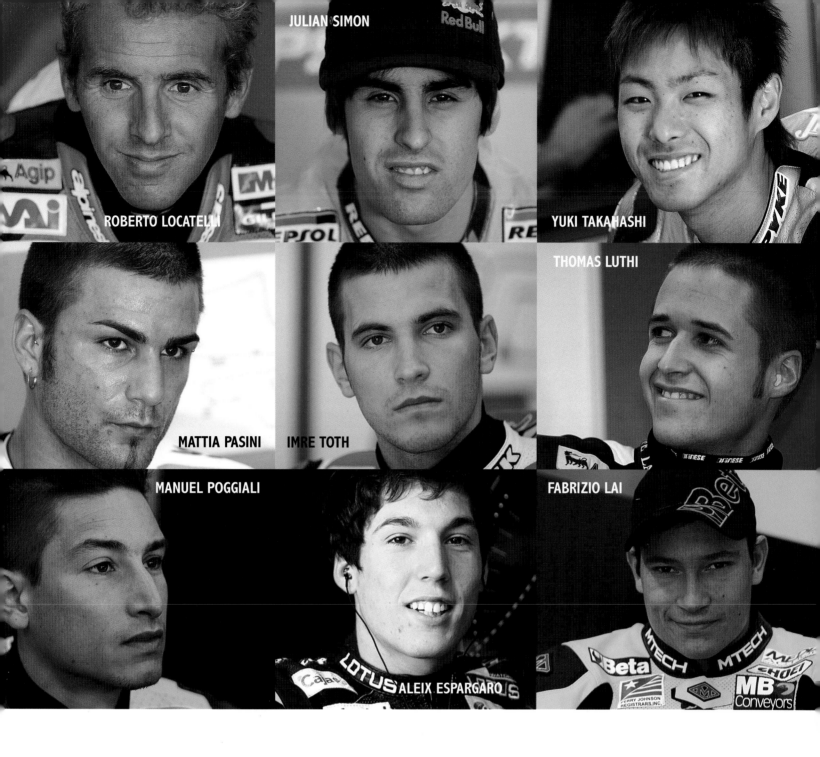

ROBERTO LOCATELLI

JULIAN SIMON

YUKI TAKAHASHI

MATTIA PASINI

IMRE TOTH

THOMAS LUTHI

MANUEL POGGIALI

ALEIX ESPARGARO

FABRIZIO LAI

went straight to the rostrum. He was replaced for the final races by 17-year-old Spanish rookie Daniel Arcas. Another Spanish rookie, Manuel Hernandez, started and ended the season with the team, being replaced for a spell mid-year by Russel Gomez, who never finished in the points.

Two high-level single-rider teams also lined up with strong backing and RSA machines. The backing only just lasted the year for Mattia Pasini. The class rookie won the opening round and was often impressive, but was jobless at year's end after Spanish property development company Polaris World withdrew its sponsorship after three years.

The other factory-bike singleton was former 125 champion Thomas Luthi, from Switzerland, for a second year with the Emmi-Caffe Latte team. Luthi had a downbeat year, relieved by second place at Assen and one other rostrum visit, but marred by injury at Indianapolis, which curtailed his season.

Czech racer Karel Abraham was back for a second year with the Cardion AB Aprilia, claiming a trio of top-ten finishes; compatriot Lukas Pesek was up from 125s, backed by Auto Kelly CP, and outpointed him overall with a marginally more consistent debut season. The final single-rider team was the well-established Matteoni

Racing squad, who fielded experienced mid-field Italian Alex Baldolini.

The Gilera is only nominally a different bike, but the Metis Gilera team was linked to the Aprilia factory and would claim the big prize. It was 21-year-old Italian Marco Simoncelli's second year in the team and his third in the 250 class. His team-mate was veteran and former 125 champion Roberto Locatelli, at 33 deserving the description 'evergreen'. He racked up a string of top tens and a best of fourth.

Two more Gileras went to the well-established Campetella squad, for Italian Fabrizio Lai, the former 125 racer completing his second year in the class, and San Marino's Manuel Poggiali. A former 125 and 250 champion with a very fragile track record, Poggiali achieved a sixth, but lasted only until melt-down at Brno, after which his place was taken by Italian Simone Grotzkyj, a class rookie with two 125 years behind him.

KTM

The official factory Red Bull team, run by Harald Bartol, had the same two riders as 2007. Mike Kallio was in his second year in the class, and the 25-year-old Finn

would mount a serious title challenge in the early part of the season. Hiro Aoyama, from Japan, was in his fifth 250 year, but would not add to his total of five wins.

The third machine was in the hands of Julian Simon. Backed by Repsol on a Honda in 2007, he'd made the switch along with the sponsor. He was often impressive, but never quite made the rostrum.

THE JAPANESE

Of the two Hondas, that of Team Scot's Yuki Takahashi was an RS250-W version, the closest thing to a factory bike, albeit from the previous season. The injury-prone Japanese rider gave the bike a fair send-off, with three rostrum visits.

Fitted with HRC kits, the second surviving Honda was not far off the same specification. Backed by Thai Honda and sponsored by PTT Sag, Ratthapark Wilairot, the 19-year-old Thai rider, was in his second season, and by the end of it was a top-ten regular.

The sole Yamaha was ridden by Indonesian rookie Doni Tata Pradita. He finished once in the points, but the new team suffered a setback when experienced principal Dieter Stappert suffered an ultimately fatal heart attack soon after the middle of the season.

MIKE DI MEGLIO

GABOR TALMACSI

STEFAN BRADL

SIMONE CORSI

JOAN OLIVE

BRADLEY SMITH

125cc: YOUTH VS EXPERIENCE

THE kindergarten class was heaving with a full grid of 34 entries, and a gaggle of young teenagers pitted against the experienced class leaders. Although Faubel, Pasini and Pesek had gone to 250s, defending champion Talmacsi had stayed, as had several other redoubtable class specialists.

The machine numbers echoed the 250 class, with Aprilia taking up the bulk of the entry list, but the number of KTMs was up from three in 2007 to seven. However, the one-time Honda hordes had dwindled to just a single bike.

There was variety up front, with eight different race winners over 17 rounds. Two would rise above the rest: champion di Meglio, who claimed four wins, the same number as his closest challenger, Corsi. Defending champion Talmacsi claimed three late in the year. Teenage son of a GP winner, Stefan Bradl took his first two career wins, the rest being shared one apiece by Terol, Iannone, Gadea and Redding.

APRILIA

Aprilia numbers stood at 21 at the start of the year, with four identical, but rebadged, Derbis alongside. The Italian bikes had won every race but one in 2007,

two falling to Pesek's Derbi.

The ranks were led by the three-rider Aspar team, companion to the 250 squad, but with a different sponsor, Bancaja. Hungarian rider Gabor Talmacsi stayed on to carry the number one, the former boxer a target for all, although early unreliability and later injury would spoil his defence. Team-mate Sergio Gadea also remained, the experienced pair being joined by 17-year-old Spaniard Pere Tutusaus, who replaced Faubel.

Strong competition would come from another smart and well-sponsored team, the two-rider Jack & Jones outfit, and especially from rising 20-year-old Roman Simone Corsi, in his second year back after a 250 season. He would win four races and challenge for the title to the end. Team-mate Nicolas Terol, from Spain, in his fourth season, would also win a race.

The next best Aprilia rider was a bit of a surprise: German Stefan Bradl, the son of former 250 winner Helmut Bradl, was in only his second full season. But his effort and the Grizzly Gas Kiefer machine he rode were to a very high standard. For team-mates, he had fellow German rookie Robin Lasser and Roumanian Robert Muresan, who was in his second season.

The successful Emmi-Caffe Latte team fielded one

rider as usual, the German Sandro Cortese, but a stronger challenge would come from another established one-rider team. Polaris World Aprilia had replaced the departed Pasini with Bradley Smith, in his third season as Britain's bright hope. It was close, but that first win stayed just out of reach.

A new British rising star would emerge, and rather unexpectedly. At 15, Scott Redding was a rank rookie, but the Blusens Aprilia Junior team rider was a gifted natural, not only winning his home GP to become the youngest ever winner, but backing it up with eight more top-tens. He far outranked his fellow rookie team-mate, 21-year-old Efren Vazquez from Spain.

There was a third candidate: Danny Webb was in his second season with the Dutch Degraaf team, but too often luck was against him, and he crashed frequently too. Degraaf was three-strong, with American hope Stevie Bonsey, in his second year after his KTM debut, and Dutchman Hugo van den Berg, the tallest rider in this or any class.

Italian Andrea Iannone would win a race in his third season; his IC Aprilia team-mate, Austrian Michael Ranseder, would end the year injured. A third team-mate was Dorna Academy graduate Takaaki Nakagami from Japan.

STEVIE BONSEY

NICOLAS TEROL

SCOTT REDDING

ANDREA IANNONE

SANDRO CORTESE

SERGIO GADEA

MARC MARQUES

POL ESPARGARO

DANNY WEBB

Three season starters would not make the finish. WTR San Marino team rider Stefano Bianco was replaced by Swiss rookie Bastien Chesaux; Roberto Lacalendola gave way to fellow Italian rookie Marco Ravaioli; while on-again/off-again Dino Lombardi, also from Italy, and his BQR team ran for only part of the season.

DERBI

Only the paint and the name on the tank are changed to turn an Aprilia into a Derbi. In 2008, two teams ran two riders apiece. One of them was a veteran of five years and one GP win, swarthy Frenchman Mike di Meglio, who had staked pretty much everything he owned to get a place in the Ajo Motorsport team. The gamble paid off with a hard-won championship.

His team-mate was Swiss rider Dominique Aegerter, in his second season, who claimed four top-ten finishes.

The second team was the Spanish Belson squad, which had a strong line-up. At 23, Joan Olive was a class veteran, but although he scored three seconds, that first win would remain out of reach. Fellow Spaniard Pol Espargaro, a 16-year-old in his second full season and following in brother Aleix's tracks, would also visit the rostrum three times.

HONDA

Once a mainstay of the class, Honda all but slipped out of the picture through lack of interest and development, former users crossing over to Aprilia. Only one remained faithful, the low-level French federation-backed FFM team, which fielded rookie Louis Rossi, from Le Mans. Name and place ticked the right boxes, but his performance was below par, and before the season was out he had been replaced by another bright French hope, Cyril Carillo, although Rossi returned to replace him after injury at year's end.

KTM

In a year without a win for the Austrian machine, there was a significant shuffle in the ranks, with cheery Japanese former race winner Tomoyoshi Koyama starting with one of the new satellite teams, ISPA KTM Aran, falling out with them mid-season and rejoining the Red Bull factory squad for the last races.

At Red Bull, Koyama joined Swiss rider Randy Krummenacher, up from the junior squad for his second full season. He'd left behind at ISPA – formerly the Seedorf team – 20-year-old Italian Lorenzo Zanetti, and his

place had been taken by Enrique Jerez.

The well-founded Repsol team had also abandoned – or had been abandoned by – Honda, and had switched to KTM with a pair of Spanish riders. Esteve Rabat was in his third year, and was joined by impressive and rostrum-bound rookie Marc Marquez.

The final KTM customer was a new team, Onde 2000, backed by a Spanish self-made millionaire and just warming up to go to MotoGP with Sete Gibernau in 2009. Run by ex-rider Angel Nieto Junior, it fielded his brother, Pablo, in his last season, and experienced Italian Raffaele de Rosa.

LONCIN

If this was the tip of an iceberg, in some ways it was deceptive. With the Chinese motorcycle name of Loncin, this was the Malaguti team reborn and running Honda RS125 clones. They were ridden by experienced Frenchmen Alex Masbou and Jules Cluzel. Masbou finished at the back of the points just three times.

A more enterprising Chinese venture was announced at the Shanghai GP: the Maxtra – an all-new design financed by China, with an engine by the architect of Aprilia's success over many years, Jan Witteveen.

GRANDS PRIX 2008

QATAR GRAND PRIX	62
SPANISH GRAND PRIX	70
PORTUGUESE GRAND PRIX	78
CHINESE GRAND PRIX	86
FRENCH GRAND PRIX	94
ITALIAN GRAND PRIX	102
CATALUNYA GRAND PRIX	110
BRITISH GRAND PRIX	118
DUTCH TT	126
GERMAN GRAND PRIX	134
U.S. GRAND PRIX	142
CZECH REPUBLIC GRAND PRIX	150
SAN MARINO GRAND PRIX	158
INDIANAPOLIS GRAND PRIX	166
JAPANESE GRAND PRIX	174
AUSTRALIAN GRAND PRIX	182
MALAYSIAN GRAND PRIX	190
VALENCIA GRAND PRIX	198

FIM WORLD CHAMPIONSHIP • ROUND 1

QATAR GP
LOSAIL CIRCUIT

Above: Reds and blues – Stoner's and Lorenzo's pit crews applaud their respective riders.

Far left: Defending champion Stoner looked set to dominate again.
Photographs: Gold & Goose

They rode by night: Qatar was the first floodlit GP on two or four wheels.
Photograph: Gold & Goose

THE desert air crackled – with electricity, noise and unfamiliarity. The first night grand prix, on two or four wheels, was a signal moment. It passed off without a hitch, which was just as well: the lighting suppliers had advised that in the rare, but not unknown, event of rain, the race would probably have to be cancelled. Floodlighting reflecting off the spray would have cut visibility dangerously.

In this way, MotoGP claimed a world first, beating Formula One by several months with the first floodlit World Championship race. It was also the largest sports floodlighting exercise ever undertaken, according to Musco Lighting, who bragged with no sense of irony that the amount of light units would have provided average city street lighting stretching from the circuit all the way to the city of Moscow.

With the phrase 'carbon footprint' consigned to oblivion, this slap in the face for the greens was radiant proof that modern MotoGP would happily ally itself with the grandiose dreams of oil-rich Arabs, as long as the price was right. Those dreams were shared by only a few of the locals, it seemed, with a crowd figure of 5,422.

Musco had excelled itself, and not only by its own account. With 44 13-megawatt generators humming almost non-stop (the lights were on all afternoon as well as after dark), there were 1,000 lamp standards at various levels connected by 500km of wiring, turning night into day for the full circuit. For the most part, the riders liked it; some of them loved it, having grown up racing dirt-track under lights. Like Colin Edwards. 'I want to do it every weekend,' he said, after qualifying on the front row. 'Could you lay that on?'

Even slow learners had adapted by race day, all having had the advantage of night tests the week before. The imagined horror of dew wetting the circuit was dispelled, as was that of temperatures too low for the tyres to operate, although the latter was certainly a factor in problems that did occur, especially for Bridgestone, in spite of winning the race.

The night tests were the culmination of a pre-season that had claimed several victims. Stoner had hurt his shoulder in the last tests of 2007 and spent the winter recuperating. Early in 2008, John Hopkins had gone flying at Phillip Island's daunting turn one while getting acquainted with his new Kawasaki, severely wrenching his groin; Dani Pedrosa was still recovering from injuries to his right hand.

The intensive test season had yielded some other surprises: Randy de Puniet had been fastest Honda rider more than once, Jorge Lorenzo had soon got up to speed, and Rossi had taken a little time to adapt to Bridgestones. Both factory M1s had been enlivened with pneumatic valve springs, although not yet the satellite-team bikes. The new system obviously paid off, as Rossi observed. In 2007, he had struggled against Stoner's Ducati with a speed differential of some 14km/h. For the new season, this had been halved.

Perhaps the biggest surprise was the confusion of Honda. The manufacturer had brought out its own pneumatic-spring motor for testing at Malaysia, but had promptly taken it away again. The protracted saga leading to its eventual return would occupy half the season. For now, while satellite teams battled with iffy handling and performance from their production version of the 2007 bike, the factory riders were in a quandary. Hayden had been fastest at the Jerez tests, but at night in the desert, they had slumped behind even satellite riders de Puniet and Dovizioso. The problem was handling on corner entry, which prompted a panic at Tokyo HQ when the riders asked for their 2007 bikes back. Staff worked day and night to reassemble machines from pensioned-off parts, the bikes being flown to Qatar in the nick of time. In the event, Pedrosa preferred the new

Right: Rookie pole-sitter Lorenzo emulated his role model, Max Biaggi.

Far right: Stoner took complete control of the desert night.

Below: Dovizioso underlined the rookie effect, beating Rossi for fourth.

Photographs: Gold & Goose

Above: Steve Parrish was never in the dark.

Left: Toseland made it two rookies on the front row and raced strongly in his MotoGP debut.

Photographs: Gold & Goose

machine after all, while Hayden chose the old. This was the start also of a long saga concerning Honda chassis and special favour for Pedrosa. His new Qatar chassis was not available to Hayden, and he would enjoy such benefits ahead of his team-mate for the whole year to come.

Suzuki also stepped backwards, starting with bodywork and some chassis parts that had been disinterred from 2007 to help the feel of the 2008 bike. Pretty soon it would be the whole chassis. Later in the year, Kawasaki would follow suit. In racing, not all progress is necessarily forwards.

Except at the sharp end. The 800s now had one year's maturity, while the electronics were similarly advanced. The lap speeds showed as much, records being broken in qualifying and the race. But by whom? By a bunch of rookies. If ever anyone sought proof that a modern MotoGP bike is too easy to ride, here it was, on the front row of the grid, with first-timer Jorge Lorenzo sitting on pole position – the first class rookie to do so since his role model, Biaggi, in 2002 – and ex-Super-bike champion James Toseland alongside. With fellow class new boys Dovizioso and de Angelis also fast, surely something was wrong.

The other end of the grid also had some surprises. It was populated by the wrong sort of people on the wrong sorts of bike. None more so than five-times MotoGP winner and former 250 champion Marco Melandri, whose move to the factory Ducati team had triggered the most extraordinary slump. He qualified two seconds slower than Stoner, setting a pattern that would not

change for the full year to come. The two satellite Dukes of Elias – another race winner – and Guintoli were down there with him, along with Anthony West's Kawasaki in plum last.

Too easy to ride?

Maybe 125s are too easy as well. At least, you might think so if you looked at British rookie Scott Redding. On an old Aprilia, Redding made the front row in his first GP – joining two other British riders in the top six, including Bradley Smith on his first pole – and all but the rostrum as well.

The first race under eased tyre restrictions demonstrated one immediate change. Tyre allocation was up from 14/17 front/rear to 18/22. This was enough to ease pressure on choice, especially given Michelin's broader-spectrum approach that was refined at the end of last year. It also allowed riders to choose three rather than two qualifying tyres – another chance to get closer to the limits of the sticky rubber, and another fillip to the already exciting single qualifying hour.

A new name in the 125 class was Loncin, the first full-time entry by a Chinese manufacturer. In fact it was a takeaway team: last year's Malaguti – already a copy Honda, with interchangeable parts – rebadged. The significance of Chinese interest was to grow as the year wore on.

Does night racing have a bright future? There was a flurry of interest, including from Malaysia, while Dorna's contract with Qatar was renewed on the weekend to run until 2016.

MOTOGP RACE – 22 laps

What a start to the season: old and new riders on the new-generation electronic 800s engaged in an early-laps brawl more like a club race. With Toseland prominent in the mix and employing what Rossi would later smilingly chide as 'a Superbike style', paint, tyre-rubber and reputations were frequently exchanged. Lorenzo's description was also apt: 'All the riders were going like crazy. Me too. It was very scary.'

Lorenzo was on pole, Toseland alongside, then Edwards; Stoner headed row two from de Puniet and Hayden. Rossi and Pedrosa were on the third, 1.2 seconds off Lorenzo's blazing time, but it was Pedrosa away in the lead into the first corner. Edwards and Toseland were jostling behind, then Lorenzo, while Rossi took fifth off Stoner at the end of lap one.

They remained all over one another, with Lorenzo and Toseland colliding after the Spaniard took the latter by surprise with his fast turn-in, cutting across the Englishman's front wheel. 'I need to learn how these guys ride,' he said later.

Any hopes Pedrosa may have had of a breakaway disappeared when a forceful Rossi took second on lap two and immediately started to close the 1.4-second gap. Three laps later, he was in the lead, the rest still close, although Dovizioso had displaced Edwards, hanging on at the back of the septet.

Stoner had kept out of trouble during the opening laps, but now was moving forward, changing places twice with Lorenzo before powering from fourth to first down the straight on lap eight. One lap later, Lorenzo also passed Rossi and set off after the Ducati. Clearly the Italian was in trouble. He explained later that it was with tyres, or more precisely unfamiliarity with the

Bridgestones. 'I could brake very strongly, but in the middle of the corner I was very slow. It looks like we don't have enough weight on the rear. I think the key is to throw away all the settings that we had with Michelin and understand how to use this type of tyre in our bike.'

He was losing half a second a lap, and after half-distance was receiving close attention from Pedrosa, with Dovizioso and Toseland less than a second behind.

From lap 14, Stoner started to push: half a second clear, and then a second, the gap stretching to the flag in a display of assured superiority from the champion. It would be the last such demonstration for a while.

The top three was settled for the youngest rostrum since France in 1976 – Sheene, Cecotto, Lucchinelli. Lorenzo was comfortably clear, Pedrosa now drawing away from Rossi, whose problems were not over yet. Dovizioso, Toseland right behind, started pushing, and on lap 20 moved briefly ahead when Rossi ran wide. He nosed ahead again over the line by mere hundredths. Toseland was never able to find a way past the Italian pair.

Edwards, second on lap one, had dropped straight to the back of the leading group, five riders slamming past every which way. It was all he could do to stay within a couple of seconds. By the finish, with the unwelcome sight of his rookie team-mate ahead of him, he'd closed up again, but not enough to attack. 'I didn't leave anything out there tonight. If you paid me a million dollars, I couldn't have gone any faster,' he said.

Hayden struggled from the start to match his performance on qualifiers, and endured a drawn-out failure to do so. He clung on to eighth for four laps, the rest piling up behind him. On lap five, both Capirossi and Hopkins got ahead, moving on for a private battle that would last

until Hopkins started to drop back. His front tyre was sliding. 'The only way to prop the bike up was with my knee.' This played hell with his groin injury, and his fight was over.

By now, de Puniet was also ahead of the fading Hayden, and then even de Angelis, although he crowned his MotoGP debut by crashing out five laps later while striving to close the two seconds on de Puniet.

Hopkins continued to drop back into the hands of the new-class no-hopers. Melandri was ahead of him by the end, but 44 seconds behind Stoner on the same motorcycle – two seconds a lap. Nakano, making a most undistinguished return to Bridgestones on a Honda, was still behind Hopkins at the flag.

Another gap, then Elias narrowly defeated new team-mate Guintoli, each on his first Ducati outing. West remained all at sea, out of the points, but not last – that went to countryman Vermeulen, a lap down after pitting early on to change a faulty Bridgestone.

250cc RACE – 20 laps

Veteran Alex Debon, on Lorenzo's old team, took his first pole in 107 starts, alongside Spanish compatriots Barbera and Bautista, and Finn Kallio on a close front row. But it was Luthi ahead from the start. Alas, his flier from the second row had anticipated the green light, and he was promptly pulled in for a ruinous ride-through penalty.

By now, on lap three, Bautista led by almost a second-and-a-half, but Barbera had got past Kallio and was closing up steadily. Before half-distance he was attacking, and on lap nine succeeded. Bautista stayed near for a while; more than 2.5 seconds behind, there was a ding-dong for third. Debon and Kallio were going back and forth, while Pasini was close, Takahashi in his

Left: Jorge Lorenzo flies low on his sensational rostrum debut.

Below: De Angelis was the only one to fall in the race.

Bottom: Class rookie Pasini took the 250 win at his first attempt.

Below right: Early 125 race action: Gadea leads Talmacsi, de la Rosa and brilliant beginner Redding.

Bottom centre: Aged 15, Redding made an instant impression in his GP debut.

Bottom right: Redding's countryman, Webb, was just one place behind.

Photographs: Gold & Goose

tracks. The Japanese soon lost touch, however, at the same time that Pasini vaulted to the front of the group.

Bautista was now running into trouble with rear grip, his tyre used up. He soon fell back into the hands of Debon and Pasini, the older Spaniard in front once more and gaining an advantage as Pasini was held up by Bautista.

It looked as though it was all settled, but in the last few laps the leading four closed up again. The race was on once more.

Debon took the lead on the second-to-last lap, and Barbera fought back at once. With the pair thus occupied, Pasini took immediate advantage to dive underneath both of them and gallop away. In his first 250 race, he did enough to hold his lead by half a second all the way to the end.

Kallio had been biding his time in familiar fashion, and now that it mattered he also joined battle, taking third from Debon just two corners after Pasini had moved into the lead.

More than ten seconds back by now, Takahashi's Honda was less than a second clear of Bautista. Abraham was another two seconds away, survivor of a battle with another ex-125 class first-timer, Pesek, until he crashed out. Simoncelli made a slow start to his season as well, chasing his Gilera team-mate, Locatelli, for an eventual eighth place, but also falling before reaching half-distance.

The field was thinly spread; Espargaro was a lonely ninth, and another 125 promotee, Faubel, a distant tenth. He'd got away 15th, but had gradually picked up places. In the closing laps, he took the lead of a trio, from Simon and Lai.

Thai rider Wilairot fell back from this group, but stayed ahead of low-key returnee Poggiali, a former champion; Luthi salvaged a point for 15th, out of just 17 finishers.

Team-mates Laverty and Hernandez made the worst possible start to their collaboration, colliding on the first lap and both crashing out as a result.

125cc RACE – 18 laps

The British revival in the smallest class was signalled by Bradley Smith's first pole, on Pasini's old light blue bike, with out-of-nowhere rookie Scott Redding on the far end of the front row, in his first GP. Talmacsi and di Meglio were sandwiched between them; another Briton, Danny Webb, led row two.

Smith inherited the Polaris World bike's frequent frailty. He led away and for the first lap, then wobbled and slowed on the second, gradually dropping away. A steering damper had failed.

Talmacsi led until lap seven, then Olive for one lap. Gadea had been coming through steadily after finishing lap one seventh, and he took over next time around, at the head of a typically volatile brawl.

Talmacsi led again at half-distance, from Gadea, de Rosa, Olive, Webb, Redding and di Meglio, all shuffling to and fro, with plenty of drama remaining. Notably that the world champion suddenly slowed, flapping at the twist-grip, his motor picking up again only after he had dropped right out of contention.

With five laps left, Redding swooped around the outside to third, and was straight back to sixth. Then de Rosa ran into the back of Olive. The former crashed out, while Olive was sent wide, promoting the English teenager to fourth, within sight of a debut rostrum.

By now Gadea had a small breathing space. Behind him, battle raged to the end. Olive quickly recovered and fought his way back through to reclaim second. Stefan Bradl had closed on the leaders, and tagged on. On the sprint to the line, the young German managed to shade di Meglio and Redding. Third to fifth was covered by less than two-tenths.

Webb had lost ground mid-race, but stayed sixth, a second ahead of Corsi, in turn battling with Espargaro Vazquez. Talmacsi was a disgruntled 12th. Smith missed the last point by less than three-tenths.

Commercialbank GRAND PRIX OF QATAR

09 MARCH 2008 • FIM WORLD CHAMPIONSHIP ROUND 1

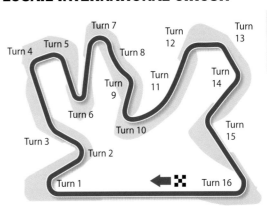

LOSAIL INTERNATIONAL CIRCUIT

Turn 1, Turn 2, Turn 3, Turn 4, Turn 5, Turn 6, Turn 7, Turn 8, Turn 9, Turn 10, Turn 11, Turn 12, Turn 13, Turn 14, Turn 15, Turn 16

Circuit 5.380km / 3.343 miles

MOTOGP

RACE: 22 laps, 73.546 miles/118.360km • Weather: Dry • Air 18°C • Humidity 58% • Track 19°C

Pos.	Rider	Nat.	No.	Entrant	Machine	Tyres	Laps	Time & speed (mph/km/h)
1	Casey Stoner	AUS	1	Ducati Marlboro Team	Ducati	B	22	42m 36.587s 103.561mph/ 166.665km/h
2	Jorge Lorenzo	SPA	48	Fiat Yamaha Team	Yamaha	M	22	42m 41.910s
3	Dani Pedrosa	SPA	2	Repsol Honda Team	Honda	M	22	42m 47.187s
4	Andrea Dovizioso	ITA	4	JiR Team Scot MotoGP	Honda	M	22	42m 49.875s
5	Valentino Rossi	ITA	46	Fiat Yamaha Team	Yamaha	B	22	42m 49.892s
6	James Toseland	GBR	52	Tech 3 Yamaha	Yamaha	M	22	42m 50.627s
7	Colin Edwards	USA	5	Tech 3 Yamaha	Yamaha	M	22	42m 51.737s
8	Loris Capirossi	ITA	65	Rizla Suzuki MotoGP	Suzuki	B	22	43m 09.092s
9	Randy de Puniet	FRA	14	LCR Honda MotoGP	Honda	M	22	43m 09.590s
10	Nicky Hayden	USA	69	Repsol Honda Team	Honda	M	22	43m 14.941s
11	Marco Melandri	ITA	33	Ducati Marlboro Team	Ducati	B	22	43m 20.871s
12	John Hopkins	USA	21	Kawasaki Racing Team	Kawasaki	B	22	43m 26.444s
13	Shinya Nakano	JPN	56	San Carlo Honda Gresini	Honda	B	22	43m 26.458s
14	Toni Elias	SPA	24	Alice Team	Ducati	B	22	43m 35.119s
15	Sylvain Guintoli	FRA	50	Alice Team	Ducati	B	22	43m 35.517s
16	Anthony West	AUS	13	Kawasaki Racing Team	Kawasaki	B	22	43m 42.230s
17	Chris Vermeulen	AUS	7	Rizla Suzuki MotoGP	Suzuki	B	21	43m 11.483s
	Alex de Angelis	RSM	15	San Carlo Honda Gresini	Honda	B	16	31m 26.773s

Fastest lap: Casey Stoner, on lap 14, 1m 55.153s, 104.510mph/168.193km/h (record).

Previous lap record: Casey Stoner, AUS (Ducati), 1m 56.528s, 103.277mph/166.208km/h (2007).

Event best maximum speed: Marco Melandri, 207.8mph/334.4km/h (race).

QUALIFYING: 8 March 2008

Weather: Dry
Air: 16°C Humidity: 45% Track: 15°C

Pos.	Rider	Time
1	Lorenzo	1m 53.927s
2	Toseland	1m 54.182s
3	Edwards	1m 54.499s
4	Stoner	1m 54.733s
5	de Puniet	1m 54.818s
6	Hayden	1m 54.880s
7	Rossi	1m 55.133s
8	Pedrosa	1m 55.170s
9	Dovizioso	1m 55.185s
10	Hopkins	1m 55.263s
11	Vermeulen	1m 55.540s
12	de Angelis	1m 55.692s
13	Capirossi	1m 56.070s
14	Elias	1m 56.251s
15	Nakano	1m 56.434s
16	Melandri	1m 56.730s
17	Guintoli	1m 57.198s
18	West	1m 57.445s

Grid order	1	2	3	4	5	6	7	8	9	10	11	12	13	14	15	16	17	18	19	20	21	22	•
48 LORENZO	2	2	2	2	46	46	46	1	1	1	1	1	1	1	1	1	1	1	1	1	1	1	1
52 TOSELAND	5	46	46	46	2	2	48	46	48	48	48	48	48	48	48	48	48	48	48	48	48	48	2
5 EDWARDS	52	52	48	48	48	48	2	48	46	46	2	46	46	2	2	2	2	2	2	2	2	2	3
1 STONER	48	48	1	1	1	1	1	2	2	2	46	2	2	46	46	46	46	46	46	46	46	4	4
14 de PUNIET	46	1	52	4	4	4	4	4	4	4	4	4	4	4	4	4	4	4	4	4	4	46	5
69 HAYDEN	1	4	4	52	52	52	52	52	52	52	52	52	52	52	52	52	52	52	52	52	52	52	6
46 ROSSI	4	5	5	5	5	5	5	5	5	5	5	5	5	5	5	5	5	5	5	5	5	5	7
2 PEDROSA	69	69	69	69	65	65	65	65	65	65	65	65	65	65	65	65	65	65	65	65	65	65	8
4 DOVISIOSO	21	21	65	65	21	21	21	21	21	21	21	21	14	14	14	14	14	14	14	14	14	14	9
21 HOPKINS	7	65	21	21	69	69	69	69	14	14	14	14	15	15	15	15	69	69	69	69	69	69	10
7 VERMEULEN	14	7	7	7	7	15	14	14	69	69	69	69	21	69	69	69	21	21	33	33	33	33	11
15 de ANGELIS	65	14	15	15	15	14	15	15	15	15	15	15	69	21	21	21	33	33	21	21	21	21	12
65 CAPIROSSI	15	15	14	14	14	7	56	56	56	56	56	56	56	56	56	56	56	56	56	56	56	56	13
24 ELIAS	24	56	56	56	56	56	7	33	33	33	33	33	33	33	33	33	50	50	50	50	24	24	14
56 NAKANO	33	24	24	33	33	33	33	7	7	24	50	50	50	50	50	24	24	24	24	24	50	50	15
33 MELANDRI	56	33	33	24	24	24	24	24	24	50	24	24	24	24	24	13	13	13	13	13	13		
50 GUINTOLI	13	50	50	50	50	50	50	50	50	13	13	13	13	13	13	7	7	7	7	7			
13 WEST	50	13	13	13	13	13	13	13	13	7	7	7	7	7	7	7							

7 lapped rider

FASTEST RACE LAPS

	Rider	Lap	Time
1	Stoner	14	1m 55.153s
2	Lorenzo	13	1m 55.528s
3	Dovizioso	4	1m 55.559s
4	Rossi	4	1m 55.693s
5	Toseland	6	1m 55.891s
6	Edwards	6	1m 55.940s
7	Pedrosa	10	1m 56.049s
8	de Puniet	7	1m 56.380s
9	Hopkins	6	1m 56.491s
10	de Angelis	7	1m 56.501s
11	Capirossi	6	1m 56.689s
12	Hayden	7	1m 56.954s
13	Melandri	15	1m 56.972s
14	Vermeulen	4	1m 57.009s
15	Nakano	3	1m 57.124s
16	Guintoli	3	1m 57.753s
17	Elias	5	1m 57.841s
18	West	8	1m 57.989s

statistics

250cc

20 laps, 66.860 miles/107.600km

Pos.	Rider (Nat.)	No.	Team	Machine	Laps	Time & speed
1	Mattia Pasini (ITA)	75	Polaris World	Aprilia	20	40m 16.202s 99.616mph/ 160.317km/h
2	Hector Barbera (SPA)	21	Team Toth Aprilia	Aprilia	20	40m 16.759s
3	Mika Kallio (FIN)	36	Red Bull KTM 250	KTM	20	40m 17.231s
4	Alex Debon (SPA)	6	Lotus Aprilia	Aprilia	20	40m 17.620s
5	Yuki Takahashi (JPN)	72	JiR Team Scot 250	Honda	20	40m 29.146s
6	Alvaro Bautista (SPA)	19	Mapfre Aspar Team	Aprilia	20	40m 30.682s
7	Karel Abraham (CZE)	17	Cardion AB Motoracing	Aprilia	20	40m 32.923s
8	Roberto Locatelli (ITA)	15	Metis Gilera	Gilera	20	40m 35.189s
9	Aleix Espargaro (SPA)	41	Lotus Aprilia	Aprilia	20	40m 48.434s
10	Hector Faubel (SPA)	55	Mapfre Aspar Team	Aprilia	20	40m 57.304s
11	Julian Simon (SPA)	60	Repsol KTM 250cc	KTM	20	40m 57.659s
12	Fabrizio Lai (ITA)	32	Campetella Racing	Gilera	20	40m 57.896s
13	Ratthapark Wilairot (THA)	14	Thai Honda PTT SAG	Honda	20	40m 59.394s
14	Manuel Poggiali (RSM)	54	Campetella Racing	Gilera	20	41m 00.430s
15	Thomas Luthi (SWI)	12	Emmi - Caffe Latte	Aprilia	20	41m 04.962s
16	Hiroshi Aoyama (JPN)	4	Red Bull KTM 250	KTM	20	41m 27.233s
17	Doni Tata Pradita (INA)	45	Yamaha Pertamina Indonesia	Yamaha	20	42m 21.663s
	Alex Baldolini (ITA)	25	Matteoni Racing	Aprilia	14	DNF
	Lukas Pesek (CZE)	52	Auto Kelly - CP	Aprilia	12	DNF
	Marco Simoncelli (ITA)	58	Metis Gilera	Gilera	7	DNF
	Imre Toth (HUN)	10	Team Toth Aprilia	Aprilia	4	DNF
	Manuel Hernandez (SPA)	43	Blusens Aprilia	Aprilia	0	DNF
	Eugene Laverty (IRL)	50	Blusens Aprilia	Aprilia	0	DNF

Fastest lap: Debon, 1m 59.379s, 100.811mph/162.239km/h (record).

Previous lap record: Alex de Angelis, RSM (Aprilia), 2m 00.121s, 100.188mph/ 161.237km/h (2007).

Event best maximum speed: Bautista, 170.4mph/274.3km/h (race).

Qualifying: 1 Debon, 1m 59.470s; 2 Barbera, 1m 59.629s; 3 Bautista, 1m 59.694s; 4 Kallio, 1m 59.814s; 5 Pasini, 1m 59.863s; 6 Simoncelli, 1m 59.911s; 7 Luthi, 2m 00.108s; 8 Takahashi, 2m 00.326s; 9 Espargaro, 2m 00.365s; 10 Locatelli, 2m 00.403s; 11 Abraham, 2m 00.517s; 12 Aoyama, 2m 00.609s; 13 Lai, 2m 00.854s; 14 Simon, 2m 00.975s; 15 Faubel, 2m 00.998s; 16 Pesek, 2m 01.000s; 17 Baldolini, 2m 01.149s; 18 Poggiali, 2m 01.391s; 19 Wilairot, 2m 01.487s; 20 Laverty, 2m 02.482s; 21 Toth, 2m 03.538s; 22 Hernandez, 2m 03.703s; 23 Pradita, 2m 05.343s.

Fastest race laps: 1 Debon, 1m 59.379s; 2 Pasini, 1m 59.447s; 3 Kallio, 1m 59.502s; 4 Barbera, 1m 59.789s; 5 Bautista, 2m 00.105s; 6 Simoncelli, 2m 00.267s; 7 Takahashi, 2m 00.415s; 8 Abraham, 2m 00.497s; 9 Locatelli, 2m 00.770s; 10 Pesek, 2m 00.913s; 11 Luthi, 2m 01.092s; 12 Espargaro, 2m 01.166s; 13 Baldolini, 2m 01.570s; 14 Poggiali, 2m 01.578s; 15 Lai, 2m 01.709s; 16 Simon, 2m 01.798s; 17 Faubel, 2m 01.951s; 18 Wilairot, 2m 02.100s; 19 Aoyama, 2m 03.378s; 20 Toth, 2m 05.334s; 21 Pradita, 2m 05.942s.

World Championship: 1 Pasini, 25; 2 Barbera, 20; 3 Kallio, 16; 4 Debon, 13; 5 Takahashi, 11; 6 Bautista, 10; 7 Abraham, 9; 8 Locatelli, 8; 9 Espargaro, 7; 10 Faubel, 6; 11 Simon, 5; 12 Lai, 4; 13 Wilairot, 3; 14 Poggiali, 2; 15 Luthi, 1.

125cc

18 laps, 60.174 miles/96.840km

Pos.	Rider (Nat.)	No.	Team	Machine	Laps	Time & speed
1	Sergio Gadea (SPA)	33	Bancaja Aspar Team	Aprilia	18	38m 09.444s 94.619mph/ 152.274km/h
2	Joan Olive (SPA)	6	Belson Derbi	Derbi	18	38m 10.376s
3	Stefan Bradl (GER)	17	Grizzly Gas Kiefer Racing	Aprilia	18	38m 11.104s
4	Mike di Meglio (FRA)	63	Ajo Motorsport	Derbi	18	38m 11.215s
5	Scott Redding (GBR)	45	Blusens Aprilia Junior	Aprilia	18	38m 11.263s
6	Danny Webb (GBR)	99	Degraaf Grand Prix	Aprilia	18	38m 17.133s
7	Simone Corsi (ITA)	24	Jack & Jones WRB	Aprilia	18	38m 18.128s
8	Pol Espargaro (SPA)	44	Belson Derbi	Derbi	18	38m 18.137s
9	Efren Vazquez (SPA)	7	Blusens Aprilia Junior	Aprilia	18	38m 18.498s
10	Nicolas Terol (SPA)	18	Jack & Jones WRB	Aprilia	18	38m 20.346s
11	Sandro Cortese (GER)	11	Emmi - Caffe Latte	Aprilia	18	38m 20.389s
12	Gabor Talmacsi (HUN)	1	Bancaja Aspar Team	Aprilia	18	38m 22.062s
13	Stefano Bianco (ITA)	27	S3+ WTR San Marino Team	Aprilia	18	38m 22.153s
14	Andrea Iannone (ITA)	29	I.C. Team	Apilia	18	38m 29.530s
15	Michael Ranseder (AUT)	60	I.C. Team	Aprilia	18	38m 33.019s
16	Bradley Smith (GBR)	38	Polaris World	Aprilia	18	38m 33.334s
17	Dominique Aegerter (SWI)	77	Ajo Motorsport	Derbi	18	38m 38.850s
18	Pablo Nieto (SPA)	22	Onde 2000 KTM	KTM	18	38m 42.335s
19	Takaaki Nakagami (JPN)	73	I.C. Team	Aprilia	18	38m 42.790s
20	Pere Tutusaus (SPA)	30	Bancaja Aspar Team	Aprilia	18	38m 43.093s
21	Lorenzo Zanetti (ITA)	8	ISPA KTM Aran	KTM	18	38m 46.140s
22	Randy Krummenacher (SWI)	34	Red Bull KTM 125	KTM	18	38m 46.198s
23	Robin Lasser (GER)	21	Grizzly Gas Kiefer Racing	Aprilia	18	38m 54.761s
24	Esteve Rabat (SPA)	12	Repsol KTM 125cc	KTM	18	39m 05.884s
25	Louis Rossi (FRA)	69	FFM Honda GP 125	Honda	18	39m 23.946s
	Raffaele de Rosa (ITA)	35	Onde 2000 KTM	KTM	15	DNF
	Dino Lombardi (ITA)	13	BQR Blusens	Aprilia	11	DNF
	Hugo van den Berg (NED)	56	Degraaf Grand Prix	Aprilia	10	DNF
	Tomoyoshi Koyama (JPN)	71	ISPA KTM Aran	KTM	8	DNF
	Stevie Bonsey (USA)	51	Degraaf Grand Prix	Aprilia	5	DNF
	Jules Cluzel (FRA)	16	Loncin Racing	Loncin	4	DNF
	Alexis Masbou (FRA)	5	Loncin Racing	Loncin	1	DNF
	Roberto Lacalendola (ITA)	19	Matteoni Racing	Aprilia	1	DNF
	Robert Muresan (ROU)	95	Grizzly Gas Kiefer Racing	Aprilia	0	DNF

Fastest lap: Redding, 2m 05.695s, 95.745mph/154.087km/h (record).

Previous lap record: Gabor Talmacsi, HUN (Aprilia), 2m 06.267s, 95.312mph/ 153.389km/h (2007).

Event best maximum speed: Bradl, 150.1mph/241.5km/h (qualifying practice no. 2).

Qualifying: 1 Smith, 2m 05.242s; 2 Talmacsi, 2m 05.308s; 3 di Meglio, 2m 05.351s; 4 Redding, 2m 05.545s; 5 Webb, 2m 05.593s; 6 de Rosa, 2m 05.618s; 7 Terol, 2m 05.833s; 8 Gadea, 2m 05.953s; 9 Olive, 2m 06.074s; 10 Corsi, 2m 06.096s; 11 Rabat, 2m 06.132s; 12 Bianco, 2m 06.205s; 13 Cortese, 2m 06.218s; 14 Bonsey, 2m 06.329s; 15 Bradl, 2m 06.347s; 16 Nieto, 2m 06.380s; 17 Iannone, 2m 06.388s; 18 Espargaro, 2m 06.402s; 19 Vazquez, 2m 06.477s; 20 Aegerter, 2m 06.585s; 21 Koyama, 2m 06.702s; 22 Ranseder, 2m 06.787s; 23 Nakagami, 2m 07.016s; 24 Zanetti, 2m 07.338s; 25 Krummenacher, 2m 07.603s; 26 Tutusaus, 2m 07.605s; 27 Lasser, 2m 08.000s; 28 Masbou, 2m 08.381s; 29 van den Berg, 2m 08.502s; 30 Cluzel, 2m 08.769s; 31 Muresan, 2m 09.257s; 32 Lombardi, 2m 09.632s; 33 Lacalendola, 2m 09.827s; 34 Rossi, 2m 10.153s.

Fastest race laps: 1 Redding, 2m 05.695s; 2 Webb, 2m 05.919s; 3 Gadea, 2m 05.953s; 4 de Rosa, 2m 06.006s; 5 di Meglio, 2m 06.024s; 6 Vazquez, 2m 06.125s; 7 Olive, 2m 06.129s; 8 Talmacsi, 2m 06.149s; 9 Bradl, 2m 06.198s; 10 Bianco, 2m 06.274s; 11 Corsi, 2m 06.285s; 12 Cortese, 2m 06.371s; 13 Espargaro, 2m 06.534s; 14 Iannone, 2m 06.709s; 15 Terol, 2m 06.775s; 16 Ranseder, 2m 06.814s; 17 Nieto, 2m 07.226s; 18 Koyama, 2m 07.232s; 19 Smith, 2m 07.408s; 20 Aegerter, 2m 07.605s; 21 Lasser, 2m 07.650s; 22 Tutusaus, 2m 07.669s; 23 Rabat, 2m 07.682s; 24 Krummenacher, 2m 07.805s; 25 Nakagami, 2m 07.900s; 26 Bonsey, 2m 07.906s; 27 Zanetti, 2m 08.275s; 28 Cluzel, 2m 08.888s; 29 van den Berg, 2m 09.226s; 30 Lombardi, 2m 09.482s; 31 Rossi, 2m 10.127s; 32 Masbou, 2m 18.590s; 33 Lacalendola, 2m 21.214s.

World Championship: 1 Gadea, 25; 2 Olive, 20; 3 Bradl, 16; 4 di Meglio, 13; 5 Redding, 11; 6 Webb, 10; 7 Corsi, 9; 8 Espargaro, 8; 9 Vazquez, 7; 10 Terol, 6; 11 Cortese, 5; 12 Talmacsi, 4; 13 Bianco, 3; 14 Iannone, 2; 15 Ranseder, 1.

RIDER STANDINGS

After 1 Round

1	Casey Stoner	25
2	Jorge Lorenzo	20
3	Dani Pedrosa	16
4	Andrea Dovizioso	13
5	Valentino Rossi	11
6	James Toseland	10
7	Colin Edwards	9
8	Loris Capirossi	8
9	Randy de Puniet	7
10	Nicky Hayden	6
11	Marco Melandri	5
12	John Hopkins	4
13	Shinya Nakano	3
14	Toni Elias	2
15	Sylvain Guintoli	1

TEAM STANDINGS

After 1 Round

1	Fiat Yamaha Team	31
2	Ducati Marlboro Team	30
3	Repsol Honda Team	22
4	Tech 3 Yamaha	19
5	JiR Team Scot MotoGP	13
6	Rizla Suzuki MotoGP	8
7	LCR Honda MotoGP	7
8	Kawasaki Racing Team	4
9 =	San Carlo Honda Gresini	3
9 =	Alice Team	3

CONSTRUCTOR STANDINGS

After 1 Round

1	Ducati	25
2	Yamaha	20
3	Honda	16
4	Suzuki	8
5	Kawasaki	4

Rossi looks glum; rostrum companions Pedrosa – winner and new points leader – and Lorenzo had just been told off by the king.
Photograph: Gold & Goose

THERE'S nothing like deadly rivalry to make racing more personal, and nobody likes it more personal than the Spanish; the first of four Iberian races was preceded by a Press-fostered spat between Lorenzo and Pedrosa. In the main, it came from Lorenzo, who complained that instead of the expected congratulations when he stood one step higher than Dani on the Qatar rostrum, his rival simply had ignored him. 'I should have thought I deserved some recognition,' he said at the time; the intervening three weeks had seen much more of the same, including (allegedly) from Lorenzo: 'The difference between me and Dani is that when he gets on to a train, nobody notices.'

By the time they got to the track, they were studiously ignoring one another, even when again obliged to share the press-conference table and then the rostrum. When each declined to comment publicly on this rift, a mischievous Spanish journalist suggested that instead they might like to give one another 'un abrazo' (an embrace, in the national custom). This too was pointedly disregarded by both.

It took the intervention of the king: not Elvis Presley, although he was well represented by a pair of paddock impersonators, but King Juan Carlos himself, who grabbed each by the arm and forced them to touch, between climbing off their bikes and heading up to the rostrum. This was the same king that another one, King Kenny Roberts (not having been introduced), snubbed all those years ago at Jarama, his interest in motorcycle racing undimmed, but his patronage now enjoyed by a much more Spanish sport than back then. Doubtless, his intervention did more to bless the feud than cool it down. Spain remains crazy about MotoGP, as attested by more than 130,000 screaming race-day fans.

On track, Pedrosa took the race and the title lead, but Lorenzo was rampant once again, gaining a second successive pole position. Not counting the obvious first year of 1949, this has been achieved only twice by rookies:

by Geoff Duke in 1950 and by Jarno Saarinen in 1973.

But the show was not only about the two bickering Spaniards. This isolated precursor to the full European season was a key weekend for other riders. For Rossi, it marked another step forward in consummating his new relationship with Bridgestone. For Stoner, it was the start of a slump. The defending champion's usual throttle-happy tactics didn't suit the circuit or the bike, and running off the track twice in the race told the whole story.

Jerez tests in not dissimilar cool temperatures had taken place barely a month before, and Hayden had been fastest in the dry. He dug into his well of optimism after acquiring a 'new' 2008 chassis. (Whether it was the same as Pedrosa's from Qatar or not was shrouded in mystery and deliberate obfuscation; even Hayden said he'd had 'a couple of different answers'.) For complex reasons of fit, this condemned him to Pedrosa's softer engine tune rather than the raspier Hayden style available for the '07 chassis, but he looked on the bright side. 'It has a lot better feel at the front. I've been enjoying riding again … it's a much better bike than I had in Qatar.' It was not quite a false dawn, because he was a contender for both front row and rostrum; but at less technical circuits, where horsepower is more important, he would find himself back in the woods again.

The puzzlement at the back of the grid continued: West and the three remaining Ducati riders struggled to avoid being stone last. West was slowest in free practice, on a bike that went sideways rather than forwards when he opened the throttle. 'I can stay on it, but the other guys are just going away,' he explained. Melandri took last spot on the grid, a first-ever embarrassment he might have avoided had he not crashed during qualifying. 'I know this is not my level,' he said.

In the power corridors, the death knell of the 250s was briefly postponed after Dorna asked the GP Commission for more time to come up with a proposal for an alternative class. On the track, a fine display of 250 two-stroke

Right: Mid-field maul: Capirossi heads Toseland, Dovizioso and Hopkins.

Below left: Edwards saved this slide in practice, but succumbed in the race.

Below centre: Former Spanish world champions: Sito Pons (top) watched his son Axel's GP debut; Alex Criville (below) is a TV commentator.

Bottom right: Stoner blamed Nakano for his second off. This is why.

Photographs: Gold & Goose

duelling ended catastrophically, with yet more bad luck for pre-season favourite, the ever-smiling Bautista. He led on the last lap; Simoncelli was poised on his back wheel for the final attack. Then the Italian ran right into the back of him, sending both flying. Given Simoncelli's reputation for forceful riding, he was immediately blamed by all and sundry. Except Bautista, who warmly gave his fallen comrade 'un abrazo' in the gravel trap, for he knew it was his engine nipping up that had caused the crash.

Randy Krummenacher took the 125 limelight for all the wrong reasons. After a heavy fall from his mountain bike in the preceding week, he arrived at the track with worsening pain, diagnosed at the Clinica Mobile as 'only nerves'. His condition worsened on the morning of practice and he went to hospital for a check-up, where he immediately underwent emergency surgery. Internal bleeding and a ruptured spleen had caused a life-threatening condition. 'Dr Costa might be alright at fixing broken bones, but he should stay away from internal injuries,' said the 18-year-old Red Bull KTM rider's angry father, Peter Krummenacher.

Angry fathers are kept under strict control and well out of the way over at the Red Bull rookies camp, open to 13-year-olds, which returned for a second year, with some of the same riders and a crop of new ones. The best from last year had moved on to the Dorna Academy, while graduates from that school, including Redding, continued to make a mark on the 125 class.

MOTOGP RACE – 27 laps

Michelin soft tyres and a dose of magic gave new boy wonder Lorenzo pole by an amazing six-tenths, in a class of his own. Pedrosa headed the rest in second,

with Edwards on the front row again. Rossi was alongside Hayden on row two after having to back out of his fast lap with an electronics glitch. Second to 13th spots were within a second.

Pedrosa got another of his jack-rabbit starts, and this time it worked all the way to the chequered flag. Tucked small behind his fairing, he didn't see another motorbike all afternoon.

Lorenzo, Hayden and Stoner shadowed him away, Stoner displacing the American by the end of the lap; Rossi was seventh behind Edwards. It all changed next time around. The champion had a big slide and lost two places, one of them to Rossi, who was making rapid progress. On the next lap, on the way into the Dry Sack hairpin, Stoner braked, but his bike wouldn't slow and he ran right out into the gravel, saving the crash to rejoin 17th and last, de Puniet having fallen on the same lap. 'Normally, braking is one of our strong points,' said Stoner. 'I wasn't quite on the limit when I ran off, but I couldn't get the bike stopped. It took me by surprise.' He set about moving forward and by lap eight was in 11th, five seconds down on Nakano at the back of a mid-field gang.

Rossi took second on lap four, 1.49 seconds off Pedrosa. Now, surely, the race was on: the seven-times Jerez winner would soon cut that back. The Yamaha had a speed advantage, and he was Valentino.

Hope lingered only for a few laps. Pedrosa was in preferred runaway mode; Rossi was not settled yet with his new tyres, still making setting changes between warm-up and race. Both were on the limit, Rossi quicker through the first section, Pedrosa regaining ground with interest on the second flatter part. On lap seven, the gap was two seconds and stretching, almost four by half-distance.

Lorenzo held station behind Rossi for a second successive rostrum; Hayden followed him, dropping by more than a second mid-race, but closing back up and readying for an attack at the start of lap 22 when 'I stayed on the brake a bit too long into Turn One, and pretty much crashed. Elbow down, I thought I was done. But the front tyre was good, so I picked it up with my knee and saved it. It's the first time I've done that.'

His countryman, Edwards, had done the same in practice, on camera, but couldn't save himself in the race, chasing after Capirossi, who had slipped ahead for fifth. The Suzuki couldn't catch the leaders, but stayed clear of the pursuit for the first half of the race. That pursuit comprised Toseland, Vermeulen, Nakano and Hopkins, trading blows and – after the race – insults. Vermeulen thought Toseland a bit uncouth for diving underneath mid-corner; the Englishman responded that, lacking speed and acceleration, corner speed was his only weapon.

Dovizioso had all but stalled on the line, and forged through the back markers rapidly to close on the midfield gang by lap four. By the seventh, he had cut through them: Hopkins and Vermeulen in one lap, then one more each for Nakano and Toseland. Capirossi was the next target, almost three seconds clear, but the silver Honda caught him in only four laps.

Now he had company: Vermeulen, Toseland and Hopkins. What followed gave the lie to complaints about processional racing. It wasn't until lap 20 that Dovizioso finally got past Capirossi, with Vermeulen now off the back and striving to fend off Nakano, ultimately in vain. The rest stayed close and dangerous for a classic Jerez last-corner showdown. Dovizioso led, but was too fast and ran wide. This carried Toseland out as well. Capirossi had an open door, Toseland was behind, then Hopkins also passed the over-enthusiastic rookie at the flag. Less than a second covered all four of them.

Stoner had caught Nakano and Vermeulen on lap 22

and was of a mind to pass at once. He speared between them under braking, only to find himself off into the gravel again, losing ten seconds, but not the position. He took the blame for the first error himself, but fingered Nakano for the second.

But for a two-second gap, it would have been a formation finish for the factory Ducatis, both this time 40 seconds adrift. Melandri had narrowly outpaced West, who had his hands full with de Angelis. Distant Elias took a joyless last point, with team-mate Guintoli five seconds behind him.

250cc RACE – 26 laps

Kallio set the early practice pace, but by the end Bautista had edged him out, by four-hundredths. Debon and Luthi completed the first row; two more KTMs – Simon and Aoyama – headed row two.

Kallio led away, but Bautista was ahead on lap two; on the fourth, he and Simoncelli were starting to stretch away. It became a two-horse race.

Bautista was circulating smoothly and fast, Simoncelli inches behind, setting the lap record on the ninth. They were six seconds clear by half-distance and ten seconds just five laps later.

Now Simoncelli turned up the heat, pushing alongside only to be consigned to second again. Two corners later, he did it once more, but by the end of the lap Bautista was in front again. And so they went on – to the final lap.

Simoncelli was poised for a final attack, but never got the chance. On the second fast left, he was inches behind when Bautista suddenly slowed. No chance. They collided, and both went down.

Kallio could hardly believe his luck. He'd been engaged with Barbera and Luthi, Simon and Takahashi in close attendance, and on lap 17 Luthi had moved ahead for a few laps. Kallio was in front again, the pair

now dropping off Takahashi, when Luthi fell victim to a giant high-side, leaving the Finn to a safe third, eight seconds adrift. Which suddenly became first as he flashed past the dust cloud in the gravel. 'I'm sorry for them, but we've also had our share of bad luck in the past,' he said later, typically deadpan.

Simon, suffering from arm pump, had dropped out of the battle for second; Pasini had been making ground rapidly after finishing lap one in 15th. By mid-distance, fellow slow starter Aoyama had tagged on; by the end, they'd caught and passed Barbera. He also joined on behind, and all three closed on Takahashi for the inevitable brawl to the line.

Pasini won it from Takahashi by a hundredth, Aoyama half a second away, with another second to Barbera.

Debon was sixth, surviving a near crash; Simon was a lonely seventh, likewise all those trailing along behind – Locatelli, Espargaro, Pesek and so on. With Faubel crashing out on lap two and three other retirements, there were only 16 finishers. Faubel's crash meant that the Aspar team had no finishers in the class in its home GP, while two out of three crashed in the 125 race as well, the survivor scoring zero points.

125cc RACE – 23 laps

Smith sprinted off from his second successive pole of the season, but by the end of the second lap, both Jack & Jones team-mates were ahead of him, Terol at the first corner, Corsi at the end of the lap.

By lap ten, the trio had doubled: Bradl, Nieto and Bonsey had closed the gap, the last-named battling to stay in touch. This was Corsi's signal to get going, and he finally made a decisive pass on his younger team-mate, the pair of them soon drawing away.

Corsi still had something to spare, however, and with three laps to go he kicked again and pulled out to win by almost three seconds. The victory gave him the lead

in the title chase.

The battle for third went to the end. Smith managed to downgrade Bradl by two-tenths, with Nieto by then a second adrift; Bonsey soldiered on with sliding tyres, staying two seconds ahead of the next trio for a career-best sixth.

Redding headed the following group, the rookie getting the better of the Derbi pair Aegerter and di Meglio. Cortese took tenth at the head of the next group; de Rosa, Rabat and Koyama were right with him, Espargaro off the back.

The first race began Aspar's day of almost complete disaster. Talmacsi was fourth on lap four when he pulled off in high dudgeon with a broken crankshaft. Three laps later, Qatar winner Gadea crashed out of a lowly 18th, after starting off 12th. Pere Tutusaus was 19th, the only teamster to finish all day.

Webb and Olive were among seven to crash out, both in the top ten. Axel Pons, 15-year-old son of former double 250 champion Sito, also crashed out of his GP debut race.

Above: Corsi takes control of the 125 race, from Terol, Bradl and Smith.

Left: Webb bites the Olive, taking them both out of the 125 race.

Facing page: Uncatchable, Pedrosa pulls away from Rossi and Lorenzo.

Top of page, clockwise: Joy unconfined for 250 winner Kallio, podium finisher Pasini's crew and third-placed Yuki Takahashi.

Photographs: Gold & Goose

GRAN PREMIO bwin.com DE ESPANA

30 MARCH 2008 • FIM WORLD CHAMPIONSHIP ROUND 2

CIRCUITO DE JEREZ

Sito Pons
Michelin
Ducados
Expo '92
Ferrari
Ayrton Senna
Angel Nieto
Dry Sack
Peluqui

Circuit 4.423km / 2.745 miles

MOTOGP

RACE: 27 laps, 74.196 miles/119.421km • Weather: Dry • Air 19°C • Humidity 26% • Track 23°C

Pos.	Rider	Nat.	No.	Team	Machine	Tyres	Laps	Time & speed (mph/km/h)
1	Dani Pedrosa	SPA	2	Repsol Honda Team	Honda	M	27	45m 35.121s 97.669mph/ 157.183km/h
2	Valentino Rossi	ITA	46	Fiat Yamaha Team	Yamaha	B	27	45m 38.004s
3	Jorge Lorenzo	SPA	48	Fiat Yamaha Team	Yamaha	M	27	45m 39.460s
4	Nicky Hayden	USA	69	Repsol Honda Team	Honda	M	27	45m 45.263s
5	Loris Capirossi	ITA	65	Rizla Suzuki MotoGP	Suzuki	B	27	46m 02.645s
6	James Toseland	GBR	52	Tech 3 Yamaha	Yamaha	M	27	46m 02.929s
7	John Hopkins	USA	21	Kawasaki Racing Team	Kawasaki	B	27	46m 03.417s
8	Andrea Dovizioso	ITA	4	JiR Team Scot MotoGP	Honda	M	27	46m 03.570s
9	Shinya Nakano	JPN	56	San Carlo Honda Gresini	Honda	B	27	46m 07.690s
10	Chris Vermeulen	AUS	7	Rizla Suzuki MotoGP	Suzuki	B	27	46m 10.212s
11	Casey Stoner	AUS	1	Ducati Marlboro Team	Ducati	B	27	46m 17.344s
12	Marco Melandri	ITA	33	Ducati Marlboro Team	Ducati	B	27	46m 19.619s
13	Anthony West	AUS	13	Kawasaki Racing Team	Kawasaki	B	27	46m 20.928s
14	Alex de Angelis	RSM	15	San Carlo Honda Gresini	Honda	B	27	46m 20.992s
15	Toni Elias	SPA	24	Alice Team	Ducati	B	27	46m 44.679s
16	Sylvain Guintoli	FRA	50	Alice Team	Ducati	B	27	46m 49.563s
	Colin Edwards	USA	5	Tech 3 Yamaha	Yamaha	M	5	9m 10.348s
	Randy de Puniet	FRA	14	LCR Honda MotoGP	Honda	M	2	3m 31.127s

Fastest lap: Dani Pedrosa, on lap 3, 1m 40.116s, 98.825mph/159.043km/h (record).

Previous lap record: Valentino Rossi, ITA (Yamaha), 1m 40.596s, 98.353mph/158.284km/h (2005).

Event best maximum speed: Loris Capirossi, 175.4mph/282.2km/h (qualifying practice).

QUALIFYING: 29 March 2008

Weather: Dry
Air: 25°C Humidity: 35% Track: 26°C

Pos.	Rider	Time
1	Lorenzo	1m 38.189s
2	Pedrosa	1m 38.789s
3	Edwards	1m 38.954s
4	Hayden	1m 39.061s
5	Rossi	1m 39.064s
6	de Puniet	1m 39.122s
7	Stoner	1m 39.286s
8	Toseland	1m 39.334s
9	Hopkins	1m 39.439s
10	Capirossi	1m 39.484s
11	Nakano	1m 39.559s
12	Vermeulen	1m 39.704s
13	Dovizioso	1m 39.767s
14	de Angelis	1m 40.037s
15	West	1m 40.088s
16	Elias	1m 40.286s
17	Guintoli	1m 40.939s
18	Melandri	1m 41.027s

Grid order	1	2	3	4	5	6	7	8	9	10	11	12	13	14	15	16	17	18	19	20	21	22	23	24	25	26	27	
48 LORENZO	2	2	2	2	2	2	2	2	2	2	2	2	2	2	2	2	2	2	2	2	2	2	2	2	2	2	2	1
2 PEDROSA	48	48	48	46	46	46	46	46	46	46	46	46	46	46	46	46	46	46	46	46	46	46	46	46	46	46	46	2
5 EDWARDS	1	69	46	48	48	48	48	48	48	48	48	48	48	48	48	48	48	48	48	48	48	48	48	48	48	48	48	3
69 HAYDEN	69	46	69	69	69	69	69	69	69	69	69	69	69	69	69	69	69	69	69	69	69	69	69	69	69	69	69	4
46 ROSSI	5	1	65	65	65	65	65	65	65	65	65	65	65	65	65	65	65	65	65	4	4	4	4	65	65	52	65	5
14 de PUNIET	46	5	5	5	52	52	4	4	4	4	4	4	4	4	4	4	4	4	4	65	65	65	65	52	52	4	52	6
1 STONER	65	65	56	56	56	4	52	7	7	7	7	7	7	7	7	7	7	52	52	52	52	52	4	4	65	21		7
52 TOSELAND	56	56	21	52	4	7	7	52	52	52	52	52	52	52	52	52	52	21	21	21	21	21	21	21	4			8
21 HOPKINS	21	21	52	7	7	56	21	21	21	21	21	21	21	21	21	21	21	7	7	7	7	7	7	56	56			9
65 CAPIROSSI	52	52	7	21	21	21	56	56	56	56	56	56	56	56	56	56	56	56	56	56	56	56	56	7	7			10
56 NAKANO	14	7	4	4	13	13	13	1	1	1	1	1	1	1	1	1	1	1	1	1	1	1	1	1	1	1	1	11
7 VERMEULEN	7	14	13	33	33	33	1	13	13	13	13	13	13	13	13	33	33	33	13	13	13	13	13	33	33	33		12
4 DOVISIOSO	13	13	33	13	15	15	33	33	33	15	15	15	15	15	33	13	13	13	33	33	33	33	33	13	13	13		13
15 de ANGELIS	33	4	15	15	1	1	15	15	15	33	33	33	33	33	15	15	15	15	15	15	15	15	15	15	15	15		14
13 WEST	24	33	24	24	24	24	24	24	24	24	24	24	24	24	24	24	24	24	24	24	24	24	24	24	24	24		15
24 ELIAS	4	15	50	1	50	50	50	50	50	50	50	50	50	50	50	50	50	50	50	50	50	50	50	50	50	50		
50 GUINTOLI	15	24	1	50	5																							
33 MELANDRI	50	50																										

FASTEST RACE LAPS

	Rider	Lap	Time
1	Pedrosa	3	1m 40.116s
2	Rossi	3	1m 40.192s
3	Capirossi	3	1m 40.402s
4	Lorenzo	3	1m 40.540s
5	Hayden	4	1m 40.671s
6	Dovizioso	3	1m 40.675s
7	Edwards	4	1m 40.700s
8	Vermeulen	3	1m 41.199s
9	Toseland	3	1m 41.327s
10	Hopkins	3	1m 41.336s
11	Stoner	5	1m 41.386s
12	Nakano	2	1m 41.560s
13	de Puniet	2	1m 41.645s
14	Melandri	2	1m 41.735s
15	West	2	1m 41.767s
16	de Angelis	4	1m 41.982s
17	Elias	6	1m 42.515s
18	Guintoli	2	1m 42.880s

statistics

OFFICIAL TIMEKEEPER

250cc

26 laps, 71.448 miles/114.998km

Pos.	Rider (Nat.)	No.	Team	Machine	Laps	Time & speed
1	Mika Kallio (FIN)	36	Red Bull KTM 250	KTM	26	45m 27.908s 94.301mph/ 151.762km/h
2	Mattia Pasini (ITA)	75	Polaris World	Aprilia	26	45m 32.185s
3	Yuki Takahashi (JPN)	72	JiR Team Scot 250	Honda	26	45m 32.195s
4	Hiroshi Aoyama (JPN)	4	Red Bull KTM 250	KTM	26	45m 32.784s
5	Hector Barbera (SPA)	21	Team Toth Aprilia	Aprilia	26	45m 33.876s
6	Alex Debon (SPA)	6	Lotus Aprilia	Aprilia	26	45m 41.541s
7	Julian Simon (SPA)	60	Repsol KTM 250cc	KTM	26	45m 44.280s
8	Roberto Locatelli (ITA)	15	Metis Gilera	Gilera	26	45m 50.479s
9	Aleix Espargaro (SPA)	41	Lotus Aprilia	Aprilia	26	45m 56.514s
10	Lukas Pesek (CZE)	52	Auto Kelly - CP	Aprilia	26	46m 00.634s
11	Alex Baldolini (ITA)	25	Matteoni Racing	Aprilia	26	46m 06.510s
12	Ratthapark Wilairot (THA)	14	Thai Honda PTT SAG	Honda	26	46m 11.279s
13	Karel Abraham (CZE)	17	Cardion AB Motoracing	Aprilia	26	46m 22.067s
14	Manuel Hernandez (SPA)	43	Blusens Aprilia	Aprilia	26	46m 49.846s
15	Imre Toth (HUN)	10	Team Toth Aprilia	Aprilia	25	45m 38.968s
16	Doni Tata Pradita (INA)	45	Yamaha Pertamina Indonesia	Yamaha	25	45m 52.650s
	Alvaro Bautista (SPA)	19	Mapfre Aspar Team	Aprilia	25	DNF
	Marco Simoncelli (ITA)	58	Metis Gilera	Gilera	25	DNF
	Thomas Luthi (SWI)	12	Emmi - Caffe Latte	Aprilia	22	DNF
	Manuel Poggiali (RSM)	54	Campetella Racing	Gilera	20	DNF
	Fabrizio Lai (ITA)	32	Campetella Racing	Gilera	17	DNF
	Eugene Laverty (IRL)	50	Blusens Aprilia	Aprilia	8	DNF
	Hector Faubel (SPA)	55	Mapfre Aspar Team	Aprilia	2	DNF

Fastest lap: Simoncelli, 1m 43.546s, 95.551mph/153.775km/h (record).

Previous lap record: Alex de Angelis, RSM (Aprilia), 1m 44.295s, 94.865mph/ 152.670km/h (2007).

Event best maximum speed: Bautista, 155.9mph/250.9km/h (free practice no. 1).

Qualifying: **1** Bautista, 1m 43.071s; **2** Kallio, 1m 43.111s; **3** Debon, 1m 43.286s; **4** Luthi, 1m 43.596s; **5** Simon, 1m 43.629s; **6** Koyama, 1m 43.640s; **7** Barbera, 1m 43.748s; **8** Locatelli, 1m 43.823s; **9** Simoncelli, 1m 43.921s; **10** Pasini, 1m 43.935s; **11** Takahashi, 1m 44.022s; **12** Lai, 1m 44.032s; **13** Faubel, 1m 44.166s; **14** Pesek, 1m 44.228s; **15** Abraham, 1m 44.249s; **16** Espargaro, 1m 44.335s; **17** Baldolini, 1m 44.754s; **18** Poggiali, 1m 44.754s; **19** Wilairot, 1m 45.753s; **20** Laverty, 1m 46.034s; **21** Toth, 1m 46.710s; **22** Hernandez, 1m 46.835s; **23** Pradita, 1m 47.989s.

Fastest race laps: **1** Simoncelli, 1m 43.546s; **2** Bautista, 1m 43.674s; **3** Luthi, 1m 44.010s; **4** Barbera, 1m 44.077s; **5** Simon, 1m 44.102s; **6** Takahashi, 1m 44.143s; **7** Pasini, 1m 44.147s; **8** Debon, 1m 44.200s; **9** Kallio, 1m 44.209s; **10** Aoyama, 1m 44.398s; **11** Pesek, 1m 44.582s; **12** Abraham, 1m 44.792s; **13** Baldolini, 1m 44.882s; **14** Locatelli, 1m 44.918s; **15** Espargaro, 1m 44.969s; **16** Wilairot, 1m 45.177s; **17** Lai, 1m 45.223s; **18** Poggiali, 1m 45.542s; **19** Faubel, 1m 45.707s; **20** Hernandez, 1m 46.804s; **21** Laverty, 1m 47.087s; **22** Toth, 1m 48.083s; **23** Pradita, 1m 48.566s.

World Championship: **1** Pasini, 45; **2** Kallio, 41; **3** Barbera, 31; **4** Takahashi, 27; **5** Debon, 23; **6** Locatelli, 16; **7** Simon, 14; **8** Espargaro, 14; **9** Aoyama, 13; **10** Abraham, 12; **11** Bautista, 10; **12** Wilairot, 7; **13** Faubel and Pesek, 6; **15** Baldolini, 5; **16** Lai, 4; **17** Hernandez and Poggiali, 2; **19** Luthi and Toth, 1.

125cc

23 laps, 63.204 miles/101.729km

Pos.	Rider (Nat.)	No.	Team	Machine	Laps	Time & speed
1	Simone Corsi (ITA)	24	Jack & Jones WRB	Aprilia	23	41m 46.100s 90.803mph/ 146.133km/h
2	Nicolas Terol (SPA)	18	Jack & Jones WRB	Aprilia	23	41m 49.306s
3	Bradley Smith (GBR)	38	Polaris World	Aprilia	23	41m 51.086s
4	Stefan Bradl (GER)	17	Grizzly Gas Kiefer Racing	Aprilia	23	41m 51.122s
5	Pablo Nieto (SPA)	22	Onde 2000 KTM	KTM	23	41m 52.354s
6	Stevie Bonsey (USA)	51	Degraaf Grand Prix	Aprilia	23	42m 06.663s
7	Scott Redding (GBR)	45	Blusens Aprilia Junior	Aprilia	23	42m 08.617s
8	Dominique Aegerter (SWI)	77	Ajo Motorsport	Derbi	23	42m 09.102s
9	Mike di Meglio (FRA)	63	Ajo Motorsport	Derbi	23	42m 10.028s
10	Sandro Cortese (GER)	11	Emmi - Caffe Latte	Aprilia	23	42m 19.641s
11	Raffaele de Rosa (ITA)	35	Onde 2000 KTM	KTM	23	42m 19.764s
12	Esteve Rabat (SPA)	12	Repsol KTM 125cc	KTM	23	42m 20.087s
13	Tomoyoshi Koyama (JPN)	71	ISPA KTM Aran	KTM	23	42m 20.526s
14	Pol Espargaro (SPA)	44	Belson Derbi	Derbi	23	42m 26.138s
15	Takaaki Nakagami (JPN)	73	I.C. Team	Aprilia	23	42m 30.615s
16	Michael Ranseder (AUT)	60	I.C. Team	Aprilia	23	42m 31.598s
17	Jules Cluzel (FRA)	16	Loncin Racing	Loncin	23	42m 35.785s
18	Andrea Iannone (ITA)	29	I.C. Team	Aprilia	23	42m 39.286s
19	Pere Tutusaus (SPA)	30	Bancaja Aspar Team	Aprilia	23	42m 44.137s
20	Roberto Lacalendola (ITA)	19	Matteoni Racing	Aprilia	23	42m 49.710s
21	Alexis Masbou (FRA)	5	Loncin Racing	Loncin	23	42m 50.832s
22	Ivan Maestro (SPA)	76	Alpo Atletico de Madrid	Honda	23	43m 05.699s
23	Daniel Saez (SPA)	78	Gaviota Prosolia Racing	Aprilia	23	43m 11.090s
24	Louis Rossi (FRA)	69	FFM Honda GP 125	Honda	23	43m 25.835s
25	Alberto Moncayo (SPA)	79	Andalucia Derbi	Derbi	23	43m 34.292s
26	Robert Muresan (ROU)	95	Grizzly Gas Kiefer Racing	Aprilia	20	43m 02.935s
	Axel Pons (SPA)	14	Jack & Jones WRB	Aprilia	22	DNF
	Lorenzo Zanetti (ITA)	8	ISPA KTM Aran	KTM	14	DNF
	Hugo van den Berg (NED)	56	Degraaf Grand Prix	Aprilia	12	DNF
	Joan Olive (SPA)	6	Belson Derbi	Derbi	9	DNF
	Danny Webb (GBR)	99	Degraaf Grand Prix	Aprilia	8	DNF
	Stefano Bianco (ITA)	27	S3+ WTR San Marino Team	Aprilia	7	DNF
	Sergio Gadea (SPA)	33	Bancaja Aspar Team	Aprilia	6	DNF
	Efren Vazquez (SPA)	7	Blusens Aprilia Junior	Aprilia	6	DNF
	Gabor Talmacsi (HUN)	1	Bancaja Aspar Team	Aprilia	3	DNF

Fastest lap: Corsi, 1m 47.999s, 91.611mph/147.434km/h.

Lap record: Lukas Pesek, CZE (Derbi), 1m 47.404s, 92.119mph/148.251km/h (2006).

Event best maximum speed: Bradl, 137.0mph/220.5km/h (qualifying practice no. 1).

Qualifying: **1** Smith, 1m 47.587s; **2** Terol, 1m 48.041s; **3** Bradl, 1m 48.070s; **4** Talmacsi, 1m 48.113s; **5** Corsi, 1m 48.128s; **6** Bonsey, 1m 48.146s; **7** di Meglio, 1m 48.165s; **8** Redding, 1m 48.315s; **9** Webb, 1m 48.333s; **10** de Rosa, 1m 48.345s; **11** Aegerter, 1m 48.348s; **12** Gadea, 1m 48.437s; **13** Nieto, 1m 48.441s; **14** Bianco, 1m 48.481s; **15** Cortese, 1m 48.510s; **16** Rabat, 1m 48.520s; **17** Espargaro, 1m 48.572s; **18** Olive, 1m 48.688s; **19** Nakagami, 1m 48.783s; **20** Iannone, 1m 48.791s; **21** Koyama, 1m 48.799s; **22** Vazquez, 1m 48.907s; **23** Pons, 1m 49.357s; **24** Ranseder, 1m 49.392s; **25** Tutusaus, 1m 49.446s; **26** Masbou, 1m 49.720s; **27** Cluzel, 1m 49.773s; **28** Lacalendola, 1m 49.879s; **29** Muresan, 1m 49.936s; **30** van den Berg, 1m 50.161s; **31** Zanetti, 1m 50.557s; **32** Saez, 1m 51.362s; **33** Rossi, 1m 51.894s; **34** Maestro, 1m 52.070s; **35** Moncayo, 1m 53.283s.

Fastest race laps: **1** Corsi, 1m 47.999s; **2** Smith, 1m 48.032s; **3** Talmacsi, 1m 48.111s; **4** Terol, 1m 48.191s; **5** Bonsey, 1m 48.202s; **6** Nieto, 1m 48.262s; **7** Bradl, 1m 48.263s; **8** Webb, 1m 48.381s; **9** Vazquez, 1m 48.429s; **10** Olive, 1m 48.473s; **11** Bianco, 1m 48.486s; **12** Redding, 1m 48.619s; **13** Aegerter, 1m 48.641s; **14** di Meglio, 1m 48.653s; **15** Cortese, 1m 48.730s; **16** Rabat, 1m 48.780s; **17** Koyama, 1m 48.813s; **18** de Rosa, 1m 48.878s; **19** Ranseder, 1m 48.886s; **20** Espargaro, 1m 49.106s; **21** Masbou, 1m 49.106s; **22** Cluzel, 1m 49.207s; **23** Pons, 1m 49.424s; **24** van den Berg, 1m 49.507s; **25** Nakagami, 1m 49.599s; **26** Lacalendola, 1m 49.839s; **27** Iannone, 1m 50.008s; **28** Tutusaus, 1m 50.192s; **29** Masbou, 1m 50.240s; **30** Zanetti, 1m 50.416s; **31** Saez, 1m 50.618s; **32** Maestro, 1m 50.735s; **33** Muresan, 1m 51.175s; **34** Rossi, 1m 51.470s; **35** Moncayo, 1m 52.510s.

World Championship: **1** Corsi, 34; **2** Bradl, 29; **3** Terol, 26; **4** Gadea, 25; **5** Olive, 20; **6** di Meglio, 20; **7** Redding, 20; **8** Smith, 16; **9** Nieto, 11; **10** Cortese, 11; **11** Bonsey and Webb, 10; **13** Espargaro, 10; **14** Aegerter, 8; **15** Vazquez, 7; **16** de Rosa, 5; **17** Rabat and Talmacsi, 4; **19** Bianco and Koyama, 3; **21** Iannone, 2; **22** Nakagami and Ranseder, 1.

RIDER STANDINGS
After 2 Rounds

1	Dani Pedrosa	41
2	Jorge Lorenzo	36
3	Valentino Rossi	31
4	Casey Stoner	30
5	Andrea Dovizioso	21
6	James Toseland	20
7	Nicky Hayden	19
8	Loris Capirossi	19
9	John Hopkins	13
10	Shinya Nakano	10
11	Colin Edwards	9
12	Marco Melandri	9
13	Randy de Puniet	7
14	Chris Vermeulen	6
15	Anthony West	3
16	Toni Elias	3
17	Alex de Angelis	2
18	Sylvain Guintoli	1

TEAM STANDINGS
After 2 Rounds

1	Fiat Yamaha Team	67
2	Repsol Honda Team	60
3	Ducati Marlboro Team	39
4	Tech 3 Yamaha	29
5	Rizla Suzuki MotoGP	25
6	JiR Team Scot MotoGP	21
7	Kawasaki Racing Team	16
8	San Carlo Honda Gresini	12
9	LCR Honda MotoGP	7
10	Alice Team	4

CONSTRUCTOR STANDINGS
After 2 Rounds

1	Honda	41
2	Yamaha	40
3	Ducati	30
4	Suzuki	19
5	Kawasaki	13

Lorenzo's line, Lorenzo's day, Lorenzo's land. It took
the rookie just three races to claim his first win.

Photographs: Gold & Goose

PORTUGUESE|GP
ESTORIL

RAIN was to become a theme of the first half of the season, and Estoril was typical: because it was not proper rain, just bad weather, blustery mini-squalls and intermittent spots. Friday morning was wet-and-dry, causing several riders to crash, including Rossi – a big one on the long, fast last corner. He walked away. Race day was very iffy, and the white flags were hung out to signify a wet race before the start, while Rossi pointed anxiously at the sky, but in fact the wet-shod bikes stayed put in the garages, kept warm, and the tyres changed from time to time for progressively softer rubber as the race wore on.

People would have to get used to these conditions. Losing a practice session had more impact on rookies. Toseland was the most acutely affected: learning a new bike, new tyres and a new circuit, he needed all the time he could get. Not all were as troubled, however, for by now, three races in, it was almost becoming normal for Jorge Lorenzo to qualify on pole.

The margin was smaller this time, but again he equalled the feat of 1974 top-class rookie Jarno Saarinen, on pole for the first three races of the year before being killed in the 250 round at the fourth. Saarinen had won his first two races as well. Lorenzo would win his third, quite clearly and definitely. It looked very much like a new chapter, and the story to unfold was full of drama. Lorenzo was the 100th winner in the premier class.

The weather also complicated the question of tyres. Michelin had come back fighting; while the increased tyre allocation had eased the pressure all round. How about Bridgestone? It had won at Qatar, but the next best runner was Rossi in fifth, then Capirossi eighth. Jerez had been a Michelin track, and it seemed Estoril would be as well. Only one of the top eight qualifiers was not on Michelin, third-placed Rossi. In the race also, he was pushed to third, fading as time wore on. Had his switch been a terrible error?

For a second race, Stoner wasn't there for a compari-son. Not a grip problem this time, as his lap times later in the race proved, but a strange one: a black box forming part of the increasingly elaborate on-bike camera equipment came loose from behind the handlebar and was flapping around outside the fairing on the left, and threatening to become mixed up with the steering. Stoner dropped back and back until he found a way to tuck it into the fairing without it blowing out again on the straight. His recovery took him from 11th to sixth, once again disproving the insistence that overtaking is difficult on the 800s. It's not, if the rider is fast enough.

Pneumatic valve springs were in the news: some with and some without.

The haves were the Yamaha B-team riders, Edwards and Toseland; the have-nots were the factory Honda pairing of Pedrosa and Hayden. The former were delighted, being more or less on a par now with Rossi and Lorenzo. With the old engine, said Edwards, shifting up through the gears to sixth was 'like letting air out of a balloon. Whereas now, every time you shift a gear, it feels like it's building more steam.' Meanwhile, team boss Hervé Poncharal was so pleased with James Toseland's strong debut that he exercised his contract option to sign him up pronto for 2009 as well. In addition to impressing with his results, Toseland had even made his French team chief (and IRTA president) coffee during testing. 'No rider's ever done that before,' he said.

As for Honda, the pneumo engine had been promised only for post-race tests, and Hayden in particular was keen. Instead, hopes were dashed – the engine was not ready even for further testing, arrival now postponed until after the French GP.

Perhaps the disappointment accounted for some peevish behaviour from paddock nice guy Hayden, whose qualifying run, heading for the front row on his third tyre, was spoiled when he found Toseland in his way. The Englishman visited the pit later to apologise, but Nicky would have none of it. 'I didn't want to hear

Right: Early laps, and Edwards heads Hayden, Vermeulen, Stoner, Capirossi and the pack.

Below: Ashleigh Hopkins put some pink into the green pit.

Bottom: Hopkins took a strong fifth.

Below right: Hayden had a rare race crash.

Bottom right: Ex-GP racer Roger Burnett, now managing Toseland.

Photographs: Gold & Goose

"sorry". He's been saying "sorry" a lot. Three races in and a lot of "sorries."' He sent Toseland packing, then was overcome with remorse and visited Tech 3 hospitality himself to apologise. 'At the time, I kind of acted like a punk.'

There was no new engine either for Kawasaki. Intriguingly, the Screamer motor, with even firing order, had run again at tests after Jerez and gained attention for the shrill pitch of the exhaust. As Anthony West, struggling to find form, commented after the test, 'The noise it makes kind of cheers you up.' But it was not race ready. Meanwhile Suzuki was finding much the same with its 2008 bike, and again was running a hybrid concoction of 2007 chassis and bodywork.

Elias, a winner at Estoril in the past, encountered extra misfortune as he continued to make difficult acquaintance with the Ducati. Running down the main straight, suddenly there was a bang and a plume of smoke; the rider pulled over hurriedly to park the bike, jumping off and clutching at his right boot. The clutch basket had flown to pieces, damaging the casings and spewing hot oil. What really hurt was a piece of shrapnel that hit his foot. At the medical centre, it transpired that no bones were broken, but it was enough to end his session and leave him limping for some time.

Countryman Lorenzo had his own appointment with pain, after the race. He'd been suffering from arm pump more severely on the bigger bikes, and had chosen to take advantage of a couple of weekends off to have remedial carpal tunnel surgery on his right arm, the worst affected. The name of his surgeon, Dr Xavier Mir, of the Barcelona Clinica Dexeus, would be mentioned increasingly in the coming months, linked to Pedrosa as well as Lorenzo.

MOTOGP RACE – 28 laps

Lorenzo, Pedrosa and Rossi lined up on the front row, the thwarted Hayden fourth, otherwise it might have been an all-Michelin trio. Edwards and Toseland completed row three, the first six barely covered by a second. Stoner was down in ninth, and troubled. 'There's just something missing in our bike, in our package. We're not just slower compared to other riders, we're slower compared to us six months ago,' he said.

Rain was spotting visors as they lined up. All were on slicks, then a wet race was decreed: if they needed to change tyres now, they would have to switch to the spare bikes being warmed in the pit lane.

Capirossi took Stoner's place on the grid, but the delay was minimal as they hastily swapped.

Pedrosa made his usual lightning start to lead into the first corner, but a combination of caution and professional recklessness in the iffy conditions made for an all-action first lap. By the end, Lorenzo had pushed past Rossi and the leader to head them over the line, Pedrosa now fourth, behind Dovizioso. A second or so off came Hopkins, Edwards and Hayden.

Rossi swept past down the straight and into the first corner, holding the lead until the 13th lap. Pedrosa had regained third second time around, when the rain was at its worst, although it soon improved again. The front group closed up gradually: after eight laps, first to sixth was covered by just over 2.5 seconds. But Hopkins was starting to lose pace as front-wheel chatter gave him several scary moments. Both his fellow Americans passed him on lap ten; next time around, Hayden had passed Edwards and set his sights on Dovizioso, almost three seconds ahead.

Up front, Pedrosa had finally mounted a successful attack on Lorenzo for second on lap 11. It triggered a new phase. Two laps later, Lorenzo did the same thing back – the favoured first-turn out-braking move – and directly started to lean on Rossi. At the tricky uphill chicane, he pounced, pushing inside and forcing Rossi wide. 'I said sorry to Valentino because it was a very crazy overtake, but I thought that it was the moment to try to go away, and that's it,' he explained.

It was well judged. Rossi knew before the start that his rear tyre wouldn't grip all race long. Two laps later, Pedrosa was also ahead of him.

Could the Honda catch the Yamaha? That question remained unanswered until lap 18, when Lorenzo laid down a new record as he stretched the gap to over a second. It had almost doubled before Pedrosa started pushing again during the closing laps, but Lorenzo was able to respond, to take a classic maiden victory. The 'Lorenzo's Land' flag was planted for the first time in the new class.

Grip-troubled Rossi was another ten seconds down, but drama in the pursuit group meant that he escaped the potential threat of two Michelin-shod Hondas.

Hayden had closed gradually on Dovizioso, leaving Edwards and Hopkins trailing, and by lap 15 was less than two seconds down. He never got the opportunity to attack, however, for the Italian lost the front end and slid off at the bottom of the hill before the chicane. Next time around, Hayden did the same thing in exactly the same spot. Dovizioso admitted that he'd been pushing to the very maximum, but Hayden was rather baffled. 'Just went down quick, quite early and no warning at all,' he said.

That left Edwards safely alone to take fifth, with Hopkins continuing to lose ground behind him, but never-theless far enough ahead of the pursuit to gain a well-earned sixth place.

The group had been headed at first by Stoner, before his flapping black box problem, and thereafter by Vermeulen. Toseland had started well and had moved ahead of the Suzuki after yet another close passing move on lap 14. He had pulled a handy little gap on de Puniet and the fading Vermeulen, but now Stoner was going again and gaining rapidly. Vermeulen succumbed directly on lap 17, de Puniet likewise next time around, tucking in behind as the Ducati quickly got on to Tose-land's back wheel.

The Englishman proved easy meat for Stoner, who left him to fend off de Puniet. The Frenchman did finally get by, the pair colliding as he did so, only to run into the gravel on the very next lap.

Vermeulen came home in eighth, Capirossi a lacklus-tre two more seconds down, followed by the equally un-exciting Nakano.

The also-rans were another 20 seconds away and, while close together, had hardly changed positions since half-distance, by which point Elias had come from last past all except group leader de Angelis, who finished 11th. Melandri and Guintoli were next of the downbeat, non-Stoner Ducatis, with de Puniet regaining solid ground to take the last point, ahead of increasingly at-sea West.

250cc RACE – 26 laps

Simoncelli led from pole, pursued by Kallio, Bautista and Debon. Estoril, however, is Bautista's track, with successive 125 and 250 wins. By the end of the lap, he was firmly in front and gradually drawing away from Simoncelli, the pair in turn gapping the pursuing pack.

This was led from lap four by Pasini, from Kallio, Taka-hashi and Aoyama, Debon having crashed out.

By lap seven, Bautista was more than two seconds clear and still going faster, setting fastest lap – slower than his own record – next time around to keep stretch-ing. At one point, he was more than nine seconds clear, and still seven at the end, after slowing his pace. 'With a few laps left, it started to drizzle at the chicane, but the advantage was big enough for me not to have to take any risks,' he said.

The pursuit may have been in vain, but it gave Simon-celli an equally healthy margin over the quartet behind, more than five seconds on lap 11. On the same lap, Kallio had taken control once and for all, and immedi-ately gained a little air as Pasini and Aoyama worried away at one another.

The KTM rider would build on it, closing gradually, but remorselessly. The mathematics added some excite-ment to a processional race up front, and as they started the last lap, he was just eight-tenths behind, and had been lapping up to half a second faster as spots of rain threatened here and there.

He would have passed over the line too, had Simon-celli not veered very firmly to the left. The bikes touched, and Kallio had to come off the throttle. 'I think without this move, for sure we could be second. But sometimes it's like this,' said the Finn, impassive as always. Simon-celli narrowly escaped official censure; Kallio's consola-tion was the lead on points.

He'd left some chaos behind him. By lap 13, Luthi and Simon had come up to join the group, the last-named only briefly, but clearly Luthi was on the move. He passed Pasini, Aoyama and finally Takahashi in one lap, the first two at the chicane. They all stayed in very close attendance. Too close.

Pasini took fifth off Aoyama three laps later, but the Japanese rider swooped back inside him at the bottom of the hill. The bikes touched, and Pasini was down. With practised ease, he ran to his blue Aprilia and jumped back on. But at the end of the back straight, he discovered he had no front brake. Down he went again, this time the bike cartwheeling to destruction.

Luthi now outpaced the two Japanese riders. Finally, with three laps left, Aoyama also passed Takahashi and pulled clear.

Simon faded behind, retaining seventh only by a second as battling Spaniards Barbera and Faubel closed, Barbera passing the latter with three laps to go.

Pesek held a lonely vigil for tenth, still two seconds clear of Espargaro, who had broken free from the next battle and closed impressively. The Chinese Zongshen 250 team finished in the points in 14th with Federico Sandi, although Chinese rider Ho Wan Chow crashed out on lap two; Laverty opened his account with a single point for 15th.

Above: Thomas Luthi was best of the rest among the 250s.

Above right: Corsi took a second straight 125 win.

Top: Simoncelli narrowly escaped censure for his blocking move on Kallio.

Left: Bautista enjoyed his first win of 2008.

Top left: Pedrosa follows the black lines to second on the podium.

Photographs: Gold & Goose

125cc RACE – 23 laps

Two new faces were on the front row, on two not very special Degraaf Aprilias: American Stevie Bonsey, in only his second year of road-racing, and English teenager Danny Webb, second and fourth. Sadly, Bonsey lost all chance of a podium when he messed up his start.

Terol led the first lap, from Webb, but the Englishman was fifth next time around, having been passed by Corsi, Olive and his own compatriot, Smith. Terol led for two more laps as a group of four moved away, Talmacsi now a lone fifth, and Webb settling in the next gang.

The four laid on the most entertaining racing for the first ten laps, Olive doing most of the leading across the line. Over the next two laps, Corsi moved forward and Terol dropped to the back of the group. Then Smith went flying – a big high-side on the exit from the double left behind the paddock, eliminating himself and costing the Spaniard almost two seconds.

At this point, the front pair started to move away, Olive in front until the 17th lap, when Corsi took over. They raced wheel to wheel, seldom further apart than the three-tenths gap as they crossed the line, but the Italian had a better exit from the last corner and kept the Spaniard at bay all the way. A second successive win extended his points lead; Corsi also set fastest lap, but not a record.

Terol was a lone third, then came a six-strong fight for fourth, admittedly rather strung out at the back by the finish. By then, it was led by Bonsey, who had finished lap one 12th, but in fighting mood. His last victims included Webb, a troubled Talmacsi with a below-par engine and Di Meglio, who finished in that order, with Bradl and Gadea just off the back.

bwin.com GRANDE PREMIO DE PORTUGAL

13 APRIL 2008 • FIM WORLD CHAMPIONSHIP ROUND 3

CIRCUITO DO ESTORIL

Turn 8, Turn 10, Turn 3, Turn 9, Turn 2, Orelha, Esses, Turn 5, Turn 6, Turn 4, Turn 1, Parabolica

Circuit 4.182km / 2.598 miles

MotoGP

RACE: 28 laps, 72.772 miles/117.096km • Weather: Dry • Air 18°C • Humidity 53% • Track 21°C

Pos.	Rider	Nat.	No.	Team	Machine	Tyres	Laps	Time & speed (mph/km/h)
1	Jorge Lorenzo	SPA	48	Fiat Yamaha Team	Yamaha	M	28	45m 53.089s 95.142mph/ 153.117km/h
2	Dani Pedrosa	SPA	2	Repsol Honda Team	Honda	M	28	45m 54.906s
3	Valentino Rossi	ITA	46	Fiat Yamaha Team	Yamaha	B	28	46m 05.812s
4	Colin Edwards	USA	5	Tech 3 Yamaha	Yamaha	M	28	46m 10.312s
5	John Hopkins	USA	21	Kawasaki Racing Team	Kawasaki	B	28	46m 16.841s
6	Casey Stoner	AUS	1	Ducati Marlboro Team	Ducati	B	28	46m 19.777s
7	James Toseland	GBR	52	Tech 3 Yamaha	Yamaha	M	28	46m 25.720s
8	Chris Vermeulen	AUS	7	Rizla Suzuki MotoGP	Suzuki	B	28	46m 29.471s
9	Loris Capirossi	ITA	65	Rizla Suzuki MotoGP	Suzuki	B	28	46m 31.357s
10	Shinya Nakano	JPN	56	San Carlo Honda Gresini	Honda	B	28	46m 32.565s
11	Alex de Angelis	RSM	15	San Carlo Honda Gresini	Honda	B	28	46m 54.395s
12	Toni Elias	SPA	24	Alice Team	Ducati	B	28	46m 56.956s
13	Marco Melandri	ITA	33	Ducati Marlboro Team	Ducati	B	28	47m 02.614s
14	Sylvain Guintoli	FRA	50	Alice Team	Ducati	B	28	47m 02.723s
15	Randy de Puniet	FRA	14	LCR Honda MotoGP	Honda	M	28	47m 04.631s
16	Anthony West	AUS	13	Kawasaki Racing Team	Kawasaki	B	28	47m 16.718s
	Nicky Hayden	USA	69	Repsol Honda Team	Honda	M	16	26m 23.675s
	Andrea Dovizioso	ITA	4	JiR Team Scot MotoGP	Honda	M	15	24m 43.870s

Fastest lap: Jorge Lorenzo, on lap 18, 1m 37.404s, 96.042mph/154.564km/h (record).

Previous lap record: Nicky Hayden, USA (Honda), 1m 37.493s, 95.954mph/154.423km/h (2007).

Event best maximum speed: Toni Elias, 200.8mph/323.2km/h (free practice no. 3).

QUALIFYING: 12 April 2008

Weather: Dry
Air: 17°C Humidity: 37% Track: 26°C

Pos.	Rider	Time
1	Lorenzo	1m 35.715s
2	Pedrosa	1m 35.948s
3	Rossi	1m 36.199s
4	Hayden	1m 36.266s
5	Edwards	1m 36.289s
6	Toseland	1m 36.790s
7	Dovizioso	1m 36.998s
8	de Puniet	1m 37.223s
9	Stoner	1m 37.253s
10	Hopkins	1m 37.346s
11	Nakano	1m 37.664s
12	Capirossi	1m 37.786s
13	Vermeulen	1m 37.843s
14	Elias	1m 38.561s
15	West	1m 38.775s
16	de Angelis	1m 38.823s
17	Melandri	1m 39.115s
18	Guintoli	1m 39.355s

Grid order

Grid order	1	2	3	4	5	6	7	8	9	10	11	12	13	14	15	16	17	18	19	20	21	22	23	24	25	26	27	28	●
48 LORENZO	48	46	46	46	46	46	46	46	46	46	46	46	48	48	48	48	48	48	48	48	48	48	48	48	48	48	48	48	1
2 PEDROSA	46	48	48	48	48	48	48	48	48	48	2	2	46	46	2	2	2	2	2	2	2	2	2	2	2	2	2	2	2
46 ROSSI	4	4	2	2	2	2	2	2	2	2	48	48	2	2	46	46	46	46	46	46	46	46	46	46	46	46	46	46	3
69 HAYDEN	2	2	4	4	4	4	4	4	4	4	4	4	4	4	69	5	5	5	5	5	5	5	5	5	5	5	5	5	4
5 EDWARDS	21	21	21	21	21	21	21	21	21	5	69	69	69	69	69	5	21	21	21	21	21	21	21	21	21	21	21	21	5
52 TOSELAND	5	5	5	5	5	5	5	5	5	69	5	5	5	21	5	21	52	52	52	52	1	1	1	1	1	1	1	1	6
4 DOVISIOSO	69	69	69	69	69	69	69	69	69	21	21	21	21	21	21	52	14	1	1	52	52	52	52	52	14	52	52		7
14 de PUNIET	7	7	7	1	1	1	7	7	7	7	7	7	7	7	52	52	14	1	14	14	14	14	14	14	52	7	7		8
1 STONER	1	1	1	7	7	7	1	52	52	52	52	52	52	7	14	7	7	7	7	7	7	7	7	7	7	65	65		9
21 HOPKINS	65	52	52	52	52	52	52	1	14	14	14	14	14	14	7	1	65	65	65	65	65	65	65	65	65	56	56		10
56 NAKANO	52	65	65	65	65	65	65	14	1	1	1	1	1	1	1	65	56	56	56	56	56	56	56	56	56	15	15		11
65 CAPIROSSI	50	56	56	56	14	14	14	65	65	65	65	65	65	65	56	15	15	15	15	15	15	15	15	15	24	24			12
7 VERMEULEN	56	50	14	14	56	56	56	56	56	56	56	56	56	56	15	24	24	24	24	24	24	24	24	33	33			13
24 ELIAS	14	14	50	15	15	15	15	15	15	15	15	15	15	15	24	33	33	33	33	33	33	33	33	50	50			14
13 WEST	15	15	13	50	50	50	50	50	50	50	33	33	33	24	33	50	50	50	50	50	50	50	50	14	14			15
15 de ANGELIS	13	13	15	13	33	33	33	33	33	33	50	50	50	33	50	13	13	13	13	13	13	13	13	13	13				
33 MELANDRI	33	33	33	33	33	13	13	13	13	13	24	24	24	50	13														
50 GUINTOLI	24	24	24	24	24	24	24	24	24	24	13	13	13	13															

FASTEST RACE LAPS

	Rider	Lap	Time
1	Lorenzo	18	1m 37.404s
2	Pedrosa	18	1m 37.471s
3	Hayden	16	1m 37.806s
4	Stoner	21	1m 37.972s
5	Rossi	17	1m 37.975s
6	Dovizioso	12	1m 37.985s
7	Edwards	19	1m 38.083s
8	Hopkins	5	1m 38.228s
9	de Puniet	20	1m 38.291s
10	Nakano	9	1m 38.666s
11	Toseland	11	1m 38.721s
12	Vermeulen	10	1m 38.750s
13	Capirossi	22	1m 38.773s
14	Melandri	21	1m 39.387s
15	Elias	20	1m 39.439s
16	de Angelis	5	1m 39.454s
17	Guintoli	26	1m 39.811s
18	West	9	1m 40.099s

statistics

250cc

26 laps, 67.574 miles/108.732km

Pos.	Rider (Nat.)	No.	Team	Machine	Laps	Time & speed
1	Alvaro Bautista (SPA)	19	Mapfre Aspar Team	Aprilia	26	44m 34.257s 90.951mph/ 146.371km/h
2	Marco Simoncelli (ITA)	58	Metis Gilera	Gilera	26	44m 41.307s
3	Mika Kallio (FIN)	36	Red Bull KTM 250	KTM	26	44m 41.320s
4	Thomas Luthi (SWI)	12	Emmi - Caffe Latte	Aprilia	26	44m 47.255s
5	Hiroshi Aoyama (JPN)	4	Red Bull KTM 250	KTM	26	44m 48.923s
6	Yuki Takahashi (JPN)	72	JiR Team Scot 250	Honda	26	44m 52.755s
7	Julian Simon (SPA)	60	Repsol KTM 250cc	KTM	26	45m 01.069s
8	Hector Barbera (SPA)	21	Team Toth Aprilia	Aprilia	26	45m 02.269s
9	Hector Faubel (SPA)	55	Mapfre Aspar Team	Aprilia	26	45m 02.545s
10	Lukas Pesek (CZE)	52	Auto Kelly - CP	Aprilia	26	45m 11.223s
11	Aleix Espargaro (SPA)	41	Lotus Aprilia	Aprilia	26	45m 12.553s
12	Alex Baldolini (ITA)	25	Matteoni Racing	Aprilia	26	45m 26.327s
13	Ratthapark Wilairot (THA)	14	Thai Honda PTT SAG	Honda	26	45m 47.560s
14	Federico Sandi (ITA)	90	Zongshen Team of China	Aprilia	26	45m 51.849s
15	Eugene Laverty (IRL)	50	Blusens Aprilia	Aprilia	26	45m 55.620s
16	Karel Abraham (CZE)	17	Cardion AB Motoracing	Aprilia	26	46m 00.612s
17	Manuel Poggiali (RSM)	54	Campetella Racing	Gilera	26	46m 01.695s
18	Imre Toth (HUN)	10	Team Toth Aprilia	Aprilia	25	45m 08.919s
19	Doni Tata Pradita (INA)	45	Yamaha Pertamina Indonesia	Yamaha	25	45m 57.795s
	Roberto Locatelli (ITA)	15	Metis Gilera	Gilera	23	DNF
	Mattia Pasini (ITA)	75	Polaris World	Aprilia	20	DNF
	Russel Gomez (SPA)	7	Blusens Aprilia	Aprilia	11	DNF
	Fabrizio Lai (ITA)	32	Campetella Racing	Gilera	4	DNF
	Alex Debon (SPA)	6	Lotus Aprilia	Aprilia	3	DNF
	Ho Wan Chow (CHN)	89	Zongshen Team of China	Aprilia	1	DNF

Fastest lap: Bautista, 1m 41.425s, 92.234mph/148.436km/h.

Lap record: Alvaro Bautista, SPA (Aprilia), 1m 40.521s, 93.063mph/149.771km/h (2007).

Event best maximum speed: Luthi, 172.3mph/277.3km/h (free practice no. 1).

Qualifying: 1 Simoncelli, 1m 40.257s; 2 Bautista, 1m 40.554s; 3 Pasini, 1m 40.653s; 4 Kallio, 1m 40.772s; 5 Takahashi, 1m 41.063s; 6 Aoyama, 1m 41.228s; 7 Debon, 1m 41.280s; 8 Luthi, 1m 41.356s; 9 Barbera, 1m 41.370s; 10 Faubel, 1m 41.470s; 11 Simon, 1m 41.820s; 12 Pesek, 1m 41.841s; 13 Espargaro, 1m 42.080s; 14 Baldolini, 1m 42.179s; 15 Poggiali, 1m 42.265s; 16 Abraham, 1m 42.360s; 17 Wilairot, 1m 42.472s; 18 Lai, 1m 42.574s; 19 Locatelli, 1m 42.813s; 20 Sandi, 1m 43.288s; 21 Laverty, 1m 43.297s; 22 Toth, 1m 44.853s; 23 Pradita, 1m 45.402s; 24 Gomez, 1m 46.051s; 25 Chow, 1m 46.594s.

Fastest race laps: 1 Bautista, 1m 41.425s; 2 Kallio, 1m 41.984s; 3 Simoncelli, 1m 42.168s; 4 Luthi, 1m 42.206s; 5 Simon, 1m 42.228s; 6 Aoyama, 1m 42.430s; 7 Pasini, 1m 42.453s; 8 Barbera, 1m 42.468s; 9 Takahashi, 1m 42.575s; 10 Faubel, 1m 42.659s; 11 Pesek, 1m 42.980s; 12 Espargaro, 1m 42.981s; 13 Debon, 1m 43.297s; 14 Locatelli, 1m 43.304s; 15 Baldolini, 1m 43.584s; 16 Wilairot, 1m 43.925s; 17 Poggiali, 1m 44.344s; 18 Sandi, 1m 44.450s; 19 Abraham, 1m 44.537s; 20 Laverty, 1m 44.813s; 21 Lai, 1m 45.748s; 22 Toth, 1m 46.481s; 23 Gomez, 1m 47.688s; 24 Pradita, 1m 47.912s; 25 Chow, 1m 58.334s.

World Championship: 1 Kallio, 57; 2 Pasini, 45; 3 Barbera, 39; 4 Takahashi, 37; 5 Bautista, 35; 6 Aoyama, 24; 7 Debon, 23; 8 Simon, 23; 9 Simoncelli, 20; 10 Espargaro, 19; 11 Locatelli, 16; 12 Luthi, 14; 13 Faubel, 13; 14 Abraham, 12; 15 Pesek, 12; 16 Wilairot, 10; 17 Baldolini, 9; 18 Lai, 4; 19 Hernandez, Poggiali and Sandi, 2; 22 Laverty and Toth, 1.

125cc

23 laps, 59.777 miles/98.186km

Pos.	Rider (Nat.)	No.	Team	Machine	Laps	Time & speed
1	Simone Corsi (ITA)	24	Jack & Jones WRB	Aprilia	23	40m 56.168s 87.600mph/ 140.979km/h
2	Joan Olive (SPA)	6	Belson Derbi	Derbi	23	40m 56.467s
3	Nicolas Terol (SPA)	18	Jack & Jones WRB	Aprilia	23	41m 02.523s
4	Stevie Bonsey (USA)	51	Degraaf Grand Prix	Aprilia	23	41m 11.141s
5	Danny Webb (GBR)	99	Degraaf Grand Prix	Aprilia	23	41m 11.700s
6	Gabor Talmacsi (HUN)	1	Bancaja Aspar Team	Aprilia	23	41m 12.036s
7	Mike di Meglio (FRA)	63	Ajo Motorsport	Derbi	23	41m 12.043s
8	Stefan Bradl (GER)	17	Grizzly Gas Kiefer Racing	Aprilia	23	41m 14.055s
9	Sergio Gadea (SPA)	33	Bancaja Aspar Team	Aprilia	23	41m 14.291s
10	Sandro Cortese (GER)	11	Emmi - Caffe Latte	Aprilia	23	41m 18.781s
11	Andrea Iannone (ITA)	29	I.C. Team	Aprilia	23	41m 23.658s
12	Dominique Aegerter (SWI)	77	Ajo Motorsport	Derbi	23	41m 23.712s
13	Pol Espargaro (SPA)	44	Belson Derbi	Derbi	23	41m 24.538s
14	Michael Ranseder (AUT)	60	I.C. Team	Aprilia	23	41m 24.585s
15	Efren Vazquez (SPA)	7	Blusens Aprilia Junior	Aprilia	23	41m 28.881s
16	Tomoyoshi Koyama (JPN)	71	ISPA KTM Aran	KTM	23	41m 30.170s
17	Stefano Bianco (ITA)	27	S3+ WTR San Marino Team	Aprilia	23	41m 43.866s
18	Marc Marquez (SPA)	93	Repsol KTM 125cc	KTM	23	41m 47.805s
19	Takaaki Nakagami (JPN)	73	I.C. Team	Aprilia	23	41m 47.847s
20	Alexis Masbou (FRA)	5	Loncin Racing	Loncin	23	41m 47.885s
21	Scott Redding (GBR)	45	Blusens Aprilia Junior	Aprilia	23	42m 04.076s
22	Pere Tutusaus (SPA)	30	Bancaja Aspar Team	Aprilia	23	42m 12.062s
23	Dino Lombardi (ITA)	13	BQR Blusens	Aprilia	23	42m 16.143s
24	Robert Muresan (ROU)	95	Grizzly Gas Kiefer Racing	Aprilia	23	42m 35.362s
25	Cyril Carrillo (FRA)	36	FFM Honda GP 125	Honda	23	42m 35.386s
26	Axel Pons (SPA)	14	Jack & Jones WRB	Aprilia	23	42m 40.124s
27	Ivan Maestro (SPA)	76	Hune Matteoni	Aprilia	22	41m 37.869s
28	Karel Pesek (CZE)	37	Czech Road Racing JNR	Aprilia	22	41m 52.604s
	Bradley Smith (GBR)	38	Polaris World	Aprilia	12	DNF
	Lorenzo Zanetti (ITA)	8	ISPA KTM Aran	KTM	12	DNF
	Pablo Nieto (SPA)	22	Onde 2000 KTM	KTM	11	DNF
	Jules Cluzel (FRA)	16	Loncin Racing	Loncin	8	DNF
	Esteve Rabat (SPA)	12	Repsol KTM 125cc	KTM	7	DNF
	Raffaele de Rosa (ITA)	35	Onde 2000 KTM	KTM	6	DNF
	Hugo van den Berg (NED)	56	Degraaf Grand Prix	Aprilia	0	DNF

Fastest lap: Corsi, 1m 45.557s, 88.624mph/142.626km/h.

Lap record: Gabor Talmacsi, HUN (Aprilia), 1m 45.027s, 89.070mph/143.345km/h (2007).

Event best maximum speed: Bradl, 148.2mph/238.5km/h (qualifying practice no. 1).

Qualifying: 1 Corsi, 1m 45.367s; 2 Bonsey, 1m 45.621s; 3 Terol, 1m 45.622s; 4 Webb, 1m 45.782s; 5 Gadea, 1m 45.808s; 6 Olive, 1m 45.854s; 7 Bradl, 1m 46.026s; 8 di Meglio, 1m 46.144s; 9 Talmacsi, 1m 46.158s; 10 Redding, 1m 46.329s; 11 Koyama, 1m 46.448s; 12 Iannone, 1m 46.491s; 13 Smith, 1m 46.523s; 14 Nieto, 1m 46.622s; 15 Vazquez, 1m 46.679s; 16 de Rosa, 1m 46.736s; 17 Bianco, 1m 46.860s; 18 Rabat, 1m 47.016s; 19 Aegerter, 1m 47.133s; 20 Cortese, 1m 47.293s; 21 Espargaro, 1m 47.300s; 22 Ranseder, 1m 47.628s; 23 Tutusaus, 1m 47.717s; 24 Nakagami, 1m 47.724s; 25 Masbou, 1m 47.734s; 26 Marquez, 1m 47.817s; 27 Cluzel, 1m 47.953s; 28 Zanetti, 1m 47.971s; 29 van den Berg, 1m 48.495s; 30 Muresan, 1m 48.840s; 31 Maestro, 1m 49.355s; 32 Pons, 1m 49.669s; 33 Lombardi, 1m 49.690s; 34 Carrillo, 1m 49.809s; 35 Pesek, 1m 50.687s.

Fastest race laps: 1 Corsi, 1m 45.557s; 2 Olive, 1m 45.965s; 3 Terol, 1m 45.966s; 4 Smith, 1m 46.063s; 5 di Meglio, 1m 46.367s; 6 Bonsey, 1m 46.382s; 7 Talmacsi, 1m 46.387s; 8 Webb, 1m 46.531s; 9 Gadea, 1m 46.602s; 10 de Rosa, 1m 46.652s; 11 Cortese, 1m 46.730s; 12 Bradl, 1m 46.743s; 13 Vazquez, 1m 46.796s; 14 Ranseder, 1m 46.844s; 15 Aegerter, 1m 46.938s; 16 Espargaro, 1m 46.957s; 17 Iannone, 1m 47.104s; 18 Koyama, 1m 47.295s; 19 Bianco, 1m 47.372s; 20 Redding, 1m 47.578s; 21 Nieto, 1m 47.580s; 22 Marquez, 1m 47.766s; 23 Zanetti, 1m 47.824s; 24 Nakagami, 1m 47.987s; 25 Masbou, 1m 48.042s; 26 Cluzel, 1m 48.133s; 27 Rabat, 1m 49.204s; 28 Tutusaus, 1m 49.229s; 29 Lombardi, 1m 49.366s; 30 Pons, 1m 49.686s; 31 Muresan, 1m 49.797s; 32 Carrillo, 1m 49.836s; 33 Pesek, 1m 50.710s; 34 Maestro, 1m 51.418s.

World Championship: 1 Corsi, 59; 2 Terol, 42; 3 Olive, 40; 4 Bradl, 37; 5 Gadea, 32; 6 di Meglio, 29; 7 Bonsey, 23; 8 Webb, 21; 9 Redding, 20; 10 Cortese, 17; 11 Smith, 16; 12 Talmacsi, 14; 13 Espargaro, 13; 14 Aegerter, 12; 15 Nieto, 11; 16 Vazquez, 8; 17 Iannone, 7; 18 de Rosa, 5; 19 Rabat, 4; 20 Bianco and Koyama, 3; 22 Ranseder, 3; 23 Nakagami, 1.

RIDER STANDINGS
After 3 Rounds

1 =	Jorge Lorenzo	61
1 =	Dani Pedrosa	61
3	Valentino Rossi	47
4	Casey Stoner	40
5	James Toseland	29
6	Loris Capirossi	26
7	John Hopkins	24
8	Colin Edwards	22
9	Andrea Dovizioso	21
10	Nicky Hayden	19
11	Shinya Nakano	16
12	Chris Vermeulen	14
13	Marco Melandri	12
14	Randy de Puniet	8
15	Alex de Angelis	7
16	Toni Elias	7
17	Anthony West	3
18	Sylvain Guintoli	3

TEAM STANDINGS
After 3 Rounds

1	Fiat Yamaha Team	108
2	Repsol Honda Team	80
3	Ducati Marlboro Team	52
4	Tech 3 Yamaha	51
5	Rizla Suzuki MotoGP	40
6	Kawasaki Racing Team	27
7	San Carlo Honda Gresini	23
8	JiR Team Scot MotoGP	21
9	Alice Team	10
10	LCR Honda MotoGP	8

CONSTRUCTOR STANDINGS
After 3 Rounds

1	Yamaha	65
2	Honda	61
3	Ducati	40
4	Suzuki	27
5	Kawasaki	24

CHINESE | GP
SHANGHAI

The man who fell to earth. Lorenzo's high-side crash was balletic and violent. Miraculously, he came back to race.
Photographs: Gold & Goose

THE forthcoming Olympic Games in Beijing had put a spotlight on international sport, politics, and the clash of Western and Chinese political systems and mores. What we had been told would be the last GP at the Shanghai circuit blundered in and out of it, causing barely a stir. In a country of more than 1.3 billion people, a crowd of 20,000 arrived, heavily reinforced by large numbers of bused-in schoolchildren.

The timing of the Chinese GP was not especially comfortable. Elsewhere in the Western world, the Olympic torch was on its controversial rounds, escorted by track-suited protectors and angry protestors, and headed, even more controversially, to Tibet. Already there had been uneasy moments at Estoril, when the top riders at the pre-race conference had been asked if they would contemplate some sort of a protest at the forthcoming race. Loris Capirossi particularly stood up for the oppressed and suggested that some action could be forthcoming; Pedrosa, Rossi and Toseland sort of went along with him. In the intervening period, however, there had been quiet warnings that the riders should stick to their day jobs, and talk about gearing and side-grip rather than civil liberties. By the time everyone arrived in Shanghai, people were more prone to apprehension than agitation. Let's just get it over with.

The welcome – once customs had been cleared, and give or take a few pairs of well-armed policemen roaming the paddock and press room – was warm and friendly, the weather muggy and changeable, with rain on race morning and gloomy overcast skies dropping track temperature by a massive 25 degrees from qualifying, making tyre choice a gamble. The track was its usual over-swirly self. To Stoner, the tight technical sections, 'on bikes, are just more of a pain than anything', while pole qualifier Edwards decried the frequent opportunity to 'lose all my time in one corner'. As happened to him in the race, when he ran on at the hairpin after braking from more than 200mph on the longest straight of the year. He dropped from third to seventh in the process, and did it again later.

Up front, the race was two-strong: a battle of fastest laps between Rossi the hare and Pedrosa the hound, with Stoner on a poor tyre choice relegated to a lonely

Left: The sparse crowd was boosted by parties of schoolchildren on a day out.

Right: The Doctor was back, with his first win for Bridgestone.

Below left: Old boys club: the launch of the Maxtra brought back some famous names, including John Surtees (*third from left*), Garry Taylor (*alongside*) and two-stroke engine designer Jan Witteveen (*right*).

Below: Edwards took his third career pole.
Photographs: Gold & Goose

Left: Marco Melandri rode a spirited race to take fifth place.
Photograph: Gold & Goose

and ultimately distant pursuit. But there was plenty of action behind them in the mid-field. Nobody did more overtaking than Lorenzo, climbing from ninth to fourth.

The Estoril winner, who turned 21 on race day, had arrived with his right arm in a compression bandage; he left in a wheelchair, with yet more accolades. The injury came on only his tenth lap, in a vicious high-side behind the massive stands, changing direction between the first long right-hander and the next left. As he flopped over, the bike flicked sideways and then gripped, catapulting the rider in a very high and graceful loop with a painfully hard landing. He sat up and clutched his right ankle. When reports came that he had suffered at least one fracture there, it seemed unlikely he would be riding.

To do so was certainly heroic; to qualify and finish fourth even more so. There was no doubt that he was injured and hurting, and it was borne out by his thin smile on the grid. But was this showman doing a bit of play-acting as well? Taking off for the sighting lap, he stalled his engine. As officials ran up and his pit crew returned with the starter, Jorge vaulted off and pushed his M1. He got it started on his own – quite a feat for a man who couldn't walk. Or perhaps just a tribute to the industrial strength of Dr Costa's pain-killing regimen.

The Ducati puzzle was deepening: how Stoner could be so competitive on a bike that the other riders had trouble lifting off the back row of the grid. SBK men Bayliss and Biaggi were scheduled to test it; there were rumours that Alex Barros would be brought back to re-

lieve Melandri. The lower orders of Ducati riders had a brief respite at Shanghai, with Melandri running particularly strongly thanks to revised traction-control settings. Elias was also in the top ten after a visit to the factory for a face-to-face with design chief Filippo Preziosi, hoping to prove the 2008 Desmosedici was not just a one-rider bike. It would be a false dawn for both.

It may have been the dying of the light for the Shanghai race, and it may have been that in four years MotoGP had learned little of the country or the culture, and vice versa. But the event had not escaped the notice of some Chinese manufacturers, who serve an enormous domestic market.

Already, Zongshen had made occasional wild-card forays, and continued to do so in 2008, fielding Aprilias; in the 125 class, Loncin had taken over the entire Malaguti team, Honda-clone bikes and all. Now came something new and different: another company with a fully original bike of its own – a 125 prototype with a novel downward-pointing cylinder and a paint job suggestive of a dragon. Admittedly, it had been designed and built in Europe, the engine by long-time Aprilia chief designer Jan Witteveen, and the chassis by England's Harris Performance. But as John Surtees pointed out, in modern car racing, it is normal practice for even major factories to out-source design and manufacture to specialist racing firms.

Surtees, the only car and motorcycle world champion, was making a rare GP appearance as patron of

the Sino-European project, launched at Shanghai under the new name of Maxtra – the company behind it is the Grand River Group, which makes Haojue motorcycles, mainly under licence from Suzuki. He spoke eloquently of how the purity of relationship between rider and machine was preserved in the 125 class, free from the interference of electronic aids. 'There needs to be an accord between manufacturers and promoters relative to where research and development finishes, and where the entertainment factor and the relationship between a machine and a rider are maintained,' he said on the controversial theme.

Long-time Suzuki team manager Garry Taylor was a founder of the project, and the Maxtra is planned for GPs in 2009. For those with long memories, this first 'toe in the water' was highly reminiscent of Honda's first racing venture, also in the 125 class, at the Isle of Man in 1959. And just look what happened next...

MOTOGP RACE – 22 laps

The usual trio – Rossi, Stoner, Pedrosa – squabbled over top time on race tyres, but on qualifiers it was Edwards from Rossi and Stoner, with the injured Lorenzo a surprise fourth. Hayden was tenth, after spoiling his chances by crashing in qualifying

On a cool, but basically dry track, it was Edwards again, who pushed past fast-starting Stoner on the way into the first corner and went on to lead the first lap

Above: Stoner was a distant third. He explains his problems to his crew.

Left: Lorenzo's fourth was a courageous come-back.

Right: Kallio conquered changeable conditions for a canny second win.

Below right: Di Meglio held off 125 champion Talmacsi for second.

Below far right: Iannone was ecstatic after his first win.

Photographs:Gold & Goose

from the Ducati rider and Pedrosa, Rossi having been pushed back to fourth.

Stoner started to run wide here and there almost at once, and dropped to the back as the quartet pulled away. Pedrosa was in the lead by lap two, and Rossi was up to second next time around, looking at a gap of eight-tenths.

Now the race was on. The Yamaha closed quickly and Rossi got ahead quite easily at the end of the 1.2km straight on lap four. But he could not escape; for the next ten laps, Pedrosa was all over him, pulling along-side on the straight, and showing a wheel on one side and then the other. At Estoril, Rossi's tyres had forced him to slacken his pace. In Shanghai, the opposite was true. The two had been exchanging fastest laps, but on the 18th Rossi raised the bar one last time. Next time around, he was more than a second clear. From there, it was plain sailing, ending a seven-race drought, his longest winless stretch since his rookie 125 year in 1996. His last had been almost eight months before, at Estoril in September. It was also his first win on Bridge-stone tyres.

There was a technical reason for Pedrosa giving up the fight at the end, to do with changed conditions. Not only had it become cooler, but also there was a strong tailwind blowing down the longest straight of the year. The way his bike was geared, he was over-revving in sixth, and engine worries decided the matter for him. 'I

was a little bit scared to not finish, and we had big gap to the next rider, so I decide to close a little bit the throt-tle,' he explained.

Stoner had been alone ever since succeeding to third on lap six, when Edwards misjudged his braking at the end of the straight and ran right off, falling to seventh. The drop in temperature had caused the Australian to choose a medium tyre for safety reasons, and it was 'the wrong one. I knew after three laps. I was pushing the tyre way too much. We should have stayed with the hard from yesterday,' he explained.

The battle for fourth was absorbing. Lorenzo had started well, but soon began dropping back, with Hay-den taking over, pursued by Dovizioso and Capirossi, until lap five, when the Suzuki rider followed the Ed-wards line at the hairpin, rejoining 12th.

Meanwhile Melandri was riding like a man trans-formed, for one race only, and moving forwards rapidly from tenth on lap one, in the wake of fellow slow-starter Dovizioso. On lap eight, the Ducati got past both Dovi and Hayden, to start a long spell at the front of a group that included the pair and Edwards, with Lorenzo a sec-ond or so adrift.

By half-distance, Lorenzo had started to close, while Hayden had dropped back. The Yamaha was ahead on lap 12; two laps later, Lorenzo took Edwards and Dovizioso, then challenged Melandri. The next lap, he was ahead of him, pulling clear by three seconds.

Melandri was left a safe fifth, while Dovizioso ran into serious grip problems with four laps to go, dropping right out of contention and later blaming his inexperience for bad set-up. Hayden had already found a second wind, moving past Edwards on lap 18 for sixth.

The Yamaha rider now found himself under pressure from a resurgent Capirossi, until the Italian repeated his hairpin misadventure, letting Elias through to eighth. The Ducati rider had been moving slowly, but steadily, all race long.

Capirossi was next, losing two places after running wide again on the last lap, from Nakano and a now-dis-tant Dovizioso. Toseland had been lapping steadily on yet another new track, after succumbing to Nakano, and managed to fend off de Puniet, who had gained speed in the last laps. Then came Hopkins, after a dire after-noon during which he became the youngest rider to complete 100 GPs in the top class. He, de Angelis and West had chosen a harder rear Bridgestone and paid the price, finishing 14th, 16th and 17th respectively. Guintoli was 15th for the last point.

Chris Vermeulen was the only non-finisher, having pit-ted after six laps with his drive chain jumping.

With four different winners in four races, on three dif-ferent marques and two different tyre brands, the omens for the coming European season were good. And Rossi put himself into the title chase as a significant third force.

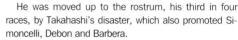

250cc RACE – 21 laps

Bautista's pole was by a confident four-tenths, but again he would find misfortune in a race made difficult by iffy conditions. The track was mostly dry as they started, and would become drier in spite of a few more wisps of rain.

Baldolini, Abraham and Poggiali crashed out on lap one, only Poggiali being unable to rejoin. The others were the first of several to fall and get back on. The most notable was Bautista.

Barbera led at first, from Simoncelli and Simon, but Bautista took all three to grab the lead on lap two. It wasn't quite settled, though, as Barbera got ahead again, while Simoncelli pushed Bautista to third. Two laps later, however, he was ahead of both and starting to move away slowly. By lap eight, he was almost 1.5 seconds clear. Then he pushed too hard in the first corner and slid off. By the time he got going again, he was 13th. 'The wet is a lottery, and it was my turn to lose,' he said philosophically.

Kallio, in a typically canny ride, had been fifth on lap one, but had picked up places gradually, and when Bautista went, he inherited a lead he was never to lose. On the same lap, team-mate Aoyama vaulted from fifth to second. The gap between the two would stretch out over the coming laps to more than three seconds: it was KTM's second one-two finish in the class.

Barbera had given way to Simoncelli and Takahashi on lap ten, and would drop back gradually as they all spaced out. Takahashi took a couple more laps to deal with Simoncelli and then moved clearly ahead, even closing to within a couple of seconds of Aoyama. By the end, he had dropped off, but seemed safe in third, starting the last lap with a cushion of more than six seconds. Then he ran wide at the penultimate corner and even wider at the next. Mechanical failure left him to freewheel over the line, dropping to seventh in the process.

Pasini had fallen to ninth on lap three, but he'd been gaining pace and, in the last laps, places as he improved his rhythm. Barbera was despatched on the 15th lap, and over the next four laps Pasini sliced away at a four-second gap to Simoncelli in fourth, flying past on the 19th.

He was moved up to the rostrum, his third in four races, by Takahashi's disaster, which also promoted Simoncelli, Debon and Barbera.

Debon? He'd come out of the blue after starting strong, then also slipping off and getting back on. That was on lap five, but he was going again so quickly that he lost only five places, dropping to 11th in an already well-spaced race. He moved forwards from then on, finally passing Barbera with two laps to go.

Wilairot was a career-best eighth, outdistancing Espargaro; Faubel headed Locatelli for tenth place. Bautista, nursing a damaged machine, was 12th, having passed Laverty in the closing corners.

125cc RACE – 19 laps

It was raining and the track was sodden at the start, but the surface dried as the race wore on. The difficult conditions triggered a crash-strewn event with several high-profile victims. One was pole starter and early leader Bradley Smith, lying third behind Iannone and Talmacsi at the time. He slumped in despair when he was unable to restart. Another was Simone Corsi, taken out at the hairpin on lap five.

Smith's fall came on lap seven, when Iannone was leading Talmacsi. The pair continued without him, the defending champion always looking for a way past. He found it over the line on lap ten, but Iannone was straight back ahead and stayed there to the finish. It was his first win in four years of trying, his previous best result being ninth.

Talmacsi was caught and passed by di Meglio on lap 13, which helped Iannone's escape. The Frenchman stayed ahead to the flag, albeit by only a tenth.

With only 19 survivors, they were well spread by the end. Espargaro was a lonely fifth, ditto Bradl in sixth and Olive in seventh, both having managed to get clear of a fierce mid-field battle. It was won at the end by Terol, from de Rosa, Vazquez, Rabat and Marquez.

Thirteen riders crashed out, among them Webb, lying eighth on lap 11; countryman Redding went five laps later, also in the points at the time. Cortese crashed and remounted twice, missing out on the points by less than a second.

PRAMAC GRAND PRIX OF CHINA

4 MAY 2008 • FIM WORLD CHAMPIONSHIP ROUND 4

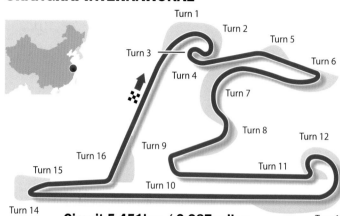

SHANGHAI INTERNATIONAL

Turn 1, Turn 2, Turn 3, Turn 4, Turn 5, Turn 6, Turn 7, Turn 8, Turn 9, Turn 10, Turn 11, Turn 12, Turn 13, Turn 14, Turn 15, Turn 16

Circuit 5.451km / 3.387 miles

MOTOGP

RACE: 22 laps, 72.182 miles/116.182km • Weather: Wet • Air 21°C • Humidity 72% • Track 21°C

Pos.	Rider	Nat.	No.	Team	Machine	Tyres	Laps	Time & speed (mph/km/h)
1	Valentino Rossi	ITA	46	*Fiat Yamaha Team*	Yamaha	B	22	44m 08.061s 98.144mph/ 157.947km/h
2	Dani Pedrosa	SPA	2	*Repsol Honda Team*	Honda	M	22	44m 11.951s
3	Casey Stoner	AUS	1	*Ducati Marlboro Team*	Ducati	B	22	44m 23.989s
4	Jorge Lorenzo	SPA	48	*Fiat Yamaha Team*	Yamaha	M	22	44m 30.555s
5	Marco Melandri	ITA	33	*Ducati Marlboro Team*	Ducati	B	22	44m 35.018s
6	Nicky Hayden	USA	69	*Repsol Honda Team*	Honda	M	22	44m 36.430s
7	Colin Edwards	USA	5	*Tech 3 Yamaha*	Yamaha	M	22	44m 37.841s
8	Toni Elias	SPA	24	*Alice Team*	Ducati	B	22	44m 38.286s
9	Loris Capirossi	ITA	65	*Rizla Suzuki MotoGP*	Suzuki	B	22	44m 39.501s
10	Shinya Nakano	JPN	56	*San Carlo Honda Gresini*	Honda	B	22	44m 44.030s
11	Andrea Dovizioso	ITA	4	*JiR Team Scot MotoGP*	Honda	M	22	44m 44.307s
12	James Toseland	GBR	52	*Tech 3 Yamaha*	Yamaha	M	22	44m 51.252s
13	Randy de Puniet	FRA	14	*LCR Honda MotoGP*	Honda	M	22	44m 51.503s
14	John Hopkins	USA	21	*Kawasaki Racing Team*	Kawasaki	B	22	44m 53.916s
15	Sylvain Guintoli	FRA	50	*Alice Team*	Ducati	B	22	44m 54.391s
16	Alex de Angelis	RSM	15	*San Carlo Honda Gresini*	Honda	B	22	44m 58.654s
17	Anthony West	AUS	13	*Kawasaki Racing Team*	Kawasaki	B	22	45m 13.654s
	Chris Vermeulen	AUS	7	*Rizla Suzuki MotoGP*	Suzuki	B	6	12m 37.734s

Fastest lap: Valentino Rossi, on lap 18, 1m 59.273s, 99.043mph/159.395km/h (record).

Previous lap record: Dani Pedrosa, SPA (Honda), 1m 59.318s, 99.006mph/159.335km/h (2006).

Event best maximum speed: Casey Stoner, 213.3mph/343.2km/h (race).

QUALIFYING: 3 May 2008

Weather: Dry
Air: 29°C Humidity: 38% Track: 46°C

Pos.	Rider	Time
1	Edwards	1m 58.139s
2	Rossi	1m 58.494s
3	Stoner	1m 58.591s
4	Lorenzo	1m 58.711s
5	Pedrosa	1m 58.855s
6	Capirossi	1m 58.941s
7	Toseland	1m 59.254s
8	Vermeulen	1m 59.325s
9	de Puniet	1m 59.357s
10	Hayden	1m 59.507s
11	Dovizioso	1m 59.559s
12	Melandri	1m 59.678s
13	Nakano	1m 59.716s
14	Hopkins	1m 59.740s
15	Elias	1m 59.933s
16	de Angelis	2m 00.316s
17	Guintoli	2m 00.760s
18	West	2m 00.838s

Grid order	1	2	3	4	5	6	7	8	9	10	11	12	13	14	15	16	17	18	19	20	21	22	●
5 EDWARDS	5	2	2	2	46	46	46	46	46	46	46	46	46	46	46	46	46	46	46	46	46	46	1
46 ROSSI	1	5	46	46	2	2	2	2	2	2	2	2	2	2	2	2	2	2	2	2	2	2	2
1 STONER	2	46	5	5	5	1	1	1	1	1	1	1	1	1	1	1	1	1	1	1	1	1	3
48 LORENZO	46	1	1	1	1	69	69	33	33	33	33	33	33	33	48	48	48	48	48	48	48	48	4
2 PEDROSA	48	69	69	69	69	4	4	69	4	4	4	4	48	33	33	33	33	33	33	33			5
65 CAPIROSSI	69	48	4	4	4	33	33	4	69	5	5	5	5	4	4	4	4	69	69	69	69	69	6
52 TOSELAND	65	65	48	65	33	5	5	5	5	69	69	48	48	5	5	5	69	69	4	5	65	5	7
7 VERMEULEN	52	4	65	33	48	48	48	48	48	48	48	69	69	69	69	69	5	5	5	65		24	8
14 de PUNIET	7	33	33	48	52	52	65	65	65	65	65	65	65	65	65	65	65	65	65	4	24	65	9
69 HAYDEN	4	52	52	52	56	65	52	52	56	56	56	56	24	24	24	24	24	24	24	4	56		10
4 DOVISIOSO	33	7	56	56	7	56	56	56	52	52	24	24	56	56	56	56	56	56	56	56	4		11
33 MELANDRI	56	56	7	7	65	24	24	24	24	24	52	52	52	52	52	52	52	52	52	52	52	52	12
56 NAKANO	50	50	50	50	24	50	50	50	50	50	50	50	50	50	50	50	50	50	14	14	14	14	13
21 HOPKINS	24	24	24	24	50	14	14	14	14	14	14	14	14	14	14	14	14	14	50	21	21	21	14
24 ELIAS	14	14	14	21	14	15	15	15	15	15	15	15	15	15	15	15	15	21	50	50	50	50	15
15 de ANGELIS	15	15	15	14	15	13	21	21	21	21	21	21	21	21	21	21	21	15	15	15	15		
50 GUINTOLI	21	21	21	15	13	21	13	13	13	13	13	13	13	13	13	13	13	13	13	13	13		
13 WEST	13	13	13	13	21	7																	

FASTEST RACE LAPS

	Rider	Lap	Time
1	Rossi	18	1m 59.273s
2	Pedrosa	18	1m 59.384s
3	Stoner	20	2m 00.056s
4	Lorenzo	19	2m 00.308s
5	Elias	21	2m 00.355s
6	Capirossi	15	2m 00.435s
7	Melandri	18	2m 00.451s
8	Hayden	15	2m 00.601s
9	Dovizioso	15	2m 00.619s
10	Edwards	11	2m 00.651s
11	de Puniet	20	2m 00.845s
12	Hopkins	10	2m 00.948s
13	Nakano	17	2m 01.023s
14	de Angelis	10	2m 01.401s
15	Toseland	20	2m 01.515s
16	Guintoli	15	2m 01.663s
17	Vermeulen	5	2m 01.742s
18	West	6	2m 02.229s

statistics

OFFICIAL TIMEKEEPER

250cc
21 laps, 68.901 miles/110.901km

Pos.	Rider (Nat.)	No.	Team	Machine	Laps	Time & speed
1	Mika Kallio (FIN)	36	Red Bull KTM 250	KTM	21	48m 12.217s 85.774mph/ 138.040km/h
2	Hiroshi Aoyama (JPN)	4	Red Bull KTM 250	KTM	21	48m 15.455s
3	Mattia Pasini (ITA)	75	Polaris World	Aprilia	21	48m 26.028s
4	Marco Simoncelli (ITA)	58	Metis Gilera	Gilera	21	48m 30.691s
5	Alex Debon (SPA)	6	Lotus Aprilia	Aprilia	21	48m 33.283s
6	Hector Barbera (SPA)	21	Team Toth Aprilia	Aprilia	21	48m 37.375s
7	Yuki Takahashi (JPN)	72	JiR Team Scot 250	Honda	21	48m 42.207s
8	Ratthapark Wilairot (THA)	14	Thai Honda PTT SAG	Honda	21	48m 52.088s
9	Aleix Espargaro (SPA)	41	Lotus Aprilia	Aprilia	21	49m 00.561s
10	Hector Faubel (SPA)	55	Mapfre Aspar Team	Aprilia	21	49m 07.687s
11	Roberto Locatelli (ITA)	15	Metis Gilera	Gilera	21	49m 08.049s
12	Alvaro Bautista (SPA)	19	Mapfre Aspar Team	Aprilia	21	49m 12.659s
13	Eugene Laverty (IRL)	50	Blusens Aprilia	Aprilia	21	49m 12.949s
14	Fabrizio Lai (ITA)	32	Campetella Racing	Gilera	21	49m 49.192s
15	Doni Tata Pradita (INA)	45	Yamaha Pertamina Indonesia	Yamaha	21	49m 49.297s
16	Imre Toth (HUN)	10	Team Toth Aprilia	Aprilia	21	49m 57.235s
17	Russel Gomez (SPA)	7	Blusens Aprilia	Aprilia	21	50m 25.935s
	Alex Baldolini (ITA)	25	Matteoni Racing	Aprilia	14	DNF
	Julian Simon (SPA)	60	Repsol KTM 250cc	KTM	5	DNF
	Thomas Luthi (SWI)	12	Emmi - Caffe Latte	Aprilia	5	DNF
	Karel Abraham (CZE)	17	Cardion AB Motoracing	Aprilia	4	DNF
	Lukas Pesek (CZE)	52	Auto Kelly - CP	Aprilia	2	DNF
	Manuel Poggiali (RSM)	54	Campetella Racing	Gilera	0	DNF

Fastest lap: Kallio, 2m 15.834s, 86.968mph/139.962km/h.

Lap record: Jorge Lorenzo, SPA (Aprilia), 2m 05.738s, 93.951mph/151.200km/h (2007).

Event best maximum speed: Aoyama, 173.8mph/279.7km/h (race).

Qualifying: 1 Bautista, 2m 04.882s; 2 Barbera, 2m 05.317s; 3 Kallio, 2m 05.402s; 4 Simon, 2m 05.651s; 5 Simoncelli, 2m 05.724s; 6 Luthi, 2m 05.853s; 7 Pasini, 2m 06.119s; 8 Poggiali, 2m 06.192s; 9 Locatelli, 2m 06.216s; 10 Takahashi, 2m 06.245s; 11 Aoyama, 2m 06.276s; 12 Debon, 2m 06.279s; 13 Faubel, 2m 06.283s; 14 Pesek, 2m 06.428s; 15 Espargaro, 2m 06.559s; 16 Lai, 2m 07.083s; 17 Abraham, 2m 07.101s; 18 Wilairot, 2m 07.114s; 19 Laverty, 2m 07.665s; 20 Baldolini, 2m 09.063s; 21 Pradita, 2m 10.254s; 22 Toth, 2m 10.509s; 23 Gomez, 2m 11.624s.

Fastest race laps: 1 Kallio, 2m 15.834s; 2 Aoyama, 2m 16.279s; 3 Debon, 2m 16.495s; 4 Takahashi, 2m 16.567s; 5 Pasini, 2m 16.607s; 6 Locatelli, 2m 16.695s; 7 Bautista, 2m 16.796s; 8 Simoncelli, 2m 17.178s; 9 Barbera, 2m 17.441s; 10 Laverty, 2m 18.068s; 11 Wilairot, 2m 18.371s; 12 Simon, 2m 18.462s; 13 Espargaro, 2m 18.800s; 14 Faubel, 2m 19.077s; 15 Luthi, 2m 19.364s; 16 Lai, 2m 19.439s; 17 Pradita, 2m 20.045s; 18 Toth, 2m 20.357s; 19 Gomez, 2m 21.480s; 20 Baldolini, 2m 22.275s; 21 Abraham, 2m 24.051s; 22 Pesek, 2m 26.688s.

World Championship: 1 Kallio, 82; 2 Pasini, 61; 3 Barbera, 49; 4 Takahashi, 46; 5 Aoyama, 44; 6 Bautista, 39; 7 Debon, 34; 8 Simoncelli, 33; 9 Espargaro, 26; 10 Simon, 23; 11 Locatelli, 21; 12 Faubel, 19; 13 Wilairot, 18; 14 Luthi, 14; 15 Abraham, 12; 16 Pesek, 12; 17 Baldolini, 9; 18 Lai, 6; 19 Laverty, 4; 20 Hernandez, Poggiali and Sandi, 2; 23 Pradita and Toth, 1.

125cc
19 laps, 62.339 miles/100.339km

Pos.	Rider (Nat.)	No.	Team	Machine	Laps	Time & speed
1	Andrea Iannone (ITA)	29	I.C. Team	Aprilia	19	46m 02.275s 81.256mph/ 130.769km/h
2	Mike di Meglio (FRA)	63	Ajo Motorsport	Derbi	19	46m 05.630s
3	Gabor Talmacsi (HUN)	1	Bancaja Aspar Team	Aprilia	19	46m 05.726s
4	Pol Espargaro (SPA)	44	Belson Derbi	Derbi	19	46m 16.303s
5	Stefan Bradl (GER)	17	Grizzly Gas Kiefer Racing	Aprilia	19	46m 26.128s
6	Joan Olive (SPA)	6	Belson Derbi	Derbi	19	46m 34.237s
7	Michael Ranseder (AUT)	60	I.C. Team	Aprilia	19	46m 36.033s
8	Nicolas Terol (SPA)	18	Jack & Jones WRB	Aprilia	19	46m 36.971s
9	Raffaele de Rosa (ITA)	35	Onde 2000 KTM	KTM	19	46m 37.113s
10	Efren Vazquez (SPA)	7	Blusens Aprilia Junior	Aprilia	19	46m 43.286s
11	Esteve Rabat (SPA)	12	Repsol KTM 125cc	KTM	19	46m 43.414s
12	Marc Marquez (SPA)	93	Repsol KTM 125cc	KTM	19	46m 45.952s
13	Tomoyoshi Koyama (JPN)	71	ISPA KTM Aran	KTM	19	46m 55.764s
14	Stevie Bonsey (USA)	51	Degraaf Grand Prix	Aprilia	19	46m 56.737s
15	Pere Tutusaus (SPA)	30	Bancaja Aspar Team	Aprilia	19	47m 00.981s
16	Sandro Cortese (GER)	11	Emmi - Caffe Latte	Aprilia	19	47m 01.729s
17	Dominique Aegerter (SWI)	77	Ajo Motorsport	Derbi	19	47m 12.979s
18	Louis Rossi (FRA)	69	FFM Honda GP 125	Honda	19	47m 50.193s
19	Hugo van den Berg (NED)	56	Degraaf Grand Prix	Aprilia	19	47m 52.681s
	Randy Krummenacher (SWI)	34	Red Bull KTM 125	KTM	16	DNF
	Scott Redding (GBR)	45	Blusens Aprilia Junior	Aprilia	15	DNF
	Lorenzo Zanetti (ITA)	8	ISPA KTM Aran	KTM	11	DNF
	Danny Webb (GBR)	99	Degraaf Grand Prix	Aprilia	10	DNF
	Robert Muresan (ROU)	95	Grizzly Gas Kiefer Racing	Aprilia	9	DNF
	Alexis Masbou (FRA)	5	Loncin Racing	Loncin	9	DNF
	Robin Lasser (GER)	21	Grizzly Gas Kiefer Racing	Aprilia	7	DNF
	Roberto Lacalendola (ITA)	19	Matteoni Racing	Aprilia	7	DNF
	Bradley Smith (GBR)	38	Polaris World	Aprilia	6	DNF
	Simone Corsi (ITA)	24	Jack & Jones WRB	Aprilia	5	DNF
	Takaaki Nakagami (JPN)	73	I.C. Team	Aprilia	4	DNF
	Sergio Gadea (SPA)	33	Bancaja Aspar Team	Aprilia	1	DNF
	Pablo Nieto (SPA)	13	Onde 2000 KTM	KTM		DNS
	Stefano Bianco (ITA)	27	S3+ WTR San Marino Team	Aprilia		DNS

Fastest lap: Ranseder, 2m 23.432s, 82.361mph/132.547km/h.

Lap record: Alvaro Bautista, SPA (Aprilia), 2m 12.131s, 89.405mph/143.884km/h (2006).

Event best maximum speed: Bradl, 150.9mph/242.9km/h (race).

Qualifying: 1 Smith, 2m 12.364s; 2 Terol, 2m 12.392s; 3 di Meglio, 2m 12.905s; 4 Talmacsi, 2m 13.012s; 5 Iannone, 2m 13.147s; 6 Olive, 2m 13.149s; 7 Espargaro, 2m 13.173s; 8 Bradl, 2m 13.184s; 9 Gadea, 2m 13.262s; 10 Webb, 2m 13.335s; 11 Corsi, 2m 13.404s; 12 Cortese, 2m 13.436s; 13 Nieto, 2m 13.744s; 14 Aegerter, 2m 13.762s; 15 de Rosa, 2m 13.800s; 16 Bianco, 2m 13.845s; 17 Bonsey, 2m 13.947s; 18 Nakagami, 2m 14.031s; 19 Ranseder, 2m 14.180s; 20 Vazquez, 2m 14.561s; 21 Tutusaus, 2m 14.629s; 22 Marquez, 2m 14.796s; 23 Rabat, 2m 14.830s; 24 Redding, 2m 15.092s; 25 Koyama, 2m 15.122s; 26 Masbou, 2m 15.325s; 27 Zanetti, 2m 15.721s; 28 Lasser, 2m 16.362s; 29 Lacalendola, 2m 16.420s; 30 van den Berg, 2m 16.501s; 31 Muresan, 2m 16.693s; 32 Krummenacher, 2m 17.034s; 33 Rossi, 2m 18.440s.

Fastest race laps: 1 Ranseder, 2m 23.432s; 2 Cortese, 2m 23.521s; 3 Iannone, 2m 23.963s; 4 di Meglio, 2m 24.118s; 5 de Rosa, 2m 24.248s; 6 Rabat, 2m 24.367s; 7 Espargaro, 2m 24.371s; 8 Bradl, 2m 24.457s; 9 Talmacsi, 2m 24.603s; 10 Vazquez, 2m 24.799s; 11 Marquez, 2m 24.999s; 12 Bonsey, 2m 25.214s; 13 Terol, 2m 25.365s; 14 Webb, 2m 25.402s; 15 Smith, 2m 25.452s; 16 Olive, 2m 25.461s; 17 Redding, 2m 25.543s; 18 Aegerter, 2m 25.961s; 19 Tutusaus, 2m 26.131s; 20 Krummenacher, 2m 26.392s; 21 Koyama, 2m 26.462s; 22 Zanetti, 2m 26.703s; 23 Muresan, 2m 27.563s; 24 Masbou, 2m 27.604s; 25 Lacalendola, 2m 27.913s; 26 Lasser, 2m 27.932s; 27 Corsi, 2m 28.352s; 28 van den Berg, 2m 28.571s; 29 Rossi, 2m 28.976s; 30 Nakagami, 2m 32.497s; 31 Gadea, 2m 34.309s.

World Championship: 1 Corsi, 59; 2 Olive, 50; 3 Terol, 50; 4 di Meglio, 49; 5 Bradl, 48; 6 Gadea, 32; 7 Iannone, 32; 8 Talmacsi, 30; 9 Espargaro, 26; 10 Bonsey, 25; 11 Webb, 21; 12 Redding, 20; 13 Cortese, 17; 14 Smith, 16; 15 Vazquez, 14; 16 Ranseder, 12; 17 Aegerter, 12; 18 de Rosa, 12; 19 Nieto, 11; 20 Rabat, 9; 21 Koyama, 6; 22 Marquez, 4; 23 Bianco, 3; 24 Nakagami and Tutusaus, 1.

RIDER STANDINGS
After 4 Rounds

1	Dani Pedrosa	81
2	Jorge Lorenzo	74
3	Valentino Rossi	72
4	Casey Stoner	56
5	Loris Capirossi	33
6	James Toseland	33
7	Colin Edwards	31
8	Nicky Hayden	29
9	Andrea Dovizioso	26
10	John Hopkins	26
11	Marco Melandri	23
12	Shinya Nakano	22
13	Toni Elias	15
14	Chris Vermeulen	14
15	Randy de Puniet	11
16	Alex de Angelis	7
17	Sylvain Guintoli	4
18	Anthony West	3

TEAM STANDINGS
After 4 Rounds

1	Fiat Yamaha Team	146
2	Repsol Honda Team	110
3	Ducati Marlboro Team	79
4	Tech 3 Yamaha	64
5	Rizla Suzuki MotoGP	47
6	Kawasaki Racing Team	29
7	San Carlo Honda Gresini	29
8	JiR Team Scot MotoGP	26
9	Alice Team	19
10	LCR Honda MotoGP	11

CONSTRUCTOR STANDINGS
After 4 Rounds

1	Yamaha	90
2	Honda	81
3	Ducati	56
4	Suzuki	34
5	Kawasaki	26

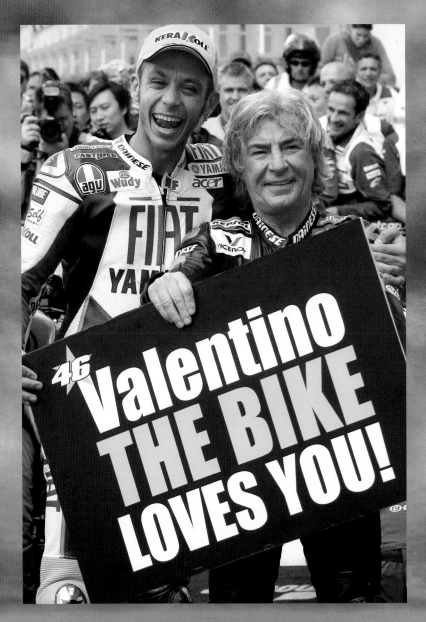

History men: Rossi's 91st win put him one
ahead of legend Angel Nieto. The pair
celebrated together.
Photographs: Gold & Goose

HISTORY was in the air at Le Mans. In 2007, adopted Frenchman Jack Findlay, the legendary Australian Prince of Privateers in the 1960s and 1970s, had died during the race weekend. In 2008, the organisers had laid on a special classic-bike race as a tribute to the rider. Run in treacherous wet conditions, fittingly it was won by Phil Read, the only man on the grid who had actually raced against Jack. Read's success, he admitted, was mainly because his Paton twin was significantly faster than the single-cylinder opposition. 'It meant I could go slowly in the corners, then get away again,' he said. Some racing truths are eternal.

History, of course, is always being made, and Rossi's second win in a row ticked off another major milestone, quite apart from putting him back in the lead on points for the first time since Jerez in 2007. 'I'm back in business,' he said. A respecter of the past, his acknowledgement was very proper. It was his 90th GP win, which put him equal with legendary 13-times 50 and 125 World Champion Angel Nieto, and also equalled Nieto's rostrum record of 130. The revered Nieto, now a commentator on Spanish TV, had donned leathers and helmet, and was waiting by the track where Rossi stopped on his victory lap. Rossi insisted that the older rider take the controls, then occupied a back seat for a further tour around the track. He held a white flag with the legend '90 plus 90'. 'It was my idea,' he explained. 'In 2006, I arranged it with Angel ... but f***, then we had to wait a long, long time!' Rossi's next target will take two years or more: his compatriot, Giacomo Agostini, has a total of 122 wins.

Alterations to the Bugatti circuit threw into focus again a changing fashion in race-track design – hard surfacing of run-off areas. More a provision for cars, this was first encountered at Istanbul, where it received a mixed, but not unfavourable, reception. Since then, it has appeared elsewhere. Le Mans followed fashion at several corners, especially at the revised Garage Vert

corner, previously a long loop now converted to a pair of 90-degree rights. This improved the run-off, with a generous gravel trap beyond the asphalt, and shortened overall distance by four metres.

The hard surface also gives bike riders a second chance. Not if they have already fallen, obviously, but now there is the opportunity to avoid falling by running off instead. This allows the rider to collect himself before rejoining little daunted.

For Stoner, however, this was a step too far. Safety's one thing, but mistakes ought not to go unpunished, he thought. 'For me, all this extra run-off is not racing. It gives people the opportunity to push beyond the limits, and if they make a mistake, pick up the bike and run off. For me, if you make a mistake, you go in the gravel and it's your problem. You made a mistake.' Stoner is by nature outspoken and uncompromising, shooting from the hip. On this point, paddock nice guy Hayden agreed. 'We're having all the rider aids, and we're having extra run-off. It's taking away ... it lets you get away with a lot more. Almost makes it too easy just to pick it up and run wide. If they didn't have all that run-off, you wouldn't have everybody running wide.' Ironically, both riders were among the many who took advantage of the facility during the weekend, Hayden in the race.

Another aspect of safety came to the top of the agenda at Le Mans: the medical standards that allow a rider with broken and damaged ankles to take part in a race. It was Jorge Lorenzo again, in another weekend of sensation, of brutal falls and magnificent recovery, and yet another rostrum finish. On his return from China, he had been prescribed complete immobilisation to both ankles, after diagnosis of a fractured astralagus bone in his right ankle and a broken ligament in his left. He was treated again by Dr Xavier Mir of the Barcelona Clinica Dexeus, increasingly filling a role for Spanish riders that is still occupied for the Americans by San Francisco's Dr Arthur Ting, who has treated riders from Kenny Roberts

Right and far right: Patched up and painful, Lorenzo survived another crash in practice, and got ahead of Edwards to finish second.

Below: At 69, multi-champion Phil Read won the wet classic Jack Findlay Tribute race.

Bottom: Trouble ahead: Stoner's misfortune was waiting in a race to forget.

Bottom left: Points leader Rossi is pillion in a million to Angel Nieto.

Photographs: Gold & Goose

Senior in the 1980s all the way through to John Hopkins in 2008.

Jorge was still wheelchair-bound at Le Mans, one leg in a special zip-up cast that he removed when riding. His adventures began on day one, with a tumble from which, incredibly, he was able to hobble away, followed by another off-track excursion later, then a fraught and scary fast one through the gravel after running on from the front straight.

It wasn't enough to stop him, amazingly; even more amazingly, he finished second – with Edwards third, it was the first all-Yamaha rostrum since 2001 – a result that quite vindicated his courage and commitment. But many were questioning whether somebody should have stopped him. Some thought it another reminder that while MotoGP is blessed with medical care and attention from Dr Costa's Clinica Mobile, it lacks a counterbalance to Costa's fast-fix philosophy, aimed at getting riders out on track just as quickly as humanly possible, and sometimes a little more so.

The paddock echoed again to the death knell of the 250 class, when Dorna presented Saturday's GP Commission meeting with its already delayed proposal for a replacement. In a short-lived attempt to sidestep opposition from SBK, this had been altered to 'between 625 and 650cc' for four-stroke engines, specified as in-line fours with a control ECU. Predictably, the reaction from KTM and Aprilia was down in the mouth, for this was another step closer to oblivion for almost 50 years of two-stroke 250 development.

Conditions were cool and frequently damp, with the rain-dance motif of the year becoming better established. Bridgestone had learned the lessons of Qatar and Jerez, and had a new rear better suited to lower temperatures. In all classes, however, there were several off-track adventures. As is so often the case, the worst of the high-sides came in the 125 class, with rising Briton Danny Webb setting height records in a massive first-day flier at the end of the back straight. 'I've had some high-sides before, though never as high as that. You feel your heart go into your mouth, but this time it all happened so quick, it was all over and done with,' he said. He was very lucky to escape without injury. Riding in pain and finishing out of the points, he was another to benefit from the efficacy of Costa's treatment and the laxity of the overall regulations.

MOTOGP RACE – 28 laps

The Yamahas had signalled their strength in free practice on race tyres: Edwards headed Rossi from Pedrosa, Stoner half a second away. The crucial final hour belonged to the Michelin qualifiers of Pedrosa and Edwards, however, with Stoner on the far end of the front row and Rossi leading the second.

The rain had stopped and the track had dried for the start, although there were ominous clouds in the sky. Stoner and Pedrosa led away, then came Edwards, Hayden and Rossi at the end of lap one. Rossi was quickly ahead of the Honda and looking for more.

His chance came on lap four, when Pedrosa mounted a vain attack on Stoner into Museum corner. He ran wide. Rossi, passing Edwards in the same place, got the Spaniard as well, to sit on Stoner's tail.

It remained that way for the next four laps, Rossi sizing him up. Then he scythed past cleanly under braking for the same looping left. Immediately he opened up a gap, a typically majestic performance, as he strove to create a comfort zone in case the threatened rain made its appearance.

It did, according to officials, at the half-way point, when the white flags were shown and spare bikes began to be revved in the pits. But it was only a sprinkling. 'I hoped it would stop, because I didn't want to change bikes,' said Rossi. In spite of a few slippery moments for all, his wish was granted.

At that point, he had some three seconds on Pedrosa, Stoner and Edwards, who were in close company. The 2007 winner, Vermeulen, had closed on them, but dropped away when the rain started.

Then came a scrapping Hayden, Capirossi and Hopkins. And behind them, Lorenzo, who later explained his philosophy: 'It is always a fight of two minds. One says, "Only finish"; the other says, "You can try and stay with them."' He'd dropped back to 11th on lap two before the second mind-set prevailed, and by lap five, he had caught up this group. On a memorable eighth lap, he passed all three of them and set off after Vermeulen, a couple of seconds away.

It took until lap 14 to catch the Australian, and Lorenzo swept straight past in a fine display of daring, cutting inside at the apex of the daunting first corner. Now the next three, disputing second place, were not far ahead. By lap 19, he was right with them.

He picked off Edwards, then had a little help from Stoner's gremlins as the Ducati slowed suddenly into the first corner on lap 21. Now there was just Pedrosa, who said later that he had been in trouble with bad front tyre grip. Lorenzo passed him easily into the first chicane for a magnificent and memorable second. Edwards followed him past the Honda one lap later.

Stoner's disaster was comprehensive. First the power

dropped off, then as he started lap 21 suddenly he slowed. The engine barely running, he nursed it back to the pits, pushing the last few metres. Rain rules meant that he could switch to his spare, on different (ie. the wrong) tyres. He kept his perfect Ducati finishing score, but not his points record, ending up 16th. At the time, the malady was said to be electronic. Later, it emerged that it was a broken crankshaft, one of a bad batch. The team had known about the problem, but taken a risk anyway, said a source. The price was very heavy.

Pedrosa was alone to the end; Vermeulen not so, for second fast rookie Dovizioso was coming through. He'd dropped to 14th on lap three after a collision with Toseland, which knocked the fast-starting Englishman out. After a couple of laps jockeying with the likes of de Puniet, Nakano and de Angelis, the Italian had taken tenth by lap seven and was closing on the next group even as Lorenzo was pushing on through it.

Dovi was saved the trouble of grabbing seventh off Hopkins when the Kawasaki rider's chain snapped and went snaking along the track as he pulled up to park angrily. That just left Vermeulen, and with another lap he might have passed him as well. As it was, he was less than half a second adrift.

Capirossi had lost touch over the last four laps, while Hayden had been close behind him throughout, but never quite close enough to prevail.

Behind de Puniet and Nakano, Elias was 11th, still unhappy with the Ducati, but the first to finish. De Angelis had slowed with chatter problems after the rain hit; Guintoli was another 15 seconds away; struggling West a further eight seconds down.

Melandri had another sad story. He'd been left on the line with a misfire and was so far behind that he welcomed the chance to change to his spare bike, even though it was on the wrong tyres. 'I hoped it really might rain,' he said. It didn't, but he was a lap ahead of Stoner and took the last point.

250cc RACE – 26 laps

At 32, Alex Debon is the most race-seasoned of 250 riders, with this his 112th start in the class. And he was on pole position, for only the second time. He had one other advantage: his Aprilia was fitted with a prototype traction control. Added together, the sum produced his first GP win in 11 years of trying.

Tyre choice was the traditional lottery. Debon chose slicks. However, most of the rest went for cut slicks or hard intermediates – safer options. The sun was out, but the track was still very wet in sections and more rain seemed imminent.

Debon led Kallio and Barbera away, and soon started to pull clear, the others riding more gingerly. After five laps, his lead was better than two seconds and stretching. He kept on for a comfortable cushion of almost five seconds at the finish. 'I've waited a long time for this,' he said.

Aoyama led the pursuit for the first two laps, but the track was drying and his intermediates were losing performance as it did so. He gave way to Takahashi on lap six, joined three laps later by Simon, who got ahead for a couple of laps after mid-distance. They stayed together until after the 20th lap, second surely in the bag for one or the other of them. But they also were running into tyre trouble, while following riders had saved their tyres better in the early laps.

Kallio, always a cunning candidate, headed the group, with Pasini, Poggiali and Simoncelli on his tail as he caught up. Over the last five laps, the battle for second was six-strong, until Simon faded badly towards the finish of the race.

Pasini was in fighting form and led the group at the start of the last lap, with Simoncelli hard behind, then Takahashi, Kallio and Poggiali, all over one another. Simoncelli pounced with his usual aggression on the way into the final tight double-rights. He held Pasini narrowly

at bay over the line; Takahashi was less than a second adrift, then Kallio and Poggiali in a flash.

Ten seconds back, Aoyama had faded earlier than Simon, but had managed to get back ahead of him over the line by two seconds.

It was rather processional behind, perhaps not surprisingly in the conditions – there was another light sprinkling of rain mid-race. Espargaro finally escaped from Faubel for ninth. Another 12 seconds away, Luthi was eleventh, having passed Barbera with seven laps to go. The Spaniard had finished lap one in third, but dropped back rapidly for the rest of the afternoon. Locatelli was only a second adrift.

Bautista never did come to terms with the conditions. Having qualified second, he had finished lap one 18th, but had climbed to 13th when an excursion on lap five lost him five places again. He was a lone 14th at the end, while Wilairot won a battle with Baldolini for the final point. Pesek, Laverty, Abraham and Pradita crashed out.

125cc RACE – Five laps

The shortest race in history couldn't have happened without the 15 laps run beforehand, until rain and several crashes brought out the red flags. It was just short of two-thirds of the scheduled 24 laps, so the race was 'neutralised'. Bad luck for clear leader Olive, for track positions counted only for the grid.

Gadea had led away from pole, giving way to Terol briefly and then to Bradl on lap nine. By now, there was a close pack of ten, slow-starting Smith having battled his way up to the back of it.

Terol led once more, but Olive took over at the front on the 14th, just as the rain started to sprinkle. He was ready to take advantage, pulling out a second lead over the next two laps. But it was only for pole, with the race about to be neutralised.

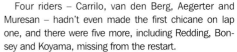

Four riders – Carrilo, van den Berg, Aegerter and Muresan – hadn't even made the first chicane on lap one, and there were five more, including Redding, Bonsey and Koyama, missing from the restart.

By now, it was very wet. Talmacsi took an immediate lead from fourth on the grid, but didn't complete the second lap, crashing in high dudgeon on the exit of the last corner. Then it was Terol, and Smith second, the latter and di Meglio having passed Espargaro.

Terol had a little slip and dropped to third. Then, with two laps left, di Meglio took over from Smith. Cautious in the conditions, the English rider was happy to follow the home hero over the line for a career-best second.

Terol was two seconds away, Espargaro clung to fourth, ahead of Iannone and Bradl. Zanetti, Olive, de Rosa and Krummenacher completed the top ten.

Gadea was swamped at the start and finished a lowly 20th. Corsi had been fourth on the first leg, but was engulfed at the re-start to finish 13th; di Meglio took over the lead on points.

Above: Pasini heads Kallio, Poggiali and Simoncelli in a fierce 250 battle.

Top: Vermeulen has the advantage, as Hayden and Capirossi follow.

Above right: Terol was delighted with his third 125 podium of the year.

Left: Alex Debon, a winner after 11 years and 112 starts.

Right: Smith heads Terol and di Meglio, en route to gaining his first win of the season.

Right: Di Meglio takes the chequered flag, having seized the lead from Smith two laps from the end.

Facing page: The gang's all here. Yamahas

ALICE GRAND PRIX DE FRANCE

18 MAY 2008 • FIM WORLD CHAMPIONSHIP ROUND 5

LE MANS – BUGATTI

Garage Vert
Chemin aux Boeufs
La Chappelle
Le Musée   "S" du Garage Bleu
Chicane Dunlop
Courbe Dunlop
Raccordement

Circuit 4.180km /2.597 miles

MOTOGP

RACE: 28 laps, 72.800 miles/117.180km • Weather: Dry • Air 20°C • Humidity 38% • Track 26°C

Pos.	Rider	Nat.	No.	Team	Machine	Tyres	Laps	Time & speed (mph/km/h)
1	Valentino Rossi	ITA	46	Fiat Yamaha Team	Yamaha	B	28	44m 30.799s 98.144mph/ 157.948km/h
2	Jorge Lorenzo	SPA	48	Fiat Yamaha Team	Yamaha	M	28	44m 35.796s
3	Colin Edwards	USA	5	Tech 3 Yamaha	Yamaha	M	28	44m 37.604s
4	Dani Pedrosa	SPA	2	Repsol Honda Team	Honda	M	28	44m 40.956s
5	Chris Vermeulen	AUS	7	Rizla Suzuki MotoGP	Suzuki	B	28	44m 52.561s
6	Andrea Dovizioso	ITA	4	JiR Team Scot MotoGP	Honda	M	28	44m 53.194s
7	Loris Capirossi	ITA	65	Rizla Suzuki MotoGP	Suzuki	B	28	44m 58.605s
8	Nicky Hayden	USA	69	Repsol Honda Team	Honda	M	28	44m 58.794s
9	Randy de Puniet	FRA	14	LCR Honda MotoGP	Honda	M	28	45m 00.143s
10	Shinya Nakano	JPN	56	San Carlo Honda Gresini	Honda	B	28	45m 01.621s
11	Toni Elias	SPA	24	Alice Team	Ducati	B	28	45m 05.953s
12	Alex de Angelis	RSM	15	San Carlo Honda Gresini	Honda	B	28	45m 07.015s
13	Sylvain Guintoli	FRA	50	Alice Team	Ducati	B	28	45m 22.837s
14	Anthony West	AUS	13	Kawasaki Racing Team	Kawasaki	B	28	46m 00.106s
15	Marco Melandri	ITA	33	Ducati Marlboro Team	Ducati	B	27	46m 10.422s
16	Casey Stoner	AUS	1	Ducati Marlboro Team	Ducati	B	26	44m 47.085s
	John Hopkins	USA	21	Kawasaki Racing Team	Kawasaki	B	16	25m 36.029s
	James Toseland	GBR	52	Tech 3 Yamaha	Yamaha	M	2	3m 19.828s

Fastest lap: Valentino Rossi, on lap 11, 1m 34.215s, 99.363mph/159.910km/h (record).

Previous lap record: New circuit.

Event best maximum speed: John Hopkins, 181.2mph/291.6km/h (qualifying practice).

QUALIFYING: 17 May 2008

Weather: Dry
Air: 21°C Humidity: 23% Track: 31°C

Pos.	Rider	Time
1	Pedrosa	1m 32.647s
2	Edwards	1m 32.774s
3	Stoner	1m 32.994s
4	Rossi	1m 33.157s
5	Lorenzo	1m 33.269s
6	Hayden	1m 33.286s
7	Toseland	1m 33.396s
8	Vermeulen	1m 33.440s
9	Hopkins	1m 33.628s
10	Dovizioso	1m 33.689s
11	Capirossi	1m 33.707s
12	de Puniet	1m 33.723s
13	Nakano	1m 34.077s
14	Elias	1m 34.561s
15	de Angelis	1m 34.670s
16	Guintoli	1m 34.747s
17	Melandri	1m 35.081s
18	West	1m 35.349s

Grid order	1	2	3	4	5	6	7	8	9	10	11	12	13	14	15	16	17	18	19	20	21	22	23	24	25	26	27	28	
2 PEDROSA	1	1	1	1	1	1	1	46	46	46	46	46	46	46	46	46	46	46	46	46	46	46	46	46	46	46	46	46	1
5 EDWARDS	2	2	2	46	46	46	46	1	1	1	2	2	2	2	2	2	2	2	2	2	48	48	48	48	48	48	48	48	2
1 STONER	5	5	5	2	2	2	2	2	2	2	1	1	1	1	1	1	1	1	1	1	2	5	5	5	5	5	5	5	3
46 ROSSI	69	46	46	5	5	5	5	5	5	5	5	5	5	5	5	5	5	5	48	5	2	2	2	2	2	2	2	2	4
48 LORENZO	46	69	69	7	7	7	7	7	7	7	7	7	7	7	48	48	48	48	48	5	7	7	7	7	7	7	7	7	5
69 HAYDEN	7	7	7	69	69	69	69	48	48	48	48	48	48	48	7	7	7	7	7	7	4	4	4	4	4	4	4	4	6
52 TOSELAND	52	65	65	65	65	65	65	69	69	69	69	69	69	21	21	21	4	4	4	4	65	65	65	65	65	65	65	65	7
7 VERMEULEN	65	21	21	21	21	21	21	65	65	65	65	65	21	4	4	4	65	65	65	65	69	69	69	69	69	69	69	69	8
21 HOPKINS	21	52	48	48	48	48	48	21	21	21	21	21	4	65	65	65	69	69	69	69	56	56	56	14	14	14	14	14	9
4 DOVISIOSO	48	4	24	24	56	56	4	4	4	4	4	4	65	69	69	69	56	56	56	56	14	14	14	56	56	56	56	56	10
65 CAPIROSSI	24	48	56	56	24	24	56	56	56	56	56	56	56	56	56	56	14	14	14	14	24	24	24	24	24	24	24	24	11
14 de PUNIET	4	24	14	14	4	14	14	15	15	15	14	14	14	14	14	14	24	24	24	15	15	15	15	15	15	15	15	15	12
56 NAKANO	56	56	15	4	14	4	24	14	14	14	15	15	15	15	15	15	15	15	15	24	50	50	50	50	50	50	50	50	13
24 ELIAS	14	14	4	15	15	15	15	24	24	24	24	24	24	24	50	50	50	50	50	50									

FASTEST RACE LAPS

	Rider	Lap	Time
1	Rossi	11	1m 34.215s
2	Edwards	6	1m 34.321s
3	Lorenzo	14	1m 34.421s
4	Pedrosa	5	1m 34.469s
5	Stoner	9	1m 34.561s
6	Vermeulen	6	1m 34.585s
7	Dovizioso	27	1m 34.727s
8	Hopkins	5	1m 34.947s
9	Capirossi	5	1m 34.992s
10	Hayden	10	1m 35.182s
11	de Puniet	9	1m 35.191s

250cc

26 laps, 67.600 miles/108.810km

Pos. Rider (Nat.)	No.	Team	Machine	Laps	Time & speed
1 Alex Debon (SPA)	6	Lotus Aprilia	Aprilia	26	47m 27.406s 85.481mph/ 137.569km/h
2 Marco Simoncelli (ITA)	58	Metis Gilera	Gilera	26	47m 32.222s
3 Mattia Pasini (ITA)	75	Polaris World	Aprilia	26	47m 32.404s
4 Yuki Takahashi (JPN)	72	JiR Team Scot 250	Honda	26	47m 33.176s
5 Mika Kallio (FIN)	36	Red Bull KTM 250	KTM	26	47m 33.603s
6 Manuel Poggiali (RSM)	54	Campetella Racing	Gilera	26	47m 33.880s
7 Hiroshi Aoyama (JPN)	4	Red Bull KTM 250	KTM	26	47m 42.315s
8 Julian Simon (SPA)	60	Repsol KTM 250cc	KTM	26	47m 44.932s
9 Aleix Espargaro (SPA)	41	Lotus Aprilia	Aprilia	26	48m 00.331s
10 Hector Faubel (SPA)	55	Mapfre Aspar Team	Aprilia	26	48m 04.125s
11 Thomas Luthi (SWI)	12	Emmi - Caffe Latte	Aprilia	26	48m 16.374s
12 Hector Barbera (SPA)	21	Team Toth Aprilia	Aprilia	26	48m 24.243s
13 Roberto Locatelli (ITA)	15	Metis Gilera	Gilera	26	48m 25.233s
14 Alvaro Bautista (SPA)	19	Mapfre Aspar Team	Aprilia	26	48m 32.813s
15 Ratthapark Wilairot (THA)	14	Thai Honda PTT SAG	Honda	26	48m 51.742s
16 Alex Baldolini (ITA)	25	Matteoni Racing	Aprilia	26	48m 51.983s
17 Federico Sandi (ITA)	90	Zongshen Team of China	Aprilia	25	47m 37.804s
18 Imre Toth (HUN)	10	Team Toth Aprilia	Aprilia	25	47m 58.293s
19 Russel Gomez (SPA)	7	Blusens Aprilia	Aprilia	25	48m 05.598s
Karel Abraham (CZE)	17	Cardion AB Motoracing	Aprilia	24	DNF
Doni Tata Pradita (INA)	45	Yamaha Pertamina Indonesia	Yamaha	24	DNF
Lukas Pesek (CZE)	52	Auto Kelly - CP	Aprilia	21	DNF
Fabrizio Lai (ITA)	32	Campetella Racing	Gilera	13	DNF
Eugene Laverty (IRL)	50	Blusens Aprilia	Aprilia	11	DNF

Fastest lap: Simoncelli, 1m 39.666s, 93.929mph/151.164km/h (record).

Previous lap record: New circuit.

Event best maximum speed: Luthi, 160.7mph/258.6km/h (qualifying practice no. 2).

Qualifying: **1** Debon, 1m 38.478s; **2** Bautista, 1m 38.479s; **3** Simoncelli, 1m 38.567s; **4** Luthi, 1m 38.648s; **5** Pasini, 1m 38.788s; **6** Kallio, 1m 38.790s; **7** Simon, 1m 39.051s; **8** Poggiali, 1m 39.064s; **9** Espargaro, 1m 39.184s; **10** Aoyama, 1m 39.197s; **11** Barbera, 1m 39.312s; **12** Takahashi, 1m 39.446s; **13** Faubel, 1m 39.450s; **14** Lai, 1m 39.724s; **15** Pesek, 1m 39.798s; **16** Wilairot, 1m 39.924s; **17** Locatelli, 1m 40.171s; **18** Laverty, 1m 40.325s; **19** Abraham, 1m 40.455s; **20** Sandi, 1m 40.595s; **21** Baldolini, 1m 40.605s; **22** Toth, 1m 41.365s; **23** Gomez, 1m 42.820s; **24** Pradita, 1m 42.847s.

Fastest race laps: **1** Simoncelli, 1m 39.666s; **2** Kallio, 1m 39.895s; **3** Poggiali, 1m 40.012s; **4** Bautista, 1m 40.020s; **5** Pasini, 1m 40.093s; **6** Takahashi, 1m 40.275s; **7** Locatelli, 1m 41.042s; **8** Luthi, 1m 41.404s; **9** Aoyama, 1m 41.452s; **10** Debon, 1m 41.584s; **11** Wilairot, 1m 41.688s; **12** Simon, 1m 41.875s; 13 Abraham, 1m 42.076s; **14** Espargaro, 1m 42.294s; **15** Baldolini, 1m 42.347s; **16** Barbera, 1m 42.612s; **17** Faubel, 1m 42.712s; **18** Sandi, 1m 43.426s; **19** Pradita, 1m 44.492s; **20** Gomez, 1m 44.900s; **21** Pesek, 1m 45.028s; **22** Toth, 1m 45.128s; **23** Laverty, 1m 52.548s; **24** Lai, 1m 55.547s.

World Championship: **1** Kallio, 93; **2** Pasini, 77; **3** Debon, 59; **4** Takahashi, 59; **5** Simoncelli, 53; **6** Aoyama, 53; **7** Barbera, 53; **8** Bautista, 41; **9** Espargaro, 33; **10** Simon, 31; **11** Faubel, 25; **12** Locatelli, 24; **13** Luthi, 19; **14** Wilairot, 19; **15** Poggiali, 12; **16** Abraham, 12; **17** Pesek, 12; **18** Baldolini, 9; **19** Lai, 6; **20** Laverty, 4; **21** Hernandez and Sandi, 2; **23** Pradita and Toth, 1.

125cc

Race Part 2: 5 laps, 13.000 miles/20.925km

Pos. Rider (Nat.)	No.	Team	Machine	Laps	Time & speed
1 Mike di Meglio (FRA)	63	Ajo Motorsport	Derbi	5	10m 08.574s 76.914mph/ 123.781km/h
2 Bradley Smith (GBR)	38	Polaris World	Aprilia	5	10m 09.374s
3 Nicolas Terol (SPA)	18	Jack & Jones WRB	Aprilia	5	10m 11.651s
4 Pol Espargaro (SPA)	44	Belson Derbi	Derbi	5	10m 18.981s
5 Andrea Iannone (ITA)	29	I.C. Team	Aprilia	5	10m 20.271s
6 Stefan Bradl (GER)	17	Grizzly Gas Kiefer Racing	Aprilia	5	10m 20.455s
7 Lorenzo Zanetti (ITA)	8	ISPA KTM Aran	KTM	5	10m 24.946s
8 Joan Olive (SPA)	6	Belson Derbi	Derbi	5	10m 25.119s
9 Raffaele de Rosa (ITA)	35	Onde 2000 KTM	KTM	5	10m 27.737s
10 Randy Krummenacher (SWI)	34	Red Bull KTM 125	KTM	5	10m 30.965s
11 Sandro Cortese (GER)	11	Emmi - Caffe Latte	Aprilia	5	10m 31.421s
12 Pere Tutusaus (SPA)	30	Bancaja Aspar Team	Aprilia	5	10m 31.769s
13 Simone Corsi (ITA)	24	Jack & Jones WRB	Aprilia	5	10m 32.127s
14 Gabor Talmacsi (HUN)	1	Bancaja Aspar Team	Aprilia	5	10m 32.269s
15 Alexis Masbou (FRA)	5	Loncin Racing	Loncin	5	10m 32.814s
16 Takaaki Nakagami (JPN)	73	I.C. Team	Aprilia	5	10m 34.770s
17 Esteve Rabat (SPA)	12	Repsol KTM 125cc	KTM	5	10m 34.985s
18 Roberto Lacalendola (ITA)	19	Matteoni Racing	Aprilia	5	10m 35.469s
19 Louis Rossi (FRA)	69	FFM Honda GP 125	Honda	5	10m 36.020s
20 Sergio Gadea (SPA)	33	Bancaja Aspar Team	Aprilia	5	10m 40.403s
21 Danny Webb (GBR)	99	Degraaf Grand Prix	Aprilia	5	10m 43.384s
22 Robert Muresan (ROU)	95	Grizzly Gas Kiefer Racing	Aprilia	5	10m 43.764s
23 Dominique Aegerter (SWI)	77	Ajo Motorsport	Derbi	5	10m 56.414s
Michael Ranseder (AUT)	60	I.C. Team	Aprilia	4	DNF
Robin Lasser (GER)	21	Grizzly Gas Kiefer Racing	Aprilia	2	DNF
Steven Le Coquen (FRA)	52	Villiers Team Competition	Honda	1	DNF
Gioele Pellino (ITA)	61	Loncin Racing	Loncin	1	DNF
Stefano Bianco (ITA)	27	S3+ WTR San Marino Team	Aprilia	0	DNF
Did not start Race Part 2:					
Cyril Carrillo (FRA)	36	FFM Honda GP 125	Honda		DNS
Tobias Siegert (GER)	41	Adac Nordbayern e.v.	Aprilia		DNS
Scott Redding (GBR)	45	Blusens Aprilia Junior	Aprilia		DNS
Stevie Bonsey (USA)	51	Degraaf Grand Prix	Aprilia		DNS
Efren Vazquez (SPA)	7	Blusens Aprilia Junior	Aprilia		DNS
Tomoyoshi Koyama (JPN)	71	ISPA KTM Aran	KTM		DNS
Marc Marquez (SPA)	93	Repsol KTM 125cc	KTM		DNS
Race Part 1:					
Pablo Nieto (SPA)	22	Onde 2000 KTM	KTM	0	DNF
Hugo van den Berg (NED)	56	Degraaf Grand Prix	Aprilia	0	DNF
Valentin Debise (FRA)	53	Racing Motoclub Circuit d'Albi	KTM		DNS

Fastest lap: Espargaro, 1m 43.918s, 90.086mph/144.979km/h (record – in Race Part 1).

Prevous lap record: New circuit.

Event best maximum speed: Bradl, 140.0mph/225.3km/h (qualifying practice no. 2).

Qualifying: **1** Gadea, 1m 43.515s; **2** Smith, 1m 43.540s; **3** Bradl, 1m 43.710s; **4** Corsi, 1m 43.711s; **5** Cortese, 1m 43.811s; **6** di Meglio, 1m 43.956s; **7** Terol, 1m 44.116s; **8** Talmacsi, 1m 44.210s; **9** Rabat, 1m 44.344s; **10** Espargaro, 1m 44.485s; **11** Olive, 1m 44.532s; **12** Redding, 1m 44.793s; **13** Bonsey, 1m 44.852s; **14** Koyama, 1m 44.864s; **15** Webb, 1m 44.874s; **16** Ranseder, 1m 44.893s; **17** de Rosa, 1m 44.945s; **18** Iannone, 1m 45.006s; **19** Masbou, 1m 45.152s; **20** Marquez, 1m 45.250s; **21** Bianco, 1m 45.268s; **22** Nakagami, 1m 45.273s; **23** Zanetti, 1m 45.361s; **24** Vazquez, 1m 45.454s; **25** Nieto, 1m 45.541s; **26** van den Berg, 1m 45.864s; **27** Aegerter, 1m 46.015s; **28** Muresan, 1m 46.140s; **29** Tutusaus, 1m 46.416s; **30** Krummenacher, 1m 46.569s; **31** Le Coquen, 1m 46.645s; **32** Carrillo, 1m 47.185s; **33** Lasser, 1m 47.259s; **34** Rossi, 1m 47.330s; **35** Pellino, 1m 47.371s; **36** Lacalendola, 1m 47.854s; **37** Debise, 1m 48.298s; **38** Siegert, 1m 50.021s.

Fastest race laps (in Race Part 2): **1** di Meglio, 1m 58.528s; **2** Smith, 1m 58.663s; **3** Talmacsi, 1m 58.691s; **4** Terol, 1m 59.361s; **5** Bradl, 2m 00.525s; **6** Corsi, 2m 01.068s; **7** Iannone, 2m 01.207s; **8** Lacalendola, 2m 01.424s; **9** Rabat, 2m 01.800s; **10** Espargaro, 2m 01.856s; **11** Olive, 2m 02.013s; **12** de Rosa, 2m 02.199s; **13** Nakagami, 2m 02.221s; **14** Zanetti, 2m 02.345s; **15** Masbou, 2m 02.563s; **16** Krummenacher, 2m 02.790s; **17** Gadea, 2m 03.202s; **18** Cortese, 2m 03.377s; **19** Muresan, 2m 03.450s; **20** Rossi, 2m 03.627s; **21** Tutusaus, 2m 03.699s; **22** Webb, 2m 03.724s; **23** Aegerter, 2m 04.838s; **24** Ranseder, 2m 06.639s; **25** Lasser, 2m 07.543s; **26** Le Coquen, 2m 17.200s.

World Championship: **1** di Meglio, 74; **2** Terol, 66; **3** Corsi, 62; **4** Olive, 58; **5** Bradl, 58; **6** Iannone, 43; **7** Espargaro, 39; **8** Smith, 36; **9** Gadea, 32; **10** Talmacsi, 32; **11** Bonsey, 25; **12** Cortese, 22; **13** Webb, 21; **14** Redding, 20; **15** de Rosa, 19; **16** Vazquez, 14; **17** Ranseder, 12; **18** Aegerter, 12; **19** Nieto, 11; **20** Zanetti, 9; **21** Rabat, 9; **22** Krummenacher, 6; **23** Koyama, 6; **24** Tutusaus, 5; **25** Marquez, 4; **26** Bianco, 3; **27** Masbou and Nakagami, 1.

RIDER STANDINGS
After 5 Rounds

1	Valentino Rossi	97
2 =	Jorge Lorenzo	94
2 =	Dani Pedrosa	94
4	Casey Stoner	56
5	Colin Edwards	47
6	Loris Capirossi	42
7	Nicky Hayden	37
8	Andrea Dovizioso	36
9	James Toseland	33
10	Shinya Nakano	28
11	John Hopkins	26
12	Chris Vermeulen	25
13	Marco Melandri	24
14	Toni Elias	20
15	Randy de Puniet	18
16	Alex de Angelis	11
17	Sylvain Guintoli	7
18	Anthony West	5

TEAM STANDINGS
After 5 Rounds

1	Fiat Yamaha Team	191
2	Repsol Honda Team	131
3	Ducati Marlboro Team	80
4	Tech 3 Yamaha	80
5	Rizla Suzuki MotoGP	67
6	San Carlo Honda Gresini	39
7	JiR Team Scot MotoGP	36
8	Kawasaki Racing Team	31
9	Alice Team	27
10	LCR Honda MotoGP	18

CONSTRUCTOR STANDINGS
After 5 Rounds

1	Yamaha	115
2	Honda	94
3	Ducati	61
4	Suzuki	45
5	Kawasaki	28

Above: Valentino Rossi drowns out the scream
with earplugs as his cheerful helpmeet, Uccio,
shows off his helmet.
Photograph: Martin Heath

Main photograph: Stoner and Pedrosa are in
hopeless pursuit of the face that launched a
thousand replicas.
Photograph: Gold & Goose

THE end of the main straight at Mugello engenders awe and respect. Approaching at more than 200mph, riders must brake hard and drop four gears for the ensuing corner, a task made more exacting because arrival at the braking zone is over a rise, the bike light and close to flying.

Watchers there in 2008 saw an extraordinary sight: an achingly familiar rider's face staring over the screen. The expression showed sheer terror – eyes and mouth wide open, tongue out in a primal scream. It was, of course, the great showman Rossi, and the face had been painted on the top of his helmet by his designer, Aldo Drudi. 'I think it's the best yet,' he said.

Rossi the showman always does something special for his home GP at Mugello; Rossi the racer likewise. He had won there for the previous six years without a break. Never mind that his Yamaha was not the fastest bike, never mind the long straight, never mind the braking terror. The track is Valentino's. So it was again in 2008 – as he reminded everybody with pole position. It was the 50th of his career, his 40th in the top class, his first for almost a year. And his first on Bridgestone tyres.

The last fact is the most significant. He may have made this a third race win in a row, but he and his team were still feeling their way with the new tyres, a fundamentally different approach than with the Michelins. His fast qualifying lap came after additional set-up changes at lunchtime, and there were more between morning warm-up and the race, a process of continual refinement that would persist for several races to come. And he was getting better all the time.

The track belongs also to Ducati, in the sense that it is the factory team's test circuit, and the Desmos have put in many laps around Mugello, both with regular rid-

Right: Here passing Toseland and Edwards, de Angelis had the race of his life to fourth.

Left: Natural grandstands at the scenic circuit in the foothills.

Clockwise from below left: Dovizioso models headgear fashions; the paddock at dusk; Rossi fan Brad Pitt; 'Gimme the money.' Rossi jokes with Capirossi; Okada steers the new Honda through the spray.

Below centre: Hopkins had another forgettable weekend.

Photographs: Gold & Goose

ers and factory testers. That made a second Italian icon for the huge crowd of more than 96,000, 10,000 up on 2007, and a big block of red on the last right-hander. They had to settle for second, although Stoner did enough to salvage some pride, keeping Rossi honest to the end. But the puzzle about the other Ducati riders continued to deepen. Even as Stoner insisted that it was not a one-rider bike – 'You just have to work on the settings.' – the other three continued to flounder. Factory man Melandri literally, into the gravel on lap five, having leapt up to 12th from his qualifying position of 18th; he was running a different-spec engine from Stoner's ultra-quick motor, aimed at smoother low- and mid-range response. Guintoli and Elias didn't even make the top ten. The facts were proving Stoner wrong; it was an echo of the complaints about Michelin tyres over the previous season – when they worked well, they were excellent, but they worked only in a narrow range of conditions and temperatures that was often hard to achieve. In the same way, it was almost as though the other riders were having trouble in getting the Ducati's figurative stress temperature up to working levels, and could not even reach the zone in which Stoner rode as a matter of habit.

Honda took some limelight too, with – at last! – the arrival of the pneumatic-valve-spring engine. It was still in experimental form and ridden by stony-faced veteran Tadayuki Okada, four times a GP winner in the 1990s and now, at 41, official factory tester. Under wraps since its unsatisfactory test debut at the beginning of the year, the development bike looked little different, but assuredly was, according to project leader Shinichi Kokubu at a special briefing. With shared mounting points, it was interchangeable in the chassis with the steel-spring engine, but was quite different in almost every other way. And different to ride, revealed Okada, who – like HRC itself – found his development time split between both versions. The rev ceiling was 1,000rpm

higher, for one thing, while reduced valve-train loading cut engine drag. The more feisty engine had made fuel consumption even more important, and electronic management – Honda's in-house system – was still under development and not perfected, as Hayden would find much to his cost at Assen.

Other electronic issues remained: Okada revealed that mid-range throttle response was still erratic. He described the difference in feel and performance as 'like with the Big Bang and the Screamer two-strokes. The different character of the engine makes the handling different, even with the same weight distribution. On the front side, the handling is improved, maybe because of less engine friction.' He had a spill on the first day, but qualified 15th and had an uneventful race to 14th to claim the first points for the new machine.

Injury was still a talking point in the paddock, after Lorenzo's heroic second place in France. The Spaniard, still in a wheelchair, was a strong supporter of the argument that riders should make their own decisions. In this, he was supported by his peers, and by ex-racer Randy Mamola, who spoke of far stricter tests for F1 drivers, but pointed out that they are subjected to much greater G-forces, both lateral and under braking. 'We sportsmen are not superhuman, but … you know the phrase, "Mind over matter."' Hayden agreed: 'I've only gotten tested one time, and it seemed pretty thorough; but it's not so much the injury, more the dope – I'm more worried about how much juice they give a guy.'

What of Lorenzo? Well, boys will be boys. He fell off once more.

It was at the beginning of the long straight that an event took place that re-opened the debate on whether racing bikes should have some sort of handlebar guard or full-width bodywork, and at the end of the 250 race. Barbera and Simoncelli had been battling it out, and the latter led on to the straight to start the last lap. Fearing a draft-past move, he veered to the left, at the precise

moment that Barbera was pulling alongside. Barbera's brake lever clipped Simoncelli's seat, the front wheel locked and he ground-looped over the handlebars at close to top speed. Amazingly, he walked away.

This was an echo of the ruinous first-corner MotoGP crash at Catalunya in 2007, when the same point was raised. But bar-guards are considered a mixed blessing, offering also the possibility of a rider's hand becoming trapped during an accident.

MOTOGP RACE – 23 laps

Bad weather spoiled every free practice session, and only the final qualifying hour was fully dry. Everyone was short of set-up time as a result. Pedrosa was just two-tenths off Rossi's time, while the pole man had given his old pal Capirossi a friendly tow for his first front row since joining Suzuki. Rossi mimed demanding payment at the post-qualifying press conference.

Pedrosa blazed away, heading Stoner and Capirossi up the hill. By the end of the lap, however, Rossi was up to third; when they reached the end of the pit straight, Stoner sailed past Pedrosa to take the lead.

Capirossi stayed on the trio's tail for the first five laps, but played only a spectator's role as Rossi moved inside Pedrosa into the last corner at the end of lap two. He followed Stoner up the hill, but as they plunged off through the Casanova-Savelli right-left combination, one of his favourite overtaking spots, he took the lead.

For the next six laps, Rossi, Stoner and Pedrosa whistled around together. By the ninth, Rossi had eked out eight-tenths and was starting to look dangerous. Stoner responded with a lunging attack into the first corner, only to run wide, giving Pedrosa the few inches of space he needed. This was the crucial moment. It took Stoner five more laps to get ahead, by which time Rossi's push had taken him all but 2.5 seconds clear, with fewer than ten laps left.

The gap stretched by another second on lap 21, and only then could Rossi relax a little. Stoner was closing by the finish, but the Maestro of Mugello had it all under control, even though it fell to Stoner to break Max Biaggi's long-standing lap record.

Pedrosa had been unable to match the pace and settled for a safe third, although in the last laps, the imminent arrival of storming rookie de Angelis forced him to turn up the wick again.

The San Marino rider had messed up the first corner and finished lap one barely in the top 15. For the rest of the race, he forced his way forwards, cutting through what had been a lively mid-field battle in the ride of his life.

Hayden had been fifth on lap one, but first Lorenzo and then Dovizioso passed him, the latter getting ahead of Lorenzo as well. Using a softer tyre, he would pay the price later in the race. For now, when Lorenzo tried to get ahead again, he crashed out instead, on lap seven.

By now, de Angelis had passed Edwards and, after some to and fro, Toseland as well. Soon afterwards, he caught Dovizioso, who was hounding Capirossi for fourth. On lap nine, he passed both of them; at the same time, the Tech 3 pair were catching up as well.

As they passed half-distance, de Angelis escaped and the rest were fully engaged. Before long, the Yamahas got ahead again, Edwards going on to pass Toseland on lap 15. He'd taken a gamble on a tyre he thought would have better endurance, without having had the chance to test it. This paid off.

They all closed up at the finish, Edwards a second clear, Toseland managing to stay ahead of Capirossi and Dovizioso, with Nakano just behind.

Vermeulen was a lonely tenth, pushed to 17th after being badly boxed on the first lap. Hayden was behind, having lost ground steadily – he had a faulty tyre, which had caused vibration and grip issues. 'It was clear from the beginning I had a problem,' he said. Both Alice Ducatis were ahead by the end, Elias grabbing 12th on the run to the line, by four-thousandths of a second.

Okada cited a lack of set-up time for not being able to exploit his bike's higher performance. 'My data recorded 327km/h, but if I had come off the corner better, it would have been 5km/h faster,' he said. The best official speed recorded was 330.8km/h, by Melandri's Ducati in practice. Okada had been battling throughout with West who, once again, had struggled to stop the wheelspin that plagued his bike. 'I'm starting to sound like a stuck record, because I'm always explaining the same problem,' he said.

Melandri and de Puniet crashed out together after four laps. The Frenchman said he'd caught his brake lever on Vermeulen's bike as he passed; Melandri was an innocent victim.

Hopkins had crashed alone on the previous lap, blaming a quick-shifter fault that had stopped him from back-shifting at the end of the front straight.

250cc RACE – 21 laps

A dramatic 250 race was punctuated by a number of crashes and a fraught finish.

Barbera claimed his first pole of the season, ousting Bautista at the last second, with Simoncelli and Kallio completing the front row. Bautista took off at breakneck speed, with Simoncelli clearly struggling to stay with him. Before long, Barbera was more than a second adrift of the pair.

Bautista kept pushing on, setting a new record on lap five to break Simoncelli's pursuit. He was eight-tenths clear next time around, but his nemesis was waiting on lap seven, when the front tucked under and he went down. 'I went into the corner exactly the same speed as before,' he said later, his title hopes badly dented.

Simoncelli now led, but his comfort zone over Barbera shrank rapidly over the next three laps. Barbera had a clear speed advantage on the long straight, and he rode past easily on lap ten.

It was the start of a bitter battle. Simoncelli made su-

Above: Capirossi leads from Dovizioso, Toseland and Edwards in the mid-field battle.

Top right: In *parc fermé*, Corsi's 125 crew celebrate his third win, and the points lead.

Top far right: Pasini mops his brow after finishing fifth in the 250 race.

Above right: A typical 125 finish at Mugello as Corsi wins by inches from Talmacsi, Espargaro, di Meglio and Smith.
Photographs: Gold & Goose

Right: Polka-dot inversion as Barbera ground-loops and Simoncelli flashes past his pit board.
Photograph: Martin Heath

perhuman efforts and led over the line more often than not. But each time, Barbera was poised on his back wheel and would sweep demoralisingly past before they got to the first corner.

So it went on, and the result seemed pre-ordained. Unless Simoncelli could make a real gap on the last lap, Barbera had only to stick behind him and power past on the run to the flag. Both riders knew this, and Simoncelli decided to act at the end of the penultimate lap.

Out of the final corner, without looking behind, he swerved across to the left so that Barbera would have to take the long way around. He hadn't realised that the Spaniard was really close – almost alongside. The pair collided and Barbera went flying through the air for his lucky escape.

'He could have killed me,' he said later. While both riders received a word of warning, Race Direction decided that it had been a 'racing incident', so the lion-maned Italian escaped official punishment.

There had been a fierce battle for what had been fourth, Debon narrowly holding off Pesek, Takahashi and Luthi, with Pasini and Faubel in very close attendance.

Both Pesek and Faubel crashed out, separately, on lap ten; Poggiali – not far behind – also fell on the next lap. Takahashi lasted another seven laps before he abandoned the party for the gravel trap.

That left Debon and Luthi scrapping to the line for what was now second place – and it almost became one better. Simoncelli had been more than 2.5 seconds clear when he started his final lap after the incident with Barbera, and thought he had ample time to celebrate in front of his home crowd. Debon was less than half a second adrift at the flag.

Pasini dropped back, ceding fourth to Kallio, who had a stolid ride to gain valuable points. Aoyama had been following his KTM team-mate, but ran off on the last lap, regaining the track behind Pasini, Locatelli and Abrams. Espargaro led the next group over the line, Wilairot and Simon almost alongside.

125cc RACE – 20 laps

Once again, the 125s laid on the race of the day, with a typical Mugello finish, the first five riders crossing the line within two-tenths, and the next two still less than a second behind. A brawling mob had been together throughout, into the corners two or three abreast – bike racing at its finest.

De Rosa had taken his first pole, another last-minute run, at the expense of Talmacsi, with di Meglio and Espargaro alongside on the front row.

The lead was in dispute from the off, changing hands several times every lap, and often several times in the same corner. Over the line, di Meglio, Talmacsi, Terol and Bradl all took a turn leading, with the first named getting most of it towards the end.

Then it was Smith, on laps 18 and 19 – to an optimist, it even looked as though the young Briton might break free for a first win. But as they began the final lap, they were all right on him again and he was mobbed into the first turn, dropping down to fifth place in the space of a few yards.

Corsi led out of the last turn, which at Mugello usually means that someone will draft past before the finish line. Not this time, however, and he fervently thanked Aprilia for the horsepower that enabled him to stay inches ahead.

Best of the drafters was Talmacsi, who timed it almost perfectly with a spurt that brought him nearly alongside the leaders. He did consign Espargaro to third, from di Meglio, Smith, Gadea and Terol. Barely four seconds away, Cortese, Olive and Bradl completed the top ten, with Bonsey just prevailing over Iannone for 11th.

AUTODROMO INTERNAZIONALE DEL MUGELLO

Arrabbiata 2 · Scarperia · Palagio · Correntaio · Biondetti 1 · Biondetti 2 · Bucine · San Donato · Savelli · Arrabbiata 1 · Materassi · Luco · Cassanova · Poggio Seco · Borgo San Lorenzo

Circuit 5.245km / 3.259 miles

MOTOGP

RACE: 23 laps, 74.957 miles/120.635km • Weather: Dry • Air 29°C • Humidity 30% • Track 42°C

Pos.	Rider	Nat.	No.	Team	Machine	Tyres	Laps	Time & speed (mph/km/h)
1	Valentino Rossi	ITA	46	Fiat Yamaha Team	Yamaha	B	23	42m 31.153s 105.777mph/ 170.231km/h
2	Casey Stoner	AUS	1	Ducati Marlboro Team	Ducati	B	23	42m 33.354s
3	Dani Pedrosa	SPA	2	Repsol Honda Team	Honda	M	23	42m 36.020s
4	Alex de Angelis	RSM	15	San Carlo Honda Gresini	Honda	B	23	42m 37.466s
5	Colin Edwards	USA	5	Tech 3 Yamaha	Yamaha	M	23	42m 43.683s
6	James Toseland	GBR	52	Tech 3 Yamaha	Yamaha	M	23	42m 44.959s
7	Loris Capirossi	ITA	65	Rizla Suzuki MotoGP	Suzuki	B	23	42m 45.600s
8	Andrea Dovizioso	ITA	4	JiR Team Scot MotoGP	Honda	M	23	42m 46.472s
9	Shinya Nakano	JPN	56	San Carlo Honda Gresini	Honda	B	23	42m 46.480s
10	Chris Vermeulen	AUS	7	Rizla Suzuki MotoGP	Suzuki	B	23	43m 01.938s
11	Sylvain Guintoli	FRA	50	Alice Team	Ducati	B	23	43m 10.774s
12	Toni Elias	SPA	24	Alice Team	Ducati	B	23	43m 21.174s
13	Nicky Hayden	USA	69	Repsol Honda Team	Honda	M	23	43m 21.593s
14	Tadayuki Okada	JPN	8	Repsol Honda Team	Honda	M	23	43m 30.002s
15	Anthony West	AUS	13	Kawasaki Racing Team	Kawasaki	B	23	43m 31.889s
	Jorge Lorenzo	SPA	48	Fiat Yamaha Team	Yamaha	M	6	11m 11.489s
	John Hopkins	USA	21	Kawasaki Racing Team	Kawasaki	B	6	11m 17.629s
	Randy de Puniet	FRA	14	LCR Honda MotoGP	Honda	M	5	9m 25.989s
	Marco Melandri	ITA	33	Ducati Marlboro Team	Ducati	B	5	9m 26.358s

Fastest lap: Casey Stoner, on lap 5, 1m 50.003s, 106.658mph/171.649km/h (record).

Previous lap record: Max Biaggi, ITA (Honda), 1m 50.117s, 106.548mph/171.472km/h (2005).

Event best maximum speed: Marco Melandri, 205.5mph/330.8km/h (race).

QUALIFYING: 31 May 2008

Weather: Dry
Air: 24°C Humidity: 44% Track: 33°C

Pos.	Rider	Time
1	Rossi	1m 48.130s
2	Pedrosa	1m 48.297s
3	Capirossi	1m 48.313s
4	Stoner	1m 48.375s
5	Edwards	1m 48.383s
6	Hayden	1m 48.666s
7	Lorenzo	1m 48.905s
8	Toseland	1m 49.025s
9	Nakano	1m 49.095s
10	de Angelis	1m 49.145s
11	Vermeulen	1m 49.220s
12	de Puniet	1m 49.246s
13	Dovizioso	1m 49.565s
14	Hopkins	1m 49.601s
15	Okada	1m 49.829s
16	Elias	1m 49.851s
17	Guintoli	1m 50.275s
18	Melandri	1m 50.465s
19	West	1m 50.889s

Grid order	1	2	3	4	5	6	7	8	9	10	11	12	13	14	15	16	17	18	19	20	21	22	23	
46 ROSSI	2	1	1	46	46	46	46	46	46	46	46	46	46	46	46	46	46	46	46	46	46	46	46	1
2 PEDROSA	1	2	46	1	1	1	1	1	1	1	1	1	1	1	1	1	1	1	1	1	1	1	1	2
65 CAPIROSSI	46	46	2	2	2	2	2	2	2	2	2	2	2	2	2	2	2	2	2	2	2	2	2	3
1 STONER	65	65	65	65	65	65	65	65	15	15	15	15	15	15	15	15	15	15	15	15	15	15	15	4
5 EDWARDS	69	69	4	4	4	4	4	4	65	65	65	52	52	52	5	5	5	5	5	5	5	5	5	5
69 HAYDEN	48	4	48	48	48	48	15	15	4	4	52	65	5	5	52	52	52	52	52	52	52	52	52	6
48 LORENZO	4	48	69	69	52	52	52	52	52	52	4	4	65	65	65	4	4	65	65	65	65	65	65	7
52 TOSELAND	5	5	5	15	15	15	5	5	5	5	5	4	4	4	65	65	4	4	4	4	4	4	4	8
56 NAKANO	14	52	52	52	5	5	56	56	56	56	56	56	56	56	56	56	56	56	56	56	56	56	56	9
15 de ANGELIS	56	56	56	5	69	69	69	7	7	7	7	7	7	7	7	7	7	7	7	7	7	7	7	10
7 VERMEULEN	52	14	15	56	56	56	7	69	69	69	69	69	69	69	69	69	69	69	69	50	50	50	50	11
14 de PUNIET	33	33	33	33	21	7	50	50	50	50	50	50	50	50	24	24	24	24	50	69	69	24	12
4 DOVISIOSO	21	15	14	14	14	21	24	24	24	24	24	24	24	24	8	8	8	8	24	24	24	69	13
21 HOPKINS	15	21	21	21	7	24	13	13	13	13	13	13	8	8	13	13	13	13	8	8	8	8	14
8 OKADA	24	7	7	7	33	50	8	8	8	8	8	8	13	13	8	13	13	13	13	13	13	15
24 ELIAS	50	24	24	24	24	13																	
50 GUINTOLI	7	50	50	50	50	8																	
33 MELANDRI	8	8	13	13	13																		
13 WEST	13	13	8	8	8																		

FASTEST RACE LAPS

	Rider	Lap	Time
1	Stoner	5	1m 50.003s
2	Rossi	5	1m 50.034s
3	Pedrosa	5	1m 50.131s
4	de Angelis	8	1m 50.179s
5	Edwards	6	1m 50.502s
6	Dovizioso	4	1m 50.511s
7	Lorenzo	6	1m 50.518s
8	Capirossi	2	1m 50.523s
9	Toseland	2	1m 50.696s
10	Nakano	11	1m 50.886s
11	Hayden	2	1m 50.909s
12	Vermeulen	3	1m 50.916s
13	Melandri	2	1m 51.181s
14	Hopkins	3	1m 51.215s
15	de Puniet	4	1m 51.510s
16	Elias	3	1m 51.793s
17	Guintoli	3	1m 51.830s
18	Okada	23	1m 52.445s
19	West	2	1m 52.565s

OFFICIAL TIMEKEEPER

250cc

21 laps, 68.439 miles/110.145km

Pos.	Rider (Nat.)	No.	Team	Machine	Laps	Time & speed
1	Marco Simoncelli (ITA)	58	Metis Gilera	Gilera	21	40m 19.910s 101.817mph 163.858km/h
2	Alex Debon (SPA)	6	Lotus Aprilia	Aprilia	21	40m 20.409s
3	Thomas Luthi (SWI)	12	Emmi - Caffe Latte	Aprilia	21	40m 20.622s
4	Mika Kallio (FIN)	36	Red Bull KTM 250	KTM	21	40m 27.313s
5	Mattia Pasini (ITA)	75	Polaris World	Aprilia	21	40m 32.452s
6	Roberto Locatelli (ITA)	15	Metis Gilera	Gilera	21	40m 32.700s
7	Karel Abraham (CZE)	17	Cardion AB Motoracing	Aprilia	21	40m 36.024s
8	Hiroshi Aoyama (JPN)	4	Red Bull KTM 250	KTM	21	40m 37.226s
9	Aleix Espargaro (SPA)	41	Lotus Aprilia	Aprilia	21	40m 39.552s
10	Ratthapark Wilairot (THA)	14	Thai Honda PTT SAG	Honda	21	40m 39.614s
11	Julian Simon (FRA)	60	Repsol KTM 250cc	KTM	21	40m 39.661s
12	Alex Baldolini (ITA)	25	Matteoni Racing	Aprilia	21	41m 07.270s
13	Eugene Laverty (IRL)	50	Blusens Aprilia	Aprilia	21	41m 07.332s
14	Fabrizio Lai (ITA)	32	Campetella Racing	Gilera	21	41m 33.333s
15	Imre Toth (HUN)	10	Team Toth Aprilia	Aprilia	21	41m 45.801s
16	Russel Gomez (SPA)	7	Blusens Aprilia	Aprilia	21	41m 56.467s
17	Doni Tata Pradita (INA)	45	Yamaha Pertamina Indonesia	Yamaha	21	42m 08.134s
	Hector Barbera (SPA)	21	Team Toth Aprilia	Aprilia	19	DNF
	Yuki Takahashi (JPN)	72	JiR Team Scot 250	Honda	17	DNF
	Lukas Pesek (CZE)	52	Auto Kelly - CP	Aprilia	9	DNF
	Hector Faubel (SPA)	55	Mapfre Aspar Team	Aprilia	9	DNF
	Manuel Poggiali (RSM)	54	Campetella Racing	Gilera	9	DNF
	Alvaro Bautista (SPA)	19	Mapfre Aspar Team	Aprilia	6	DNF

Fastest lap: Bautista, 1m 53.669s, 103.218mph/166.113km/h (record).

Previous lap record: Hector Barbera, SPA (Aprilia), 1m 54.061s, 102.863mph/165.542km/h (2007).

Event best maximum speed: Luthi, 173.1mph/278.6km/h (race).

Qualifying: **1** Barbera, 1m 52.675s; **2** Bautista, 1m 53.447s; **3** Simoncelli, 1m 53.611s; **4** Kallio, 1m 53.635s; **5** Pesek, 1m 53.928s; **6** Poggiali, 1m 54.144s; **7** Debon, 1m 54.271s; **8** Luthi, 1m 54.376s; **9** Pasini, 1m 54.489s; **10** Aoyama, 1m 54.516s; **11** Takahashi, 1m 54.546s; **12** Faubel, 1m 54.578s; **13** Simon, 1m 54.626s; **14** Espargaro, 1m 54.712s; **15** Lai, 1m 54.735s; **16** Abraham, 1m 54.838s; **17** Wilairot, 1m 55.549s; **18** Locatelli, 1m 55.888s; **19** Toth, 1m 56.325s; **20** Laverty, 1m 56.990s; **21** Baldolini, 1m 57.305s; **22** Gomez, 1m 58.069s; **23** Pradita, 1m 58.731s.

Fastest race laps: **1** Bautista, 1m 53.669s; **2** Simoncelli, 1m 53.734s; **3** Barbera, 1m 53.840s; **4** Debon, 1m 54.132s; **5** Luthi, 1m 54.241s; **6** Pesek, 1m 54.254s; **7** Takahashi, 1m 54.331s; **8** Kallio, 1m 54.420s; **9** Locatelli, 1m 54.692s; **10** Espargaro, 1m 54.701s; **11** Pasini, 1m 54.727s; **12** Aoyama, 1m 54.730s; **13** Faubel, 1m 54.830s; **14** Abraham, 1m 54.902s; **15** Simon, 1m 54.925s; **16** Poggiali, 1m 54.939s; **17** Wilairot, 1m 55.103s; **18** Laverty, 1m 56.172s; **19** Lai, 1m 56.275s; **20** Baldolini, 1m 56.422s; **21** Toth, 1m 57.763s; **22** Gomez, 1m 58.622s; **23** Pradita, 1m 58.756s.

World Championship: **1** Kallio, 106; **2** Pasini, 88; **3** Debon, 79; **4** Simoncelli, 78; **5** Aoyama, 61; **6** Takahashi, 59; **7** Barbera, 53; **8** Bautista, 41; **9** Espargaro, 40; **10** Simon, 36; **11** Luthi, 35; **12** Locatelli, 34; **13** Wilairot, 25; **14** Faubel, 25; **15** Abraham, 21; **16** Baldolini, 13; **17** Poggiali, 12; **18** Pesek, 12; **19** Lai, 8; **20** Laverty, 7; **21** Hernandez and Sandi, 2; **23** Toth, 2; **24** Pradita, 1.

125cc

20 laps, 65.180 miles/104.900km

Pos.	Rider (Nat.)	No.	Team	Machine	Laps	Time & speed
1	Simone Corsi (ITA)	24	Jack & Jones WRB	Aprilia	20	39m 59.020s 97.813mph/ 157.414km/h
2	Gabor Talmacsi (HUN)	1	Bancaja Aspar Team	Aprilia	20	39m 59.039s
3	Pol Espargaro (SPA)	44	Belson Derbi	Derbi	20	39m 59.056s
4	Mike di Meglio (FRA)	63	Ajo Motorsport	Derbi	20	39m 59.155s
5	Bradley Smith (GBR)	38	Polaris World	Aprilia	20	39m 59.198s
6	Sergio Gadea (SPA)	33	Bancaja Aspar Team	Aprilia	20	39m 59.510s
7	Nicolas Terol (SPA)	18	Jack & Jones WRB	Aprilia	20	39m 59.852s
8	Sandro Cortese (GER)	11	Emmi - Caffe Latte	Aprilia	20	40m 02.885s
9	Joan Olive (SPA)	6	Belson Derbi	Derbi	20	40m 02.948s
10	Stefan Bradl (GER)	17	Grizzly Gas Kiefer Racing	Aprilia	20	40m 04.459s
11	Stevie Bonsey (USA)	51	Degraaf Grand Prix	Aprilia	20	40m 09.264s
12	Andrea Iannone (ITA)	29	I.C. Team	Aprilia	20	40m 09.467s
13	Raffaele de Rosa (ITA)	35	Onde 2000 KTM	KTM	20	40m 17.386s
14	Scott Redding (GBR)	45	Blusens Aprilia Junior	Aprilia	20	40m 22.221s
15	Michael Ranseder (AUT)	60	I.C. Team	Aprilia	20	40m 23.460s
16	Takaaki Nakagami (JPN)	73	I.C. Team	Aprilia	20	40m 25.651s
17	Randy Krummenacher (SWI)	34	Red Bull KTM 125	KTM	20	40m 29.649s
18	Efren Vazquez (SPA)	7	Blusens Aprilia Junior	Aprilia	20	40m 29.750s
19	Marc Marquez (SPA)	93	Repsol KTM 125cc	KTM	20	40m 32.888s
20	Lorenzo Zanetti (ITA)	8	ISPA KTM Aran	KTM	20	40m 35.948s
21	Pere Tutusaus (SPA)	30	Bancaja Aspar Team	Aprilia	20	40m 48.971s
22	Lorenzo Savadori (ITA)	40	RCGM	Aprilia	20	40m 49.058s
23	Jules Cluzel (FRA)	16	Loncin Racing	Loncin	20	40m 49.060s
24	Dominique Aegerter (SWI)	77	Ajo Motorsport	Derbi	20	40m 49.072s
25	Esteve Rabat (SPA)	12	Repsol KTM 125cc	KTM	20	40m 55.380s
26	Riccardo Moretti (ITA)	47	CRP Racing	Honda	20	41m 05.267s
27	Alexis Masbou (FRA)	5	Loncin Racing	Loncin	20	41m 05.586s
28	Robin Lasser (GER)	21	Grizzly Gas Kiefer Racing	Aprilia	20	41m 06.002s
29	Hugo van den Berg (NED)	56	Degraaf Grand Prix	Aprilia	20	41m 08.286s
30	Luca Vitali (ITA)	42	RCGM	Aprilia	20	41m 09.571s
31	Gabriele Ferro (ITA)	43	Metasystems RS	Honda	20	41m 09.587s
32	Louis Rossi (FRA)	69	FFM Honda GP 125	Honda	20	41m 35.471s
33	Ferruccio Lamborghini (ITA)	39	Junior GP Racing Dream	Aprilia	20	41m 38.903s
34	Robert Muresan (ROU)	95	Grizzly Gas Kiefer Racing	Aprilia	18	40m 57.755s
	Danny Webb (GBR)	99	Degraaf Grand Prix	Aprilia	19	DNF
	Tomoyoshi Koyama (JPN)	71	ISPA KTM Aran	KTM	16	DNF
	Roberto Lacalendola (ITA)	19	Matteoni Racing	Aprilia	11	DNF
	Pablo Nieto (SPA)	22	Onde 2000 KTM	KTM	8	DNF
	Stefano Bianco (ITA)	27	S3+ WTR San Marino Team	Aprilia	2	DNF

Fastest lap: di Meglio, 1m 58.570s, 98.951mph/159.247km/h (record).

Previous lap record: Sergio Gadea, SPA (Aprilia), 1m 58.636s, 98.897mph/159.159km/h (2007).

Event best maximum speed: Smith, 148.7mph/239.3km/h (race).

Qualifying: **1** de Rosa, 1m 58.302s; **2** Talmacsi, 1m 58.467s; **3** di Meglio, 1m 58.490s; **4** Espargaro, 1m 58.572s; **5** Gadea, 1m 58.631s; **6** Cortese, 1m 58.658s; **7** Smith, 1m 58.816s; **8** Corsi, 1m 58.895s; **9** Terol, 1m 59.065s; **10** Koyama, 1m 59.328s; **11** Bradl, 1m 59.351s; **12** Iannone, 1m 59.382s; **13** Bonsey, 1m 59.395s; **14** Olive, 1m 59.485s; **15** Nakagami, 1m 59.580s; **16** Redding, 1m 59.700s; **17** Webb, 1m 59.880s; **18** Ranseder, 1m 59.938s; **19** Krummenacher, 2m 00.341s; **20** Rabat, 2m 00.540s; **21** Bianco, 2m 00.562s; **22** Savadori, 2m 00.916s; **23** Marquez, 2m 01.384s; **24** Cluzel, 2m 01.657s; **25** Vazquez, 2m 01.762s; **26** Aegerter, 2m 01.799s; **27** Nieto, 2m 01.823s; **28** van den Berg, 2m 01.873s; **29** Lacalendola, 2m 01.900s; **30** Muresan, 2m 02.097s; **31** Zanetti, 2m 02.161s; **32** Tutusaus, 2m 02.195s; **33** Lasser, 2m 02.242s; **34** Ferro, 2m 02.344s; **35** Moretti, 2m 02.566s; **36** Lamborghini, 2m 02.779s; **37** Rossi, 2m 03.414s; **38** Vitali, 2m 04.221s; **39** Masbou, 2m 21.359s.

Fastest race laps: **1** di Meglio, 1m 58.570s; **2** Smith, 1m 58.637s; **3** Espargaro, 1m 58.798s; **4** Bradl, 1m 58.808s; **5** Terol, 1m 58.835s; **6** Talmacsi, 1m 58.872s; **7** Cortese, 1m 58.925s; **8** Corsi, 1m 58.932s; **9** Gadea, 1m 58.936s; **10** Iannone, 1m 58.955s; **11** Olive, 1m 59.084s; **12** de Rosa, 1m 59.324s; **13** Bonsey, 1m 59.457s; **14** Ranseder, 1m 59.791s; **15** Krummenacher, 1m 59.954s; **16** Webb, 1m 59.982s; **17** Bianco, 2m 00.075s; **18** Redding, 2m 00.152s; **19** Vazquez, 2m 00.165s; **20** Nakagami, 2m 00.228s; **21** Zanetti, 2m 00.333s; **22** Koyama, 2m 00.373s; **23** Marquez, 2m 00.400s; **24** Savadori, 2m 00.742s; **25** Tutusaus, 2m 00.765s; **26** Cluzel, 2m 00.831s; **27** Lacalendola, 2m 00.960s; **28** Aegerter, 2m 01.054s; **29** Rabat, 2m 01.432s; **30** Nieto, 2m 01.455s; **31** Masbou, 2m 01.550s; **32** Ferro, 2m 01.720s; **33** Lasser, 2m 01.723s; **34** van den Berg, 2m 01.844s; **35** Moretti, 2m 02.001s; **36** Vitali, 2m 02.025s; **37** Muresan, 2m 02.350s; **38** Lamborghini, 2m 02.754s; **39** Rossi, 2m 03.512s.

World Championship: **1** Corsi, 87; **2** di Meglio, 87; **3** Terol, 75; **4** Olive, 65; **5** Bradl, 64; **6** Espargaro, 55; **7** Talmacsi, 52; **8** Iannone, 47; **9** Smith, 47; **10** Gadea, 42; **11** Bonsey, 30; **12** Cortese, 30; **13** Redding, 22; **14** de Rosa, 22; **15** Webb, 21; **16** Vazquez, 14; **17** Ranseder, 13; **18** Aegerter, 12; **19** Nieto, 11; **20** Zanetti, 9; **21** Rabat, 9; **22** Krummenacher, 6; **23** Koyama, 6; **24** Tutusaus, 5; **25** Marquez, 4; **26** Bianco, 3; **27** Masbou and Nakagami, 1.

RIDER STANDINGS
After 6 Rounds

1	Valentino Rossi	122
2	Dani Pedrosa	110
3	Jorge Lorenzo	94
4	Casey Stoner	76
5	Colin Edwards	58
6	Loris Capirossi	51
7	Andrea Dovizioso	44
8	James Toseland	43
9	Nicky Hayden	40
10	Shinya Nakano	35
11	Chris Vermeulen	31
12	John Hopkins	26
13	Alex de Angelis	24
14	Marco Melandri	24
15	Toni Elias	24
16	Randy de Puniet	18
17	Sylvain Guintoli	12
18	Anthony West	6
19	Tadayuki Okada	2

TEAM STANDINGS
After 6 Rounds

1	Fiat Yamaha Team	216
2	Repsol Honda Team	150
3	Tech 3 Yamaha	101
4	Ducati Marlboro Team	100
5	Rizla Suzuki MotoGP	82
6	San Carlo Honda Gresini	59
7	JiR Team Scot MotoGP	44
8	Alice Team	36
9	Kawasaki Racing Team	32
10	LCR Honda MotoGP	18

CONSTRUCTOR STANDINGS
After 6 Rounds

1	Yamaha	140
2	Honda	110
3	Ducati	81
4	Suzuki	54
5	Kawasaki	29

FIM WORLD CHAMPIONSHIP • ROUND 7

CATALUNYA|GP
BARCELONA

Packed grandstands and a home boy doing them
proud: Pedrosa leads from Stoner, Dovizioso,
Edwards, de Puniet and Hayden. Rossi, in unfamiliar
blue and white, heads the next batch.
Photograph: Gold & Goose

WHEN the last finisher crossed the line at Catalunya, it highlighted a problem to which everyone had been turning a blind eye – a severe shortage of MotoGP entries. He was Sylvain Guintoli, and he finished 13th. There was nobody else left to take the final points.

On a good day, without any wild-cards, there are only 18 starters. At Catalunya, Lorenzo was out after a crash in practice, Elias had been disqualified and three others had fallen. Lose a couple more and even Randy Mamola would have been able to take a top-ten finish, with a passenger on the Ducati two-seater. Time, thought some, to stop awarding points all the way to 15th.

The conversation before the race had been about another matter, however, the forthcoming 250 replacement class. The latest news was that the manufacturers had rejected Dorna's proposal of 625–650cc production-based engines on the reasonable grounds that nobody made engines of that size; they preferred to stick with 600s. This would bring the proposed class into direct conflict with the Flammini Group's World Supersport series, which clearly Dorna had been trying to sidestep; the new situation put CEO Ezpeleta in a difficult position. Doorstepped by the Anglophone media, he was soon splutteringly explaining that even with engines bearing serial numbers, the new bikes would still be prototypes. Even MotoGP bikes, he said, shared many components with street bikes. Which components? The clutches, he said. This was contradicted firmly. Well then, the chains, he insisted.

A wider controversy threatened this particular weekend: a transport strike had blocked some roads and forced an early start on Sunday – 05.30 or even before – for those who had to be sure to be at the track outside Barcelona in good time. Whatever the perpetrators had hoped for or imagined, it didn't deter the crowds, more than 113,000 turning up for the second Spanish race of the year.

They were well rewarded by Dani Pedrosa, who, in spite of the long straight, proved he had no need of Honda's pneumatic-valve-spring engine. Team-mate Hayden had wanted it rather more than the Spaniard, but he too was denied. All would have to wait until the test days after the race, when the American managed to persuade Honda, against its will, to let him have a go with the engine at the following round.

Another talking point had been Lorenzo and his willingness, or capacity, to race while injured. The fast but unfortunate rookie had another big crash in practice, and this one actually did stop him, thanks to a dose of concussion and memory loss, as well as injuries to his right hand. He was one of seven people to crash in practice at yet another race where bad weather played a hand, albeit indirectly, with heavy rain on Thursday and Saturday night. It wasn't actually wet for the race, but rubber had been rinsed off the surface, and grip was a problem. De Puniet actually fell twice in practice, but the only other injured rider was Hopkins, who suffered damaged vertebrae. He was able to ride on, although severely detuned.

The endemic bumps and lack of grip failed to halt the inexorable progress of lap times, however. The first six qualifiers were inside Rossi's pole time of 2007, and TV viewers had a better than ever opportunity to watch how they did it, with a plethora of on-bike cameras offering the most comprehensive coverage yet. Every MotoGP bike was fitted with three mini-cams, and seven of them carried a fourth. Standard angles of view were forward,

Right: Tanned and fit, Sete Gibernau was ready for come-back rumours.

Far right: Rossi forces a gap to seize second place from Stoner.
Photographs: Gold & Goose

Below right: Rossi had his own 'Euro 2008' football collector card on his windscreen.
Photograph: Martin Heath

Bottom right: The fans were ecstatic, but Elias had a disastrous weekend.

Below: Yet another crunching impact for Lorenzo. This one actually stopped him.
Photographs: Gold & Goose

back and the rider from the tail – for those intimate views of Rossi tugging at the seat of his leathers. Additional angles included Rossi's clutch hand, Pedrosa's throttle and front brake, the front tyres of Stoner and Edwards, and for some reason Capirossi's right knee. The largesse extended to the 250 class, the four top runners each having a pair of cameras. Given the close racing, some thought it high time the 125 class had some more.

The start of the European Football Championship during the weekend prompted Rossi to make a change in livery – the first time in living memory that he had not worn yellow at least somewhere on his leathers. Instead, he was kitted up as an Italian footballer, with the blue of the 'Azzuri' set off by a lurid pink on arms and legs to simulate shorts and a football shirt; his helmet was painted to resemble a football. His bike was also in blue and white, the idea of Fiat, he said, although the leathers had been his own choice.

The Italian was already talking about the renewal of his contract with Yamaha. Discussions were at a fairly advanced stage, he revealed, adding – no doubt to the dismay of his rivals – that possibly he would stay on in MotoGP for four or five more years. Aged 29, he said, 'Age is not a problem. Look at Troy Bayliss – he is very, very fast and he is 38. And Loris Capirossi is 35 and is still very hungry.'

Rossi made his life harder by qualifying only ninth, while Stoner took his first pole of the year. At the other end of the grid, hapless fellow Australian Anthony West continued to struggle with a Kawasaki more prone to wheelspin than forward motion, at the track where he had ridden the bike for the first time in 2007. West was last qualifier for the fifth time in the season – his frequent adversary for this uncoveted position, Marco Melandri, was alongside, while injured team-mate Hopkins was just two places ahead. But he showed he had not quite lost his sense of humour. When the TV cameras came to him on the grid, he gestured that they should perhaps run the race in the opposite direction. Then, he pointed out, he would be on pole.

There were more electronic advances in the 250 class, with Hector Barbera being the latest Aprilia rider to be given traction control, pioneered two races previously by Debon. He complained that the period of adjustment required in practice had distracted him from the important task of testing tyres, which proved costly during the race when he faded from contention in the closing stages.

MOTOGP RACE – 25 laps

Stoner's pole put the Hondas second and third on the grid, Hayden's first time on the front row all season. Both satellite Yamahas were on the second row, but Rossi was on the far end of the third – he explained that corner entry problems had spoiled his set-up.

Pedrosa's race was simple enough, at least to watch. He got the jump off the start and led through the first right-left and up the hill. Stoner was in hot pursuit, but had a major wobble under braking for the tight left-hander once they'd run down the hill again, and Dovizioso took advantage to grab second.

This helped Pedrosa's escape. If he needed any help, for he was lapping like a metronome set on *prestissimo*, setting a new record on lap four. By then, Stoner had got back to second, but was almost three seconds adrift. It was a gap that would continue to grow as the Australian ran wide again into the tight left on lap eight, letting Dovi through once more for another lap.

Rossi had been eighth on lap one, but he picked his way through the field remorselessly – past Toseland on lap two, Hayden on the fourth, then de Puniet and Edwards on the sixth and seventh. On lap nine, he ran around the outside of Dovizioso over the hill, then blitzed Stoner as well on the Australian's bogey corner.

De Puniet crashed out of sixth shortly before half-distance, while Edwards hung on behind the battling trio, until he too started to lose ground. Likewise Dovizioso, although it wasn't until the 19th lap that the gap grew to more than a second.

This left Rossi and Stoner hard at it, much as they had been a year before, and the outcome was equally uncertain. That time, it had gone Stoner's way by six-hundredths. Now he got ahead on lap 17 and seemed able to hold Rossi at bay over the next six tours, in spite of the Yamaha rider's best efforts. When Rossi did make a decisive attack, however, into the first corner at the start of the penultimate lap, it was clear that he had been biding his time. He crossed the line only half a second ahead, but firmly out of reach of the Ducati

Meanwhile, Pedrosa had slackened his pace over the last five laps, letting a gap of eight seconds shrink to a still-decisive 2.8 for his second win of the year.

Dovi finished almost ten seconds down, Edwards another five behind him.

The battle for sixth had been fierce almost from the start, and became more so by the finish. Hayden had lost touch with the lead group bit by bit, a second adrift of de Puniet by lap seven, and then well out of touch when the Frenchman crashed out on the 12th lap. Meanwhile, Vermeulen had moved through to head the pursuit, team-mate Capirossi ceding the lead of the group to him on lap eight, two laps before he and de Angelis crashed out together, each blaming the other. Capirossi came off the worse, sustaining fractures in his right hand and a dislocation that would spoil the next several races.

By this stage, Nakano had lost touch with them, while Toseland was engaged with the Australian, and ahead of him again on lap 15 as they all closed up on the fading Hayden. Both passed the factory bike on lap 21, but the American stayed with them as Nakano joined up again. Over the line, Toseland just managed to stay ahead of Vermeulen, with Hayden and Nakano right up behind.

Further back, Hopkins had a pained and lonely race, and then there was another big gap to Melandri, who had started well to finish the first lap tenth, but soon dropped back until he was engaged with West. The pair changed places over and over, but Melandri had the straight-line speed to head the Kawasaki over the line every time except once, including the crucial last lap. Guintoli was a second behind at the end, never quite a threat to them.

There were only 13 finishers from a mere 17 starters. As well as the three crashers, Elias capped a dreary afternoon by taking a black flag, having missed the sign calling him in for a jumped-start ride-through penalty: a more than disappointing home GP.

Right: Dani Pedrosa celebrates a second runaway home win.

Below: Dovizioso impressed again, on the way to fourth.

Bottom: Thomas Luthi would work his way through to fifth from the middle of the grid.

Photographs: Gold & Goose

250cc RACE — 23 laps

Bautista took his third pole of the year, heading Debon, Barbera and Simoncelli; points leader Kallio was in an unusual third-row spot at a track where the Aprilias and even Takahashi's Honda had the legs on the KTMs. He was 5km/h down on the 278.4km/h top speed clocked by Barbera during the race, when slipstreaming tends to even out the figures.

Bautista and Debon led away, hotly pursued by Locatelli, Takahashi and Simoncelli. Only the last-named would reach the end of the lap unscathed, however, a collision in the final stadium section taking out Locatelli and putting a remounted Takahashi last.

Simoncelli gained the lead from Bautista on lap two, and Barbera consigned Debon to fourth next time around. From there, the first three forged ahead, setting one fastest lap after another. Bautista was fastest of all, on lap 21, but still a couple of tenths short of 2007's

record by de Angelis. The Spaniard headed them over the line on every lap from the third, except for the sixth. And, as it turned out, the last.

Barbera had held a long-term watching brief on Simoncelli's back wheel. From the 16th lap, however, he was losing touch rapidly, blaming a poor tyre choice because of time spent during practice adapting to his new traction control. Third was safe enough, however, with Debon more than ten seconds behind him and also losing speed.

Bautista was faster over the first half of the track; Simoncelli would close up again over the second part, several times coming within inches of the Spaniard's rear wheel going into the left-hander at the end of the back straight. Perhaps it was this that unsettled the former 125 champion, who until then had appeared to have the race under control.

Last time into that turn, he held it tight on the entry

and left his braking as late as he dared. Too late, as it turned out. A little slip as he tipped it in forced him wide; Simoncelli was right there and ready to dive into the apex. Finally he was in front, and able to resist every attempt by his rival. He took a crucial second win of the season by less than four-hundredths.

Kallio had dropped back to seventh at mid-distance from a fast start, then closed up again to within less than two seconds of fourth-placed Debon. Whether he would attack would never be known, for with less than five laps to go, he suddenly sat up and slowed, shaking his head. A piston ring had failed, and as he cruised back to the pits he almost crashed when he crossed a kerb to get out of the way of the pursuit.

Luthi held off a last-lap challenge for fifth from long-time pursuer Pasini; almost ten seconds behind, Aoyama steadfastly resisted Faubel and Simon, the order stable almost all race long. Pesek was a lone tenth; Takahashi came through from last to 12th, still four seconds behind Wilairot's Honda.

125cc RACE – 22 laps

The younger Espargaro brother took a maiden pole at the circuit that lies adjacent to his home town of Grano-liers, adding youngest pole qualifier to a CV that includes youngest points scorer and youngest podium finisher. He turned 17 two days after the race. Di

Meglio, Terol and Redding, on the front row for a second time, were alongside.

Young Pol failed to take a first GP victory by just over a quarter of a second, after a race in which the usual big-lead gang had been trimmed down to just three by the finish.

Terol led Espargaro on lap one; next time around, Gadea was in front, chased by Terol, Olive, Espargaro, di Meglio, Redding and Iannone.

Di Meglio took over on lap five, then Gadea again for a lap. The Spaniard was disputing second with Terol when the two collided, sending Gadea off across the gravel, to rejoin way down in 24th place.

Terol chased on and took over up front again briefly on lap 18, but it was di Meglio ahead over the line every other time, the pair making a small break. Two laps from the end, it was Terol's turn for a slip, at the corner at the end of the back straight where he had sent Gadea flying. He crashed out alone.

By now, the chase group – Espargaro, Olive, Talmacsi and Corsi – was catching up again. Then Olive also slid out, breaking them up a bit and leaving the first three unmolested from there to the flag.

Corsi, in pain from a heavy crash during morning warm-up, faded to fifth, having ceded fourth place to Bradl; Redding was a second adrift. Bonsey led the next group, from Cortese and Gadea, who had stormed all the way through to ninth in a remarkable recovery.

Above: Hair bigger by the week, Simoncelli took a second win in a row.

Above right: Gilera team-mates Poggiali and Lai sandwich Laverty in a battle for the last points.

Right: A second 125 victory gave di Meglio the points lead.

Photographs: Gold & Goose

GRAN PREMI CINZANO DE CATALUNYA

08 JUNE 2008 • FIM WORLD CHAMPIONSHIP ROUND 7

CIRCUIT DE CATALUNYA

Renault · Repsol · Seat · Campsa · Banc Sabadel · Europcar · Würth · Elf · La Caixa · New Holland

Circuit:
2.892 miles/4.655 km

MOTOGP

RACE: 25 laps, 73.425 miles/118.175km • Weather: Dry • Air 27°C • Humidity 34% • Track 39°C

Pos.	Rider	Nat.	No.	Team	Machine	Tyres	Laps	Time & speed (mph/km/h)
1	Dani Pedrosa	SPA	2	Repsol Honda Team	Honda	M	25	43m 02.175s 102.375mph/ 164.756km/h
2	Valentino Rossi	ITA	46	Fiat Yamaha Team	Yamaha	B	25	43m 04.981s
3	Casey Stoner	AUS	1	Ducati Marlboro Team	Ducati	B	25	43m 05.518s
4	Andrea Dovizioso	ITA	4	JiR Team Scot MotoGP	Honda	M	25	43m 13.068s
5	Colin Edwards	USA	5	Tech 3 Yamaha	Yamaha	M	25	43m 18.601s
6	James Toseland	GBR	52	Tech 3 Yamaha	Yamaha	M	25	43m 23.657s
7	Chris Vermeulen	AUS	7	Rizla Suzuki MotoGP	Suzuki	B	25	43m 23.723s
8	Nicky Hayden	USA	69	Repsol Honda Team	Honda	M	25	43m 24.455s
9	Shinya Nakano	JPN	56	San Carlo Honda Gresini	Honda	B	25	43m 24.550s
10	John Hopkins	USA	21	Kawasaki Racing Team	Kawasaki	B	25	43m 49.010s
11	Marco Melandri	ITA	33	Ducati Marlboro Team	Ducati	B	25	44m 00.166s
12	Anthony West	AUS	13	Kawasaki Racing Team	Kawasaki	B	25	44m 01.343s
13	Sylvain Guintoli	FRA	50	Alice Team	Ducati	B	25	44m 02.954s
	Randy de Puniet	FRA	14	LCR Honda MotoGP	Honda	M	11	19m 01.576s
	Alex de Angelis	RSM	15	San Carlo Honda Gresini	Honda	B	10	17m 23.460s
	Loris Capirossi	ITA	65	Rizla Suzuki MotoGP	Suzuki	B	10	17m 23.501s
	Toni Elias	SPA	24	Alice Team	Ducati	B		EXC

Fastest lap: Dani Pedrosa, on lap 4, 1m 42.358s, 103.304mph/166.251km/h (record).

Previous lap record: Nicky Hayden, USA (Honda), 1m 43.048s, 102.612mph/165.138km/h (2006).

Event best maximum speed: Marco Melandri, 204.2mph/328.7km/h (free practice no. 3).

QUALIFYING: 7 June 2008

Weather: Dry
Air: 21°C Humidity: 41% Track: 34°C

Pos.	Rider	Time
1	Stoner	1m 41.186s
2	Pedrosa	1m 41.269s
3	Hayden	1m 41.437s
4	de Puniet	1m 41.571s
5	Edwards	1m 41.609s
6	Toseland	1m 41.820s
7	Dovizioso	1m 42.053s
8	Vermeulen	1m 42.365s
9	Rossi	1m 42.427s
10	de Angelis	1m 42.580s
11	Nakano	1m 42.643s
12	Capirossi	1m 42.648s
13	Elias	1m 42.808s
14	Hopkins	1m 42.819s
15	Guintoli	1m 43.204s
16	Melandri	1m 43.719s
17	West	1m 44.558s

Grid order	1	2	3	4	5	6	7	8	9	10	11	12	13	14	15	16	17	18	19	20	21	22	23	24	25	
1 STONER	2	2	2	2	2	2	2	2	2	2	2	2	2	2	2	2	2	2	2	2	2	2	2	2	2	1
2 PEDROSA	4	4	1	1	1	1	1	4	46	46	46	46	46	46	46	46	1	1	1	1	1	1	1	46	46	2
69 HAYDEN	1	1	4	4	4	4	4	1	1	1	1	1	1	1	1	1	46	46	46	46	46	46	46	1	1	3
14 de PUNIET	5	5	5	5	5	5	5	46	4	4	4	4	4	4	4	4	4	4	4	4	4	4	4	4	4	4
5 EDWARDS	14	14	14	14	14	14	46	5	5	5	5	5	5	5	5	5	5	5	5	5	5	5	5	5	5	5
52 TOSELAND	69	69	69	69	46	46	14	14	14	14	14	69	69	69	69	69	69	69	69	69	52	52	52	52	52	6
4 DOVISIOSO	52	46	46	46	69	69	69	69	69	69	69	7	7	7	52	52	52	52	52	52	7	7	7	7	7	7
7 VERMEULEN	46	65	65	65	65	65	65	7	7	7	7	52	52	52	7	7	7	7	7	7	69	69	69	69	69	8
46 ROSSI	65	52	52	52	52	7	7	65	65	52	52	56	56	56	56	56	56	56	56	56	56	56	56	56	56	9
15 de ANGELIS	33	7	7	7	7	52	52	15	52	15	56	21	21	21	21	21	21	21	21	21	21	21	21	21	21	10
56 NAKANO	56	15	15	15	15	15	15	52	15	65	21	33	33	33	33	33	13	33	33	33	33	33	33	33	33	11
65 CAPIROSSI	15	56	56	56	56	56	56	56	56	56	13	13	13	13	33	13	33	13	13	13	13	13	13	13	13	12
24 ELIAS	7	33	21	21	21	21	21	21	21	21	33	50	50	50	50	50	50	50	50	50	50	50	50	50	50	13
21 HOPKINS	21	21	33	13	13	13	13	33	33	33	50															
50 GUINTOLI	13	13	13	33	33	24	24	13	13	13																
33 MELANDRI	24	24	24	24	24	33	33	24	50	50																
13 WEST	50	50	50	50	50	50	50	50																		

FASTEST RACE LAPS

	Rider	Lap	Time
1	Pedrosa	4	1m 42.358s
2	Rossi	5	1m 42.555s
3	Stoner	5	1m 42.831s
4	Capirossi	3	1m 42.871s
5	Edwards	4	1m 42.924s
6	de Puniet	5	1m 42.935s
7	Dovizioso	5	1m 42.990s
8	de Angelis	4	1m 43.047s
9	Nakano	5	1m 43.146s
10	Vermeulen	4	1m 43.165s
11	Hayden	2	1m 43.172s
12	Toseland	5	1m 43.323s
13	Hopkins	5	1m 43.792s
14	West	3	1m 44.413s
15	Elias	3	1m 44.520s
16	Guintoli	3	1m 44.548s
17	Melandri	7	1m 44.694s

250cc

23 laps, 67.551 miles/108.721km

Pos.	Rider (Nat.)	No.	Team	Machine	Laps	Time & speed
1	Marco Simoncelli (ITA)	58	Metis Gilera	Gilera	23	41m 01.859s 98.787mph/ 158.983km/h
2	Alvaro Bautista (SPA)	19	Mapfre Aspar Team	Aprilia	23	41m 01.898s
3	Hector Barbera (SPA)	21	Team Toth Aprilia	Aprilia	23	41m 13.150s
4	Alex Debon (SPA)	6	Lotus Aprilia	Aprilia	23	41m 23.232s
5	Thomas Luthi (SWI)	12	Emmi - Caffe Latte	Aprilia	23	41m 28.480s
6	Mattia Pasini (ITA)	75	Polaris World	Aprilia	23	41m 28.579s
7	Hiroshi Aoyama (JPN)	4	Red Bull KTM 250	KTM	23	41m 37.677s
8	Hector Faubel (SPA)	55	Mapfre Aspar Team	Aprilia	23	41m 38.180s
9	Julian Simon (SPA)	60	Repsol KTM 250cc	KTM	23	41m 38.823s
10	Lukas Pesek (CZE)	52	Auto Kelly - CP	Aprilia	23	41m 43.096s
11	Ratthapark Wilairot (THA)	14	Thai Honda PTT SAG	Honda	23	41m 54.250s
12	Yuki Takahashi (JPN)	72	JiR Team Scot 250	Honda	23	41m 58.515s
13	Alex Baldolini (ITA)	25	Matteoni Racing	Aprilia	23	42m 01.141s
14	Manuel Poggiali (RSM)	54	Campetella Racing	Gilera	23	42m 04.362s
15	Fabrizio Lai (ITA)	32	Campetella Racing	Gilera	23	42m 04.515s
16	Eugene Laverty (IRL)	50	Blusens Aprilia	Aprilia	23	42m 09.277s
17	Russel Gomez (SPA)	7	Blusens Aprilia	Aprilia	22	41m 21.386s
18	Doni Tata Pradita (INA)	45	Yamaha Pertamina Indonesia	Yamaha	22	41m 27.310s
	Mika Kallio (FIN)	36	Red Bull KTM 250	KTM	19	DNF
	Imre Toth (HUN)	10	Team Toth Aprilia	Aprilia	9	DNF
	Karel Abraham (CZE)	17	Cardion AB Motoracing	Aprilia	7	DNF
	Aleix Espargaro (SPA)	41	Lotus Aprilia	Aprilia	2	DNF
	Daniel Arcas (SPA)	92	Team Honda Merson	Honda	2	DNF
	Roberto Locatelli (ITA)	15	Metis Gilera	Gilera	0	DNF

Fastest lap: Bautista, 1m 46.143s, 99.620mph/160.323km/h.

Lap record: Alex de Angelis, RSM (Aprilia), 1m 45.925s, 99.825mph/160.653km/h (2007).

Event best maximum speed: Barbera, 173.0mph/278.4km/h (race).

Qualifying: **1** Bautista, 1m 45.636s; **2** Debon, 1m 45.767s; **3** Barbera, 1m 46.062s; **4** Simoncelli, 1m 46.295s; **5** Pasini, 1m 46.363s; **6** Faubel, 1m 46.594s; **7** Takahashi, 1m 46.668s; **8** Aoyama, 1m 46.856s; **9** Kallio, 1m 46.952s; **10** Simon, 1m 47.121s; **11** Locatelli, 1m 47.190s; **12** Luthi, 1m 47.207s; **13** Espargaro, 1m 47.422s; **14** Wilairot, 1m 47.510s; **15** Abraham, 1m 47.510s; **16** Pesek, 1m 47.666s; **17** Poggiali, 1m 47.728s; **18** Lai, 1m 47.818s; **19** Baldolini, 1m 49.272s; **20** Laverty, 1m 49.392s; **21** Gomez, 1m 49.618s; **22** Toth, 1m 49.776s; **23** Arcas, 1m 50.186s; **24** Pradita, 1m 50.450s.

Fastest race laps: **1** Bautista, 1m 46.143s; **2** Simoncelli, 1m 46.166s; **3** Barbera, 1m 46.440s; **4** Luthi, 1m 47.078s; **5** Debon, 1m 47.329s; **6** Kallio, 1m 47.530s; **7** Pasini, 1m 47.683s; **8** Faubel, 1m 47.717s; **9** Simon, 1m 47.806s; **10** Wilairot, 1m 47.887s; **11** Abraham, 1m 47.927s; **12** Pesek, 1m 47.968s; **13** Aoyama, 1m 47.982s; **14** Takahashi, 1m 48.191s; **15** Baldolini, 1m 48.453s; **16** Lai, 1m 48.481s; **17** Poggiali, 1m 48.893s; **18** Laverty, 1m 48.999s; **19** Espargaro, 1m 49.247s; **20** Gomez, 1m 50.263s; **21** Pradita, 1m 51.430s; **22** Arcas, 1m 51.727s; **23** Toth, 1m 52.565s.

World Championship: **1** Kallio, 106; **2** Simoncelli, 103; **3** Pasini, 98; **4** Debon, 92; **5** Aoyama, 70; **6** Barbera, 69; **7** Takahashi, 63; **8** Bautista, 61; **9** Luthi, 46; **10** Simon, 43; **11** Espargaro, 40; **12** Locatelli, 34; **13** Faubel, 33; **14** Wilairot, 30; **15** Abraham, 21; **16** Pesek, 18; **17** Baldolini, 16; **18** Poggiali, 14; **19** Lai, 9; **20** Laverty, 7; **21** Hernandez and Sandi, 2; **23** Toth, 2; **24** Pradita, 1.

125cc

22 laps, 64.614 miles/103.994km

Pos.	Rider (Nat.)	No.	Team	Machine	Laps	Time & speed
1	Mike di Meglio (FRA)	63	Ajo Motorsport	Derbi	22	41m 08.708s 94.230mph/ 151.649km/h
2	Pol Espargaro (SPA)	44	Belson Derbi	Derbi	22	41m 08.976s
3	Gabor Talmacsi (HUN)	1	Bancaja Aspar Team	Aprilia	22	41m 09.046s
4	Stefan Bradl (GER)	17	Grizzly Gas Kiefer Racing	Aprilia	22	41m 17.473s
5	Simone Corsi (ITA)	24	Jack & Jones WRB	Aprilia	22	41m 18.849s
6	Scott Redding (GBR)	45	Blusens Aprilia Junior	Aprilia	22	41m 19.886s
7	Stevie Bonsey (USA)	51	Degraaf Grand Prix	Aprilia	22	41m 22.379s
8	Sandro Cortese (GER)	11	Emmi - Caffe Latte	Aprilia	22	41m 22.463s
9	Sergio Gadea (SPA)	33	Bancaja Aspar Team	Aprilia	22	41m 24.249s
10	Marc Marquez (SPA)	93	Repsol KTM 125cc	KTM	22	41m 27.670s
11	Danny Webb (GBR)	99	Degraaf Grand Prix	Aprilia	22	41m 31.361s
12	Dominique Aegerter (SWI)	77	Ajo Motorsport	Derbi	22	41m 33.636s
13	Tomoyoshi Koyama (JPN)	71	ISPA KTM Aran	KTM	22	41m 33.721s
14	Bradley Smith (GBR)	38	Polaris World	Aprilia	22	41m 33.767s
15	Randy Krummenacher (SWI)	34	Red Bull KTM 125	KTM	22	41m 33.896s
16	Efren Vazquez (SPA)	7	Blusens Aprilia Junior	Aprilia	22	41m 34.060s
17	Michael Ranseder (AUT)	60	I.C. Team	Aprilia	22	41m 34.249s
18	Stefano Bianco (ITA)	27	S3+ WTR San Marino Team	Aprilia	22	41m 40.073s
19	Pere Tutusaus (SPA)	30	Bancaja Aspar Team	Aprilia	22	41m 51.607s
20	Jules Cluzel (FRA)	16	Loncin Racing	Loncin	22	41m 52.177s
21	Hugo van den Berg (NED)	56	Degraaf Grand Prix	Aprilia	22	42m 05.638s
22	Takaaki Nakagami (JPN)	73	I.C. Team	Aprilia	22	42m 10.026s
23	Roberto Lacalendola (ITA)	19	Matteoni Racing	Aprilia	22	42m 11.575s
24	Robert Muresan (ROU)	95	Grizzly Gas Kiefer Racing	Aprilia	22	42m 26.078s
25	Louis Rossi (FRA)	69	FFM Honda GP 125	Honda	22	42m 27.498s
26	Ricard Cardus (SPA)	75	Andalucia Derbi	Derbi	22	42m 36.058s
27	Daniel Saez (SPA)	78	Gaviota Prosolia Racing	Aprilia	22	42m 37.444s
	Axel Pons (SPA)	14	Jack & Jones WRB	Aprilia	21	DNF
	Nicolas Terol (SPA)	18	Jack & Jones WRB	Aprilia	20	DNF
	Raffaele de Rosa (ITA)	35	Onde 2000 KTM	KTM	20	DNF
	Joan Olive (SPA)	6	Belson Derbi	Derbi	19	DNF
	Andrea Iannone (ITA)	29	I.C. Team	Aprilia	17	DNF
	Robin Lasser (GER)	21	Grizzly Gas Kiefer Racing	Aprilia	17	DNF
	Lorenzo Zanetti (ITA)	8	ISPA KTM Aran	KTM	14	DNF
	Alexis Masbou (FRA)	5	Loncin Racing	Loncin	13	DNF
	Jordi Dalmau (SPA)	31	SAG Castrol	Honda	11	DNF
	Ivan Maestro (SPA)	76	Hune Matteoni	Aprilia	10	DNF
	Pablo Nieto (SPA)	22	Onde 2000 KTM	KTM	1	DNF

Fastest lap: Olive, 1m 51.271s, 95.029mph/152.934km/h.

Lap record: Randy Krummenacher, SWI (KTM), 1m 50.732s, 95.492mph/153.679km/h (2007).

Event best maximum speed: Talmacsi, 150.2mph/241.7km/h (race).

Qualifying: **1** Espargaro, 1m 50.557s; **2** di Meglio, 1m 50.696s; **3** Terol, 1m 50.740s; **4** Redding, 1m 51.101s; **5** Corsi, 1m 51.365s; **6** Gadea, 1m 51.399s; **7** Talmacsi, 1m 51.436s; **8** Smith, 1m 51.439s; **9** Iannone, 1m 51.500s; **10** Olive, 1m 51.518s; **11** Cortese, 1m 51.564s; **12** de Rosa, 1m 51.566s; **13** Bradl, 1m 51.593s; **14** Marquez, 1m 51.650s; **15** Vazquez, 1m 51.780s; **16** Bonsey, 1m 51.932s; **17** Aegerter, 1m 51.976s; **18** Krummenacher, 1m 52.074s; **19** Nakagami, 1m 52.076s; **20** Nieto, 1m 52.080s; **21** Webb, 1m 52.161s; **22** Koyama, 1m 52.250s; **23** Masbou, 1m 52.428s; **24** Zanetti, 1m 52.428s; **25** Lasser, 1m 52.474s; **26** Bianco, 1m 52.593s; **27** Ranseder, 1m 52.769s; **28** Tutusaus, 1m 52.806s; **29** Cluzel, 1m 53.345s; **30** Pons, 1m 53.532s; **31** van den Berg, 1m 53.560s; **32** Muresan, 1m 53.607s; **33** Cardus, 1m 53.698s; **34** Lacalendola, 1m 54.090s; **35** Rossi, 1m 54.190s; **36** Dalmau, 1m 54.944s; **37** Saez, 1m 55.022s; **38** Maestro, 1m 55.681s.

Fastest race laps: **1** Olive, 1m 51.271s; **2** di Meglio, 1m 51.280s; **3** Corsi, 1m 51.285s; **4** Terol, 1m 51.343s; **5** Talmacsi, 1m 51.364s; **6** Espargaro, 1m 51.507s; **7** Bradl, 1m 51.515s; **8** Redding, 1m 51.531s; **9** Cortese, 1m 51.636s; **10** Gadea, 1m 51.640s; **11** Marquez, 1m 51.680s; **12** de Rosa, 1m 51.721s; **13** Bonsey, 1m 51.766s; **14** Smith, 1m 51.773s; **15** Webb, 1m 52.064s; **16** Iannone, 1m 52.073s; **17** Vazquez, 1m 52.086s; **18** Ranseder, 1m 52.124s; **19** Krummenacher, 1m 52.191s; **20** Bianco, 1m 52.207s; **21** Nakagami, 1m 52.219s; **22** Koyama, 1m 52.239s; **23** Aegerter, 1m 52.326s; **24** Masbou, 1m 52.639s; **25** Cluzel, 1m 52.674s; **26** Zanetti, 1m 52.805s; **27** Tutusaus, 1m 53.184s; **28** van den Berg, 1m 53.548s; **29** Lasser, 1m 53.820s; **30** Lacalendola, 1m 54.089s; **31** Muresan, 1m 54.158s; **32** Pons, 1m 54.172s; **33** Saez, 1m 54.525s; **34** Dalmau, 1m 54.624s; **35** Rossi, 1m 54.849s; **36** Cardus, 1m 55.174s; **37** Maestro, 1m 57.252s.

World Championship: **1** di Meglio, 112; **2** Corsi, 98; **3** Bradl, 77; **4** Terol, 75; **5** Espargaro, 75; **6** Talmacsi, 68; **7** Olive, 65; **8** Gadea, 49; **9** Smith, 49; **10** Iannone, 47; **11** Bonsey, 39; **12** Cortese, 38; **13** Redding, 32; **14** Webb, 26; **15** de Rosa, 22; **16** Aegerter, 16; **17** Vazquez, 14; **18** Ranseder, 13; **19** Nieto, 11; **20** Marquez, 10; **21** Zanetti, 9; **22** Rabat, 9; **23** Koyama, 9; **24** Krummenacher, 7; **25** Tutusaus, 5; **26** Bianco, 3; **27** Masbou and Nakagami, 1.

RIDER STANDINGS
After 7 Rounds

1	Valentino Rossi	142
2	Dani Pedrosa	135
3	Jorge Lorenzo	94
4	Casey Stoner	92
5	Colin Edwards	69
6	Andrea Dovizioso	57
7	James Toseland	53
8	Loris Capirossi	51
9	Nicky Hayden	48
10	Shinya Nakano	42
11	Chris Vermeulen	40
12	John Hopkins	32
13	Marco Melandri	29
14	Alex de Angelis	24
15	Toni Elias	24
16	Randy de Puniet	18
17	Sylvain Guintoli	15
18	Anthony West	10
19	Tadayuki Okada	2

TEAM STANDINGS
After 7 Rounds

1	Fiat Yamaha Team	236
2	Repsol Honda Team	183
3	Tech 3 Yamaha	122
4	Ducati Marlboro Team	121
5	Rizla Suzuki MotoGP	91
6	San Carlo Honda Gresini	66
7	JiR Team Scot MotoGP	57
8	Kawasaki Racing Team	42
9	Alice Team	39
10	LCR Honda MotoGP	18

CONSTRUCTOR STANDINGS
After 7 Rounds

1	Yamaha	160
2	Honda	135
3	Ducati	97
4	Suzuki	63
5	Kawasaki	35

BRITISH | GP
DONINGTON PARK

A new hero for British fans, 125 rookie Scott Redding made history as the youngest ever winner of a World Championship race. It was an assured performance.

Photographs: Gold & Goose

BRITAIN'S relationship with GP racing has been on the mend for a decade or more. The nation once dominated and by the 2008 running of the British Grand Prix still held third in the tally of premier-class wins. But it had been seven years since the last win – by Jeremy McWilliams on a 250 at Assen – and more than 30 years since the late Barry Sheene had won the World Championship. In the intervening period, a national affair with World Superbikes had been consummated repeatedly by Carl Fogarty and more recently by James Toseland, and the health of the British GP itself had slumped, and then revived again. A crowd of 88,000 braved uncertain weather in 2008.

Only the most jingoistic could have hoped for another win, however. Toseland was now in the top class and doing well enough for a rookie, but even with the home-circuit effect, victory was a long shot.

But there was a win, by a rider few had ever heard of, and who had never raced at Donington Park before, a teenager from Gloucestershire, too young to enjoy the rostrum champagne. His planned celebration, he revealed, was 'to go straight home so my dad can get hammered'. Scott Redding had been schooled by the Dorna Academy, and driven by a natural talent that meant his sweeping lines and sheer speed were enough to catch and then harry leader Iannone into a headlong crash. It was a fine display of precocious mastery from the youngest ever GP winner – at 15 years and 170 days, he displaced Marco Melandri by 154 days.

Redding was the first British 125 winner since Chas Mortimer in Spain in 1973, the first ever British solo winner in 22 years at Donington Park and the first Briton to win his home GP since Ian McConnachie at Silverstone in 1986 (80cc).

As for Toseland, the keenly anticipated home weekend was an unmitigated disaster. He fell twice during qualifying and ended up 16th on the grid. Then he fell at the first corner, remounting to soldier on dutifully without a right footpeg; he finished a lap down and last. It was, he said later, 'the worst day of my life'.

It was almost the other way around for Stoner, fresh from tests at Barcelona that had revived his season.

Right: Pole position and a runaway win marked the start of Stoner's mid-season come-back.

Below: Hayden persuaded Honda to let him ride the new bike, but it played him false.

Below left: Jim Redman aboard a replica of his 350 Honda Six, launched at the GP.

Photographs: Gold & Goose

Bottom: Toseland hoped for glory at home, but it all went wrong at the very first corner.

Photograph: Martin Heath

This was the start of an impressive charge, after dominating all dry practice sessions. A new electronic setting had made the motor 'sweeter at the bottom end. We've had trouble getting power to the ground. Every time I opened the throttle, the bike wanted to buck, and that made the chassis look a lot worse than it was,' he said.

Over at HRC, the sidelining of its only world champion since Rossi left at the end of 2003 had been an undercurrent ever since Pedrosa had joined the team in 2006. That was Hayden's year of victory, but even then he'd been given a test-rider role, pedalling a diminutive forerunner of the following year's 800. And that next bike, a tiny thing, appeared to have been built around Dani rather than the brawny American.

Had things changed at Donington Park? It seemed so, for at last HRC had acceded to Hayden's request to be allowed to race the long-delayed, pneumatic-valve-spring engine that he had tested at Barcelona. Reluctantly, it appeared, for Honda's engineers felt that the engine was not yet ready – in this, they would prove justified. But Hayden had been insistent, beguiled by the main characteristic of the revvier engine: more top-end power. 'You pick it up, open the throttle and you go somewhere,' he said.

Yet even now there was some sidelining. He was given a revised chassis, one he hadn't even known of. It was the same one that Pedrosa had used to take the win at Catalunya.

West was also hoping for some improvement to his dire season. He'd been out to Kawasaki's Autopolis test track in Japan for some one-on-one with the factory engineers. There the bike had been through a number of changes, mainly in shortening the wheelbase and swing-arm, moving his seating position forward and incorporating engine software changes that softened the initial

response. His wheelspin problems had been improved, he said – rather optimistically, as it would transpire – and he was prepared to accept the return of chatter and wheelying in exchange. 'I've been riding the bike speedway style all year, while the other guys accelerate away,' he continued.

Yet again, bad weather hit race weekend, this time on a soaking Saturday, which left everyone short of dry set-up time. That was a particular problem for a new face on the grid – double and soon-to-be treble AMA Superbike Champion Ben Spies. The Texan had long hungered for a GP chance, having run 30-odd testing laps at Valencia in 2007. His luck was at the expense of Capirossi, ruled out by hand injuries sustained at Catalunya. Spies came jetting over pronto, and impressed, running eighth in wet practice. He opined that compared with his Superbike, there was not that much difference in speed and power – at least not at this low-speed and low-geared track – but that it felt 'like a completely different brand of bike. They don't compare in one way.' That rather gave the lie to Dorna CEO Ezpeleta's opinion of the similarity between street bikes and the MotoGP variants.

It was as well that race day was dry, for in spite of a new track treatment, sections were still so slippery that Stoner described it as 'one of the most dangerous we use'. There had been 23 crashes in the 45-minute morning 125 session alone. The new treatment had taken the form of high-pressure cleaning by a specialist firm called Ringway, after investigations had exonerated the old suspect of jet fuel settling from the adjacent East Midlands Airport. Ringway blamed increased stress in braking areas and treated these with Trackjet. For 2009, suggested Rossi, they should treat the whole track in similar fashion.

The weekend began with the annual Day of Champions charity bash, which netted £186,000 for Riders for Health, an impressive total, although £31,000 short of 2007's record. Then came the first of a series of 60th anniversary ceremonies to honour past champions – the presentation of replicas of the World Championship trophy, dubbed 'Champions' Towers'. Phil Read was the only champion present, however, Geoff Duke and John Surtees having sent apologies, while the sons of the first champion, Les Graham, and the great Mike Hailwood accepted awards on behalf of their late fathers. Britain had been chosen for the first of these presentations for two reasons: because it was closest in date to the 60th anniversary of the first-ever GP and, as Dorna chief Ezpeleta said, because 'it is the spiritual home of the sport'. Which is where we came in.

MOTOGP RACE – 30 laps

Stoner dominated in the dry, then timed it right in the damp qualifying session for his second pole in succession. Rossi, lining up for his 200th start, was more than half a second adrift, while Vermeulen was alongside for his first front row of the season, then Hayden with his new engine.

Pedrosa was ninth after a high-side crash in dry practice, his second in a fortnight; the returned Lorenzo was way down in 17th and in careful mode.

The track was dry, but conditions blustery and difficult, as Stoner made the perfect start to lead into the first corner. He was never headed, pulling out two- or three-tenths a lap on Rossi; he was more than two seconds ahead before ten laps were up. Rossi's own pace quickened, but Stoner kept on pulling away, his lead up to 6.4 seconds with four laps to go, whereupon he was

able to relax for a secure second win. It was a majestic performance and the start of a major fight-back, and if he was dismayed at being booed on the rostrum – he is a pet-hate figure in England – he managed to hide it pretty well.

At first, it had been Dovizioso chasing Rossi, Hayden behind him, but Pedrosa had made his usual lightning start to finish the first lap in fifth. By the fourth lap, he had moved ahead of his team-mate, although he took another five laps before he could get in front of impressive rookie Dovizioso.

At that point, the gap to Rossi was still less than a second, and Pedrosa was soon challenging hard. Faster through the tight sections, he got ahead several times in a protracted battle, but never for long enough to lead over the line, Rossi always passing him straight back.

'Then I made a mistake at the chicane,' said Pedrosa later, and for the last three laps he dropped away, secure in third and finishing more than two seconds adrift.

Dovizioso continued to lose ground, and by the 12th lap, Hayden was ahead, five seconds adrift of his team-mate. But the new bike had a trap in store. 'Things were going decent, then I had a warning light on the dash. With the electronics, if something's wrong, you can go into a corner and have no engine brake system or no traction control.' Unsettled, his rhythm broken, he started to lose positions again – first to Dovizioso on lap 16, and then to Edwards, who had been making steady progress after earlier falling behind Vermeulen.

One lap later, the American Yamaha rider was ahead of Dovizioso as well. While the latter stayed close for several more laps, eventually Edwards got away for a safe fourth, with Dovizioso fifth.

All the while, Lorenzo was on the march. A good start saw him finish the first lap tenth, and two laps later he was ahead of West for ninth. There he stayed until there were just ten laps to go. By then, he had caught up to Nakano, lapping steadily at the back of the mid-field battle. On lap 21, Lorenzo was ahead of the Japanese rider, then he picked off Vermeulen and Hayden for an excellent sixth. 'My number-one aim was to finish the race without crashing or hurting myself, but I started to feel more confident, and at the end I realised I could do a good race,' he explained happily.

Vermeulen lost pace at the end, ceding seventh again to Hayden and losing touch, although safe enough

from the fading Nakano. West was a long way back by the finish, tenth his best result so far. Elias pounced to snitch 11th from de Puniet on the final lap.

A couple of seconds back came Guintoli and Spies, the American closing over the last laps. He had lost places after the start, still learning bike, tyres and track after the abbreviated dry practice. Then he picked up pace. 'That's the best track time I've got on the bike all weekend – like a third dry practice session. I turned my fastest lap with two to go,' he said.

A distant de Angelis took the final point, having slipped off, remounted and passed the perennially fading Melandri.

Toseland was a lap down and distraught. It had all gone wrong as he tipped it into the first corner, and he'd taken Hopkins out wide as he'd slithered into the Redgate gravel. He picked the Yamaha up and remounted, persisting to the end without a right footpeg, determined at least to finish.

Hopkins was the only rider not to do so. He had just passed West after regaining the tarmac on lap one in last place, but for Toseland, when an engine failure led to a third non-finish.

250cc RACE – 27 laps

The wet Saturday mixed up the qualifying order. The usual suspects – Bautista, Simoncelli and Barbera – were joined on row one by Luthi, but Debon was 11th and Kallio 14th, all on Friday times. Kallio was getting used to a brand-new chassis and decided to take the risk of using it in the race.

Simoncelli led the first lap from Takahashi, Bautista and Simon, but Bautista had moved up to second by the fourth lap, and over the next two, the Japanese also fell behind Simon and Barbera. By then, the two up front were almost two seconds clear, Bautista harrying his rival constantly, although it wasn't until just before half-distance that he led over the line for the first time, for two laps.

All the while, Kallio was gaining places. Tenth behind slow-starter Luthi on the first lap, he was ahead of him next time around, and in front of Espargaro one lap later, sticking behind team-mate Aoyama for the next three.

On lap six, he passed him and Debon as well. Over the next two, he picked off Takahashi and Barbera, and

was poised on Simon's back wheel. With the lead two pulling clear, there was no time to waste, and the orange KTM was third just one lap later. The leaders were still just over two seconds away, but they proved harder to catch. It wasn't until lap 19 that the canny Finn upped his pace again.

Barbera, on his tail, couldn't match him, but he was three seconds ahead of Luthi, with Debon a safe distance behind him, while Simon was losing pace and places steadily.

Bautista took the lead again on lap 20 and held it for the next five laps. But by now, it had become a three-way battle, Kallio tight behind the pair, although still biding his time.

The decisive move came at the final hairpin on the penultimate lap. As leader Bautista peeled across to the left, Simoncelli made an impetuous dive up the inside. Too fast, he ran wide. Bautista had no option but to run even wider. Without having to make any extra effort, Kallio nipped past both of them and fended off Simoncelli to the flag. He was the first rider to take three wins in 2008, usefully extending his title lead.

Bautista's recovery had left him more than a second behind, and fuming. He called for action to be taken. 'Simoncelli came to apologise, and I told him he can't keep riding like that. It's not normal to pass if you aren't able to. He is very aggressive, and one for whom what he wants to do exceeds what he can do.' Such spats were becoming a keynote of the season.

Barbera and Luthi were spaced out behind; Aoyama regained sixth from Debon at the last gasp. Simon was a couple more seconds adrift, with a distant Takahashi and then Espargaro completing the top ten.

Pasini was the only rider to crash, after climbing from 15th on lap one to tenth.

125cc RACE – 25 laps

History-making rookie Redding took his second front-row start in succession and his third of the year, with Corsi, Talmacsi and Gadea ahead on the grid. But it was Iannone away first, from the second row, and he had an eight-tenths lead over Corsi and the gang at the end of lap one, with Redding fifth.

To the delight of the crowd, the English teen had swept past his rivals to take second next time around,

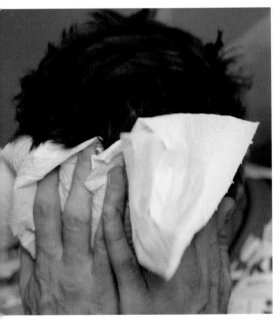

Above: Kallio leads Simon and Barbera. The Finn escaped to win.

Above left: Hands unmarked by the years, Rossi made his 200th GP start at Donington.

Left: Toseland hides his shame at 'the worst weekend of my life'.

Below: Chasing Redding – Marquez (93) and di Meglio completed the 125 rostrum.

Facing page: AMA Champion Ben Spies, heading de Puniet, made a long-awaited GP debut.
Photographs: Gold & Goose

Right: Bautista complains, Simoncelli shrugs. Such incidents were common in 2008.
Photograph: Clive Challinor

but the gap was now 1.8 seconds, and it stayed there until lap six. But Redding had easily outpaced the group in pursuit, led by Gadea from de Rosa, Marquez, Koyama and the rest. Now the youngster started to close the gap by a few tenths each lap. Iannone kicked again and held his advantage at about a second right up until lap 14. Then Redding put in a couple of fliers, and he was less than four-tenths behind.

By lap 20, the pressure had become more than Iannone could bear, and Redding had a grandstand seat as the Italian pushed a fraction too hard on the run down the hill and went flying. The English rider was not only in the lead, but also ahead by miles – better than six seconds over the tussling gang behind, now led by di Meglio. His only remaining task, not necessarily easy as he explained later, was to keep his focus and run on to his first chequered flag.

Di Meglio narrowly hung on to second, ahead of another fast rookie, Repsol KTM's Marquez. Gadea pulled a couple of seconds clear in fourth, with Corsi fifth at the head of the rest of a huge gang – fifth to 11th covered by 2.1 seconds.

bwin.com BRITISH GRAND PRIX

22 JUNE 2008 • FIM WORLD CHAMPIONSHIP ROUND 8

DONINGTON PARK

Craner
Hollywood
Old Hairpin
Redgate
Starkey's Bridge
McLear Corner
Wheatcroft Straight
Schwantz
Melborne Hairpin
Goddards
Fogarty Esses
Coppice
Starkey's Straight

Circuit 4.023km / 2.500 miles

MOTOGP

RACE: 30 laps, 75.000 miles/120.690km • Weather: Dry • Air 20°C • Humidity 22% • Track 26°C

Pos.	Rider	Nat.	No.	Team	Machine	Tyres	Laps	Time & speed (mph/km/h)
1	Casey Stoner	AUS	1	Ducati Marlboro Team	Ducati	B	30	44m 44.982s 100.550mph/ 161.820km/h
2	Valentino Rossi	ITA	46	Fiat Yamaha Team	Yamaha	B	30	44m 50.771s
3	Dani Pedrosa	SPA	2	Repsol Honda Team	Honda	M	30	44m 53.329s
4	Colin Edwards	USA	5	Tech 3 Yamaha	Yamaha	M	30	44m 57.660s
5	Andrea Dovizioso	ITA	4	JiR Team Scot MotoGP	Honda	M	30	44m 59.783s
6	Jorge Lorenzo	SPA	48	Fiat Yamaha Team	Yamaha	M	30	45m 00.672s
7	Nicky Hayden	USA	69	Repsol Honda Team	Honda	M	30	45m 03.178s
8	Chris Vermeulen	AUS	7	Rizla Suzuki MotoGP	Suzuki	B	30	45m 06.648s
9	Shinya Nakano	JPN	56	San Carlo Honda Gresini	Honda	B	30	45m 14.336s
10	Anthony West	AUS	13	Kawasaki Racing Team	Kawasaki	B	30	45m 26.012s
11	Toni Elias	SPA	24	Alice Team	Ducati	B	30	45m 29.408s
12	Randy de Puniet	FRA	14	LCR Honda MotoGP	Honda	M	30	45m 31.181s
13	Sylvain Guintoli	FRA	50	Alice Team	Ducati	B	30	45m 33.713s
14	Ben Spies	USA	11	Rizla Suzuki MotoGP	Suzuki	B	30	45m 34.573s
15	Alex de Angelis	RSM	15	San Carlo Honda Gresini	Honda	B	30	46m 07.168s
16	Marco Melandri	ITA	33	Ducati Marlboro Team	Ducati	B	30	46m 15.003s
17	James Toseland	GBR	52	Tech 3 Yamaha	Yamaha	M	29	45m 32.234s
	John Hopkins	USA	21	Kawasaki Racing Team	Kawasaki	B	16	24m 18.021s

Fastest lap: Casey Stoner, on lap 5, 1m 28.773s, 101.373mph/163.144km/h.

Lap record: Dani Pedrosa, SPA (Honda), 1m 28.714s, 101.440mph/163.252km/h (2006).

Event best maximum speed: Casey Stoner, 170.9mph/275.0km/h (warm-up).

QUALIFYING: 21 June 2008

Weather: Wet
Air: 12°C Humidity: 81% Track: 15°C

Pos.	Rider	Time
1	Stoner	1m 38.232s
2	Rossi	1m 38.881s
3	Vermeulen	1m 39.018s
4	Hayden	1m 39.270s
5	Edwards	1m 39.601s
6	Dovizioso	1m 39.783s
7	West	1m 39.995s
8	Spies	1m 40.244s
9	Pedrosa	1m 40.350s
10	Nakano	1m 40.417s
11	Hopkins	1m 40.539s
12	Guintoli	1m 40.595s
13	de Angelis	1m 40.667s
14	de Puniet	1m 41.110s
15	Melandri	1m 41.379s
16	Toseland	1m 41.751s
17	Lorenzo	1m 41.873s
18	Elias	1m 42.933s

Grid order	1	2	3	4	5	6	7	8	9	10	11	12	13	14	15	16	17	18	19	20	21	22	23	24	25	26	27	28	29	30	
1 STONER	1	1	1	1	1	1	1	1	1	1	1	1	1	1	1	1	1	1	1	1	1	1	1	1	1	1	1	1	1	1	1
46 ROSSI	46	46	46	46	46	46	46	46	46	46	46	46	46	46	46	46	46	46	46	46	46	46	46	46	46	46	46	46	46	46	2
7 VERMEULEN	4	4	4	4	4	4	2	2	2	2	2	2	2	2	2	2	2	2	2	2	2	2	2	2	2	2	2	2	2	2	3
69 HAYDEN	69	69	69	2	2	2	4	4	4	4	69	69	69	69	4	4	5	5	5	5	5	5	5	5	5	5	5	5			4
5 EDWARDS	2	2	2	69	69	69	69	69	69	69	69	4	4	4	69	5	4	4	4	4	4	4	4	4	4	4	4	4	4	4	5
4 DOVISIOSO	7	7	7	7	7	7	7	7	7	7	5	5	5	69	69	7	7	7	7	7	7	69	48	48	48	48	48	48			6
13 WEST	5	5	5	5	5	5	5	5	5	5	5	5	5	7	7	7	7	7	69	69	69	69	69	69	69	69	69	69	69	69	7
11 SPIES	56	56	56	56	56	56	56	56	56	56	56	56	56	56	56	56	56	56	48	48	48	48	7	7	7	7	7	7			8
2 PEDROSA	13	13	48	48	48	48	48	48	48	48	48	48	48	48	48	48	48	48	48	56	56	56	56	56	56	56	56	56			9
56 NAKANO	48	48	13	13	13	13	13	13	13	13	13	13	21	21	21	21	13	13	13	13	13	13	13	13	13	13	13	13			10
21 HOPKINS	50	50	50	50	50	50	21	21	21	21	21	21	13	13	13	14	14	14	14	14	14	14	14	14	14	14	24				11
50 GUINTOLI	15	11	11	11	14	14	14	14	14	14	14	14	14	14	24	24	24	24	24	24	24	24	24	24	24	24	14				12
15 de ANGELIS	11	14	14	14	21	50	50	50	50	50	50	24	24	24	50	50	50	50	50	50	50	50	50	50	50	50	50				13
14 de PUNIET	14	33	33	21	21	11	11	24	24	24	24	50	50	50	11	11	11	11	11	11	11	11	11	11	11	11	11				14
33 MELANDRI	33	24	21	33	24	24	24	11	11	11	11	11	11	11	15	15	15	15	15	15	15	15	15	15	15	15	15				15
52 TOSELAND	24	21	24	24	33	33	33	33	33	33	33	15	15	15	33	33	33	33	33	33	33	33	33	33	33	33	33				
48 LORENZO	21	15	15	15	15	15	15	15	15	15	15	33	33	33	33	52	52	52	52	52	52	52	52	52	52	52	52				
24 ELIAS	52	52	52	52	52	52	52	52	52	52	52	52	52	52	52																

52 lapped rider

FASTEST RACE LAPS

	Rider	Lap	Time
1	Stoner	5	1m 28.773s
2	Pedrosa	4	1m 28.823s
3	Dovizioso	6	1m 29.053s
4	Rossi	7	1m 29.080s
5	Hayden	6	1m 29.136s
6	Edwards	21	1m 29.138s
7	Lorenzo	30	1m 29.275s
8	Vermeulen	19	1m 29.373s
9	Nakano	11	1m 29.534s
10	Hopkins	10	1m 29.827s
11	Elias	21	1m 29.834s
12	West	23	1m 30.024s
13	de Angelis	11	1m 30.059s
14	de Puniet	15	1m 30.084s
15	Spies	21	1m 30.106s
16	Guintoli	15	1m 30.441s
17	Melandri	6	1m 30.750s
18	Toseland	21	1m 31.658s

statistics

250cc
27 laps, 67.500 miles/108.621km

Pos.	Rider (Nat.)	No.	Team	Machine	Laps	Time & speed
1	Mika Kallio (FIN)	36	Red Bull KTM 250	KTM	27	42m 14.410s 95.871mph/ 154.290km/h
2	Marco Simoncelli (ITA)	58	Metis Gilera	Gilera	27	42m 14.763s
3	Alvaro Bautista (SPA)	19	Mapfre Aspar Team	Aprilia	27	42m 15.647s
4	Hector Barbera (SPA)	21	Team Toth Aprilia	Aprilia	27	42m 23.285s
5	Thomas Luthi (SWI)	12	Emmi - Caffe Latte	Aprilia	27	42m 25.769s
6	Hiroshi Aoyama (JPN)	4	Red Bull KTM 250	KTM	27	42m 30.534s
7	Alex Debon (SPA)	6	Lotus Aprilia	Aprilia	27	42m 30.546s
8	Julian Simon (SPA)	60	Repsol KTM 250cc	KTM	27	42m 32.417s
9	Yuki Takahashi (JPN)	72	JiR Team Scot 250	Honda	27	42m 47.681s
10	Aleix Espargaro (SPA)	41	Lotus Aprilia	Aprilia	27	43m 04.091s
11	Roberto Locatelli (ITA)	15	Metis Gilera	Gilera	27	43m 06.944s
12	Karel Abraham (CZE)	17	Cardion AB Motoracing	Aprilia	27	43m 09.721s
13	Lukas Pesek (CZE)	52	Auto Kelly - CP	Aprilia	27	43m 11.809s
14	Manuel Poggiali (RSM)	54	Campetella Racing	Gilera	27	43m 12.051s
15	Hector Faubel (SPA)	55	Mapfre Aspar Team	Aprilia	27	43m 18.739s
16	Ratthapark Wilairot (THA)	14	Thai Honda PTT SAG	Honda	27	43m 20.566s
17	Fabrizio Lai (ITA)	32	Campetella Racing	Gilera	27	43m 30.222s
18	Russel Gomez (SPA)	7	Blusens Aprilia	Aprilia	26	42m 51.084s
19	Doni Tata Pradita (INA)	45	Yamaha Pertamina Indonesia	Yamaha	26	43m 06.332s
	Eugene Laverty (IRL)	50	Blusens Aprilia	Aprilia	19	DNF
	Alex Baldolini (ITA)	25	Matteoni Racing	Aprilia	13	DNF
	Mattia Pasini (ITA)	75	Polaris World	Aprilia	12	DNF
	Imre Toth (HUN)	10	Team Toth Aprilia	Aprilia	11	DNF

Fastest lap: Simoncelli, 1m 32.474s, 97.315mph/156.614km/h (record).

Previous lap record: Andrea Dovizioso, ITA (Honda), 1m 33.029s, 96.735mph/155.680km/h (2006).

Event best maximum speed: Debon, 149.1mph/239.9km/h (race).

Qualifying: 1 Bautista, 1m 31.834s; 2 Simoncelli, 1m 32.004s; 3 Barbera, 1m 32.353s; 4 Luthi, 1m 32.835s; 5 Takahashi, 1m 32.853s; 6 Aoyama, 1m 32.983s; 7 Simon, 1m 33.063s; 8 Espargaro, 1m 33.116s; 9 Pesek, 1m 33.276s; 10 Lai, 1m 33.281s; 11 Debon, 1m 33.297s; 12 Pasini, 1m 33.302s; 13 Locatelli, 1m 33.379s; 14 Kallio, 1m 33.595s; 15 Poggiali, 1m 33.660s; 16 Abraham, 1m 33.859s; 17 Faubel, 1m 33.954s; 18 Wilairot, 1m 34.039s; 19 Baldolini, 1m 34.074s; 20 Laverty, 1m 34.285s; 21 Toth, 1m 35.571s; 22 Gomez, 1m 37.081s; 23 Pradita, 1m 38.170s.

Fastest race laps: 1 Simoncelli, 1m 32.474s; 2 Kallio, 1m 32.500s; 3 Bautista, 1m 32.659s; 4 Barbera, 1m 33.116s; 5 Luthi, 1m 33.205s; 6 Debon, 1m 33.471s; 7 Aoyama, 1m 33.507s; 8 Simon, 1m 33.625s; 9 Pasini, 1m 33.949s; 10 Takahashi, 1m 34.085s; 11 Espargaro, 1m 34.169s; 12 Locatelli, 1m 34.307s; 13 Poggiali, 1m 34.509s; 14 Abraham, 1m 34.703s; 15 Pesek, 1m 34.755s; 16 Lai, 1m 35.097s; 17 Faubel, 1m 35.267s; 18 Laverty, 1m 35.409s; 19 Wilairot, 1m 35.451s; 20 Baldolini, 1m 35.814s; 21 Gomez, 1m 37.153s; 22 Pradita, 1m 38.527s; 23 Toth, 1m 39.098s.

World Championship: 1 Kallio, 131; 2 Simoncelli, 123; 3 Debon, 101; 4 Pasini, 98; 5 Barbera, 82; 6 Aoyama, 80; 7 Bautista, 77; 8 Takahashi, 70; 9 Luthi, 57; 10 Simon, 51; 11 Espargaro, 46; 12 Locatelli, 39; 13 Faubel, 34; 14 Wilairot, 30; 15 Abraham, 25; 16 Pesek, 21; 17 Poggiali, 16; 18 Baldolini, 16; 19 Lai, 9; 20 Laverty, 7; 21 Hernandez and Sandi, 2; 23 Toth, 2; 24 Pradita, 1.

125cc
25 laps, 62.500 miles/100.575km

Pos.	Rider (Nat.)	No.	Team	Machine	Laps	Time & speed
1	Scott Redding (GBR)	45	Blusens Aprilia Junior	Aprilia	25	41m 39.472s 90.011mph/ 144.858km/h
2	Mike di Meglio (FRA)	63	Ajo Motorsport	Derbi	25	41m 44.796s
3	Marc Marquez (SPA)	93	Repsol KTM 125cc	KTM	25	41m 45.278s
4	Sergio Gadea (SPA)	33	Bancaja Aspar Team	Aprilia	25	41m 53.462s
5	Simone Corsi (ITA)	24	Jack & Jones WRB	Aprilia	25	41m 56.327s
6	Tomoyoshi Koyama (JPN)	71	ISPA KTM Aran	KTM	25	41m 56.653s
7	Joan Olive (SPA)	6	Belson Derbi	Derbi	25	41m 57.486s
8	Takaaki Nakagami (JPN)	73	I.C. Team	Aprilia	25	41m 57.694s
9	Sandro Cortese (GER)	11	Emmi - Caffe Latte	Aprilia	25	41m 57.876s
10	Bradley Smith (GBR)	38	Polaris World	Aprilia	25	41m 58.363s
11	Esteve Rabat (SPA)	12	Repsol KTM 125cc	KTM	25	41m 58.448s
12	Michael Ranseder (AUT)	60	I.C. Team	Aprilia	25	42m 07.741s
13	Randy Krummenacher (SWI)	34	Red Bull KTM 125	KTM	25	42m 07.819s
14	Raffaele de Rosa (ITA)	35	Onde 2000 KTM	KTM	25	42m 08.875s
15	Lorenzo Zanetti (ITA)	8	ISPA KTM Aran	KTM	25	42m 15.235s
16	Jules Cluzel (FRA)	16	Loncin Racing	Loncin	25	42m 15.340s
17	Stevie Bonsey (USA)	51	Degraaf Grand Prix	Aprilia	25	42m 17.630s
18	Nicolas Terol (SPA)	18	Jack & Jones WRB	Aprilia	25	42m 22.238s
19	Dominique Aegerter (SWI)	77	Ajo Motorsport	Derbi	25	42m 22.396s
20	Stefano Bianco (ITA)	27	S3+ WTR San Marino Team	Aprilia	25	42m 45.768s
21	Robin Lasser (GER)	66	Grizzly Gas Kiefer Racing	Aprilia	25	42m 49.630s
22	Pere Tutusaus (SPA)	30	Bancaja Aspar Team	Aprilia	25	42m 50.377s
23	Louis Rossi (FRA)	69	FFM Honda GP 125	Honda	25	43m 08.741s
24	Robert Muresan (ROU)	95	Grizzly Gas Kiefer Racing	Aprilia	24	41m 42.744s
25	Hugo van den Berg (NED)	56	Degraaf Grand Prix	Aprilia	24	41m 43.631s
26	Lee Costello (GBR)	67	Vent-Axia	Honda	24	41m 47.686s
27	Roberto Lacalendola (ITA)	19	Matteoni Racing	Aprilia	24	41m 48.261s
	Andrea Iannone (ITA)	29	I.C. Team	Aprilia	19	DNF
	Stefan Bradl (GER)	17	Grizzly Gas Kiefer Racing	Aprilia	18	DNF
	Matthew Hoyle (GBR)	64	SP 125 Racing/Mackrory Demol	Honda	14	DNF
	Connor Behan (GBR)	66	Connor Behan Racing	Honda	14	DNF
	Paul Jordan (IRL)	68	KRP	Honda	14	DNF
	Alexis Masbou (FRA)	5	Loncin Racing	Loncin	5	DNF
	Luke Hinton (GBR)	65	Buildbase/Knotts	Honda	4	DNF
	Gabor Talmacsi (HUN)	1	Bancaja Aspar Team	Aprilia	1	DNF
	Pablo Nieto (SPA)	22	Onde 2000 KTM	KTM	0	DNF
	Danny Webb (GBR)	99	Degraaf Grand Prix	Aprilia	0	DNF

Fastest lap: Redding, 1m 38.704s, 91.173mph/146.729km/h.

Lap record: Alvaro Bautista, SPA (Aprilia), 1m 37.312s, 92.477mph/148.828km/h (2006).

Event best maximum speed: Gadea, 130.5mph/210.0km/h (qualifying practice no. 1).

Qualifying: 1 Corsi, 1m 37.488s; 2 Talmacsi, 1m 37.520s; 3 Gadea, 1m 37.649s; 4 Redding, 1m 37.766s; 5 Iannone, 1m 37.950s; 6 Terol, 1m 38.034s; 7 Marquez, 1m 38.044s; 8 Nieto, 1m 38.104s; 9 Koyama, 1m 38.153s; 10 de Rosa, 1m 38.186s; 11 Smith, 1m 38.347s; 12 Rabat, 1m 38.355s; 13 Webb, 1m 38.473s; 14 Olive, 1m 38.554s; 15 Bonsey, 1m 38.606s; 16 Cortese, 1m 38.724s; 17 Bradl, 1m 38.775s; 18 Krummenacher, 1m 38.856s; 19 Ranseder, 1m 38.916s; 20 di Meglio, 1m 38.938s; 21 Nakagami, 1m 39.007s; 22 Bianco, 1m 39.037s; 23 Zanetti, 1m 39.386s; 24 Tutusaus, 1m 39.538s; 25 Cluzel, 1m 39.760s; 26 Aegerter, 1m 39.806s; 27 Masbou, 1m 39.986s; 28 van den Berg, 1m 40.357s; 29 Lasser, 1m 40.525s; 30 Muresan, 1m 41.070s; 31 Rossi, 1m 41.320s; 32 Lacalendola, 1m 42.182s; 33 Hoyle, 1m 42.316s; 34 Behan, 1m 42.593s; 35 Hinton, 1m 42.966s; 36 Costello, 1m 43.149s; 37 Jordan, 1m 43.227s.

Fastest race laps: 1 Redding, 1m 38.704s; 2 Marquez, 1m 38.841s; 3 di Meglio, 1m 38.930s; 4 Gadea, 1m 38.933s; 5 Bradl, 1m 39.120s; 6 Iannone, 1m 39.133s; 7 Corsi, 1m 39.147s; 8 Nakagami, 1m 39.289s; 9 Cortese, 1m 39.302s; 10 Olive, 1m 39.322s; 11 Smith, 1m 39.351s; 12 Koyama, 1m 39.437s; 13 de Rosa, 1m 39.588s; 14 Rabat, 1m 39.596s; 15 Ranseder, 1m 39.836s; 16 Krummenacher, 1m 39.843s; 17 Zanetti, 1m 39.976s; 18 Bonsey, 1m 39.999s; 19 Terol, 1m 40.151s; 20 Aegerter, 1m 40.181s; 21 Cluzel, 1m 40.316s; 22 Tutusaus, 1m 40.881s; 23 Bianco, 1m 41.254s; 24 Lasser, 1m 41.431s; 25 Masbou, 1m 41.725s; 26 Rossi, 1m 42.110s; 27 Hoyle, 1m 42.514s; 28 Muresan, 1m 42.617s; 29 Costello, 1m 42.618s; 30 van den Berg, 1m 42.648s; 31 Lacalendola, 1m 42.823s; 32 Behan, 1m 43.716s; 33 Jordan, 1m 44.374s; 34 Hinton, 1m 44.639s; 35 Talmacsi, 1m 48.259s.

World Championship: 1 di Meglio, 132; 2 Corsi, 109; 3 Bradl, 77; 4 Terol, 75; 5 Espargaro, 75; 6 Olive, 74; 7 Talmacsi, 68; 8 Gadea, 62; 9 Redding, 57; 10 Smith, 55; 11 Iannone, 47; 12 Cortese, 45; 13 Bonsey, 39; 14 Marquez, 26; 15 Webb, 26; 16 de Rosa, 24; 17 Koyama, 19; 18 Ranseder, 17; 19 Aegerter, 16; 20 Vazquez, 14; 21 Rabat, 14; 22 Nieto, 11; 23 Zanetti, 10; 24 Krummenacher, 10; 25 Nakagami, 9; 26 Tutusaus, 5; 27 Bianco, 3; 28 Masbou, 1.

RIDER STANDINGS
After 8 Rounds

1	Valentino Rossi	162
2	Dani Pedrosa	151
3	Casey Stoner	117
4	Jorge Lorenzo	104
5	Colin Edwards	82
6	Andrea Dovizioso	68
7	Nicky Hayden	57
8	James Toseland	53
9	Loris Capirossi	51
10	Shinya Nakano	49
11	Chris Vermeulen	48
12	John Hopkins	32
13	Marco Melandri	29
14	Toni Elias	29
15	Alex de Angelis	25
16	Randy de Puniet	22
17	Sylvain Guintoli	18
18	Anthony West	16
19 =	Tadayuki Okada	2
19 =	Ben Spies	2

TEAM STANDINGS
After 8 Rounds

1	Fiat Yamaha Team	266
2	Repsol Honda Team	208
3	Ducati Marlboro Team	146
4	Tech 3 Yamaha	135
5	Rizla Suzuki MotoGP	101
6	San Carlo Honda Gresini	74
7	JiR Team Scot MotoGP	68
8	Kawasaki Racing Team	48
9	Alice Team	47
10	LCR Honda MotoGP	22

CONSTRUCTOR STANDINGS
After 8 Rounds

1	Yamaha	180
2	Honda	151
3	Ducati	122
4	Suzuki	71
5	Kawasaki	41

Adriana and Casey Stoner. The defending champion
was all-dominant.
Photograph: Gold & Goose

DUTCH | TT

ASSEN

WHAT makes a grand prix circuit? According to the late Jack Findlay, the answer was simple: 'Top-gear corners'. The modern trend is different. Look at Valencia, Shanghai, Sachsenring – almost any new circuit, with the honourable exception of Istanbul: keep 'em slow, lean 'em low and let them squabble like dogs over a rat.

Assen used to be the opposite, until it was emasculated in 2006. A few of the old sections remained, however, in particular the last run back towards the paddock and the final chicane, where a few magic names and magic corners were preserved. Through the double rights of Mandeveen and Duikersloot, a faster right through Meeuwenmeer, hard on the gas and eyes narrowed, steering heavy with speed as you aim at the daunting and thrilling right-hand kink at Hoge Heide. Flat out, over the white line on the inside, the suspension compressing at the apex, and then on the brakes as it settles – even a little before – and heave it across again, the steering heavy once more, to pull it around into the long left of Ramshoek. Real racing.

It was at this point, or a little after, that Capirossi lost control. He fell in the Ramshoek, tumbling with his bike, the footrest digging a great big hole in his right arm. In 2007, Elias fell at the same spot, sustaining a truly nasty spiral fracture of his femur; in 2006, it was Rossi, who broke his wrist. And again in 2008, during the tricky high-speed transition phase before braking, John Hopkins also lost control.

It happened so fast that it looked as though his brakes might have failed. Not so. It was very early in the corner, so the green-clad rider went flying across the newly paved start of the run-off area and then the gravel, before slamming into an advertising hoarding. He was

stretchered off with costly injuries, including a fractured ankle, an aggravated old tibia fracture and knee damage – yet more pain in a hurtful season. He would miss this and the next two races, including his home US GP.

Hitting the barrier was a blow to fans of the old track who might have hoped that further depredations to the circuit would be avoided. Air-fence was promptly installed, but the real problem was the speed. Fifth- and sixth-gear corners certainly sort the men from the boys, but falling off at these speeds is almost inevitably injurious. Can it be long before this blissful, but menacing, section of old-time religion has a chicane installed?

The GP Commission was busy also on other business: accepting the proposal for the 250-class replacement for 2011, with some rationalisation and a deadline of just over a month for manufacturers to indicate interest. It was another step in the gestation of the so-called 'Dornatypes' and the assassination of 250s. Little wonder that people were talking about murder at the cathedral.

In addition, Dorna wielded the axe on what had become another racing institution, the free-to-view Eurosport channel. For Britain, this would mean the end not only of a popular commentating team – Julian Ryder, Toby Moody and Randy Mamola – but also full coverage of qualifying in all classes as well as the race itself. The loss of coverage throughout the rest of Europe, and especially the Eastern bloc, would be even greater, there being no alternative terrestrial channel. It was all part of the increasing professionalism within the sport – Dorna felt that now it was big enough for more mainstream coverage, such as that provided by the BBC, with its massive staffing levels and elaborate production values. And, of course, much larger audiences.

Capirossi's crash on day one clearly ruled him out of

Above: Melandri was close to melt-down at Ducati. Here he confers with race engineer Cristhian Pupulin.

Right: Rossi's sole mistake of the season: he remounted, but was too far behind to make any difference.

Photographs: Gold & Goose

Left: A rare view of Pedrosa's race face: bad weather meant a clear helmet visor.
Photograph: Gold & Goose

Below: Ben Spies went home early, turning down the chance to race.
Photograph: Martin Heath

Bottom: Kevin Schwantz, whose old-track lap record still stands, beneath a portrait of the re-injured Capirossi.

Bottom right: Stoner took complete control.
Photograph: Gold & Goose

his comeback event. Fortuitously, Ben Spies was at the circuit, fresh from his British GP debut, along with his mentor, Kevin Schwantz. The solution seemed obvious to all, including the 1993 World Champion – and still all-time lap-record holder at the old Assen. Ben had his leathers and helmet with him, and a degree of bike familiarity. He was offered the chance to take up the empty saddle immediately.

To the surprise of all, he declined, instead leaving the circuit almost directly and looking very glum indeed. His expression suggested that there had been some outside intervention, but the decision had been his own: 'If I'd have gotten just one practice session today, I'd have done it. But tomorrow they say will be wet, then the race may be dry. To get out and learn the track in the rain with these guys who are already up to speed, then have it different again on race day – I decided it wasn't worth it.' Schwantz was also surprised. 'My initial thought was it's a couple more hours' track time. But with the weather, I guess he felt like there were more cons than there were pros,' he said.

Equally glum was Marco Melandri, although few noticed since he was keeping himself to himself, and his team was blocking any approaches from the Press. His inability to get to grips with the bike on which Stoner was starting to dominate had become more than a puzzle, and his immediate future with the team was open to public speculation. At the track where he had become the youngest GP winner, he qualified fully three seconds slower than his team-mate. Sete Gibernau, who had reluctantly retired after losing his Ducati ride to Stoner after 2005, had been drafted in to test after the Catalunya GP and had made a good impression. Now he was down for more tests at Mugello, and at least tentatively earmarked to take over from Marco, as team chief Livio Suppo acknowledged: 'We are all so sorry, but sooner or later we will have to seriously consider replacing him. It is not easy to find anyone at this time of

year. Sete will test again this week, and we will see if he can be consistent.'

The puzzlement at Marco's problems was universal, and shared by former friend Rossi. Asked what he would be looking for if he was three seconds slower than his team-mate, he said, 'I would look in the mirror, because the problem comes from inside.' Rossi, by the way, was lining up for his 201st consecutive grand prix start, having never missed a race, equalling his old rival, Biaggi.

Spies's concerns about the weather were wrongly timed, but not misplaced. There was rain on the morning of day two, then high winds in the afternoon; race day was awful, the 125 race being interrupted by rain, robbing a heartbroken Bradley Smith of a massive lead when the first running was 'neutralised'. Rain further delayed the 250 race and frequently threatened to stop that as well. Mercifully, it dried up for the big bikes.

MOTOGP RACE – 26 laps

There were two key passages. One was Rossi's rare error. On the first lap, scrambling to recover from a poor start, he crashed at the ultra-tight first left, taking a hapless de Puniet down with him. At the other end of the race, Hayden lost a secure third on the last corner when his pneumatic-valve-spring Honda ran out of fuel.

And perhaps a third: Stoner's sheer dominance, which put his title defence well back on track.

Only one free practice session was spoiled by the weather, on Friday morning. It was the only one Stoner didn't command, leaving it to Pedrosa and de Puniet. And the increasingly rampant defending champion was in firm control of qualifying, being joined on the front row by Pedrosa and Rossi, while Hayden led the second.

The rain that had spoiled the earlier races held off, and the 95,000-strong crowd watched Pedrosa make a trade-mark flying start to lead away. At the chicane for the first time, Stoner swept past and was never troubled

again. He pulled away from Pedrosa, who was equally alone all race, by eight- or more tenths on some laps to win by a commanding ten seconds.

Hayden had been close to Pedrosa for a couple of laps before the return of the electronic glitches – rogue warning lights and rough running – that had plagued him during the British GP at Donington and in practice. He'd even considered changing bikes after the sighting lap, but recalled that he 'hadn't been going anywhere on that other bike.' Now he was having to use extra gas to keep the speed. This hurt the fuel consumption in a way that the control program couldn't manage, and he paid a heavy price. He had a safe third in the bag, but when he got to the chicane, he was without an engine. Out of fuel, all he could do was coast over the line, powerless to resist as a jubilant Edwards soared past to claim the last rostrum spot.

It was revenge for 2006, when Edwards had crashed out of the lead at the same place, handing the race to Nicky. Edwards dubbed the chicane 'Karma Corner' and joked, 'Not one single shred of me feels sorry for Nicky. After what happened two years ago, screw him.'

Third was also the reward for an epic ride, for the American had been a third victim of Rossi's first-lap indiscretion, forced – along with West – to come to a virtual stop; he had finished the first lap 12th.

Nakano had been fourth at the end of lap one, from Dovizioso, Vermeulen and Lorenzo, although he would lose touch. Both Dovizioso and Vermeulen were ahead on lap five, the trio staying together. At the same time, Edwards was attacking Guintoli and Toseland, having quickly got ahead of Elias and Melandri. Then he caught and passed Lorenzo on lap ten, and quickly closed on the battling threesome. On top form, he picked them off over just two laps and was fourth on lap 14, Dovizioso tagging on behind for a couple more laps.

Hayden was out of touch, six seconds ahead. Until he ran out of gas…

Dovizioso had gained a comfort zone by the time Nakano got back ahead of Vermeulen on lap 17, the Suzuki running out of speed as the tyres faded. By now, however, Lorenzo had gained pace to become a factor. Three laps later, he was ahead of Vermeulen, and Nakano also next time around; he was barely a second off old 250 rival Dovizioso at the finish.

Vermeulen was back ahead of Nakano by the flag, Toseland less than three seconds adrift, having stayed ahead of Guintoli. He had expected better, at a second successive track where he had previous circuit knowledge.

De Puniet's race had ended on lap one, but his assailant, Rossi, had rejoined almost 25 seconds adrift. It wasn't until lap 19 that he caught and passed Melandri, for he'd had to adjust to riding with only the stub of a gear pedal. His lap times began falling, however, and on the 23rd, he set third-fastest lap of the race. By then, he'd also passed Elias, but was still seven seconds behind Guintoli, and not even in the top ten.

De Angelis had crashed out one corner after Rossi; West had pulled through to 11th after he'd regained momentum, but then also crashed out.

Again, there was not a full quorum for points – just 13 finishers. And the name at the top of the table once more was that of Pedrosa, while Stoner's second win in a row put him fewer than 30 points behind. The title battle was well and truly alive.

250cc RACE – 24 laps

Bautista took a fifth pole, ahead of Barbera. Simoncelli and Debon, completing the front row, were among a handful who managed to improve in high winds on Friday.

The start, already delayed, was deferred by another

Left: Hayden was denied the rostrum by an electronic glitch.

Below left: Bautista took a fine second 250 win of the year.

Below: Alberto Puig, a sombre presence at Honda.

Below centre: Olive at the head of the gang in the second 125 race.

Bottom: Tough guy Talmacsi celebrates his first 2008 win.

Below right: Unlucky Bradley Smith nurses his injured arm.

Photographs: Gold & Goose

five minutes as a light sprinkling of rain passed. There would be more of the same, with wild variations in lap times and much shuffling.

Debon led them into the tightening first corner, where there were several minor collisions. One of the victims was Simoncelli, off the track on the outside. He finished lap one in 12th; Bautista was eighth.

Luthi had taken over by the end of the lap and started to pull clear. There was already a gap to the pursuing pack, which was led by Simon.

Bautista was running even faster, gaining places hand over fist to close on Debon by the fourth lap; he was ahead of him two laps later. Luthi was 3.1 seconds away, but the track was fully dry and the Spaniard set a new record on lap 12. Now he was right on Luthi's tail, and straight past him, almost a second clear on lap 14.

The rain returned – half-hearted, but menacing all the same – and the 'Wet Race' flag was shown at the end of lap 15. Now it turned into what Bautista would describe as 'a crazy race'. Cautiously he backed off; two laps later, the bolder Luthi was ahead once more and pulling clear at a second a lap.

Like the rain, this was short-lived. It started to dry once more, and Bautista judged the changing conditions best. He closed rapidly to regain the lead with five laps left, charging off to take his second win by more than 4.5 seconds.

Simoncelli took a little longer to get going, but by lap six, he had tagged on to the five-strong group disputing fourth, a little way behind Debon. It was led by Kallio and Barbera, going back and forth, from Aoyama, Espargaro and the fading Simon. He finally got to the front on lap 14. Barbera and the KTMs were with him, but Simon and Espargaro had faded. And they had all caught Debon.

The next shuffle pushed Debon to the back, triggered by a headlong Barbera when he took to the escape road

at the end of the back straight for the first of three occasions, almost colliding with Kallio as he rejoined. At the same time, Aoyama took third for four laps.

The final decision came on lap 18, when Simoncelli pushed past both KTMs at the tight hairpin and moved away to make sure of an important rostrum finish, which put him within one point of overall leader Kallio.

Debon came back strongly to head Barbera over the line. Kallio had faded with tyre problems, ceding sixth to his team-mate. By the end, Takahashi was also closing on the Finn.

The experienced Locatelli had made the most of the wet confusion to pull through from 14th to ninth; Simon had dropped some way behind, well clear of Faubel, Wilairot, Lai and Baldolini. A distant Pesek took the last point; Espargaro fell all the way back to 17th.

Pasini had pulled through from 13th to eighth when he crashed out with 13 laps remaining.

125cc RACE – Five laps

Corsi was on pole from Smith, Olive and di Meglio, and the race started dry. Smith took off at amazing speed, leading Olive by 1.3 seconds after just one lap and stretching away steadily. When the even faster Terol took over on lap seven, he was still more than three seconds clear.

It was all for nothing; his efforts would be neutralised, for the sake of a very localised shower on lap ten.

Smith arrived there first, and crashed. The red flags came out at once, but not soon enough to save Marquez and four others from going down.

The positions at the end of lap nine were Smith, Terol, Olive, Vazquez, Cortese, Marquez, Bradl, Iannone, Corsi – but they counted only for the grid for a winner-takes-all, five-lap gallop. Talmacsi and di Meglio were 11th and 12th. Redding had been 15th, but was missing: a fractured exhaust valve meant he couldn't make the restart.

It was a brutal brawl. Olive led almost to the end, with Corsi holding second from Talmacsi and Rabat. Smith was overwhelmed, finishing lap one seventh.

They were all so close, however, that anything could happen on the final lap.

Rabat made a lunge at the end of the back straight, gaining an impressive lead, but was swamped on the last run towards Ramshoek and the chicane.

The decisive moves came under the final braking. A combination of brawn and brains gave Talmacsi his first win of the year, by 0.128 second from Olive, Corsi right behind. Sandro Cortese was fourth, with Smith almost alongside in fifth, then Rabat, di Meglio and Iannone. Terol was less than half a second adrift, while de Rosa completed the top ten.

A-STYLE TT ASSEN

28 JUNE 2008 • FIM WORLD CHAMPIONSHIP ROUND 9

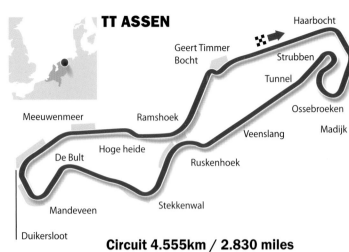

TT ASSEN

Haarbocht
Geert Timmer Bocht
Strubben
Tunnel
Ossebroeken
Meeuwenmeer
Ramshoek
Madijk
Veenslang
Hoge heide
De Bult
Ruskenhoek
Mandeveen
Stekkenwal
Duikersloot

Circuit 4.555km / 2.830 miles

MOTOGP

RACE: 26 laps, 73.580 miles/118.430km • Weather: Dry • Air 20°C • Humidity 62% • Track 24°C

Pos.	Rider	Nat.	No.	Team	Machine	Tyres	Laps	Time & speed (mph/km/h)
1	Casey Stoner	AUS	1	Ducati Marlboro Team	Ducati	B	26	42m 12.337s 104.615mph/ 168.361km/h
2	Dani Pedrosa	SPA	2	Repsol Honda Team	Honda	M	26	42m 23.647s
3	Colin Edwards	USA	5	Tech 3 Yamaha	Yamaha	M	26	42m 29.462s
4	Nicky Hayden	USA	69	Repsol Honda Team	Honda	M	26	42m 32.814s
5	Andrea Dovizioso	ITA	4	JiR Team Scot MotoGP	Honda	M	26	42m 39.683s
6	Jorge Lorenzo	SPA	48	Fiat Yamaha Team	Yamaha	M	26	42m 40.945s
7	Chris Vermeulen	AUS	7	Rizla Suzuki MotoGP	Suzuki	B	26	42m 44.667s
8	Shinya Nakano	JPN	56	San Carlo Honda Gresini	Honda	B	26	43m 47.229s
9	James Toseland	GBR	52	Tech 3 Yamaha	Yamaha	M	26	42m 50.903s
10	Sylvain Guintoli	FRA	50	Alice Team	Ducati	B	26	42m 51.154s
11	Valentino Rossi	ITA	46	Fiat Yamaha Team	Yamaha	B	26	42m 58.362s
12	Toni Elias	SPA	24	Alice Team	Ducati	B	26	43m 00.550s
13	Marco Melandri	ITA	33	Ducati Marlboro Team	Ducati	B	26	43m 11.931s
	Anthony West	AUS	13	Kawasaki Racing Team	Kawasaki	B	7	11m 41.383s
	Randy de Puniet	FRA	14	LCR Honda MotoGP	Honda	M	0	DNF
	Alex de Angelis	RSM	15	San Carlo Honda Gresini	Honda	B	0	DNF

Fastest lap: Casey Stoner, on lap 5, 1m 36.738s, 105.328mph/169.509km/h (record).

Previous lap record: Nicky Hayden, USA (Honda), 1m 37.106s, 104.929mph/168.867km/h (2006).

Event best maximum speed: Casey Stoner, 184.7mph/297.2km/h (qualifying practice).

QUALIFYING: 27 June 2008

Weather: Dry
Air: 20°C Humidity: 44% Track: 29°C

Pos.	Rider	Time
1	Stoner	1m 35.520s
2	Pedrosa	1m 35.552s
3	Rossi	1m 35.659s
4	Hayden	1m 35.975s
5	de Puniet	1m 35.985s
6	Edwards	1m 36.278s
7	Lorenzo	1m 36.532s
8	Vermeulen	1m 36.768s
9	Nakano	1m 36.804s
10	Guintoli	1m 36.823s
11	Dovizioso	1m 36.899s
12	de Angelis	1m 36.948s
13	Toseland	1m 36.978s
14	Elias	1m 37.287s
15	West	1m 37.793s
16	Melandri	1m 38.726s

Grid order	1	2	3	4	5	6	7	8	9	10	11	12	13	14	15	16	17	18	19	20	21	22	23	24	25	26	
1 STONER	1	1	1	1	1	1	1	1	1	1	1	1	1	1	1	1	1	1	1	1	1	1	1	1	1	1	1
2 PEDROSA	2	2	2	2	2	2	2	2	2	2	2	2	2	2	2	2	2	2	2	2	2	2	2	2	2	2	2
46 ROSSI	69	69	69	69	69	69	69	69	69	69	69	69	69	69	69	69	69	69	69	69	69	69	69	69	69	5	3
69 HAYDEN	56	56	56	56	4	4	7	7	7	7	7	4	5	5	5	5	5	5	5	5	5	5	5	5	5	69	4
14 de PUNIET	4	4	4	4	7	7	4	4	4	4	7	7	4	4	4	4	4	4	4	4	4	4	4	4	4	4	5
5 EDWARDS	7	7	7	7	56	56	56	56	56	56	56	56	7	7	7	56	56	56	56	48	48	48	48	48	48		6
48 LORENZO	48	48	48	48	48	48	48	48	48	5	5	5	56	56	56	56	7	7	7	48	56	56	56	7	7	7	7
7 VERMEULEN	52	52	52	52	52	52	5	5	48	48	48	48	48	48	48	48	48	48	7	7	7	7	56	56	56		8
56 NAKANO	50	50	50	50	5	5	52	52	52	52	52	52	52	52	52	52	52	52	52	52	52	52	52	52	52		9
50 GUINTOLI	33	5	5	5	50	50	50	50	50	50	50	50	50	50	50	50	50	50	50	50	50	50	50	50	50		10
4 DOVISIOSO	24	33	13	13	13	13	13	24	24	24	24	24	24	24	24	24	24	24	46	46	46	46	46	46	46		11
15 de ANGELIS	5	13	33	33	24	24	33	33	33	33	33	33	33	33	33	46	46	46	46	46	24	24	24	24	24		12
52 TOSELAND	13	24	24	24	33	33	46	46	46	46	46	46	46	46	46	33	33	33	33	33	33	33	33	33	33		13
24 ELIAS	46	46	46	46	46	46	46																				
65 CAPIROSSI																											
21 HOPKINS																											
13 WEST																											
33 MELANDRI																											
65 CAPIROSSI																											

FASTEST RACE LAPS

	Rider	Lap	Time
1	Stoner	5	1m 36.738s
2	Edwards	18	1m 37.034s
3	Rossi	20	1m 37.173s
4	Pedrosa	8	1m 37.208s
5	Hayden	3	1m 37.346s
6	Vermeulen	3	1m 37.629s
7	Dovizioso	15	1m 37.662s
8	Elias	25	1m 37.705s
9	Toseland	8	1m 37.846s
10	Lorenzo	23	1m 37.853s
11	Nakano	11	1m 37.854s
12	Guintoli	25	1m 37.982s
13	West	5	1m 38.270s
14	Melandri	8	1m 38.676s

statistics

250cc

24 laps, 67.920 miles/109.320km

Pos.	Rider (Nat.)	No.	Team	Machine	Laps	Time & speed
1	Alvaro Bautista (SPA)	19	Mapfre Aspar Team	Aprilia	24	40m 54.117s 99.645mph/ 160.363km/h
2	Thomas Luthi (SWI)	12	Emmi - Caffe Latte	Aprilia	24	40m 58.714s
3	Marco Simoncelli (ITA)	58	Metis Gilera	Gilera	24	41m 00.120s
4	Alex Debon (SPA)	6	Lotus Aprilia	Aprilia	24	41m 03.151s
5	Hector Barbera (SPA)	21	Team Toth Aprilia	Aprilia	24	41m 03.196s
6	Hiroshi Aoyama (JPN)	4	Red Bull KTM 250	KTM	24	41m 05.632s
7	Mika Kallio (FIN)	36	Red Bull KTM 250	KTM	24	41m 06.991s
8	Yuki Takahashi (JPN)	72	JiR Team Scot 250	Honda	24	41m 07.739s
9	Roberto Locatelli (ITA)	15	Metis Gilera	Gilera	24	41m 15.285s
10	Julian Simon (SPA)	60	Repsol KTM 250cc	KTM	24	41m 22.906s
11	Hector Faubel (SPA)	55	Mapfre Aspar Team	Aprilia	24	41m 31.724s
12	Ratthapark Wilairot (THA)	14	Thai Honda PTT SAG	Honda	24	41m 31.858s
13	Fabrizio Lai (ITA)	32	Campetella Racing	Gilera	24	41m 32.846s
14	Alex Baldolini (ITA)	25	Matteoni Racing	Aprilia	24	41m 33.282s
15	Lukas Pesek (CZE)	52	Auto Kelly - CP	Aprilia	24	41m 37.154s
16	Eugene Laverty (IRL)	50	Blusens Aprilia	Aprilia	24	41m 48.288s
17	Aleix Espargaro (SPA)	41	Lotus Aprilia	Aprilia	24	41m 48.451s
18	Frederik Watz (SWE)	64	Jaap Kingma Racing	Aprilia	24	42m 18.547s
19	Doni Tata Pradita (INA)	45	Yamaha Pertamina Indonesia	Yamaha	23	41m 22.050s
20	Imre Toth (HUN)	10	Team Toth Aprilia	Aprilia	23	41m 50.516s
	Manuel Poggiali (RSM)	54	Campetella Racing	Gilera	17	DNF
	Mattia Pasini (ITA)	75	Polaris World	Aprilia	11	DNF
	Russel Gomez (SPA)	7	Blusens Aprilia	Aprilia	0	DNF
	Karel Abraham (CZE)	17	Cardion AB Motoracing	Aprilia		DNS

Fastest lap: Bautista, 1m 40.340s, 101.547mph/163.424km/h (record).

Previous lap record: Alex de Angelis, RSM (Aprilia), 1m 40.354s, 101.533mph/ 163.401km/h (2007).

Event best maximum speed: Luthi, 156.3mph/251.6km/h (qualifying practice no. 2).

Qualifying: **1** Bautista, 1m 39.510s; **2** Barbera, 1m 39.741s; **3** Simoncelli, 1m 39.854s; **4** Debon, 1m 40.059s; **5** Espargaro, 1m 40.210s; **6** Luthi, 1m 40.455s; **7** Simon, 1m 40.686s; **8** Pesek, 1m 40.742s; **9** Locatelli, 1m 40.759s; **10** Takahashi, 1m 40.796s; **11** Kallio, 1m 40.849s; **12** Lai, 1m 40.862s; **13** Aoyama, 1m 40.914s; **14** Pasini, 1m 40.936s; **15** Faubel, 1m 40.972s; **16** Poggiali, 1m 41.180s; **17** Wilairot, 1m 41.543s; **18** Abraham, 1m 41.680s; **19** Baldolini, 1m 42.121s; **20** Laverty, 1m 42.943s; **21** Toth, 1m 43.108s; **22** Watz, 1m 44.481s; **23** Gomez, 1m 44.639s; **24** Pradita, 1m 45.400s.

Fastest race laps: **1** Bautista, 1m 40.340s; **2** Luthi, 1m 40.881s; **3** Simoncelli, 1m 41.039s; **4** Barbera, 1m 41.234s; **5** Aoyama, 1m 41.288s; **6** Kallio, 1m 41.325s; **7** Pasini, 1m 41.462s; **8** Debon, 1m 41.476s; **9** Takahashi, 1m 41.709s; **10** Locatelli, 1m 41.840s; **11** Simon, 1m 41.926s; **12** Espargaro, 1m 41.961s; **13** Lai, 1m 42.248s; **14** Faubel, 1m 42.398s; **15** Pesek, 1m 42.403s; **16** Wilairot, 1m 42.412s; **17** Laverty, 1m 42.469s; **18** Baldolini, 1m 42.519s; **19** Poggiali, 1m 43.730s; **20** Watz, 1m 44.364s; **21** Toth, 1m 45.648s; **22** Pradita, 1m 45.829s.

World Championship: **1** Kallio, 140; **2** Simoncelli, 139; **3** Debon, 114; **4** Bautista, 102; **5** Pasini, 98; **6** Barbera, 93; **7** Aoyama, 90; **8** Takahashi, 78; **9** Luthi, 77; **10** Simon, 57; **11** Locatelli, 46; **12** Espargaro, 46; **13** Faubel, 39; **14** Wilairot, 34; **15** Abraham, 25; **16** Pesek, 22; **17** Baldolini, 18; **18** Poggiali, 16; **19** Lai, 12; **20** Laverty, 7; **21** Hernandez and Sandi, 2; **23** Toth, 2; **24** Pradita, 1.

125cc

Race Part 2: 5 laps, 14.150 miles/22.775km

Pos.	Rider (Nat.)	No.	Team	Machine	Laps	Time & speed
1	Gabor Talmacsi (HUN)	1	Bancaja Aspar Team	Aprilia	5	9m 04.520s 93.561mph/ 150.572km/h
2	Joan Olive (SPA)	6	Belson Derbi	Derbi	5	9m 04.648s
3	Simone Corsi (ITA)	24	Jack & Jones WRB	Aprilia	5	9m 04.775s
4	Sandro Cortese (GER)	11	Emmi - Caffe Latte	Aprilia	5	9m 04.860s
5	Bradley Smith (GBR)	38	Polaris World	Aprilia	5	9m 04.945s
6	Esteve Rabat (SPA)	12	Repsol KTM 125cc	KTM	5	9m 05.088s
7	Mike di Meglio (FRA)	63	Ajo Motorsport	Derbi	5	9m 05.366s
8	Andrea Iannone (ITA)	29	I.C. Team	Aprilia	5	9m 05.448s
9	Nicolas Terol (SPA)	18	Jack & Jones WRB	Aprilia	5	9m 05.958s
10	Raffaele de Rosa (ITA)	35	Onde 2000 KTM	KTM	5	9m 07.074s
11	Stefano Bianco (ITA)	27	S3+ WTR San Marino Team	Aprilia	5	9m 07.349s
12	Stefan Bradl (GER)	17	Grizzly Gas Kiefer Racing	Aprilia	5	9m 07.541s
13	Tomoyoshi Koyama (JPN)	71	ISPA KTM Aran	KTM	5	9m 07.721s
14	Michael Ranseder (AUT)	60	I.C. Team	Aprilia	5	9m 08.120s
15	Hugo van den Berg (NED)	56	Degraaf Grand Prix	Aprilia	5	9m 09.067s
16	Dominique Aegerter (SWI)	77	Ajo Motorsport	Derbi	5	9m 09.112s
17	Stevie Bonsey (USA)	51	Degraaf Grand Prix	Aprilia	5	9m 09.339s
18	Jules Cluzel (FRA)	16	Loncin Racing	Loncin	5	9m 15.068s
19	Randy Krummenacher (SWI)	34	Red Bull KTM 125	KTM	5	9m 15.163s
20	Pablo Nieto (SPA)	22	Onde 2000 KTM	KTM	5	9m 15.369s
21	Pere Tutusaus (SPA)	30	Bancaja Aspar Team	Aprilia	5	9m 15.614s
22	Robin Lasser (GER)	21	Grizzly Gas Kiefer Racing	Aprilia	5	9m 16.374s
23	Alexis Masbou (FRA)	5	Loncin Racing	Loncin	5	9m 18.236s
24	Louis Rossi (FRA)	69	FFM Honda GP 125	Honda	5	9m 18.348s
25	Robert Muresan (ROU)	95	Grizzly Gas Kiefer Racing	Aprilia	5	9m 20.675s
26	Michael van der Mark (NED)	82	Dutch Racing Team	Honda	5	9m 22.721s
27	Robert Gull (SWE)	84	Ajo Motorsports Jnr Project	Derbi	5	9m 30.212s
28	Jasper Iwema (NED)	81	Abbink Bos Racing	Seel	5	9m 33.728s
29	Ernst Dubbink (NED)	89	RV Racing Team	Honda	5	9m 34.469s
30	Jerry van de Bunt (NED)	83	Degraaf Grand Prix	Aprilia	5	9m 40.939s
	Takaaki Nakagami (JPN)	73	I.C. Team	Aprilia	3	DNF
	Lorenzo Zanetti (ITA)	8	ISPA KTM Aran	KTM	3	DNF
Did not start:	Race Part 2					
	Roberto Lacalendola (ITA)	19	Matteoni Racing	Aprilia		DNS
	Sergio Gadea (SPA)	33	Bancaja Aspar Team	Aprilia		DNS
	Scott Redding (GBR)	45	Blusens Aprilia Junior	Aprilia		DNS
	Efren Vazquez (SPA)	7	Blusens Aprilia Junior	Aprilia		DNS
	Joey Litjens (NED)	80	Abbink Bos Racing	Seel		DNS
	Marc Marquez (SPA)	93	Repsol KTM 125cc	KTM		DNS

Fastest lap: Vazquez, 1m 46.445s, 95.723mph/154.051km/h (in Race Part 1).

Lap record: Sergio Gadea, SPA (Aprilia), 1m 45.098s, 96.949mph/156.025km/h (2006).

Event best maximum speed: Bradl, 134.3mph/216.2km/h (Race Part 2).

Qualifying: **1** Corsi, 1m 45.533s; **2** Smith, 1m 45.873s; **3** Olive, 1m 45.896s; **4** di Meglio, 1m 45.897s; **5** Cortese, 1m 45.935s; **6** Redding, 1m 46.028s; **7** de Rosa, 1m 46.105s; **8** Terol, 1m 46.139s; **9** Gadea, 1m 46.318s; **10** Bradl, 1m 46.329s; **11** Krummenacher, 1m 46.396s; **12** Aegerter, 1m 46.444s; **13** Talmacsi, 1m 46.532s; **14** Bianco, 1m 46.554s; **15** Rabat, 1m 46.700s; **16** Bonsey, 1m 46.714s; **17** Koyama, 1m 46.760s; **18** Marquez, 1m 46.863s; **19** Zanetti, 1m 46.935s; **20** Nieto, 1m 46.956s; **21** Ranseder, 1m 47.019s; **22** Vazquez, 1m 47.106s; **23** Iannone, 1m 47.243s; **24** Tutusaus, 1m 47.354s; **25** van den Berg, 1m 47.458s; **26** Nakagami, 1m 47.502s; **27** Cluzel, 1m 47.617s; **28** Litjens, 1m 47.670s; **29** Masbou, 1m 47.795s; **30** Muresan, 1m 48.027s; **31** Lacalendola, 1m 48.037s; **32** van der Mark, 1m 49.173s; **33** Lasser, 1m 49.207s; **34** Rossi, 1m 49.995s; **35** Dubbink, 1m 50.126s; **36** Iwema, 1m 50.574s; **37** Gull, 1m 50.598s; **38** van de Bunt, 1m 51.560s.

Fastest race laps (in Race Part 1): **1** Vazquez, 1m 46.445s; **2** Terol, 1m 46.515s; **3** Cortese, 1m 46.548s; **4** di Meglio, 1m 46.659s; **5** Smith, 1m 46.814s; **6** Corsi, 1m 46.892s; **7** Marquez, 1m 47.147s; **8** Iannone, 1m 47.210s; **9** Redding, 1m 47.220s; **10** Koyama, 1m 47.279s; **11** Rabat, 1m 47.331s; **12** Bianco, 1m 47.352s; **13** Nakagami, 1m 47.499s; **14** Olive, 1m 47.502s; **15** Bradl, 1m 47.603s; **16** Bonsey, 1m 47.654s; **17** Talmacsi, 1m 47.674s; **18** van den Berg, 1m 48.256s; **19** Masbou, 1m 48.615s; **20** Ranseder, 1m 48.635s; **21** Aegerter, 1m 48.635s; **22** Zanetti, 1m 48.699s; **23** Tutusaus, 1m 49.261s; **24** Rossi, 1m 49.442s; **25** Cluzel, 1m 49.497s; **26** Lasser, 1m 49.501s; **27** Krummenacher, 1m 49.658s; **28** Nieto, 1m 49.989s; **29** de Rosa, 1m 50.210s; **30** van der Mark, 1m 50.424s; **31** Lacalendola, 1m 50.767s; **32** Muresan, 1m 50.778s; **33** Gull, 1m 51.355s; **34** Dubbink, 1m 51.382s; **35** Iwema, 1m 52.433s; **36** Gadea, 1m 52.968s; **37** van de Bunt, 1m 53.085s.

World Championship: **1** di Meglio, 141; **2** Corsi, 125; **3** Olive, 94; **4** Talmacsi, 93; **5** Terol, 82; **6** Bradl, 81; **7** Espargaro, 75; **8** Smith, 66; **9** Gadea, 62; **10** Cortese, 58; **11** Redding, 57; **12** Iannone, 55; **13** Bonsey, 39; **14** de Rosa, 30; **15** Marquez, 26; **16** Webb, 26; **17** Rabat, 24; **18** Koyama, 22; **19** Ranseder, 19; **20** Aegerter, 16; **21** Vazquez, 14; **22** Nieto, 11; **23** Zanetti, 10; **24** Krummenacher, 10; **25** Nakagami, 9; **26** Bianco, 8; **27** Tutusaus, 5; **28** Masbou and van den Berg

RIDER STANDINGS

After 9 Rounds

1	Dani Pedrosa	171
2	Valentino Rossi	167
3	Casey Stoner	142
4	Jorge Lorenzo	114
5	Colin Edwards	98
6	Andrea Dovizioso	79
7	Nicky Hayden	70
8	James Toseland	60
9	Chris Vermeulen	57
10	Shinya Nakano	57
11	Loris Capirossi	51
12	Toni Elias	33
13	John Hopkins	32
14	Marco Melandri	32
15	Alex de Angelis	25
16	Sylvain Guintoli	24
17	Randy de Puniet	22
18	Anthony West	16
19 =	Tadayuki Okada	2
19 =	Ben Spies	2

TEAM STANDINGS

After 9 Rounds

1	Fiat Yamaha Team	281
2	Repsol Honda Team	241
3	Ducati Marlboro Team	174
4	Tech 3 Yamaha	158
5	Rizla Suzuki MotoGP	110
6	San Carlo Honda Gresini	82
7	JiR Team Scot MotoGP	79
8	Alice Team	57
9	Kawasaki Racing Team	48
10	LCR Honda MotoGP	22

CONSTRUCTOR STANDINGS

After 9 Rounds

1	Yamaha	196
2	Honda	171
3	Ducati	147
4	Suzuki	80
5	Kawasaki	41

Wet specialists Vermeulen and West
sandwich erratically brilliant class
rookie de Angelis. West fell, Vermeulen
made the rostrum, de Angelis chased
him all the way.

Photograph: Gold & Goose

FIM WORLD CHAMPIONSHIP • ROUND 10
GERMAN GP
SACHSENRING

THERE was another runaway win at the Sachsenring, the tightest, though not quite the slowest, track of the year – that is Laguna Seca. This was the trend, it seemed, of the 800 class – as much because of the grip of the new-generation tyres as the advance in electronics, thought Rossi. Overtaking was becoming increasingly difficult: 'The last part was big slides with the tyres finished. It was possible make a bit more difference. Now everybody has great pace for all the race.'

Actually there were two runaways, but the first one didn't go all the way. That was by Dani Pedrosa, who had amassed a huge advantage after just five laps – some 7.5 seconds. He never made the sixth. As he touched the brakes for the first tight corner, he slammed into the ground so suddenly it seemed he'd hit a trip wire. Travelling at speed, he went head first into the air-fence, while his Honda broke several large bits off itself before ending up on top of the barrier. He was left with ankle injuries and a broken finger on his left hand, and it ruined the erstwhile points leader's season.

The runaway that mattered was Stoner's for a third race in a row, with a lead almost as large until he slackened his pace with four laps remaining. As at the previous two races, he had all but dominated free practice – Pedrosa was fractionally faster in the third – and qualified with a big advantage. Rossi took over the points lead from the fallen Dani, but Stoner had closed to within 20 points and was starting to look as invincible as he had been in 2007. 'You know, three weeks ago, basically, we were counted out of the championship. Now we believe that we can actually be in with a fight,' he said.

The weather was becoming a major theme of the season. There were showers on Saturday morning and a deluge almost all day on Sunday. Not enough to dampen the ardour of the 98,000-strong sell-out crowd, but enough that the racers were becoming rather tired of it. And enough to show the first major cracks in Michelin's façade, at least in the wet. As well as Pedrosa, Lorenzo and Edwards also crashed out, while Hayden pitted to change his too-hard rear rather than follow suit. The best of the French company's survivors, Dovizioso, was more than 40 seconds adrift and only fifth. Some front-end crashes in practice also raised questions about the front tyres. Problems at one race would be forgivable, but this would turn out to be the beginning of a serious rot, which ultimately would have devastating consequences.

Grim rumours were circulating in the wake of tests at Indianapolis. No full-time riders had taken part, but testers, including Olivier Jacque, reported mixed surfaces, ultra-tight corners and a worrying proximity to the oval-track wall. There was muttering and an assumption that there were big problems to come. Even Hayden was guarded: he was the only regular to have lapped the new track, which ran in the opposite direction and was slightly altered from the F1 circuit, albeit only on a CBR1000 street bike – and a 1909 Indian.

Contract talk had already surfaced, somewhat early, and Hayden's name was linked to a move to Ducati. In real terms, this was very premature, but would turn out to be true. There was still some doubt that Melandri would see out his Ducati season, and he was already earmarked for Kawasaki for 2009. And there were questions over whether satellite-team Ducati struggler Toni Elias would see out the season. These turned out to be well wide of the mark. In fact, Ducati had come up with a revised rear suspension link he'd been asking for since Le Mans, and while it took a little time to adjust, this would signal a major return to form.

There was serious trouble of another kind at his Alice-backed team, with the abrupt departure of the principal,

former GP racer Luis d'Antin. The Spaniard had 're-signed' on race eve, amid rumours of serious financial irregularities, including an unpaid team hotel bill from earlier in the season. D'Antin would not be seen again.

Capirossi was back, his ugly arm injury from Assen still heavily dressed, but his determination undimmed. He qualified and raced strongly, proving once again that he is at least as tough as he looks, if not more so.

There were a number of crashes during the weekend, of which Stoner's was the fastest – on the 250km/h right-hander before the so-called waterfall back straight. Two years before, a tumble there had ruled him out of the race with suspected concussion, a decision that he still disputes. This time, he escaped unhurt. The next-fastest crash was by countryman West, whose 230km/h fall left him with a painful back, while it snapped his Kawasaki clean in half. Pedrosa also fell in practice as well as in the race, as did Edwards. Dovizioso and Toseland were two more Friday victims.

Simoncelli, his hair now so big and wild that it was causing widespread comment, claimed a third win and took over the 250 title lead from Kallio, the only other rider with three wins. The Italian did it thanks to some new weaponry: his progress had earned him the 2008 factory Aprilia – albeit dubbed 'Gilera' in his case – in place of the 2007 bike he'd had so far, putting him on equal footing with Bautista, Barbera, Pasini, Luthi and Debon, riders he had been beating regularly. The new bike had a shorter engine, thanks to a higher forward crankshaft, allowing a longer swing-arm. Although he'd

Left, right and below: Pedrosa's crash out of a seven-second lead ruined his championship chances, and demonstrated the effectiveness of the air-fence. The machine hit the safety barrier way up high and fell back to the top of the air-fence; Pedrosa slammed into it very hard indeed.

Photos: Gold & Goose (left) and Martin Heath (right and below)

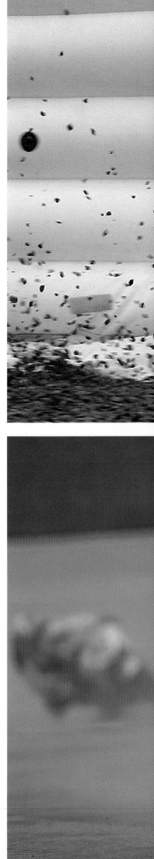

Above: Simoncelli grins out from his personal mane after taking his third 250 win and the points lead.

Right: Randy de Puniet was the second Michelin rider home.

Photographs: Gold & Goose

tested it successfully at Brno, he had to be persuaded to use it for this race. A risk that paid off handsomely.

Finally, electronics are blamed for making the big bikes too easy to ride. But consider the case – and the obvious, though often underrated, skill – of Ducati battler Sylvain Guintoli. His engine management system malfunctioned on only the third lap of the race, leaving him to revert to traditional manual throttle and gear-shifting control. Was he thrown straight off? Far from it. He took sixth, by far his best result of the season.

MOTOGP RACE – 28 laps

Stoner's pace in qualifying gave him his fourth pole in a row. Equally demoralising was his capacity for stringing fast laps together. Pedrosa and Edwards were along-side, but with Dovizioso, Lorenzo and de Puniet filling the second row, Rossi and Hayden were only on the third, and somewhat concerned, at a track where over-taking possibilities are limited.

Although Saturday morning had been partially damp, there had been no fully wet practice. Now the rain was pouring down steadily, making tyre choice a gamble. As usual, some got it right – like Pedrosa; others did not. Like the Spaniard's team-mate, Hayden, who discovered at the first corner that his bike's rear grip was virtually non-existent: 'just sideways ... wouldn't even let the electronics work'. He finished the first lap stone last and was almost a full minute behind the leaders when he pitted to change the tyre after seven laps.

The first lap also was enough to show Pedrosa's strength. He led into the first corner and galloped off, almost two seconds clear after just one lap.

Dovizioso led the pursuit, from Stoner, with Edwards, Lorenzo, Toseland and Rossi behind.

Stoner was up to second next time around, while Rossi had passed Toseland and Lorenzo. Neither of these would last much longer. Toseland was also in tyre trouble and dropping back rapidly; Lorenzo likewise, but paying a different price as he tried to overcome the disadvantage. He high-sided out of the looping Omega curve on lap three.

By lap six, after Pedrosa's abrupt departure, Stoner was starting to pull clear of Dovizioso, while Rossi was about to get ahead of Edwards. A couple of seconds further back, wet specialist Vermeulen had come through steadily from 11th on lap one. Right behind was de Angelis, showing similar strong style in his first wet MotoGP race, and barely a second adrift of him another rainmaster, West, was closing. He too had come charging through after finishing lap one in 14th, but he was

Above: Bautista came through for a fourth successive rostrum.

Above left: Guintoli heads come-back man Capirossi. He was riding without the aid of electronics.

Top: Di Meglio's third win stretched his points lead.

Left: MotoGP top three: Rossi took the points lead, smiling Stoner was closing fast, Vermeulen was happy to be on the rostrum again.

Far left: Kawasaki's race director, Ichiro Yoda.

Photographs: Gold & Goose

heading for trouble. He slipped off on the eighth lap, scrambling back on board to rejoin at the back, with only the struggling Elias and Hayden behind him.

Ambition would be thwarted also one lap later for Melandri, who had made similarly impressive progress, from 15th to seventh; he crashed out on lap ten.

Rossi had gained second on lap nine, 3.2 seconds behind Stoner. He would take seven-tenths off this next time around, but Stoner got the message at once and slashed more than a second off his own lap time to re-open the gap and drive home the fact that he didn't intend being caught. For these two, there was little more to be done except press on. Especially for Rossi, since there was more pressure coming from behind.

That pressure came from Vermeulen and his constant companion, de Angelis. They had caught the Edwards/Dovizioso duet on lap nine, and the Australian had promptly led the way past both of them. Within two laps, both had succeeded, while Edwards had got ahead of Dovizioso in the process.

Now Vermeulen started to close on Rossi, coming to within less than 1.5 seconds at half-distance, before Rossi also turned up the wick slightly to escape once more. From there to the finish, the order of the top four remained unchanged, with Vermeulen more than ten seconds behind over the line, and the remarkable de Angelis just over a tenth behind him, having pushed and probed at his more experienced rival all the way.

Edwards was losing ground slowly on this pair, Dovizioso close behind, but never close enough to challenge. In the end, he didn't have to, for Edwards was the final victim of the treacherous conditions, after 20 laps, still striving to be at least top Michelin finisher.

The order remained basically the same for the last ten uncomfortable laps. Dovizioso had faded by more than 40 seconds at the end, but not quite enough for Guintoli to catch him. Riding without the benefit of electronics, but with the advantage of Bridgestones, the Frenchman had caught Capirossi by lap ten and taken seventh off him by lap 12. He not only pulled away steadily, but also was only four seconds behind Dovizioso at the finish. Wet races really do make heroes of the forgotten men of racing.

Nor was Capirossi's ride much less heroic. Still in pain, he had kept pushing and also seen off a persistent challenge from de Puniet, regaining seventh place on the last lap, by a tenth over the line. Nakano was ninth, while a disappointed West was back up to tenth by the end, the last rider to complete the full 30 laps.

Again, there were points for all finishers – only 13 of them, with Toseland and Elias trailing in one lap down, and Hayden another lap away.

250cc RACE – 29 laps

It was raining, but that was no problem for Simoncelli, who started from pole and was never troubled. After only ten laps, his lead was better than seven seconds, and later it grew to more than eight, although by the end he'd slackened his pace, winning by a still commanding 2.2 seconds. More than enough to give him the points lead over Kallio, who was fourth.

Simon, Barbera and Kallio were alongside the Gilera on the front row, Bautista and Debon heading the second. The front-row men followed him away in that order for the first three laps, but then started swapping, with Barbera up to second for a spell, and then Kallio from lap ten to 22.

Debon lasted only one lap in pursuit, falling on the second and rejoining last, only to pit and retire.

On lap nine, Aoyama took fifth from Pasini and gave chase to the three up front, some five seconds away.

Bautista had started slowly, finishing lap one way down in the pack, in 17th, as he came to terms with the tricky conditions. He was soon up to 11th, however, behind Takahashi, and ahead of him on lap four. Over the next two laps, he passed both Lai and Luthi, but he became stuck in seventh until lap 16, gradually closing a three-second gap to Pasini.

Next time around, they were both promoted when Aoyama slipped off. He remounted hurriedly, losing 20 seconds, but only three places in a by-now well-spread mid-field. At this point, Kallio, Barbera and Simon were still locked in combat, with Pasini and Bautista another four seconds adrift, and Luthi almost 15 seconds down.

With the advantage of something to aim at, Pasini and his shadow were the fastest of all, and over the next five laps, they steadily cut away at the gap. By lap 22, they were less than a second off the group; on the 23rd, Bautista put in a flier to pass the Italian.

At the same time, Barbera found a way ahead of Kallio into the Omega curve. The group was now five-strong and fierce, covered over the line by less than eight-tenths of a second. With Simoncelli still away alone, the fans had something to keep them on the edges of their wet seats.

Kallio slipped to fifth on lap 24; two laps later, Bautista put a strong move on Simon, while Kallio and Pasini were back and forth at the back of the gang.

There would be just one more change, Kallio moving inside Simon under braking at the bottom of the hill to secure fourth with one lap to go. Striving mightily, but to no avail, they stayed in the same order to the finish, from second to fifth covered by a couple of seconds, with Pasini just out of touch in sixth.

Luthi was seventh; Aoyama managed to hold Takahashi at bay to the flag, with Locatelli closing at the finish.

Abraham, Pesek and Sandi joined a remarkably short crash list, given the nature of the track and the dire weather conditions.

125cc RACE – 27 laps

Talmacsi was on pole for the first time in the season, from Smith, Bradl and Corsi, with points leader di Meglio behind Olive on row two.

Bradl thrilled the home crowd by leading the first two laps – on a dry track and before the rain started falling. By the time he succumbed to Corsi on lap three, there were four out in front, with Olive, Bradl and Smith swapping back and forth through the twists.

Bradl, Olive and Corsi all led again over the line, until Smith took over from lap nine to 17. By now, rain was sprinkling down, although not enough to bring out the white flags or even slow the lap times much. Talmacsi, Terol and di Meglio had closed up to join the lead pack, while the unfortunate Olive had slowed suddenly with a mechanical problem, eventually pitting after 14 laps.

Smith pulled away in the tricky conditions, his lead up to almost 1.7 seconds on lap 14. Di Meglio had come to head the pursuit, however, and he was soon closing up again. On lap 18, he took the lead when Smith ran wide and on to the rumble strip. A lap later, Bradl also passed the Englishman, at the same spot.

Talmacsi was now fourth and soon began leaning on Smith, pushing past on lap 21.

Over the last laps, the rain began again, still patchy and dry at the start-finish, but troublesome over the back of the circuit, making conditions very difficult; all the riders were waiting for the red flag, but it never came. The experienced di Meglio made the most of the situation, taking the win by two seconds.

Bradl, Talmacsi and Smith flashed over the line almost together; then came Corsi, Cortese and Terol, seven seconds down, but even closer together.

Redding escaped from the next group for eighth, while Rabat headed a huge gang separated by inches, all the way down to Nieto in 15th, and even a little beyond.

ALICE MOTORRAD GRAND PRIX DEUTSCHLAND

13 JULY 2008 • FIM WORLD CHAMPIONSHIP ROUND 10

SACHSENRING GP CIRCUIT

Castrol Omega

Coca Cola Kurve

Sternquell

Quickenburgkurve

Sachsenkurve

Circuit 3.671km /2.281 miles

MOTOGP

RACE: 30 laps, 68.430 miles/110.130km • Weather: Wet • Air 14°C • Humidity 82% • Track 17°C

Pos.	Rider	Nat.	No.	Team	Machine	Tyres	Laps	Time & speed (mph/km/h)
1	Casey Stoner	AUS	1	Ducati Marlboro Team	Ducati	B	30	47m 30.057s 86.438mph/ 139.108km/h
2	Valentino Rossi	ITA	46	Fiat Yamaha Team	Yamaha	B	30	47m 33.765s
3	Chris Vermeulen	AUS	7	Rizla Suzuki MotoGP	Suzuki	B	30	47m 44.059s
4	Alex de Angelis	RSM	15	San Carlo Honda Gresini	Honda	B	30	47m 44.181s
5	Andrea Dovizioso	ITA	4	JiR Team Scot MotoGP	Honda	M	30	48m 12.079s
6	Sylvain Guintoli	FRA	50	Alice Team	Ducati	B	30	48m 16.705s
7	Loris Capirossi	ITA	65	Rizla Suzuki MotoGP	Suzuki	B	30	48m 34.540s
8	Randy de Puniet	FRA	14	LCR Honda MotoGP	Honda	M	30	48m 34.645s
9	Shinya Nakano	JPN	56	San Carlo Honda Gresini	Honda	B	30	48m 46.830s
10	Anthony West	AUS	13	Kawasaki Racing Team	Kawasaki	B	30	48m 59.332s
11	James Toseland	GBR	52	Tech 3 Yamaha	Yamaha	M	29	47m 41.757s
12	Toni Elias	SPA	24	Alice Team	Ducati	B	29	47m 43.954s
13	Nicky Hayden	USA	69	Repsol Honda Team	Honda	M	28	48m 13.749s
	Colin Edwards	USA	5	Tech 3 Yamaha	Yamaha	M	20	32m 10.373s
	Marco Melandri	ITA	33	Ducati Marlboro Team	Ducati	B	9	14m 50.161s
	Dani Pedrosa	SPA	2	Repsol Honda Team	Honda	M	5	8m 05.615s
	Jorge Lorenzo	SPA	48	Fiat Yamaha Team	Yamaha	M	2	3m 23.795s

Fastest lap: Casey Stoner, on lap 23, 1m 32.749s, 88.537mph/142.487km/h.

Lap record: Dani Pedrosa, SPA (Honda), 1m 23.082s, 98.839mph/159.066km/h (2007).

Event best maximum speed: Dani Pedrosa, 177.3mph/285.4km/h (qualifying practice).

QUALIFYING: 12 July 2008

Weather: Dry
Air: 20°C Humidity: 48% Track: 27°C

Pos.	Rider	Time
1	Stoner	1m 21.067s
2	Pedrosa	1m 21.420s
3	Edwards	1m 21.519s
4	Dovizioso	1m 21.656s
5	Lorenzo	1m 21.795s
6	de Puniet	1m 21.821s
7	Rossi	1m 21.845s
8	Hayden	1m 21.876s
9	Nakano	1m 21.920s
10	de Angelis	1m 21.977s
11	Toseland	1m 22.126s
12	Elias	1m 22.256s
13	Capirossi	1m 22.542s
14	Vermeulen	1m 22.601s
15	Guintoli	1m 22.938s
16	Melandri	1m 23.131s
17	West	1m 23.158s

Grid order	1	2	3	4	5	6	7	8	9	10	11	12	13	14	15	16	17	18	19	20	21	22	23	24	25	26	27	28	29	30	°
1 STONER	2	2	2	2	2	1	1	1	1	1	1	1	1	1	1	1	1	1	1	1	1	1	1	1	1	1	1	1	1	1	1
2 PEDROSA	4	1	1	1	1	4	4	4	46	46	46	46	46	46	46	46	46	46	46	46	46	46	46	46	46	46	46	46	46	46	2
5 EDWARDS	1	4	4	4	4	5	5	46	5	7	7	7	7	7	7	7	7	7	7	7	7	7	7	7	7	7	7	7	7	7	3
4 DOVISIOSO	5	5	5	5	5	46	46	5	4	5	15	15	15	15	15	15	15	15	15	15	15	15	15	15	15	15	15	15	15	15	
48 LORENZO	48	46	46	46	46	7	7	7	7	15	5	5	5	5	5	5	5	5	5	5	4	4	4	4	4	4	4	4	4	4	5
14 de PUNIET	52	48	15	7	7	15	15	15	15	4	4	4	4	4	4	4	4	4	4	4	50	50	50	50	50	50	50	50	50	50	6
46 ROSSI	46	14	7	15	15	13	13	65	33	65	65	50	50	50	50	50	50	50	50	50	14	14	14	14	14	14	14	14	14	65	7
69 HAYDEN	14	15	14	13	13	14	14	33	65	50	50	65	65	65	65	65	65	65	65	65	14	65	65	65	65	65	65	65	65	14	8
56 NAKANO	50	7	13	14	65	65	50	50	14	14	14	14	14	14	14	14	14	14	65	56	56	56	56	56	56	56	56	56			9
15 de ANGELIS	15	50	50	65	65	50	33	14	14	56	56	56	56	56	56	56	56	56	14	13	13	13	13	13	13	13	13	13			10
52 TOSELAND	7	52	65	50	50	33	50	56	56	52	52	52	13	13	13	13	13	13	13	52	52	52	52	52	52	52	52	52			11
24 ELIAS	65	65	52	33	33	56	56	52	52	13	13	13	13	52	52	52	52	52	52	52	24	24	24	24	24	24	24	24			12
65 CAPIROSSI	56	103	56	52	56	52	52	13	13	24	24	24	24	24	24	24	24	24	24	69	69	69	69	69	69	69	69	69			13
7 VERMEULEN	13	56	33	56	52	24	24	24	24	69	69	69	69	69	69	69	69	69	69												
50 GUINTOLI	33	33	24	24	24	69	69	69	69																						
33 MELANDRI	24	24	69	69	69																										
13 WEST	69	69																													

69 lapped rider

FASTEST RACE LAPS

	Rider	Lap	Time
1	Stoner	23	1m 32.749s
2	Rossi	20	1m 33.041s
3	de Angelis	30	1m 33.405s
4	Vermeulen	30	1m 33.446s
5	Dovizioso	19	1m 33.923s
6	Edwards	20	1m 34.066s
7	Guintoli	19	1m 34.316s
8	West	20	1m 35.191s
9	Capirossi	30	1m 35.274s
10	de Puniet	15	1m 35.343s
11	Elias	29	1m 35.631s
12	Nakano	18	1m 35.710s
13	Melandri	8	1m 35.750s
14	Pedrosa	5	1m 35.954s
15	Toseland	29	1m 36.239s
16	Hayden	18	1m 36.789s
17	Lorenzo	2	1m 40.562s

statistics

MotoGP · TISSOT · SWISS WATCHES SINCE 1853 · OFFICIAL TIMEKEEPER

RIDER STANDINGS

After 10 Rounds

1	Valentino Rossi	187
2	Dani Pedrosa	171
3	Casey Stoner	167
4	Jorge Lorenzo	114
5	Colin Edwards	98
6	Andrea Dovizioso	90
7	Chris Vermeulen	73
8	Nicky Hayden	73
9	James Toseland	65
10	Shinya Nakano	64
11	Loris Capirossi	60
12	Alex de Angelis	38
13	Toni Elias	37
14	Sylvain Guintoli	34
15	John Hopkins	32
16	Marco Melandri	32
17	Randy de Puniet	30
18	Anthony West	22
19 =	Tadayuki Okada	2
19 =	Ben Spies	2

TEAM STANDINGS

After 10 Rounds

1	Fiat Yamaha Team	301
2	Repsol Honda Team	244
3	Ducati Marlboro Team	199
4	Tech 3 Yamaha	163
5	Rizla Suzuki MotoGP	135
6	San Carlo Honda Gresini	102
7	JiR Team Scot MotoGP	90
8	Alice Team	71
9	Kawasaki Racing Team	54
10	LCR Honda MotoGP	30

CONSTRUCTOR STANDINGS

After 10 Rounds

1	Yamaha	216
2	Honda	184
3	Ducati	172
4	Suzuki	96
5	Kawasaki	47

250cc

29 laps, 66.149 miles/106.459km

Pos.	Rider (Nat.)	No.	Team	Machine	Laps	Time & speed
1	Marco Simoncelli (ITA)	58	*Metis Gilera*	Gilera	29	45m 36.703s 87.017mph/ 140.041km/h
2	Hector Barbera (SPA)	21	*Team Toth Aprilia*	Aprilia	29	45m 38.960s
3	Alvaro Bautista (SPA)	19	*Mapfre Aspar Team*	Aprilia	29	45m 39.126s
4	Mika Kallio (FIN)	36	*Red Bull KTM 250*	KTM	29	45m 40.853s
5	Julian Simon (SPA)	60	*Repsol KTM 250cc*	KTM	29	45m 41.549s
6	Mattia Pasini (ITA)	75	*Polaris World*	Aprilia	29	45m 44.835s
7	Thomas Luthi (SWI)	12	*Emmi - Caffe Latte*	Aprilia	29	46m 15.005s
8	Hiroshi Aoyama (JPN)	4	*Red Bull KTM 250*	KTM	29	46m 25.629s
9	Yuki Takahashi (JPN)	72	*JiR Team Scot 250*	Honda	29	46m 26.765s
10	Roberto Locatelli (ITA)	15	*Metis Gilera*	Gilera	29	46m 28.373s
11	Alex Baldolini (ITA)	25	*Matteoni Racing*	Aprilia	29	46m 45.499s
12	Fabrizio Lai (ITA)	32	*Campetella Racing*	Gilera	29	46m 45.665s
13	Aleix Espargaro (SPA)	41	*Lotus Aprilia*	Aprilia	29	46m 48.054s
14	Hector Faubel (SPA)	55	*Mapfre Aspar Team*	Aprilia	29	46m 48.357s
15	Eugene Laverty (IRL)	50	*Blusens Aprilia*	Aprilia	29	46m 50.559s
16	Ratthapark Wilairot (THA)	14	*Thai Honda PTT SAG*	Honda	29	47m 06.679s
17	Imre Toth (HUN)	10	*Team Toth Aprilia*	Aprilia	28	45m 54.806s
18	Alen Gyorfi (HUN)	93	*Motorcycle Competition Service*	Honda	28	46m 13.583s
19	Doni Tata Pradita (INA)	45	*Yamaha Pertamina Indonesia*	Yamaha	28	46m 24.376s
20	Toni Wirsing (GER)	94	*Racing Team Germany*	Honda	27	46m 16.021s
	Federico Sandi (ITA)	90	*Zongshen Team of China*	Aprilia	22	DNF
	Lukas Pesek (CZE)	52	*Auto Kelly - CP*	Aprilia	18	DNF
	Karel Abraham (CZE)	17	*Cardion AB Motoracing*	Aprilia	3	DNF
	Alex Debon (SPA)	6	*Lotus Aprilia*	Aprilia	3	DNF
	Russel Gomez (SPA)	7	*Blusens Aprilia*	Aprilia	0	DNF
	Manuel Poggiali (RSM)	54	*Campetella Racing*	Gilera		DNS

Fastest lap: Barbera, 1m 32.551s, 88.727mph/142.792km/h.

Lap record: Mika Kallio, FIN (KTM), 1m 24.762s, 96.880mph/155.914km/h (2007).

Event best maximum speed: Luthi, 151.3mph/243.5km/h (qualifying practice no. 2).

Qualifying: **1** Simoncelli, 1m 23.399s; **2** Simon, 1m 24.057s; **3** Barbera, 1m 24.077s; **4** Kallio, 1m 24.084s; **5** Bautista, 1m 24.253s; **6** Debon, 1m 24.398s; **7** Lai, 1m 24.460s; **8** Locatelli, 1m 24.502s; **9** Aoyama, 1m 24.544s; **10** Takahashi, 1m 24.652s; **11** Faubel, 1m 24.709s; **12** Espargaro, 1m 24.785s; **13** Pasini, 1m 24.797s; **14** Luthi, 1m 24.811s; **15** Pesek, 1m 24.847s; **16** Abraham, 1m 24.865s; **17** Wilairot, 1m 25.331s; **18** Sandi, 1m 25.492s; **19** Laverty, 1m 25.840s; **20** Poggiali, 1m 25.889s; **21** Baldolini, 1m 26.197s; **22** Toth, 1m 26.862s; **23** Gomez, 1m 27.291s; **24** Pradita, 1m 27.388s; **25** Wirsing, 1m 27.836s; **26** Gyorfi, 1m 29.134s.

Fastest race laps: **1** Barbera, 1m 32.551s; **2** Bautista, 1m 32.554s; **3** Kallio, 1m 33.005s; **4** Simon, 1m 33.217s; **5** Pasini, 1m 33.494s; **6** Simoncelli, 1m 33.539s; **7** Aoyama, 1m 33.655s; **8** Luthi, 1m 34.150s; **9** Takahashi, 1m 34.352s; **10** Locatelli, 1m 34.678s; **11** Sandi, 1m 34.895s; **12** Espargaro, 1m 35.252s; **13** Faubel, 1m 35.260s; **14** Pesek, 1m 35.326s; **15** Baldolini, 1m 35.358s; **16** Lai, 1m 35.360s; **17** Laverty, 1m 35.414s; **18** Wilairot, 1m 36.079s; **19** Toth, 1m 36.283s; **20** Gyorfi, 1m 37.379s; **21** Abraham, 1m 37.387s; **22** Pradita, 1m 37.603s; **23** Wirsing, 1m 38.842s; **24** Debon, 1m 40.114s.

World Championship: **1** Simoncelli, 164; **2** Kallio, 153; **3** Bautista, 118; **4** Debon, 114; **5** Barbera, 113; **6** Pasini, 108; **7** Aoyama, 98; **8** Luthi, 86; **9** Takahashi, 85; **10** Simon, 68; **11** Locatelli, 52; **12** Espargaro, 49; **13** Faubel, 41; **14** Wilairot, 34; **15** Abraham, 25; **16** Baldolini, 23; **17** Pesek, 22; **18** Poggiali, 16; **19** Lai, 16; **20** Laverty, 8; **21** Hernandez and Sandi, 2; **23** Toth, 2; **24** Pradita, 1.

125cc

27 laps, 61.587 miles/99.117km

Pos.	Rider (Nat.)	No.	Team	Machine	Laps	Time & speed
1	Mike di Meglio (FRA)	63	*Ajo Motorsport*	Derbi	27	40m 03.710s 92.240mph/ 148.446km/h
2	Stefan Bradl (GER)	17	*Grizzly Gas Kiefer Racing*	Aprilia	27	40m 05.720s
3	Gabor Talmacsi (HUN)	1	*Bancaja Aspar Team*	Aprilia	27	40m 06.443s
4	Bradley Smith (GBR)	38	*Polaris World*	Aprilia	27	40m 06.557s
5	Simone Corsi (ITA)	24	*Jack & Jones WRB*	Aprilia	27	40m 12.827s
6	Sandro Cortese (GER)	11	*Emmi - Caffe Latte*	Aprilia	27	40m 12.959s
7	Nicolas Terol (SPA)	18	*Jack & Jones WRB*	Aprilia	27	40m 12.967s
8	Scott Redding (GBR)	45	*Blusens Aprilia Junior*	Aprilia	27	40m 34.488s
9	Marc Marquez (SPA)	93	*Repsol KTM 125cc*	KTM	27	40m 36.744s
10	Dominique Aegerter (SWI)	77	*Ajo Motorsport*	Derbi	27	40m 36.831s
11	Andrea Iannone (ITA)	29	*I.C. Team*	Aprilia	27	40m 36.844s
12	Pere Tutusaus (SPA)	30	*Bancaja Aspar Team*	Aprilia	27	40m 36.881s
13	Marcel Schrotter (GER)	87	*Toni Mang Team*	Honda	27	40m 36.918s
14	Pablo Nieto (SPA)	22	*Onde 2000 KTM*	KTM	27	40m 37.465s
15	Efren Vazquez (SPA)	7	*Blusens Aprilia Junior*	Aprilia	27	40m 38.264s
16	Pol Espargaro (SPA)	44	*Belson Derbi*	Derbi	27	40m 41.486s
17	Stevie Bonsey (USA)	51	*Degraaf Grand Prix*	Aprilia	27	40m 41.582s
18	Takaaki Nakagami (JPN)	73	*I.C. Team*	Aprilia	27	40m 57.950s
19	Marvin Fritz (GER)	85	*Kiefer Bos Sotin Jnr Team*	Seel	27	41m 01.959s
20	Alexis Masbou (FRA)	5	*Loncin Racing*	Loncin	27	41m 17.912s
21	Louis Rossi (FRA)	69	*FFM Honda GP 125*	Honda	27	41m 18.965s
22	Robert Muresan (ROU)	95	*Grizzly Gas Kiefer Racing*	Aprilia	27	41m 20.066s
23	Marco Ravaioli (ITA)	72	*Matteoni Racing*	Aprilia	27	41m 20.564s
24	Tobias Siegert (GER)	41	*Adac Nordbayern e.v.*	Aprilia	26	40m 59.273s
	Lorenzo Zanetti (ITA)	8	*ISPA KTM Aran*	KTM	25	DNF
	Tomoyoshi Koyama (JPN)	71	*ISPA KTM Aran*	KTM	24	DNF
	Raffaele de Rosa (ITA)	35	*Onde 2000 KTM*	KTM	22	DNF
	Jules Cluzel (FRA)	16	*Loncin Racing*	Loncin	19	DNF
	Sergio Gadea (SPA)	33	*Bancaja Aspar Team*	Aprilia	15	DNF
	Robin Lasser (GER)	21	*Grizzly Gas Kiefer Racing*	Aprilia	15	DNF
	Joan Olive (SPA)	6	*Belson Derbi*	Derbi	14	DNF
	Sebastian Kreuziger (GER)	88	*RZT-Racing*	Honda	14	DNF
	Michael Ranseder (AUT)	60	*I.C. Team*	Aprilia	12	DNF
	Bastien Chesaux (SWI)	48	*S3+ WTR San Marino Team*	Aprilia	9	DNF
	Danny Webb (GBR)	99	*Degraaf Grand Prix*	Aprilia	5	DNF
	Hugo van den Berg (NED)	56	*Degraaf Grand Prix*	Aprilia	4	DNF
	Randy Krummenacher (SWI)	34	*Red Bull KTM 125*	KTM	3	DNF
	Eric Hubsch (GER)	86	*Team Sachsenring*	Aprilia	2	DNF
	Esteve Rabat (SPA)	12	*Repsol KTM 125cc*	KTM	27	EXC

Fastest lap: di Meglio, 1m 27.584s, 93.759mph/150.890km/h.

Lap record: Gabor Talmacsi, HUN (Aprilia), 1m 26.909s, 94.487mph/152.062km/h (2007).

Event best maximum speed: Talmacsi, 130.6mph/210.1km/h (qualifying practice no. 2).

Qualifying: **1** Talmacsi, 1m 27.552s; **2** Smith, 1m 27.645s; **3** Bradl, 1m 27.921s; **4** Corsi, 1m 28.038s; **5** Olive, 1m 28.045s; **6** di Meglio, 1m 28.123s; **7** Koyama, 1m 28.363s; **8** de Rosa, 1m 28.410s; **9** Cortese, 1m 28.465s; **10** Rabat, 1m 28.499s; **11** Webb, 1m 28.535s; **12** Gadea, 1m 28.559s; **13** Bonsey, 1m 28.572s; **14** Terol, 1m 28.622s; **15** Espargaro, 1m 28.702s; **16** Redding, 1m 28.732s; **17** Krummenacher, 1m 28.754s; **18** Nieto, 1m 28.759s; **19** Marquez, 1m 28.831s; **20** Schrotter, 1m 28.852s; **21** Aegerter, 1m 28.870s; **22** Ranseder, 1m 28.935s; **23** Vazquez, 1m 28.944s; **24** Iannone, 1m 28.964s; **25** Nakagami, 1m 29.007s; **26** Cluzel, 1m 29.231s; **27** Zanetti, 1m 29.232s; **28** Lasser, 1m 29.307s; **29** van den Berg, 1m 29.308s; **30** Fritz, 1m 29.552s; **31** Tutusaus, 1m 29.618s; **32** Muresan, 1m 29.638s; **33** Masbou, 1m 29.821s; **34** Kreuziger, 1m 30.074s; **35** Ravaioli, 1m 30.739s; **36** Hubsch, 1m 30.947s; **37** Siegert, 1m 30.971s; **38** Chesaux, 1m 30.983s; **39** Rossi, 1m 31.308s.

Fastest race laps: **1** di Meglio, 1m 27.584s; **2** Smith, 1m 27.681s; **3** Corsi, 1m 27.865s; **4** Talmacsi, 1m 27.950s; **5** Bradl, 1m 28.042s; **6** Terol, 1m 28.321s; **7** de Rosa, 1m 28.551s; **8** Cortese, 1m 28.586s; **9** Olive, 1m 28.650s; **10** Redding, 1m 28.667s; **11** Rabat, 1m 28.800s; **12** Bonsey, 1m 28.944s; **13** Nieto, 1m 28.999s; **14** Tutusaus, 1m 29.035s; **15** Schrotter, 1m 29.050s; **16** Espargaro, 1m 29.068s; **17** Iannone, 1m 29.144s; **18** Marquez, 1m 29.156s; **19** Aegerter, 1m 29.164s; **20** Vazquez, 1m 29.178s; **21** Koyama, 1m 29.259s; **22** Gadea, 1m 29.302s; **23** Nakagami, 1m 29.385s; **24** Fritz, 1m 29.845s; **25** Lasser, 1m 29.855s; **26** Ranseder, 1m 29.880s; **27** Cluzel, 1m 29.904s; **28** Webb, 1m 30.233s; **29** Muresan, 1m 30.584s; **30** Masbou, 1m 30.639s; **31** Rossi, 1m 30.697s; **32** Ravaioli, 1m 30.725s; **33** Zanetti, 1m 30.864s; **34** Krummenacher, 1m 31.467s; **35** Chesaux, 1m 31.491s; **36** van den Berg, 1m 31.726s; **37** Siegert, 1m 31.788s; **38** Kreuziger, 1m 32.463s; **39** Hubsch, 1m 33.847s.

World Championship: **1** di Meglio, 166; **2** Corsi, 136; **3** Talmacsi, 109; **4** Bradl, 101; **5** Olive, 94; **6** Terol, 91; **7** Smith, 79; **8** Espargaro, 75; **9** Cortese, 68; **10** Redding, 65; **11** Gadea, 62; **12** Iannone, 60; **13** Bonsey, 39; **14** Marquez, 33; **15** de Rosa, 30; **16** Webb, 26; **17** Rabat, 24; **18** Koyama, 22; **19** Aegerter, 22; **20** Ranseder, 19; **21** Vazquez, 15; **22** Nieto, 13; **23** Zanetti, 10; **24** Krummenacher, 10; **25** Nakagami, 9; **26** Tutusaus, 9; **27** Bianco, 8; **28** Schrotter, 3; **29** Masbou and van den Berg, 1.

UNITED STATES | GP
LAGUNA SECA

Above: A kiss for the Corkscrew. Rossi celebrates a classic win.

Right: Right: Respect lost? Stoner's expression says it all.
Photographs: Gold & Goose

Far right: A move too far. Rossi had missed the Corkscrew entry and was within a hair's breadth of crashing. Stoner had no choice but to let him by.
Photograph: Andrew Wheeler/ automotophoto

THE importance of the 2008 US GP can hardly be exaggerated. For the MotoGP class only and the last round before the summer break, it proved to be a cornerstone of the year, and certainly the fulcrum of the championship.

Racing first – and what a race: the showdown between Rossi and Stoner that reinforced the former's reputation as one of the greatest of all time, and showed the latter to be ... well, still a rookie by comparison. Rossi, on a slower motorcycle, thrilled a crowd of almost 50,000 as he used every trick in the book and invented a few new ones. His Yamaha was as wide as a bus and always in the way. Whenever the Ducati did find a way past, it suddenly became as narrow as a wraith and slipped ahead again. Stoner was undone, and there was no other reason than the rider himself. The result was that he ran off the track, although really he shouldn't have fallen – that was because of an unexpectedly soft patch of gravel. It was only fair that he was able to remount and still finish second. If nothing else, it showed by how much the pair of them had outclassed everybody else in the race.

The other story was all about tyres – Michelin tyres. The French company was undone too, this time by its own hand and with far-reaching consequences.

The story goes back almost to 1973, when Michelin entered GP racing. Three years later, it won the title for the first time with Barry Sheene. Since then, it has done so on 25 other occasions, including a run of several years of domination leading up to Hayden's win in 2006. It saw off rival Dunlop, and for a long period MotoGP ran under an effective single-tyre rule. It was dur-

ing this time that the company's reputation for arrogance and for manipulative control was cemented. It was obvious that Michelin would win every race, and it seemed that the company's operatives could decide which rider that would be. Perhaps that is putting it too strongly, but only slightly.

The 2008 Laguna disaster had its roots in the previous year's race, when blazing heat and an abrasive surface had ripped tyres to shreds. A more recent key event had occurred three weeks before the race, when Hayden arranged for a tyre test with ex-GP racer Doug Chandler on a Superbike. Michelin declined the invitation. It would cost the company dear. Instead, engineers based the selection of tyres on 2007's experience, allowing for the increase in overall bike performance. It was all wrong. Not only were the temperatures much lower – 30°C in 2007 compared to 18°C in 2008 – but also the track surface had mellowed.

It would be a considerable understatement to say that the hopeful US riders, former winner Hayden and wannabe Edwards, were dismayed when presented with the range of tyres from which to make their pre-race selection. Edwards's favoured front wasn't on the menu, neither was Hayden's preferred rear. Nicky had looked at the range, he explained, and said, 'This is way too hard. And they said, "Well we don't have nothing softer."'

Such was the difficulty in getting the rubber to a working temperature that on the second day, some riders even resorted to treaded intermediate tyres to get a lap time.

By then, Pedrosa had left, not only because of his

growing lack of confidence in the tyres, but also, more importantly, because his left hand and wrist injuries made it impossible to ride on this intensely physical track. He'd struggled to a lowly 15th on day one and left the next morning, explaining his departure in a written statement. Pain killing pills in the morning had had little effect; an injection for the afternoon was little better. 'I did a nine-lap run and it felt like 40 laps. When I woke, I had a lot of pain and the fingers were very swollen. I knew I couldn't finish the race,' he said, adding, 'At least I tried. If I had stayed at home, I would never have known if I could have ridden.'

It was too late for anyone to take his place, but there were two US hopefuls already on track. Ben Spies was a scheduled wild-card for Suzuki, and although he blotted his copybook in practice with a first-ever MotoGP tumble, and was somewhat swamped in the early laps, he pushed through impressively to eighth, and almost seventh. It was not enough to secure the full-time place he sought with the team, however.

The other US rider was Jamie Hacking, actually British born, on the Kawasaki in place of the injured Hopkins. Aged 37, the AMA rider realised that his own GP hopes were long past, but he raced strongly, finishing well ahead of his erstwhile team-mate, West, who had been the most spectacular victim in practice of the tricky entrance to Turn Three, injuring his back. Spies and Nakano fell at the same place, while de Angelis tumbled later on the lap, fracturing his thumb. Hopkins attended the race in a golf cart, having been told to keep weight off his recovering leg.

The shortest, and in some ways trickiest, track of the

Left: Part-time GP men Spies and Hacking head Elias's Ducati.
Photograph: Gold & Goose

Right: Pioneers and heroes: American world champions are (*standing, from left*) Eddie Lawson, Freddie Spencer, Kenny Roberts Junior, Nicky Hayden and (*seated*) Wayne Rainey, Kenny Roberts, Kevin Schwantz.
Photograph: Martin Heath

Below right: English-born US veteran Jamie Hacking confers with crew chief Fiorenzo Fanali.

Below far right: Top guns – actor Tom Cruise wishes real racer Nicky Hayden luck.
Photographs: Gold & Goose

year made its usual impact on the ex-250 new boys. Lorenzo cited the blind and fast Turn One as having made the biggest impression; Dovizioso picked the Corkscrew. 'It is a mad track, in both a good and bad way,' said the Italian. The Corkscrew 'gives you so much fear at first. You do not see the descent to the left, but you have to keep the gas on as long as possible. I followed Valentino Rossi for a while to learn the correct trajectory.' This corner remained tricky, in spite of the approach having been flattened at the behest of the Safety Commission.

There were smiles at Yamaha, as it was announced that not only had Edwards's contract been renewed for one more year, but also, more importantly, the somewhat protracted negotiations with Rossi had reached a conclusion. In the American's case, he had been flirting with Kawasaki and hinting broadly about how the unsponsored team needed to up its offer. Now he joked that the 'deciding factor was probably in Sachsenring when Hervé [Poncharal] come to my motor home and he was on his hands and knees, and he was crying a little bit, and he was just begging me to stay, and he pulled his wallet out and he had five euros in it. And I took it.'

Rossi, without his long-standing management team following 2007's tax problems, had done his own negotiating, and had spoken often at the preceding races of how it was progressing, step by step. All the same, he took everyone by surprise with the announcement that he had signed up for not one more year, but two. Those rivals hoping that the end of his career was in sight sighed a sigh of something like despair. Rossi would un-

derline those feelings on Sunday.

The ceremony of the Champions' Towers, begun in Britain, was a reminder of an era of racing when US riders could do no wrong. The presentation hosted a galaxy of stars, from Kenny Roberts in the 1970s to Kevin Schwantz in the 1990s, encompassing Freddie Spencer, Eddie Lawson and Wayne Rainey, and adding Kenny Roberts Junior and Nicky Hayden as a postscript. Star-struck, Hayden said, 'Even sitting here it doesn't seem real to be on this line-up. I'm almost embarrassed because of the results I've put up the last two years. I mean, Kenny is the godfather of this whole thing.'

MOTOGP RACE – 32 laps

In effect, this was two races: a spellbinding one up front, and a fairly exciting second race, only devalued by being so far away from the action.

The battle for the lead will be remembered for years: a protracted, but ultimately decisive, fight between the two main title contenders. Speed versus craftiness, youth versus experience. And a quite astonishing level of aggression from Rossi, whom many thought might now be old enough to know better. To entertain such thoughts, however, would be to seriously underestimate not only his sheer talent, but also the extraordinary depth of his determination.

Stoner had claimed a record-breaking pole, his fifth in a row, by almost half a second from Rossi, with Hayden completing the front row and Lorenzo leading the second. Stoner had dominated every session, and everyone expected him to run away. Asked on race eve what he

would need to beat him, Rossi quipped, 'A 30-second start. Or a gun.' As it turned out, all he needed was never to give Stoner the chance to run off ahead.

Stoner did take off in the lead, but first time into the Corkscrew, Rossi forced his way past. The race was on, and over the line Rossi led all 32 laps except for the 13th. But the lap chart does not tell the whole story. Stoner overtook Rossi several times, but on each occasion the Italian came straight back at him.

Lap four was typical. Stoner got a good drive out of the last corner and used his speed to find a faster entry into the tight Turn Two. Rossi daringly and narrowly outbraked him into Turn Five; Stoner came back on the run into the Corkscrew; Rossi tried to hold him off, ran off the outside of the tricky downhill plunge, almost crashed as he ran across the dirt inside the second apex, but recovered to regain the lead, forcing Stoner to slow and run wide to avoid a collision.

There was more of the same, sporadically: Stoner passing, Rossi fighting straight back. Until Stoner seemed to settled for a while, to await his chance to make a decisive move. It all came to a head on lap 24.

Once again, Stoner surged past through the daunting Turn One. Astonishingly, Rossi managed to get inside under braking for Turn Two, forcing Stoner wide. But the Australian attacked immediately once more into the right-hand Turn Three. With his inside line, it looked as though he had the corner. Rossi simply wouldn't concede, however, holding on to the outside line even though it took him across the kerb on the exit. It was almost an invitation to Stoner to nudge him just that little bit wider.

For the rest of the lap, Stoner stared at the Yamaha's back wheel – all the way to the hard braking zone for the final corner. Then it all went wrong. He was a little later on the brakes and his Ducati wriggled, then he swerved to the left to avoid hitting the back of the Yamaha. He went off on the exit, and he might have made it back to the track but for running into a patch of deeper gravel. At walking speed, he was down, remounting directly to rejoin without losing second. Even if he hadn't fallen, however, it would have made little difference. The race of the year was over.

Was it the Corkscrew incident or the last-corner brake check that made the young Australian spitting mad, or just the taste of a thorough drubbing by a rider on a slower bike? Stoner commented after the race that Rossi's riding had been beyond sporting. 'I've been racing for many years, but for me some passes went past the point. I was disappointed by the way he was riding. I frigging nearly went into the gravel so many times. I'd have preferred a bit of a cleaner battle,' he said. 'I've lost a bit of respect for him.'

Rossi took the criticism with a winner's grin. 'After a hard race, it's normal,' he said. 'Every overtake was very clear for me. We never touched. I was stronger in braking, so I tried to use that to my advantage. For me, it was fun, like old-style racing.' Certainly it was one of his hardest-fought and finest wins ever, and when the pair met again after the summer break, a more reflective Stoner apologised privately for his comments.

Behind this pair, a lively race was depleted on only the fifth of the track's 11 turns when Lorenzo had another of his spectacular, trade-mark high-side crashes. He had just moved into fourth, behind Hayden. The Spaniard would need the forthcoming break to recover from fresh ankle injuries.

That left Hayden hotly pursued by track novice Dovizioso, fast-starting Vermeulen and Elias, with another off-the-line flier, Toseland, disputing the next slot with de Puniet.

Elias, enjoying the benefit of the new rear suspension link received in Germany, left the group on lap six after running off the track and dropping to ninth. By now, Hayden, Vermeulen and Dovizioso were clear of the pursuit; two laps later, Vermeulen was ahead of Hayden as well, moving away for a long and lonely ride to third, his second successive rostrum at the track.

Hayden managed to hold off the hard-pressing Dovizioso until lap 21, by which time de Puniet was closing up on the pair, although he never got close enough to challenge. The American had moved up again to attack the Italian in the closing laps, but was deeply disappointed – at a race he had previously won – to fail by seven-tenths of a second.

Toseland, pushed hard by Nakano, had led the next group for most of the race; behind him, Ben Spies had succumbed early to temporary team-mate Capirossi, and then found himself behind Elias and a resurgent Melandri, for once having a strong ride. By lap seven, the American was down in 12th, but from then on he started moving forward steadily, being promoted on lap ten when Melandri spoiled his rare good afternoon by running off and dropping right to the back.

The AMA triple champion repassed Edwards and got Elias also on lap nine, then benefited as Capirossi dropped back. By half-distance, he was closing a five-second gap to Nakano; by then, second wild-card Jamie Hacking, in a mighty impressive ride, was with him, although thereafter he was unable to match his pace.

By the penultimate lap, Spies was up to seventh, ahead of Toseland, but by then Elias had also found a closing burst, reversing the positions on the last lap. Toseland was ninth, Nakano dropping away at the end, followed by Hacking.

A long way back, Guintoli had come through from last on lap one and headed de Angelis, pushing hard in spite of his broken thumb. A disconsolate Edwards had fallen back by some five seconds; the pained Capirossi took the last point; while Melandri was closing fast on him by the finish.

West was a lap down, also in pain after his tumble in practice and slowed by his off-track excursion.

Above: Whenever Stoner got ahead, Rossi made sure it was never for long.
Photograph: Martin Heath

Left: Stoner recovers in the gravel trap, so far ahead that he still took an easy second.

Far left: Corkscrew unplugged. Capirossi heads Spies, Elias, Edwards and Hacking into the dizzy plunge.

Below: Almost unoticed, Chris Vermeulen finished third for Suzuki
Photographs: Gold & Goose

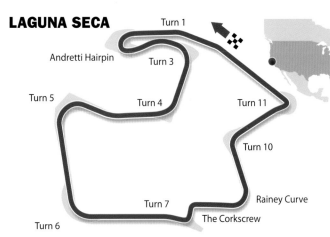

LAGUNA SECA

Andretti Hairpin · Turn 1 · Turn 3 · Turn 5 · Turn 4 · Turn 11 · Turn 10 · Rainey Curve · Turn 7 · The Corkscrew · Turn 6

Circuit 3.602km /2.238 miles

MOTOGP

RACE: 32 laps, 71.776 miles/115.520km • Weather: Dry • Air 21°C • Humidity 42% • Track 34°C

Pos.	Rider	Nat.	No.	Team	Machine	Tyres	Laps	Time & speed (mph/km/h)
1	Valentino Rossi	ITA	46	Fiat Yamaha Team	Yamaha	B	32	44m 04.311s 97.723mph/ 157.270km/h
2	Casey Stoner	AUS	1	Ducati Team	Ducati	B	32	44m 17.312s
3	Chris Vermeulen	AUS	7	Rizla Suzuki MotoGP	Suzuki	B	32	44m 30.920s
4	Andrea Dovizioso	ITA	4	JiR Team Scot MotoGP	Honda	M	32	44m 39.212s
5	Nicky Hayden	USA	69	Repsol Honda Team	Honda	M	32	44m 39.974s
6	Randy de Puniet	FRA	14	LCR Honda MotoGP	Honda	M	32	44m 41.979s
7	Toni Elias	SPA	24	Alice Team	Ducati	B	32	44m 45.940s
8	Ben Spies	USA	11	Rizla Suzuki MotoGP	Suzuki	B	32	44m 46.238s
9	James Toseland	GBR	52	Tech 3 Yamaha	Yamaha	M	32	44m 47.330s
10	Shinya Nakano	JPN	56	San Carlo Honda Gresini	Honda	B	32	44m 48.702s
11	Jamie Hacking	USA	12	Kawasaki Racing Team	Kawasaki	B	32	44m 50.569s
12	Sylvain Guintoli	FRA	50	Alice Team	Ducati	B	32	44m 59.584s
13	Alex de Angelis	RSM	15	San Carlo Honda Gresini	Honda	B	32	44m 59.832s
14	Colin Edwards	USA	5	Tech 3 Yamaha	Yamaha	M	32	45m 06.691s
15	Loris Capirossi	ITA	65	Rizla Suzuki MotoGP	Suzuki	B	32	45m 12.518s
16	Marco Melandri	ITA	33	Ducati Team	Ducati	B	32	45m 15.273s
17	Anthony West	AUS	13	Kawasaki Racing Team	Kawasaki	B	31	44m 34.872s
	Jorge Lorenzo	SPA	48	Fiat Yamaha Team	Yamaha	M	0	DNF

Fastest lap: Casey Stoner, on lap 15, 1m 21.488s, 99.098mph/159.483km/h (record).

Previous lap record: Casey Stoner, AUS (Ducati), 1m 22.542s, 97.833mph/157.447km/h (2007).

Event best maximum speed: Casey Stoner, 163.3mph/262.8km/h (qualifying practice).

QUALIFYING: 19 July 2008

Weather: Dry

Air: 23°C Humidity: 42% Track: 36°C

Pos.	Rider	Time
1	Stoner	1m 20.700s
2	Rossi	1m 21.147s
3	Hayden	1m 21.430s
4	Lorenzo	1m 21.636s
5	Toseland	1m 21.848s
6	de Puniet	1m 21.921s
7	Edwards	1m 21.947s
8	Vermeulen	1m 21.971s
9	Dovizioso	1m 21.974s
10	Elias	1m 21.999s
11	Capirossi	1m 22.039s
12	Nakano	1m 22.092s
13	Spies	1m 22.127s
14	Guintoli	1m 22.719s
15	Melandri	1m 22.957s
16	de Angelis	1m 23.035s
17	Hacking	1m 23.309s
18	West	1m 24.525s

Grid order	1	2	3	4	5	6	7	8	9	10	11	12	13	14	15	16	17	18	19	20	21	22	23	24	25	26	27	28	29	30	31	32	
1 STONER	46	46	46	46	46	46	46	46	46	46	46	46	1	46	46	46	46	46	46	46	46	46	46	46	46	46	46	46	46	46	46	46	1
46 ROSSI	1	1	1	1	1	1	1	1	1	1	1	1	46	1	1	1	1	1	1	1	1	1	1	1	1	1	1	1	1	1	1	1	2
69 HAYDEN	69	69	69	69	69	69	69	7	7	7	7	7	7	7	7	7	7	7	7	7	7	7	7	7	7	7	7	7	7	7	7	7	3
48 LORENZO	4	4	7	7	7	7	7	69	69	69	69	69	69	69	69	69	69	69	69	69	4	4	4	4	4	4	4	4	4	4	4	4	4
52 TOSELAND	7	7	4	4	4	4	4	4	4	4	4	4	4	4	4	4	4	4	69	69	69	69	69	69	69	69	69	69	69	69	69	69	5
14 de PUNIET	24	24	24	24	24	52	52	52	52	52	52	14	14	14	14	14	14	14	14	14	14	14	14	14	14	14	14	14	14	14	14	14	6
5 EDWARDS	52	52	52	52	14	14	14	14	14	14	52	52	52	52	52	52	52	52	52	52	52	52	52	52	52	52	11	11	24	7
7 VERMEULEN	52	14	14	14	14	56	65	56	56	56	56	56	56	56	56	56	56	56	56	56	56	56	56	56	56	56	56	56	52	24	11		8
4 DOVISIOSO	56	56	56	56	56	65	56	65	33	65	65	11	11	11	11	11	11	11	11	11	11	11	11	11	11	11	11	24	52	52		9
24 ELIAS	11	11	11	65	65	24	24	33	65	11	11	24	12	12	12	12	12	12	12	12	12	12	24	24	24	24	56	56	56		10
65 CAPIROSSI	5	65	65	11	11	11	33	5	11	24	5	12	24	24	24	24	24	24	24	12	12	12	12	12	12	12	12	12	12		11
56 NAKANO	65	33	33	33	33	13	11	24	24	5	24	65	65	65	5	5	5	5	5	5	5	50	50	50	50	50	50	50	50		12
11 SPIES	33	5	5	5	5	5	11	12	5	12	12	5	5	5	65	65	65	65	50	50	50	50	50	15	15	15	15	15	15		13
50 GUINTOLI	13	13	13	12	12	12	12	12	12	13	13	50	50	50	50	50	50	50	50	65	15	15	15	15	15	5	5	5	5	5		14
33 MELANDRI	15	12	12	13	13	13	13	15	50	13	15	15	15	15	15	15	15	65	65	65	65	65	65	65	65	65	65	65	65		15
15 de ANGELIS	12	15	15	15	15	15	15	15	50	15	50	13	13	13	13	13	13	33	33	33	33	33	33	33	33	33	33	33	33		16
12 HACKING	50	50	50	50	50	50	50	50	33	33	33	33	33	33	33	33	33	13	13	13	13	13	13	13	13	13	13				
13 WEST																															

FASTEST RACE LAPS

	Rider	Lap	Time
1	Stoner	15	1m 21.488s
2	Rossi	17	1m 21.713s
3	Vermeulen	11	1m 22.499s
4	Elias	29	1m 22.795s
5	Hayden	11	1m 22.915s
6	Spies	27	1m 22.966s
7	Nakano	10	1m 23.014s
8	Dovizioso	11	1m 23.047s
9	Hacking	18	1m 23.063s
10	de Puniet	14	1m 23.070s
11	de Angelis	30	1m 23.107s
12	Melandri	25	1m 23.142s
13	Toseland	8	1m 23.216s
14	Guintoli	30	1m 23.332s
15	Capirossi	4	1m 23.378s
16	Edwards	17	1m 23.394s
17	West	10	1m 24.226s

OFFICIAL TIMEKEEPER

RIDER STANDINGS

After 11 Rounds

1	Valentino Rossi	212
2	Casey Stoner	187
3	Dani Pedrosa	171
4	Jorge Lorenzo	114
5	Andrea Dovizioso	103
6	Colin Edwards	100
7	Chris Vermeulen	89
8	Nicky Hayden	84
9	James Toseland	72
10	Shinya Nakano	70
11	Loris Capirossi	61
12	Toni Elias	46
13	Alex de Angelis	41
14	Randy de Puniet	40
15	Sylvain Guintoli	38
16	John Hopkins	32
17	Marco Melandri	32
18	Anthony West	22
19	Ben Spies	10
20	Jamie Hacking	5
21	Tadayuki Okada	2

TEAM STANDINGS

After 11 Rounds

1	Fiat Yamaha Team	326
2	Repsol Honda Team	255
3	Ducati Team	219
4	Tech 3 Yamaha	172
5	Rizla Suzuki MotoGP	152
6	San Carlo Honda Gresini	111
7	JiR Team Scot MotoGP	103
8	Alice Team	84
9	Kawasaki Racing Team	59
10	LCR Honda MotoGP	40

CONSTRUCTOR STANDINGS

After 11 Rounds

1	Yamaha	241
2	Honda	197
3	Ducati	192
4	Suzuki	112
5	Kawasaki	52

CZECH REPUBLIC|GP
BRNO

Stoner has already gone as they jostle into the first corner. Hopkins (21) will come out of it ahead of Rossi (46). West is right behind his team-mate.
Photograph: Gold & Goose

AFTER the summer break, the change of direction Rossi had initiated at Laguna Seca continued, more strongly than he could have hoped or expected. His points lead doubled to 50 as Stoner crashed out for a second race in succession. This time, he had been in the lead, and this time he wasn't able to restart. Zero points.

Later the Australian would deny that he'd caved in under pressure: 'I've never been rattled in my life. Why would I be rattled now?' But it looked like it. He'd dominated practice and qualifying, and led away, but Rossi had been remorseless in pursuit. Subsequently, and rather obliquely, Stoner blamed a tyre problem for the crash, which happened as he entered a downhill right-hander at exactly the same speed as before. Either way, he was going too fast and paid a severe price.

If the previous two races had been incendiary devices in the tyre war, Brno was the big bomb. Central to the issue was a third successive problem race for Michelin. A fully resurfaced track proved a killer to the French front tyres: those that gripped wouldn't last more than 12 laps, according to Edwards; those that lasted the race wouldn't grip.

The consequences on track were obvious. In free practice, the best Michelin man was Edwards in seventh, the rest all languishing and complaining. In qualifying, which was streaming wet (like 'a change of season', as Rossi put it), two Michelin users failed to make the 107-per-cent cut. Both were double world champions, Jorge Lorenzo and James Toseland. They were allowed to start all the same, not least because their exclusion would have dropped the numbers to just 15. In the race,

the top Michelin finisher, Dovisioso, was ninth. The worst off was Pedrosa, still nursing left-wrist and index-finger injuries. He had qualified 12th and had a dismal race to 15th, blaming the tyres and saying afterwards, 'I felt impotent and ashamed.' All weekend it had been obvious that he had been in more trouble than his lingering injuries: using conspicuously more traction control out of the corners and clearly thoroughly unsettled.

Individually, it was Pedrosa, or rather his mentor and manager, Alberto Puig, who caused the most trouble. The latter, with the surprising backing of HRC, had tried to foment a rebellion among the Michelin users, insisting that they should refuse even to go to the starting grid. In this, he was unsuccessful, sowing instead the seeds of increasingly bitter personal feuds that would grow as the season progressed. Even as the grid was forming up, Puig was still attempting to convince the likes of Tech 3 to pull out. This caused some disquiet within the Honda team, since he was wearing Repsol Honda uniform.

The disquiet was not shared at the top. One day later, HRC President Masumi Hamane gave a blistering interview to *MOTOCOURSE* technical correspondent Neil Spalding, saying that the loyalty to Michelin expressed less than a year before had come to an end, and that he would be switching the factory team to Bridgestone. Nobody could know quite how soon.

There was a clue, however, in the provision of a full factory RS212V for Nakano, in the Gresini team. Shinya was not the most obvious candidate in terms of performance – that would have been rookie Dovizioso. Importantly, though, the Japanese veteran, able to talk to

Left: Erratic, but explosive – Elias scored a surprise second place.

Below left: Colin Edwards and crew chief Gary Reynders present a study in frustration.

Bottom left: Pedrosa and Puig on the grid. The rider was left 'impotent and ashamed'.

Bottom right: Stoner's race ended abruptly.

Photographs: Gold & Goose

factory engineers in their native language, used Bridge-stones, giving the factory a head start in determining how settings would need to be revised.

Collectively, the Michelin riders also played a signifi-cant role in the ultimate introduction of a one-tyre rule. Increasing safety concerns prompted Dorna's Ezpeleta to call a MotoGP riders' meeting to discuss ways of cut-ting the rise in corner speed, although such a rise was disputed by many and hardly supported by data. (In fact, the smaller classes had a higher mid-corner speed, al-though tyre advances had much improved MotoGP entry and exit speeds.)

Many suggestions were forthcoming. The only one to attract universal support, Rossi said later, was to bring back 990s. Another was to switch to a single-tyre rule. Rossi thought that this had received more votes for than against; Vermeulen's memory differed. 'There were only about five for it, all on Michelins … and they hadn't been saying that earlier in the season, when it was Bridgestone having problems.' Nonetheless, Ezpeleta gave this as a major reason in support of the single-tyre move later in the year.

The tide was going that way. With the first eight fin-ishers on Bridgestone – and five different makes in the top five – Rossi's 15.004-second winning margin was the biggest ever in the four-stroke era in the dry. The last time a race had been won by more than 15 sec-onds had been in 1997 in Australia, where Mick Doohan had done so by 22.077 seconds.

Tyres and politics aside, the summer break had left riders not only refreshed, but also in many cases recu-perated. Pedrosa, as we've observed, was still in pain. Compatriot Lorenzo was limping again after his US mis-adventure and pronounced himself only 60 per cent re-covered 'for walking, but 90 per cent for riding'. Hopkins was also back and upbeat, although perhaps a little over-optimistic, since pain and fatigue caused him to sit out much of the wet free practice. Even so, he said he was enjoying Kawasaki's latest engine and chassis up-grades. Capirossi, his ugly arm injury all but fully healed,

had more right to be bullish and went on to claim his first rostrum for Suzuki.

But there was a fresh victim – Nicky Hayden had frac-tured his heel taking part in a so-called 'fun' event, the X Games for ESPN at Los Angeles. He'd been expecting to race in a Supermoto, '80 per cent pavement and 20 per cent dirt', and to be competitive, he said. Instead he had found the track to be more like Supercross, com-plete with a triple jump. He had soldiered on, but a heavy landing from said jump had injured his foot and kept him out of the Brno post-summer return. 'I'm really bummed out for HRC,' he said, in absentia.

A vignette of history repeating itself came in the 125 class when Stefan Bradl, twice on the rostrum already, took a very convincing maiden win. Stefan is the son of former 250 challenger Helmut Bradl, who had been the last German to win at Brno, back in 1991.

MOTOGP RACE – 22 laps

Stoner, although complaining of a virus, dominated in the dry on Friday, and in the damp on Saturday morn-ing. Qualifying was complicated by a sodden start, and those who waited for conditions to improve were pun-ished, for the rain only got worse. It was Stoner again for a sixth pole in succession, ahead of Rossi by better than a second. And Hopkins timed it just right for his first Kawasaki front row.

The erratically surprising rookie de Angelis was in the middle of the second row, flanked by wet specialists Ver-meulen and West, also his best on a Kawasaki. West had set his time late in the session, when standing water and fearsome aquaplaning had consigned most to the pits.

Pedrosa ended up a gloomy 12th, Dovizioso and Ed-wards languished at the back of the legitimate grid, and special provision was made for non-qualifiers Toseland and Lorenzo.

Mercifully, race day was dry, with 146,000 packing the hillsides. They saw Stoner set off like the avenging angel, better than a second ahead of the pursuing Rossi

at the end of one lap. He set a new record on lap five, but had only got away by a couple more tenths. The pressure was on as Rossi took two of them back on lap six. And then it happened. Running into the first downhill right, Stoner's front wheel tucked, the rear spun out simultaneously and he was down. As Rossi flashed past, he scrambled to his bike and ran on down the hill, trying in vain to restart it. Later he reported that a perfectly shaped stone had found its way into a perfectly shaped hole in the fuel injection system. His race was done.

Rossi might have attacked earlier had Hopkins not nipped inside into the first corner to delay him. But by the time this happened, he was ten seconds clear of the rest. By now, Vermeulen was ahead of Hopkins, with Capirossi behind. A second back came Elias all in a rush, his new rear suspension coming good and his progress spectacular. He had already passed West and Dovizioso in one lap, after moving through from tenth on lap one – he'd started 13th.

The first three were hard at it, especially the Suzuki team-mates with their identical bikes, but different styles: on one lap, they changed places three times. This helped Elias to close up, West on his heels. By lap nine, Elias had made it four scrapping over what had become second place.

The Spaniard was at his erratic best, going from fifth to second on lap ten and pulling away immediately. Rossi was more than 16 seconds clear, however, with 12 laps left. Elias would get no closer. In the same lap, a slip made by Vermeulen dropped him to the back of the group.

Capirossi hung on to third to the end, while West was ahead of Hopkins, whose tyre choice was starting to turn bad on him. As the American slowed, Nakano was also closing, the pair changing places on lap 16. On his new factory bike, the latter kept on moving by for fourth unchallenged, his best of the year; West's fifth was also his best by far. There would be more for Elias, but in the Australian's case it was a false dawn.

Vermeulen had closed a little by the end, but Hopkins had carried on slipping away backwards. On lap 20, slow-starting de Angelis, Dovizioso and Guintoli had caught up, while Melandri had also enjoyed a temporary revival of enthusiasm as he moved forwards. By the end, he'd passed all of them, including de Angelis on the last lap. Dovizioso was a couple of seconds behind, while Lorenzo was ahead of Hopkins, the first Michelin runners to finish and the trio close over the line. Guintoli was 12th, another second back.

The rest trailed in with various shades of the same Michelin story: tyres that wouldn't allow them to do more than tour around and around in the hope of staying on board to the chequered flag. Toseland was 30 seconds down, Edwards another ten and Pedrosa five more – a sorry parade.

De Puniet was the last finisher, missing points by less than a second after a typically up-and-down afternoon. He'd fallen early in the race to rejoin miles behind. Pushing on as ever, he would have been ahead of Pedrosa had there been one more lap.

250cc RACE – 20 laps

The 250s did a little better where the weather was concerned: wet on the first day, but drier for qualifying. Simoncelli took his second pole in succession, third of the year, from Debon, Barbera and Pasini.

The increasingly hirsute Italian led off pole, from Luthi, Debon, Kallio and Pasini. As so often, Bautista was a bit slower with a full tank.

Luthi was not there for long. On lap five, he ran wide out of the stadium section, over the kerb and on to a

patch of Astroturf, which is no more grippy than real turf. His bike snapped sideways, throwing him into the gravel.

Bautista had got past Pasini, who was losing touch. The Spaniard was almost two seconds adrift of the leaders, but closing. He'd cut it by a third when Debon made his first bid for the lead, on lap seven. Simoncelli seized it back on lap ten, and Bautista was on the move, having taken third off Kallio. At the same time, Barbera had followed along and soon would be challenging the Finn.

Debon took the lead once more on lap 12; now it was Bautista in second with Simoncelli third, and Kallio almost a second behind as he fought off Barbera. It looked as though the last five laps would be contested by just the three. With two laps to go, however, as Simoncelli led once more, Barbera had passed the KTM and both closed quickly, but not quite quickly enough to take part in the final battle. It was intense enough without them.

The last lap began with Simoncelli in front. Bautista dived past at once, but Simoncelli got him back on the run down to the bottom corner. He led up the final climb and on the run into the crucial last corner set – 90 degrees left and then 90 degrees right, but far too wide and fast to be called a chicane, and the scene of many last-lap dramas.

As they got there, Debon forced his way inside, putting the Gilera slightly off line – enough for Bautista to find a little gap as well.

They crossed the line in just over three-tenths of a second, Debon taking his second win by a quarter of a second. Barbera had a grandstand seat, just half a second behind, with Kallio trailing him. Simoncelli may have been robbed, but he had the consolation of extending his points lead.

Pasini had fallen back gradually to a group led at first by Aoyama and latterly by Takahashi, with Faubel and for a while Espargaro and Locatelli also involved. Only on the last lap did Takahashi get ahead of Pasini. Faubel was next, three seconds back; a similar distance away, Locatelli held off Espargaro for ninth.

Almost ten seconds behind, Wilairot managed to stay just ahead of Simon all the way. Both of them passed the fading Aoyama, who was struck by tyre problems on the last lap.

125cc RACE – 19 laps

Saturday's qualifying session was effectively rained off, but Friday had seen Talmacsi fulfil his spoken commitment to the swathe of Hungarian fans he expected with his second pole of the year. Terol, Iannone and Smith were alongside.

Smith led away and for two laps. On the third, however, Bradl leapt from fourth, past Talmacsi and Terol as well as the Briton, and led for the first time. But for a brief interruption by di Meglio on lap five, he held it to the end. By then, the Frenchman was his only remaining challenger, less than a second behind. It was a convincing maiden win.

Bradl had been under severe pressure from a big gang of ten for the first half of the race, until time whittled away his competitors. The first to drop back were Corsi and Redding, at half-distance. Soon afterwards, Cortese and Smith also fell away.

Talmacsi, Olive, di Meglio and Terol were still fiercely engaged, and their frantic combat helped the leader to draw away by more than 1.5 seconds on lap 14. At that point, di Meglio was in front and he managed to escape – but it was too late for him to get back on terms.

With Terol also losing touch, this left a massive scrap between Olive and Talmacsi for the last rostrum place. It lasted to the line, the Spaniard taking third by less than five-hundredths.

Terol, Smith and Cortese followed along; Espargaro led the next group from Iannone, Corsi and Redding.

Above: Like father, like son – Stefan Bradl took a convincing first 125 win.

Top left: West gained his best result of the year with fifth, but it was a false dawn.

Bottom left: The final countdown for a 250 thriller: Debon heads Simoncelli (58) and Bautista (19), with Barbera close behind.

Photographs: Gold & Goose

AUTODROM BRNO

Turn 5
Turn 6
Turn 9
Turn 1
Turn 4
Turn 7
Turn 8
Turn 3
Turn 12
Turn 11
Turn 2
Turn 13
Turn 1
Turn 14

Circuit 5.403km / 3.357 miles

MOTOGP

RACE: 22 laps, 73.854 miles/118.866km • Weather: Dry • Air 20°C • Humidity 33% • Track 29°C

Pos.	Rider	Nat.	No.	Team	Machine	Tyres	Laps	Time & speed (mph/km/h)
1	Valentino Rossi	ITA	46	*Fiat Yamaha Team*	Yamaha	B	22	43m 28.841s 101.920mph/ 164.025km/h
2	Toni Elias	SPA	24	*Alice Team*	Ducati	B	22	43m 43.845s
3	Loris Capirossi	ITA	65	*Rizla Suzuki MotoGP*	Suzuki	B	22	43m 50.530s
4	Shinya Nakano	JPN	56	*San Carlo Honda Gresini*	Honda	B	22	43m 54.700s
5	Anthony West	AUS	13	*Kawasaki Racing Team*	Kawasaki	B	22	43m 58.306s
6	Chris Vermeulen	AUS	7	*Rizla Suzuki MotoGP*	Suzuki	B	22	43m 59.449s
7	Marco Melandri	ITA	33	*Ducati Marlboro Team*	Ducati	B	22	44m 05.294s
8	Alex de Angelis	RSM	15	*San Carlo Honda Gresini*	Honda	B	22	44m 05.591s
9	Andrea Dovizioso	ITA	4	*JiR Team Scot MotoGP*	Honda	M	22	44m 07.663s
10	Jorge Lorenzo	SPA	48	*Fiat Yamaha Team*	Yamaha	M	22	44m 08.414s
11	John Hopkins	USA	21	*Kawasaki Racing Team*	Kawasaki	B	22	44m 08.451s
12	Sylvain Guintoli	FRA	50	*Alice Team*	Ducati	B	22	44m 09.733s
13	James Toseland	GBR	52	*Tech 3 Yamaha*	Yamaha	M	22	44m 40.331s
14	Colin Edwards	USA	5	*Tech 3 Yamaha*	Yamaha	M	22	44m 49.974s
15	Dani Pedrosa	SPA	2	*Repsol Honda Team*	Honda	M	22	45m 05.879s
16	Randy de Puniet	FRA	14	*LCR Honda MotoGP*	Honda	M	22	45m 07.248s
	Casey Stoner	USA	1	*Ducati Marlboro Team*	Ducati	B	6	11m 49.228s

Fastest lap: Casey Stoner, on lap 5, 1m 57.199s, 103.125mph/165.963km/h (record).

Previous lap record: Loris Capirossi, ITA (Ducati), 1m 58.157s, 102.289mph/164.618km/h (2006).

Event best maximum speed: Toni Elias, 187.0mph/301.0km/h (race).

QUALIFYING: 16 August 2008

Weather: Wet
Air: 12°C Humidity: 96% Track: 14°C

Pos.	Rider	Time
1	Stoner	2m 11.657s
2	Rossi	2m 12.846s
3	Hopkins	2m 12.959s
4	Vermeulen	2m 13.002s
5	de Angelis	2m 13.352s
6	West	2m 14.064s
7	de Puniet	2m 14.535s
8	Nakano	2m 14.718s
9	Capirossi	2m 14.805s
10	Guintoli	2m 14.861s
11	Melandri	2m 15.880s
12	Pedrosa	2m 16.032s
13	Elias	2m 16.510s
14	Dovizioso	2m 17.632s
15	Edwards	2m 20.074s
16	Toseland	2m 23.303s
17	Lorenzo	2m 23.701s

Grid order	1	2	3	4	5	6	7	8	9	10	11	12	13	14	15	16	17	18	19	20	21	22	
1 STONER	1	1	1	1	1	1	46	46	46	46	46	46	46	46	46	46	46	46	46	46	46	46	1
46 ROSSI	46	46	46	46	46	46	7	7	65	24	24	24	24	24	24	24	24	24	24	24	24	24	2
21 HOPKINS	21	21	21	21	7	7	65	65	7	65	65	65	65	65	65	65	65	65	65	65	65	65	3
7 VERMEULEN	13	7	7	7	21	21	21	21	21	13	13	13	13	13	13	13	56	56	56	56	56	56	4
15 de ANGELIS	7	13	65	65	65	65	24	24	24	13	21	21	21	21	21	56	56	13	13	13	13	13	5
13 WEST	2	4	13	13	24	24	13	13	13	7	7	7	7	7	56	21	7	7	7	7	7	7	6
14 de PUNIET	4	65	4	4	13	13	4	4	4	4	4	56	56	56	7	7	21	21	21	21	15	33	7
56 NAKANO	14	2	24	24	4	4	50	50	50	50	56	4	4	4	4	50	50	15	15	33	15	8
65 CAPIROSSI	65	24	2	50	50	50	56	56	56	56	50	50	50	50	50	15	15	4	4	21	4	9
50 GUINTOLI	50	14	50	2	15	56	15	15	15	15	15	15	15	15	15	4	4	50	33	4	48	10
33 MELANDRI	24	50	14	56	56	15	33	33	33	33	33	33	33	33	33	33	33	33	50	50	21	11
2 PEDROSA	56	56	56	15	14	33	2	48	48	48	48	48	48	48	48	48	48	48	48	48	50	12
24 ELIAS	15	15	15	14	2	2	48	2	52	52	52	52	52	52	52	52	52	52	52	52	52	13
4 DOVISIOSO	52	52	52	33	33	48	5	52	5	5	5	5	5	5	5	5	5	5	5	5	5	14
5 EDWARDS	5	33	33	52	52	5	52	5	2	2	2	2	2	2	2	2	2	2	2	2	2	15
52 TOSELAND	33	5	48	48	48	52	14	14	14	14	14	14	14	14	14	14	14	14	14	14	14	
48 LORENZO	48	48	5	5	5	14																

FASTEST RACE LAPS

Rider	Lap	Time
1	Stoner	5	1m 57.199s
2	Rossi	6	1m 57.228s
3	Nakano	15	1m 58.174s
4	Elias	16	1m 58.414s
5	Melandri	19	1m 58.441s
6	Capirossi	15	1m 58.497s
7	Vermeulen	3	1m 58.757s
8	Lorenzo	21	1m 58.995s
9	West	7	1m 59.136s
10	Hopkins	6	1m 59.230s
11	Guintoli	8	1m 59.306s
12	de Angelis	10	1m 59.336s
13	Dovizioso	20	1m 59.368s
14	de Puniet	21	1m 59.855s
15	Pedrosa	2	2m 00.320s
16	Edwards	6	2m 00.801s
17	Toseland	5	2m 00.953s

statistics

250cc
20 laps, 67.140 miles/108.060km

Pos. Rider (Nat.)	No.	Team	Machine	Laps	Time & speed
1 Alex Debon (SPA)	6	Lotus Aprilia	Aprilia	20	41m 08.168s 97.936mph/ 157.613km/h
2 Alvaro Bautista (SPA)	19	Mapfre Aspar Team	Aprilia	20	41m 08.448s
3 Marco Simoncelli (ITA)	58	Metis Gilera	Gilera	20	41m 08.493s
4 Hector Barbera (SPA)	21	Team Toth Aprilia	Aprilia	20	41m 08.995s
5 Mika Kallio (FIN)	36	Red Bull KTM 250	KTM	20	41m 09.417s
6 Yuki Takahashi (JPN)	72	JiR Team Scot 250	Honda	20	41m 21.881s
7 Mattia Pasini (ITA)	75	Polaris World	Aprilia	20	41m 21.994s
8 Hector Faubel (SPA)	55	Mapfre Aspar Team	Aprilia	20	41m 24.194s
9 Roberto Locatelli (ITA)	15	Metis Gilera	Gilera	20	41m 27.252s
10 Aleix Espargaro (SPA)	41	Lotus Aprilia	Aprilia	20	41m 28.860s
11 Ratthapark Wilairot (THA)	14	Thai Honda PTT SAG	Honda	20	41m 37.663s
12 Julian Simon (SPA)	60	Repsol KTM 250cc	KTM	20	41m 37.940s
13 Hiroshi Aoyama (JPN)	4	Red Bull KTM 250	KTM	20	41m 40.112s
14 Lukas Pesek (CZE)	52	Auto Kelly - CP	Aprilia	20	41m 44.482s
15 Alex Baldolini (ITA)	25	Matteoni Racing	Aprilia	20	41m 51.919s
16 Eugene Laverty (IRL)	50	Blusens Aprilia	Aprilia	20	41m 54.732s
17 Fabrizio Lai (ITA)	32	Campetella Racing	Gilera	20	42m 03.759s
18 Federico Sandi (ITA)	90	Matteoni Racing	Aprilia	20	42m 03.872s
19 Doni Tata Pradita (INA)	45	Yamaha Pertamina Indonesia	Yamaha	20	42m 32.492s
20 Toni Wirsing (GER)	94	Racing Team Germany	Honda	20	42m 47.591s
21 Russel Gomez (SPA)	7	Blusens Aprilia	Aprilia	20	43m 08.158s
Thomas Luthi (SWI)	12	Emmi - Caffe Latte	Aprilia	3	DNF
Karel Abraham (CZE)	17	Cardion AB Motoracing	Aprilia	2	DNF
Manuel Poggiali (RSM)	54	Campetella Racing	Gilera		DNS

Fastest lap: Debon, 2m 02.354s, 98.780mph/158.971km/h.

Lap record: Jorge Lorenzo, SPA (Aprilia), 2m 02.299s, 98.825mph/159.043km/h (2007).

Event best maximum speed: Barbera, 159.3mph/256.4km/h (race).

Qualifying: 1 Simoncelli, 2m 10.723s; 2 Debon, 2m 11.489s; 3 Barbera, 2m 11.578s; 4 Pasini, 2m 12.168s; 5 Luthi, 2m 12.762s; 6 Simon, 2m 13.074s; 7 Kallio, 2m 13.698s; 8 Takahashi, 2m 13.944s; 9 Pesek, 2m 13.970s; 10 Bautista, 2m 14.577s; 11 Baldolini, 2m 14.664s; 12 Laverty, 2m 14.918s; 13 Lai, 2m 15.103s; 14 Faubel, 2m 15.416s; 15 Abraham, 2m 15.659s; 16 Aoyama, 2m 15.785s; 17 Locatelli, 2m 15.836s; 18 Espargaro, 2m 16.552s; 19 Sandi, 2m 17.550s; 20 Wilairot, 2m 18.009s; 21 Wirsing, 2m 18.764s; 22 Pradita, 2m 19.018s; 23 Gomez, 2m 21.402s; 24 Poggiali, 2m 34.770s.

Fastest race laps: 1 Debon, 2m 02.354s; 2 Barbera, 2m 02.476s; 3 Bautista, 2m 02.534s; 4 Kallio, 2m 02.555s; 5 Simoncelli, 2m 02.618s; 6 Takahashi, 2m 03.025s; 7 Pasini, 2m 03.158s; 8 Faubel, 2m 03.219s; 9 Wilairot, 2m 03.244s; 10 Luthi, 2m 03.279s; 11 Locatelli, 2m 03.347s; 12 Espargaro, 2m 03.570s; 13 Simon, 2m 03.664s; 14 Aoyama, 2m 03.678s; 15 Pesek, 2m 04.032s; 16 Abraham, 2m 04.442s; 17 Laverty, 2m 04.603s; 18 Baldolini, 2m 04.731s; 19 Sandi, 2m 05.244s; 20 Lai, 2m 05.289s; 21 Pradita, 2m 06.461s; 22 Wirsing, 2m 06.937s; 23 Gomez, 2m 08.293s.

World Championship: 1 Simoncelli, 180; 2 Kallio, 164; 3 Debon, 139; 4 Bautista, 138; 5 Barbera, 126; 6 Pasini, 117; 7 Aoyama, 101; 8 Takahashi, 95; 9 Luthi, 86; 10 Simon, 72; 11 Locatelli, 59; 12 Espargaro, 55; 13 Faubel, 49; 14 Wilairot, 39; 15 Abraham, 25; 16 Pesek, 24; 17 Baldolini, 24; 18 Poggiali, 16; 19 Lai, 16; 20 Laverty, 8; 21 Hernandez and Sandi, 2; 23 Toth, 2; 24 Pradita, 1.

125cc
19 laps, 63.783 miles/102.657km

Pos. Rider (Nat.)	No.	Team	Machine	Laps	Time & speed
1 Stefan Bradl (GER)	17	Grizzly Gas Kiefer Racing	Aprilia	19	41m 05.176s 93.152mph/ 149.914km/h
2 Mike di Meglio (FRA)	63	Ajo Motorsport	Derbi	19	41m 06.057s
3 Joan Olive (SPA)	6	Belson Derbi	Derbi	19	41m 09.246s
4 Gabor Talmacsi (HUN)	1	Bancaja Aspar Team	Aprilia	19	41m 09.294s
5 Nicolas Terol (SPA)	18	Jack & Jones WRB	Aprilia	19	41m 12.224s
6 Bradley Smith (GBR)	38	Polaris World	Aprilia	19	41m 14.510s
7 Sandro Cortese (GER)	11	Emmi - Caffe Latte	Aprilia	19	41m 17.989s
8 Pol Espargaro (SPA)	44	Belson Derbi	Derbi	19	41m 21.667s
9 Andrea Iannone (ITA)	29	I.C. Team	Aprilia	19	41m 22.813s
10 Simone Corsi (ITA)	24	Jack & Jones WRB	Aprilia	19	41m 23.031s
11 Scott Redding (GBR)	45	Blusens Aprilia Junior	Aprilia	19	41m 24.140s
12 Sergio Gadea (SPA)	33	Bancaja Aspar Team	Aprilia	19	41m 35.096s
13 Esteve Rabat (SPA)	12	Repsol KTM 125cc	KTM	19	41m 43.621s
14 Dominique Aegerter (SWI)	77	Ajo Motorsport	Derbi	19	41m 59.813s
15 Robin Lasser (GER)	21	Grizzly Gas Kiefer Racing	Aprilia	19	41m 59.973s
16 Pablo Nieto (SPA)	22	Onde 2000 KTM	KTM	19	42m 00.899s
17 Lukas Sembera (CZE)	96	Matteoni Racing	Aprilia	19	42m 01.962s
18 Efren Vazquez (SPA)	7	Blusens Aprilia Junior	Aprilia	19	42m 04.342s
19 Lorenzo Zanetti (ITA)	8	ISPA KTM Aran	KTM	19	42m 04.506s
20 Pere Tutusaus (SPA)	30	Bancaja Aspar Team	Aprilia	19	42m 04.516s
21 Michael Ranseder (AUT)	60	I.C. Team	Aprilia	19	42m 05.483s
22 Marco Ravaioli (ITA)	72	Matteoni Racing	Aprilia	19	42m 12.577s
23 Randy Krummenacher (SWI)	34	Red Bull KTM 125	KTM	19	42m 16.877s
24 Jules Cluzel (FRA)	16	Loncin Racing	Loncin	19	42m 24.519s
25 Hugo van den Berg (NED)	56	Degraaf Grand Prix	Aprilia	19	42m 36.164s
26 Alexis Masbou (FRA)	5	Loncin Racing	Loncin	19	42m 36.194s
27 Robert Muresan (ROU)	95	Grizzly Gas Kiefer Racing	Aprilia	19	42m 36.325s
28 Bastien Chesaux (SWI)	48	S3+ WTR San Marino Team	Aprilia	19	42m 38.398s
29 Louis Rossi (FRA)	69	FFM Honda GP 125	Honda	19	42m 38.776s
30 Michael Prasek (CZE)	97	Roha'c & Fetja Motoracing	Honda	18	41m 49.282s
31 Andrea Touskova (CZE)	98	Eurowag Junior Racing	Honda	18	41m 49.573s
Karel Pesek (CZE)	37	Czech Road Racing Jnr Team	Aprilia	17	DNF
Stevie Bonsey (USA)	51	Degraaf Grand Prix	Aprilia	15	DNF
Marc Marquez (SPA)	93	Repsol KTM 125cc	KTM	6	DNF
Jonas Folger (GER)	94	Red Bull MotoGP Academy	KTM	1	DNF
Raffaele de Rosa (ITA)	35	Onde 2000 KTM	KTM	0	DNF
Tomoyoshi Koyama (JPN)	71	ISPA KTM Aran	KTM	0	DNF
Takaaki Nakagami (JPN)	73	I.C. Team	Aprilia	0	DNF
Danny Webb (GBR)	99	Degraaf Grand Prix	Aprilia	0	DNF

Fastest lap: di Meglio, 2m 08.391s, 94.135mph/151.496km/h.

Lap record: Lucio Cecchinello, ITA (Aprilia), 2m 07.836s, 94.544mph/152.154km/h (2003).

Event best maximum speed: Gadea, 137.0mph/220.5km/h (qualifying practice no. 1).

Qualifying: 1 Talmacsi, 2m 09.870s; 2 Terol, 2m 10.588s; 3 Iannone, 2m 10.589s; 4 Smith, 2m 10.652s; 5 di Meglio, 2m 10.791s; 6 Cortese, 2m 11.024s; 7 Espargaro, 2m 11.030s; 8 Corsi, 2m 11.227s; 9 Gadea, 2m 11.276s; 10 Olive, 2m 11.341s; 11 de Rosa, 2m 11.353s; 12 Marquez, 2m 11.353s; 13 Bradl, 2m 11.515s; 14 Koyama, 2m 11.518s; 15 Rabat, 2m 11.676s; 16 Webb, 2m 11.688s; 17 Redding, 2m 11.719s; 18 Bonsey, 2m 11.776s; 19 Vazquez, 2m 12.256s; 20 Zanetti, 2m 12.277s; 21 Nakagami, 2m 12.286s; 22 Lasser, 2m 12.675s; 23 Folger, 2m 12.921s; 24 Aegerter, 2m 13.033s; 25 Ranseder, 2m 13.099s; 26 Krummenacher, 2m 13.119s; 27 Cluzel, 2m 13.755s; 28 Nieto, 2m 13.782s; 29 Pesek, 2m 14.033s; 30 Tutusaus, 2m 14.192s; 31 Muresan, 2m 14.590s; 32 Masbou, 2m 14.631s; 33 Ravaioli, 2m 14.769s; 34 Chesaux, 2m 15.131s; 35 van den Berg, 2m 15.285s; 36 Sembera, 2m 15.909s; 37 Rossi, 2m 16.321s; 38 Prasek, 2m 16.744s; 39 Touskova, 2m 18.214s.

Fastest race laps: 1 di Meglio, 2m 08.391s; 2 Bradl, 2m 08.480s; 3 Terol, 2m 08.742s; 4 Olive, 2m 08.744s; 5 Talmacsi, 2m 08.755s; 6 Cortese, 2m 09.162s; 7 Smith, 2m 09.215s; 8 Iannone, 2m 09.549s; 9 Redding, 2m 09.622s; 10 Espargaro, 2m 09.661s; 11 Corsi, 2m 09.796s; 12 Gadea, 2m 10.027s; 13 Rabat, 2m 10.118s; 14 Marquez, 2m 10.306s; 15 Aegerter, 2m 10.624s; 16 Lasser, 2m 10.656s; 17 Sembera, 2m 10.810s; 18 Nieto, 2m 11.046s; 19 Ranseder, 2m 11.269s; 20 Tutusaus, 2m 11.277s; 21 Zanetti, 2m 11.277s; 22 Vazquez, 2m 11.336s; 23 Ravaioli, 2m 11.815s; 24 Bonsey, 2m 12.122s; 25 Muresan, 2m 12.246s; 26 Pesek, 2m 12.322s; 27 Krummenacher, 2m 12.439s; 28 Masbou, 2m 12.499s; 29 Cluzel, 2m 12.605s; 30 van den Berg, 2m 12.824s; 31 Chesaux, 2m 13.272s; 32 Rossi, 2m 13.372s; 33 Touskova, 2m 17.338s; 34 Prasek, 2m 17.404s.

World Championship: 1 di Meglio, 186; 2 Corsi, 142; 3 Bradl, 126; 4 Talmacsi, 122; 5 Olive, 110; 6 Terol, 102; 7 Smith, 89; 8 Espargaro, 83; 9 Cortese, 77; 10 Redding, 70; 11 Iannone, 67; 12 Gadea, 66; 13 Bonsey, 39; 14 Marquez, 33; 15 de Rosa, 29; 16 Rabat, 27; 17 Webb, 26; 18 Aegerter, 24; 19 Koyama, 22; 20 Ranseder, 19; 21 Vazquez, 15; 22 Nieto, 13; 23 Zanetti, 10; 24 Krummenacher, 10; 25 Nakagami, 9; 26 Tutusaus, 9; 27 Bianco, 8; 28 Schrotter, 3; 29 Lasser, Masbou and van den Berg, 1.

RIDER STANDINGS
After 12 Rounds

1	Valentino Rossi	237
2	Casey Stoner	187
3	Dani Pedrosa	172
4	Jorge Lorenzo	120
5	Andrea Dovizioso	110
6	Colin Edwards	102
7	Chris Vermeulen	99
8	Nicky Hayden	84
9	Shinya Nakano	83
10	Loris Capirossi	77
11	James Toseland	75
12	Toni Elias	66
13	Alex de Angelis	49
14	Sylvain Guintoli	42
15	Marco Melandri	41
16	Randy de Puniet	40
17	John Hopkins	37
18	Anthony West	33
19	Ben Spies	10
20	Jamie Hacking	5
21	Tadayuki Okada	2

TEAM STANDINGS
After 12 Rounds

1	Fiat Yamaha Team	357
2	Repsol Honda Team	256
3	Ducati Marlboro Team	228
4	Rizla Suzuki MotoGP	178
5	Tech 3 Yamaha	177
6	San Carlo Honda Gresini	132
7	JiR Team Scot MotoGP	110
8	Alice Team	108
9	Kawasaki Racing Team	75
10	LCR Honda MotoGP	40

CONSTRUCTOR STANDINGS
After 12 Rounds

1	Yamaha	266
2	Ducati	212
3	Honda	210
4	Suzuki	128
5	Kawasaki	63

Home is the hunter. Rossi gave the locals the victory they craved.
Photograph: Gold & Goose

THE long and the short of the Misano GP is that Stoner did it again. Crashed out of the lead, that is. At Brno, he had been under severe pressure. At the circuit near the Adriatic coast, the Ducati rider had been in a stronger position, with a healthier lead of three seconds, but again he had been caught out. He had known he had a front grip problem, but slowing down hadn't helped, and he'd decided to press on regardless.

The championship, towards which he had been clawing his way back, slipped away for sure. Most definitely because another problem surfaced in the Italian sunshine: a grimace in the pits on the first day of practice revealed pain in his left wrist. He had broken the scaphoid in 2003, and surgery had stapled the shattered bone together. But it had never healed fully – a poor blood supply is why racers dread scaphoid injury – and now it was coming to pieces. He said that it had nothing to do with his two recent crashes: there had been no impact. 'I was just adjusting my back protector this afternoon when I felt some pain,' he said. He soldiered on until the end of the season and first post-season tests, then went under the knife again.

Amid all these problems, Stoner shrugged off a newspaper attack in his home country, where an anti-smoking group had labelled him 'a high-speed drug pusher'. The only thing that did seem to be going his way was a chassis setting they'd found at tests after Brno, which stopped the bike from 'bucking so much'.

Another story eclipsed Stoner's wrist agony. This came after the race and took everyone who attended an extremely lively Press briefing by surprise. The meeting had been called by Repsol Honda to announce that from the next race, Pedrosa would be switching to Bridgestone tyres. This had been in the wind since Brno; the surprise was the speed with which it had happened. And had it been initiated by Honda, or railroaded through by what people were nicknaming the Spanish Mafia: Pedrosa's manager Puig, sponsor Repsol and Dorna?

HRC MD Kosuke Yasutake was at pains to deny that Honda had ceded its authority over its own team, but had been moved because 'there is not a good match between Dani and Michelin.' But Repsol motorcycle sponsorship manager Arturo Sus described how discussions between Honda and Michelin had been proceeding too slowly for his liking. 'Our role as sponsor is to push riders and teams to get results,' he said. Talks between Honda and Michelin were 'not moving as fast as we expected. So we decided to intervene this weekend.' Both Michelin and Bridgestone gave the same reason for their acquiescence: they wanted to avoid a single-tyre rule.

Everybody was shocked, for Michelin had come back strong, with Lorenzo taking second. 'I'm riding again with flow,' he'd said, after narrowly missing out on pole. 'The tyres give me the confidence I need.' Hayden was as surprised as anyone: 'I didn't even know about it. I wish they'd given me the chance!' He had returned, but too soon. His heel injury meant that he couldn't use the rear brake properly, and he withdrew from the race.

Rossi's third win in a row, which put him equal in premier-class wins with Agostini on 68, was just what the highly partisan crowd of 51,000 had come to see. The track is close to his Tavullia home, and the civic digni-

Above: A welcome return to form for both Lorenzo and Michelin.

Right: Agostini was on hand to see his 68 premier-class wins record equalled.

Below: An inauspicious weekend for Hopkins.

Photographs: Gold & Goose

Below: HRC's Kosuke Yasutake took the heat as he announced Honda's defection to Bridgestone.

Below centre: Start 277 for Capirossi made him the most experienced GP racer of all time.

Bottom centre: An empty grid slot for Hayden – he qualified, but did not race.

Bottom right: Strike three for Stoner saw him scootered back to the pits again.

Photographs: Gold & Goose

taries had paid tribute by holding a town council meeting, presided over by the robed mayor, in one of the grandstands on Friday morning. Rossi is not the only one, however, for this is the heartland of Italian motorcycling and home to a galaxy of other stars, including Melandri, Simoncelli, Pasini, Dovizioso and many others past and present.

Hopkins was in disgrace, both professionally and personally. He missed the first day of practice completely, spending it behind closed doors, and found the rest of the weekend 'a headache', according to his innuendo-rich team information. This attributed his absence to an injury sustained 'in a light training session' the previous evening. Paddock rumours told a different story: an argument with his wife had triggered her abrupt, although temporary, departure, and John had consoled himself by some some 'light training' which had ended with him racketing loudly around among the motorhomes late into Thursday night. His Kawasaki contract survived, but not without reprimand.

Contract talk at Suzuki finally came to a conclusion for Chris Vermeulen, who had been played like a fish for some time. Team management had been threatening to invoke a contract clause that specified he be in the top six by the mid-point of the year. He had missed by a handful of points, but after two non-finishes with machine problems. Now Suzuki relented, having already confirmed that Capirossi would stay. The team brought a new chassis, which had been tested after Brno, with weight moved to the rear, mainly by shifting the fuel tank further back beneath the seat. Both riders preferred it immediately. Capirossi made his 277th start at Misano, putting him one ahead of the retired Alex Barros. All the top scorers in this regard are from the modern era: Carlos Checa (220), Max Biaggi (214), Valentino Rossi (204) and Roberto Locatelli (203). But the legendary Mike Hailwood comes close, having racked up 203 starts over just 85 events, sometimes racing in three classes in one day.

Celebrity guests are celebrated by Dorna, but there was a special one at Misano, who impressed even

Rossi. It was footballer Diego Maradonna, who paid supplication to the Italian star by kissing his hand on the grid. 'I was embarrassed,' Rossi related. 'I said, "I should kiss your foot!"'

MOTOGP Race – 28 laps

Stoner's chassis change allowed him, he explained, to pick up the bike earlier on to the fat part of the tyre. It worked through two baking days of practice and into the start of an equally baking race – the first race since Qatar without at least some rain. He dominated free practice on race tyres and took his seventh successive pole by half a second. Again it was Rossi behind, by half a second, narrowly pushing Michelin-shod team-mate Lorenzo to third. De Puniet led row two from Elias, who was continuing to enjoy a revival, and Pedrosa.

It was Stoner who led away again, while Pedrosa flew past Rossi into second, helping the Australian take a full 1.7-second lead on lap one. Rossi escaped from one scary moment as he tried to get back ahead on the first lap, and by the time he did pass Pedrosa on the second, Stoner was three seconds away.

Over the next five laps, the gap shrunk and grew by mere tenths lap by lap. 'At Brno, I was sure I could catch him. This time I was not so sure,' Rossi said later. Then for a second race, he arrived at a right-hander to see the Ducati kicking up dust on its side in the gravel. Stoner tried to pick it up again, but the clip-on handlebar had snapped. He was a spectator once more. Surprisingly calm afterwards, he explained how he had tried to scrub in his front tyre during morning warm-up, so that he could go fast from the first lap. 'And something happened to it as a result,' he said.

Rossi had little more to do but keep going. On lap five, Lorenzo had also got ahead of Pedrosa, but was two seconds adrift. The gap stretched to three seconds and stayed there. Try as he might, Lorenzo found that his efforts to close up entailed too much risk, he said.

Elias passed Pedrosa on the sixth lap, and he closed to within a second of Lorenzo next time around. He

never did get any closer, however, and by half-distance his efforts were slowing him down and Pedrosa was on his tail again. Elias explained how he had taken a few deep breaths to calm down, before pushing on again. Pedrosa kept breathing down his neck, but on lap 22 his challenge was over and he started to fade. He blamed his softer tyre choice, made on the grid.

If this was processional, the mid-field made up for it.

Nakano had led the pursuit first, but after five laps tyre chatter dropped his pace. Now Dovizioso and Toseland were closing fast, and on laps eight and ten respectively each passed him as he faded backwards.

Vermeulen was also on the charge, after finishing lap one 13th. Before half-distance, he was past Nakano and closing rapidly on the pair ahead. By lap 17, they were together and fighting hard.

The Australian was ahead of Toseland five laps later, by which time Capirossi had joined the back of the group. Vermeulen pulled clear quickly, but the other three battled to the end. Capirossi got ahead of Toseland for the first time on lap 27, only for the English rider to reverse the positions a couple of corners later. The same thing happened next time around, with Toseland better than half a second clear over the line, and Dovizioso a little further behind Capirossi.

Trailing them, Melandri and Guintoli were also closing, separated on lap 22 when they caught Nakano and Melandri got by. At the same time, Edwards had gained speed after some dire early laps when he hadn't been able to get his rear tyre hot enough to work. He'd picked his way past the Kawasakis, the subdued Hopkins shadowing West, and set off after Melandri. He didn't catch him, but with four laps left he consigned Guintoli to 11th. Although he made the top ten for the first time in four races, this was still his worst run of results since joining Yamaha

De Puniet had got off the line slowly from the second row. Trying his utmost to get back on terms, he had crashed heavily on the first lap, injuring his right arm too badly to continue. Only later did he learn that he had sustained a fracture. De Angelis had crashed out on the next lap.

250cc RACE – 26 laps

Barbera was on pole, for the second time in the season, heading a slightly unusual front row from Simoncelli, Espargaro and Takahashi. Kallio and Bautista were back on row three.

The race was wild and volatile, and yet another strong argument for not killing off the 250 two-strokes – especially on tight tracks. Slow corners and the extensive use of paved run-off areas – allowing riders to get away with mistakes – encouraged different lines, and some aggressive and (mostly) safe manoeuvres.

Barbera led away, Simoncelli in tow, with Takahashi and Espargaro behind. Bautista was already up to sixth, behind Aoyama. Next time around, an unusually bullish Kallio was ahead of him and leaning hard on his teammate. Too hard, because on lap four he ran right into the back of him. The orange-on-orange incident took out both of them, to the despair of those in the KTM pit.

At this stage, Simoncelli led over the line for the first time, but they were changing back and fourth at various points on the track, a heaving gang of seven riders now that Pasini had come blazing through, after finishing the first lap 11th.

Simoncelli and Barbera were paying close attention to one another once again, but Takahashi took the lead on laps eight and nine, after a particularly daring move by the Spaniard sent both of them on to the run-off area.

Pasini took the lead from the Japanese rider next time around, but could not escape the gang. Two laps later, as he peeled into a right-hander, Barbera came flying past on the inside. The polka-dot bike was marginally ahead as Pasini moved towards the apex. They collided, and Pasini went flying. He was livid, but his team's protest was quashed before it had got under way, when race direction said that it would be overruled.

Barbera was under attack by Simoncelli again, and over the next seven laps the pair exchanged the lead and much fairing paint several times, swapping back and forth in a desperate battle.

On lap nine, Bautista finally got ahead of Espargaro and soon began moving forward. At half-distance, he

Above: A second rostrum in a row completely changed Elias's prospects.

Above right: 125 points leader di Meglio crashes out.

Above far right: Smith received a 125 masterclass from champion Talmacsi.

Right: Takahashi briefly leads a volatile 250 pack, from Barbera (21) and Simoncelli (58), with Bautista close behind.

Left: Bautista celebrates a return to the top step.

Photographs: Gold & Goose

was disputing the lead, ahead now and then on the back section as he, Simoncelli, Barbera and Takahashi started to move away up front.

Another clash with Barbera on lap 22 put Simoncelli on to the hard standing again, but he regained the track in fourth, with Barbera third. A couple of corners later, Simoncelli crashed all by himself on a slow corner. He kept hold of the handlebars with the clutch in, however, and was straight back in the saddle, but by now he had dropped to sixth, behind team-mate Locatelli and Simon, who had been shadowing the veteran.

As the end drew nigh, Bautista was able to pull clear by a couple of seconds, while Takahashi managed to keep a safe distance between himself and Barbera, whose tyres were shot. Locatelli was next, comfortably clear of Simon, then Simoncelli in sixth. Eight seconds away came Luthi.

Wilairot kept his Honda a second ahead of Pesek;

Abraham rounded out the top ten.

With Debon and Faubel crashing out together in the early stages, there were only 16 finishers, and with Kallio not among them, Simoncelli extended his points lead in spite of his own misfortune.

125cc RACE – 23 laps

Talmacsi qualified on pole and pledged to win every other race tin 2008 to revive his title defence. Smith was alongside, Redding on the far end of the row.

The Hungarian made good his promise, while points leader di Meglio crashed out for zero points. Perhaps there was a chance after all.

Talmacsi led every lap except for three at half-distance, after he missed a gear-change and his shadow, Smith, was able to get by. But he was soon back in

front, and the Englishman settled for a safe second.

All the action was in a seven-strong battle for third. Redding was not involved, having crashed out on the second lap. By half-distance, it had shrunk to four, Corsi heading di Meglio, up from 11th after a slow start, Bradl and Olive.

Di Meglio went on lap 15, sliding out alone two laps after passing Corsi. Later that same lap, Bradl slowed and stopped out on the track, his race done.

Olive got past Corsi on lap 16, but the Italian stayed close, awaiting the last lap. He attacked at the end of the triple right-hand corners at the end of the back straight. Olive tried too hard to get back and fell a couple of corners later, remounting for a disconsolate 12th.

Marquez nipped through to lead the next group over the line, from Terol, Iannone, Cortese, impressive rookie Aegerter and Rabat.

GP CINZANO DI SAN MARINO E RIVIERA DI RIMINI

31 AUGUST 2008 • FIM WORLD CHAMPIONSHIP ROUND 13

MISANO WORLD CIRCUIT

Tramonto · Rio · Curvone · Quercia · Rimini · Misano · Variante del Parco · Carro

Circuit 4.226km /2.626 miles

MOTOGP

RACE: 28 laps, 73.528 miles/118.328km • Weather: Dry • Air 35°C • Humidity 29% • Track 48°C

Pos.	Rider	Nat.	No.	Team	Machine	Tyres	Laps	Time & speed (mph/km/h)
1	Valentino Rossi	ITA	46	Fiat Yamaha Team	Yamaha	B	28	44m 41.884s 98.696mph/ 158.836km/h
2	Jorge Lorenzo	SPA	48	Fiat Yamaha Team	Yamaha	M	28	44m 45.047s
3	Toni Elias	SPA	24	Alice Team	Ducati	B	28	44m 53.589s
4	Dani Pedrosa	SPA	2	Repsol Honda Team	Honda	M	28	44m 59.354s
5	Chris Vermeulen	AUS	7	Rizla Suzuki MotoGP	Suzuki	B	28	45m 05.293s
6	James Toseland	GBR	52	Tech 3 Yamaha	Yamaha	M	28	45m 08.092s
7	Loris Capirossi	ITA	65	Rizla Suzuki MotoGP	Suzuki	B	28	45m 08.708s
8	Andrea Dovizioso	ITA	4	JiR Team Scot MotoGP	Honda	B	28	45m 09.475s
9	Marco Melandri	ITA	33	Ducati Marlboro Team	Ducati	B	28	45m 15.053s
10	Colin Edwards	USA	5	Tech 3 Yamaha	Yamaha	M	28	45m 18.413s
11	Sylvain Guintoli	FRA	50	Alice Team	Ducati	B	28	45m 23.965s
12	Shinya Nakano	JPN	56	San Carlo Honda Gresini	Honda	B	28	45m 25.692s
13	Anthony West	AUS	13	Kawasaki Racing Team	Kawasaki	B	28	45m 36.758s
14	John Hopkins	USA	21	Kawasaki Racing Team	Kawasaki	B	28	45m 37.038s
	Casey Stoner	AUS	1	Ducati Marlboro Team	Ducati	B	7	11m 11.968s
	Alex de Angelis	RSM	15	San Carlo Honda Gresini	Honda	B	1	1m 46.395s
	Randy de Puniet	FRA	14	LCR Honda MotoGP	Honda	M	0	
	Nicky Hayden	USA	69	Repsol Honda Team	Honda	M		DNS

Fastest lap: Valentino Rossi, on lap 6, 1m 34.904s, 99.609mph/160.305km/h (record).

Previous lap record: New circuit.

Event best maximum speed: Sylvain Guintoli, 172.3mph/277.3km/h (free practice no. 1).

QUALIFYING: 30 August 2008

Weather: Dry
Air: 31°C Humidity: 37% Track: 46°C

Pos.	Rider	Time
1	Stoner	1m 33.378s
2	Rossi	1m 33.888s
3	Lorenzo	1m 33.964s
4	de Puniet	1m 34.236s
5	Elias	1m 34.322s
6	Pedrosa	1m 34.398s
7	Vermeulen	1m 34.461s
8	Nakano	1m 34.494s
9	Toseland	1m 34.652s
10	Edwards	1m 34.795s
11	Capirossi	1m 34.926s
12	Guintoli	1m 34.961s
13	de Angelis	1m 35.153s
14	Dovizioso	1m 35.381s
15	Melandri	1m 35.418s
16	Hayden	1m 35.584s
17	Hopkins	1m 35.980s
18	West	1m 37.047s

FASTEST RACE LAPS

	Rider	Lap	Time
1	Rossi	6	1m 34.904s
2	Stoner	6	1m 34.988s
3	Lorenzo	23	1m 35.167s
4	Elias	19	1m 35.221s
5	Pedrosa	10	1m 35.479s
6	Melandri	17	1m 35.681s
7	Vermeulen	25	1m 35.741s
8	Edwards	26	1m 35.766s
9	Capirossi	21	1m 35.832s
10	Dovizioso	9	1m 35.911s
11	Toseland	18	1m 35.972s
12	Guintoli	11	1m 36.175s
13	Nakano	4	1m 36.351s
14	Hopkins	20	1m 36.710s
15	West	20	1m 36.862s
16	de Angelis	1	1m 46.395s

Grid order / Lap chart

Grid order	1	2	3	4	5	6	7	8	9	10	11	12	13	14	15	16	17	18	19	20	21	22	23	24	25	26	27	28	•
1 STONER	1	1	1	1	1	1	1	46	46	46	46	46	46	46	46	46	46	46	46	46	46	46	46	46	46	46	46	46	1
46 ROSSI	2	46	46	46	46	46	46	48	48	48	48	48	48	48	48	48	48	48	48	48	48	48	48	48	48	48	48	48	2
48 LORENZO	46	2	2	2	48	48	48	24	24	24	24	24	24	24	24	24	24	24	24	24	24	24	24	24	24	24	24	24	3
14 de PUNIET	48	48	48	48	2	24	24	2	2	2	2	2	2	2	2	2	2	2	2	2	2	2	2	2	2	2	2	2	4
24 ELIAS	24	24	24	24	24	2	2	4	4	4	4	4	4	4	4	52	52	52	7	7	7	7	7	7	7	7	7	7	5
2 PEDROSA	56	56	56	56	56	56	56	56	56	52	52	52	52	52	52	52	52	4	52	52	52	52	52	52	52	52	52	52	6
7 VERMEULEN	52	4	4	4	4	4	4	52	52	56	56	56	7	7	7	7	7	7	4	4	4	4	4	65	65	65	65	65	7
56 NAKANO	4	52	52	52	52	52	52	65	7	7	7	7	56	56	56	56	65	65	65	65	65	65	65	65	65	65	4	4	8
52 TOSELAND	65	50	50	50	65	65	65	7	65	65	65	65	65	65	65	56	56	56	33	33	33	33	33	33	33	33	33	33	9
5 EDWARDS	50	65	65	65	50	50	50	50	50	50	50	50	50	50	50	50	33	33	56	56	50	50	5	5	5	5	5	5	10
65 CAPIROSSI	15	13	7	7	7	7	7	33	33	33	33	33	33	33	33	33	33	50	50	50	50	56	5	50	50	50	50	50	11
50 GUINTOLI	13	7	13	13	33	33	33	13	13	5	5	5	5	5	5	5	5	5	50	50	50	56	56	56	56	56	56	56	12
15 de ANGELIS	7	21	33	33	13	13	13	21	5	13	13	13	13	13	13	13	13	13	13	13	13	13	13	13	13	13	13	13	13
4 DOVISIOSO	21	33	21	21	21	21	21	5	21	21	21	21	21	21	21	21	21	21	21	21	21	21	21	21	21	21	21	21	14
33 MELANDRI	5	5	5	5	5	5	5																						15
69 HAYDEN	33																												
21 HOPKINS																													
13 WEST																													

statistics

250cc
26 laps, 68.276 miles/109.876km

Pos.	Rider (Nat.)	No.	Team	Machine	Laps	Time & speed
1	Alvaro Bautista (SPA)	19	Mapfre Aspar Team	Aprilia	26	43m 15.831s 94.685mph/ 152.380km/h
2	Yuki Takahashi (JPN)	72	JiR Team Scot 250	Honda	26	43m 17.919s
3	Hector Barbera (SPA)	21	Team Toth Aprilia	Aprilia	26	43m 19.583s
4	Roberto Locatelli (ITA)	15	Metis Gilera	Gilera	26	43m 23.303s
5	Julian Simon (SPA)	60	Repsol KTM 250cc	KTM	26	43m 26.693s
6	Marco Simoncelli (ITA)	58	Metis Gilera	Gilera	26	43m 37.011s
7	Thomas Luthi (SWI)	12	Emmi - Caffe Latte	Aprilia	26	43m 45.271s
8	Ratthapark Wilairot (THA)	14	Thai Honda PTT SAG	Honda	26	43m 49.713s
9	Lukas Pesek (CZE)	52	Auto Kelly - CP	Aprilia	26	43m 50.882s
10	Karel Abraham (CZE)	17	Cardion AB Motoracing	Aprilia	26	44m 01.236s
11	Fabrizio Lai (ITA)	32	Campetella Racing	Gilera	26	44m 03.091s
12	Federico Sandi (ITA)	90	Matteoni Racing	Aprilia	26	44m 26.495s
13	Manuel Hernandez (SPA)	43	Blusens Aprilia	Aprilia	26	44m 26.713s
14	Toni Wirsing (GER)	94	Racing Team Germany	Honda	26	44m 49.163s
15	Simone Grotzkyj (ITA)	35	Campetella Racing	Gilera	25	43m 29.476s
16	Doni Tata Pradita (INA)	45	Yamaha Pertamina Indonesia	Yamaha	25	43m 44.942s
	Aleix Espargaro (SPA)	41	Lotus Aprilia	Aprilia	19	DNF
	Eugene Laverty (IRL)	50	Blusens Aprilia	Aprilia	14	DNF
	Imre Toth (HUN)	10	Team Toth Aprilia	Aprilia	12	DNF
	Mattia Pasini (ITA)	75	Polaris World	Aprilia	11	DNF
	Hiroshi Aoyama (JPN)	4	Red Bull KTM 250	KTM	3	DNF
	Mika Kallio (FIN)	36	Red Bull KTM 250	KTM	3	DNF
	Hector Faubel (SPA)	55	Mapfre Aspar Team	Aprilia	2	DNF
	Alex Debon (SPA)	6	Lotus Aprilia	Aprilia	2	DNF
	Alex Baldolini (ITA)	25	Matteoni Racing	Aprilia	1	DNF

Fastest lap: Simoncelli, 1m 38.993s, 95.494mph/153.683km/h (record).

Previous lap record: New circuit.

Event best maximum speed: Faubel, 144.8mph/233.1km/h (race).

Qualifying: 1 Barbera, 1m 38.047s; 2 Simoncelli, 1m 38.124s; 3 Espargaro, 1m 38.813s; 4 Takahashi, 1m 38.822s; 5 Aoyama, 1m 38.869s; 6 Luthi, 1m 38.961s; 7 Simon, 1m 39.009s; 8 Faubel, 1m 39.058s; 9 Pasini, 1m 39.130s; 10 Kallio, 1m 39.165s; 11 Bautista, 1m 39.217s; 12 Debon, 1m 39.402s; 13 Pesek, 1m 39.749s; 14 Locatelli, 1m 39.828s; 15 Wilairot, 1m 39.875s; 16 Lai, 1m 39.963s; 17 Laverty, 1m 40.317s; 18 Abraham, 1m 40.360s; 19 Baldolini, 1m 40.732s; 20 Sandi, 1m 41.205s; 21 Hernandez, 1m 41.513s; 22 Wirsing, 1m 42.620s; 23 Grotzkyj, 1m 42.756s; 24 Pradita, 1m 42.992s; 25 Toth, 1m 43.841s.

Fastest race laps: 1 Simoncelli, 1m 38.993s; 2 Barbera, 1m 39.066s; 3 Bautista, 1m 39.116s; 4 Takahashi, 1m 39.168s; 5 Pasini, 1m 39.248s; 6 Locatelli, 1m 39.291s; 7 Simon, 1m 39.305s; 8 Luthi, 1m 39.306s; 9 Espargaro, 1m 39.374s; 10 Kallio, 1m 39.526s; 11 Aoyama, 1m 39.564s; 12 Pesek, 1m 40.205s; 13 Lai, 1m 40.225s; 14 Wilairot, 1m 40.262s; 15 Debon, 1m 40.405s; 16 Faubel, 1m 40.409s; 17 Abraham, 1m 40.651s; 18 Laverty, 1m 40.758s; 19 Hernandez, 1m 41.580s; 20 Sandi, 1m 41.689s; 21 Wirsing, 1m 42.282s; 22 Grotzkyj, 1m 43.002s; 23 Pradita, 1m 43.687s; 24 Toth, 1m 45.422s; 25 Baldolini, 1m 50.835s.

World Championship: 1 Simoncelli, 190; 2 Kallio, 164; 3 Bautista, 163; 4 Barbera, 142; 5 Debon, 139; 6 Pasini, 117; 7 Takahashi, 115; 8 Aoyama, 101; 9 Luthi, 95; 10 Simon, 83; 11 Locatelli, 72; 12 Espargaro, 55; 13 Faubel, 49; 14 Wilairot, 47; 15 Abraham, 31; 16 Pesek, 31; 17 Baldolini, 24; 18 Lai, 21; 19 Poggiali, 16; 20 Laverty, 8; 21 Sandi, 6; 22 Hernandez, 5; 23 Wirsing, 2; 24 Toth, 2; 25 Grotzkyj and Pradita, 1.

125cc
23 laps, 60.398 miles/97.198km

Pos.	Rider (Nat.)	No.	Team	Machine	Laps	Time & speed
1	Gabor Talmacsi (HUN)	1	Bancaja Aspar Team	Aprilia	23	40m 03.679s 90.455mph/ 145.573km/h
2	Bradley Smith (GBR)	38	Polaris World	Aprilia	23	40m 09.081s
3	Simone Corsi (ITA)	24	Jack & Jones WRB	Aprilia	23	40m 18.067s
4	Marc Marquez (SPA)	93	Repsol KTM 125cc	KTM	23	40m 20.737s
5	Nicolas Terol (SPA)	18	Jack & Jones WRB	Aprilia	23	40m 21.000s
6	Andrea Iannone (ITA)	29	I.C. Team	Aprilia	23	40m 21.161s
7	Sandro Cortese (GER)	11	Emmi - Caffe Latte	Aprilia	23	40m 21.164s
8	Dominique Aegerter (SWI)	77	Ajo Motorsport	Derbi	23	40m 22.336s
9	Esteve Rabat (SPA)	12	Repsol KTM 125cc	KTM	23	40m 22.827s
10	Sergio Gadea (SPA)	33	Bancaja Aspar Team	Aprilia	23	40m 38.329s
11	Efren Vazquez (SPA)	7	Blusens Aprilia Junior	Aprilia	23	40m 38.534s
12	Joan Olive (SPA)	6	Belson Derbi	Derbi	23	40m 43.073s
13	Michael Ranseder (AUT)	60	I.C. Team	Aprilia	23	40m 50.983s
14	Danny Webb (GBR)	99	Degraaf Grand Prix	Aprilia	23	40m 56.920s
15	Jonas Folger (GER)	94	Red Bull MotoGP Academy	KTM	23	40m 57.028s
16	Jules Cluzel (FRA)	16	Loncin Racing	Loncin	23	41m 05.582s
17	Marco Ravaioli (ITA)	72	Matteoni Racing	Aprilia	23	41m 07.844s
18	Tomoyoshi Koyama (JPN)	71	ISPA KTM Aran	KTM	23	41m 09.914s
19	Takaaki Nakagami (JPN)	73	I.C. Team	Aprilia	23	41m 09.939s
20	Robin Lasser (GER)	21	Grizzly Gas Kiefer Racing	Aprilia	23	41m 10.879s
21	Gabriele Ferro (ITA)	43	Metasystems RS	Honda	23	41m 25.493s
22	Bastien Chesaux (SWI)	48	WTR San Marino Team	Aprilia	23	41m 26.200s
23	Louis Rossi (FRA)	69	FFM Honda GP 125	Honda	23	41m 38.926s
24	Hugo van den Berg (NED)	56	Degraaf Grand Prix	Aprilia	23	41m 43.402s
25	Luca Vitali (ITA)	42	Grizzly Gas Kiefer Racing	Aprilia	22	40m 19.907s
26	Randy Krummenacher (SWI)	34	Red Bull KTM 125	KTM	21	41m 00.200s
	Mike di Meglio (FRA)	63	Ajo Motorsport	Derbi	14	DNF
	Stefan Bradl (GER)	17	Grizzly Gas Kiefer Racing	Aprilia	14	DNF
	Lorenzo Zanetti (ITA)	8	ISPA KTM Aran	KTM	14	DNF
	Pol Espargaro (SPA)	44	Belson Derbi	Derbi	12	DNF
	Lorenzo Savadori (ITA)	40	RCGM	Aprilia	12	DNF
	Raffaele de Rosa (ITA)	35	Onde 2000 KTM	KTM	10	DNF
	Alexis Masbou (FRA)	5	Loncin Racing	Loncin	6	DNF
	Gennaro Sabatino (ITA)	49	Junior GP Racing Dream	Aprilia	6	DNF
	Pablo Nieto (SPA)	22	Onde 2000 KTM	KTM	4	DNF
	Stevie Bonsey (USA)	51	Degraaf Grand Prix	Aprilia	3	DNF
	Scott Redding (GBR)	45	Blusens Aprilia Junior	Aprilia	1	DNF
	Adrian Martin (SPA)	26	Bancaja Aspar Team	Aprilia	0	DNF
	Riccardo Moretti (ITA)	47	CRP Racing	Honda	0	DNF

Fastest lap: Talmacsi, 1m 43.839s, 91.038mph/146.511km/h (record).

Previous lap record: New circuit.

Event best maximum speed: Corsi, 127.6mph/205.3km/h (free practice no. 2).

Qualifying: 1 Talmacsi, 1m 43.729s; 2 Smith, 1m 43.920s; 3 Espargaro, 1m 44.334s; 4 Redding, 1m 44.339s; 5 Corsi, 1m 44.450s; 6 di Meglio, 1m 44.543s; 7 Cortese, 1m 44.555s; 8 Marquez, 1m 44.668s; 9 Terol, 1m 44.706s; 10 Olive, 1m 44.821s; 11 Bradl, 1m 44.840s; 12 Gadea, 1m 45.033s; 13 Iannone, 1m 45.082s; 14 Aegerter, 1m 45.119s; 15 de Rosa, 1m 45.324s; 16 Moretii, 1m 45.370s; 17 Bonsey, 1m 45.394s; 18 Vazquez, 1m 45.418s; 19 Rabat, 1m 45.539s; 20 Webb, 1m 45.566s; 21 Ranseder, 1m 45.607s; 22 Koyama, 1m 45.641s; 23 Savadori, 1m 46.017s; 24 Cluzel, 1m 46.099s; 25 Nakagami, 1m 46.136s; 26 Zanetti, 1m 46.278s; 27 Lasser, 1m 46.310s; 28 Folger, 1m 46.341s; 29 Masbou, 1m 46.410s; 30 Sabatino, 1m 46.500s; 31 Ferro, 1m 46.559s; 32 Ravaioli, 1m 46.670s; 33 Rossi, 1m 46.781s; 34 Nieto, 1m 46.801s; 35 Martin, 1m 47.023s; 36 Vitali, 1m 47.078s; 37 Krummenacher, 1m 47.100s; 38 Chesaux, 1m 47.863s; 39 van den Berg, 1m 47.891s.

Fastest race laps: 1 Talmacsi, 1m 43.839s; 2 Corsi, 1m 43.956s; 3 Smith, 1m 43.964s; 4 di Meglio, 1m 44.025s; 5 Cortese, 1m 44.104s; 6 Olive, 1m 44.107s; 7 Aegerter, 1m 44.136s; 8 Terol, 1m 44.192s; 9 Marquez, 1m 44.221s; 10 Iannone, 1m 44.320s; 11 Bradl, 1m 44.371s; 12 Rabat, 1m 44.379s; 13 Espargaro, 1m 44.538s; 14 Vazquez, 1m 44.723s; 15 Gadea, 1m 44.966s; 16 Ranseder, 1m 45.274s; 17 Folger, 1m 45.548s; 18 Zanetti, 1m 45.727s; 19 Webb, 1m 45.777s; 20 Savadori, 1m 45.800s; 21 Bonsey, 1m 45.850s; 22 Koyama, 1m 46.100s; 23 Krummenacher, 1m 46.128s; 24 Cluzel, 1m 46.209s; 25 Ravaioli, 1m 46.234s; 26 Nakagami, 1m 46.266s; 27 Lasser, 1m 46.287s; 28 de Rosa, 1m 46.438s; 29 Chesaux, 1m 46.769s; 30 Ferro, 1m 46.876s; 31 Nieto, 1m 47.286s; 32 Masbou, 1m 47.344s; 33 Rossi, 1m 47.357s; 34 van den Berg, 1m 47.441s; 35 Sabatino, 1m 48.109s; 36 Vitali, 1m 48.631s; 37 Redding, 1m 52.952s.

World Championship: 1 di Meglio, 186; 2 Corsi, 158; 3 Talmacsi, 147; 4 Bradl, 126; 5 Olive, 114; 6 Terol, 113; 7 Smith, 109; 8 Cortese, 86; 9 Espargaro, 83; 10 Iannone, 77; 11 Gadea, 72; 12 Redding, 70; 13 Marquez, 46; 14 Bonsey, 39; 15 Rabat, 34; 16 Aegerter, 32; 17 de Rosa, 30; 18 Webb, 28; 19 Koyama, 22; 20 Ranseder, 22; 21 Vazquez, 20; 22 Nieto, 13; 23 Zanetti, 10; 24 Krummenacher, 10; 25 Nakagami, 9; 26 Tutusaus, 9; 27 Bianco, 8; 28 Schrotter, 3; 29 Folger, Lasser, Masbou and van den Berg, 1.

RIDER STANDINGS
After 13 Rounds

1	Valentino Rossi	262
2	Casey Stoner	187
3	Dani Pedrosa	185
4	Jorge Lorenzo	140
5	Andrea Dovizioso	118
6	Chris Vermeulen	110
7	Colin Edwards	108
8	Shinya Nakano	87
9	Loris Capirossi	86
10	James Toseland	85
11	Nicky Hayden	84
12	Toni Elias	82
13	Alex de Angelis	49
14	Marco Melandri	48
15	Sylvain Guintoli	47
16	Randy de Puniet	40
17	John Hopkins	39
18	Anthony West	36
19	Ben Spies	10
20	Jamie Hacking	5
21	Tadayuki Okada	2

TEAM STANDINGS
After 13 Rounds

1	Fiat Yamaha Team	402
2	Repsol Honda Team	269
3	Ducati Marlboro Team	235
4	Rizla Suzuki MotoGP	198
5	Tech 3 Yamaha	193
6	San Carlo Honda Gresini	136
7	Alice Team	129
8	JiR Team Scot MotoGP	118
9	Kawasaki Racing Team	80
10	LCR Honda MotoGP	40

CONSTRUCTOR STANDINGS
After 13 Rounds

1	Yamaha	291
2	Ducati	228
3	Honda	223
4	Suzuki	139
5	Kawasaki	66

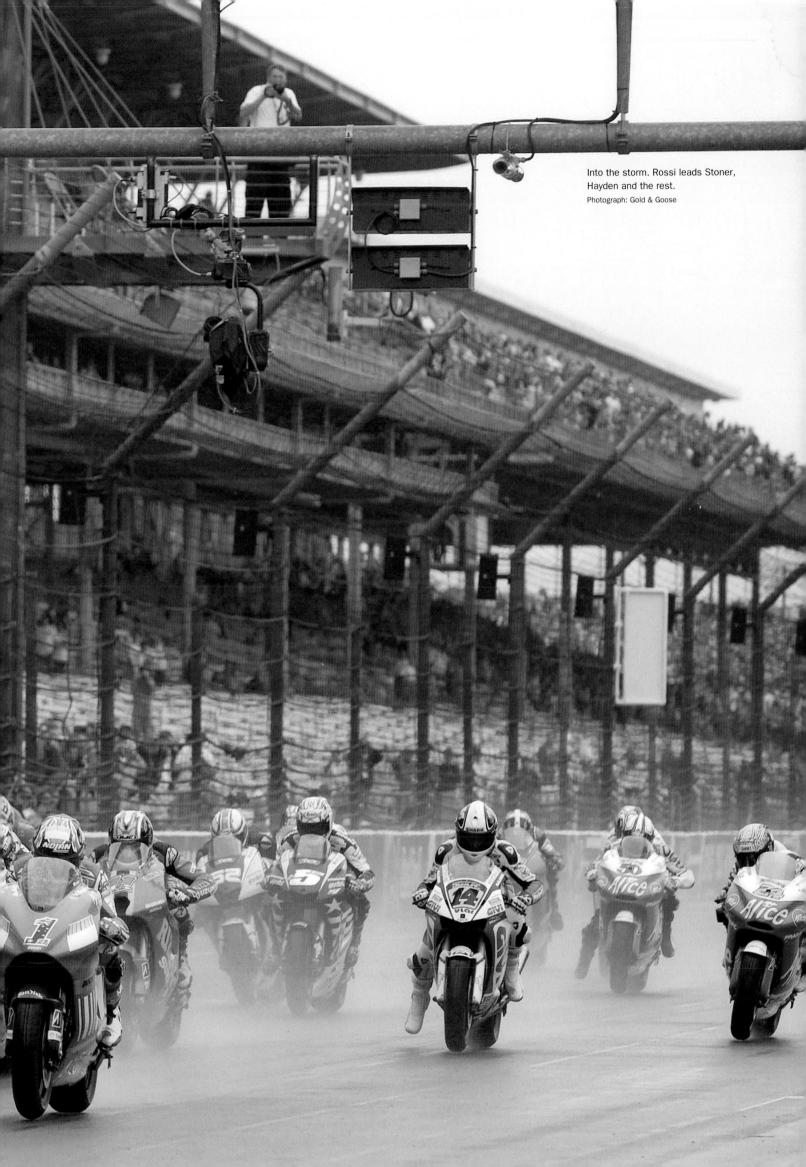

Into the storm. Rossi leads Stoner,
Hayden and the rest.

Photograph: Gold & Goose

THERE had been much apprehension about the first visit to Indianapolis. Trials by test riders before the summer break had yielded tales of a bumpy track with a terrifying run by the wall; previous experiences at Laguna Seca had been far from reassuring in terms of the understanding of MotoGP and the quality of track-side officials.

All that was overturned during the weekend. There was a wall by the straight, yes, but the layout neutralised its menace. The track was bumpy and the surface mixed, but not terminally so, and there was every reassurance that these things would be attended to before the next visit. There were rather a lot of corners, but the layout was not displeasing, reminding Rossi of Rio – 'and I loved Rio: a lot of difficult corners in a row'. And the organisation and facilities at the oldest permanent track in America displayed undreamt of degrees of experience and professionalism.

The problems, and there were plenty, came from quite another source. Off the coast of Africa, to be precise, some two weeks before, when a depression that had moved across the continent started to build into a category-5.6 hurricane. By the time the eye of the storm made landfall at Galveston, Texas, which had been evacuated, the second day of practice was getting under way at Indianapolis, more than 1,000 miles away. The storm moved on to the northwest, but its effects were felt over a far wider area. By the time the MotoGP race had been cut short in torrential rain, amid power cuts and violent winds, the cancellation of the 250 race was a bagatelle compared with the destruction wrought upon the United States. Eighty-two people had lost their lives, while more than 200 were missing.

The scale of the destruction makes the events at the Brickyard seem insignificant, but motorbike racing is our business, and they were important in that respect. Two out of three races did take place, and although strictly speaking the abbreviated MotoGP race should have been restarted and run as an eight-lap sprint, there can be few cases where *force majeure* was more applicable, and there were no complaints that the results after 20 of 28 scheduled laps were declared valid. Amazingly, and a tribute to effective electronics and excellent tyres, not a single rider crashed.

Indianapolis may have been peripheral to the path of the hurricane, but the weather was very profound. The first day of practice was wet, and the track drainage was not up to the job in several places. Day two developed into a deceptively sunny afternoon for qualifying. Race day was dire, as we shall see.

There was much to prick the interest. Pedrosa had tested Bridgestones the day after the Misano race and instantly cut a second off his best lap time. He was also using the pneumatic-valve-spring engine for the first time. Hayden was back, again, and if his foot was still troublesome, the facts that Indy was within driving distance of his Kentucky home and that he badly wanted to beat his turncoat team-mate meant that he wouldn't let it slow him down. Ben Spies was wild-carding again on the Suzuki, and ready to rumble.

And then the history: the Indianapolis Motor Speedway may be better known for car racing and the famous 2.5-mile banked oval, but it had been inaugurated in 1909 with a motorcycle race. The upstart MotoGP track was a 2.621-mile, 16-corner swerver on the grassy infield. A modification of the former F1 circuit, it was run in the opposite direction. One change was to the final corner, now a very slow right-left to avoid launching riders too fast on to the straight, with its adjacent wall – shared with the oval and running across the famous yard of bricks.

Unusually, it was a first-time track for all except wild-card Spies. In these circumstances, riders frequently turn to the Sony Playstation for familiarity, but the reverse direction prevented that, as Stoner pointed out. Average speed in dry practice of 150.6km/h made it the slowest of the year. Riders found it interesting when there were no puddles, although the change of grip levels of the different surfaces was a concern.

Stoner was one of many to fall victim, crashing unhurt in the wet on the first day. Three riders in the smaller classes were not so lucky. Luthi and Eugene Laverty both fell in the dry on Saturday morning. The Swiss rider suffered concussion and a thumb injury; Laverty broke bones in both feet. Both riders were out of the race, and Laverty for the rest of the season – tiring of the unequal struggle on a below-par bike, he finished his year in World Supersport instead. Talmacsi fell in the first 125

Above: Fairground attraction – the Indy Mile was a highlight for the visitors.

Right: Strapped for action, Stoner's left wrist injury was becoming a problem.

Below: The famous yard of bricks.

Photographs: Gold & Goose

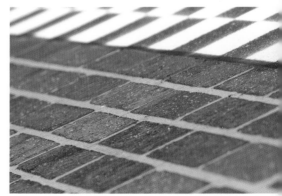

Left: Michelin men Hayden and Lorenzo dispute second. The Yamaha rider got ahead, but too late.

Below: Marshals batten down the hatches as Hurricane Ike kicks in.

Bottom: The pit-lane puddle ran the full length.

Bottom right: Jostling for the last points – Toseland leads de Puniet and Nakano.

Photographs: Gold & Goose

qualifying practice and fractured the scaphoid in his left wrist. Bravely, he rode on, undergoing surgery directly after the race.

Kawasaki confirmed the long-expected signing of Melandri on Sunday morning, at the expense of incumbent West. The Australian complained that his MotoGP chance had been spoiled by a bike that was not up to the task. 'It's a bit unfair. Even Hopkins is struggling. If he was winning races and I was last, then I could understand, but he's in the back with me, and it's hard work.' Few would disagree.

The 250 race cancellation was the first since 1980, when the Austrian GP at the Salzburgring had been rained off. The race had already been postponed from 13.15 to 16.15, after the MotoGP, which had been cut short, not only because of the dangerous conditions, but also because of debris blowing across the track. This included signage and patches of Astroturf, while Yamaha's hospitality marquee also blew down. Race director Paul Butler explained the decision: 'We couldn't have fixed the track in a reasonable time, and not knowing what the weather would do we couldn't say we'd wait for another two hours.' Worsening conditions and a major power cut proved the decision right, and most riders supported it, although Simoncelli was one to express disappointment.

One of the most eagerly anticipated events took place several miles away from the track, at the Indiana State Fairgrounds – the revived Indy Mile. All mile-long, oval dirt tracks are awe inspiring; this one is especially famous as the scene of the race that Kenny Roberts still regards as his best, when he out-slid the factory Harley-Davidsons on a flat-tracker powered by Yamaha's TZ750 four-cylinder two-stroke engine – the bike was later banned, at Roberts's behest, as too dangerous. Roberts was at the track, along with other US racing luminaries, including Nicky Hayden on crutches and famed tuner Kel Carruthers; so too a large contingent from the MotoGP paddock. The 25-lap race was red-flagged twice, and the final five-lap dash was won by veteran Chris Carr from defending dirt-track champion Kenny Coolbeth by just 0.03 second.

Another point of interest was the intercontinental match race between European and American Red Bull rookies. Europe triumphed by 114 points to 26. The winner was Norwegian Sturla Fagerhaug, from South African Matthew Scholz and Briton Matthew Hoyle, but only after Hayden Gillim from Georgia had crashed out while battling for the lead. The best placed US rider was Jake Gagne in eighth.

MOTOGP RACE – 20 laps

An impressive 91,000 fans braved the weather conditions on Sunday, not far short of double the Laguna Seca figure. They saw Rossi make history. His 69th victory overtook Agostini's record as the winner of most races in the premier class.

The race started on a damp track, under ominous skies, with the weather radar promising worse to come. In fact, conditions stayed merely very wet for the first 14 of the 28 scheduled laps, although lap times were almost ten seconds off the dry qualifying time.

Rossi headed Stoner and Lorenzo on a close grid, with Hayden disappointed to be knocked to fourth, to lead row two.

The first laps were all action. Rossi led away, Stoner took over directly and Hayden pushed through to second. Then Dovizioso – who had started from the third row – blitzed past all of them to lead by the ninth corner.

When they crossed the yard of bricks, Hayden was second, and on the second lap he drafted past into the lead. At this point, Lorenzo was third, and Rossi fifth behind Stoner. Rossi soon started moving forwards, however, his pace increasing with one fastest lap after another. He was ahead of Stoner on lap three, and Dovizioso two laps later. On the sixth, he passed Lorenzo as well. He was just under a second behind Hayden and the chase was on.

Hayden had a crucial advantage – he was faster out of the last corner and down the front straight. It was enough to keep him ahead until the 14th lap, but he was living in hope, for he knew Rossi wouldn't give up. 'I tried to be smooth and not destroy my tyre. At least I would make him work for it.'

The pass came on the left, at the end of the infield straight, Rossi slipping inside under braking and setting the fastest lap as he tried to pull away. In this, ultimately

he was successful, but at the same time the rain became heavier and lap times slowed again. Before much longer, Rossi was 'looking for the red flag every time I crossed the finish line'. Everyone was having trouble aquaplaning and getting blown around, and Rossi all but crashed on one occasion. The flag was shown finally as the leaders finished their 21st lap, the results being taken from the previous lap.

Hayden had stayed valiantly within a second or so for five laps, the gap see-sawing. But he had punished his tyres in the effort. On lap 19, he slowed radically and started what would have been a dispiriting slide backwards, had the race not been stopped.

Behind them, Lorenzo and Dovizioso had battled until the Italian had lost touch after nine laps. At this point, Lorenzo was just a couple of seconds behind the leaders. The gap would grow to some seven seconds by lap 18. Then he saw Hayden getting closer rapidly and redoubled his efforts. He had passed the slowing Honda by the time the red flags came out, but was delighted nevertheless with his first ever wet rostrum, in any form of racing.

Dovizioso fell back into the hands of Stoner, a couple of seconds behind, and began his second battle of the afternoon. They changed places several times and were still closely engaged when the red flag came out. Luckily for Stoner, he was ahead on lap 20.

A little way back, Spies had moved up to sixth after passing Pedrosa on lap four. But the American had problems with his visor misting, which forced him to battle poor vision as well as bad conditions. All the same, he gradually closed up to the pair ahead of him. He was less than a second behind Dovizioso at the finish.

Pedrosa had dropped almost ten seconds behind the wild-card American when a pair of fast, wet riders, Guintoli and Vermeulen, caught him. They had come through in more or less close formation, their last victim being Toseland by lap seven. Six laps later, both were on Pedrosa, and on the 17th were ahead of him.

Guintoli made it stick, but Pedrosa was back ahead of the Suzuki when it mattered.

The remaining riders were spread out at the finish. West had got up to tenth, but then his tyre started to shed chunks, and de Angelis got by him three laps from the end.

Elias, Hopkins, Toseland, de Puniet, Nakano, Capirossi, Edwards and Melandri had all been together on the tenth lap, then spaces appeared. Hopkins lost 13th to de Puniet with three laps to go. Edwards was two seconds behind for the last point. Another five seconds away, Capirossi narrowly managed to fend off Nakano. Toseland was a solitary 18th, Melandri even further back.

125 RACE – 16 laps

Espargaro took pole for a second time in 2008, with Webb making his second front-row start, di Meglio and Bradl between them.

The race began dry, but that didn't last.

Espargaro led away and was almost 2.5 seconds clear by lap five. Terol and Redding were in hot pursuit, di Meglio in the thick of a big gang disputing fourth. Webb had been left on the line and finished the first lap way down in 20th.

Terol closed rapidly on his compatriot and took the lead on lap ten, when Espargaro ran wide at the last corner. He was pulling clear as spots of rain brought out the warning flags on lap 13.

First one, then the other slowed cautiously as the spots turned into drops. Now Espargaro made another run, fully aware that the race was unlikely to go the full distance of 24 laps. With a final lunge, he got ahead at the end of lap 17, but it was too late. The red flags came out simultaneously, and the results were taken from the previous lap.

Redding had dropped back with gear-shifting problems, and on lap 16 he was caught by a group of four. Only Bradl was ahead over the line, and although the rest piled past going into Turn One, it was too late for them as well.

The luckless trio comprised Cortese, Marquez and Corsi. Two seconds back, Smith had come through to eighth after being forced off track after the start to finish the first lap 25th. Bonsey was just ahead of di Meglio to round out the top ten.

Full of pain killers, Talmacsi had run with the chase group in the early laps, but dropped back to 14th; Webb was one place behind for the final point.

Right: Endurance racing? Pedrosa and Nakano keep on keeping on.

Below: Close to home, Hayden claimed his first rostrum in over a year.

Photographs: Gold & Goose

Left: Conditions had gone black and white by the time the 250 race was cancelled.

Right: First-time winner Terol celebrates his good timing in the abbreviated 125 race.

Photographs: Gold & Goose

RED BULL INDIANAPOLIS GRAND PRIX

14 SEPTEMBER 2008 • FIM WORLD CHAMPIONSHIP ROUND 14

INDIANAPOLIS MOTOR SPEEDWAY

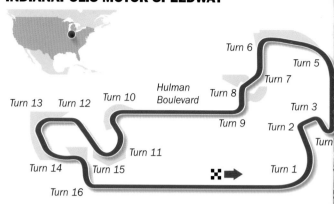

Turn 6
Turn 5
Turn 7
Turn 8
Hulman Boulevard
Turn 13 Turn 12 Turn 10
Turn 3
Turn 9 Turn 2
Turn
Turn 11
Turn 14 Turn 15
Turn 1
Turn 16

Circuit 4.218km / 2.621 miles

MOTOGP

RACE: 20 laps, 52.400 miles/84.320km • Weather: Wet • Air 21°C • Humidity 89% • Track 20°C

Pos.	Rider	Nat.	No.	Team	Machine	Tyres	Laps	Time & speed (mph/km/h)
1	Valentino Rossi	ITA	46	Fiat Yamaha Team	Yamaha	B	20	37m 20.095s 84.201mph/ 135.508km/h
2	Nicky Hayden	USA	69	Repsol Honda Team	Honda	M	20	37m 26.067s
3	Jorge Lorenzo	SPA	48	Fiat Yamaha Team	Yamaha	M	20	37m 27.953s
4	Casey Stoner	AUS	1	Ducati Team	Ducati	B	20	37m 48.257s
5	Andrea Dovizioso	ITA	4	JiR Team Scot Honda	Honda	M	20	37m 48.919s
6	Ben Spies	USA	11	Rizla Suzuki MotoGP	Suzuki	B	20	37m 49.740s
7	Sylvain Guintoli	FRA	50	Alice Team	Ducati	B	20	37m 56.318s
8	Dani Pedrosa	SPA	2	Repsol Honda Team	Honda	B	20	37m 57.353s
9	Chris Vermeulen	AUS	7	Rizla Suzuki MotoGP	Suzuki	B	20	37m 58.537s
10	Alex de Angelis	RSM	15	San Carlo Honda Gresini	Honda	B	20	38m 02.532s
11	Anthony West	AUS	13	Kawasaki Racing Team	Kawasaki	B	20	38m 07.274s
12	Toni Elias	SPA	24	Alice Team	Ducati	B	20	38m 16.057s
13	Randy de Puniet	FRA	14	LCR Honda MotoGP	Honda	M	20	38m 17.461s
14	John Hopkins	USA	21	Kawasaki Racing Team	Kawasaki	B	20	38m 18.448s
15	Colin Edwards	USA	5	Tech 3 Yamaha	Yamaha	M	20	38m 20.708s
16	Loris Capirossi	ITA	65	Rizla Suzuki MotoGP	Suzuki	B	20	38m 25.715s
17	Shinya Nakano	JPN	56	San Carlo Honda Gresini	Honda	B	20	38m 25.949s
18	James Toseland	GBR	52	Tech 3 Yamaha	Yamaha	M	20	38m 28.063s
19	Marco Melandri	ITA	33	Ducati Team	Ducati	B	20	38m 41.118s

Fastest lap: Valentino Rossi, on lap 15, 1m 49.668s, 85.995mph/138.395km/h (record).

Previous lap record: New circuit.

Event best maximum speed: Marco Melandri, 196.0mph/315.5km/h (warm-up).

QUALIFYING: 13 September 2008

Weather: Dry
Air: 34°C Humidity: 44% Track: 40°C

Pos.	Rider	Time
1	Rossi	1m 40.776s
2	Stoner	1m 40.860s
3	Lorenzo	1m 41.177s
4	Hayden	1m 41.271s
5	Spies	1m 41.464s
6	de Puniet	1m 41.492s
7	Dovizioso	1m 41.744s
8	Pedrosa	1m 41.754s
9	Elias	1m 41.886s
10	Toseland	1m 41.897s
11	Edwards	1m 41.934s
12	de Angelis	1m 41.969s
13	Capirossi	1m 42.305s
14	Guintoli	1m 42.405s
15	Vermeulen	1m 42.551s
16	Hopkins	1m 42.673s
17	Nakano	1m 42.732s
18	Melandri	1m 43.807s
19	West	1m 43.931s

Grid order	1	2	3	4	5	6	7	8	9	10	11	12	13	14	15	16	17	18	19	20	
46 ROSSI	4	69	69	69	69	69	69	69	69	69	69	69	69	46	46	46	46	46	46	46	1
1 STONER	69	4	4	4	4	46	46	46	46	46	46	46	46	69	69	69	69	69	69	69	2
48 LORENZO	1	48	48	46	46	4	4	48	48	48	48	48	48	48	48	48	48	48	48	48	3
69 HAYDEN	46	1	46	48	48	48	48	4	4	4	4	4	1	1	1	1	4	4	1	1	4
11 SPIES	48	46	1	1	1	1	1	1	1	1	1	1	4	4	4	4	1	1	4	4	5
14 de PUNIET	2	2	2	11	11	11	11	11	11	11	11	11	11	11	11	11	11	11	11	11	6
4 DOVISIOSO	11	11	11	2	2	2	2	2	2	2	2	2	2	2	2	2	50	50	50	50	7
2 PEDROSA	52	52	52	52	52	50	50	50	50	50	50	50	50	50	50	50	7	7	2	2	8
24 ELIAS	24	21	21	7	50	52	7	7	7	7	7	7	7	7	7	7	2	2	7	7	9
52 TOSELAND	21	24	7	50	7	7	52	13	13	13	13	13	13	13	13	13	15	15	15	15	10
5 EDWARDS	14	15	24	21	21	21	13	15	15	15	15	15	15	15	15	15	13	13	13	13	11
15 de ANGELIS	56	50	50	15	15	15	15	52	52	24	24	24	24	24	24	24	24	24	24	24	12
65 CAPIROSSI	15	14	15	13	13	13	21	21	21	21	21	21	21	21	21	21	14	14	14	14	13
50 GUINTOLI	50	7	13	24	24	24	24	24	24	52	52	14	14	14	14	14	21	21	21	21	14
7 VERMEULEN	13	13	14	14	14	14	14	14	14	14	14	52	5	5	5	5	5	5	5	5	15
21 HOPKINS	7	65	56	56	56	56	56	56	56	56	56	5	52	65	65	65	65	65	65	65	
56 NAKANO	65	56	65	65	65	65	65	65	65	65	5	56	65	33	33	33	56	56	56	56	
33 MELANDRI	5	5	5	5	5	5	5	5	5	5	65	65	33	52	52	56	52	52	52	52	
13 WEST	33	33	33	33	33	33	33	33	33	33	33	33	56	56	56	52	33	33	33	33	

FASTEST RACE LAPS

	Rider	Lap	Time
1	Rossi	15	1m 49.668s
2	Hayden	11	1m 50.057s
3	Lorenzo	12	1m 50.418s
4	Dovizioso	12	1m 50.926s
5	Stoner	11	1m 50.989s
6	de Angelis	12	1m 51.040s
7	Spies	10	1m 51.219s
8	Guintoli	11	1m 51.265s
9	West	10	1m 51.524s
10	Vermeulen	9	1m 51.761s
11	Pedrosa	7	1m 51.789s
12	de Puniet	14	1m 51.945s
13	Elias	12	1m 51.962s
14	Edwards	13	1m 52.070s
15	Hopkins	12	1m 52.075s
16	Melandri	10	1m 52.451s
17	Nakano	8	1m 52.830s
18	Capirossi	8	1m 52.905s
19	Toseland	12	1m 53.385s

statistics

OFFICIAL TIMEKEEPER

250cc

Race cancelled due to adverse weather conditions

Rider (Nat.)	No.	Team	Machine
Hiroshi Aoyama (JPN)	4	Red Bull KTM 250	KTM
Alex Debon (SPA)	6	Lotus Aprilia	Aprilia
Imre Toth (HUN)	10	Team Toth Aprilia	Aprilia
Thomas Luthi (SWI)	12	Emmi - Caffe Latte	Aprilia
Ratthapark Wilairot (THA)	14	Thai Honda PTT SAG	Honda
Roberto Locatelli (ITA)	15	Metis Gilera	Gilera
Karel Abraham (CZE)	17	Cardion AB Motoracing	Aprilia
Alvaro Bautista (SPA)	19	Mapfre Aspar Team	Aprilia
Hector Barbera (SPA)	21	Team Toth Aprilia	Aprilia
Alex Baldolini (ITA)	25	Matteoni Racing	Aprilia
Stefano Bianco (ITA)	27	Campetella Racing	Gilera
Barrett Long (USA)	29	Longevity Racing	Yamaha
Simone Grotzkyj (ITA)	35	Campetella Racing	Gilera
Mika Kallio (FIN)	36	Red Bull KTM 250	KTM
Kyle Ferris (USA)	38	Team Infinity Replicast	Yamaha
Aleix Espargaro (SPA)	41	Lotus Aprilia	Aprilia
Manuel Hemandez (SPA)	43	Blusens Aprilia	Aprilia
Doni Tata Pradita (INA)	45	Yamaha Pertamina Indonesia	Yamaha
Eugene Laverty (IRL)	50	Blusens Aprilia	Yamaha
Lukas Pesek (CZE)	52	Auto Kelly - CP	Aprilia
Hector Faubel (SPA)	55	Mapfre Aspar Team	Aprilia
Marco Simoncelli (ITA)	58	Metis Gilera	Gilera
Julian Simon (SPA)	60	Repsol KTM 250cc	KTM
Yuki Takahashi (JPN)	72	JiR Team Scot 250	Honda
Mattia Pasini (ITA)	75	Polaris World	Aprilia

Qualifying: **1** Simoncelli, 1m 45.168s; **2** Barbera, 1m 45.537s; **3** Kallio, 1m 45.563s; **4** Debon, 1m 45.601s; **5** Aoyama, 1m 45.850s; **6** Bautista, 1m 46.174s; **7** Pasini, 1m 46.322s; **8** Faubel, 1m 46.360s; **9** Pesek, 1m 46.370s; **10** Simon, 1m 46.687s; **11** Takahashi, 1m 46.739s; **12** Espargaro, 1m 46.835s; **13** Wilairot, 1m 46.847s; **14** Locatelli, 1m 47.049s; **15** Abraham, 1m 47.974s; **16** Bianco, 1m 48.620s; **17** Hemandez, 1m 49.024s; **18** Pradita, 1m 49.089s; **19** Grotzkyj, 1m 49.666s; **20** Toth, 1m 49.758s; **21** Baldolini, 1m 50.694s; **22** Laverty, 1m 51.097s; **23** Long, 1m 1m 52.384s; **24** Ferris, 1m 53.899s; **25** Luthi, 2m 06.570s.

World Championship: **1** Simoncelli, 190; **2** Kallio, 164; **3** Bautista, 163; **4** Barbera, 142; **5** Debon, 139; **6** Pasini, 117; **7** Takahashi, 115; **8** Aoyama, 101; **9** Luthi, 95; **10** Simon, 83; **11** Locatelli, 72; **12** Espargaro, 55; **13** Faubel, 49; **14** Wilairot, 47; **15** Abraham, 31; **16** Pesek, 31; **17** Baldolini, 24; **18** Lai, 21; **19** Poggiali, 16; **20** Laverty, 8; **21** Sandi, 6; **22** Hemandez, 5; **23** Wirsing, 2; **24** Toth, 2; **25** Grotzkyj and Pradita, 1.

125cc

16 laps, 41.920 miles/67.456km

Pos.	Rider (Nat.)	No.	Team	Machine	Laps	Time & speed
1	Nicolas Terol (SPA)	18	Jack & Jones WRB	Aprilia	16	29m 51.350s 84.235mph/ 135.563km/h
2	Pol Espargaro (SPA)	44	Belson Derbi	Derbi	16	29m 53.058s
3	Stefan Bradl (GER)	17	Grizzly Gas Kiefer Racing	Aprilia	16	29m 55.334s
4	Scott Redding (GBR)	45	Blusens Aprilia Junior	Aprilia	16	29m 55.627s
5	Sandro Cortese (GER)	11	Emmi - Caffe Latte	Aprilia	16	29m 55.763s
6	Marc Marquez (SPA)	93	Repsol KTM 125cc	KTM	16	29m 55.804s
7	Simone Corsi (ITA)	24	Jack & Jones WRB	Aprilia	16	29m 57.611s
8	Bradley Smith (GBR)	38	Polaris World	Aprilia	16	29m 59.132s
9	Stevie Bonsey (USA)	51	Degraaf Grand Prix	Aprilia	16	30m 03.385s
10	Mike di Meglio (FRA)	63	Ajo Motorsport	Derbi	16	30m 03.601s
11	Dominique Aegerter (SWI)	77	Ajo Motorsport	Derbi	16	30m 06.815s
12	Joan Olive (SPA)	6	Belson Derbi	Derbi	16	30m 09.662s
13	Raffaele de Rosa (ITA)	35	Onde 2000 KTM	KTM	16	30m 11.487s
14	Gabor Talmacsi (HUN)	1	Bancaja Aspar Team	Aprilia	16	30m 16.001s
15	Danny Webb (GBR)	99	Degraaf Grand Prix	Aprilia	16	30m 18.942s
16	Jules Cluzel (FRA)	16	Loncin Racing	Loncin	16	30m 26.782s
17	Robin Lasser (GER)	21	Grizzly Gas Kiefer Racing	Aprilia	16	30m 28.432s
18	Sergio Gadea (SPA)	33	Bancaja Aspar Team	Aprilia	16	30m 29.899s
19	Tomoyoshi Koyama (JPN)	71	ISPA KTM Aran	KTM	16	30m 29.921s
20	Efren Vazquez (SPA)	7	Blusens Aprilia Junior	Aprilia	16	30m 32.341s
21	Hugo van den Berg (NED)	56	Degraaf Grand Prix	Aprilia	16	30m 57.547s
22	PJ Jacobsen (USA)	54	Bancaja Aspar Team	Aprilia	16	30m 57.677s
23	Bastien Chesaux (SWI)	48	WTR San Marino Team	Aprilia	16	30m 58.417s
24	Jonas Folger (GER)	94	Red Bull KTM 125	KTM	16	31m 06.059s
25	Robert Muresan (ROU)	95	Grizzly Gas Kiefer Racing	Aprilia	16	31m 11.763s
26	Alexis Masbou (FRA)	5	Loncin Racing	Loncin	16	31m 13.230s
27	Davide Stirpe (ITA)	74	ISPA KTM Aran	KTM	16	31m 13.376s
28	Cyril Carrillo (FRA)	36	FFM Honda GP 125	Honda	16	31m 13.509s
29	Kristian Lee Turner (USA)	90	Veloce Racing	Aprilia	16	32m 02.874s
	Lorenzo Zanetti (ITA)	8	ISPA KTM Aran	KTM	12	DNF
	Marco Ravaioli (ITA)	72	Matteoni Racing	Aprilia	9	DNF
	Pablo Nieto (SPA)	22	Onde 2000 KTM	KTM	8	DNF
	Michael Ranseder (AUT)	60	I.C. Team	Aprilia	6	DNF
	Takaaki Nakagami (JPN)	73	I.C. Team	Aprilia	5	DNF
	Andrea Iannone (ITA)	29	I.C. Team	Aprilia	4	DNF
	Esteve Rabat (SPA)	12	Repsol KTM 125cc	KTM	1	DNF

Fastest lap: Bradl, 1m 50.460s, 85.378mph/137.403km/h (record).

Previous lap record: New circuit.

Event best maximum speed: Corsi, 141.7mph/228.1km/h (race).

Qualifying: **1** Espargaro, 1m 50.475s; **2** di Meglio, 1m 50.844s; **3** Bradl, 1m 50.878s; **4** Webb, 1m 51.000s; **5** Iannone, 1m 51.031s; **6** Terol, 1m 51.179s; **7** Corsi, 1m 51.211s; **8** Aegerter, 1m 51.260s; **9** Redding, 1m 51.274s; **10** Cortese, 1m 51.551s; **11** Smith, 1m 51.572s; **12** Olive, 1m 51.985s; **13** Marquez, 1m 52.069s; **14** Nakagami, 1m 52.076s; **15** Bonsey, 1m 52.086s; **16** Talmacsi, 1m 52.170s; **17** de Rosa, 1m 52.358s; **18** Koyama, 1m 52.635s; **19** Ranseder, 1m 52.759s; **20** Nieto, 1m 53.053s; **21** Rabat, 1m 53.115s; **22** Lasser, 1m 53.137s; **23** Gadea, 1m 53.140s; **24** Vazquez, 1m 53.155s; **25** Jacobsen, 1m 53.209s; **26** Ravaioli, 1m 53.239s; **27** Masbou, 1m 53.478s; **28** Zanetti, 1m 53.683s; **29** Folger, 1m 53.774s; **30** van den Berg, 1m 53.931s; **31** Cluzel, 1m 54.414s; **32** Muresan, 1m 54.732s; **33** Stirpe, 1m 55.279s; **34** Chesaux, 1m 55.440s; **35** Carrillo, 1m 55.697s; **36** Turner, 1m 56.703s.

Fastest race laps: **1** Bradl, 1m 50.460s; **2** Smith, 1m 50.484s; **3** Terol, 1m 50.528s; **4** Corsi, 1m 50.710s; **5** Cortese, 1m 50.856s; **6** Espargaro, 1m 50.918s; **7** Bonsey, 1m 50.974s; **8** di Meglio, 1m 50.991s; **9** Redding, 1m 51.077s; **10** Marquez, 1m 51.127s; **11** Webb, 1m 51.151s; **12** de Rosa, 1m 51.371s; **13** Olive, 1m 51.475s; **14** Talmacsi, 1m 51.666s; **15** Aegerter, 1m 51.776s; **16** Gadea, 1m 51.893s; **17** Vazquez, 1m 51.963s; **18** Ravaioli, 1m 52.002s; **19** Iannone, 1m 52.301s; **20** Cluzel, 1m 52.351s; **21** Lasser, 1m 52.423s; **22** Nakagami, 1m 52.514s; **23** Masbou, 1m 52.607s; **24** Koyama, 1m 52.646s; **25** Ranseder, 1m 53.278s; **26** Nieto, 1m 53.304s; **27** Jacobsen, 1m 53.824s; **28** van den Berg, 1m 53.921s; **29** Muresan, 1m 54.123s; **30** Folger, 1m 54.158s; **31** Chesaux, 1m 54.237s; **32** Zanetti, 1m 54.242s; **33** Stirpe, 1m 54.759s; **34** Carrillo, 1m 55.407s; **35** Turner, 1m 55.490s; **36** Rabat, 2m 03.773s.

World Championship: **1** di Meglio, 192; **2** Corsi, 167; **3** Talmacsi, 149; **4** Bradl, 142; **5** Terol, 138; **6** Olive, 118; **7** Smith, 117; **8** Espargaro, 103; **9** Cortese, 97; **10** Redding, 83; **11** Iannone, 77; **12** Gadea, 72; **13** Marquez, 56; **14** Bonsey, 46; **15** Aegerter, 37; **16** Rabat, 34; **17** de Rosa, 33; **18** Webb, 29; **19** Koyama, 22; **20** Ranseder, 22; **21** Vazquez, 20; **22** Nieto, 13; **23** Zanetti, 10; **24** Krummenacher, 10; **25** Nakagami, 9; **26** Tutusaus, 9; **27** Bianco, 8; **28** Schrotter, 3; **29** Folger, Lasser, Masbou and van den Berg, 1.

RIDER STANDINGS
After 14 Rounds

1	Valentino Rossi	287
2	Casey Stoner	200
3	Dani Pedrosa	193
4	Jorge Lorenzo	156
5	Andrea Dovizioso	129
6	Chris Vermeulen	117
7	Colin Edwards	109
8	Nicky Hayden	104
9	Shinya Nakano	87
10	Toni Elias	86
11	Loris Capirossi	86
12	James Toseland	85
13	Sylvain Guintoli	56
14	Alex de Angelis	55
15	Marco Melandri	48
16	Randy de Puniet	43
17	John Hopkins	41
18	Anthony West	41
19	Ben Spies	20
20	Jamie Hacking	5
21	Tadayuki Okada	2

TEAM STANDINGS
After 14 Rounds

1	Fiat Yamaha Team	443
2	Repsol Honda Team	297
3	Ducati Team	248
4	Rizla Suzuki MotoGP	205
5	Tech 3 Yamaha	194
6	Alice Team	142
7	San Carlo Honda Gresini	142
8	JiR Team Scot MotoGP	129
9	Kawasaki Racing Team	87
10	LCR Honda MotoGP	43

CONSTRUCTOR STANDINGS
After 14 Rounds

1	Yamaha	316
2	Honda	243
3	Ducati	241
4	Suzuki	149
5	Kawasaki	71

Main photograph: Foot dangling, front wheel angled – Rossi is pushing hard.

Inset right: Post-race celebration included a visit to a lawyer.
Photographs: Gold & Goose

Above: Scusati Ritardo.
Photograph: Gold & Goose

FIM WORLD CHAMPIONSHIP • ROUND 15

JAPANESE | GP
MOTEGI

Above: Hayden went local with banzai bandana.

Right: Casey and Adriana share a joke on the grid.

Far right: Dovizioso was announced as Hayden's replacement at Honda.

Bottom right: Akiyoshi prepared for the start. The unlucky wild card didn't finish the first lap.

Opposite page: Rossi's 'World Soup' recipe was spelled out on his crew's T-shirts.

Photographs: Gold & Goose

THERE was a sense of inevitability at Motegi. On all sides. It was certainly inevitable that Rossi would win his eighth world championship, his sixth in the premier class, either in Japan or at the next round. And inevitable that he would celebrate his fine race and title victory with his unique style: on this occasion, a super-cheesy pantomime involving one of his fan club dressed as a lawyer at his desk by the track. Rossi stopped off to have his title deed officially notarised. TV producers and, indeed, viewers were miffed that the performance took so long that Valentino missed the post-race interviews; and especially that Dorna had been complicit by providing him with a pen fitted with a mini-camera to film his signature in close-up. It added extra meaning to his T-shirt message: 'Scusati Ritardo' (sorry for the delay).

And it had long seemed inevitable that the tyre situation would be resolved in favour of a single-tyre rule. Now it all came in a rush: the MSMA meeting on the eve of the event voted unanimously in favour, and the GP Commission followed up on Saturday, although it delayed the final decision until Sunday morning while Michelin, Ducati, Kawasaki, Suzuki, and satellite teams JIR-Scot Honda and Tech 3 engaged in a sort of last waltz – if enough riders could have been persuaded to choose Michelin, the decision would have been reversed. Ducati was keen at one point, encouraged by Stoner, and offered five bikes; two or three more would have been enough. The Kawasaki team also was interested, but this was scotched at factory level. The plans were too complex and too diverse to gel, and the time limit too short; on Sunday morning, the axe fell. There would be a single tyre supplier, but there was less than a week for tyre companies to declare an interest and submit a tender.

The final sense of inevitability concerned the 250 replacement, with broad technical regulations agreed at the MSMA, including a rev limit, a proposal for a 20,000-euro claiming rule and the possibility of a control ECU. The regs looked, said KTM's technical chief, Harald Bartol, 'as though they were drawn up by Karl Marx – like communism. From what I saw, the street-bike engines will have to be detuned. The next thing is that the 125s will be faster.' This conclusion carried with it a sense of approaching doom for the 125 two-strokes, in spite of assurances to the contrary.

Until this race, Rossi had stuck to a policy of trying to win each time: 'When you try and finish second, things can go wrong.' Now he admitted he would abandon this ploy. 'When you have the first match point, it's important to play well,' he said. His target would be the podium. Or was he just lulling his rivals with false promises?

Honda chose its own circuit to announce long-expected changes. Dovizioso was welcomed officially into the factory team alongside Pedrosa for 2009. He said that he hoped he would have a good relationship with the Spaniard, 'but if he doesn't want that, it's not such a problem for me.' HRC President Masao Hamane was on hand to promise that both riders would start off with equal equipment, 'but as the season progresses, we will give modified parts and new parts to the rider with a better points standing.' If this was a veiled threat to Pedrosa, it was not softened when he went on to reveal that, with or without a single-tyre rule (this happened before the announcement), both riders would be on the same make.

Soon afterwards, Dovi's replacement at Team Scot was announced: Yuki Takahashi, the latest home-country rider to be favoured by Honda's eternal hope for a Japanese world champion. At the same time, it was confirmed that Team Scot would split its short-lived partnership with JiR Racing. This triggered some claims from passed-over JiR manager Luca Montiron, who com-

plained that the team's application for a MotoGP bike from Honda had been refused, in spite of past successes with Pramac, racing with Camel and Max Biaggi, and GP wins with Tamada. Pramac promptly responded, pointing out that Montiron had been merely a fellow employee at that time and that JiR could claim no such credit. It made little difference either way.

Alex Criville took himself and the GP old-timers on a sentimental journey with two demonstration laps on the two-stroke Repsol Honda NSR500 with which he had won the 1999 World Championship. The bike looked light, delicate and brutal, lifting its front wheel with almost every gear-change and flicking rather too unexpectedly sideways out of the corner after the second Motegi underpass. The shrill note was a wistful counterpoint to the MotoGP bikes warming up in the pit lane, reminding one why they had been dubbed 'diesels' when they first arrived in 2002.

Polaris World became the first high-profile paddock casualty of the world financial crisis, the Spanish property developer announcing that it would cease sponsorship in the 125 and 250 classes. This left Qatar winner Mattia Pasini still without a ride at the end of the season, but 125 rider Bradley Smith was already planning a move to the Aspar team.

Hector Barbera suffered a potentially dangerous back injury in a heavy crash on Saturday morning. Amazingly, he went out on track again in the same session, before pain sent him to the medical centre. With two fractured vertebrae, he was flown straight home to Spain for treatment, and would not return.

His deadly rival, Simoncelli, who later would win Dun-

lop's 200th consecutive 125/250 GP, had some kind words: 'He is not very nice to me, and on the track we always have a great fight. But he's bad, and I hope he comes good again.'

Of course, it rained, as at almost every race in 2008, but only on the first day, leaving a bit of a scramble for qualifying on the second.

MOTOGP RACE – 24 laps

With a touch of rubbery irony, Michelin dominated the front row, with Lorenzo on his fourth pole of the year and Hayden third. Stoner, between them, might have changed that, had he not taken a great big bug on the visor at the start of his final qualifying lap. 'I struggled and struggled, but for some reason I couldn't remove the tear-off,' he said.

Hayden's lap had been his second on the same qualifier after traffic had spoiled the first, and as a result it had been rather adventurous. Enough to put Rossi fourth, from Pedrosa and 2007's winner, Capirossi.

Stoner led away, the factory Hondas of Pedrosa and Hayden in pursuit, then came Lorenzo and Rossi. The Italian pounced on his team-mate into the first corner of the second lap, taking Hayden also two corners later; the first three started to move away immediately.

Stoner had chosen a harder rear tyre and was still battling to get some heat in it, admitting later that 'I nearly spilled it.' Pedrosa led the second lap and the next three, fending off Stoner as the Australian made a strong attack.

The next attack was by mistake, into the corner

before the first underpass. Stoner misjudged his braking and had to push inside Pedrosa, waving an arm in apology. But the Spaniard had been pushed wide all the same, and Rossi took advantage, nipping through into second. Pedrosa started to lose touch immediately.

Rossi seemed content to follow until lap 14. Now he moved past cleanly under braking for the second corner and pulled clear at once.

Stoner had a problem: not only had his injured wrist curtailed his training, but also it had forced him to ride differently, using his upper body more. The effort on the fast changes of direction had left him exhausted, he admitted later.

Rossi was almost two seconds clear by lap 21, when Stoner rallied briefly for two laps, but then the Yamaha rider began inching away again for a fifth win in succession, his eighth of the year. And enough to win the title with style.

Hayden had dropped more than three seconds behind the leaders when Lorenzo went past on lap eight. The Spaniard had the other factory Honda as his next target. Within five laps, he'd turned a gap of two seconds into half a second, but catching would prove easier than passing. He pushed and pushed, while Pedrosa did everything he could to keep him back. The latter had a slight, but clear advantage under acceleration; Lorenzo was stronger on corner entry. On the last lap, the Yamaha man tried to use this asset into the hairpin at the end of the back straight. Pedrosa slammed the door in his face and they collided. The Honda rider managed to stay on board and on course, but Lorenzo wobbled and ran wide, his last chance gone.

Hayden had little relief as he dropped back. Capirossi caught up and hounded him until lap 12, when the Suzuki slid wide at the bottom of the hill. This dropped the Italian back into the hands of Edwards and Nakano, and the three pressed on together. In the closing stages, Hayden's pace dropped further, and with two laps to go, all three were on them. Meanwhile, Dovizioso had picked his way past Melandri, Hopkins and then Toseland, and was closing also at the end.

Hayden's tyres were shot, but he concentrated on keeping smooth and riding defensively; he kept the pack behind him and in the same order, fifth to ninth covered by less than 1.5-seconds.

Toseland had lost ninth to Dovizioso on lap nine; at the same time, Hopkins had got ahead of Melandri when the Italian ran out of braking power and took a trip

Top: Stoner waves an apology to Pedrosa.

Left: Simoncelli took Dunlop's 200th straight win.

Above right: Rizla Suzuki fans provided colourful support in the gloomy conditions.

Right: Out of the shadows: Bradl heads di Meglio and Talmacsi through one of Motegi's two underpasses.

Photographs: Gold & Goose

through the gravel. Soon the Kawasaki was on the Englishman's tail, but Hopkins left it to the final lap before finding a place to outbrake and get ahead. By then, de Puniet, riding with a fractured right arm, had closed up and dropped away a couple of times. He finished right behind Toseland.

Melandri had got going again, finally passing Guintoli just after half-distance and leaving the Frenchman behind. Ten seconds back, West had also been battling braking problems, at a circuit of drag strips and U-turns, where braking is of prime importance. No matter how many times he adjusted it, he said, 'the lever kept coming back to the bars.'

He took to the gravel at the bottom of the hill, as did Elias, four seconds away, and last-placed de Angelis. Vermeulen had been running in a steady 13th when he also had a brake failure, running off at the first corner and then going straight to the pits to retire. His temporary Suzuki team-mate, wild-card Kousuke Akiyoshi, crashed on the third corner of the first lap.

250cc RACE – 23 laps

Simoncelli was on pole for the second time in a row, with more hope of actually having a race on this occasion. Aoyama, Debon and Kallio completed row one; Bautista led the next from Faubel, with half a second covering the first six.

Debon got the jump, but Simoncelli was soon in front and pulling away rapidly, almost a full second clear after two laps. Debon had Simon, Aoyama, Espargaro, Kallio and Takahashi brawling on his back wheel. Bautista was behind them, but would complain again of too much weight on the front with a full tank.

Simon took second on lap three, and by the fifth had closed on Simoncelli, the pair continuing to escape little by little, with a two-second advantage. By now, Bautista was more comfortable and was pushing Debon hard.

On lap ten, Bautista was up to third and closing. It took him only three more to catch up and displace Simon, who at once started to lose ground, falling back to become involved once more with Debon.

Up front, it was a familiar scenario, but for the absence of Barbera. Simoncelli was pushing, Bautista poised threateningly behind him. He didn't seem quite able to make a decisive attack – until lap 20, when he tried an outbraking move up the inside. Simoncelli, who later told MOTOCOURSE that his greatest strength was 'I never give a present to the other rider', firmly moved across to close the apex and they almost collided.

It was still far from settled, but the final battle never came. On lap 21, they came up to lap wild-card Takumi Endoh and Spanish Blusens Aprilia replacement Daniel Arcas at the first underpass. Simoncelli dived past, but Bautista couldn't follow. 'They closed the corner line in front of me,' he said.

It broke the tow, and Bautista tried everything to get back, including setting a new lap record on the last lap, but Simoncelli had started that with an advantage of almost seven-tenths, which was just enough. He was 0.348 second ahead at the finish and took one more step towards the title.

Debon had passed Simon with seven laps to go and was ahead by six-tenths at the flag. Kallio had got the better of Espargaro and, on lap ten, also Aoyama; he pulled away gradually for a lonely second half of the race.

The next group had battled almost to the end, with Pasini joining in before half-distance as Faubel dropped to the back. Takahashi led it for the last five laps, from Espargaro, while with three laps left, Pasini regained eighth from Aoyama. The Japanese rider was over a second behind at the line, kept busy by Locatelli, who had held a watching brief at the back of the group all race and who all but overtook the KTM over the line.

Faubel was ten seconds away at the end.

All starters finished except for Grotzkyj, who crashed on lap one.

125cc RACE – 20 laps

Points leader di Meglio took a career-first pole. almost four-tenths clear of Bradl, Terol and Cortese. Talmacsi led the second row from Redding; earlier leader Smith had ended up 14th after crashing on his fast qualifying lap. It was part of an unlucky weekend for the Briton: in the race, he would fight his way up to seventh before breaking down and retiring.

Two multiple crashes on the first lap eliminated six riders. Among them were Rabat, Iannone, Espargaro and Marquez.

Terol led two laps, then Bradl took over. By the eighth, he was narrowly in control of a group of six, with di Meglio, Talmacsi, Olive, Terol and Cortese right behind; Smith and Corsi were some four seconds adrift.

Soon Terol and Cortese began losing touch, while the four leaders swapped back and fourth several times a lap. After half-distance, di Meglio took to the front for a long spell, and with five laps left, Olive dropped off the back, leaving just three.

Bradl moved to the front with three laps remaining and ran a near-perfect last lap to win by the narrowest of margins from di Meglio and Talmacsi. The first three crossed the line within three-tenths.

Olive hung on to fourth, with Terol and Cortese on his tail by the end, and Corsi right up behind them. Redding managed to keep the lead of the next group, while Gadea had taken ninth from Webb (riding with a broken collar bone, unknown to his team) with two laps to go.

A-STYLE GRAND PRIX OF JAPAN

28 SEPTEMBER 2008 • FIM WORLD CHAMPIONSHIP ROUND 15

TWIN RING MOTEGI

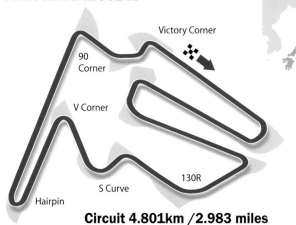

Circuit 4.801km / 2.983 miles

MOTOGP

RACE: 24 laps, 71.592 miles/115.224km • Weather: Dry • Air 19°C • Humidity 51% • Track 23°C

Pos.	Rider	Nat.	No.	Team	Machine	Tyres	Laps	Time & speed (mph/km/h)
1	Valentino Rossi	ITA	46	Fiat Yamaha Team	Yamaha	B	24	43m 09.599s 99.532mph/ 160.181km/h
2	Casey Stoner	AUS	1	Ducati Marlboro Team	Ducati	B	24	43m 11.542s
3	Dani Pedrosa	SPA	2	Repsol Honda Team	Honda	B	24	43m 14.465s
4	Jorge Lorenzo	SPA	48	Fiat Yamaha Team	Yamaha	M	24	43m 15.764s
5	Nicky Hayden	USA	69	Repsol Honda Team	Honda	M	24	43m 34.192s
6	Loris Capirossi	ITA	65	Rizla Suzuki MotoGP	Suzuki	B	24	43m 35.284s
7	Colin Edwards	USA	5	Tech 3 Yamaha	Yamaha	M	24	43m 35.517s
8	Shinya Nakano	JPN	56	San Carlo Honda Gresini	Honda	B	24	43m 35.602s
9	Andrea Dovizioso	ITA	4	JiR Team Scot MotoGP	Honda	M	24	43m 35.818s
10	John Hopkins	AUS	21	Kawasaki Racing Team	Kawasaki	B	24	43m 46.730s
11	James Toseland	GBR	52	Tech 3 Yamaha	Yamaha	M	24	43m 47.173s
12	Randy de Puniet	FRA	14	LCR Honda Moto GP	Honda	M	24	43m 47.619s
13	Marco Melandri	ITA	33	Ducati Marlboro Team	Ducati	B	24	43m 49.367s
14	Sylvain Guintoli	FRA	50	Alice Team	Ducati	B	24	43m 55.445s
15	Anthony West	AUS	13	Kawasaki Racing Team	Kawasaki	B	24	44m 05.347s
16	Toni Elias	SPA	24	Alice Team	Ducati	B	24	44m 08.919s
17	Alex de Angelis	RSM	15	San Carlo Honda Gresini	Honda	B	24	44m 21.997s
	Chris Vermeulen	AUS	7	Rizla Suzuki MotoGP	Suzuki	B	16	29m 15.247s
	Kousuke Akiyoshi	JPN	64	Rizla Suzuki MotoGP	Suzuki	B	0	DNF

Fastest lap: Casey Stoner, on lap 9, 1m 47.091s, 100.284mph/161.391km/h (record).

Previous lap record: Valentino Rossi, ITA (Yamaha), 1m 47.288s, 100.099mph/161.095km/h (2006).

Event best maximum speed: Toni Elias, 182.4mph/293.6km/h (free practice no. 3).

QUALIFYING: 27 September 2008

Weather: Dry
Air: 25°C Humidity: 25% Track: 40°C

Pos.	Rider	Time
1	Lorenzo	1m 45.543s
2	Stoner	1m 45.831s
3	Hayden	1m 45.971s
4	Rossi	1m 46.060s
5	Pedrosa	1m 46.303s
6	Capirossi	1m 46.450s
7	Edwards	1m 46.496s
8	de Puniet	1m 46.554s
9	Nakano	1m 46.616s
10	Toseland	1m 46.863s
11	Hopkins	1m 46.888s
12	Vermeulen	1m 46.904s
13	Dovizioso	1m 46.907s
14	Elias	1m 46.958s
15	Guintoli	1m 47.400s
16	Melandri	1m 47.475s
17	West	1m 47.669s
18	de Angelis	1m 47.680s
19	Akiyoshi	1m 48.671s

Grid order

Grid order	1	2	3	4	5	6	7	8	9	10	11	12	13	14	15	16	17	18	19	20	21	22	23	24	●
48 LORENZO	1	2	2	2	2	1	1	1	1	1	1	1	1	46	46	46	46	46	46	46	46	46	46	46	1
1 STONER	2	1	1	1	1	46	46	46	46	46	46	46	46	1	1	1	1	1	1	1	1	1	1	1	2
69 HAYDEN	69	46	46	46	46	2	2	2	2	2	2	2	2	2	2	2	2	2	2	2	2	2	2	2	3
46 ROSSI		69	69	69	69	69	69	48	48	48	48	48	48	48	48	48	48	48	48	48	48	48	48	48	4
2 PEDROSA	46	48	48	48	48	48	48	69	69	69	69	69	69	69	69	69	69	69	69	69	69	69	69	69	5
65 CAPIROSSI	65	65	65	65	65	65	65	65	65	65	65	65	65	65	65	65	65	65	65	65	65	65	65	65	6
5 EDWARDS	5	5	5	5	5	5	5	5	5	5	5	5	5	5	5	5	5	5	5	5	5	5	5	5	7
14 de PUNIET	52	56	56	56	56	56	56	56	56	56	56	56	56	56	56	56	56	56	56	56	56	56	56	56	8
56 NAKANO	56	52	52	52	52	52	52	4	4	4	4	4	4	4	4	4	4	4	4	4	4	4	4	4	9
52 TOSELAND	21	21	21	4	4	4	4	52	52	52	52	52	52	52	52	52	52	52	52	52	52	52	52	21	10
21 HOPKINS	33	33	4	21	21	21	33	33	21	21	21	14	14	14	14	14	14	14	14	14	14	14	14	52	11
7 VERMEULEN	4	4	33	33	33	33	21	21	14	14	14	21	21	21	21	21	21	21	21	21	21	21	14	14	12
4 DOVISIOSO	7	7	7	7	14	14	14	14	7	7	7	7	7	33	33	33	33	33	33	33	33	33	33	33	13
24 ELIAS	14	14	14	14	7	7	7	7	13	50	50	50	33	33	33	33	50	50	50	50	50	50	50	50	14
50 GUINTOLI	50	50	50	50	50	13	13	13	50	33	33	33	50	50	50	50	13	13	13	13	13	13	13	13	15
33 MELANDRI	13	13	13	13	13	24	50	50	33	13	13	13	13	13	13	15	24	24	24	24	24	24	24	24	
13 WEST	24	24	24	24	24	50	15	15	15	15	15	15	15	15	24	24	15	15	15	15	15	15	15		
15 de ANGELIS	15	15	15	15	15	15	24	24	24	24	24	24	24	24	15										
64 AKIYOSHI																									

FASTEST RACE LAPS

	Rider	Lap	Time
1	Stoner	9	1m 47.091s
2	Rossi	12	1m 47.215s
3	Pedrosa	16	1m 47.354s
4	Lorenzo	9	1m 47.418s
5	Capirossi	3	1m 47.800s
6	Hayden	5	1m 47.823s
7	Edwards	8	1m 48.174s
8	Nakano	8	1m 48.197s
9	Dovizioso	13	1m 48.208s
10	Melandri	8	1m 48.293s
11	Elias	24	1m 48.301s
12	Toseland	8	1m 48.404s
13	Hopkins	6	1m 48.421s
14	West	8	1m 48.441s
15	de Puniet	7	1m 48.503s
16	Vermeulen	8	1m 48.567s
17	Guintoli	15	1m 48.600s
18	de Angelis	6	1m 49.011s

statistics

250cc

23 laps, 68.609 miles/110.423km

Pos. Rider (Nat.)	No.	Team	Machine	Laps	Time & speed
1 Marco Simoncelli (ITA)	58	Metis Gilera	Gilera	23	43m 09.385s 95.393mph/ 153.520km/h
2 Alvaro Bautista (SPA)	19	Mapfre Aspar Team	Aprilia	23	43m 09.733s
3 Alex Debon (SPA)	6	Lotus Aprilia	Aprilia	23	43m 17.799s
4 Julian Simon (SPA)	60	Repsol KTM 250cc	KTM	23	43m 18.536s
5 Mika Kallio (FIN)	36	Red Bull KTM 250	KTM	23	43m 26.426s
6 Yuki Takahashi (JPN)	72	JiR Team Scot 250	Honda	23	43m 29.017s
7 Aleix Espargaro (SPA)	41	Lotus Aprilia	Aprilia	23	43m 29.277s
8 Mattia Pasini (ITA)	75	Polaris World	Aprilia	23	43m 29.827s
9 Hiroshi Aoyama (JPN)	4	Red Bull KTM 250	KTM	23	43m 31.688s
10 Roberto Locatelli (ITA)	15	Metis Gilera	Gilera	23	43m 31.772s
11 Hector Faubel (SPA)	55	Mapfre Aspar Team	Aprilia	23	43m 42.236s
12 Lukas Pesek (CZE)	52	Auto Kelly - CP	Aprilia	23	43m 58.006s
13 Ratthapark Wilairot (THA)	14	Thai Honda PTT SAG	Honda	23	43m 58.188s
14 Shoya Tomizawa (JPN)	66	Project U FRS	Honda	23	43m 58.957s
15 Fabrizio Lai (ITA)	32	Campetella Racing	Gilera	23	44m 07.430s
16 Alex Baldolini (ITA)	25	Matteoni Racing	Aprilia	23	44m 07.747s
17 Takumi Takahashi (JPN)	65	Burning Blood Racing Team	Honda	23	44m 24.447s
18 Doni Tata Pradita (INA)	45	Yamaha Pertamina Indonesia	Yamaha	23	44m 59.315s
19 Manuel Hernandez (SPA)	43	Blusens Aprilia	Aprilia	23	45m 07.988s
20 Daniel Arcas (SPA)	92	Blusens Aprilia	Aprilia	22	43m 25.958s
21 Takumi Endoh (JPN)	69	Ser.Spruce/Pro-Tec	Yamaha	22	43m 26.261s
22 Imre Toth (HUN)	10	Team Toth Aprilia	Aprilia	22	44m 05.874s
23 Yuuki Ito (JPN)	68	Dog Fight Racing	Yamaha	20	43m 39.227s
Simone Grotzkyj (ITA)	35	Campetella Racing	Gilera	0	DNF

Fastest lap: Bautista, 1m 51.412s, 96.395mph/155.132km/h (record).

Previous lap record: Shinya Nakano, JPN (Yamaha), 1m 52.253s, 95.673mph/ 153.970km/h (2000).

Event best maximum speed: Bautista, 159.7mph/257.0km/h (race).

Qualifying: **1** Simoncelli, 1m 51.473s; **2** Aoyama, 1m 51.719s; **3** Debon, 1m 51.758s; **4** Kallio, 1m 51.765s; **5** Bautista, 1m 51.821s; **6** Faubel, 1m 51.973s; **7** Simon, 1m 52.033s; **8** Y. Takahashi, 1m 52.197s; **9** Espargaro, 1m 52.228s; **10** Locatelli, 1m 52.259s; **11** Pasini, 1m 52.464s; **12** Pesek, 1m 53.130s; **13** Tomizawa, 1m 53.289s; **14** Wilairot, 1m 53.356s; **15** Lai, 1m 53.496s; **16** T. Takahashi, 1m 53.660s; **17** Baldolini, 1m 54.276s; **18** Grotzkyj, 1m 54.688s; **19** Pradita, 1m 55.015s; **20** Hemandez, 1m 55.675s; **21** Arcas, 1m 56.283s; **22** Ito, 1m 57.053s; **23** Toth, 1m 57.115s; **24** Endoh, 1m 57.451s.

Fastest race laps: **1** Bautista, 1m 51.412s; **2** Simoncelli, 1m 51.748s; **3** Debon, 1m 51.987s; **4** Simon, 1m 52.086s; **5** Kallio, 1m 52.443s; **6** Pasini, 1m 52.500s; **7** Espargaro, 1m 52.580s; **8** Locatelli, 1m 52.588s; **9** Aoyama, 1m 52.678s; **10** Y. Takahashi, 1m 52.702s; **11** Faubel, 1m 53.091s; **12** Pesek, 1m 53.574s; **13** Wilairot, 1m 53.618s; **14** Tomizawa, 1m 53.635s; **15** Lai, 1m 54.051s; **16** Baldolini, 1m 54.081s; **17** T. Takahashi, 1m 54.903s; **18** Pradita, 1m 56.278s; **19** Hemandez, 1m 56.569s; **20** Endoh, 1m 57.061s; **21** Toth, 1m 57.075s; **22** Arcas, 1m 57.230s; **23** Ito, 1m 57.545s.

World Championship: **1** Simoncelli, 215; **2** Bautista, 183; **3** Kallio, 175; **4** Debon, 155; **5** Barbera, 142; **6** Pasini, 125; **7** Y. Takahashi, 125; **8** Aoyama, 108; **9** Simon, 96; **10** Luthi, 95; **11** Locatelli, 78; **12** Espargaro, 64; **13** Faubel, 54; **14** Wilairot, 50; **15** Pesek, 35; **16** Abraham, 31; **17** Baldolini, 24; **18** Lai, 22; **19** Poggiali, 16; **20** Laverty, 8; **21** Sandi, 6; **22** Hernandez, 5; **23** Tomizawa and Wirsing, 2; **25** Toth, 2; **26** Grotzkyj and Pradita, 1.

125cc

20 laps, 59.660 miles/96.020km

Pos. Rider (Nat.)	No.	Team	Machine	Laps	Time & speed
1 Stefan Bradl (GER)	17	Grizzly Gas Kiefer Racing	Aprilia	20	39m 57.228s 89.599mph/ 144.196km/h
2 Mike di Meglio (FRA)	63	Ajo Motorsport	Derbi	20	39m 57.379s
3 Gabor Talmacsi (HUN)	1	Bancaja Aspar Team	Aprilia	20	39m 57.509s
4 Joan Olive (SPA)	6	Belson Derbi	Derbi	20	40m 03.173s
5 Nicolas Terol (SPA)	18	Jack & Jones WRB	Aprilia	20	40m 03.300s
6 Sandro Cortese (GER)	11	Emmi - Caffe Latte	Aprilia	20	40m 03.363s
7 Simone Corsi (ITA)	24	Jack & Jones WRB	Aprilia	20	40m 03.683s
8 Scott Redding (GBR)	45	Blusens Aprilia Junior	Aprilia	20	40m 22.621s
9 Sergio Gadea (SPA)	33	Bancaja Aspar Team	Aprilia	20	40m 22.765s
10 Danny Webb (GBR)	99	Degraaf Grand Prix	Aprilia	20	40m 23.420s
11 Tomoyoshi Koyama (JPN)	71	ISPA KTM Aran	KTM	20	40m 24.535s
12 Raffaele de Rosa (ITA)	35	Onde 2000 KTM	KTM	20	40m 36.764s
13 Takaaki Nakagami (JPN)	73	I.C. Team	Aprilia	20	40m 40.973s
14 Efren Vazquez (SPA)	7	Blusens Aprilia Junior	Aprilia	20	40m 48.857s
15 Alexis Masbou (FRA)	5	Loncin Racing	Loncin	20	40m 49.127s
16 Jonas Folger (GER)	94	Red Bull KTM 125	KTM	20	40m 49.159s
17 Lorenzo Zanetti (ITA)	8	ISPA KTM Aran	KTM	20	40m 49.190s
18 Pablo Nieto (SPA)	22	Onde 2000 KTM	KTM	20	40m 49.817s
19 Dominique Aegerter (SWI)	77	Ajo Motorsport	Derbi	20	40m 54.065s
20 Stevie Bonsey (USA)	51	Degraaf Grand Prix	Aprilia	20	40m 54.205s
21 Marco Ravaioli (ITA)	72	Matteoni Racing	Aprilia	20	40m 55.854s
22 Yuuichi Yanagisawa (JPN)	58	18 Garage Racing	Honda	20	40m 57.154s
23 Robin Lasser (GER)	21	Grizzly Gas Kiefer Racing	Aprilia	20	41m 07.010s
24 Hiroki Ono (JPN)	59	Battle Factory	Honda	20	41m 12.111s
25 Adrian Martin (SPA)	26	Bancaja Aspar Team	Aprilia	20	41m 23.348s
26 Cyril Carrillo (FRA)	36	FFM Honda GP 125	Honda	20	41m 26.358s
Bradley Smith (GBR)	38	Polaris World	Aprilia	16	DNF
Kazuma Watanabe (JPN)	62	Team Plus One	Honda	16	DNF
Michael Ranseder (AUT)	60	I.C. Team	Aprilia	14	DNF
Iori Namihira (JPN)	57	Honda Suzuka Racing	Honda	11	DNF
Hiroomi Iwata (JPN)	50	DYDO Miu Racing	Honda	10	DNF
Bastien Chesaux (SWI)	48	WTR San Marino Team	Aprilia	8	DNF
Robert Muresan (ROU)	95	Grizzly Gas Kiefer Racing	Aprilia	6	DNF
Esteve Rabat (SPA)	12	Repsol KTM 125cc	KTM	0	DNF
Jules Cluzel (FRA)	16	Loncin Racing	Loncin	0	DNF
Andrea Iannone (ITA)	29	I.C. Team	Aprilia	0	DNF
Pol Espargaro (SPA)	44	Belson Derbi	Derbi	0	DNF
Hugo van den Berg (NED)	56	Degraaf Grand Prix	Aprilia	0	DNF
Marc Marquez (SPA)	93	Repsol KTM 125cc	KTM	0	DNF

Fastest lap: Talmacsi, 1m 58.815s, 90.388mph/145.466km/h.

Lap record: Mika Kallio, FIN (KTM), 1m 57.666s, 91.271mph/146.886km/h (2006).

Event best maximum speed: Bradl, 138.6mph/223.0km/h (qualifying practice no. 2).

Qualifying: **1** di Meglio, 1m 58.678s; **2** Bradl, 1m 59.059s; **3** Terol, 1m 59.104s; **4** Cortese, 1m 59.132s; **5** Talmacsi, 1m 59.179s; **6** Redding, 1m 59.351s; **7** Aegerter, 1m 59.463s; **8** Espargaro, 1m 59.562s; **9** Iannone, 1m 59.565s; **10** Gadea, 1m 59.695s; **11** Koyama, 1m 59.739s; **12** Olive, 1m 59.756s; **13** Marquez, 1m 59.783s; **14** Smith, 1m 59.784s; **15** Corsi, 1m 59.919s; **16** Vazquez, 1m 59.956s; **17** Bonsey, 2m 00.112s; **18** Webb, 2m 00.125s; **19** de Rosa, 2m 00.404s; **20** Nakagami, 2m 00.434s; **21** Rabat, 2m 01.121s; **22** Masbou, 2m 01.247s; **23** Zanetti, 2m 01.279s; **24** Ranseder, 2m 01.395s; **25** Lasser, 2m 01.458s; **26** Namihira, 2m 01.944s; **27** Iwata, 2m 01.946s; **28** Nieto, 2m 02.000s; **29** Martin, 2m 02.069s; **30** Ravaioli, 2m 02.148s; **31** Folger, 2m 02.270s; **32** Yanagisawa, 2m 02.488s; **33** Muresan, 2m 02.656s; **34** Watanabe, 2m 02.708s; **35** Ono, 2m 02.833s; **36** Cluzel, 2m 03.058s; **37** Carrillo, 2m 03.426s; **38** van den Berg, 2m 03.494s; **39** Chesaux, 2m 04.091s.

Fastest race laps: **1** Talmacsi, 1m 58.815s; **2** Bradl, 1m 58.900s; **3** di Meglio, 1m 58.949s; **4** Smith, 1m 59.075s; **5** Corsi, 1m 59.094s; **6** Olive, 1m 59.210s; **7** Cortese, 1m 59.348s; **8** Terol, 1m 59.374s; **9** Gadea, 1m 59.712s; **10** Aegerter, 1m 59.904s; **11** Webb, 2m 00.115s; **12** Redding, 2m 00.139s; **13** de Rosa, 2m 00.148s; **14** Koyama, 2m 00.227s; **15** Nakagami, 2m 00.632s; **16** Zanetti, 2m 00.693s; **17** Bonsey, 2m 00.699s; **18** Vazquez, 2m 00.699s; **19** Nieto, 2m 00.836s; **20** Folger, 2m 00.909s; **21** Masbou, 2m 01.181s; **22** Ranseder, 2m 01.283s; **23** Yanagisawa, 2m 01.435s; **24** Ravaioli, 2m 01.600s; **25** Lasser, 2m 01.979s; **26** Ono, 2m 02.113s; **27** Namihira, 2m 02.261s; **28** Martin, 2m 02.528s; **29** Chesaux, 2m 02.836s; **30** Muresan, 2m 02.955s; **31** Carrillo, 2m 03.133s; **32** Watanabe, 2m 03.833s; **33** Iwata, 2m 04.191s.

World Championship: **1** di Meglio, 212; **2** Corsi, 176; **3** Bradl, 167; **4** Talmacsi, 165; **5** Terol, 149; **6** Olive, 131; **7** Smith, 117; **8** Cortese, 107; **9** Espargaro, 103; **10** Redding, 91; **11** Gadea, 79; **12** Iannone, 77; **13** Marquez, 56; **14** Bonsey, 46; **15** Aegerter, 37; **16** de Rosa, 37; **17** Webb, 35; **18** Rabat, 34; **19** Koyama, 27; **20** Ranseder, 22; **21** Vazquez, 22; **22** Nieto, 13; **23** Nakagami, 12; **24** Zanetti, 10; **25** Krummenacher, 10; **26** Tutusaus, 9; **27** Bianco, 8; **28** Schrotter, 3; **29** Masbou, 2; **30** Folger, Lasser and van den Berg, 1.

RIDER STANDINGS

After 15 Rounds

1	Valentino Rossi	312
2	Casey Stoner	220
3	Dani Pedrosa	209
4	Jorge Lorenzo	169
5	Andrea Dovizioso	136
6	Colin Edwards	118
7	Chris Vermeulen	117
8	Nicky Hayden	115
9	Loris Capirossi	96
10	Shinya Nakano	95
11	James Toseland	90
12	Toni Elias	86
13	Sylvain Guintoli	58
14	Alex de Angelis	55
15	Marco Melandri	51
16	John Hopkins	47
17	Randy de Puniet	47
18	Anthony West	42
19	Ben Spies	20
20	Jamie Hacking	5
21	Tadayuki Okada	2

TEAM STANDINGS

After 15 Rounds

1	Fiat Yamaha Team	481
2	Repsol Honda Team	324
3	Ducati Marlboro Team	271
4	Rizla Suzuki MotoGP	215
5	Tech 3 Yamaha	208
6	San Carlo Honda Gresini	150
7	Alice Team	144
8	JiR Team Scot MotoGP	136
9	Kawasaki Racing Team	94
10	LCR Honda MotoGP	47

CONSTRUCTOR STANDINGS

After 15 Rounds

1	Yamaha	341
2	Ducati	261
3	Honda	259
4	Suzuki	159
5	Kawasaki	77

AUSTRALIAN GP
PHILLIP ISLAND

Clear focus. Stoner is away up front, from Hayden,
while Rossi is mired in the pack. The Australian would
never be troubled seriously.
Photograph: Gold & Goose

FRESH from Japan and with the news that Michelin had bowed out gracefully, having declined to submit a tender to supply, only now were the implications of the single-tyre decision starting to sink in. The French tyre company had disagreed in principle and had not been willing to take part in a top-level series without the essential element of competition. Meanwhile, Bridgestone boss Hiroshi Yamada had withstood a barrage of hostile questioning when he had met the Press, explaining that Bridgestone was also opposed in principle, but had agreed to take part out of respect for the GP Commission's decision.

It was easier to find riders, team bosses and general racing folk opposed to the change than for it, and even feeling stricken by it. Crocodile tears or not, the atmosphere was very sober as people began to realise what would soon be lost. The familiar blue and yellow Michelin awnings and uniforms, and the staff of fitters and tyre engineers were unexpectedly making a farewell appearance. Agonising over tyre choice would soon be a thing of the past. And – nobody had really thought about this before – there would be no more qualifying tyres.

The qualifying hour will never be the same – those contests where one, then another rider flings on a qualifying tyre and lops a big margin at the top of the time sheets. Most riders had three and maybe four such one-lap rear tyres; Michelin runners had front qualifiers too. And such was their potential that even on the third, riders were still going faster, still looking for the limit. Hay-

den was the first to mourn the loss. 'They had so much grip. Sometimes after a good qualifying lap, you'd come into the pit shaking, because it was that intense.' Others would echo his lament later in the year; for all, there was a realisation that they must enjoy the tyres while they could.

Of course it rained – why would it not, in a rainy year and at this beautiful, but exposed circuit overlooking an icy ocean? It was heavy and cold, but luckily confined to Friday afternoon.

At the fastest track of the year, there are always spectacular crashes. The most elegant was that of Sylvain Guintoli on Saturday morning, the Frenchman riding as if comfortably seated on the side of his sliding bike – with a footpeg jabbing his thigh, it wasn't as smooth as it looked. The most synchronised struck the other three Ducati riders – Stoner, Melandri and Elias – each having an identical tumble under downhill braking on the approach to tight MG Corner. Some Ducati mechanical quirk triggered in an identical manner perhaps? Something even slightly mystical? Stoner thought it more likely that they'd each hit the same slippery patch; the truth is out there.

The most significant befell the new world champion. It happened on the approach to the third corner, a sort of prolonged kink on the fast run out of the Southern Loop. Rossi ran wide on the exit from that corner and kept trying, but failing, to get himself back on to the track. Eventually, and still travelling at a fair lick, he ran into the gravel, grappled for an instant and was thrown hard.

He rose to his feet, looking a tad dazed, but went out again before the end of the session. At the same corner that had ended SBK multi-champion Fogarty's career, Rossi's luck held again, but it condemned him to a poor starting position, and a fraught and exciting race.

The same corner, by the way, was picked out by Stoner when asked what it felt like to have clocked up the highest top speed of the weekend – 328.1km/h, with Pedrosa at 326.1, Rossi's Yamaha 2km/h slower, and the 'Slowzuki' of Vermeulen at 314.0. 'It's not that exciting. For me, the third corner is the one,' he said. 'You approach in fifth gear on the rev limiter, peel it in and then slide. That's the one that gives me a thrill.'

His predecessor, Mick Doohan, had been another with a matter-of-fact way of describing a fast corner that could give you goose-bumps. He and the first Australian champion, Wayne Gardner, were on hand to pick up their 'Champion's Tower' replicas, along with Barry Sheene's son, Freddie. Gardner used the chance to evangelise for the preservation of Australian junior dirt-tracking, where he, Doohan, Stoner and almost all the other fast Australians had spent their pre-teen years. His two sons are already at it, but the sport is being allowed to die over much of Australia, he said.

Tyre turncoat Pedrosa was still something of a paddock pariah, and when race two of his Bridgestone adventure ended with an unforced crash on only the second corner, only those closest to him grieved. Sidelined team-mate Hayden, cast by contrast as defender of the faith for Michelin, was fastest in the wet and on Saturday morning, storming to his second rostrum of the year, and in the last 22 races. He was full of glee, laughing at the post-race conference as he described the discomfort of 'my Michelin guy' when he opted on the grid for a softer tyre. 'I was worried about his well-being. He aged about ten years. I thought somebody better get him some air. Or water.' Then MOTOCOURSE asked how he felt about Pedrosa's misfortune. He tried to keep a straight face and said, 'I won't say he's just another rider to me, because you know I'd be lying,' before dissolving into spontaneous laughter that infected the whole room.

Just for the history books, the doomed 250 class produced another nail-biting classic, with Simoncelli riding like a demon to defeat Bautista, the championship still inches from his grasp. Motorcycle racing's forthcoming loss was again keenly felt at this most classic of all grand prix circuits.

MOTOGP RACE – 27 laps

With Phillip Island's circuit length, high speeds and left-hand bias, the question is whether a qualifying tyre can give of its best over a full lap. Stoner had to nurse his, 'standing the bike up to use the bigger part of the tyre to have grip for the last corners. This has been one of my hardest poles.' It was his eighth of 2008.

He displaced Lorenzo from what would have been his fifth, with Hayden alongside, the first eight within a second and some lesser-favoured proving that skill and courage – and Michelins – were as important as horsepower here. De Puniet was fourth, Toseland fifth and only then came Pedrosa.

Rossi was 12th after his misadventure. He had won at Assen from 11th in 2007, but this would be too tall an order.

Stoner led away from Hayden and Toseland; Pedrosa was third by the second corner, but on the way in, he slipped under braking, ran wide on to the grass and fell. From the back of the pack, Guintoli and Vermeulen followed him without falling, the latter claiming a knock-on effect, although it was not easy to see quite why.

Over the first four laps, Stoner and Hayden gained three seconds, the Honda rider pushing hard. On lap nine, the pace started to tell on his softer tyres. By the end of the tenth, he was a second down, 1.7 seconds next time around. So it would go on, leaving Stoner to a majestic second home win in succession.

Rossi had finished the first lap eighth, having very narrowly avoided hitting de Angelis when he slid off at MG – that luck again. Next time around, he was ahead of de Puniet, and quickly caught Nakano and Edwards to blow by them on the third time down the straight. It took one more lap to close up on Toseland and Lorenzo, the Englishman just having regained third from the young Spaniard, but this was a tougher barrier.

He passed Lorenzo; Lorenzo passed him back into the first corner as they started lap eight. Rossi's next pass was successful, but now he had Toseland to deal with, and the Englishman was at his best. Rossi led him over the line on lap eight, but Toseland went straight back under him into the Southern Loop and stayed in front for the next four laps. Rossi did it again at Turn One on lap 12, but Toseland came back under him once more. Next time around, Rossi managed to make the move stick, but took another lap before he could move away.

Now his target was Hayden. By lap 16, he was within five seconds, and it stayed that way next time around. Then he started gaining, and with five laps to go, he was 2.9 seconds adrift. Hayden had no response as Rossi closed rapidly, blowing by into Turn One as they started the last lap.

Lorenzo found Toseland equally difficult, after both he and Dovizioso got ahead on lap 25. Nakano had been right up close, waiting his chance. It came on the last lap at the hairpin, as Toseland seized the lead of the group only to run wide, taking Dovizioso with him. Lorenzo, Nakano and Toseland finished within seven-tenths, a complaining Dovizioso another six-tenths away.

Edwards had dropped away by ten seconds, but regained eighth from de Puniet with three laps to go and was a tenth clear over the line.

Capirossi was close behind, while Elias had closed to within a couple of tenths by the finish.

Another 20 seconds down came the Kawasakis, West working hard to fend off Hopkins at his home GP, having passed Melandri soon after the start.

Guintoli and Vermeulen had rejoined at the back and circulated in close company; with another lap, they might have passed the Kawasakis. However, the Ducati's speed allowed Guintoli to take 14th from Vermeulen over the line. Almost half a minute behind, Melandri was last.

250cc RACE – 25 laps

Simoncelli had claimed pole by better than three-quarters of a second, while Kallio, Bautista and Aoyama were with him on the front row. The race would quickly be between just him and Bautista, but it was an absorbing contest to the very end.

Bautista led away, with Simoncelli, Aoyama, Kallio, Faubel and Simon chasing. By lap two, Simoncelli had escaped, and was attacking the leader. When he got ahead with a daring out-braking move into Siberia, Simon and Kallio closed up again. But they were never close enough to make a difference, as Bautista took the lead again for laps six and seven. Faubel had gone, sliding off unhurt on lap five.

The leaders were swapping constantly, in a high-level battle of creative riding – 250 racing at its finest. The passing moves were close, artful, daring and frequent, the outcome in doubt to the last.

After half-distance, they had broken free, Simoncelli holding a narrow lead. But obviously Bautista was waiting for his chance.

He thought it had come as they went into the long left-handers for the last time. He pushed inside, hoping to make space, but Simoncelli slammed the door. Bautista ran up on to the inside kerb, had a scary wobble – and was beaten, crossing the line just over two-tenths adrift. This time, there were no recriminations. 'I am happy because we had a good race,' said the beaten Spaniard. Simoncelli concurred: 'We had a fantastic battle, from the first corner to the last.' It was his fifth win of the year; Bautista was stuck on three.

KTM rivals Simon and Kallio were having a similar fight, Aoyama losing touch after half-distance. In a lap or two, he slowed dramatically and cruised to the pits, a piston ring broken. Furious, he strode to the back of the pit and punched a Red Bull hoarding to the ground, all faithfully filmed.

Simon led on to the last lap, but Kallio had his plan: 'He was very good in braking, but I knew I was faster out of the last corner.' Accordingly, he waited his chance, and pulled alongside and inches ahead. He took the last rostrum slot by three-hundredths.

There was a good fight for fifth. Pasini had led the group from Takahashi and Espargaro, while Debon and Locatelli closed from behind. Pasini crashed on lap 16, but the other three stayed together to finish almost side by side: Debon, Locatelli and Takahashi. Espargaro had dropped back to a safe eighth.

Wilairot was equally lonely in ninth. Pesek had been ahead, but ran off on the last lap, to rejoin 14th. Lai prevailed over the next gang for tenth, two seconds clear of Abraham, Baldolini and Toth, who were still scrapping to the line.

Not much could stop Simoncelli from prevailing overall now, but there were still only 12 points between Bautista and Kallio for second.

125cc RACE – 23 laps

Twenty-year-old Frenchman Mike di Meglio took his second successive pole and scored a runaway win to secure the title. In a gamble that paid off, he had sunk his life savings into the Ajo Derbi team at the start of the year.

Smith, Bradl and Terol were alongside him on the front row, and the Briton took off at high speed. His lead lasted only until the hairpin, where he slid off under braking. He was the first of many in a crash-strewn race.

Cortese took over, but he fell on lap two. Now di Meglio was up front, with Talmacsi and Iannone behind. Di Meglio cleared off directly.

Bradl soon joined the gang disputing second, as did Olive, with riders running into Turn One three or more abreast and positions changing frequently. Just after half-distance, Olive slipped off at Honda Hairpin. Bradl narrowly escaped involvement, but quickly got back to the front of the group and pulled away.

Talmacsi and Iannone battled to the end, the defending champion taking the rostrum spot by less than a tenth. Espargaro led a close quintet over the line, from the remounted Cortese, Rabat, Marquez and Corsi. But Marquez had elbowed Corsi on to the grass at top speed on the run to the line. He was demoted to ninth, behind the Italian, after Race Direction added a punitive second to his race time.

Redding was a lone tenth; Smith had remounted, but had not made it back into the points when he fell again with two laps left. Masbou, de Rosa, Aegerter and Terol joined him on the crash list, de Rosa also remounting to fall again. Five other riders tumbled and there were only 21 finishers.

Bonsey had been up to seventh when his engine seized with 11 laps left.

Above: Di Meglio, here leading Talmacsi and the pack, claimed the title with a win.

Left: If the cap fits – the new 125 World Champion.

Opposite, top: Toseland and Lorenzo fight it out ahead of Nakano, with Rossi still catching up in the background.

Opposite, bottom: Simoncelli heads Bautista and Simon; victory was not enough to secure the title.

Main photograph: Stoner continued a tradition of home-rider wins in Australia.

Photographs: Gold & Goose

AUSTRALIAN GRAND PRIX

05 OCTOBER 2008 • FIM WORLD CHAMPIONSHIP ROUND 16

PHILLIP ISLAND

Southern Loop
Gardner Straight
Turn 12
Doohan
Bass Straight
Honda Corner
Turn 10
Turn 3
Turn 11
Turn 5
Siberia
Turn 8
Turn 7
Lukey Hieghts

Circuit 4.448km / 2.764 miles

MOTOGP

RACE: 27 laps, 74.628 miles/120.096km • Weather: Dry • Air 17°C • Humidity 45% • Track 27°C

Pos.	Rider	Nat.	No.	Team	Machine	Tyres	Laps	Time & speed (mph/km/h)
1	Casey Stoner	AUS	1	Ducati Marlboro Team	Ducati	B	27	40m 56.643s 109.355mph/ 175.990km/h
2	Valentino Rossi	ITA	46	Fiat Yamaha Team	Yamaha	B	27	41m 03.147s
3	Nicky Hayden	USA	69	Repsol Honda Team	Honda	M	27	41m 03.848s
4	Jorge Lorenzo	SPA	48	Fiat Yamaha Team	Yamaha	M	27	41m 08.143s
5	Shinya Nakano	JPN	56	San Carlo Honda Gresini	Honda	B	27	41m 08.557s
6	James Toseland	GBR	52	Tech 3 Yamaha	Yamaha	M	27	41m 08.886s
7	Andrea Dovizioso	ITA	4	JiR Team Scot MotoGP	Honda	M	27	41m 09.423s
8	Colin Edwards	USA	5	Tech 3 Yamaha	Yamaha	M	27	41m 22.563s
9	Randy de Puniet	FRA	14	LCR Honda MotoGP	Honda	M	27	41m 22.680s
10	Loris Capirossi	ITA	65	Rizla Suzuki MotoGP	Suzuki	B	27	41m 23.442s
11	Toni Elias	SPA	24	Alice Team	Ducati	B	27	41m 23.670s
12	Anthony West	AUS	13	Kawasaki Racing Team	Kawasaki	B	27	41m 44.451s
13	John Hopkins	USA	21	Kawasaki Racing Team	Kawasaki	B	27	41m 44.976s
14	Sylvain Guintoli	FRA	50	Alice Team	Ducati	B	27	41m 45.542s
15	Chris Vermeulen	AUS	7	Rizla Suzuki MotoGP	Suzuki	B	27	41m 45.542s
16	Marco Melandri	ITA	33	Ducati Marlboro Team	Ducati	B	27	42m 08.410s
	Alex de Angelis	RSM	15	San Carlo Honda Gresini	Honda	B	0	DNF
	Dani Pedrosa	SPA	2	Repsol Honda Team	Honda	B	0	DNF

Fastest lap: Nicky Hayden, on lap 3, 1m 30.059s, 110.482mph/177.803km/h (record).

Previous lap record: Marco Melandri, ITA (Honda), 1m 30.332s, 110.148mph/177.266km/h (2005).

Event best maximum speed: Casey Stoner, 205.1mph/330.1km/h (free practice no. 1).

QUALIFYING: 4 October 2008

Weather: Dry
Air: 18°C Humidity: 36% Track: 30°C

Pos.	Rider	Time
1	Stoner	1m 28.665s
2	Lorenzo	1m 28.734s
3	Hayden	1m 28.756s
4	de Puniet	1m 28.808s
5	Toseland	1m 29.031s
6	Pedrosa	1m 29.277s
7	Edwards	1m 29.513s
8	Dovizioso	1m 29.558s
9	Nakano	1m 29.710s
10	de Angelis	1m 29.925s
11	Capirossi	1m 29.942s
12	Rossi	1m 30.014s
13	Elias	1m 30.202s
14	Guintoli	1m 30.297s
15	Vermeulen	1m 30.545s
16	Hopkins	1m 31.157s
17	Melandri	1m 31.939s
18	West	1m 31.995s

Grid order	1	2	3	4	5	6	7	8	9	10	11	12	13	14	15	16	17	18	19	20	21	22	23	24	25	26	27	
1 STONER	1	1	1	1	1	1	1	1	1	1	1	1	1	1	1	1	1	1	1	1	1	1	1	1	1	1	1	1
48 LORENZO	69	69	69	69	69	69	69	69	69	69	69	69	69	69	69	69	69	69	69	69	69	69	69	69	69	69	46	2
69 HAYDEN	52	52	48	48	52	52	52	46	52	52	52	52	46	46	46	46	46	46	46	46	46	46	46	46	46	46	69	3
14 de PUNIET	48	48	52	52	48	46	46	52	46	46	46	46	52	52	52	52	52	52	52	52	52	52	52	52	48	48	48	4
52 TOSELAND	5	5	5	46	46	48	48	48	48	48	48	48	4	4	4	4	4	48	48	48	48	48	48	48	4	4	56	5
2 PEDROSA	56	56	56	56	56	56	56	56	56	56	4	4	48	48	48	48	48	4	4	4	4	4	4	4	52	52	52	6
5 EDWARDS	14	46	46	5	4	4	4	4	4	4	56	56	56	56	56	56	56	56	56	56	56	56	56	56	56	56	4	7
4 DOVISIOSO	46	14	4	4	5	5	5	5	5	5	5	14	14	14	14	14	14	14	14	14	14	14	14	14	5	5	5	8
56 NAKANO	65	4	14	14	14	14	14	14	14	14	14	5	5	65	65	5	5	5	5	5	5	5	5	14	14	14	14	9
15 de ANGELIS	4	65	65	65	65	65	65	65	65	65	65	65	65	65	5	5	65	65	65	65	65	65	65	65	65	65	65	10
65 CAPIROSSI	21	21	24	24	24	24	24	24	24	24	24	24	24	24	24	24	24	24	24	24	24	24	24	24	24	24	24	11
46 ROSSI	13	24	21	13	13	13	13	13	13	13	13	13	13	13	13	13	13	13	13	13	13	13	13	13	13	13	13	12
24 ELIAS	24	13	13	21	21	21	21	21	21	21	21	21	21	21	21	21	21	21	21	21	21	21	21	21	21	21	21	13
50 GUINTOLI	33	33	33	33	33	33	33	33	7	7	7	7	7	7	7	7	7	7	7	7	7	7	7	7	7	7	50	14
7 VERMEULEN	7	7	50	50	50	50	50	7	33	50	50	50	50	50	50	50	50	50	50	50	50	50	50	50	50	50	7	15
21 HOPKINS	50	50	7	7	7	7	7	50	50	33	33	33	33	33	33	33	33	33	33	33	33	33	33	33	33	33		
33 MELANDRI																												
13 WEST																												

FASTEST RACE LAPS

	Rider	Lap	Time
1	Hayden	3	1m 30.059s
2	Stoner	3	1m 30.067s
3	Rossi	5	1m 30.284s
4	Dovizioso	7	1m 30.585s
5	Nakano	6	1m 30.595s
6	Lorenzo	7	1m 30.702s
7	Toseland	4	1m 30.802s
8	de Puniet	4	1m 30.873s
9	Capirossi	4	1m 30.971s
10	Edwards	6	1m 31.083s
11	Elias	17	1m 31.201s
12	Vermeulen	8	1m 31.313s
13	Guintoli	21	1m 31.528s
14	West	3	1m 31.915s
15	Hopkins	2	1m 32.010s
16	Melandri	23	1m 32.519s

statistics

250cc

25 laps, 69.100 miles/111.200km

Pos.	Rider (Nat.)	No.	Team	Machine	Laps	Time & speed
1	Marco Simoncelli (ITA)	58	Metis Gilera	Gilera	25	39m 02.553s 106.186mph/ 170.890km/h
2	Alvaro Bautista (SPA)	19	Mapfre Aspar Team	Aprilia	25	39m 02.776s
3	Mika Kallio (FIN)	36	Red Bull KTM 250	KTM	25	39m 17.003s
4	Julian Simon (SPA)	60	Repsol KTM 250cc	KTM	25	39m 17.031s
5	Alex Debon (SPA)	6	Lotus Aprilia	Aprilia	25	39m 28.779s
6	Roberto Locatelli (ITA)	15	Metis Gilera	Gilera	25	39m 28.945s
7	Yuki Takahashi (JPN)	72	JiR Team Scot 250	Honda	25	39m 28.987s
8	Aleix Espargaro (SPA)	41	Lotus Aprilia	Aprilia	25	39m 43.099s
9	Ratthapark Wilairot (THA)	14	Thai Honda PTT SAG	Honda	25	40m 02.772s
10	Fabrizio Lai (ITA)	32	Campetella Racing	Gilera	25	40m 23.378s
11	Karel Abraham (CZE)	17	Cardion AB Motoracing	Aprilia	25	40m 25.355s
12	Alex Baldolini (ITA)	25	Matteoni Racing	Aprilia	25	40m 25.417s
13	Imre Toth (HUN)	10	Team Toth Aprilia	Aprilia	25	40m 26.548s
14	Lukas Pesek (CZE)	52	Auto Kelly - CP	Aprilia	25	40m 42.293s
15	Simone Grotzkyj (ITA)	35	Campetella Racing	Gilera	24	39m 21.775s
16	Daniel Arcas (SPA)	92	Blusens Aprilia	Aprilia	24	39m 31.738s
17	Doni Tata Pradita (INA)	45	Yamaha Pertamina Indonesia	Yamaha	24	39m 31.909s
	Hiroshi Aoyama (JPN)	4	Red Bull KTM 250	KTM	15	DNF
	Mattia Pasini (ITA)	75	Polaris World	Aprilia	15	DNF
	Hector Faubel (SPA)	55	Mapfre Aspar Team	Aprilia	4	DNF
	Federico Sandi (ITA)	90	Zongshen Team of China	Aprilia	1	DNF
	Manuel Hernandez (SPA)	43	Blusens Aprilia	Aprilia	1	DNF

Fastest lap: Bautista, 1m 32.710s, 107.323mph/172.719km/h (record).

Previous lap record: Sebastian Porto, ARG (Aprilia), 1m 33.381s, 106.551mph/ 171.478km/h (2004).

Event best maximum speed: Debon, 171.4mph/275.8km/h (warm-up).

Qualifying: 1 Simoncelli, 1m 32.075s; 2 Kallio, 1m 32.862s; 3 Bautista, 1m 32.917s; 4 Aoyama, 1m 33.048s; 5 Faubel, 1m 33.167s; 6 Simon, 1m 33.250s; 7 Takahashi, 1m 33.294s; 8 Debon, 1m 33.349s; 9 Espargaro, 1m 33.368s; 10 Pasini, 1m 33.376s; 11 Locatelli, 1m 33.508s; 12 Wilairot, 1m 33.538s; 13 Lai, 1m 33.696s; 14 Pesek, 1m 33.871s; 15 Sandi, 1m 34.544s; 16 Toth, 1m 34.997s; 17 Abraham, 1m 35.464s; 18 Baldolini, 1m 36.036s; 19 Hernandez, 1m 36.116s; 20 Arcas, 1m 36.921s; 21 Grotzkyj, 1m 37.006s; 22 Pradita, 1m 37.050s.

Fastest race laps: 1 Bautista, 1m 32.710s; 2 Simoncelli, 1m 32.777s; 3 Kallio, 1m 33.253s; 4 Simon, 1m 33.274s; 5 Aoyama, 1m 33.391s; 6 Takahashi, 1m 33.875s; 7 Pasini, 1m 33.926s; 8 Debon, 1m 33.970s; 9 Locatelli, 1m 34.006s; 10 Faubel, 1m 34.038s; 11 Pesek, 1m 34.064s; 12 Espargaro, 1m 34.147s; 13 Wilairot, 1m 34.342s; 14 Lai, 1m 35.632s; 15 Abraham, 1m 35.745s; 16 Toth, 1m 35.984s; 17 Baldolini, 1m 36.122s; 18 Grotzkyj, 1m 37.125s; 19 Arcas, 1m 37.378s; 20 Pradita, 1m 37.469s; 21 Sandi, 1m 43.561s; 22 Hernandez, 1m 50.629s.

World Championship: 1 Simoncelli, 240; 2 Bautista, 203; 3 Kallio, 191; 4 Debon, 166; 5 Barbera, 142; 6 Takahashi, 134; 7 Pasini, 125; 8 Simon, 109; 9 Aoyama, 108; 10 Luthi, 95; 11 Locatelli, 88; 12 Espargaro, 72; 13 Wilairot, 57; 14 Faubel, 54; 15 Pesek, 37; 16 Abraham, 36; 17 Lai, 28; 18 Baldolini, 28; 19 Poggiali, 16; 20 Laverty, 8; 21 Sandi, 6; 22 Hernandez, 5; 23 Toth, 5; 24 Tomizawa and Wirsing, 2; 26 Grotzkyj, 2; 27 Pradita, 1.

125cc

23 laps, 63.572 miles/102.304km

Pos.	Rider (Nat.)	No.	Team	Machine	Laps	Time & speed
1	Mike di Meglio (FRA)	63	Ajo Motorsport	Derbi	23	37m 55.589s 100.566mph/ 161.845km/h
2	Stefan Bradl (GER)	17	Grizzly Gas Kiefer Racing	Aprilia	23	38m 05.844s
3	Gabor Talmacsi (HUN)	1	Bancaja Aspar Team	Aprilia	23	38m 08.695s
4	Andrea Iannone (ITA)	29	I.C. Team	Aprilia	23	38m 08.738s
5	Pol Espargaro (SPA)	44	Belson Derbi	Derbi	23	38m 22.385s
6	Sandro Cortese (GER)	11	Emmi - Caffe Latte	Aprilia	23	38m 22.712s
7	Esteve Rabat (SPA)	12	Repsol KTM 125cc	KTM	23	38m 22.770s
8	Simone Corsi (ITA)	24	Jack & Jones WRB	Aprilia	23	38m 23.460s
9	Marc Marquez (SPA)	93	Repsol KTM 125cc	KTM	23	38m 23.876s
10	Scott Redding (GBR)	45	Blusens Aprilia Junior	Aprilia	23	38m 30.676s
11	Efren Vazquez (SPA)	7	Blusens Aprilia Junior	Aprilia	23	38m 52.981s
12	Lorenzo Zanetti (ITA)	8	ISPA KTM Aran	KTM	23	38m 53.002s
13	Pablo Nieto (SPA)	22	Onde 2000 KTM	KTM	23	38m 53.040s
14	Joan Olive (SPA)	6	Belson Derbi	Derbi	23	38m 53.128s
15	Robin Lasser (GER)	21	Grizzly Gas Kiefer Racing	Aprilia	23	39m 01.907s
16	Marco Ravaioli (ITA)	72	Matteoni Racing	Aprilia	23	39m 01.909s
17	Adrian Martin (SPA)	26	Bancaja Aspar Team	Aprilia	23	39m 38.030s
18	Cyril Carrillo (FRA)	36	FFM Honda GP 125	Honda	23	39m 38.044s
19	Enrique Jerez (SPA)	28	ISPA KTM Aran	KTM	23	39m 39.381s
20	Jed Metcher (AUS)	91	Angelo's Aluminium Racing	Honda	22	38m 10.914s
21	Randy Krummenacher (SWI)	34	Red Bull KTM 125	KTM	21	39m 19.340s
	Bradley Smith (GBR)	38	Polaris World	Aprilia	21	DNF
	Bastien Chesaux (SWI)	48	WTR San Marino Team	Aprilia	14	DNF
	Sergio Gadea (SPA)	33	Bancaja Aspar Team	Aprilia	13	DNF
	Stevie Bonsey (USA)	51	Degraaf Grand Prix	Aprilia	12	DNF
	Rhys Moller (AUS)	70	Rhys Moller Racing	Honda	10	DNF
	Jules Cluzel (FRA)	16	Loncin Racing	Loncin	8	DNF
	Brad Gross (AUS)	46	Gross Racing	Yamaha	8	DNF
	Hugo van den Berg (NED)	56	Degraaf Grand Prix	Aprilia	7	DNF
	Robert Muresan (ROU)	95	Grizzly Gas Kiefer Racing	Aprilia	2	DNF
	Raffaele de Rosa (ITA)	35	Onde 2000 KTM	KTM	2	DNF
	Alexis Masbou (FRA)	5	Loncin Racing	Loncin	1	DNF
	Nicolas Terol (SPA)	18	Jack & Jones WRB	Aprilia	1	DNF
	Takaaki Nakagami (JPN)	73	I.C. Team	Aprilia	0	DNF
	Dominique Aegerter (SWI)	77	Ajo Motorsport	Derbi	0	DNF

Fastest lap: Bradl, 1m 37.908s, 101.625mph/163.549km/h.

Lap record: Alvaro Bautista, SPA (Aprilia), 1m 36.927s, 102.653mph/165.204km/h (2006).

Event best maximum speed: Bradl, 152.8mph/245.9km/h (free practice no. 1).

Qualifying: 1 di Meglio, 1m 37.553s; 2 Smith, 1m 37.791s; 3 Bradl, 1m 38.034s; 4 Terol, 1m 38.110s; 5 Iannone, 1m 38.242s; 6 Cortese, 1m 38.361s; 7 de Rosa, 1m 38.473s; 8 Corsi, 1m 38.476s; 9 Talmacsi, 1m 38.501s; 10 Aegerter, 1m 38.600s; 11 Redding, 1m 38.767s; 12 Marquez, 1m 38.822s; 13 Bonsey, 1m 38.848s; 14 Gadea, 1m 38.864s; 15 Espargaro, 1m 38.928s; 16 Nieto, 1m 38.935s; 17 Rabat, 1m 38.986s; 18 Olive, 1m 39.109s; 19 Zanetti, 1m 39.688s; 20 Krummenacher, 1m 39.860s; 21 van den Berg, 1m 39.960s; 22 Masbou, 1m 39.969s; 23 Lasser, 1m 40.163s; 24 Muresan, 1m 40.352s; 25 Vazquez, 1m 40.441s; 26 Nakagami, 1m 40.480s; 27 Cluzel, 1m 41.365s; 28 Chesaux, 1m 41.473s; 29 Ravaioli, 1m 41.477s; 30 Martin, 1m 41.694s; 31 Carrillo, 1m 41.821s; 32 Jerez, 1m 41.856s; 33 Metcher, 1m 42.805s; 34 Moller, 1m 43.802s; 35 Gross, 1m 43.946s.

Fastest race laps: 1 Bradl, 1m 37.908s; 2 Olive, 1m 38.046s; 3 Iannone, 1m 38.055s; 4 di Meglio, 1m 38.170s; 5 Talmacsi, 1m 38.288s; 6 Gadea, 1m 38.412s; 7 Cortese, 1m 38.426s; 8 Rabat, 1m 38.566s; 9 Bonsey, 1m 38.626s; 10 Espargaro, 1m 38.636s; 11 Redding, 1m 38.701s; 12 Marquez, 1m 38.847s; 13 Corsi, 1m 38.870s; 14 Smith, 1m 39.667s; 15 de Rosa, 1m 39.784s; 16 Nieto, 1m 39.848s; 17 Vazquez, 1m 39.931s; 18 van den Berg, 1m 40.180s; 19 Zanetti, 1m 40.261s; 20 Krummenacher, 1m 40.620s; 21 Lasser, 1m 40.624s; 22 Cluzel, 1m 40.755s; 23 Ravaioli, 1m 40.797s; 24 Carrillo, 1m 41.585s; 25 Chesaux, 1m 41.732s; 26 Metcher, 1m 41.890s; 27 Martin, 1m 42.114s; 28 Jerez, 1m 42.357s; 29 Muresan, 1m 42.641s; 30 Moller, 1m 43.087s; 31 Gross, 1m 44.790s; 32 Masbou, 2m 08.715s; 33 Terol, 2m 14.678s.

World Championship: 1 di Meglio, 237; 2 Bradl, 187; 3 Corsi, 184; 4 Talmacsi, 181; 5 Terol, 149; 6 Olive, 133; 7 Smith, 117; 8 Cortese, 117; 9 Espargaro, 114; 10 Redding, 97; 11 Iannone, 90; 12 Gadea, 79; 13 Marquez, 63; 14 Bonsey, 46; 15 Rabat, 43; 16 Aegerter, 37; 17 de Rosa, 37; 18 Webb, 35; 19 Koyama, 27; 20 Vazquez, 27; 21 Ranseder, 22; 22 Nieto, 16; 23 Zanetti, 14; 24 Nakagami, 12; 25 Krummenacher, 10; 26 Tutusaus, 9; 27 Bianco, 8; 28 Schrotter, 3; 29 Lasser and Masbou, 2; 31 Folger and van den Berg, 1.

RIDER STANDINGS

After 16 Rounds

1	Valentino Rossi	332
2	Casey Stoner	245
3	Dani Pedrosa	209
4	Jorge Lorenzo	182
5	Andrea Dovizioso	145
6	Nicky Hayden	131
7	Colin Edwards	126
8	Chris Vermeulen	118
9	Shinya Nakano	106
10	Loris Capirossi	102
11	James Toseland	100
12	Toni Elias	91
13	Sylvain Guintoli	60
14	Alex de Angelis	55
15	Randy de Puniet	54
16	Marco Melandri	51
17	John Hopkins	50
18	Anthony West	46
19	Ben Spies	20
20	Jamie Hacking	5
21	Tadayuki Okada	2

TEAM STANDINGS

After 16 Rounds

1	Fiat Yamaha Team	514
2	Repsol Honda Team	340
3	Ducati Marlboro Team	296
4	Tech 3 Yamaha	226
5	Rizla Suzuki MotoGP	222
6	San Carlo Honda Gresini	161
7	Alice Team	151
8	JiR Team Scot MotoGP	145
9	Kawasaki Racing Team	101
10	LCR Honda MotoGP	54

CONSTRUCTOR STANDINGS

After 16 Rounds

1	Yamaha	361
2	Ducati	286
3	Honda	275
4	Suzuki	165
5	Kawasaki	81

Sweat soaked and beaming,
Rossi celebrates his ninth of
the year.
Photograph: Gold & Goose

FIM WORLD CHAMPIONSHIP • ROUND 17

MALAYSIAN | GP

SEPANG

THINGS got a bit heated in Malaysia. Not least the riders, on a punishing Sunday with temperatures soaring to 40-plus degrees. In the best argument yet for night racing in the tropics, 250 Qatar winner Mattia Pasini all but collapsed mid-race with heat fatigue and was fortunate to make it back to the pits, while new champion Marco Simoncelli – he did it with another blazing victory – was so stricken after the race that he was barely able to speak. Rossi, who won with a clinical display of dominance, said afterwards that at times his vision had 'gone to black and white' in the punishing conditions.

There were other feverish events. Especially a spat at Honda, between Nicky Hayden and Pedrosa's manager, Alberto Puig. After the Australian race, the big Spanish daily *El País* had published an interview with the outgoing American, in which he suggested that it was really Puig who ran the Honda team: the latest of the ex-racer's feats having been to engineer Pedrosa's embarrassing switch to Bridgestone tyres.

Puig responded badly, but in character, in a damning interview of his own, in which he said that Hayden had been unable to set up a bike without copying Dani's data, accused him of lying and called him 'a hypocrite'. Extraordinarily, this was published by Puig's compatriots at Dorna, on its own website, MotoGP.com. Generally this steers away from controversy and concentrates on more positive aspects of promoting the sport. Running Puig's one-sided rant word for word clearly abandoned that principal, and it was a measure of his influence in Spain. But it was not a good move in terms of public relations: attacking the most popular rider in the paddock was bound to have some repercussions.

Nicky retained his sense of humour, but fought his corner. 'I guess I've got to stop being a hypocrite,' he said, before insisting that, in fact, all the flow of data had gone the other way. 'I haven't seen his data for a long time, and he sees everybody's data. Be clear about that. If it's me going fastest or if it's Dovi going fastest, he sees everything.' He added later, 'It's funny. Talking about tyre compounds is boring, let's face it. When it gets personal, it's certainly something exciting. I mean, guys calling out team-mates…'

There was some heat also shown by the riders, confronted with the new realities of the single-tyre rule – Bridgestone's tender had been accepted and some details had been revealed. The one that stung was that each rider would get only 20 tyres for a race weekend. Not enough, they said, to run four hours of practice plus the race. It would mean down-time in the pits and a shortage of set-up time. Stoner and Rossi led a chorus of complaint that was aired at the regular safety commission meeting and discussed by the GP Commission, and then again when Rossi went to see Ezpeleta privately. Bridgestone's response was to promise otherwise. Trust us, they said – and the race authorities did. Ezpeleta had cited (spuriously) the request of the riders as a major reason for the change, but if that had given them the notion that they had played a significant part in the decision making process, now they were disillusioned. 'We don't have enough power,' said Rossi. 'It is something about politics and not just safety. It is something above us.'

KTM dropped a bomb on race eve, announcing that it would be quitting the 250 class forthwith to concentrate only on 125, two years in advance of the extinction of the two-strokes. Outspoken critic of the move, KTM had joined the 250 class in 2005, and in 2008 rider Kallio had made a serious championship challenge. That left, at the time of writing, just 14 entries for 2009's 250 series, which thus will be effectively an Aprilia one-make championship.

With the season winding down, there was more ac-

tion in and out of the managers' makeshift offices than on the track. Much of it concerned Kawasaki and Jorge 'Aspar' Martinez. The two had been close to agreement to run a third Kawasaki in 2009, but now it was foundering. The Spanish sponsor wanted a Spanish – preferably Valencian – rider, but after Elias decided to return to Honda, and Bautista to stay in 250s for one more year, there were few candidates. One was 600 Supersport rider Angel Rodriguez; another, late-blossoming 250 rider Alex Debon. For the Kawasaki factory, however, the former lacked experience and credentials, while the latter, at 33 in March 2009, was simply too old. But Nakano had become available and, as an ex-factory team rider, was very acceptable to Kawasaki. Not so to the sponsor, however, who cut the budget. During the weekend, the proposed team crumbled away. Only a post-season miracle could revive it.

Deposed rider Anthony West brought some kind of cheer to the current Kawasaki team, where he pointed out that since Hopkins's return from injury, he had beaten him four times out of five. 'It's a bit unfair,' he thought, of being dropped by the team in favour of Melandri. 'It's not as though I've been at the back and my team-mate's been at the front.' Now he announced a reluctant return to World 600 Supersport with ex-250 rider Johan Stigefelt's Honda team, celebrating by fitting a qualifying tyre on Saturday morning to top the time sheets. When the other riders did the same in qualifying, however, he was back down in 13th.

Right: It didn't matter how hard Hayden tried, Dovizioso made himself unbeatable.

Below left: Rossi checks Pedrosa's tyres in parc fermé after the race.

Below left: Under a shroud. The covered KTMs in the 250 pit symbolise the marque's withdrawal from the class.

Below centre left: Under a shroud – the covered KTMs in the 250 pit symbolise the marque's withdrawal from the class.

Bottom left: Rossi's bulldog, Guido, had joined the heavenly host.

Photographs: Gold & Goose

Marc Marquez, a fast 125 rookie, fell victim to a nasty crash at the end of Friday's first practice. He and Carrillo had a coming together, followed by a simple-looking spill at relatively low speed. But the 15-year-old's legs became trapped by his rear wheel and his feet were pulled into the suspension mechanism as a result. It took 15 minutes to free him, and he flew home with foot fractures.

MOTOGP RACE – 21 laps

Rain at the start of qualifying made for an extraordinary hour, with tyre choice ranging from full wets to qualifiers by the end as the track dried. Conditions changed so quickly that the fastest lap was set 37 times by 11 different riders. The best timed run came right at the very end from Pedrosa, who took his second pole of the year and his first on Bridgestones.

Rossi was alongside, then Lorenzo; Hayden headed the second row, and Stoner the third.

A crowd of 38,560 sweltered as Pedrosa got his usual jack-rabbit start, Dovizioso following from the far end of the second row. Rossi, Hayden and Stoner were next, then Nakano, who had been 15th on the grid. Lorenzo dropped back from the front row to finish the first lap eighth.

Rossi attacked Dovizioso going into the final corner, but ran wide. No matter. He dived inside into the sharp right at the far end of the front straight, then took off after Pedrosa.

On the same lap, Toseland crashed out, trying too hard, he admitted later, to make up for his 12th-placed starting position at a track where at least he had the benefit of plenty of testing.

Pedrosa was lapping steadily, Rossi on his tail, although they only gapped Dovizioso slowly. Rossi stalked the Honda until lap 11, when he moved firmly inside at the uphill left-hand Turn Nine and blocked Pedrosa into the following right.

From there, he concentrated only on reeling off the laps, a feat of endurance in itself. He pulled away at half a second a lap or better, and he was all but five seconds clear when he pulled up the front wheel to wheelie down the front straight for his ninth win of the year.

Pedrosa was a similar distance ahead of what finally became a fierce two-bike battle for third. For most of the race, Dovizioso and Hayden had close company. At first, it was Stoner in pursuit, Nakano harrying him and even briefly getting ahead on lap nine. All the while, Lorenzo dropped away slightly, then came back at half-distance. He nosed ahead of Nakano, but half a lap later lost the front into the first corner. He was able to remount at the back, retiring a lap later.

By now, Stoner was running into physical problems because of his wrist – the same upper-body fatigue that had struck in Motegi, which had been exacerbated considerably by the heat and a bike that 'wasn't working right'. 'Quite a lot of the time, I was thinking about coming in,' he confessed later. On lap 16, he backed off to let Nakano past once and for all. He soldiered on, thinking he may as well try and keep sixth, 'but I was absolutely rooted after that.'

Up front, Hayden was bashing his head against a brick wall with Dovizioso. A week later, he was still wondering why 'I couldn't draft my pneumatic bike past his stock bike. Maybe we went a bit conservative on the fuel. We still had enough for a lap or two at the end.'

He did manage to power past once, on the 18th lap, and to lead into the first corner. Dovizioso attacked straight back, Hayden defended for the next corner, and then it was over – the Italian was ahead again. And no matter how hard Hayden tried, all the way to the flag, he couldn't reverse the positions. A fine first podium was a fitting prize for the Italian.

Edwards had passed Capirossi for eighth early on the fourth lap, the Italian staying close and menacing, then getting back ahead on lap 15, where his next target was Stoner, a second ahead and circulating slower. His first attack failed when he ran wide; immediately afterwards, on lap 18, he touched the back of the Ducati as he ran into a corner much faster and lost a couple of seconds recovering.

On lap 15, with threatening skies, the white flags were shown. The rain didn't develop, however, and although a light shower fell on lap 17, it wasn't enough to affect lap times.

Edwards in eighth had dropped back with bad grip in the heat, as had Vermeulen another five seconds back, although with three laps left, the Suzuki man had managed to regain ninth from de Puniet, whose fractured wrist from Misano was playing up.

The rest trailed in, an embarrassed Melandri losing the last points-scoring place to Elias with three laps to go – the Spaniard had called in for a jump-start penalty and still got back ahead. Nobu Aoki was even further back, on a wild-card Suzuki.

250cc RACE, 20 Laps

Aoyama's first pole put him ahead of Bautista, Simoncelli and Kallio, with an inspired Wilairot leading the second – from Thailand, this was effectively his home race. All attention was on Simoncelli. He needed a top-three finish to tie up the title, whether Bautista won or not. Both fulfilled that destiny.

Espargaro led the first two laps, Simoncelli slotting into second; Simon passed both of them to lead for one lap on lap three. Then Simoncelli took over up front for three more.

By now, Bautista – seventh on lap one – was gaining speed. On lap seven, as Aoyama took over up front, he snatched third off Simon.

Simoncelli dropped to fourth as Bautista set about Aoyama a little way ahead. They swapped places once on the Turn Nine-Ten left-right, then Bautista got ahead for good on lap ten. He wouldn't be headed, but he tried his best to control the race all the same.

'I tried to slow the pace, so that some other riders

Left: Dovizioso enjoyed his first podium in the premier class.

Right: Bautista takes water any way he can get it after his 250 victory.

Below left: Exhausted, Simoncelli completed his slow-down lap as champion without a helmet – and paid the price.

Below right: Talmacsi kept his hopes of second overall alive with victory.

Bottom right: Another second place had Smith wreathed in smiles.

Photographs: Gold & Goose

could catch up and come into play, and maybe beat Simoncelli for the rostrum,' he said. But there were no candidates: the next group had Takahashi heading Pasini and Espargaro, but four seconds away.

With four laps left, Bautista decided to go away and win, and he did so, rapidly drawing clear of Aoyama to finished 2.5 seconds ahead.

Simoncelli kept the pressure on Aoyama until the last four laps. By now, the gap to the pursuit was seven seconds, and he slowed to make sure of the title. He stopped on the slow-down lap, removed his helmet, had water thrown over his mop of hair and rode back to enjoy his triumph – although he was 'too hot' to speak much. All the same, he was fined $1,000 for the helmetless victory lap.

Takahashi was kept fighting to the end to hang on to fourth, all the more when Debon joined his team-mate in the battle. Debon did get ahead, but Espargaro took back fifth on the last lap.

Locatelli had been ahead of Debon, but was behind at the end; Wilairot closed up to within a second over the last three laps.

Luthi was ninth, making a low-key comeback after his Indianapolis injuries; Pesek was a safe distance behind, while Lai managed to regain 11th from Abrahams on the final corner.

Simon had lost his place in the front group after half-distance, slowing and then stopping out on the track with yet more KTM woes. Kallio finished lap one fourth, but slowed almost immediately and pitted after four laps – clutch problems at first, then a seize.

Faubel was the only crasher, going out after four laps while lying 15th.

The other non-finisher was Pasini, who ran into trouble after half-distance. He lost his place in the group tussling with Takahashi, dropped back and then pulled off. When he returned to his pit, he had to be helped off his bike.

125cc RACE – 16 laps

Because of the midday rain on Saturday, grid positions were decided on Friday times, with Iannone heading Talmacsi, Webb and Espargaro. Webb would not take any advantage, however. His bike wouldn't start for the warm-up lap, and while his crew did eventually get him going and he caught up the pace car to take his place on the grid, this was against the rules. He should have started either from the pit lane or the back of the grid, but nobody in the team realised that. As a result, he was judged to have jumped the start and given a ride-through penalty; soon after, he pitted to retire, in an understandably foul temper.

Talmacsi shot away, Iannone in pursuit, with a pack of five left behind. On only the second lap, Talmacsi shook off the Italian and sped away in dominant style.

Iannone soon came under pressure from Smith, from 13th on the grid. He took second on lap nine, the gap to Talmacsi all but five seconds. The Englishman also would break away from the pack in a lone pursuit, and he was closing – to within almost 2.5 seconds with two laps to go – before settling for second.

At mid-distance, the pursuit comprised Iannone, Bradl, Cortese, di Meglio, Espargaro and Corsi. Then Bradl slowed dramatically, an electronic fault forcing him to park by the barrier. His chance of second overall had disappeared.

An all-action last lap among the group, with several changes of lead, was resolved when di Meglio left an opening into the final corner. Corsi nipped through for third, and Cortese for fourth.

Espargaro had lost touch, then came Olive narrowly heading Aegerter and Terol, with Iannone battling Koyama for tenth.

POLINI MALAYSIAN MOTORCYCLE GRAND PRIX

19 OCTOBER 2008 • FIM WORLD CHAMPIONSHIP ROUND 17

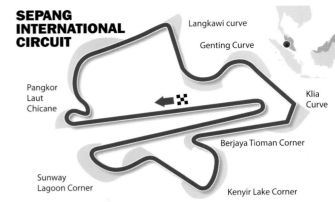

SEPANG INTERNATIONAL CIRCUIT

Langkawi curve
Genting Curve
Pangkor Laut Chicane
Klia Curve
Berjaya Tioman Corner
Sunway Lagoon Corner
Kenyir Lake Corner

Circuit 5.548km /3.447 miles

MOTOGP

RACE: 21 laps, 72.38 miles/116.508km • Weather: Dry • Air 39°C • Humidity 25% • Track 42°C

Pos.	Rider	Nat.	No.	Team	Machine	Tyres	Laps	Time & speed (mph/km/h)
1	Valentino Rossi	ITA	46	Fiat Yamaha Team	Yamaha	B	21	43m 06.007s 100.781mph/ 162.191km/h
2	Dani Pedrosa	SPA	2	Repsol Honda Team	Honda	B	21	43m 10.015s
3	Andrea Dovizioso	ITA	4	JiR Team Scot MotoGP	Honda	M	21	43m 14.543s
4	Nicky Hayden	USA	69	Repsol Honda Team	Honda	M	21	43m 14.865s
5	Shinya Nakano	JPN	56	San Carlo Honda Gresini	Honda	B	21	43m 16.590s
6	Casey Stoner	AUS	1	Ducati Marlboro Team	Ducati	B	21	43m 19.647s
7	Loris Capirossi	ITA	65	Rizla Suzuki MotoGP	Suzuki	B	21	43m 21.943s
8	Colin Edwards	USA	5	Tech 3 Yamaha	Yamaha	M	21	43m 24.809s
9	Chris Vermeulen	AUS	7	Rizla Suzuki MotoGP	Suzuki	B	21	43m 29.181s
10	Randy de Puniet	FRA	14	LCR Honda MotoGP	Honda	M	21	43m 31.523s
11	John Hopkins	USA	21	Kawasaki Racing Team	Kawasaki	B	21	43m 33.616s
12	Antony West	AUS	13	Kawasaki Racing Team	Kawasaki	B	21	43m 47.406s
13	Sylvain Guintoli	FRA	50	Alice Team	Ducati	B	21	43m 51.624s
14	Alex de Angelis	RSM	15	San Carlo Honda Gresini	Honda	B	21	43m 55.010s
15	Toni Elias	SPA	24	Alice Team	Ducati	B	21	44m 05.146s
16	Marco Melandri	ITA	33	Ducati Marlboro Team	Ducati	B	21	44m 09.335s
17	Nobuatsu Aoki	JPN	9	Rizla Suzuki MotoGP	Suzuki	B	21	44m 54.370s
	Jorge Lorenzo	SPA	48	Fiat Yamaha Team	Yamaha	M	12	25m 38.557s
	James Toseland	GBR	52	Tech 3 Yamaha	Yamaha	M	2	4m 19.122s

Fastest lap: Valentino Rossi, on lap 2, 2m 02.249s, 101.518mph/163.378km/h.

Lap record: Casey Stoner, AUS (Ducati), 2m 02.108s, 101.635mph/163.566km/h (2007).

Event best maximum speed: Casey Stoner, 193.6mph/311.5km/h (warm-up).

QUALIFYING: 18 October 2008

Weather: Dry
Air: 29°C Humidity: 54% Track: 31°C

Pos.	Rider	Time
1	Pedrosa	2m 01.548s
2	Rossi	2m 01.957s
3	Lorenzo	2m 02.171s
4	Hayden	2m 02.192s
5	Edwards	2m 02.245s
6	Dovizioso	2m 02.836s
7	Stoner	2m 02.953s
8	Capirossi	2m 03.078s
9	de Puniet	2m 03.110s
10	Hopkins	2m 03.184s
11	Vermeulen	2m 03.271s
12	Toseland	2m 03.282s
13	West	2m 03.392s
14	Melandri	2m 03.835s
15	Nakano	2m 04.001s
16	Guintoli	2m 04.378s
17	de Angelis	2m 04.679s
18	Aoki	2m 04.835s
19	Elias	2m 05.120s

Grid order	1	2	3	4	5	6	7	8	9	10	11	12	13	14	15	16	17	18	19	20	21	
2 PEDROSA	2	2	2	2	2	2	2	2	2	2	46	46	46	46	46	46	46	46	46	46	46	1
46 ROSSI	4	46	46	46	46	46	46	46	46	46	2	2	2	2	2	2	2	2	2	2	2	2
48 LORENZO	46	4	4	4	4	4	4	4	4	4	4	4	4	4	4	4	4	4	4	4	4	3
69 HAYDEN	69	69	69	69	69	69	69	69	69	69	69	69	69	69	69	69	69	69	69	69	69	4
5 EDWARDS	1	1	1	1	1	56	1	1	1	1	1	1	1	1	1	56	56	56	56	56	56	5
4 DOVISIOSO	56	56	56	56	56	1	56	56	56	56	48	56	56	56	56	1	1	1	1	1	1	6
1 STONER	48	48	48	48	48	48	48	48	48	48	56	5	5	65	65	65	65	65	65	65	65	7
65 CAPIROSSI	65	65	65	5	5	5	5	5	5	5	65	65	65	5	5	5	5	5	5	5	5	8
14 de PUNIET	5	5	5	65	65	65	65	65	65	65	14	14	14	14	14	14	14	7	7	7	7	9
21 HOPKINS	7	7	7	7	7	7	7	7	14	14	14	7	7	7	7	7	7	14	14	14	14	10
7 VERMEULEN	21	21	21	14	14	14	14	14	7	7	7	21	21	21	21	21	21	21	21	21	21	11
52 TOSELAND	52	14	14	14	21	21	21	21	21	21	13	13	13	13	13	13	13	13	13	13	13	12
13 WEST	14	24	14	21	13	13	13	13	13	13	15	15	15	15	15	15	15	50	50	50		13
33 MELANDRI	13	13	13	33	15	15	15	15	15	15	50	50	50	50	50	50	50	15	15	15		14
56 NAKANO	24	9	9	15	33	33	50	50	50	50	33	33	33	33	33	33	33	24	24			15
50 GUINTOLI	33	52	15	50	50	50	33	33	33	33	24	24	24	24	24	24	24	33	33			
15 de ANGELIS	9	15	33	9	9	9	9	9	9	9	9	9	9	9	9	9	9	9	9			
9 AOKI	15	33	50	24	24	24	24	24	24	24	48											
24 ELIAS	50	50																				

FASTEST RACE LAPS

	Rider	Lap	Time
1	Rossi	2	2m 02.249s
2	Pedrosa	9	2m 02.379s
3	Lorenzo	5	2m 02.748s
4	Hayden	3	2m 02.758s
5	Stoner	8	2m 02.759s
6	Nakano	6	2m 02.797s
7	Dovizioso	3	2m 02.881s
8	Edwards	4	2m 02.898s
9	Capirossi	6	2m 02.927s
10	de Puniet	6	2m 03.032s
11	Elias	19	2m 03.330s
12	Vermeulen	7	2m 03.371s
13	Hopkins	4	2m 03.543s
14	West	7	2m 04.127s
15	Guintoli	13	2m 04.229s
16	de Angelis	11	2m 04.292s
17	Melandri	13	2m 04.412s
18	Aoki	2	2m 05.100s
19	Toseland	2	2m 06.389s

statistics

OFFICIAL TIMEKEEPER

250cc
20 laps, 68.940 miles/110.960km

Pos.	Rider (Nat.)	No.	Team	Machine	Laps	Time & speed
1	Alvaro Bautista (SPA)	10	Mapfre Aspar Team	Aprilia	20	42m 56.428s 96.339mph/ 155.042km/h
2	Hiroshi Aoyama (JPN)	4	Red Bull KTM 250	KTM	20	42m 59.014s
3	Marco Simoncelli (ITA)	58	Metis Gilera	Gilera	20	43m 04.771s
4	Yuki Takahashi (JPN)	72	JiR Team Scot 250	Honda	20	43m 07.460s
5	Aleix Espargaro (SPA)	41	Lotus Aprilia	Aprilia	20	43m 10.274s
6	Alex Debon (SPA)	6	Lotus Aprilia	Aprilia	20	43m 10.702s
7	Roberto Locatelli (ITA)	15	Metis Gilera	Gilera	20	43m 11.529s
8	Ratthapark Wilairot (THA)	14	Thai Honda PTT SAG	Honda	20	43m 13.415s
9	Thomas Luthi (SWI)	12	Emmi - Caffe Latte	Aprilia	20	43m 21.784s
10	Lukas Pesek (CZE)	52	Auto Kelly - CP	Aprilia	20	43m 23.274s
11	Fabrizio Lai (ITA)	32	Campetella Racing	Gilera	20	43m 46.335s
12	Karel Abraham (CZE)	17	Cardion AB Motoracing	Aprilia	20	43m 46.516s
13	Alex Baldolini (ITA)	25	Matteoni Racing	Aprilia	20	44m 02.244s
14	Simone Grotzkyj (ITA)	35	Campetella Racing	Gilera	20	44m 11.972s
15	Imre Toth (HUN)	10	Team Toth Aprilia	Aprilia	20	44m 16.333s
16	Manuel Hemandez (SPA)	43	Blusens Aprilia	Aprilia	20	44m 32.318s
17	Daniel Arcas (SPA)	92	Blusens Aprilia	Aprilia	20	44m 57.145s
18	Doni Tata Pradita (INA)	45	Yamaha Pertamina Indonesia	Yamaha	20	45m 25.270s
	Mattia Pasini (ITA)	75	Polaris World	Aprilia	15	DNF
	Julian Simon (SPA)	60	Repsol KTM 250cc	KTM	11	DNF
	Mika Kallio (FIN)	36	Red Bull KTM 250	KTM	5	DNF
	Hector Faubel (SPA)	55	Mapfre Aspar Team	Aprilia	4	DNF

Fastest lap: Bautista, 2m 08.012s, 96.948mph/156.022km/h (record).

Previous lap record: Dani Pedrosa, SPA (Honda), 2m 08.015s, 96.946mph/156.019km/h (2004).

Event best maximum speed: Luthi, 164.3mph/264.4km/h (race).

Qualifying: **1** Aoyama, 2m 06.893s; **2** Bautista, 2m 07.073s; **3** Simoncelli, 2m 07.109s; **4** Kallio, 2m 07.118s; **5** Wilairot, 2m 07.410s; **6** Espargaro, 2m 07.455s; **7** Simon, 2m 07.668s; **8** Takahashi, 2m 07.766s; **9** Debon, 2m 07.920s; **10** Faubel, 2m 08.009s; **11** Pasini, 2m 08.386s; **12** Lai, 2m 08.483s; **13** Pesek, 2m 08.649s; **14** Luthi, 2m 08.653s; **15** Locatelli, 2m 09.150s; **16** Toth, 2m 09.301s; **17** Baldolini, 2m 09.759s; **18** Abraham, 2m 10.060s; **19** Grotzkyj, 2m 10.490s; **20** Pradita, 2m 11.437s; **21** Hemandez, 2m 11.665s; **22** Arcas, 2m 13.770s.

Fastest race laps: **1** Bautista, 2m 08.012s; **2** Simoncelli, 2m 08.017s; **3** Simon, 2m 08.069s; **4** Aoyama, 2m 08.155s; **5** Pasini, 2m 08.313s; **6** Kallio, 2m 08.341s; **7** Takahashi, 2m 08.395s; **8** Locatelli, 2m 08.511s; **9** Debon, 2m 08.553s; **10** Espargaro, 2m 08.597s; **11** Wilairot, 2m 08.668s; **12** Luthi, 2m 08.869s; **13** Pesek, 2m 09.424s; **14** Faubel, 2m 09.600s; **15** Lai, 2m 09.710s; **16** Baldolini, 2m 10.205s; **17** Abraham, 2m 10.314s; **18** Toth, 2m 10.870s; **19** Grotzkyj, 2m 11.124s; **20** Pradita, 2m 12.205s; **21** Hemandez, 2m 12.517s; **22** Arcas, 2m 12.599s.

World Championship: **1** Simoncelli, 256; **2** Bautista, 228; **3** Kallio, 191; **4** Debon, 176; **5** Takahashi, 147; **6** Barbera, 142; **7** Aoyama, 128; **8** Pasini, 125; **9** Simon, 109; **10** Luthi, 102; **11** Locatelli, 97; **12** Espargaro, 83; **13** Wilairot, 65; **14** Faubel, 54; **15** Pesek, 43; **16** Abraham, 40; **17** Lai, 33; **18** Baldolini, 31; **19** Poggiali, 16; **20** Laverty, 8; **21** Sandi, 6; **22** Toth, 6; **23** Hemandez, 5; **24** Grotzkyj, 4; **25** Tomizawa and Wirsing, 2; **27** Pradita, 1.

125cc
19 laps, 65.493 miles/105.412km

Pos.	Rider (Nat.)	No.	Team	Machine	Laps	Time & speed
1	Gabor Talmacsi (HUN)	1	Bancaja Aspar Team	Aprilia	19	43m 00.716s 91.370mph/ 147.045km/h
2	Bradley Smith (GBR)	38	Polaris World	Aprilia	19	43m 04.132s
3	Simone Corsi (ITA)	24	Jack & Jones WRB	Aprilia	19	43m 07.612s
4	Sandro Cortese (GER)	11	Emmi - Caffe Latte	Aprilia	19	43m 07.641s
5	Mike di Meglio (FRA)	63	Ajo Motorsport	Derbi	19	43m 07.831s
6	Pol Espargaro (SPA)	44	Belson Derbi	Derbi	19	43m 15.838s
7	Joan Olive (SPA)	6	Belson Derbi	Derbi	19	43m 22.521s
8	Dominique Aegerter (SWI)	77	Ajo Motorsport	Derbi	19	43m 22.585s
9	Nicolas Terol (SPA)	18	Jack & Jones WRB	Aprilia	19	43m 22.674s
10	Andrea Iannone (ITA)	29	I.C. Team	Aprilia	19	43m 24.331s
11	Tomoyoshi Koyama (JPN)	71	Red Bull KTM 125	KTM	19	43m 24.367s
12	Sergio Gadea (SPA)	33	Bancaja Aspar Team	Aprilia	19	43m 35.940s
13	Lorenzo Zanetti (ITA)	8	ISPA KTM Aran	KTM	19	43m 41.218s
14	Pablo Nieto (SPA)	22	Onde 2000 KTM	KTM	19	43m 52.120s
15	Adrian Martin (SPA)	26	Bancaja Aspar Team	Aprilia	19	43m 56.442s
16	Jules Cluzel (FRA)	16	Loncin Racing	Loncin	19	43m 57.253s
17	Jonas Folger (GER)	94	Red Bull MotoGP Academy	KTM	19	44m 07.856s
18	Marco Ravaioli (ITA)	72	Matteoni Racing	Aprilia	19	44m 08.289s
19	Randy Krummenacher (SWI)	34	Red Bull KTM 125	KTM	19	44m 08.457s
20	Robin Lasser (GER)	21	Grizzly Gas Kiefer Racing	Aprilia	19	44m 09.565s
21	Bastien Chesaux (SWI)	48	WTR San Marino Team	Aprilia	18	44m 47.325s
22	Robert Muresan (ROU)	95	Grizzly Gas Kiefer Racing	Aprilia	18	43m 37.123s
	Esteve Rabat (SPA)	12	Repsol KTM 125cc	KTM	17	DNF
	Stevie Bonsey (USA)	51	Degraaf Grand Prix	Aprilia	12	DNF
	Stefan Bradl (GER)	17	Grizzly Gas Kiefer Racing	Aprilia	11	DNF
	Scott Redding (GBR)	45	Blusens Aprilia Junior	Aprilia	11	DNF
	Hugo van den Berg (NED)	56	Degraaf Grand Prix	Aprilia	11	DNF
	Raffaele de Rosa (ITA)	35	Onde 2000 KTM	KTM	8	DNF
	Danny Webb (GBR)	99	Degraaf Grand Prix	Aprilia	8	DNF
	Enrique Jerez (SPA)	28	ISPA KTM Aran	KTM	8	DNF
	Alexis Masbou (FRA)	5	Loncin Racing	Loncin	6	DNF
	Takaaki Nakagami (JPN)	73	I.C. Team	Aprilia	3	DNF
	Efren Vazquez (SPA)	7	Blusens Aprilia Junior	Aprilia		DNS

Fastest lap: Cortese, 2m 14.589s, 92.210mph/148.398km/h.

Lap record: Alvaro Bautista, SPA (Aprilia), 2m 13.118s, 93.229mph/150.038km/h (2006).

Event best maximum speed: Talmacsi, 140.4mph/226.0km/h (qualifying practice no. 1).

Qualifying: **1** Iannone, 2m 14.676s; **2** Talmacsi, 2m 15.206s; **3** Webb, 2m 15.365s; **4** Espargaro, 2m 15.676s; **5** Gadea, 2m 15.684s; **6** Olive, 2m 15.860s; **7** Koyama, 2m 15.922s; **8** Corsi, 2m 16.001s; **9** di Meglio, 2m 16.030s; **10** Bradl, 2m 16.263s; **11** Redding, 2m 16.272s; **12** Terol, 2m 16.314s; **13** Smith, 2m 16.397s; **14** Masbou, 2m 16.517s; **15** Bonsey, 2m 16.557s; **16** Vazquez, 2m 16.586s; **17** Nieto, 2m 16.678s; **18** Cortese, 2m 16.731s; **19** de Rosa, 2m 16.849s; **20** Zanetti, 2m 17.272s; **21** Nakagami, 2m 17.418s; **22** Aegerter, 2m 17.622s; **23** Cluzel, 2m 18.296s; **24** Ravaioli, 2m 18.303s; **25** Rabat, 2m 18.334s; **26** Martin, 2m 18.655s; **27** Lasser, 2m 19.002s; **28** Folger, 2m 19.576s; **29** van den Berg, 2m 19.612s; **30** Muresan, 2m 19.688s; **31** Krummenacher, 2m 19.735s; **32** Jerez, 2m 19.963s; **33** Chesaux, 2m 20.115s.

Fastest race laps: **1** Cortese, 2m 14.589s; **2** Talmacsi, 2m 14.862s; **3** Iannone, 2m 14.886s; **4** di Meglio, 2m 14.912s; **5** Corsi, 2m 15.190s; **6** Smith, 2m 15.199s; **7** Bradl, 2m 15.328s; **8** Espargaro, 2m 15.449s; **9** Terol, 2m 15.580s; **10** Olive, 2m 15.653s; **11** Aegerter, 2m 15.668s; **12** Koyama, 2m 15.761s; **13** Bonsey, 2m 15.803s; **14** Gadea, 2m 16.084s; **15** de Rosa, 2m 16.179s; **16** Nieto, 2m 16.374s; **17** Zanetti, 2m 16.409s; **18** Redding, 2m 16.591s; **19** Nakagami, 2m 16.616s; **20** Webb, 2m 16.856s; **21** Folger, 2m 17.075s; **22** Masbou, 2m 17.147s; **23** Rabat, 2m 17.200s; **24** Cluzel, 2m 17.296s; **25** Martin, 2m 17.388s; **26** Krummenacher, 2m 17.844s; **27** Lasser, 2m 17.934s; **28** Ravaioli, 2m 18.077s; **29** Jerez, 2m 18.676s; **30** van den Berg, 2m 18.708s; **31** Chesaux, 2m 19.236s; **32** Muresan, 2m 19.461s.

World Championship: **1** di Meglio, 248; **2** Talmacsi, 206; **3** Corsi, 200; **4** Bradl, 187; **5** Terol, 156; **6** Olive, 142; **7** Smith, 137; **8** Cortese, 130; **9** Espargaro, 124; **10** Redding, 97; **11** Iannone, 96; **12** Gadea, 83; **13** Marquez, 63; **14** Bonsey, 46; **15** Aegerter, 45; **16** Rabat, 43; **17** de Rosa, 37; **18** Webb, 35; **19** Koyama, 32; **20** Vazquez, 27; **21** Ranseder, 22; **22** Nieto, 18; **23** Zanetti, 17; **24** Nakagami, 12; **25** Krummenacher, 10; **26** Tutusaus, 9; **27** Bianco, 8; **28** Schrotter, 3; **29** Lasser and Masbou, 2; **31** Folger, Martin and van den Berg, 1.

RIDER STANDINGS
After 17 Rounds

1	Valentino Rossi	357
2	Casey Stoner	255
3	Dani Pedrosa	229
4	Jorge Lorenzo	182
5	Andrea Dovizioso	161
6	Nicky Hayden	144
7	Colin Edwards	134
8	Chris Vermeulen	125
9	Shinya Nakano	117
10	Loris Capirossi	111
11	James Toseland	100
12	Toni Elias	92
13	Sylvain Guintoli	63
14	Randy de Puniet	60
15	Alex de Angelis	57
16	John Hopkins	55
17	Marco Melandri	51
18	Anthony West	50
19	Ben Spies	20
20	Jamie Hacking	5
21	Tadayuki Okada	2

TEAM STANDINGS
After 17 Rounds

1	Fiat Yamaha Team	539
2	Repsol Honda Team	373
3	Ducati Marlboro Team	306
4	Rizla Suzuki MotoGP	238
5	Tech 3 Yamaha	234
6	San Carlo Honda Gresini	174
7	JiR Team Scot MotoGP	161
8	Alice Team	155
9	Kawasaki Racing Team	110
10	LCR Honda MotoGP	60

CONSTRUCTOR STANDINGS
After 17 Rounds

1	Yamaha	386
2	Ducati	296
3	Honda	295
4	Suzuki	174
5	Kawasaki	86

Stoner leads Pedrosa and Hayden, their Hondas looking quaint in 1960s Repsol livery.

Photograph: Gold & Goose

WITH all championships decided and just three days of the 2008 season to go, it was more than just the end of term. For a number of riders and paddock personnel, it was the end of an era. The sentiments varied according to position. Certainly there were long faces in the Michelin compound. And Nicky Hayden admitted to feeling a lot of emotion in his last Honda ride after nine years with the manufacturer.

Mattia Pasini was sober as he considered the prospect of GP unemployment after the collapse of his Polaris World 250 team – in spite of his win at Qatar, retirement through heat fatigue in Malaysia hadn't enhanced his reputation. KTM's 250 pit was also a sombre place, in the last race for the semi-injected twin, although rider Kallio was excited to be moving to MotoGP. And Anthony West was downbeat about his last GP; he considered his move to World Supersport to be a major backward step.

By contrast, Marco Melandri could hardly wait to park his factory Ducati for the last time. Even the prospect of Kawasaki was more attractive, and he was clinging to the belief that the stiffer-chassis style of Japanese bike manufacture would be the ingredient he needed to save his career. Elias, likewise, was delighted to be going back to the Gresini Honda team, where he was due to ride a factory bike for 2009.

Hayden spoke respectfully of Honda and his team, but couldn't resist a last jibe at Alberto Puig, having the name sticker on his bike's screen changed for Saturday

morning from 'N HAYDEN' to 'N HYPOCRITE'. It was removed at lunchtime at Honda's behest, he explained, adding, 'It was just meant to be funny – not being a big punk or anything.'

He would ride the Ducati the next day, finding it a sobering experience, although he did run fastest during Tuesday's depleted wet session. He meant to make his last race a good one, heading the lists in (damp) free practice and starting from his fifth front row of the year. The race was another nightmare, however, as Dovizioso showed him the way home yet again.

Sete Gibernau was back in the paddock to launch the new Onde 2000 team, and on Monday to test the black and white Ducati he was set to race in 2009. An unfortunate translation in the literature caused titters at the launch, the switch from 125s to MotoGP being described as moving up to 'the queen's class'. With big-name brothers Gelete and Pablo Nieto to run the team, however, and the backing of hugely wealthy property magnate Francisco Hernando, a former teenage sewer worker from the same slums of Madrid as their father, Angel, the Spanish at least were taking it seriously.

The end of the season was celebrated by several special liveries. Lorenzo had his Fiat Yamaha painted white and adorned with the flags of all the countries where he had won GPs: the Lorenzo's Land theme still had space for one at Valencia, where he never had stood on the top step. Repsol Honda revived a retro scheme from 1969 to celebrate 40 years of motorsport sponsorship

Above: Lorenzo, here heading Toseland, Guintoli and West, had a downbeat final race to eighth.

Right and far right: Hayden's last race on a Honda ended a nine-year partnership.

Bottom right: Michelins lined up for one last MotoGP race.

Photographs: Gold & Goose

Below: So many questions – motif on Gibernau's bike for his MotoGP return.

Below: Graziano Rossi smiles for the camera.

Photographs: Gold & Goose

by the Spanish petrol company The fairings were white with two stripes, one blue and one orange. Gilera also chose to celebrate its centenary – and its new 250 title – with another retro fairing for Simoncelli, which was unveiled at a special party for Dunlop to celebrate an unbroken run of 200 wins, in the 125 and 250 classes, starting in 1996.

The race was something of a disaster for MotoGP fans, and something to laugh about for the rivals in the Superbike paddock, after their year of close racing. There was an almost complete absence of overtaking once Rossi had got up to third from his fourth-row starting position, which happened on the sixth of 30 laps. From there to the end, the field gradually spread out, with not a single change of position in the top six, and precious few behind them. It was a dire demonstration of how bad it can be in the new 800cc era.

With control tyres coming the very next day, *MOTOCOURSE* asked the top three in the parade whether they thought this would solve the problem. Stoner reserved judgement, but thought probably not; Rossi blamed the track and the electronics for the processional race; but Pedrosa held out some hope. 'My feeling is that before maybe the races were not so fast from the start. Riders took some laps to warm up tyres, to watch each other, and then maybe started pulling. Then you can see some closer riding. But when the 800s came, from the start everybody goes full. So if one rider is able to go a little faster than the other, the gaps start, and then it's like this all the race. When I came to MotoGP, the race start was not that fast. Now the tyres have improved a lot, so from the beginning you can go fast. Maybe with this new regulation, the tyres are not such high performance, everybody has to warm up the tyres more, and maybe it will be better.'

The hope didn't last 24 hours. Bridgestone had brought enough of what it expected would be 2009's tyres for testing, and to the surprise of all, they turned out to be very little different from the tyres most of their customers had used for the race the day before. In fact, each of the top three actually improved on his best race time by a tenth or so, although this was put down to slightly better track conditions more than anything else.

Nor did the new tyres have the effect of making times more even – certainly not at first, anyway. While Rossi and co noticed little different about the new tyres, the Kawasaki riders and at least one of the Suzuki men, Chris Vermeulen, had been using a different front, and it would take a bit of work to adapt to the new one. Melandri and Elias, both previously worried about the change, could not make a direct comparison, having switched bikes as well

And there was a problem on Tuesday, when the morning was damp. So far, intermediate tyres are not included in the allocation, and it wasn't until it started raining properly in the afternoon that a handful of riders were able to go out on full wet tyres.

It wasn't a flawless start to the new regime, and it had been a dire race. A disappointing way to wrap up what at times had been a brilliant season.

MOTOGP RACE – 30 laps

Free practice had been cold and damp, and the qualifying hour started much the same, although there was no actual rain until a light shower brought the white flags out at the mid-point. By the finish, it was dry. This left riders with a dilemma – how much of this first dry time to use towards race set-up, and how much to devote to qualifying.

All compromised one way or another, and it was Stoner on top at the end, from Pedrosa and long-time wet leader Hayden. Michelin qualifiers did well by satellite-team riders Edwards, Toseland and de Puniet, who filled row three. Rossi was tenth, leading row four, and not confident. 'We're fast in the wet, but in the dry, corner speed is bad and acceleration also. The situation is quite difficult, but we know what the problem is,' he said. 'Now we have to find out how to fix it.'

The track was dry and the sun shining for the race. The story does not take long to tell. Pedrosa led into the first corner, but Stoner moved inside him into the second, then rode away. With a series of fast laps, he set a new record on lap five. Pedrosa followed along.

At the start, Edwards had been third, trailed by Hayden, Dovizioso, Capirossi and then Rossi. Hayden moved to third on the second lap, but was already behind by almost a second, and lost another four-tenths, on lap three. He was holding up the pack, while Rossi was about to move past Dovizioso at the prime passing spot, braking into the first corner; he did the same to Edwards two laps later, his compatriot following.

Later on the same lap, both Italians moved past Hayden. The order was set.

Hayden and Edwards soon began dropping away from the leaders, and by half-distance from one another. Not one of the first seven was closer than a couple of seconds to the next, Capirossi at the back of it.

There was a flutter of excitement when Nakano caught Capirossi. He passed him quite easily on lap 14, and they too carried on. By lap 16, the two-second rule ran all the way down to eighth. Then a yawning five-second emptiness preceded what had become a closer gang, at least for a while.

At this point, it was led by Lorenzo, who had just got ahead of de Angelis. Toseland was behind, and then came Melandri, going quite well for once. Hopkins was next, having led the group in the earlier stages and then succumbed to a lack of turning potential; that meant he was wearing out his rear tyre too quickly.

Lorenzo was the fast one, and he left the gang behind, closing up what had become a four-second gap to Capirossi. He passed him as well with one lap left. Pushing on, he came within a second of Nakano and would have been on him in another lap. It wasn't that exciting, however: it was only for a distant eighth place.

Capirossi was ninth and de Angelis tenth, but Toseland had faded, to be caught at the end by Guintoli and Vermeulen. The Englishman narrowly held them at bay.

Hopkins was close behind, and then came de Puniet, who rode valiantly to claim the last point. He had been forced off the track on the first lap and had rejoined a distant last.

Melandri's run had not lasted the full distance. He'd fought through to tenth, behind Lorenzo, with three laps left, when he too ran off, dropping out of the points again in his last Ducati ride.

West and Elias were further back, the former blighted by a poor tyre choice, and Elias all out of enthusiasm.

One couldn't really blame the riders for the poor display, although Rossi's crew chief, Burgess, was among many who remembered a time when Rossi had been confident enough to make a bit of a show for the fans before driving off and winning the race. Perhaps the new generation lacks that confidence, possibly with good reason. Neither Stoner nor Pedrosa, observed Burgess, 'seem very keen to get in a fight'.

There were no significant changes to the championship. Dovizioso didn't do enough to displace Lorenzo as top rookie, while Hayden's thwarted ambitions meant that, in turn, he wasn't able to take fifth off the young Italian, nor to produce a strong final race. In this, he wasn't helped by having wrecked his number-one bike in a crash during morning warm-up. 'It didn't feel as smooth. I definitely liked my first bike better,' he said.

250cc RACE – 27 laps

If the MotoGP race illustrated what was wrong with the big class, the doomed 250s showed clearly why they will be so sorely missed.

The class was hit also by poor weather in practice, and Simoncelli took his seventh pole at the last minute, ousting Debon by just one-hundredth. Simon and Kallio completed the front row; Aoyama led the second from Bautista, Wilairot and Locatelli.

Kallio took off in the lead, pursued by crowd favourite Simon, Locatelli, Debon and only then Simoncelli, with Faubel behind. Then came Bautista in seventh.

The front-runners were going at each other from the start. Simon took a short-lived lead into the first corner on lap three, only for Kallio to do the same to him next time around. Locatelli stayed close, but there was a little gap to the next quartet, which had been swapping around. Simoncelli had dropped behind, Bautista had come to the front, while Takahashi had displaced Debon, who would soon drop away.

The first three started to close on the leaders, and Simoncelli was making his presence strongly felt, his tactics as fierce as ever. Bautista took third off Locatelli on lap six; next time around, the new champion passed not only Takahashi and Locatelli, but also Bautista.

On lap nine, he assumed the lead for the first time with another double overtake – first Simon and then Kallio. And he was pushing on hard.

Kallio stayed with him, but Simon lost third to Takahashi almost directly. Then the Spaniard began dropping away lap by lap, his KTM losing power. He lasted until lap 19 before losing fourth to Bautista, some five seconds behind, whereupon he slowed right up, flung his arms up in frustration and toured to the pits to retire.

Takahashi had joined the battle up front, but by lap 23 his pace was dropping and he was a second adrift. For the last four laps, it was just the two of them.

Kallio set fastest lap on the 24th, but could do no more than harry Simoncelli. As they started the last lap, the Italian had a couple of tenths in hand. Kallio meant to end his 250 career with a bang, and half-way around he held off the brakes as long as he dared. Then came the wrong kind of bang as he slid off into the gravel. Simoncelli, unaware of his departure, kept hunkered down to the flag.

Takahashi was more than five seconds behind, with Bautista and Locatelli spread out further back.

Debon had been holding sixth under constant pressure from Faubel, Aoyama and Espargaro, until he too lost the front and slid off on lap 22. The remaining three fought almost to the end, with Aoyama and Faubel back and forth until the Japanese managed to escape. A little way back, Espargaro had come under attack from the increasingly impressive Wilairot.

Pasini and Luthi were a long way adrift, with an even bigger gap behind them, into which Kallio had managed to slot after remounting. Lai and Pesek also crashed out.

Again, there were no significant changes to the championship order.

125cc RACE – 24 laps

Talmacsi, bound for 250s in 2009, took pole in his last 125 race, with Gadea, Corsi and Terol alongside, Smith leading row two. The fight was between Talmacsi and Corsi for second overall. Talmacsi needed to finish not only ahead of Corsi, but also in the top three to secure the position.

It wouldn't happen that way. He leapt off the start to lead the first lap, until they got to the straight. His gear lever had snapped off short and he was struggling.

Terol took over as the Hungarian dropped five more places in the next lap. He would carry on losing places until lap seven, when his gear-shifting problems cost him enough concentration that he missed his braking point and crashed.

Corsi took the lead off his team-mate on lap two, still a pack up front, with Bradl moving through it fast after finishing lap one seventh. Half-way around lap three, he pushed past Gadea into third and promptly flicked sideways into a big high-side crash, which took both out of the race.

Corsi and Terol had a bit of a gap, but di Meglio was up to third on lap five, pulling Cortese and Smith back up with him. Before half-distance, five were disputing the lead again.

Di Meglio and Corsi shared most of the leading, while Smith lost a little ground at the back of the group. Then he closed up again for the last laps; on the 18th, he was up to third, after Terol and Cortese had had a coming together and slowed.

Terol was on form at home and pushed his way back to third. Then on the penultimate lap, di Meglio, leading at the time, lost the front going into a hairpin and ran wide. This let Corsi and Terol by, although the champion had narrowly missed catching them by the finish. Smith was fourth, then Cortese.

Some 15 seconds back came Iannone, who had been tussling with an on-form Bonsey until the American had crashed out at two-thirds distance. Bonsey's team-mate, Webb, had already fallen, after crashing also in morning warm-up.

Koyama defeated Redding by inches for seventh; some way back, Nieto, in his last race, held off young compatriot Rabat for ninth, with Zanetti close behind. Espargaro did not start, after a heavy crash in practice.

With his fourth win of the season, Corsi comfortably secured second overall.

Above: Stoner's dominant win was a warning for the season to come.

Top right: KTM race chief Harald Bartol gives rider Kallio a final briefing.

Right: Tomoyoshi Koyama was back again on the factory KTM 125.

Far right: Team-mates Corsi and Terol lead di Meglio. Corsi's win made sure of second overall.

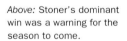
Photographs: Gold & Goose

GP PARTS EUROPE DE LA COMUNITAT VALENCIANA

26 OCTOBER 2008 • FIM WORLD CHAMPIONSHIP ROUND 18

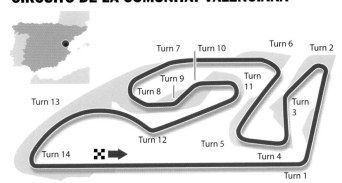

CIRCUITO DE LA COMUNITAT VALENCIANA

Circuit 4.051km /2.517 miles

MOTOGP

RACE: 30 laps, 74.670 miles/120.150km • Weather: Dry • Air 26°C • Humidity 41% • Track 34°C

Pos.	Rider	Nat.	No.	Team	Machine	Tyres	Laps	Time & speed (mph/km/h)
1	Casey Stoner	AUS	1	Ducati Marlboro Team	Ducati	B	30	46m 46.114s 95.779mph/ 154.141km/h
2	Dani Pedrosa	SPA	2	Repsol Honda Team	Honda	B	30	46m 49.504s
3	Valentino Rossi	ITA	46	Fiat Yamaha Team	Yamaha	B	30	46m 58.308s
4	Andrea Dovizioso	ITA	4	JiR Team Scot MotoGP	Honda	M	30	47m 10.273s
5	Nicky Hayden	USA	69	Repsol Honda Team	Honda	M	30	47m 12.346s
6	Colin Edwards	USA	5	Tech 3 Yamaha	Yamaha	M	30	47m 18.323s
7	Shinya Nakano	JPN	56	San Carlo Honda Gresini	Honda	B	30	47m 20.685s
8	Jorge Lorenzo	SPA	48	Fiat Yamaha Team	Yamaha	M	30	47m 21.775s
9	Loris Capirossi	ITA	65	Rizla Suzuki MotoGP	Suzuki	B	30	47m 24.342s
10	Alex de Angelis	RSM	15	San Carlo Honda Gresini	Honda	B	30	47m 33.697s
11	James Toseland	GBR	52	Tech 3 Yamaha	Yamaha	M	30	47m 38.221s
12	Sylvain Guintoli	FRA	50	Alice Team	Ducati	B	30	47m 38.464s
13	Chris Vermeulen	AUS	7	Rizla Suzuki MotoGP	Suzuki	B	30	47m 38.947s
14	John Hopkins	USA	21	Kawasaki Racing Team	Kawasaki	B	30	47m 39.341s
15	Randy de Puniet	FRA	14	LCR Honda MotoGP	Honda	M	30	47m 39.525s
16	Marco Melandri	ITA	33	Ducati Marlboro Team	Ducati	B	30	47m 54.501s
17	Anthony West	AUS	13	Kawasaki Racing Team	Kawasaki	B	30	47m 57.295s
18	Toni Elias	SPA	24	Alice Team	Ducati	B	30	48m 23.169s

Fastest lap: Casey Stoner, on lap 5, 1m 32.582s, 96.767mph/155.732km/h (record).

Previous lap record: Dani Pedrosa, SPA (Honda), 1m 32.748s, 96.594mph/155.453km/h (2007).

Event best maximum speed: Marco Melandri, 193.3mph/311.1km/h (race).

QUALIFYING: 25 October 2008

Weather: Dry
Air: 19°C Humidity: 62% Track: 18°C

Pos.	Rider	Time
1	Stoner	1m 31.502s
2	Pedrosa	1m 31.555s
3	Hayden	1m 31.703s
4	Edwards	1m 32.212s
5	Toseland	1m 32.518s
6	de Puniet	1m 32.572s
7	Lorenzo	1m 32.594s
8	Capirossi	1m 32.614s
9	Dovizioso	1m 32.734s
10	Rossi	1m 32.962s
11	Elias	1m 32.983s
12	Vermeulen	1m 33.017s
13	Guintoli	1m 33.352s
14	Hopkins	1m 33.681s
15	Nakano	1m 33.767s
16	de Angelis	1m 33.848s
17	West	1m 33.879s
18	Melandri	1m 34.174s

Grid order / lap-by-lap

Grid order	1	2	3	4	5	6	7	8	9	10	11	12	13	14	15	16	17	18	19	20	21	22	23	24	25	26	27	28	29	30	
1 STONER	1	1	1	1	1	1	1	1	1	1	1	1	1	1	1	1	1	1	1	1	1	1	1	1	1	1	1	1	1	1	1
2 PEDROSA	2	2	2	2	2	2	2	2	2	2	2	2	2	2	2	2	2	2	2	2	2	2	2	2	2	2	2	2	2	2	2
69 HAYDEN	5	69	69	69	69	46	46	46	46	46	46	46	46	46	46	46	46	46	46	46	46	46	46	46	46	46	46	46	46	46	3
5 EDWARDS	69	5	5	5	5	4	4	4	4	4	4	4	4	4	4	4	4	4	4	4	4	4	4	4	4	4	4	4	4	4	4
52 TOSELAND	4	4	4	46	46	69	69	69	69	69	69	69	69	69	69	69	69	69	69	69	69	69	69	69	69	69	69	69	69	69	5
14 de PUNIET	65	65	46	4	4	5	5	5	5	5	5	5	5	5	5	5	5	5	5	5	5	5	5	5	5	5	5	5	5	5	6
48 LORENZO	46	46	65	65	65	65	65	65	65	65	65	65	65	56	56	56	56	56	56	56	56	56	56	56	56	56	56	56	56	56	7
65 CAPIROSSI	21	21	21	56	56	56	56	56	56	56	56	56	56	65	65	65	65	65	65	65	65	65	65	65	65	65	65	65	48	48	8
4 DOVISIOSO	48	56	56	21	21	21	21	21	21	21	15	15	15	15	48	48	48	48	48	48	48	48	48	48	48	48	48	48	65	65	9
46 ROSSI	56	15	15	15	15	15	15	15	15	15	21	21	48	15	15	15	15	15	15	15	33	33	33	33	33	15	15	15	15	15	10
24 ELIAS	15	48	48	48	48	48	48	48	48	48	48	48	21	52	52	52	33	33	33	33	15	15	15	15	15	52	52	52	52	52	11
7 VERMEULEN	52	52	52	52	52	52	52	52	52	52	52	52	52	52	33	33	52	52	52	52	52	52	52	52	52	50	50	50	50	50	12
50 GUINTOLI	50	50	13	13	13	13	50	50	33	33	33	33	33	33	21	21	21	21	21	21	21	21	21	21	50	21	7	7	7	7	13
21 HOPKINS	13	13	50	50	50	50	13	33	50	50	50	50	50	50	50	50	50	50	50	50	50	50	50	50	21	7	21	21	14		14
56 NAKANO	7	7	7	7	33	33	33	13	13	7	7	7	7	7	7	7	7	7	7	7	7	7	7	7	7	14	14	14			15
15 de ANGELIS	24	24	33	33	7	7	7	7	13	14	14	14	14	14	14	14	14	14	14	14	14	14	14	14	33	33	33				
13 WEST	33	33	24	24	24	24	24	14	14	13	13	13	24	24	24	24	24	24	24	24	24	24	13	13	13	13	13				
33 MELANDRI	14	14	14	14	14	14	14	24	24	24	24	24	13	13	13	13	13	13	13	13	13	13	24	24	24	24	24	24			

FASTEST RACE LAPS

	Rider	Lap	Time
1	Stoner	5	1m 32.582s
2	Pedrosa	13	1m 32.796s
3	Rossi	10	1m 33.075s
4	Dovizioso	7	1m 33.313s
5	Hayden	3	1m 33.393s
6	Edwards	4	1m 33.399s
7	Nakano	7	1m 33.550s
8	Capirossi	5	1m 33.626s
9	de Angelis	5	1m 33.839s
10	Lorenzo	30	1m 33.884s
11	Hopkins	5	1m 34.035s
12	Melandri	22	1m 34.117s
13	Toseland	7	1m 34.150s
14	de Puniet	3	1m 34.225s
15	Guintoli	8	1m 34.462s
16	Vermeulen	17	1m 34.595s
17	Elias	5	1m 34.634s
18	West	5	1m 34.715s

statistics

250cc

27 laps, 67.203 miles/108.135km

Pos.	Rider (Nat.)	No.	Team	Machine	Laps	Time & speed
1	Marco Simoncelli (ITA)	58	Metis Gilera	Gilera	27	43m 29.003s 92.714mph/ 149.208km/h
2	Yuki Takahashi (JPN)	72	Jir Team Scot 250	Honda	27	43m 34.167s
3	Alvaro Bautista (SPA)	19	Mapfre Aspar Team	Aprilia	27	43m 37.651s
4	Roberto Locatelli (ITA)	15	Metis Gilera	Gilera	27	43m 44.608s
5	Hiroshi Aoyama (JPN)	4	Red Bull KTM 250	KTM	27	43m 49.994s
6	Hector Faubel (SPA)	55	Mapfre Aspar Team	Aprilia	27	43m 51.215s
7	Aleix Espargaro (SPA)	41	Lotus Aprilia	Aprilia	27	43m 52.202s
8	Ratthapark Wilairot (THA)	14	Thai Honda PTT SAG	Honda	27	43m 52.324s
9	Mattia Pasini (ITA)	75	Polaris World	Aprilia	27	44m 06.427s
10	Thomas Luthi (SWI)	12	Emmi - Caffe Latte	Aprilia	27	44m 07.890s
11	Mika Kallio (FIN)	36	Red Bull KTM 250	KTM	27	44m 13.068s
12	Alex Baldolini (ITA)	25	Matteoni Racing	Aprilia	27	44m 40.002s
13	Imre Toth (HUN)	10	Team Toth Aprilia	Aprilia	27	45m 00.953s
14	Daniel Arcas (SPA)	92	Blusens Aprilia	Aprilia	27	45m 08.113s
15	Simone Grotzkyj (ITA)	35	Campetella Racing	Gilera	27	45m 10.212s
16	Manuel Hernandez (SPA)	43	Blusens Aprilia	Aprilia	26	43m 30.468s
17	Karel Abraham (CZE)	17	Cardion AB Motoracing	Aprilia	26	43m 46.647s
18	Federico Sandi (ITA)	90	Zongshen AOS Racing	Aprilia	26	43m 59.590s
19	Doni Tata Pradita (INA)	45	Yamaha Pertamina Indonesia	Yamaha	26	44m 03.379s
	Alen Gyorfi (HUN)	93	Team Toth Aprilia	Aprilia	24	DNF
	Alex Debon (SPA)	6	Lotus Aprilia	Aprilia	21	DNF
	Julian Simon (SPA)	60	Repsol KTM 250cc	KTM	19	DNF
	Fabrizio Lai (ITA)	32	Campetella Racing	Gilera	12	DNF
	Lukas Pesek (CZE)	52	Auto Kelly - CP	Aprilia	11	DNF
	Toni Wirsing (GER)	94	Racing Team Germany	Honda	11	DNF

Fastest lap: Kallio, 1m 35.890s, 93.429mph/150.359km/h.

Lap record: Mika Kallio, FIN (KTM), 1m 35.659s, 93.654mph/150.722km/h (2007).

Event best maximum speed: Debon, 162.8mph/262.0km/h (qualifying practice no. 2).

Qualifying: **1** Simoncelli, 1m 35.408s; **2** Debon, 1m 35.418s; **3** Simon, 1m 35.964s; **4** Kallio, 1m 36.194s; **5** Aoyama, 1m 36.267s; **6** Bautista, 1m 36.419s; **7** Wilairot, 1m 36.568s; **8** Locatelli, 1m 36.573s; **9** Faubel, 1m 36.635s; **10** Takahashi, 1m 36.654s; **11** Luthi, 1m 36.832s; **12** Espargaro, 1m 36.841s; **13** Pesek, 1m 36.892s; **14** Pasini, 1m 37.047s; **15** Lai, 1m 37.400s; **16** Baldolini, 1m 37.455s; **17** Grotzkyj, 1m 37.803s; **18** Toth, 1m 38.245s; **19** Sandi, 1m 38.592s; **20** Abraham, 1m 38.641s; **21** Hernandez, 1m 38.874s; **22** Arcas, 1m 39.182s; **23** Pradita, 1m 40.593s; **24** Gyorfi, 1m 41.075s; **25** Wirsing, 1m 41.974s.

Fastest race laps: **1** Kallio, 1m 35.890s; **2** Takahashi, 1m 35.944s; **3** Simoncelli, 1m 35.995s; **4** Bautista, 1m 36.014s; **5** Simon, 1m 36.152s; **6** Locatelli, 1m 36.381s; **7** Espargaro, 1m 36.659s; **8** Aoyama, 1m 36.672s; **9** Wilairot, 1m 36.686s; **10** Pesek, 1m 36.765s; **11** Debon, 1m 36.769s; **12** Faubel, 1m 36.780s; **13** Luthi, 1m 36.874s; **14** Pasini, 1m 37.240s; 15 Lai, 1m 38.202s; **16** Baldolini, 1m 38.248s; **17** Grotzkyj, 1m 38.544s; **18** Toth, 1m 38.772s; **19** Sandi, 1m 38.994s; **20** Arcas, 1m 39.142s; **21** Abraham, 1m 39.513s; **22** Hernandez, 1m 39.662s; **23** Gyorfi, 1m 39.803s; **24** Pradita, 1m 40.578s; **25** Wirsing, 1m 41.700s.

Final World Championship Standings: **See table on page 207.**

125cc

24 laps, 59.736 miles/96.120km

Pos.	Rider (Nat.)	No.	Team	Machine	Laps	Time & speed
1	Simone Corsi (ITA)	24	Jack & Jones WRB	Aprilia	24	40m 45.715s 87.915mph/ 141.485km/h
2	Nicolas Terol (SPA)	18	Jack & Jones WRB	Aprilia	24	40m 45.821s
3	Mike di Meglio (FRA)	63	Ajo Motorsport	Derbi	24	40m 45.938s
4	Bradley Smith (GBR)	38	Polaris World	Aprilia	24	40m 46.491s
5	Sandro Cortese (GER)	11	Emmi - Caffe Latte	Aprilia	24	40m 47.048s
6	Andrea Iannone (ITA)	29	I.C. Team	Aprilia	24	41m 07.293s
7	Tomoyoshi Koyama (JPN)	71	Red Bull KTM 125	KTM	24	41m 15.102s
8	Scott Redding (GBR)	45	Blusens Aprilia Junior	Aprilia	24	41m 15.134s
9	Pablo Nieto (SPA)	22	Onde 2000 KTM	KTM	24	41m 23.774s
10	Esteve Rabat (SPA)	12	Repsol KTM 125cc	KTM	24	41m 24.196s
11	Lorenzo Zanetti (ITA)	8	ISPA KTM Aran	KTM	24	41m 24.656s
12	Efren Vazquez (SPA)	7	Blusens Aprilia Junior	Aprilia	24	41m 34.181s
13	Lorenzo Savadori (ITA)	40	I.C. Team	Aprilia	24	41m 34.517s
14	Alexis Masbou (FRA)	5	Loncin Racing	Loncin	24	41m 36.055s
15	Enrique Jerez (SPA)	28	ISPA KTM Aran	KTM	24	41m 36.290s
16	Takaaki Nakagami (JPN)	73	I.C. Team	Aprilia	24	41m 37.935s
17	Randy Krummenacher (SWI)	34	Red Bull KTM 125	KTM	24	41m 40.762s
18	Jonas Folger (GER)	94	Red Bull KTM 125	KTM	24	41m 40.854s
19	Jules Cluzel (FRA)	16	Loncin Racing	Loncin	24	41m 41.261s
20	Marco Ravaioli (ITA)	72	Matteoni Racing	Aprilia	24	41m 46.004s
21	Robert Muresan (ROU)	95	Grizzly Gas Kiefer Racing	Aprilia	24	41m 55.857s
22	Bastien Chesaux (SWI)	48	WTR San Marino Team	Aprilia	24	42m 11.880s
23	Louis Rossi (FRA)	69	FFM Honda GP 125	Honda	24	42m 12.122s
24	Daniel Saez (SPA)	78	Gaviota Prosolia Racing	Aprilia	24	42m 27.435s
25	Cristian Trabalon (SPA)	25	Alpo Atletico de Madrid	Aprilia	23	41m 06.206s
	Pere Tutusaus (SPA)	30	Alpo Atletico de Madrid	Aprilia	23	DNF
	Stevie Bonsey (USA)	51	Degraaf Grand Prix	Aprilia	15	DNF
	Joan Olive (SPA)	6	Belson Derbi	Derbi	14	DNF
	Adrian Martin (SPA)	26	Bancaja Aspar Team	Aprilia	11	DNF
	Raffaele de Rosa (ITA)	35	Onde 2000 KTM	KTM	8	DNF
	Gabor Talmacsi (HUN)	1	Bancaja Aspar Team	Aprilia	6	DNF
	Danny Webb (GBR)	99	Degraaf Grand Prix	Aprilia	6	DNF
	Robin Lasser (GER)	21	Grizzly Gas Kiefer Racing	Aprilia	6	DNF
	Dominique Aegerter (SWI)	77	Ajo Motorsport	Derbi	3	DNF
	Sergio Gadea (SPA)	33	Bancaja Aspar Team	Aprilia	2	DNF
	Stefan Bradl (GER)	17	Grizzly Gas Kiefer Racing	Aprilia	2	DNF
	Hugo van den Berg (NED)	56	Degraaf Grand Prix	Aprilia	0	DNF
	Ricard Cardus (SPA)	75	Andalucia Derbi	Derbi	0	DNF
	Julian Miralles (SPA)	23	Bancaja Mir CEV	Aprilia		DSQ
	Pol Espargaro (SPA)	44	Belson Derbi	Derbi		DNS

Fastest lap: di Meglio, 1m 40.901s, 88.789mph/142.892km/h.

Lap record: Hector Faubel, SPA (Aprilia), 1m 39.380s, 90.148mph/145.079km/h (2007).

Event best maximum speed: Bradl, 140.6mph/226.3km/h (race).

Qualifying: **1** Talmacsi, 1m 41.451s; **2** Gadea, 1m 41.641s; **3** Corsi, 1m 41.951s; **4** Terol, 1m 42.049s; **5** Smith, 1m 42.095s; **6** Bonsey, 1m 42.099s; **7** di Meglio, 1m 42.163s; **8** Iannone, 1m 42.237s; **9** Aegerter, 1m 42.503s; **10** Bradl, 1m 42.589s; **11** Cortese, 1m 42.636s; **12** Rabat, 1m 42.654s; **13** Webb, 1m 42.908s; **14** Olive, 1m 42.969s; **15** Koyama, 1m 43.017s; **16** Zanetti, 1m 43.037s; **17** Redding, 1m 43.133s; **18** Nieto, 1m 43.358s; **19** de Rosa, 1m 43.499s; **20** Nakagami, 1m 43.706s; **21** Krummenacher, 1m 43.843s; **22** Vazquez, 1m 44.018s; **23** Masbou, 1m 44.061s; **24** Martin, 1m 44.193s; **25** Cluzel, 1m 44.232s; **26** Savadori, 1m 44.333s; **27** Jerez, 1m 44.405s; **28** Cardus, 1m 44.530s; **29** Miralles, 1m 44.785s; **30** Espargaro, 1m 44.954s; **31** Ravaioli, 1m 45.132s; **32** Lasser, 1m 45.231s; **33** Saez, 1m 45.290s; **34** Muresan, 1m 45.380s; **35** Rossi, 1m 45.495s; **36** Tutusaus, 1m 45.774s; **37** Folger, 1m 45.976s; **38** van den Berg, 1m 46.098s; **39** Chesaux, 1m 46.749s; **40** Trabalon, 1m 48.306s.

Fastest race laps: **1** di Meglio, 1m 40.901s; **2** Cortese, 1m 41.019s; **3** Smith, 1m 41.043s; **4** Corsi, 1m 41.165s; **5** Talmacsi, 1m 41.171s; **6** Terol, 1m 41.187s; **7** Bonsey, 1m 41.361s; **8** Iannone, 1m 41.553s; **9** Bradl, 1m 41.688s; **10** Koyama, 1m 41.960s; **11** de Rosa, 1m 42.148s; **12** Redding, 1m 42.173s; **13** Nieto, 1m 42.217s; **14** Olive, 1m 42.356s; **15** Zanetti, 1m 42.445s; **16** Rabat, 1m 42.580s; **17** Gadea, 1m 42.672s; **18** Martin, 1m 42.757s; **19** Savadori, 1m 42.916s; **20** Nakagami, 1m 43.004s; **21** Ravaioli, 1m 43.026s; **22** Vazquez, 1m 43.074s; **23** Krummenacher, 1m 43.092s; **24** Folger, 1m 43.210s; **25** Masbou, 1m 43.212s; **26** Jerez, 1m 43.217s; **27** Webb, 1m 43.322s; **28** Cluzel, 1m 43.355s; **29** Muresan, 1m 43.404s; **30** Aegerter, 1m 43.525s; **31** Lasser, 1m 43.616s; **32** Tutusaus, 1m 43.765s; **33** Chesaux, 1m 44.293s; **34** Rossi, 1m 44.312s; **35** Miralles, 1m 44.339s; **36** Saez, 1m 44.848s; **37** Trabalon, 1m 45.847s.

Final World Championship Standings: **See table on page 207.**

RIDER STANDINGS

After 18 Rounds

1	Valentino Rossi	373
2	Casey Stoner	280
3	Dani Pedrosa	249
4	Jorge Lorenzo	190
5	Andrea Dovizioso	174
6	Nicky Hayden	155
7	Colin Edwards	144
8	Chris Vermeulen	128
9	Shinya Nakano	126
10	Loris Capirossi	118
11	James Toseland	105
12	Toni Elias	92
13	Sylvain Guintoli	67
14	Alex de Angelis	63
15	Randy de Puniet	61
16	John Hopkins	57
17	Marco Melandri	51
18	Anthony West	50
19	Ben Spies	20
20	Jamie Hacking	5
21	Tadayuki Okada	2

TEAM STANDINGS

After 18 Rounds

1	Fiat Yamaha Team	563
2	Repsol Honda Team	404
3	Ducati Marlboro Team	331
4	Tech 3 Yamaha	249
5	Rizla Suzuki MotoGP	248
6	San Carlo Honda Gresini	189
7	JiR Team Scot MotoGP	174
8	Alice Team	159
9	Kawasaki Racing Team	112
10	LCR Honda MotoGP	61

CONSTRUCTOR STANDINGS

After 18 Rounds

1	Yamaha	402
2	Ducati	321
3	Honda	315
4	Suzuki	181
5	Kawasaki	88

2008 MotoGP World Champions

WORLD CHAMPIONSHIP POINTS 2008

MOTOGP

Position	Rider	Nationality	Machine	Qatar	Spain	Portugal	China	France	Italy	Catalunya	Great Britain	Netherlands	Germany	United States	Czech Republic	San Marino	Indianapolis	Japan	Australia	Malaysia	Valencia	Points total
1	Valentino Rossi	ITA	Yamaha	11	20	16	25	25	25	20	20	5	20	25	25	25	25	25	20	25	16	373
2	Casey Stoner	AUS	Ducati	25	5	10	16	–	20	16	25	25	25	20	–	–	13	20	25	10	25	280
3	Dani Pedrosa	SPA	Honda	16	25	20	20	13	16	25	16	20	–	–	1	13	8	16	–	20	20	249
4	Jorge Lorenzo	SPA	Yamaha	20	16	25	13	20	–	–	10	10	–	–	6	20	16	13	13	–	8	190
5	Andrea Dovizioso	ITA	Honda	13	8	–	5	10	8	13	11	11	11	13	7	8	11	7	9	16	13	174
6	Nicky Hayden	USA	Honda	6	13	–	10	8	3	8	9	13	3	11	–	–	20	11	16	13	11	155
7	Colin Edwards	USA	Yamaha	9	–	13	9	16	11	11	13	16	–	2	2	6	1	9	8	8	10	144
8	Chris Vermeulen	AUS	Suzuki	–	6	8	–	11	6	9	8	9	16	16	10	11	7	–	1	7	3	128
9	Shinya Nakano	JPN	Honda	3	7	6	6	6	7	7	7	8	7	6	13	4	–	8	11	11	9	126
10	Loris Capirossi	ITA	Suzuki	8	11	7	7	9	9	–	–	–	9	1	16	9	–	10	6	9	7	118
11	James Toseland	GBR	Yamaha	10	10	9	4	–	10	10	–	7	5	7	3	10	–	5	10	–	5	105
12	Toni Elias	SPA	Ducati	2	1	4	8	5	4	–	5	4	4	9	20	16	4	–	5	1	–	92
13	Sylvain Guintoli	FRA	Ducati	1	–	2	1	3	5	3	3	6	10	4	4	5	9	2	2	3	4	67
14	Alex de Angelis	RSM	Honda	–	2	5	–	4	13	–	1	–	13	3	8	–	6	–	–	2	6	63
15	Randy de Puniet	FRA	Honda	7	–	1	3	7	–	–	4	–	8	10	–	–	3	4	7	6	1	61
16	John Hopkins	USA	Kawasaki	4	9	11	2	–	–	6	–	–	–	–	5	2	2	6	3	5	2	57
17	Marco Melandri	ITA	Ducati	5	4	3	11	1	–	5	–	3	–	–	9	7	–	3	–	–	–	51
18	Anthony West	AUS	Kawasaki	–	3	–	–	2	1	4	6	–	6	–	11	3	5	1	4	4	–	50
19	Ben Spies	USA	Suzuki	–	–	–	–	–	–	–	–	2	–	–	8	–	–	10	–	–	–	20
20	Jamie Hacking	USA	Kawasaki	–	–	–	–	–	–	–	–	–	–	–	–	5	–	–	–	–	–	5
21	Tadayuki Okada	JPN	Honda	–	–	–	–	–	2	–	–	–	–	–	–	–	–	–	–	–	–	2

Above: Two thumbs and one finger: 2008 champions di Meglio, Rossi and Simoncelli at Valencia.

Photograph: Gold & Goose

250cc

Position	Rider	Nationality	Machine	Qatar	Spain	Portugal	China	France	Italy	Catalunya	Great Britain	Netherlands	Germany	Czech Republic	San Marino	Indianapolis	Japan	Australia	Malaysia	Valencia	Points total
1	Marco Simoncelli	ITA	Gilera	–	–	20	13	20	25	25	20	16	25	16	10	–	25	25	16	25	281
2	Alvaro Bautista	SPA	Aprilia	10	–	25	4	2	–	20	16	25	16	20	25	–	20	20	25	16	244
3	Mika Kallio	FIN	KTM	16	25	16	25	11	13	–	25	9	13	11	–	–	11	16	–	5	196
4	Alex Debon	SPA	Aprilia	13	10	–	11	25	20	13	9	13	–	25	–	–	16	11	10	–	176
5	Yuki Takahashi	JPN	Honda	11	16	10	9	13	–	4	7	8	7	10	20	–	10	9	13	20	167
6	Hector Barbera	SPA	Aprilia	20	11	8	10	4	–	16	13	11	20	13	16	–	–	–	–	–	142
7	Hiroshi Aoyama	JPN	KTM	–	13	11	20	9	8	9	10	10	8	3	–	–	7	–	20	11	139
8	Mattia Pasini	ITA	Aprilia	25	20	–	16	16	11	10	–	–	10	9	–	–	8	–	–	7	132
9	Roberto Locatelli	ITA	Gilera	8	8	–	5	3	10	–	5	7	6	7	13	–	6	10	9	13	110
10	Julian Simon	SPA	KTM	5	9	9	–	8	5	7	8	6	11	4	11	–	13	13	–	–	109
11	Thomas Luthi	SWI	Aprilia	1	–	13	–	5	16	11	11	20	9	–	9	–	–	–	7	6	108
12	Aleix Espargaro	SPA	Aprilia	7	7	5	7	7	7	–	6	–	3	6	–	–	9	8	11	9	92
13	Ratthapark Wilairot	THA	Honda	3	4	3	8	1	6	5	–	4	–	5	8	–	3	7	8	8	73
14	Hector Faubel	SPA	Aprilia	6	–	7	6	6	–	8	1	5	2	8	–	–	5	–	–	10	64
15	Lukas Pesek	CZE	Aprilia	–	6	6	–	–	–	6	3	1	–	2	7	–	4	2	6	–	43
16	Karel Abraham	CZE	Aprilia	9	3	–	–	–	9	–	4	–	–	6	–	–	5	4	–	–	40
17	Alex Baldolini	ITA	Aprilia	–	5	4	–	–	4	3	–	2	5	1	–	–	–	4	3	4	35
18	Fabrizio Lai	ITA	Gilera	4	–	–	2	–	2	1	–	3	4	–	5	–	1	6	5	–	33
19	Manuel Poggiali	RSM	Gilera	2	–	–	–	10	–	2	2	–	–	–	–	–	–	–	–	–	16
20	Imre Toth	HUN	Aprilia	–	1	–	–	–	1	–	–	–	–	–	–	–	–	3	1	3	9
21	Eugene Laverty	IRL	Aprilia	–	–	1	3	–	3	–	–	–	1	–	–	–	–	–	–	–	8
22	Federico Sandi	ITA	Aprilia	–	–	2	–	–	–	–	–	–	–	4	–	–	–	–	–	–	6
23	Manuel Hernandez	SPA	Aprilia	–	2	–	–	–	–	–	–	–	–	3	–	–	–	–	–	–	5
24	Simone Grotzkyj	ITA	Gilera	–	–	–	–	–	–	–	–	–	–	–	1	–	–	1	2	1	5
25=	Daniel Arcas	SPA	Aprilia	–	–	–	–	–	–	–	–	–	–	–	–	–	–	–	–	2	2
25=	Shoya Tomizawa	JPN	Honda	–	–	–	–	–	–	–	–	–	–	–	–	–	2	–	–	–	2
25=	Toni Wirsing	GER	Honda	–	–	–	–	–	–	–	–	–	–	–	2	–	–	–	–	–	2
28	Doni Tata Pradita	INA	Yamaha	–	–	–	1	–	–	–	–	–	–	–	–	–	–	–	–	–	1

125cc

Position	Rider	Nationality	Machine	Qatar	Spain	Portugal	China	France	Italy	Catalunya	Great Britain	Netherlands	Germany	Czech Republic	San Marino	Indianapolis	Japan	Australia	Malaysia	Valencia	Points total
1	Mike di Meglio	FRA	Derbi	13	7	9	20	25	13	25	20	9	25	20	–	6	20	25	11	16	264
2	Simone Corsi	ITA	Aprilia	9	25	25	–	3	25	11	11	16	11	6	16	9	9	8	16	25	225
3	Gabor Talmacsi	HUN	Aprilia	4	–	10	16	2	20	16	–	25	16	13	25	2	16	16	25	–	206
4	Stefan Bradl	GER	Aprilia	16	13	8	11	10	6	13	–	4	20	25	–	16	25	20	–	–	187
5	Nicolas Terol	SPA	Aprilia	6	20	16	8	16	9	–	–	7	9	11	11	25	11	–	7	20	176
6	Bradley Smith	GBR	Aprilia	–	16	–	–	20	11	2	6	11	13	10	20	8	–	–	20	13	150
7	Joan Olive	SPA	Derbi	20	–	20	10	8	7	–	9	20	–	16	4	4	13	2	9	–	142
8	Sandro Cortese	GER	Aprilia	5	6	6	–	5	8	8	7	13	10	9	9	11	10	10	13	11	141
9	Pol Espargaro	SPA	Derbi	8	2	3	13	13	16	20	–	–	–	8	–	20	–	11	10	–	124
10	Andrea Iannone	ITA	Aprilia	2	–	5	25	11	4	–	8	5	7	10	–	–	13	6	10	–	106
11	Scott Redding	GBR	Aprilia	11	9	–	–	–	2	10	25	–	8	5	–	13	8	6	–	8	105
12	Sergio Gadea	SPA	Aprilia	25	–	7	–	–	10	7	13	–	–	4	6	–	7	–	4	–	83
13	Marc Marquez	SPA	KTM	–	–	–	4	–	–	6	16	–	7	–	13	10	–	7	–	–	63
14	Esteve Rabat	SPA	KTM	–	4	–	5	–	–	5	10	–	3	7	–	–	9	–	6	–	49
15	Stevie Bonsey	USA	Aprilia	–	10	13	2	–	5	9	–	–	–	–	–	7	–	–	–	–	46
16	Dominique Aegerter	SWI	Derbi	–	8	4	–	–	–	4	–	6	2	8	5	–	–	–	8	–	45
17	Tomoyoshi Koyama	JPN	KTM	–	3	–	3	–	3	10	3	–	–	–	–	5	–	5	9	–	41
18	Raffaele de Rosa	ITA	KTM	–	5	–	7	7	3	–	2	6	–	–	3	4	–	–	–	–	37
19	Danny Webb	GBR	Aprilia	10	–	11	–	–	–	5	–	–	–	2	1	6	–	–	–	–	35
20	Efren Vazquez	SPA	Aprilia	7	–	1	6	–	–	–	–	1	–	5	–	2	5	–	–	4	31
21	Pablo Nieto	SPA	KTM	–	11	–	–	–	–	–	–	–	–	2	–	–	–	3	2	7	25
22=	Michael Ranseder	AUT	Aprilia	1	–	2	9	–	1	–	4	2	–	–	–	3	–	–	–	–	22
22=	Lorenzo Zanetti	ITA	KTM	–	–	–	–	9	–	–	1	–	–	–	–	–	–	4	3	5	22
24	Takaaki Nakagami	JPN	Aprilia	–	1	–	–	–	–	–	8	–	–	–	–	–	3	–	–	–	12
25	Randy Krummenacher	SWI	KTM	–	–	–	–	6	–	1	3	–	–	–	–	–	–	–	–	–	10
26	Pere Tutusaus	SPA	Aprilia	–	–	–	1	4	–	–	–	–	4	–	–	–	–	–	–	–	9
27	Stefano Bianco	ITA	Aprilia	3	–	–	–	–	–	–	5	–	–	–	–	–	–	–	–	–	8
28	Alexis Masbou	FRA	Loncin	–	–	–	–	1	–	–	–	–	–	–	–	1	–	–	–	2	4
29=	Lorenzo Savadori	ITA	Aprilia	–	–	–	–	–	–	–	–	–	–	–	–	–	–	–	3	–	3
29=	Marcel Schrotter	GER	Honda	–	–	–	–	–	–	–	–	–	3	–	–	–	–	–	–	–	3
31	Robin Lasser	GER	Aprilia	–	–	–	–	–	–	–	–	–	–	1	–	–	–	1	–	–	2
32=	Jonas Folger	GER	KTM	–	–	–	–	–	–	–	–	–	–	–	–	1	–	–	–	–	1
32=	Enrique Jerez	SPA	KTM	–	–	–	–	–	–	–	–	–	–	–	–	–	–	–	–	1	1
32=	Adrian Martin	SPA	Aprilia	–	–	–	–	–	–	–	–	–	–	–	–	–	–	–	1	–	1
32=	Hugo van den Berg	NED	Aprilia	–	–	–	–	–	–	–	–	1	–	–	–	–	–	–	–	–	1

CHAMPION PROFILE: TROY BAYLISS
OUT ON TOP

FROM spray painter to champagne sprayer, this particular working-class hero is quite something. Now a three-time WSB champion, Troy Bayliss has joined another exclusive club. Not many riders ever retire as world champion, but the Australian will be one of those lucky few to leave the frenetic world of competition without major injury or lack of steam.

Bayliss came to world prominence through two dazzling displays on home ground at Phillip Island: a pair of fifths on his regular Aussie Ansett Freight Suzuki as a WSB wild-card in 1997, and sixth on a Suzuki 250GP machine at that year's Australian GP. But, at 28, was he already too old to go global?

Evidently not.

Darrell Healey, eventually to become his personal manager and joint career planner, drafted him into the GSE Racing team in 1998 for a Ducati-borne assault on BSB racing. Troy left the UK scene as champion in 1999 and was a sensation in his very short AMA career in 2000, taking two poles before being brought into WSB to replace the injured Carl Fogarty, albeit after one false start at Sugo. He was right on the pace from Monza onwards, but simply in the mix too late to challenge for the championship title.

As one Ducati legend passed into history, Bayliss soon installed himself in the vacant role with on-track brio and bravado to spare. He won his first WSB title in

2001, riding a 996F01, but kept his feet on the ground. As always.

Arguably, Bayliss's most appealing virtue, to the fans at least, is his ability to win championships, even allowing for his occasional errors, the result of putting the desire for victory in each and every individual race ahead of any grand master plan.

This approach let him down in 2002, allowing Colin Edwards to make the most remarkable comeback in WSB history and win the title in a classic man-to-man fight at Imola in the final round. It was legendary stuff, but had Bayliss not made an unforced error at Assen, it would have been World Championship number four in 2008, not three.

But even his defeat in 2002 did nothing to tarnish his reputation as a battling rider, scared of nothing and nobody. And still a normal bloke off track. Just the kind of rider to upset the apple cart in GPs, perhaps?

His GP experiences, like all his other racing endeavours, were punctuated by extremes. His first 990cc Ducati Marlboro year, 2003, was not particularly highly regarded in the GP paddock, but it looks better with every passing season, at least when you consider the disappointments of some of Ducati's more recent secondary riders. Sixth, in the toughest year imaginable and with many tracks new to him, was a good rookie innings.

Ultimately, his second GP year was just as forgettable for him as for team-mate Loris Capirossi. And his single year on a too-stiff Camel Pramac Honda saw him simply unable to ride in his most effective, all-action fashion. He left GPs feeling that he could have done more. Fifteenth in the points? It was a depressing exit indeed.

Winning the WSB title again in 2006 on the 999 F06 was a dream comeback to a paddock that was easier on him, his family and his leisure time at his new home in Monaco. With title number two, he was well cast as the saviour of Ducati's slipping WSB pre-eminence, and not for the first time. To cap a remarkable year, he was finally able to silence his MotoGP critics when he turned up at Valencia for the last round and hammered the self-proclaimed best riders in the world in a winning style as comprehensive as it was unexpected. Another ambition achieved.

Statistically, Bayliss is the second-best rider in WSB history, in terms of outright championships and race wins. That's remarkable, as he has only five full WSB seasons and one partial season to his credit.

In 2000, Bayliss hit the WSB arena running; in 2008, he'll leave it running, and at almost 40, he'll deserve all the praise that comes his way.

Everyman and extraordinary man, Bayliss will be long remembered as the people's WSB champion.

Left: Living doll. Ducati's victorious factory team manhandle the outgoing multi-champion.

Right: Typical action: Bayliss on his own line and going for the win.

Below centre: Family racer Troy with wife Kim.

Below centre right: Bayliss after securing his third Superbike title.
Photographs: Gold & Goose

Above: Bayliss and the Ducati were made for one another.

Left: In front again at Laguna.
Photographs: Gold & Goose

Jakub Smrz

Lorenzo Lanzi

Carlos Checa

Max Biaggi

2008 TEAMS & RIDERS

DUCATI

Ducati Xerox

WSB legend Troy Bayliss (38) was the only one who could win with any level of consistency on the remarkably adept 1098 F08, sponsored for the fourth year by Xerox. The team was headed by Davide Tardozzi and Technical Director Ernesto Marinelli, and this most successful squad was certainly well equipped to win the title. It did this in not quite flawless fashion, but came close. Factory rider Michel Fabrizio (23) was just as amazingly talented and prone to hot-headedness as he ever had been as a privateer. Seven podiums and eight DNFs were a perfect summary of what he brought to bear in works guise.

Niccolò Canepa (20) joined in on a semi-development bike for the Vallelunga race and was fast in practice, less so in the race.

RG Team

Lorenzo Lanzi (26) was a surprise winner at Valencia on the 1098 RS, finally delivering again as a privateer after some unhappy times in the factory squad. His new team was delighted, but cash-strapped towards the end. When the owner fell ill shortly before Portimao, RG opted to miss the last round.

Sterilgarda Go Eleven

According to the riders, Max Biaggi (36) and Ruben Xaus (30), this was an almost completely private team on the new 1098 RS. According to the team manager and Ducati factory sources, it was only a step or two behind in development, from race to race. It was a strong effort all the same from ex-rider Marco Borciani's latest race team. Arguably, it had the strongest rider line-up, behind Troy Corser and Noriyuki Haga.

Guandalini Racing by Grifo's

Jakub Smrz (24) enjoyed little more success on the new 1098 RS than he had done on the old 999, but the latest pairing had pace for one lap on many occasions. A good new team, stepping up from Italian national racing and providing a space for a fast Czech rider. Thus it was welcomed by all.

HONDA

Hannspree Ten Kate

The World Championship winner of 2007 had an all-new star cast on the all-new Fireblade, in the same Hannspree colours. Carlos Checa (35) is well known to MOTOCOURSE readers from his times in MotoGP; Ryuichi Kiyonari (25) is a double BSB champion and Honda favourite; and reigning WSS champion Kenan Sofuoglu (23) completed the trio.

Receiving bikes only as Christmas presents is not ideal when the series begins on 23 February, but they won five races, shared between Kiyonari and Checa. Sofuoglu had a miserable time, suffering all the more when his brother was killed in a racing accident back home in Turkey, only a couple of years after the loss of his other brother. He swapped places with the Ten Kate WSS rider Jonathan Rea (21) for the final round, and Kenan won the Portimao race. When Kiyonari broke his collarbone in a crash during testing, Martin Bauer (32) was his one-race replacement in France.

DF Racing

Karl Muggeridge (33) was the all-season signing, but struggled on both the old and the new Fireblade, even after Magneti Marelli electronics had been installed. The cause was hardly helped by the induction of various team-mates after the exit of Russell Holland (24); the list was long and seemingly ever changing. Luca Morelli (22), Matej Smrz (23), Jiri Drazdak (29), Luca Scassa (25) and Ivan Silva (26) all had a go before the season's end.

Alto Evolution

Shuhei Aoyama (23) was in the doldrums as he tried to make the transition from 250GP to WSB. His tiny frame looked out of place on the team's original 2007-spec bikes; even on the smaller 2008 version, the marriage was an unhappy one. There would be several number-two riders in Marco Nicotari's squad. Luca Morelli (20) joined in at one time; Jason Pridmore (39) was also signed, but fled before the end; and Matt Lynn (24) struggled as well, having followed Pridmore's lead from America.

Regis Laconi

Michel Fabrizio

Ruben Xaus

Hannspree Althea

A strong WSS team still, and a desperately unlucky WSB rookie effort, with good backing on two fronts and a good rider in Roby Rolfo (27). It was still a good team at season's end, and it should have had better results. Giovanni Bussei (36) was drafted in to ride when Rolfo injured himself while cycling, but Bussei himself was also injured.

Vent-Axia VK

Gregorio Lavilla (34) and the highly respected BSB outfit should have been a dream team, sponsored by UK companies and owner Paul Bird. The fact that the team ended up as the first 'proper' privateer effort did not help dispel the air of general disappointment that was evident on occasion, and which most others found mystifying. The squad brought in Chris Walker (36) after Brno, poaching him from his WSS Kawasaki ride.

SUZUKI

Suzuki Alstare

Losing ten year's worth of Corona sponsorship could have been a hangover for the whole Alstare set-up, but mobile-phone money from Spain and energy-drink money from Germany kept them in SIM cards and fizzy pop. In the Giacomo Guidotti side of the garage, Fonsi Nieto (29) and Yukio Kagayama (33) shared space and machine spec, even though Kagayama missed an early round or two with injury.

Max Neukirchner (24) was Alstare's star turn on Francis Batta's home-tuned machines. He was first a real threat, then a real winner.

YAMAHA

Yamaha Motor Italia

The second year of the same rider line-up and same machine, in the last year of Santander sponsorship. Troy Corser (36) and Noriyuki Haga (33) made the strongest combo on paper, and it proved that way in the end. Run by the Italian importer, this was Euro-distributor factory racing at the highest level.

YZF Team

The 2008 season was the end of the road for Shinichi Nakatomi (29) in Martial Garcia's team, charged with testing racing parts for Yamaha by running them in World Championship competition.

GMT 94 Ipone

For Sébastien Gimbert (30) and David Checa (27), the start of the year promised much, but points were hard to come by for this oil-sponsored outfit. The Endurance-based team received more Superbike parts as the season progressed, and its enthusiasm for the new racing world was unbounded. Michael Beck (24) replaced Checa temporarily at Monza after he was injured.

Grillini Team

The back-marker of 2008, Grillini ran Loïc Napoleone (22) first and foremost, but then gave saddle time to Nino Brignola (35) for Misano, and Christian Zaiser (35) from Brno onwards.

KAWASAKI

Kawasaki PSG1

The PSG-1 Kawasaki team had two riders again in 2008, one of its own choice, the other nominated by Japan: Regis Laconi (32) and Makoto Tamada (31) respectively. With sponsorship from the mountain-top city-state of San Marino, ultimately the best intentions of Pierguido Pagani's squad were frustrated. Early technical issues with what had looked to be a good new bike ruined a potentially positive year, and before the end of the season there were recriminations between manufacturer and team. The relationship with Kawasaki will be no more, officially at least.

Pedercini

Ayrton Badovini (21) and Vittorio Iannuzzo (25) ran year-old machinery, direct from PSG-1's stock of 2007 works equipment, and often outperformed the newer machines in qualifying. A very Italian effort all round, which, in its first Kawasaki year, had a much greater air of confidence and outward glitz than many of its recent Ducati incarnations.

Makoto Tamada

Max Neukirchner

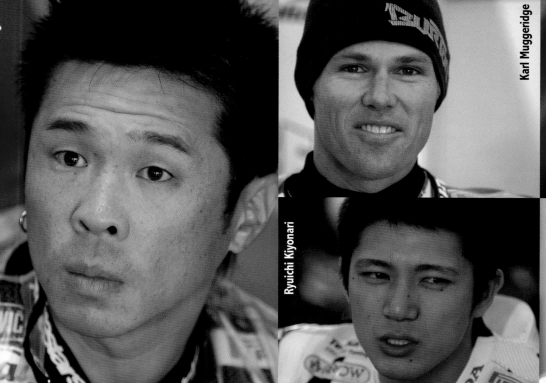

Ryuichi Kiyonari

Karl Muggeridge

Troy Corser

Yukio Kagayama

THE BIKES OF 2008

DUCATI 1098 F08

L IKE every new generation of Ducati since the original belt-driven Pantah 90-degree Vee, the latest offering was a complete change, but still very much to the same basic formula. The extra 200cc over the old models, taking the only current WSB twin to 1198cc, came via a small increase in bore, from 104mm to 106mm, and a larger increase in stroke, from 58.8mm to 67.9mm.

Ducati did not release figures for what the new bike would pump out if it were unfettered by its FIM-sanctioned 50mm air-intake restrictor, but in real race trim, the machine made a claimed 198bhp at a much reduced 11,000rpm. Part of this reduction came from the greater reciprocating mass of the larger pistons and longer piston stroke, but the restrictors also played a part.

The twin had a higher minimum weight than the fours: 168kg compared to 162. With less need for high revs and likewise to pare weight, apparently the Ducati engine had never been more standard inside – partly by regulation, but also because modifications proved to be simply unnecessary.

The new engine and its bigger torque pulses created new challenges for the mapping of the Magneti Marelli Marvel 4 ECU/EFI, which vaporised fuel through two differentially sized injectors.

Ducati did not use the new electronic suspension from Öhlins, opting instead for forks 1mm fatter than 2007: gas-pressurized TTX20 upside-down units and a TTX36 shock. The return to a single-sided swing-arm apparently imbued the new bike with no nasty habits, but the greater torque made former traction-control sceptic Troy Bayliss glad of the system towards the end of races. He said the 999 hardly needed TC, but he admitted that on occasion the 1098 could be a handful without it.

With an all-new, 200cc larger 1098 RS available, the other Ducati teams – RG, Sterilgarda Go Eleven and Guandalini – opted for the greater power, and some riders even won with it.

The return of 'real' privateer Ducatis, instead of year-old factory material for the next best team in the series, meant that everybody started out the same. Max Biaggi and Ruben Xaus received some updates in software and the benefit of works personnel in their garages, but the Sterilgarda guys still took the opportunity to try their own exhausts and other internal tuning parts.

HONDA CBR1000RR

A NEW Ducati was followed by an all-new and much more race orientated CBR1000RR. The team's explanation was by analogy: the big jump that had turned the 2002 CBR600FS Honda roadster into the subsequent CBR600RR street-legal race bike had finally happened in the Fireblade camp.

Hannspree Ten Kate looked after the most official new bike, and although it was not really any faster than the old one in terms of its engine, it was a much more densely packed, more responsive machine overall. That said, it could be wrong on race day – sometimes achieving the correct set-up was a delicate business.

While other teams simply buy in or follow the understandably well-worn Brembo/Magneti Marelli/Öhlins path, Ten Kate is well known for finding its own individualistic engineering solutions. To this end, the team continued its co-operation with PI Research/Pectel for electronics and ignition modules. Although lots of the hardware was the same as the 2007 version, there was endless development of the software. And there is still more to come in 2009, apparently.

Despite its streak of individuality, Ten Kate still relies on lots of parts straight from the HRC kit box, but then works on improving or replacing them. The team ran either HRC kit or KR rear swing-arms, depending on rider preference at the time.

With a full-time WP technician at home and abroad, and similar support from Nissin brakes, Ten Kate simply plough a different furrow, combining successful racing ventures with its race preparation and engineering business. The WP forks were slimmer and lighter around the bottoms than 2007 versions.

Team sources put the bike's race development at 90 per cent near the end of the season, so 2009 may be the real chance for a much more race-ready Fireblade.

The Alto Evolution Honda team suffered a litany of problems again, and without financial support from Europe, it went back to the home factory in Japan for basic electronic systems and other parts.

DFX Honda brought in a well-proven Magneti Marelli EFI system for one of its machines, but found out that new hardware without the latest software and an expert to run it sometimes can be counter-productive.

New boys for 2008 were Hannspree Althea Honda and Vent-Axia Honda. The Althea team swapped to Magneti Marelli mid-season, while the well-prepped and fettled Paul Bird bikes were as good as a lack of testing and mid-season equipment dilution between two riders allowed. The skeleton of a proper factory team was there, and the squad was deservedly top of the 'real' privateers in its first year in WSB.

YAMAHA YZF-R1

WITH a bike that was largely the same as in 2007, the biggest step for Yamaha was to make improvements in the electronics and some of the cycle parts. The 2008 factory bike had an extra electronics sensor, to measure lean angle, which helped a lot with the traction control aspect of the Magneti Marelli Marvel 4 ECU.

The injector bodies were changed from standard to the more expensive Marelli version, as used in MotoGP, and the Yamaha road-bike's variable-length intake trumpet was finally ditched by Noriyuki Haga. It was retained by Troy Corser, however, mainly because he wanted more bottom-end power and smoother transitions during throttle application.

A new camshaft design was used for three or four races, then rejected. Although it gave more top-end power, it was simply too peaky.

The airbox on the R1 was bigger and fabricated in carbon fibre, while the fuel tank was given an extra litre of capacity and was positioned out of sight in the bowels of the machine.

A new swing-arm, customisable for Haga and Corser's individual riding styles, appeared and weighed a whopping 1kg less than the previous year's version.

Factory Öhlins suspension with electronic variable damping control was truly leading edge. It was used during the Vallelunga test and soon after tried out in races from Donington onwards. Both riders employed the suspension at both ends of the bike initially, but Haga reverted to the original air forks, although he did continue to use the electronic unit at the rear. Corser, at first a convert to the new units, went back to the conventional factory TTX units front and rear. Ironically, the new electronic damping system came along just in time for it to be banned in WSB for 2009.

Corser's front Brembo brake rotors were regular 320mm versions, but Haga had special 314mm units made up, to help him make fast changes of direction at some races.

KAWASAKI ZX-10R

THE new ZX-10R offered much in theory, but was still somewhat imperfect in practice. Basic chassis design was blamed, something the GP observers also had seen in the ZX-RR. Most worryingly, the new bike was frequently outperformed by the old one, which was still around in works form and run by the combined PSG-1/Pedercini outfit.

With works riders of the calibre of Regis Laconi and GP/WSB race winner Makoto Tamada, the results should have been better.

Bore and stroke dimensions of 76 x 55mm made for a 998cc engine that was just as peaky as it had been in 2007, causing the bike to wheelie – or for the new Magneti Marelli Marvel 4 electronics package to cut in – too often to stop its unruly tendencies, thus reducing ultimate push down the straights.

The factory Öhlins input in respect of the suspension ended prematurely after a dispute at Magny-Cours, but with or without the extra support, the suspension set-up could not completely mask some fundamental problem or other. PSG-1 tried a total of six different rear swing-arm designs, or modifications, but it is thought that budget restraints prevented the wholesale adoption of new material.

An unhappy year for the factory Kawasaki team and the new WSB machine.

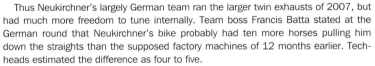

THE three-rider Suzuki team for 2008 made for a split garage. Yukio Kagayama and Fonsi Nieto were running the latest updates from the factory on the K8; the Alstare team did its own development on Max Neukirchner's ex-Biaggi 2007 factory-spec machine, which provided some obvious differences between the Suzuki Alstare duo and the Alstare Suzuki singleton.

Thus Neukirchner's largely German team ran the larger twin exhausts of 2007, but had much more freedom to tune internally. Team boss Francis Batta stated at the German round that Neukirchner's bike probably had ten more horses pulling him down the straights than the supposed factory machines of 12 months earlier. Techheads estimated the difference as four to five.

One major external difference between the Alstare and Suzuki machines was the small bore/big noise of the factory machine's twin exhausts, which had been designed for better performance at high rpm, to reduce weight in areas away from the centre of mass and to improve aerodynamics. Several other items, like the battery and electronics processors, were centralised, while the fuel tank was moved and modded, again to centralise weight.

The Marelli ECU was retained, but to ensure clear communication with Japan, the team went back to a 2D data acquisition system, as used in MotoGP and Japanese Superbike.

The most 'factory' of the Japanese offerings, the Nieto/Kagayama machines eventually (at Vallelunga) received new Showa forks, as used by Hondas in MotoGP. The fork stroke was extended from 120mm to 130, all adjustments being done from the fork tops. All riders who used them said that the new forks provided much better feedback.

SUZUKI GSX-R1000K8/K7

The factory bike was simply easier to set up than in 2007, and tyre life generally was improved. The first part of the race seemed to be more difficult for the factory machines, but they would finish stronger. Neukirchner's experience was the opposite.

The K8 weighed 162kg, right on the minimum – indeed it needed ballast on occasions – whereas Max's bike was around 3kg heavier. Front-wheel chatter was reduced by breaking the basic tenet of racing and making the front axle heavier than before, not lighter.

LOSAIL
QATAR

P RE-SEASON preambles completed, and with many a rider on an old bike in the well-populated Honda encampment, the Qatari desert blossomed once more with the sight and muted sound of WSB's February hordes. The traditional season opener had a traditional name topping the Superpole qualifying sessions, Troy Corser, who set a new lap record of 1m 58.053s on his year-old Yamaha.

One day later, we had another Aussie SBK superstar, Troy Bayliss, taking win number one on the new Ducati 1098F08. Running with a weight penalty and power-sapping air restrictors, and with less tuning allowed than previous Ducati Superbikes, made no difference to Bayliss or his demon desmo. Moreover, Biaggi was second by only 0.3 second, on a privateer 1098RS Ducati. Oh dear.

The paddock held its breath as fears of the dominance of the new 1200cc twins were instantly realised – and then quickly undermined by Fonsi Nieto's first ever WSB race win in race two, on a year-old Suzuki four. Corser, meanwhile, had been third in race one by only 1.8 seconds on a similarly 'old' Yamaha.

Or did the consistently strong early form of Ducati privateers Max Biaggi – second and then third – and Ruben Xaus – fourth and second, the latter when 0.3 second behind Nieto – mean that it was hammer time for those riders with greater numbers of smaller-displacement cylinders inside their engines?

Whatever else was happening in WSB racing, Qatar proved that 2008 was set to be no normal season. Not with Fonsi Nieto winning first time out from 11th on the grid, while double BSB champion Ryuichi Kiyonari was 22nd and 19th. Carlos Checa was sixth and 11th on the new four-blade Fireblade, putting all the more perspective on Kiyo's dismal debut rides. With the Spaniards very much in the ascendancy, Nieto just edged out Biaggi's old lap record with a 1m 59.156s in race two.

What seemed particularly improbable at Qatar, however, was Noriyuki Haga finishing only 14th and then 13th, despite participating in winter tests at the Losail venue.

There was a degree of corporate chafing in the Yamaha garage, particularly as Corser followed his splendid third with a poor seventh, eventually blamed on tyres.

Less of a mystery was the early form of the new Kawasaki ZX-10R, campaigned by Regis Laconi and new WSB full-timer – albeit three-times WSB wild-card race winner – Makoto Tamada. Early days, benefit of the doubt, lack of development time; the old adages were all wheeled out as the sharp looking Ninja went slow, but looked quick standing still. Indeed, it scrabbled for the leavings from the points table on race day.

Among the privateers, the Ducati RS riders had it all their own way. Those on fours had something old, few things new, plenty of things borrowed and moods that were blue.

The simple fact, as had been the case in so many previous seasons, was that the Ducati riders started the campaign on all-new bikes that had a year's worth of development powering them onwards, rather than all of the year's forthcoming development holding them back.

Honda staff viewed the Ducatis almost enviously, Yamaha people looked inwards quizzically, Suzuki bods wore expressions of relief and Kawasaki personnel looked on hopefully. Hope was all the green men had to cling to after round one, however, as relative WSB extras Ayrton Badovini and Vittorio Iannuzzo out-qualified the new Ninja stars, despite being on the cast-off 2007 factory versions, in Pedercini colours. On race day, Badovini – in his second ever WSB race – finished right on Laconi's tail in the second 18-lapper.

There was a lot to think of at 35,000ft as the members of the WSB paddock winged their way to Australia.

Left: Bayliss took the first race of the year.

Above right: Biaggi on his new Ducati, twice on the rostrum.

Right: Fonsi Nieto's second race win was a surprise.

Below left: Xaus was on the rostrum.

Below centre: Corser made a fair start.

Bottom: Kiyonari and crew – zero points.

Photographs: Gold & Goose

Round 1
LOSAIL, Qatar
23 February 2008, 3.343-mile/5.380km circuit

Race 1 18 laps, 60.174 miles/96.840km

Dry, Air 24°C Humidity 30% Track 37°C

Pl.	Name Nat. (*Machine*)	No.	Time & gap	Laps
1	Troy Bayliss, AUS (*Ducati*)	21	36m 11.468s	18
			99.760mph/160.548km/h	
2	Max Biaggi, ITA (*Ducati*)	3	0.396s	18
3	Troy Corser, AUS (*Yamaha*)	11	1.878s	18
4	Ruben Xaus, SPA (*Ducati*)	111	4.487s	18
5	Max Neukirchner, GER (*Suzuki*)	76	7.505s	18
6	Carlos Checa, SPA (*Honda*)	7	9.639s	18
7	Fonsi Nieto, SPA (*Suzuki*)	10	9.725s	18
8	Yukio Kagayama, JPN (*Suzuki*)	34	19.537s	18
9	Michel Fabrizio, ITA (*Ducati*)	84	23.156s	18
10	Jakub Smrz, CZE (*Ducati*)	96	24.429s	18
11	Roberto Rolfo, ITA (*Honda*)	44	27.595s	18
12	Kenan Sofuoglu, TUR (*Honda*)	54	27.979s	18
13	Gregorio Lavilla, SPA (*Honda*)	36	28.237s	18
14	Noriyuki Haga, JPN (*Yamaha*)	41	30.205s	18
15	Regis Laconi, FRA (*Kawasaki*)	55	31.882s	18
16	Lorenzo Lanzi, ITA (*Ducati*)	57	32.067s	18
17	Karl Muggeridge, AUS (*Honda*)	31	40.745s	18
18	Ayrton Badovini, ITA (*Kawasaki*)	86	41.280s	18
19	Vittorio Iannuzzo, ITA (*Kawasaki*)	13	41.333s	18
20	Sébastien Gimbert, FRA (*Yamaha*)	194	41.743s	18
21	Shinichi Nakatomi, JPN (*Yamaha*)	38	43.183s	18
22	Ryuichi Kiyonari, JPN (*Honda*)	23	43.569s	18
23	David Checa, SPA (*Yamaha*)	94	43.892s	18
24	Russell Holland, AUS (*Honda*)	83	50.380s	18
25	Shuhei Aoyama, JPN (*Honda*)	88	1m 12.884s	18

DNF: Luca Morelli, ITA (*Honda*) 22, 12 laps; Loic Napoleone, FRA (*Yamaha*) 77, 12 laps; Makoto Tamada, JPN (*Kawasaki*) 100, 5 laps.

Fastest lap: Haga, 1m 59.217s, 100.948mph/162.460km/h.

Superpole: Corser, 1m 58.053s, 101.943mph/164.062km/h.

Lap record: Max Biaggi, ITA (*Suzuki*), 1m 59.194s, 100.967mph/162.491km/h (2007).

Race 2 18 laps, 60.174 miles/96.840km

Dry, Air 22°C Humidity 30% Track 36°C

Pl.	Name Nat. (*Machine*)	No.	Time & gap	Laps
1	Fonsi Nieto, SPA (*Suzuki*)	10	36m 12.963s	18
			99.691mph/160.437km/h	
2	Ruben Xaus, SPA (*Ducati*)	111	0.301s	18
3	Max Biaggi, ITA (*Ducati*)	3	1.321s	18
4	Troy Bayliss, AUS (*Ducati*)	21	6.452s	18
5	Michel Fabrizio, ITA (*Ducati*)	84	7.627s	18
6	Lorenzo Lanzi, ITA (*Ducati*)	57	9.117s	18
7	Troy Corser, AUS (*Yamaha*)	11	10.806s	18
8	Max Neukirchner, GER (*Suzuki*)	76	11.661s	18
9	Jakub Smrz, CZE (*Ducati*)	96	13.269s	18
10	Kenan Sofuoglu, TUR (*Honda*)	54	14.563s	18
11	Carlos Checa, SPA (*Honda*)	7	15.953s	18
12	Makoto Tamada, JPN (*Kawasaki*)	100	16.748s	18
13	Noriyuki Haga, JPN (*Yamaha*)	41	18.356s	18
14	Gregorio Lavilla, SPA (*Honda*)	36	26.311s	18
15	Roberto Rolfo, ITA (*Honda*)	44	26.560s	18
16	Regis Laconi, FRA (*Kawasaki*)	55	26.683s	18
17	Ayrton Badovini, ITA (*Kawasaki*)	86	26.821s	18
18	Sébastien Gimbert, FRA (*Yamaha*)	194	28.650s	18
19	Ryuichi Kiyonari, JPN (*Honda*)	23	33.150s	18
20	Karl Muggeridge, AUS (*Honda*)	31	36.656s	18
21	Russell Holland, AUS (*Honda*)	83	42.633s	18
22	Shuhei Aoyama, JPN (*Honda*)	88	55.352s	18

DNF: Vittorio Iannuzzo, ITA (*Kawasaki*) 13, 17 laps; Shinichi Nakatomi, JPN (*Yamaha*) 38, 11 laps; Loic Napoleone, FRA (*Yamaha*) 77, 9 laps; David Checa, SPA (*Yamaha*) 94, 8 laps; Luca Morelli, ITA (*Honda*) 22, 4 laps; Yukio Kagayama, JPN (*Suzuki*) 34, 0 laps.

Fastest lap: Nieto, 1m 59.156s, 100.999mph/162.543km/h (record).

Championship points: 1 Bayliss, 38; 2 Biaggi, 36; 3 Nieto, 34; 4 Xaus, 33; 5 Corser, 25; 6 Neukirchner, 19; 7 Fabrizio, 18; 8 C. Checa, 15; 9 Smrz, 13; 10 Lanzi, 10; 11 Sofuoglu, 10; 12 Kagayama, 8; 13 Rolfo, 6; 14 Haga and Lavilla, 5.

PHILLIP ISLAND
AUSTRALIA

OVER the course of the Phillip Island weekend there were a claimed 65,400 spectators inside the naturally sculpted race facility, and other than the odd foreign interloper, almost all of them got more than they bargained for, usually in a good way. They enjoyed their own red-letter day when Troy Bayliss and his factory Ducati scored in Superpole and then took both race wins.

The races themselves were very different affairs, held on a track that started out at 30°C in race one, then rose dramatically to 47°C in race two. Pirelli had said that its aim with 2008's race tyres was to give good performance over an even wider range of temperatures than before. Thus nobody beat Corser's 2007 lap record, but many more riders were able to race harder for longer.

Race one, 22 laps, was an eventual straightforward win for Bayliss, by four seconds from Corser, Fabrizio, Xaus, Nieto, Checa and Neukirchner. That lot were covered by only 1.7 seconds, after a belting fight between them all.

At the start, the drama unfolded rapidly as Fabrizio stalled at the light. David Checa came through unsighted and glanced off him, then Vittorio Iannuzzo smashed into the right side of Fabrizio's machine. The impact was so hard that Vittorio crashed and collided with another rider trackside, while Fabrizio's boot was knocked clean off, hurting his ankle and foot.

The remainder of the field, most of whom had got away before the impact, carried on largely oblivious of the accident. Entering Lukey Heights as the race was being stopped, new WSB regular Russell Holland lost the front and barrelled into Carlos Checa, sending both riders hurtling into the run-off area. Checa had to nip back to make the restart, suitably fired up.

Remarkably, Fabrizio restarted in the delayed race as well, and was a podium finisher in third. Iannuzzo had broken his wrist and dislodged all the main bones in his left hand in the start-line crash, a nasty and

complicated injury, but eventually he would overcome it.

The second event, also over 22-laps, saw the remarkable sight of Carlos Checa, nursing a sore elbow and ankle, coming through to take second by only 1.1 seconds from that man Bayliss, and three seconds ahead of continuing podium threat Nieto.

It was proving to be a bumper season's start for the Spanish. Xaus was fourth and Gregorio Lavilla, the best privateer Honda rider by a mile – on a year-old machine, was tenth.

Indeed, the fours in general rallied hard at Phillip Island, only Bayliss being dominant on his Ducati. The remainder of the podium occupants looked evenly matched whatever machine they rode.

One high-profile Ducati rider was down and out for a while after the Australian round. Max Biaggi, who had qualified last in Superpole due to a dodgy gear lever, had attempted a dubious race-two pass on Nieto at the ultra-fast turn one, but only succeeded in being thrown from his bike. During a fast and sustained tumble, he broke his left radius. He had already fallen in race one, from second place to boot, after a brilliant charge from row four.

Haga was in bother of another kind in Australia, dropping back from his race-one prominence to leave with an eventual eighth and seventh. He lost pace at an alarming rate as the laps unwound.

His team-mate, Corser, fell on lap five of race two, making it another up-and-downer for his side of the garage.

A slew of jump-start penalties affected a few top riders: Michel Fabrizio received one on lap three of race two, as did Corser shortly afterwards – although he ignored it before crashing; then Smrz and Laconi were singled out for pit-lane excursions. It was something of a minor tragedy for Kawasaki man Laconi, who had been forced out in race one with electrical problems. His race-two penalty killed a potential top-six finish.

Above: Checa was knocked off after the red flag.

Top: Close quarters for Corser and new boy Checa.

Right: Bayliss stood on the top step twice.

Centre right: The double winner was invincible.

Right: The Yamaha girls.
Photographs: Gold & Goose

Left: Nieto was a podium threat again.

Right: Xaus took a double fourth.

Below: Fabrizio was hurt in a start-line crash, but raced on.

Photographs: Gold & Goose

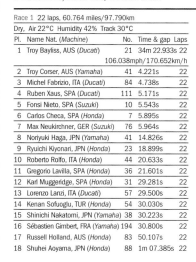

Round 2
PHILLIP ISLAND, Australia
2 March 2008, 2.762-mile/4.445km circuit

Race 1 22 laps, 60.764 miles/97.790km			
Dry, Air 22°C Humidity 42% Track 30°C			
Pl. Name Nat. (*Machine*)	No.	Time & gap	Laps
1 Troy Bayliss, AUS (*Ducati*)	21	34m 22.933s	22
		106.038mph/170.652km/h	
2 Troy Corser, AUS (*Yamaha*)	41	4.221s	22
3 Michel Fabrizio, ITA (*Ducati*)	84	4.738s	22
4 Ruben Xaus, SPA (*Ducati*)	111	5.171s	22
5 Fonsi Nieto, SPA (*Suzuki*)	10	5.543s	22
6 Carlos Checa, SPA (*Honda*)	7	5.895s	22
7 Max Neukirchner, GER (*Suzuki*)	76	5.964s	22
8 Noriyuki Haga, JPN (*Yamaha*)	41	14.826s	22
9 Ryuichi Kiyonari, JPN (*Honda*)	23	18.899s	22
10 Roberto Rolfo, ITA (*Honda*)	44	20.633s	22
11 Gregorio Lavilla, SPA (*Honda*)	36	21.601s	22
12 Karl Muggeridge, SPA (*Honda*)	31	29.281s	22
13 Lorenzo Lanzi, ITA (*Ducati*)	57	29.500s	22
14 Kenan Sofuoglu, TUR (*Honda*)	54	30.030s	22
15 Shinichi Nakatomi, JPN (*Yamaha*)	38	30.223s	22
16 Sébastien Gimbert, FRA (*Yamaha*)	194	30.800s	22
17 Russell Holland, AUS (*Honda*)	83	50.107s	22
18 Shuhei Aoyama, JPN (*Honda*)	88	1m 07.385s	22

Race 2 22 laps, 60.764 miles/97.790km			
Dry, Air 28°C Humidity 29% Track 47°C			
Pl. Name Nat. (*Machine*)	No.	Time & gap	Laps
1 Troy Bayliss, AUS (*Ducati*)	21	34m 35.284s	22
		105.408mph/169.637km/h	
2 Carlos Checa, SPA (*Honda*)	7	1.127s	22
3 Fonsi Nieto, SPA (*Suzuki*)	10	4.395s	22
4 Ruben Xaus, SPA (*Ducati*)	111	6.621s	22
5 Max Neukirchner, GER (*Suzuki*)	76	11.550s	22
6 Ryuichi Kiyonari, JPN (*Honda*)	23	11.620s	22
7 Noriyuki Haga, JPN (*Yamaha*)	41	12.049s	22
8 Gregorio Lavilla, SPA (*Honda*)	36	12.134s	22
9 Russell Holland, AUS (*Honda*)	83	13.462s	22
10 Karl Muggeridge, AUS (*Honda*)	31	15.519s	22
11 Kenan Sofuoglu, TUR (*Honda*)	54	16.225s	22
12 David Checa, SPA (*Yamaha*)	94	21.959s	22
13 Sébastien Gimbert, FRA (*Yamaha*)	194	21.989s	22
14 Makoto Tamada, JPN (*Kawasaki*)	100	29.106s	22
15 Shinichi Nakatomi, JPN (*Yamaha*)	38	29.219s	22
16 Roberto Rolfo, ITA (*Honda*)	44	32.994s	22
17 Regis Laconi, FRA (*Kawasaki*)	55	34.380s	22
18 Jakub Smrz, CZE (*Ducati*)	96	42.537s	22
19 Michel Fabrizio, ITA (*Ducati*)	84	46.623s	22
20 Lorenzo Lanzi, ITA (*Ducati*)	57	47.030s	22
21 Ayrton Badovini, ITA (*Kawasaki*)	86	1m 08.601s	22

DNF: Max Biaggi, ITA (*Ducati*) 3, 15 laps; Makoto Tamada, JPN (*Kawasaki*) 100, 12 laps; Ayrton Badovini, ITA (*Kawasaki*) 86, 9 laps; Loic Napoleone, FRA (*Yamaha*) 77, 7 laps; Regis Laconi, FRA (*Kawasaki*) 55, 6 laps; Jakub Smrz, CZE (*Ducati*) 96, 2 laps; Luca Morelli, ITA (*Honda*) 22, 0 laps; Vittorio Iannuzzo, ITA (*Kawasaki*) 13, 0 laps; David Checa, SPA (*Yamaha*) 94, 0 laps.

Fastest lap: Bayliss, 1m 32.516s, 107.475mph/172.965km/h.

DNF: Max Biaggi, ITA (*Ducati*) 3, 6 laps; Troy Corser, AUS (*Yamaha*) 11, 4 laps; Shuhei Aoyama, JPN (*Honda*) 88, 3 laps; Loic Napoleone, FRA (*Yamaha*) 77, 3 laps.

Fastest lap: Biaggi, 1m 33.477s, 106.370mph/171.186km/h.

Superpole: Bayliss, 1m 31.493s, 108.677mph/174.899km/h.

Lap record: Troy Corser, AUS (*Yamaha*), 1m 31.826s, 108.283mph/174.264km/h (2007).

Championship points: 1 Bayliss, 88; 2 Nieto, 61; 3 Xaus, 59; 4 Corser, 45; 5 C. Checa, 45; 6 Neukirchner, 39; 7 Biaggi, 36; 8 Fabrizio, 34; 9 Haga, 22; 10 Lavilla, 18; 11 Kiyonari, 17; 12 Sofuoglu, 17; 13 Lanzi, 13; 14 Smrz, 13; 15 Rolfo, 12.

VALENCIA
SPAIN

IT was all Max Neukirchner at Valencia. Only, ultimately, it wasn't. In the first two rounds of the championship, Suzuki's junior hopeful had been fifth, eighth, seventh and then fifth again. From his first ever WSB Superpole win to the final corner of the first race, however, there was only one real class act at Valencia. Masterful wasn't in it: he was unstoppable as he secured the lead from lap one and then eased his way clear, heading for a sure-fire win. And perhaps a second a few hours later.

It was shocking, therefore, to see the closing and increasingly desperate Carlos Checa, who had been down in 13th early on, make an impossible final-lap attempt at overtaking at the infamous last corner. He was miles too far back, but in front of a healthy home crowd.

Later, Checa claimed that he had been capitalising on the opportunity Neukirchner had left him by setting such a slow final lap, but his attempted pass was destined for the tyre wall until Neukirchner began to make the final corner. Tipping in earlier or later might have saved the German, but Checa was never going to make it around unless he used Max as his personal pinball flipper.

The crash tangled the Suzuki and Honda, which hit and cracked a rumble strip on the outside of the circuit. Another impact broke Neukirchner's collarbone.

Thus, Max – the 'real Max' or 'Max I' as some cruel types dubbed him after Biaggi was only 16th and eighth – was not only robbed of his first win, but also a probable second as well. Checa cheekily remounted to score fifth and then take a podium for third in race two.

He apologised later, and Neukirchner accepted the apology. At the time, the incident almost masked an opportunistic, but nonetheless remarkably adept win by RG Ducati privateer Lorenzo Lanzi. Out of the factory Ducati picture after two fruitless years, he was back in the winning frame in probably the most unlikely private Ducati team in the paddock, after only five races. Good tyre choices played a part, but few would have denied the new WSB team and its long-suffering rider an early highlight.

Ten riders failed to finish, but Lanzi broke the challenge of Bayliss – on a fading set-up – to record his win, with Corser seven seconds back and puzzled as to why he was not challenging for wins. He was only a

tad more than seven seconds from the victory in race two, but this time around, it was his team-mate, Haga, recovering from his fast first-race fall at turn one, who won from Bayliss, after taking the lead on lap 12 on his number-two bike.

After suffering a technical retirement in the opener, Ryuichi Kiyonari enjoyed a positive result from the usual pre-race official tests at Valencia. If sixth in Australia had been good, fourth in Valencia was a more than lime-green shoot of recovery.

Valencia 2008 was simply messy and unfathomable on many levels, partly because on a track that should have favoured the twins, the fours were in the ascendant. Moreover, the race-one incident involving Checa and Neukirchner caused a delay while the cracked and shattered kerb stone was fixed.

The most important outcome at the very end of the sixth race in succession was not Bayliss's extended championship lead, but whether or not the complicated handicapping rules designed to ensure fair play between the twins and fours would kick-in. The figures added up to the same no matter how often you counted them, and the final result was … absolutely no weight penalties for Ducati riders.

Above: 'The Real Max' Neukirchner was cruelly robbed of victory.

Middle column, from top: Lanzi wheelies in victory; Haga took a first win of the year; Bayliss and Lanzi hug on the rostrum.

Top right: Corser was a lonely third in race one.

Centre right: Checa, close to home, celebrates his second Superbike rostrum.

Photographs: Gold & Goose

Round 3
VALENCIA, Spain
6 April 2008, 2.489-mile/4.005km circuit

Race 1	23 laps, 57.247 miles/92.115km			
Dry, Air 24°C Humidity 27% Track 29°C				
Pl.	Name Nat. (*Machine*)	No.	Time & gap	Laps
1	Lorenzo Lanzi, ITA (*Ducati*)	57	37m 01.894s	23
			92.738mph/149.248km/h	
2	Troy Bayliss, AUS (*Ducati*)	21	2.987s	23
3	Troy Corser, AUS (*Yamaha*)	11	7.287s	23
4	Fonsi Nieto, SPA (*Suzuki*)	10	11.992s	23
5	Carlos Checa, SPA (*Honda*)	7	12.824s	23
6	Karl Muggeridge, AUS (*Honda*)	31	13.125s	23
7	Gregorio Lavilla, SPA (*Honda*)	36	13.191s	23
8	Regis Laconi, FRA (*Kawasaki*)	55	13.906s	23
9	Makoto Tamada, JPN (*Kawasaki*)	100	17.254s	23
10	Roberto Rolfo, ITA (*Honda*)	44	18.606s	23
11	Shinichi Nakatomi, JPN (*Yamaha*)	38	19.858s	23
12	Kenan Sofuoglu, TUR (*Honda*)	54	23.350s	23
13	Russell Holland, AUS (*Honda*)	83	23.577s	23
14	Jakub Smrz, CZE (*Ducati*)	96	24.082s	23
15	David Checa, SPA (*Yamaha*)	94	26.611s	23
16	Max Biaggi, ITA (*Ducati*)	3	41.168s	23
17	Ayrton Badovini, ITA (*Kawasaki*)	86	44.405s	23
18	Luca Morelli, ITA (*Honda*)	22	57.045s	23
19	Diego Lozano Ortiz, SPA (*Honda*)	37	1m 05.173s	23
20	Loic Napoleone, FRA (*Yamaha*)	77	5 laps	18

DNF: Max Neukirchner, GER (*Suzuki*) 76, 22 laps; Ruben Xaus, SPA (*Ducati*) 111, 10 laps; Ryuichi Kiyonari, JPN (*Honda*) 23, 9 laps; Michel Fabrizio, ITA (*Ducati*) 84, 4 laps; Noriyuki Haga, JPN (*Yamaha*) 41, 3 laps; Yukio Kagayama, JPN (*Suzuki*) 34, 3 laps; Carmelo Morales, SPA (*Yamaha*) 131, 3 laps; Sébastien Gimbert, FRA (*Yamaha*) 194, 1 lap; Sergio Fuertes, SPA (*Suzuki*) 16, 1 lap; Shuhei Aoyama, JPN (*Honda*) 88, 1 lap.

Fastest lap: Haga, 1m 35.131s, 94.174mph/151.559km/h.

Race 2	23 laps, 57.247 miles/92.115km			
Dry, Air 30°C Humidity 21% Track 37°C				
Pl.	Name Nat. (*Machine*)	No.	Time & gap	Laps
1	Noriyuki Haga, JPN (*Yamaha*)	41	37m 03.759s	23
			92.661mph/149.123km/h	
2	Troy Bayliss, AUS (*Ducati*)	21	1.551s	23
3	Carlos Checa, SPA (*Honda*)	7	2.903s	23
4	Ryuichi Kiyonari, JPN (*Honda*)	23	7.277s	23
5	Troy Corser, AUS (*Yamaha*)	11	8.051s	23
6	Yukio Kagayama, JPN (*Suzuki*)	34	9.223s	23
7	Ruben Xaus, SPA (*Ducati*)	111	10.164s	23
8	Max Biaggi, ITA (*Ducati*)	3	10.614s	23
9	Regis Laconi, FRA (*Kawasaki*)	55	17.234s	23
10	Fonsi Nieto, SPA (*Suzuki*)	10	18.100s	23
11	Gregorio Lavilla, SPA (*Honda*)	36	18.288s	23
12	Lorenzo Lanzi, ITA (*Ducati*)	57	18.826s	23
13	Michel Fabrizio, ITA (*Ducati*)	84	21.770s	23
14	Jakub Smrz, CZE (*Ducati*)	96	22.872s	23
15	Kenan Sofuoglu, TUR (*Honda*)	54	25.224s	23
16	Shinichi Nakatomi, JPN (*Yamaha*)	38	25.301s	23
17	Roberto Rolfo, ITA (*Honda*)	44	25.509s	23
18	David Checa, SPA (*Yamaha*)	94	25.615s	23
19	Russell Holland, AUS (*Honda*)	83	26.503s	23
20	Karl Muggeridge, AUS (*Honda*)	31	35.171s	23
21	Ayrton Badovini, ITA (*Kawasaki*)	86	53.624s	23
22	Diego Lozano Ortiz, SPA (*Honda*)	37	54.672s	23
23	Luca Morelli, ITA (*Honda*)	22	1m 00.537s	23
24	Shuhei Aoyama, JPN (*Honda*)	88	1m 24.952s	23
25	Carmelo Morales, SPA (*Yamaha*)	131	1 lap	22

DNF: Makoto Tamada, JPN (*Kawasaki*) 100, 7 laps; Loic Napoleone, FRA (*Yamaha*) 77, 6 laps.

Fastest lap: Checa, 1m 35.322s, 93.986mph/151.256km/h.

Superpole: Neukirchner, 1m 33.805s, 95.506mph/153.702km/h.

Lap record: Neil Hodgson, GBR (*Ducati*), 1m 35.007s, 94.297mph/151.757km/h (2003).

Championship points: 1 Bayliss, 128; 2 Nieto, 80; 3 Corser, 72; 4 C. Checa, 72; 5 Xaus, 68; 6 Haga, 47; 7 Biaggi, 44; 8 Lanzi, 42; 9 Neukirchner, 39; 10 Fabrizio, 37; 11 Lavilla, 32; 12 Kiyonari, 30; 13 Sofuoglu, 22; 14 Muggeridge, 20; 15 Kagayama and Rolfo, 18.

WORLD SUPERBIKE CHAMPIONSHIP · ROUND 4
ASSEN
HOLLAND

WITH no further regulatory handicap burdening his machine going into Assen, Bayliss managed to give himself a bit of extra ballast anyway. A silly bicycle crash near his Monaco home the day before he left saw him battered and bruised, with swellings on the small of his back so large that he had to cut away parts of his body armour to get into a racing tuck.

He was sore, he said, but his rivals were the ones who left Assen with bloodied noses and more wounds to their championship hopes. Particularly Haga and Xaus, who had collided at the end of lap two – Haga went right out, but Xaus made it back in eventually, only to finish 16th and out of the points.

Pole position and two wins – it was all too easy for Bayliss, wasn't it? Well, no. He was made to work in both races.

In race one, Kagayama led from lap five to lap 11, while the recuperating Neukirchner and Checa pressurised Bayliss for a time, until they dropped to a couple of seconds off the win, Checa taking second and Neukirchner third. Their anticipated grudge match came to little, but provided great entertainment, the gap between them being only 0.057 second at the flag. After Valencia, third place felt like a win for the injured German rider.

He even carried out a bizarre, post-race, Rossi-style 'victory' ritual, although like every other rider who attempts this kind of trick, it wasn't quite in the same orbit of wit. He had set up a fishing stool and rod near one of Assen's many drainage ditches, and took time out for an impromptu piscatorial pause on the slow-down lap. After his impressive ride with a recently broken collarbone, his tomfoolery was not begrudged, particularly as he had set a new lap record of 1m 39.395s on lap three.

Kagayama headed up a fight for fourth with Corser

and the enigmatic Jakub Smrz; all three were within a second across the line.

Race two was more of a final-lap workout for Bayliss, with Haga pushing him all the way to a margin of victory of 0.082 second, having moved in to pounce near the end. It was a typical Haga weekend: in the dirt in race one; recovering to post a strong result in race two.

Third went to Checa, and fourth to Xaus, who overcame a flagging Neukirchner and his over-tired front tyre by half a second.

Kagayama, starting to get back to normality, was sixth, while Lavilla made good privateer progress to seventh after a race-one ninth.

Michel Fabrizio had a double DNF to go with team-mate Bayliss's double victory, putting more question marks against his name for all but his rabid defenders in the Italian media. They were distracted this particular weekend, however, as talk of Max Biaggi being drafted by the factory Ducati team for 2009 appeared to affect the four-time 250cc champion, and he finished tenth and 12th, while Xaus looked set for a podium at one stage. Biaggi blamed his old Phillip Island injury in part, but he didn't even make Superpole in a great qualifying circuit for the Ducatis, which had Bayliss, Xaus and Smrz in the top three beforehand. Bizarrely, Suzuki's top three riders were fourth to sixth at the same juncture.

Lorenzo Lanzi could not follow his Valencia race win with another, or even a finish, as he had broken his left elbow in the second of two crashes on day one.

The Kawasaki PSG-1 team had a glimmer of hope at Assen, where Tamada used his track knowledge and another swing-arm development to grab sixth in first qualifying. Tenth into Superpole, tenth out of it, and then eighth and ninth in the races showed that this may have been a flash in the dry pan. It seemed a long time since Chris Walker had won a race for the green guys, in the wet at this very circuit in 2006.

Above: Kagayama wheeled the big Suzuki to fourth and sixth.

Right: Fabrizio on the grid. He failed to finish twice.

Left: Haga chased Bayliss hard in race two.

Top left: Bayliss heads Haga and Neukirchner through the chicane.

Bottom: Taking the piscator. Neukirchner celebrated third place.

Photographs: Gold & Goose

Round 4
ASSEN, Holland
27 April 2008, 2.830-mile/4.555km circuit

Race 1 22 laps, 62.260 miles/100.210km			
Dry, Air 19°C Humidity 39% Track 23°C			
Pl. Name Nat. (*Machine*)	No.	Time & gap	Laps
1 Troy Bayliss, AUS (*Ducati*)	21	36m 50.907s	22
		101.390mph/163.171km/h	
2 Carlos Checa, SPA (*Honda*)	7	2.132s	22
3 Max Neukirchner, GER (*Suzuki*)	76	2.179s	22
4 Yukio Kagayama, JPN (*Suzuki*)	34	10.919s	22
5 Troy Corser, AUS (*Yamaha*)	11	11.051s	22
6 Jakub Smrz, CZE (*Ducati*)	96	11.979s	22
7 Ryuichi Kiyonari, JPN (*Honda*)	23	15.184s	22
8 Makoto Tamada, JPN (*Kawasaki*)	100	18.395s	22
9 Gregorio Lavilla, SPA (*Honda*)	36	18.634s	22
10 Max Biaggi, ITA (*Ducati*)	3	20.699s	22
11 Regis Laconi, FRA (*Kawasaki*)	55	25.759s	22
12 Kenan Sofuoglu, TUR (*Honda*)	54	26.064s	22
13 Ayrton Badovini, ITA (*Kawasaki*)	86	35.582s	22
14 Karl Muggeridge, AUS (*Honda*)	31	36.266s	22
15 Shinichi Nakatomi, JPN (*Yamaha*)	38	37.215s	22
16 Ruben Xaus, SPA (*Ducati*)	111	37.286s	22
17 Sébastien Gimbert, FRA (*Yamaha*)	194	39.037s	22
18 Russell Holland, AUS (*Honda*)	83	45.162s	22
19 Shuhei Aoyama, JPN (*Honda*)	88	1m 04.895s	22
20 Arie Vos, NED (*Ducati*)	28	1m 05.022s	22
21 Loic Napoleone, FRA (*Yamaha*)	77	1m 22.777s	22
22 Roberto Rolfo, ITA (*Honda*)	44	2 laps	20

Race 2 22 laps, 62.260 miles/100.210km			
Dry, Air 22°C Humidity 31% Track 31°C			
Pl. Name Nat. (*Machine*)	No.	Time & gap	Laps
1 Troy Bayliss, AUS (*Ducati*)	21	36m 46.238s	22
		101.604mph/163.516km/h	
2 Noriyuki Haga, JPN (*Yamaha*)	41	0.082s	22
3 Carlos Checa, SPA (*Honda*)	7	6.336s	22
4 Ruben Xaus, SPA (*Ducati*)	111	7.575s	22
5 Max Neukirchner, GER (*Suzuki*)	76	8.011s	22
6 Yukio Kagayama, JPN (*Suzuki*)	34	13.999s	22
7 Gregorio Lavilla, SPA (*Honda*)	36	15.215s	22
8 Jakub Smrz, CZE (*Ducati*)	96	16.376s	22
9 Makoto Tamada, JPN (*Kawasaki*)	100	17.269s	22
10 Troy Corser, AUS (*Yamaha*)	11	18.380s	22
11 Fonsi Nieto, SPA (*Suzuki*)	10	18.926s	22
12 Max Biaggi, ITA (*Ducati*)	3	21.452s	22
13 Karl Muggeridge, AUS (*Honda*)	31	23.794s	22
14 Roberto Rolfo, ITA (*Honda*)	44	29.847s	22
15 Shinichi Nakatomi, JPN (*Yamaha*)	38	30.252s	22
16 Regis Laconi, FRA (*Kawasaki*)	55	31.249s	22
17 Sébastien Gimbert, FRA (*Yamaha*)	194	31.328s	22
18 Ayrton Badovini, ITA (*Kawasaki*)	86	39.814s	22
19 Kenan Sofuoglu, TUR (*Honda*)	54	49.956s	22
20 Russell Holland, AUS (*Honda*)	83	51.554s	22
21 Shuhei Aoyama, JPN (*Honda*)	88	51.642s	22
22 Loic Napoleone, FRA (*Yamaha*)	77	1m 02.682s	22
23 Arie Vos, NED (*Ducati*)	28	1m 02.729s	22

DNF: Michel Fabrizio, ITA (*Ducati*) 84, 9 laps; Fonsi Nieto, SPA (*Suzuki*) 10, 9 laps; David Checa, SPA (*Yamaha*) 94, 6 laps; Luca Morelli, ITA (*Honda*) 22, 6 laps; Noriyuki Haga, JPN (*Yamaha*) 41, 1 lap.

DNS: Vittorio Iannuzzo, ITA (*Kawasaki*) 13.

Fastest lap: Neukirchner, 1m 39.395s, 102.513mph/164.978km/h (record).

Superpole: Bayliss, 1m 38.428s, 103.519mph/166.599km/h.

DNF: Michel Fabrizio, ITA (*Ducati*) 84, 10 laps; Ryuichi Kiyonari, JPN (*Honda*) 23, 8 laps; Luca Morelli, ITA (*Honda*) 22, 4 laps.

Fastest lap: Bayliss, 1m 39.562s, 102.340mph/164.701km/h.

Lap record: Noriyuki Haga, JPN (*Yamaha*), 1m 39.770s, 102.127mph/164.358km/h (2007).

Championship points: 1 Bayliss, 178; 2 C. Checa, 108; 3 Corser, 89; 4 Nieto, 85; 5 Xaus, 81; 6 Haga, 67; 7 Neukirchner, 66; 8 Biaggi, 54; 9 Lavilla, 48; 10 Lanzi, 42; 11 Kagayama, 41; 12 Kiyonari, 39; 13 Fabrizio, 37; 14 Smrz, 35; 15 Tamada, 28.

MONZA
ITALY

THE spectacle of racing at Monza is always helped by the high-speed nature of the track and – dare we say such a thing? – the heavy braking for the chicanes. In their own different ways, these opposites attract close race finishes more often than not. This year, we had two absolute belters, right to the final metre.

In race one, the top four were separated by only 0.771 second, and the winner to second by only 0.058 second. Race two saw first to third covered by only 0.051 second, while the winning margin was thinner than a parmesan shaving in the paddock hospitality units, only 0.009 second.

The ever-smiling Max Neukirchner, largely repaired physically and seemingly doubled in his determination, despite his awful Spanish disappointments, put the worst behind him by just managing to keep Noriyuki Haga at bay in race one. Troy Bayliss was only 0.672 second adrift, while Yukio Kagayama was in the Ducati rider's wheel tracks, despite almost pulling in because his brakes were playing up occasionally. It was a flavour of what was to come in race two.

In the second race, the equal fifth closest finish in WSB history gave Haga a win that had looked doubtful when his Yamaha had proved to be up to 10km/h slower than the best during the early part of the weekend. His early-season woes seemingly behind him, he pushed the surprise contender Ryuichi Kiyonari to the white stripe on the exit of the final Parabolica corner, and in doing so allowed Neukirchner to slip past the rookie to record second place.

Suzuki man Kagayama had put himself out of race two before the last lap, having crashed by high-siding at full pace at the exit of the second chicane. He slid to an abrupt stop against the air-fence.

The twins-vs-fours debate, still raging in some quarters – mostly outside the WSB paddock by this stage – looked very biased towards the fours at this particular track on race day, despite Bayliss having taken his 21st career pole on the day before, finally matching his race number. In the races, the Australian battled on effectively, and with his nearest rivals having poor weekends, even a race-two DNF made no impact on his runaway lead in the championship.

An engine oil leak had sidelined Bayliss in race two, and the rider who had pointed this out to him, Haga, looked like he would be black-flagged himself when blue smoke suddenly came off his machine. It started and puffed, but then stopped almost completely. Then it returned and stopped again. Later it was diagnosed as a loose fender rubbing on the tyre and eventually wearing a groove in the rubber.

In an occasionally combative race weekend, Troy Corser and Carlos Checa collided with each other in race two, while Jakub Smrz snagged Max Biaggi's handlebar and punted him off, breaking his finger in the process. It was proving to be a painful season for the Italian after his big Phillip Island crash and fracture.

The fastest speeds ever recorded officially in WSB history were set in qualifying, when both Neukirchner and Karl Muggeridge (DFX Honda) hit 324km/h (201.3mph). Astonishing as it may seem, Neukirchner's race-one win was the first race victory for a German rider in 21 years of World Superbike competition. For him, it was worth the wait, particularly after his violent mugging in Valencia.

After a good early qualifying session on Friday, Kenan Sofuoglu's Monza weekend performances faded into irrelevance with the news that his brother had been killed in a racing accident back home in Turkey, and he immediately withdrew from the meeting to be with his family. The Sofuoglu clan had endured the loss of his other brother in a road accident a short while before, and this desperately sad event had a sombre effect on the whole paddock.

Above: Second-race podium: Haga flanked by Neukirchner and Kiyonari.
Top: Clearly, Neukirchner was fully recovered.

Centre right: Fonsi Nieto skims the kerb.

Right: Blue Max. Neukirchner celebrated his win with a wig.

Far right: Kagayama survived this moment, but crashed later.
Photographs: Gold & Goose

Left: Haga psyches himself up into victory mode.

Below: Race one finishers Neukirchner, Haga and Bayliss were still this close at the finish.

Photographs: Gold & Goose

Round 5
MONZA, Italy
11 May 2008, 3.600-mile/5.793km circuit

Race 1 18 laps, 64.800 miles/104.274km
Dry, Air 22°C Humidity 43% Track 36°C

Pl.	Name Nat. (Machine)	No.	Time & gap	Laps
1	Max Neukirchner, GER (Suzuki)	76	32m 02.851s	18
			121.307mph/195.224km/h	
2	Noriyuki Haga, JPN (Yamaha)	41	0.058s	18
3	Troy Bayliss, AUS (Ducati)	21	0.672s	18
4	Yukio Kagayama, JPN (Suzuki)	34	0.771s	18
5	Max Biaggi, ITA (Ducati)	3	3.869s	18
6	Ryuichi Kiyonari, JPN (Honda)	23	5.995s	18
7	Fonsi Nieto, SPA (Suzuki)	10	8.788s	18
8	Carlos Checa, SPA (Honda)	7	9.374s	18
9	Michel Fabrizio, ITA (Ducati)	84	10.667s	18
10	Jakub Smrz, CZE (Ducati)	96	10.771s	18
11	Gregorio Lavilla, SPA (Honda)	36	12.180s	18
12	Troy Corser, AUS (Yamaha)	11	14.719s	18
13	Shinichi Nakatomi, JPN (Yamaha)	38	32.734s	18
14	Lorenzo Lanzi, ITA (Ducati)	57	36.550s	18
15	Sébastien Gimbert, FRA (Yamaha)	194	36.607s	18
16	Russell Holland, AUS (Honda)	83	52.464s	18
17	Luca Morelli, ITA (Honda)	22	56.929s	18
18	Shuhei Aoyama, JPN (Honda)	88	1m 27.543s	18
19	Michael Beck, USA (Yamaha)	49	1m 28.342s	18

DNF: Makoto Tamada, JPN (Kawasaki) 100, 16 laps; Lorenzo Mauri, ITA (Ducati) 110, 14 laps; Vittorio Iannuzzo, ITA (Kawasaki) 13, 13 laps; Ayrton Badovini, ITA (Kawasaki) 86, 8 laps; Ruben Xaus, SPA (Ducati) 111, 7 laps; Regis Laconi, FRA (Kawasaki) 55, 3 laps; Loic Napoleone, FRA (Yamaha) 77, 1 lap; Karl Muggeridge, AUS (Honda) 31, 0 laps.

Fastest lap: Haga, 1m 45.882s, 122.387mph/196.963km/h (record).

Race 2 18 laps, 64.800 miles/104.274km
Dry, Air 21°C Humidity 55% Track 40°C

Pl.	Name Nat. (Machine)	No.	Time & gap	Laps
1	Noriyuki Haga, JPN (Yamaha)	41	32m 07.576s	18
			121.009mph/194.745km/h	
2	Max Neukirchner, GER (Suzuki)	76	0.009s	18
3	Ryuichi Kiyonari, JPN (Honda)	23	0.051s	18
4	Fonsi Nieto, SPA (Suzuki)	10	4.489s	18
5	Michel Fabrizio, ITA (Ducati)	84	10.272s	18
6	Karl Muggeridge, AUS (Honda)	31	10.376s	18
7	Ruben Xaus, SPA (Ducati)	111	10.496s	18
8	Troy Corser, AUS (Yamaha)	11	12.498s	18
9	Ayrton Badovini, ITA (Kawasaki)	86	19.429s	18
10	Gregorio Lavilla, SPA (Honda)	36	26.373s	18
11	Lorenzo Lanzi, ITA (Ducati)	57	26.544s	18
12	Shinichi Nakatomi, JPN (Yamaha)	38	26.895s	18
13	Russell Holland, AUS (Honda)	83	27.761s	18
14	Sébastien Gimbert, FRA (Yamaha)	194	29.661s	18
15	Michael Beck, USA (Yamaha)	49	1m 29.001s	18
16	Shuhei Aoyama, JPN (Honda)	88	3 laps	15

DNF: Makoto Tamada, JPN (Kawasaki) 100, 17 laps; Max Biaggi, ITA (Ducati) 3, 15 laps; Jakub Smrz, CZE (Ducati) 96, 15 laps; Carlos Checa, SPA (Honda) 7, 9 laps; Loic Napoleone, FRA (Yamaha) 77, 9 laps; Troy Bayliss, AUS (Ducati) 21, 8 laps; Regis Laconi, FRA (Kawasaki) 55, 6 laps; Yukio Kagayama, JPN (Suzuki) 34, 4 laps; Vittorio Iannuzzo, ITA (Kawasaki) 13, 3 laps; Luca Morelli, ITA (Honda) 22, 1 lap.

Fastest lap: Haga, 1m 46.363s, 121.833mph/196.072km/h.

Superpole: Bayliss, 1m 44.931s, 123.496mph/198.748km/h.

Lap record: Noriyuki Haga, JPN (Yamaha), 1m 46.064s, 122.177mph/196.625km/h (2007).

Championship points: 1 Bayliss, 194; 2 C. Checa, 116; 3 Nieto, 94; 4 Corser, 93; 5 Neukirchner, 91; 6 Haga, 87; 7 Xaus, 81; 8 Biaggi, 65; 9 Kagayama, 54; 10 Lavilla, 53; 11 Kiyonari, 49; 12 Lanzi, 44; 13 Fabrizio, 44; 14 Smrz, 41; 15 Tamada, 28.

MILLER MOTORSPORTS PARK

UNITED STATES

A NEW beginning at an almost brand-new circuit in America was a real shot in the arm for World Superbike, even if the track was some way from downtown Salt Lake City, and SLC itself was a long way from pretty much anywhere else.

The former Winter Olympic venue was welcoming enough, heartily so, matching the generous facilities, layout and attitude of the Miller Motorsports Park and its staff. There was even a special mayoral reception and parade from the Capitol building to downtown. All that was needed was a crowd on Sunday – in fact, more spectators turned out to watch Carlos Checa win both races than some had feared.

With AMA classes and no WSS class, the weekend was doubly unusual. The prize for weirdness, however, has to go to those who named the corners. Dreamboat, Knock Out, Wind Up, Release, Scream, Bad Attitude and Right Hook were just some of the nonsensical monikers given to the curves and bends that snaked around the 4.905km circuit set out on the desert floor and surrounded by mountains.

But don't let the idea of a desert floor fool you. The circuit is 1,358 metres above sea level, which robbed machines of power and prompted the installation of specially fabricated, enlarged air-boxes.

For Checa, the two wins were his first outside Spain, and they drew him closer to Troy Bayliss in the championship fight, as the series leader had had one of his more peculiar race days. Having fallen in race one and retired with bike problems in race two, he had recorded three no-scores on the trot. A glimmer of hope for the Spaniard and his still-developing Honda perhaps? Both looked like the real deal in America.

Previous bright star Max Neukirchner recovered from a poor set-up in race one to take second in race two. Third was Michel Fabrizio, who recorded a double

podium finish, having been just behind Troy Corser in race one.

The fact of the matter, however, was that nobody else mattered in America except Checa, who set every lap record and took the maximum points. So it was incongruous that his performance probably wasn't the most attention worthy, even though he had had to use his number-two bike in both races, after gremlins struck during the crucial pre-race moments.

Noriyuki Haga, having made one of his hot-headed attacks up the inside of Kenan Sofuoglu in practice, fell and smashed his right collarbone into four jagged and seriously displaced pieces. He was declared unfit immediately. But he did ride again, with only surgical bandages and a homemade brace across his shoulders – no plates, no pins, just drugs and determination.

In Superpole next day, Haga went from 16th to tenth on the grid. Then he fell in race one, luckily on the other collarbone, but still he would not admit defeat. He lined up for race two and finished sixth in a ride that was one step removed from the impossible. He received surgery on the following day. The fact that this was the first time he had broken a bone in 22 years of racing simply added to the mystique of it all. Haga's MMP experience was awesome to witness.

Yamaha's weekend was saved in race one by Corser's second place. Until, that is, he fell at high speed in race two, after losing the front on the penultimate corner. His bike had been given revised fork settings that produced better performance but ultimately less front-end feel.

From the fourth row of the grid, Fonsi Nieto took fifth in race one, while Max Biaggi, having another troublesome day in the privateer ranks, was ninth to start and fourth in race two, having been muscled out of the way by fellow Roman Michel Fabrizio.

Above: Fine new desert-floor circuit saw Checa out on his own.

Right: His collar-bone shattered, Haga refused to stop racing.

Below: Jakub Smrz was battling for fifth.
Photographs: Gold & Goose

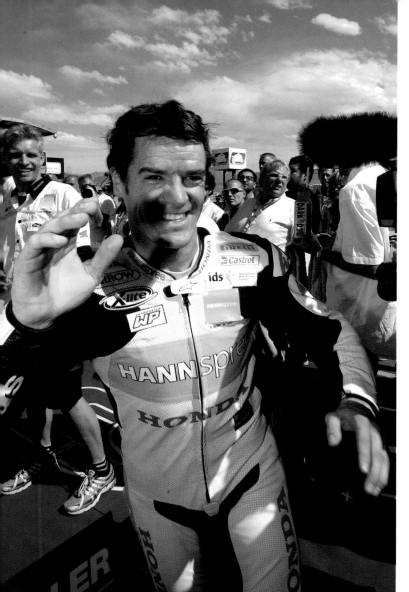

Left: Checa beams after his first ever double race win.

Below: Fabrizio took two third places.

Photographs: Gold & Goose

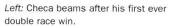

Round 6
MILLER MOTORSPORTS PARK, United States
1 June 2008, 3.049-mile/4.907km circuit

Race 1	20 laps, 60.980 miles/98.140km		
Dry, Air 27°C Humidity 20% Track 39°C			
Pl.	Name Nat. (Machine)	No.	Time & gap Laps
1	Carlos Checa, SPA (Honda)	7	37m 04.991s 20
			98.667mph/158.789km/h
2	Troy Corser, AUS (Yamaha)	11	2.809s 20
3	Michel Fabrizio, ITA (Ducati)	84	6.546s 20
4	Max Neukirchner, GER (Suzuki)	76	7.764s 20
5	Fonsi Nieto, SPA (Suzuki)	10	16.475s 20
6	Jakub Smrz, CZE (Ducati)	96	17.126s 20
7	Karl Muggeridge, AUS (Honda)	31	17.284s 20
8	Yukio Kagayama, JPN (Suzuki)	34	17.416s 20
9	Max Biaggi, ITA (Ducati)	3	18.117s 20
10	Ryuichi Kiyonari, JPN (Honda)	23	20.467s 20
11	Lorenzo Lanzi, ITA (Ducati)	57	21.742s 20
12	Kenan Sofuoglu, TUR (Honda)	54	27.533s 20
13	Gregorio Lavilla, SPA (Honda)	36	32.609s 20
14	Ruben Xaus, SPA (Ducati)	111	33.165s 20
15	Russell Holland, AUS (Honda)	83	34.182s 20
16	Shinichi Nakatomi, JPN (Yamaha)	38	34.500s 20
17	Ayrton Badovini, ITA (Kawasaki)	86	36.155s 20
18	Sébastien Gimbert, FRA (Yamaha)	194	41.685s 20
19	Makoto Tamada, JPN (Kawasaki)	100	43.579s 20
20	Roberto Rolfo, ITA (Honda)	44	54.195s 20
21	Jason Pridmore, USA (Honda)	43	1m 00.388s 20
22	Vittorio Iannuzzo, ITA (Kawasaki)	13	1m 02.104s 20
23	Scott Jensen, USA (Suzuki)	61	1m 09.953s 20
24	Loic Napoleone, FRA (Yamaha)	77	1m 12.258s 20

DNF: Shuhei Aoyama, JPN (Honda) 88, 14 laps; David Checa, SPA (Yamaha) 94, 6 laps; Noriyuki Haga, JPN (Yamaha) 41, 5 laps; Troy Bayliss, AUS (Ducati) 21, 4 laps; Regis Laconi, FRA (Kawasaki) 55, 4 laps.

Fastest lap: C. Checa, 1m 50.091s, 99.705mph/160.460km/h (record).

Superpole: C. Checa, 1m 48.193s, 101.454mph/163.275km/h.

Lap record: New circuit.

Race 2	21 laps, 64.029 miles/103.047km		
Dry, Air 28°C Humidity 26% Track 49°C			
Pl.	Name Nat. (Machine)	No.	Time & gap Laps
1	Carlos Checa, SPA (Honda)	7	38m 44.105s 21
			99.182mph/159.618km/h
2	Max Neukirchner, GER (Suzuki)	76	3.547s 21
3	Michel Fabrizio, ITA (Ducati)	84	6.613s 21
4	Max Biaggi, ITA (Ducati)	3	7.878s 21
5	Yukio Kagayama, JPN (Suzuki)	34	10.568s 21
6	Noriyuki Haga, JPN (Yamaha)	41	11.539s 21
7	Ryuichi Kiyonari, JPN (Honda)	23	18.381s 21
8	Fonsi Nieto, SPA (Suzuki)	10	20.646s 21
9	Regis Laconi, FRA (Kawasaki)	55	21.264s 21
10	Lorenzo Lanzi, ITA (Ducati)	57	24.863s 21
11	Karl Muggeridge, AUS (Honda)	31	25.672s 21
12	Ayrton Badovini, ITA (Kawasaki)	86	31.711s 21
13	Makoto Tamada, JPN (Kawasaki)	100	35.628s 21
14	Kenan Sofuoglu, TUR (Honda)	54	42.816s 21
15	Gregorio Lavilla, SPA (Honda)	36	45.034s 21
16	Roberto Rolfo, ITA (Honda)	44	50.220s 21
17	Sébastien Gimbert, FRA (Yamaha)	194	50.653s 21
18	Jason Pridmore, USA (Honda)	43	51.188s 21
19	Vittorio Iannuzzo, ITA (Kawasaki)	13	1m 04.533s 21
20	Scott Jensen, USA (Suzuki)	61	1m 12.049s 21
21	Loic Napoleone, FRA (Yamaha)	77	1m 19.221s 21
22	Troy Bayliss, AUS (Ducati)	21	2 laps 19

DNF: Troy Corser, AUS (Yamaha) 11, 16 laps; Shuhei Aoyama, JPN (Honda) 88, 14 laps; Shinichi Nakatomi, JPN (Yamaha) 38, 13 laps; Ruben Xaus, SPA (Ducati) 111, 5 laps; Russell Holland, AUS (Honda) 83, 1 lap.

DSQ: Jakub Smrz, CZE (Ducati) 96, 4 laps.

Fastest lap: C. Checa, 1m 49.703s, 100.058mph/161.028km/h (record).

Championship points: 1 Bayliss, 194; 2 C. Checa, 166; 3 Neukirchner, 144; 4 Nieto, 126; 5 Haga, 122; 6 Corser, 121; 7 Xaus, 92; 8 Fabrizio, 87; 9 Biaggi, 85; 10 Kiyonari, 80; 11 Kagayama, 73; 12 Lavilla, 63; 13 Lanzi, 60; 14 Smrz, 51; 15 Muggeridge, 49.

NÜRBURGRING

GERMANY

THE enigmatic Noriyuki Haga has always been an unpredictable WSB entity: brilliant one week, inexplicably off the pace the next. But finally one Haga characteristic has shown itself to be repeatable: pace under pressure. Adversity seems to be his biggest power source.

With the adrenaline of his American escapades behind him, and a pin-and-plate job holding his right collarbone together, Haga got down to business on race day, holding off Troy Bayliss in race one, then benefiting from the reappearance of the rain in race two. In the latter, it had looked as though Troy Corser had the better set-up and physical stamina to go the full 20 laps, but the end came early when the rain started to fall. Thus Haga took an unexpected double win, and not for the first time in his career.

Championship leader Bayliss had recovered from his recent upsets in Germany, but still made a small error that allowed Haga to make his escape in race one; second best was all he could manage. He took fourth in race two, and thus his results mirrored those of Corser.

Both third places went to local hero Max Neukirchner, who was not quite able to match his ambitions for a home win to a set-up that would allow him to do just that, due to handling imperfections in race one and braking issues in race two. This was curious, considering how dominant he had been in winning Superpole from Bayliss by 0.320 second.

Neukirchner's performance on Saturday probably convinced some locals to brave the elements and come along on race day after all; his double podiums were some reward for their perseverance in the occasionally-grim weather conditions. In fact, the first race was delayed because of a sudden and vicious hailstorm, which added to the misery of the return to a venue that otherwise was popular with the riders.

The Nürburgring circuit had been altered somewhat since the last WSB visit to the Eifel region, the first and now exceptionally tight downhill hairpin providing passing opportunities aplenty – and encouraging the riders to make mistakes in braking judgement. Bayliss did just that on lap 18 of race one, which allowed Haga to escape.

In race two, Corser seemed determined to make a break, but Bayliss and Haga found his pace. Eventually, however, it was left to the two Yamaha riders to swap the lead in crowd-pleasing fashion after Bayliss ran on to the gravel. He restarted in sixth and admitted later that he had been riding too hard.

Understandably, the Yamaha Motor Italia team was on edge, given the sometimes tactile passes their riders made on each other. That said, both Haga and Corser described the race as hard, but fair – and fun.

In the end, it was the weather that decided everything, not some classic, last-lap sort-out. The first raindrops fell on the leaders' visors on lap 12, and Haga was declared the winner, by 0.150 second, on lap 14.

Behind the podium places, Carlos Checa scored two fifths, surprisingly far away from the wins he had taken in America. He blamed a lack of grip.

When WSB visited the circuit in 2008, it was undergoing massive changes to make the entire facility a more year-round venue; next time we trust there will be less of a building-site atmosphere. Nonetheless, it was good to be back at such a historic venue, particularly after the soulless and vast Lausitzring.

The circuit in the Eifel had attracted similar accusations in the past, at least in comparison to the old Nordschleife. With all the main contending machines evenly matched once more, however, the 'new' Nürburgring may have been occasionally rain lashed and windswept, but it certainly was interesting.

Left: Pinned and plated, Haga was uncatchable – twice.

Below: Bayliss slipped up, but still led the points comfortably.

Right: The class of the field: Corser leads Neukirchner, Bayliss and Haga.

Photograph: Gold & Goose

Above: Checa got a double fifth.

Left: Neukirchner's hopes of a home win were dashed.

Photographs: Gold & Goose

Round 7
NÜRBURGRING, Germany
15 June 2008, 3.192-mile/5.137km circuit

Race 1 20 laps, 63.840 miles /102.740km			
Dry, Air 13°C Humidity 63% Track 21°C			
Pl. Name Nat. (*Machine*)	No.	Time & gap	Laps
1 Noriyuki Haga, JPN (*Yamaha*)	41	39m 19.427s	20
		97.406mph/156.760km/h	
2 Troy Bayliss, AUS (*Ducati*)	21	2.025s	20
3 Max Neukirchner, GER (*Suzuki*)	76	2.792s	20
4 Troy Corser, AUS (*Yamaha*)	11	5.458s	20
5 Carlos Checa, SPA (*Honda*)	7	10.225s	20
6 Ruben Xaus, SPA (*Ducati*)	111	10.462s	20
7 Michel Fabrizio, ITA (*Ducati*)	84	17.018s	20
8 Fonsi Nieto, SPA (*Suzuki*)	10	20.520s	20
9 Makoto Tamada, JPN (*Kawasaki*)	100	21.162s	20
10 Karl Muggeridge, AUS (*Honda*)	31	22.650s	20
11 Jakub Smrz, CZE (*Ducati*)	96	22.845s	20
12 Ryuichi Kiyonari, JPN (*Honda*)	23	25.555s	20
13 Max Biaggi, ITA (*Ducati*)	3	25.879s	20
14 Regis Laconi, FRA (*Kawasaki*)	55	26.288s	20
15 Sébastien Gimbert, FRA (*Yamaha*)	194	32.824s	20
16 Roberto Rolfo, ITA (*Honda*)	44	42.157s	20
17 Ayrton Badovini, ITA (*Kawasaki*)	86	42.486s	20
18 Shinichi Nakatomi, JPN (*Yamaha*)	38	52.232s	20
19 Russell Holland, AUS (*Honda*)	83	52.387s	20
20 Vittorio Iannuzzo, ITA (*Kawasaki*)	13	1m 00.099s	20

DNF: Loic Napoleone, FRA (*Yamaha*) 77, 16 laps; Lorenzo Lanzi, ITA (*Ducati*) 57, 16 laps; Jason Pridmore, USA (*Honda*) 43, 12 laps; Kenan Sofuoglu, TUR (*Honda*) 54, 6 laps; David Checa, SPA (*Yamaha*) 94, 5 laps; Shuhei Aoyama, JPN (*Honda*) 88, 3 laps; Gregorio Lavilla, SPA (*Honda*) 36, 0 laps.

Fastest lap: Bayliss, 1m 57.276s, 97.984mph/157.690km/h (record).

Race 2 14 laps, 44.688 miles/71.918km			
Dry, Air 19°C Humidity 36% Track 44°C			
Pl. Name Nat. (*Machine*)	No.	Time & gap	Laps
1 Noriyuki Haga, JPN (*Yamaha*)	41	27m 26.594s	14
		97.703mph/157.237km/h	
2 Troy Corser, AUS (*Yamaha*)	11	0.150s	14
3 Max Neukirchner, GER (*Suzuki*)	76	5.316s	14
4 Troy Bayliss, AUS (*Ducati*)	21	7.651s	14
5 Carlos Checa, SPA (*Honda*)	7	7.951s	14
6 Michel Fabrizio, ITA (*Ducati*)	84	9.027s	14
7 Max Biaggi, ITA (*Ducati*)	3	9.420s	14
8 Ruben Xaus, SPA (*Ducati*)	111	9.916s	14
9 Fonsi Nieto, SPA (*Suzuki*)	10	12.862s	14
10 Regis Laconi, FRA (*Kawasaki*)	55	13.559s	14
11 Ryuichi Kiyonari, JPN (*Honda*)	23	13.960s	14
12 Karl Muggeridge, AUS (*Honda*)	31	16.172s	14
13 Makoto Tamada, JPN (*Kawasaki*)	100	17.946s	14
14 Gregorio Lavilla, SPA (*Honda*)	36	22.815s	14
15 David Checa, SPA (*Yamaha*)	94	23.758s	14
16 Sébastien Gimbert, FRA (*Yamaha*)	194	24.127s	14
17 Roberto Rolfo, ITA (*Honda*)	44	24.421s	14
18 Shinichi Nakatomi, JPN (*Yamaha*)	38	25.356s	14
19 Russell Holland, AUS (*Honda*)	83	25.729s	14
20 Lorenzo Lanzi, ITA (*Ducati*)	57	28.846s	14
21 Kenan Sofuoglu, TUR (*Honda*)	54	33.107s	14
22 Loic Napoleone, FRA (*Yamaha*)	77	54.255s	14
23 Jason Pridmore, USA (*Honda*)	43	1m 04.877s	14
24 Shuhei Aoyama, JPN (*Honda*)	88	1 lap	13

DNF: Jakub Smrz, CZE (*Ducati*) 96, 6 laps; Ayrton Badovini, ITA (*Kawasaki*) 86, 5 laps; Vittorio Iannuzzo, ITA (*Kawasaki*) 13, 5 laps.

Fastest lap: Haga, 1m 56.892s, 98.306mph/158.208km/h (record).

Superpole: Neukirchner, 1m 55.471s, 99.515mph/160.154km/h.

Previous record: New circuit.

Championship points: 1 Bayliss, 227; 2 C. Checa, 188; 3 Neukirchner, 176; 4 Haga, 172; 5 Corser, 154; 6 Nieto, 141; 7 Xaus, 110; 8 Fabrizio, 106; 9 Biaggi, 97; 10 Kiyonari, 89; 11 Kagayama, 73; 12 Lavilla, 65; 13 Lanzi, 60; 14 Muggeridge, 59; 15 Smrz, 56.

S INCE its reversal of direction a couple of years ago, Misano has been polished around the edges, but it's still the tight, street-fighting kind of circuit it's always been. It's flat, invariably boiling hot, humid, too, as it's so close to the sea, and packed with spectators desperate for a win from anyone riding a Ducati.

It was no different in 2008, but after qualifying and Superpole, nobody could have predicted that the two race winners on Sunday would be Max Neukirchner and Ruben Xaus. The latter had been fast in practice, not so Neukirchner, but each race win was a season's high point in terms of personal satisfaction.

We had the unlikely scenario of Troy Bayliss being beaten up by several riders on the way past the hole-shot man in race one, including Superpole winner Troy Corser, who had been forced to run wide himself in Turn One. The first few laps were dramatic, with Regis Laconi out early, and both Roberto Rolfo and Ryuichi Kiyonari being handed ride-through penalties for jump-starting.

Xaus took his turn to lead, as did Corser, but Max Biaggi's race one ended when Michel Fabrizio skittled them both.

Neukirchner worked his way from an off-podium place to take the lead for seven laps; crucially, the last one kept him half a second up on Corser. Not long before the end, Bayliss passed Xaus for third. The latter was a close fourth, while Carlos Checa got the better of re-ignited Valencia race winner Lorenzo Lanzi, who was sixth. With Jakub Smrz seventh, there were a lot of Ducatis in the top places, their best result of the year.

It may have taken eight rounds to do it, but finally we had a whole podium's worth of Ducati 1200s in the second race at Misano; suddenly the hitherto muted voices of protest against the whole idea of a differential capacity rule in WSB cleared their throats and sang for a foul.

Xaus, who added to his career total in race two by leading GP legend Biaggi and second best WSB rider ever Troy Bayliss over the line, unwittingly may have made an argument for big-twin supremacy more convincing. However, the fact that two privateer Ducatis beat the factory bike of Bayliss certainly raised a few eyebrows – and later reduced Ducati's help, according to Xaus.

On the way to the top two places, Xaus and Biaggi had been beating each other up in fine style, passing and re-passing in endless games of bluff and personal rivalry.

The second race was stopped and re-started, after Muggeridge's engine dumped oil and water on the track at Turn One. It was half an hour late in finishing.

Noriyuki Haga recovered in this race from a bad qualifying place of 14th and a first-race finish of only tenth, having tangled with faller Laconi. Poor bump absorption had been his cry all weekend, but with Corser winning Superpole and challenging up front in race one, his early showings had been close to inexplicable. He did beat Corser for fourth in race two, but he was a tired red shadow compared to the Nürburgring.

Lanzi was sixth in race two, while race-one winner Neukirchner was only seventh as the track temperatures hit 58°C. His team had changed nothing between races, so the six-degree increase compared to race one was seen as the only factor at play.

Checa had qualified 11th in Superpole; he went on to record a fifth in race one and an eighth in race two.

Another hard weekend in the Kawasaki camp saw neither PSG-1 factory rider, Laconi or Makoto Tamada, finish a single race. Not ideal when the Republic of San Marino is one of your main sponsors and you are racing in their blue and white colours, in their very own race.

The heat was intense in Misano, and all the riders felt it. The race-two false start and extra downtime on the grid simply added to the pressure-cooker temperatures.

Left: Laconi in practice, but he failed to finish twice.

Far left: Xaus was on unbeatable form in race two.

Right: Race-one winner Neukirchner moved to second overall.

Below right: No win, but two rostrums for Bayliss.

Photographs: Gold & Goose

Above: Lanzi was struggling to repeat his success.

Left: Biaggi's first podium was an all-Ducati affair, raising some eyebrows.

Photographs: Gold & Goose

Round 8
MISANO, Italy
29 June 2008, 2.626-mile/4.226km circuit

Race 1 24 laps, 63.024 miles/101.424km			
Dry, Air 31°C Humidity 48% Track 52°C			
Pl. Name Nat. (Machine)	No.	Time/gap	Laps
1 Max Neukirchner, GER (Suzuki)	76	39m 27.918s	24
		95.814mph/154.197km/h	
2 Troy Corser, AUS (Yamaha)	11	0.542s	24
3 Troy Bayliss, AUS (Ducati)	21	2.249s	24
4 Ruben Xaus, SPA (Ducati)	111	3.028s	24
5 Carlos Checa, SPA (Honda)	7	5.408s	24
6 Lorenzo Lanzi, ITA (Ducati)	57	5.518s	24
7 Jakub Smrz, CZE (Ducati)	96	6.202s	24
8 Gregorio Lavilla, SPA (Honda)	36	18.279s	24
9 Shinichi Nakatomi, JPN (Yamaha)	38	19.072s	24
10 Noriyuki Haga, JPN (Yamaha)	41	19.132s	24
11 Yukio Kagayama, JPN (Suzuki)	34	28.098s	24
12 Fonsi Nieto, SPA (Suzuki)	10	34.385s	24
13 Shuhei Aoyama, JPN (Honda)	88	34.572s	24
14 Ryuichi Kiyonari, JPN (Honda)	23	34.902s	24
15 David Checa, SPA (Yamaha)	94	39.979s	24
16 Sébastien Gimbert, FRA (Yamaha)	194	44.669s	24
17 Roberto Rolfo, ITA (Honda)	44	49.290s	24
18 Kenan Sofuoglu, TUR (Honda)	54	59.304s	24

Race 2 24 laps, 63.024 miles/101.424km			
Dry, Air 30°C Humidity 58% Track 58°C			
Pl. Name Nat. (Machine)	No.	Time & gap	Laps
1 Ruben Xaus, SPA (Ducati)	111	39m 19.710s	24
		96.147mph/154.734km/h	
2 Max Biaggi, ITA (Ducati)	3	1.035s	24
3 Troy Bayliss, AUS (Ducati)	21	4.158s	24
4 Noriyuki Haga, JPN (Yamaha)	41	5.466s	24
5 Troy Corser, AUS (Yamaha)	11	6.759s	24
6 Lorenzo Lanzi, ITA (Ducati)	57	13.468s	24
7 Max Neukirchner, GER (Suzuki)	76	15.221s	24
8 Carlos Checa, SPA (Honda)	7	16.687s	24
9 Jakub Smrz, CZE (Ducati)	96	17.030s	24
10 Fonsi Nieto, SPA (Suzuki)	10	17.681s	24
11 Michel Fabrizio, ITA (Ducati)	84	21.356s	24
12 Yukio Kagayama, JPN (Suzuki)	34	28.676s	24
13 Ryuichi Kiyonari, JPN (Honda)	23	31.304s	24
14 Gregorio Lavilla, SPA (Honda)	36	32.339s	24
15 Shinichi Nakatomi, JPN (Yamaha)	38	33.716s	24
16 David Checa, SPA (Yamaha)	94	34.171s	24
17 Ayrton Badovini, ITA (Kawasaki)	86	40.638s	24
18 Roberto Rolfo, ITA (Honda)	44	41.136s	24
19 Shuhei Aoyama, JPN (Honda)	88	49.699s	24

DNF: Ayrton Badovini, ITA (Kawasaki) 86, 19 laps; Karl Muggeridge, AUS (Honda) 31, 17 laps; Max Biaggi, ITA (Ducati) 3, 11 laps; Michel Fabrizio, ITA (Ducati) 84, 11 laps; Makoto Tamada, JPN (Kawasaki) 100, 6 laps; Jason Pridmore, USA (Honda) 43, 6 laps; Vittorio Iannuzzo, ITA (Kawasaki) 13, 3 laps; Regis Laconi, FRA (Kawasaki) 55, 0 laps.

Fastest lap: Smrz, 1m 37.694s, 96.764mph/155.727km/h (record).

DNF: Jason Pridmore, USA (Honda) 43, 23 laps; Sébastien Gimbert, FRA (Yamaha) 194, 14 laps; Vittorio Iannuzzo, ITA (Kawasaki) 13, 8 laps; Regis Laconi, FRA (Kawasaki) 55, 5 laps; Makoto Tamada, JPN (Kawasaki) 100, 2 laps; Karl Muggeridge, AUS (Honda) 31, 2 laps; Kenan Sofuoglu, TUR (Honda) 54, 0 laps.

Fastest lap: Corser, 1m 37.580s, 96.877mph/155.909km/h (record).

Superpole: Corser, 1m 35.993s, 98.479mph/158.487km/h.

Lap record: New circuit.

Championship points: 1 Bayliss, 259; 2 Neukirchner, 210; 3 C. Checa, 207; 4 Haga, 191; 5 Corser, 185; 6 Nieto, 151; 7 Xaus, 148; 8 Biaggi, 117; 9 Fabrizio, 111; 10 Kiyonari, 94; 11 Kagayama, 82; 12 Lanzi, 80; 13 Lavilla, 75; 14 Smrz, 72; 15 Muggeridge, 59.

BRNO
CZECH REPUBLIC

A pair of thirds had been the hand dealt to Troy Bayliss at Misano; a full house was his reward at Brno a few weeks later, when a Superpole victory preceded a double win on race day, despite the attentions of many potential challengers. The margins of victory were 1.4 seconds and 0.9 second; five riders finished within 3.7 seconds in race one; four within 1.7 seconds in race two. Not up to Monza's standard, but not bad.

Few weekends feature WSB and MotoGP races on the same day, so it was interesting to compare and contrast the Laguna Seca GP and Brno. Unlike the MotoGP race – one of the best races some ringside commentators claimed ever to have seen – the two SBK races were contests all the way to the end, involving multiple riders to boot. And just to underline how hard they were flaying the throttles, the new Brno WSB lap record of 1m 59.970s came about on the 18th lap of race two, courtesy of Michel Fabrizio.

Flag-to-flag racing, in the real sense of the term.

Double winner Bayliss sparred with the wild bunch early in race one, but punched his way to the front on lap 13. It was combative stuff up front, with Troy Corser and Max Biaggi swapping the early lead on several occasions. The slow, fast, then slowing Neukirchner was also at the sharp end for a time, until he slipped back to seventh.

Bayliss, waiting his turn, watched Corser and Biaggi go at it like eager novices rather than veterans in their thirties. Eventually Biaggi ended up in a scrap with Fabrizio behind the two Troys. The younger man proved the more effective and aggressive, however, taking third spot after holding off a final chicane charge by Biaggi.

Ryuichi Kiyonari was back in shape at this meeting,

and his fifth place in race one, only 3.7 seconds adrift of Bayliss, was a sign of things to come in the next round. He could have achieved more had he not had such slow starts in each race.

In race two, Bayliss made a better start than in race one, but Corser was determined once more, passing him on lap two and leading over the line for another seven laps, until the Australian finally freed himself of his immediate rivals. At one stage, those rivals were Corser and Max Neukirchner, but after ten laps, it was Corser and Biaggi giving little and not happy to sit behind.

The passing opportunities at Brno are seemingly endless; such is the width of the track and the frequency of the chicanes. The trick as always, however, is to make an entry overtake count on the exit.

Corser ended up gently slipping back from contention, even for a podium place, but only after he and Fabrizio had slugged it out for a time. Shortly afterwards, the latter lined up Biaggi for a second assault.

Fabrizio helped team-mate Bayliss by taking an eventual second place, but the Australian's series rivals were all in trouble anyway. Neukirchner was eased backwards yet again, this time to fifth, while Carlos Checa had to retire in the second race with electronic problems, having been a lonely seventh in race one after losing front grip. He had been 13th in Superpole. Haga had qualified 12th on the grid and was unhappy. Fighting back from his poor grid slots, he took sixth in race one and seventh in race two.

Brno had seen another two belting WSB races, the best rider and bike package winning each of them, but not without a real fight. Just another day in the 2008 WSB office, at one of the best 'modern' tracks ever devised.

Above: Carlos Checa had a downbeat weekend.

Above centre right: Somewhere in there Laconi and Smrz loop into the air-fence.

Above far right: Fabrizio made the rostrum in both outings.

Right: Corser, Bayliss and Fabrizio after race one.
Photographs: Gold & Goose

Left: Australian duel: Corser leads Bayliss into the first turn. Biaggi, Neukirchner (hidden) and Fabrizio (84) are in close attendance.

Below: Biaggi savoured the bubbly at a favourite track.

Photograph: Gold & Goose

Round 9
BRNO, Czech Republic
20 July 2008, 3.357-mile/5.403km circuit

Race 1 20 laps, 67.140 miles/108.060km				Race 2 20 laps, 67.140 miles/108.060km			
Dry, Air 25°C Humidity 32% Track 43°C				Dry, Air 26°C Humidity 30% Track 45°C			
Pl. Name Nat. (*Machine*)	No.	Time & gap	Laps	Pl. Name Nat. (*Machine*)	No.	Time & gap	Laps
1 Troy Bayliss, AUS (*Ducati*)	21	40m 22.724s	20	1 Troy Bayliss, AUS (*Ducati*)	21	40m 16.436s	20
		99.774mph/160.570km/h				100.033mph/160.988km/h	
2 Troy Corser, AUS (*Yamaha*)	11	1.468s	20	2 Michel Fabrizio, ITA (*Ducati*)	84	0.928s	20
3 Michel Fabrizio, ITA (*Ducati*)	84	3.272s	20	3 Max Biaggi, ITA (*Ducati*)	3	1.259s	20
4 Max Biaggi, ITA (*Ducati*)	3	3.475s	20	4 Troy Corser, AUS (*Yamaha*)	11	1.785s	20
5 Ryuichi Kiyonari, JPN (*Honda*)	23	3.791s	20	5 Max Neukirchner, GER (*Suzuki*)	76	3.942s	20
6 Noriyuki Haga, JPN (*Yamaha*)	41	9.120s	20	6 Ryuichi Kiyonari, JPN (*Honda*)	23	7.910s	20
7 Max Neukirchner, GER (*Suzuki*)	76	9.358s	20	7 Noriyuki Haga, JPN (*Yamaha*)	41	11.297s	20
8 Carlos Checa, SPA (*Honda*)	7	11.787s	20	8 Fonsi Nieto, SPA (*Suzuki*)	10	11.375s	20
9 Yukio Kagayama, JPN (*Suzuki*)	34	17.228s	20	9 Yukio Kagayama, JPN (*Suzuki*)	34	13.103s	20
10 Kenan Sofuoglu, TUR (*Honda*)	54	17.705s	20	10 Kenan Sofuoglu, TUR (*Honda*)	54	18.978s	20
11 Karl Muggeridge, AUS (*Honda*)	31	22.347s	20	11 Jakub Smrz, CZE (*Ducati*)	96	19.106s	20
12 Shinichi Nakatomi, JPN (*Yamaha*)	38	25.563s	20	12 Roberto Rolfo, ITA (*Honda*)	44	20.556s	20
13 Niccolò Canepa, ITA (*Ducati*)	59	25.699s	20	13 Lorenzo Lanzi, ITA (*Ducati*)	57	21.775s	20
14 Fonsi Nieto, SPA (*Suzuki*)	10	34.064s	20	14 Gregorio Lavilla, SPA (*Honda*)	36	26.372s	20
15 Gregorio Lavilla, SPA (*Honda*)	36	36.545s	20	15 Shinichi Nakatomi, JPN (*Yamaha*)	38	26.922s	20
16 Makoto Tamada, JPN (*Kawasaki*)	100	43.934s	20	16 David Checa, SPA (*Yamaha*)	94	27.109s	20
17 Ayrton Badovini, ITA (*Kawasaki*)	86	44.339s	20	17 Makoto Tamada, JPN (*Kawasaki*)	100	39.711s	20
18 Shuhei Aoyama, JPN (*Honda*)	88	50.092s	20	18 Shuhei Aoyama, JPN (*Honda*)	88	39.953s	20
19 Jason Pridmore, USA (*Honda*)	43	58.827s	20	19 Jason Pridmore, USA (*Honda*)	43	56.812s	20
20 Jiri Drasdak, CZE (*Honda*)	113	59.928s	20	20 Christian Zaiser, AUT (*Yamaha*)	73	1m 44.073s	20
21 Christian Zaiser, AUT (*Yamaha*)	73	1m 21.587s	20	21 Milos Cihak, CZE (*Suzuki*)	15	1m 46.620s	20

DNF: Sébastien Gimbert, FRA (*Yamaha*) 194, 18 laps; Vittorio Iannuzzo, ITA (*Kawasaki*) 13, 9 laps; Roberto Rolfo, ITA (*Honda*) 44, 8 laps; Ruben Xaus, SPA (*Ducati*) 111, 8 laps; Milos Cihak, CZE (*Suzuki*) 15, 5 laps; David Checa, SPA (*Yamaha*) 94, 3 laps; Lorenzo Lanzi, ITA (*Ducati*) 57, 3 laps; Regis Laconi, FRA (*Kawasaki*) 55, 3 laps; Jakub Smrz, CZE (*Ducati*) 96, 3 laps.

DNF: Karl Muggeridge, AUS (*Honda*) 31, 15 laps; Sébastien Gimbert, FRA (*Yamaha*) 194, 14 laps; Ruben Xaus, SPA (*Ducati*) 111, 11 laps; Carlos Checa, SPA (*Honda*) 7, 11 laps; Niccolò Canepa, ITA (*Ducati*) 59, 6 laps; Vittorio Iannuzzo, ITA (*Kawasaki*) 13, 6 laps; Ayrton Badovini, ITA (*Kawasaki*) 86, 5 laps; Jiri Drasdak, CZE (*Honda*) 113, 2 laps; Regis Laconi, FRA (*Kawasaki*) 55, 1 lap.

Fastest lap: Bayliss, 2m 00.298s, 100.468mph/161.688km/h.

Fastest lap: Fabrizio, 1m 59.979s, 100.735mph/162.118km/h (record).

Superpole: Bayliss, 1m 58.345s, 102.127mph/164.357km/h.

Lap record: Troy Corser, AUS (*Yamaha*), 2m 00.674s, 100.156mph/161.185km/h (2007).

Championship points: 1 Bayliss, 309; 2 Neukirchner, 230; 3 Corser, 218; 4 C. Checa, 215; 5 Haga, 210; 6 Nieto, 161; 7 Xaus, 148; 8 Fabrizio, 147; 9 Biaggi, 146; 10 Kiyonari, 115; 11 Kagayama, 96; 12 Lanzi, 83; 13 Lavilla, 78; 14 Smrz, 77; 15 Muggeridge, 64.

BRANDS HATCH
GREAT BRITAIN

NOBODY knew at the start of the weekend that this may have been the last Brands Hatch round of all time, but if that is the way it turns out, at least it proved to be a classic. There was even a new power in WSB to put a smile on local faces. The fact that he was from Japan seemed immaterial to a crowd recently robbed of top-level British entrants to cheer in 2008. Ryuichi Kiyonari was the reigning BSB gold medal holder (and bar) and thus was claimed by the crowd as being at least partially one of their own.

On the other hand, Brands Hatch 2008 will also be a meeting to forget, due to a fatal accident involving rising WSS star Craig Jones.

In a year of delays and false starts, we had another one in England, when the rain arrived shortly before the noon start of WSB race one. It abated quickly, however, and the race got under way in dry conditions.

Troy Bayliss started from pole position, with Noriyuki Haga, Kiyonari and Jakub Smrz alongside.

Bayliss, Troy Corser, Haga and Max Biaggi were the immediate leaders, but local wild-card Tom Sykes, on the Rizla Suzuki, was also in the leading echelon. His

opening race did not last, however, as his radiator was holed when another rider's rear tyre kicked up a stone.

Haga had gone out even before Sykes, losing the rear on full lean on the entry to the uphill left-hander of Surtees.

At mid-race distance, there were ten riders within seven seconds of the lead, while at the finish there were six riders – Kiyonari, Bayliss, Biaggi, the bouncing ball that is Yukio Kagayama, Fonsi Nieto and Max Neukirchner – all within 6.9 seconds of the chequered flag. Bayliss had led for 21 laps, but not when it mattered most.

Heading it up after 25 laps was Kiyonari, 0.137 second ahead of Bayliss and 0.180 second faster than the rapidly closing Biaggi. A typical Brands race, with yet another coming up.

With his eye well in, Kiyonari may have dominated race two, but he couldn't, as Bayliss led five laps, and Haga the next five. But from lap 11 to 25, Kiyo was in front each time over the line. He had constant and impressive pressure applied to him by Haga, who had bounced back to form at one of his favourite circuits.

Their fight was impressive, Kiyonari continually passing Haga at the bottom of Pilgrim's Drop, and Haga claiming every other opportunity to get past again.

To the surprise of some, it was Haga who broke, and with a lap left to run, Kiyonari was well clear, becoming the eighth different rider to score a WSB race win in 2008, with 20 races of 28 completed. Haga was second and Corser some eight seconds adrift in third.

Bayliss had been slowing dramatically after mistakenly changing from his race-one tyre choice. He would finish only 11th, just ahead of Biaggi, who had run way off track at Graham Hill Bend.

Corser was another with rear grip issues, and had the race finished a bit earlier, Sykes would have been in with a shout of going much higher than seventh. A pair of fifth places for Nieto showed that he was back in the mix, even though he had lost the second duel of the day to team-mate Neukirchner.

For most of the right reasons, and some of the wrong, Brands 2008 will be hard to shake from the memory.

Above: Bayliss leads around Druids in race one.

Left: Crowd favourite Haga made the podium.

Far left: Double British champion Kiyonari won both 'home' races.

Right: Wild-card Tom Sykes made a big impression.

Below: Kiyonari had come home.

Bottom: Kagayama was fourth in race one.

Photographs: Gold & Goose

Round 10
BRANDS HATCH, Great Britain
3 August 2008, 2.301-mile/3.702km circuit

Race 1 25 laps, 57.525 miles/92.550km
Dry, Air 21°C Humidity 77% Track 23°C

Pl.	Name Nat. (Machine)	No.	Time & gap	Laps
1	Ryuichi Kiyonari, JPN (*Honda*)	23	36m 18.607s	25
			95.028mph/152.933km/h	
2	Troy Bayliss, AUS (*Ducati*)	21	0.137s	25
3	Max Biaggi, ITA (*Ducati*)	3	0.180s	25
4	Yukio Kagayama, JPN (*Suzuki*)	34	5.733s	25
5	Fonsi Nieto, SPA (*Suzuki*)	10	6.499s	25
6	Carlos Checa, SPA (*Honda*)	7	6.984s	25
7	Max Neukirchner, GER (*Suzuki*)	76	8.300s	25
8	Troy Corser, AUS (*Yamaha*)	11	10.732s	25
9	Jakub Smrz, CZE (*Ducati*)	96	16.547s	25
10	Roberto Rolfo, ITA (*Honda*)	44	16.569s	25
11	Lorenzo Lanzi, ITA (*Ducati*)	57	18.366s	25
12	Michel Fabrizio, ITA (*Ducati*)	84	22.308s	25
13	Kenan Sofuoglu, TUR (*Honda*)	54	26.788s	25
14	Gregorio Lavilla, SPA (*Honda*)	36	26.856s	25
15	Chris Walker, GBR (*Honda*)	9	32.877s	25
16	Karl Muggeridge, AUS (*Honda*)	31	38.329s	25
17	David Checa, SPA (*Yamaha*)	94	46.868s	25
18	Makoto Tamada, JPN (*Kawasaki*)	100	48.417s	25
19	Noriyuki Haga, JPN (*Yamaha*)	41	58.986s	25
20	Vittorio Iannuzzo, ITA (*Kawasaki*)	13	1m 06.028s	25
21	Luca Morelli, ITA (*Honda*)	22	1m 09.376s	25
22	Jason Pridmore, USA (*Honda*)	43	1m 09.475s	25
23	Christian Zaiser, AUT (*Yamaha*)	73	1m 22.214s	25

DNF: Regis Laconi, FRA (*Kawasaki*) 55, 22 laps; Ayrton Badovini, ITA (*Kawasaki*) 86, 16 laps; Sébastien Gimbert, FRA (*Yamaha*) 194, 12 laps; Tom Sykes, GBR (*Suzuki*) 66, 9 laps; Tristan Palmer, GBR (*Yamaha*) 17, 7 laps; Shuhei Aoyama, JPN (*Honda*) 88, 3 laps.

Fastest lap: Kiyonari, 1m 26.560s, 95.669mph/ 153.965km/h.

Superpole: Bayliss, 1m 25.656s, 96.679mph/155.590km/h.

Lap record: James Toseland, GBR (*Honda*), 1m 26.351s, 95.927mph/154.379km/h (2006).

Race 2 25 laps, 57.525 miles/92.550km
Dry, Air 20°C Humidity 74% Track 22°C

Pl.	Name Nat. (Machine)	No.	Time & gap	Laps
1	Ryuichi Kiyonari, JPN (*Honda*)	23	36m 14.904s	25
			95.190mph/153.193km/h	
2	Noriyuki Haga, JPN (*Yamaha*)	41	1.848s	25
3	Troy Corser, AUS (*Yamaha*)	11	8.883s	25
4	Max Neukirchner, GER (*Suzuki*)	76	11.180s	25
5	Fonsi Nieto, SPA (*Suzuki*)	10	12.928s	25
6	Michel Fabrizio, ITA (*Ducati*)	84	13.696s	25
7	Tom Sykes, GBR (*Suzuki*)	66	13.872s	25
8	Carlos Checa, SPA (*Honda*)	7	14.009s	25
9	Jakub Smrz, CZE (*Ducati*)	96	19.065s	25
10	Lorenzo Lanzi, ITA (*Ducati*)	57	19.864s	25
11	Troy Bayliss, AUS (*Ducati*)	21	20.479s	25
12	Max Biaggi, ITA (*Ducati*)	3	20.621s	25
13	Gregorio Lavilla, SPA (*Honda*)	36	20.722s	25
14	Roberto Rolfo, ITA (*Honda*)	44	24.512s	25
15	Chris Walker, GBR (*Honda*)	9	32.090s	25
16	Regis Laconi, FRA (*Kawasaki*)	55	32.207s	25
17	Kenan Sofuoglu, TUR (*Honda*)	54	32.815s	25
18	Makoto Tamada, JPN (*Kawasaki*)	100	33.648s	25
19	Sébastien Gimbert, FRA (*Yamaha*)	194	35.382s	25
20	David Checa, SPA (*Yamaha*)	94	44.866s	25
21	Ayrton Badovini, ITA (*Kawasaki*)	86	53.969s	25
22	Shuhei Aoyama, JPN (*Honda*)	88	1m 00.875s	25
23	Jason Pridmore, USA (*Honda*)	43	1m 01.104s	25
24	Luca Morelli, ITA (*Honda*)	22	1m 04.329s	25
25	Yukio Kagayama, JPN (*Suzuki*)	34	1 lap	24

DNF: Karl Muggeridge, AUS (*Honda*) 31, 17 laps; Vittorio Iannuzzo, ITA (*Kawasaki*) 13, 15 laps; Tristan Palmer, GBR (*Yamaha*) 17, 9 laps; Christian Zaiser, AUT (*Yamaha*) 73, 4 laps.

Fastest lap: Fabrizio, 1m 26.362s, 95.889mph/154.318km/h.

Championship points: 1 Bayliss, 334; 2 Neukirchner, 252; 3 Corser, 242; 4 C. Checa, 233; 5 Haga, 230; 6 Nieto, 183; 7 Biaggi, 166; 8 Kiyonari, 165; 9 Fabrizio, 161; 10 Xaus, 148; 11 Kagayama, 109; 12 Lanzi, 94; 13 Smrz, 91; 14 Lavilla, 83; 15 Muggeridge, 64.

DONINGTON PARK
GREAT BRITAIN

SADLY, the biggest factor in many race weekends in 2008 was adverse weather. It proved to be that way yet again as Donington swapped 2007's April freeze for a cold and miserable September drenching. Dry practice time was a mirage through the mire for most riders, although ultimately practice was not affected to any great degree, despite many areas of the UK suffering significant flooding.

Donington was largely spared that particular fate, but the first race was still a tough trial by oil and then water – so much so that after an aggregate race of 19 combined laps instead of the expected 23, only 14 riders finished. Considering that 33 had started, that indicated a spectacular casualty rate. Many riders' settings were guesswork, as the track dried shortly before the first start, and most made quick swaps to dry tyres from intermediates.

Off the line, Ryuichi Kiyonari demonstrated track knowledge and aggression yet again, with local lad Tom Sykes and Troy Bayliss just behind. That lasted a lap until Kiyonari crashed, having lost the front on a drying track surface that was still running five seconds off record pace. Then it was Bayliss being chased by Sykes, followed by Leon Haslam, Carlos Checa, privateer Gregorio Lavilla, Max Neukirchner, Max Biaggi, Chris Walker and Yukio Kagayama. Sykes would soon take the lead and press on to a fine three-second advantage.

Oil from Noriyuki Haga's machine coated the track in places and brought down a few riders, including his team-mate, Troy Corser. As Haga had ignored a black and orange flag indicating that he should stop immediately, he was punished with disqualification from the restart. He and Corser attempted to restart anyway, but they were stopped from doing so, Haga on the line.

With nine laps completed in the first leg, the game for Bayliss was to use the next 14 to get a real lead over Sykes, and he delivered, but only after fending off several opponents in the initial laps. With rain spotting some riders' visors early in the second leg, Haslam put his hand up on the way down Craner, but Bayliss just took this as a chance to overtake. He passed Haslam, then Sykes, who had slowed his leading pace, having more to lose than Bayliss.

Heavier rain finally stopped things for good on the 19th aggregate lap, but not before a wild pass on Haslam by Roby Rolfo at the Esses put both of them out.

After a messy first race, there was an even messier podium ceremony, as Ruben Xaus was disqualified for falling on the final lap and failing to get back to the pit lane on his own machine in time for the ceremony. He protested – convincingly – that this was irrelevant, and despite angry and occasionally tactile disagreements with Biaggi and the officials, he was led away, Biaggi taking third place, behind Bayliss and Sykes. Xaus was awarded a DNF.

Race two, held in atrociously wet weather conditions, saw Haga punished with a ride-through penalty, which he took at the wrong time, leading to him being black-flagged again. Two races, nil points. A disaster for him, but Corser provided a redemptive miracle. He had crashed six times already at Donington, but instead of hiding from the pain in the pits, or just making up the numbers, he was a gritty third on the slippery track.

The rain had returned five minutes before the start of the second race, causing yet more delays, but from flag to flag, Kiyonari was the conqueror, albeit somewhat alarmed, thanks to the progress of Cal Crutchlow, an early casualty of race one's madness. The local HM Plant Honda rider pressurised Kiyo all the way, finishing only 2.2 seconds down.

Over ten seconds from Corser, another wild-card rider, James Ellison (Hydrex Honda), splashed his way to fourth, some seven seconds up on Michel Fabrizio.

It was like British rounds of old: wild-cards scoring strongly, lots of drama and action, and all carried out under changeable track conditions.

Left: Local knowledge helped Crutchlow take his BSB Honda to the rostrum.

Below left: Kiyonari leads Bayliss through the flood.

Below: Late to the rostrum, Xaus eventually found himself excluded.

Photographs: Gold & Goose

Above: Conditions, atrocious; Bayliss, triumphant.

Above right: James Ellison, fourth in race two, was a wild-card who benefited from the rain.

Right: Wild-card Cal Crutchlow joined Kiyonari and Corser on the race-two rostrum.

Photographs: Gold & Goose

Round 11
DONINGTON PARK, Great Britain
7 September 2008, 2.500-mile/4.023km circuit

Race 1 19 laps, 47.500 miles/76.437km (aggregated result)
Dry/Wet, Air 16°C Humidity 87% Track 16°C

Pl.	Name Nat. (Machine)	No.	Time & gap	Laps
1	Troy Bayliss, AUS (Ducati)	21	29m 55.384s	19
			95.236mph/153.267km/h	
2	Tom Sykes, GBR (Suzuki)	66	1.266s	19
3	Max Biaggi, ITA (Ducati)	3	28.636s	19
4	Gregorio Lavilla, SPA (Honda)	36	33.566s	19
5	Yukio Kagayama, JPN (Suzuki)	34	35.966s	19
6	Jakub Smrz, CZE (Ducati)	96	36.034s	19
7	Fonsi Nieto, SPA (Suzuki)	10	36.442s	19
8	Leon Haslam, GBR (Honda)	91	41.633s	19
9	Karl Muggeridge, AUS (Honda)	31	42.075s	19
10	James Ellison, GBR (Honda)	80	43.476s	19
11	David Checa, SPA (Yamaha)	94	1m 12.578s	19
12	Ayrton Badovini, ITA (Kawasaki)	86	1m 13.147s	19
13	Shinichi Nakatomi, JPN (Yamaha)	38	1m 34.664s	19
14	Shuhei Aoyama, JPN (Honda)	88	1m 56.726s	19

DNF: Ruben Xaus, SPA (Ducati) 111, 19 laps; Vittorio Iannuzzo, ITA (Kawasaki) 13, 19 laps; Christian Zaiser, AUT (Yamaha) 73, 19 laps; Lorenzo Lanzi, ITA (Ducati) 57, 14 laps; Roberto Rolfo, ITA (Honda) 44, 12 laps; Michel Fabrizio, ITA (Ducati) 84, 10 laps; Troy Corser, AUS (Yamaha) 11, 9 laps; Makoto Tamada, JPN (Kawasaki) 100, 9 laps; Noriyuki Haga, JPN (Yamaha) 41, 9 laps; Carlos Checa, SPA (Honda) 7, 9 laps; Sébastien Gimbert, FRA (Yamaha) 194, 6 laps; Max Neukirchner, GER (Suzuki) 76, 5 laps; Chris Walker, GBR (Honda) 9, 5 laps; Regis Laconi, FRA (Kawasaki) 55, 5 laps; Matt Lynn, USA (Honda) 50, 3 laps; Luca Morelli, ITA (Honda) 22, 3 laps; Cal Crutchlow, GBR (Honda) 35, 2 laps; Ryuichi Kiyonari, JPN (Honda) 23, 1 lap; Kenan Sofuoglu, TUR (Honda) 54, 1 lap.

Fastest lap: Bayliss, 1m 31.814s, 98.016mph/157.741km/h.

Superpole: Bayliss, 1m 42.013s, 88.216mph/141.970km/h.

Race 2 23 laps, 57.500 miles/92.529km
Wet, Air 20°C Humidity 70% Track 18°C

Pl.	Name Nat. (Machine)	No.	Time & gap	Laps
1	Ryuichi Kiyonari, JPN (Honda)	23	40m 26.508s	23
			85.300mph/137.277km/h	
2	Cal Crutchlow, GBR (Honda)	35	2.261s	23
3	Troy Corser, AUS (Yamaha)	11	9.727s	23
4	James Ellison, GBR (Honda)	80	20.227s	23
5	Michel Fabrizio, ITA (Ducati)	84	27.475s	23
6	Max Biaggi, ITA (Ducati)	3	28.051s	23
7	Gregorio Lavilla, SPA (Honda)	36	30.922s	23
8	Ruben Xaus, SPA (Ducati)	111	38.353s	23
9	Carlos Checa, SPA (Honda)	7	50.196s	23
10	Tom Sykes, GBR (Suzuki)	66	57.346s	23
11	Lorenzo Lanzi, ITA (Ducati)	57	1m 03.093s	23
12	Jakub Smrz, CZE (Ducati)	96	1m 06.697s	23
13	Roberto Rolfo, ITA (Honda)	44	1m 08.057s	23
14	Max Neukirchner, GER (Suzuki)	76	1m 15.276s	23
15	Regis Laconi, FRA (Kawasaki)	55	1m 38.848s	23
16	Makoto Tamada, JPN (Kawasaki)	100	1 lap	22
17	Shuhei Aoyama, JPN (Honda)	88	1 lap	22
18	Shinichi Nakatomi, JPN (Yamaha)	38	1 lap	22
19	Yukio Kagayama, JPN (Suzuki)	34	1 lap	22

DNF: Karl Muggeridge, AUS (Honda) 31, 21 laps; Leon Haslam, GBR (Honda) 91, 20 laps; David Checa, SPA (Yamaha) 94, 18 laps; Fonsi Nieto, SPA (Suzuki) 10, 18 laps; Matt Lynn, USA (Honda) 50, 18 laps; Chris Walker, GBR (Honda) 9, 16 laps; Troy Bayliss, AUS (Ducati) 21, 12 laps; Noriyuki Haga, JPN (Yamaha) 41, 9 laps; Christian Zaiser, AUT (Yamaha) 73, 7 laps; Ayrton Badovini, ITA (Kawasaki) 86, 6 laps; Luca Morelli, ITA (Honda) 22, 3 laps; Sébastien Gimbert, FRA (Yamaha) 194, 2 laps; Vittorio Iannuzzo, ITA (Kawasaki) 13, 2 laps.

Fastest lap: Ellison, 1m 43.405s, 87.029mph/140.059km/h.

Lap record: Troy Bayliss, AUS (Ducati), 1m 31.575s, 98.271mph/158.152km/h (2007).

Championship points: 1 Bayliss, 359; 2 Corser, 258; 3 Neukirchner, 254; 4 C. Checa, 240; 5 Haga, 230; 6 Nieto, 192; 7 Biaggi, 192; 8 Kiyonari, 190; 9 Fabrizio, 172; 10 Xaus, 156; 11 Kagayama, 120; 12 Lavilla and Smrz, 105; 14 Lanzi, 99; 15 Muggeridge, 71.

VALLELUNGA
ITALY

YET again, the weather played its malevolent tricks, this time lashing with constant rain early on, in a very un-Roman fashion. Noriyuki Haga had crashed in the first wet qualifying session – a rapid and pounding, low-orbit high-side, followed by a short freestyle bike wrestle, his head hitting the ground with some force. Partly because of this, Troy Bayliss was in good shape to do it come Sunday, having won Superpole once more, even though his immediate rivals for the championship surrounded him on the grid.

Beaten and battered, with ice packs all over him, Haga went on to finish third in Superpole on day two, even if he was only tenth after the second qualifying session, which was held in the dry, finally.

On a warmish and dry race day, Bayliss was fastest away, and how the crowd cheered. Or at least those who didn't hang pro-Biaggi banners in front of the official Ducati pit garage, accusing the manufacturer of treason for not signing their own Roman home-town hero for the official team in 2009.

Despite his start, Bayliss struggled with too hard a tyre choice in race one and was seven seconds down on eventual winner Haga, who was involved in a late

and thrilling game of cat and mouse with the closing Max Biaggi. The latter, having been finally rejected by the factory team, rode manfully on his private 1098RS, and second in the opener was close to his first 2008 win. Troy Corser was only 0.053 second from winner Haga, but seemingly no closer to a win here than at any other race.

The leading trio were followed home by Max Neukirchner, Carlos Checa and – only then – Bayliss. A whopping 16 seconds back, Michel Fabrizio was seventh, Roberto Rolfo eighth.

In race two, a gigantic lap-one crash ensued after Biaggi's brake lever was bashed in a collision with Corser. The initial impact produced a big fishtail slide from Biaggi's machine as they all thundered down the hill from Curvone to Cimini. The Italian veered dramatically right at very high speed, all the while fighting for control. Checa saw him, was hard on the brakes and did well to avoid him. The unsighted Kenan Sofuoglu, running flat out, had no chance and simply smashed into the side of Biaggi's bike as it suddenly appeared on his line. The black Ducati was almost side-on to him at the time of impact.

This bizarre crash was a huge and destructive colli-

sion, flinging Sofuoglu over the bars and a long way down the track. Biaggi was lucky to be missed by the main pack of riders as he also slid down the hill at high speed. The two riders ended up crumpled near their wrecked machines; astonishingly, neither suffered any significant injury.

The race continued, and once in the lead, Haga was not to be headed over the line. But Bayliss, being Bayliss, decided that winning the title by finishing second was not good enough. An attempted pass went wrong half-way around the final lap and he ran wide. It was too late to recover any chance of the win, but Bayliss didn't see it that way. One final lunge to make up ground on Haga at the tight infield hairpin corner saw him lose the front, right at the apex under braking, and fall, his titanium armour striking sparks all the way to the grass run-off.

Paradoxically, Bayliss didn't even need to try to pass Haga, as his team-mate had just passed Corser, which was enough to give the Australian the crown.

It was a stunning moment, never to be forgotten.

Fabrizio was second, Corser third, only a couple of seconds behind another win that got away.

Right: Heading for a clash: Lanzi (57) and Iannuzzo's Kawasaki.

Below right: Gimbert's Yamaha heads Rolfo's Honda – temporarily.

Below left: Roman hero Biaggi came close to winning at home.

Facing page: Bayliss crashed. If he hadn't done so, he'd have been champion.

Photographs: Gold & Goose

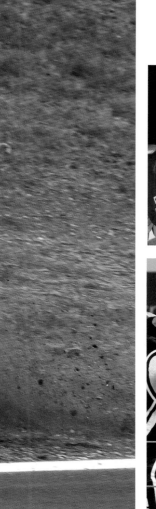

Above: Veteran rivals Bayliss, Haga and Corser – new boy Fabrizio looks on.

Left: Haga came back for the wreath after a big crash in practice.

Facing page, from left: On the grid: Regis Laconi, Karl Muggeridge, late-comer Chris Walker.

Photographs: Gold & Goose

Round 12
VALLELUNGA, Italy
21 September 2008, 2.554-mile/4.110km circuit

Race 1	24 laps, 61.296 miles/98.640km			
Dry, Air 19°C Humidity 44% Track 31°C				
Pl.	Name Nat. (*Machine*)	No.	Time/gap	Laps
1	Noriyuki Haga, JPN (*Yamaha*)	41	39m 25.030s	24
			93.298mph/150.148km/h	
2	Max Biaggi, ITA (*Ducati*)	3	0.129s	24
3	Troy Corser, AUS (*Yamaha*)	11	0.535s	24
4	Max Neukirchner, GER (*Suzuki*)	76	5.188s	24
5	Carlos Checa, SPA (*Honda*)	7	6.693s	24
6	Troy Bayliss, AUS (*Ducati*)	21	7.993s	24
7	Michel Fabrizio, ITA (*Ducati*)	84	16.976s	24
8	Roberto Rolfo, ITA (*Honda*)	44	18.359s	24
9	Yukio Kagayama, JPN (*Suzuki*)	34	19.214s	24
10	Shinichi Nakatomi, JPN (*Yamaha*)	38	19.386s	24
11	Lorenzo Lanzi, ITA (*Ducati*)	57	21.230s	24
12	Fonsi Nieto, SPA (*Suzuki*)	10	24.956s	24
13	Jakub Smrz, CZE (*Ducati*)	96	25.186s	24
14	Gregorio Lavilla, SPA (*Honda*)	36	31.799s	24
15	Ayrton Badovini, ITA (*Kawasaki*)	86	33.949s	24
16	Regis Laconi, FRA (*Kawasaki*)	55	34.050s	24
17	David Checa, SPA (*Yamaha*)	94	34.665s	24
18	Chris Walker, GBR (*Honda*)	9	52.420s	24
19	Shuhei Aoyama, JPN (*Honda*)	88	1m 02.555s	24
20	Makoto Tamada, JPN (*Kawasaki*)	100	1m 06.475s	24
21	Matej Smrz, CZE (*Honda*)	122	1m 16.985s	24
22	Matt Lynn, USA (*Honda*)	50	1 lap	23

DNF: Sébastien Gimbert, FRA (*Yamaha*) 194, 17 laps; Vittorio Iannuzzo, ITA (*Kawasaki*) 13, 14 laps; Ruben Xaus, SPA (*Ducati*) 111, 6 laps; Christian Zaiser, AUT (*Yamaha*) 73, 5 laps; Ryuichi Kiyonari, JPN (*Honda*) 23, 3 laps; Kenan Sofuoglu, TUR (*Honda*) 54, 2 laps; Karl Muggeridge, AUS (*Honda*) 31, 2 laps.

Fastest lap: Checa, 1m 37.537s, 94.260mph/151.696km/h.

Superpole: Bayliss, 1m 36.606s, 95.168mph/153.158km/h.

Race 2	24 laps, 61.296 miles/98.640km			
Dry, Air 21°C Humidity 35% Track 30°C				
Pl.	Name Nat. (*Machine*)	No.	Time/gap	Laps
1	Noriyuki Haga, JPN (*Yamaha*)	41	39m 10.265s	24
			93.884mph/151.091km/h	
2	Michel Fabrizio, ITA (*Ducati*)	84	1.507s	24
3	Troy Corser, AUS (*Yamaha*)	11	2.268s	24
4	Max Neukirchner, GER (*Suzuki*)	76	11.813s	24
5	Carlos Checa, SPA (*Honda*)	7	17.922s	24
6	Fonsi Nieto, SPA (*Suzuki*)	10	18.281s	24
7	Yukio Kagayama, JPN (*Suzuki*)	34	19.368s	24
8	Shinichi Nakatomi, JPN (*Yamaha*)	38	19.717s	24
9	Regis Laconi, FRA (*Kawasaki*)	55	23.868s	24
10	Roberto Rolfo, ITA (*Honda*)	44	24.198s	24
11	Jakub Smrz, CZE (*Ducati*)	96	25.426s	24
12	Ruben Xaus, SPA (*Ducati*)	111	28.384s	24
13	Ryuichi Kiyonari, JPN (*Honda*)	23	30.436s	24
14	Sébastien Gimbert, FRA (*Yamaha*)	194	36.490s	24
15	Chris Walker, GBR (*Honda*)	9	42.903s	24
16	Troy Bayliss, AUS (*Ducati*)	21	43.758s	24
17	Shuhei Aoyama, JPN (*Honda*)	88	44.993s	24
18	Lorenzo Lanzi, ITA (*Ducati*)	57	48.469s	24
19	Makoto Tamada, JPN (*Kawasaki*)	100	58.868s	24
20	David Checa, SPA (*Yamaha*)	94	1m 18.547s	24
21	Matej Smrz, CZE (*Honda*)	122	1m 42.272s	24
22	Matt Lynn, USA (*Honda*)	50	1 lap	23

DNF: Ayrton Badovini, ITA (*Kawasaki*) 86, 15 laps; Vittorio Iannuzzo, ITA (*Kawasaki*) 13, 13 laps; Gregorio Lavilla, SPA (*Honda*) 36, 6 laps; Christian Zaiser, AUT (*Yamaha*) 73, 5 laps; Karl Muggeridge, AUS (*Honda*) 31, 2 laps; Kenan Sofuoglu, TUR (*Honda*) 54, 0 laps; Max Biaggi, ITA (*Ducati*) 3, 0 laps.

Fastest lap: Corser, 1m 37.072s, 94.711mph/152.423km/h (record).

Lap record: Noriyuki Haga, JPN (*Yamaha*), 1m 37.419s, 94.374mph/151.880km/h (2007).

Championship points: 1 Bayliss, 369; 2 Corser, 290; 3 Haga, 280; 4 Neukirchner, 280; 5 Checa, 262; 6 Biaggi, 212; 7 Nieto, 206; 8 Fabrizio, 201; 9 Kiyonari, 193; 10 Xaus, 160; 11 Kagayama, 136; 12 Smrz, 113; 13 Lavilla, 107; 14 Lanzi, 104; 15 Muggeridge, 71.

MAGNY-COURS
FRANCE

A FTER the first race at Magny-Cours, Troy Bayliss had finally done enough to win the title for himself and Ducati. But the man who would replace him in 2009, Noriyuki Haga, spoiled the party once more, if just a little bit. The Japanese rider won race one, but Bayliss would get him back in race two, in what was his 150th race start in WSB. That win was also his 50th WSB success.

It was a classic fight between some major Superbike players at Magny-Cours, and those in the crowd with weekend tickets were glad of something to get the circulation going again.

Once more, the weather was the main talking point in practice, as the heavens opened on Friday, bringing devilishly unpredictable rain and even hail. Even the British contingent was unused to such completely iffy weather, and it did not bring out the best in anyone's mood at the start.

Superpole was run in the dry, and Haga set a new track best for Superbikes with his pole win. In 228 WSB race starts, he had scored only five poles before Magny-Cours in 2008 – an amazingly small ratio for a rider with 32 previous race wins to his credit.

Fonsi Nieto was a remarkably fast second in Superpole, not his favourite discipline it must be said, with Bayliss and Carlos Checa behind. Yamaha, Suzuki, Ducati, Honda: four different bikes in the top four places.

In the opener, Bayliss took the lead early once more, but Haga moved to the front on lap two. He had it all under control and was an easy winner. Michel Fabrizio was a high-profile faller on lap 20, while Nieto reappeared on the podium for the first time since round two. Bayliss was a safe third, finally choosing caution and safety to get the bigger job done.

As he lifted the extraordinarily heavy WSB championship trophy over his head on the podium, it was easy to forget that there was still one race left on the

day, and one round to go in a whole month's time.

Race two was taken by Bayliss, appropriately enough, from the two riders who would finish the day behind him in the points total, Haga and Troy Corser. It was a superb race between them all – there were moments of recklessness and naked competitiveness throughout.

Bayliss almost fell twice on the way out of the final left hander of the start-line chicane, once when he ran over the rumble strip on the inside, losing rear grip, and the second time when his foot came off the peg and dragged on the ground as he headed towards the tyre wall.

Corser also overcooked it on the brakes in one corner and had to run wide on the last downhill right, narrowly missing Bayliss.

Fabrizio's reputation as a block passer was enhanced in race two, but he would finish only 14th. His race day was still better than Ryuichi Kiyonari's, however. Since his Brands and Donington brilliance, the Japanese rider had posted only one 13th place – in Vallelunga – and he didn't even make it to Magny-Cours for the race weekend. During testing at the French venue in readiness for the race, he had fallen in the same session that had seen F1 record breaker Michael Schumacher get a ride on the Ten Kate Honda. Kiyo broke his right collarbone for the fourth time and was withdrawn from the 13th round to allow him to have another plate fitted, before returning for the final round at Portimao.

Checa had his best single race finish since his double win at Miller, posting fourth in race two. Meanwhile, Corser had eventful races, having fallen in Superpole and been forced to start from 12th. Only sixth in race one, he was a quite brilliant third in race two, just under three seconds from Bayliss and right in the mix for long periods.

Max Biaggi was fourth in race one, having chased Bayliss in vain.

Above: Sofuoglu on the grid – a hard first year.

Above right: Lanzi's Ducati (57) in combat again, this time with David Checa's Yamaha.

Right: The championship top three: Haga, Bayliss, Corser.

Photographs: Gold & Goose

Left: Bayliss leads the pack into the first corner. He would end race one as champion.

Far right: Roby Rolfo got just one tenth – in race two.

Below right: Bayliss paints the track black as he stays clear of Corser and Haga.

Photographs: Gold & Goose

Round 13
MAGNY-COURS, France
5 October 2008, 2.741-mile/4.411km circuit

Race 1 23 laps, 63.043 miles/101.453km
Dry, Air 12°C Humidity 56% Track 14°C

Pl.	Name Nat. (Machine)	No.	Time/gap	Laps
1	Noriyuki Haga, JPN (*Yamaha*)	41	38m 33.367s	23
			98.101mph/157.878km/h	
2	Fonsi Nieto, SPA (*Suzuki*)	10	6.223s	23
3	Troy Bayliss, AUS (*Ducati*)	21	6.875s	23
4	Max Biaggi, ITA (*Ducati*)	3	7.237s	23
5	Max Neukirchner, GER (*Suzuki*)	76	8.925s	23
6	Troy Corser, AUS (*Yamaha*)	11	10.714s	23
7	Carlos Checa, SPA (*Honda*)	7	16.176s	23
8	Yukio Kagayama, JPN (*Suzuki*)	34	22.661s	23
9	Kenan Sofuoglu, TUR (*Honda*)	54	27.224s	23
10	Gregorio Lavilla, SPA (*Honda*)	36	31.300s	23
11	Regis Laconi, FRA (*Kawasaki*)	55	35.558s	23
12	Karl Muggeridge, AUS (*Honda*)	31	35.774s	23
13	Sébastien Gimbert, FRA (*Yamaha*)	194	36.078s	23
14	Shinichi Nakatomi, JPN (*Yamaha*)	38	36.289s	23
15	Chris Walker, GBR (*Honda*)	9	40.472s	23
16	Ayrton Badovini, ITA (*Kawasaki*)	86	40.497s	23
17	Martin Bauer, AUT (*Honda*)	32	43.350s	23
18	Makoto Tamada, JPN (*Kawasaki*)	100	54.263s	23
19	Shuhei Aoyama, JPN (*Honda*)	88	54.382s	23
20	Ivan Silva, SPA (*Honda*)	69	54.513s	23

DNF: Jakub Smrz, CZE (*Ducati*) 96, 22 laps; Christian Zaiser, AUT (*Yamaha*) 73, 21 laps; Lorenzo Lanzi, ITA (*Ducati*) 57, 20 laps; Michel Fabrizio, ITA (*Ducati*) 84, 19 laps; David Checa, SPA (*Yamaha*) 94, 17 laps; Roberto Rolfo, ITA (*Honda*) 44, 16 laps; Ruben Xaus, SPA (*Ducati*) 111, 14 laps; Vittorio Iannuzzo, ITA (*Kawasaki*) 13, 6 laps.

Fastest lap: Checa, 1m 39.834s, 98.835mph/159.060km/h (record).

Superpole: Haga, 1m 38.444s, 100.231mph/161.306km/h.

Race 2 23 laps, 63.043 miles/101.453km
Dry, Air 17°C Humidity 38% Track 20°C

Pl.	Name Nat. (Machine)	No.	Time/gap	Laps
1	Troy Bayliss, AUS (*Ducati*)	21	38m 33.579s	23
			98.092mph/157.864km/h	
2	Noriyuki Haga, JPN (*Yamaha*)	41	0.909s	23
3	Troy Corser, AUS (*Yamaha*)	11	2.966s	23
4	Carlos Checa, SPA (*Honda*)	7	7.175s	23
5	Ruben Xaus, SPA (*Ducati*)	111	12.822s	23
6	Max Biaggi, ITA (*Ducati*)	3	13.004s	23
7	Yukio Kagayama, JPN (*Suzuki*)	34	18.876s	23
8	Fonsi Nieto, SPA (*Suzuki*)	10	19.512s	23
9	Max Neukirchner, GER (*Suzuki*)	76	19.627s	23
10	Roberto Rolfo, ITA (*Honda*)	44	21.425s	23
11	Lorenzo Lanzi, ITA (*Ducati*)	57	25.133s	23
12	Gregorio Lavilla, SPA (*Honda*)	36	30.538s	23
13	Jakub Smrz, CZE (*Ducati*)	96	35.334s	23
14	Michel Fabrizio, ITA (*Ducati*)	84	38.453s	23
15	Chris Walker, GBR (*Honda*)	9	40.008s	23
16	Shinichi Nakatomi, JPN (*Yamaha*)	38	40.802s	23
17	Ayrton Badovini, ITA (*Kawasaki*)	86	46.941s	23
18	Makoto Tamada, JPN (*Kawasaki*)	100	50.172s	23
19	Kenan Sofuoglu, TUR (*Honda*)	54	58.616s	23
20	Regis Laconi, FRA (*Kawasaki*)	55	1m 00.422s	23
21	Ivan Silva, SPA (*Honda*)	69	1m 02.852s	23
22	Shuhei Aoyama, JPN (*Honda*)	88	1m 21.378s	23
23	Vittorio Iannuzzo, ITA (*Kawasaki*)	13	1m 32.289s	23

DNF: Karl Muggeridge, AUS (*Honda*) 31, 22 laps; Christian Zaiser, AUT (*Yamaha*) 73, 11 laps; David Checa, SPA (*Yamaha*) 94, 10 laps; Sébastien Gimbert, FRA (*Yamaha*) 194, 4 laps; Martin Bauer, AUT (*Honda*) 32, 3 laps.

Fastest lap: Bayliss, 1m 39.818s, 98.851mph/159.086km/h (record).

Previous record: Max Neukirchner, GER (*Suzuki*), 1m 39.844s, 98.825mph/159.044km/h (2007).

Championship points: 1 Bayliss, 410; 2 Haga, 325; 3 Corser, 316; 4 Neukirchner, 298; 5 Checa, 284; 6 Biaggi, 235; 7 Nieto, 234; 8 Fabrizio, 203; 9 Kiyonari, 193; 10 Xaus, 171; 11 Kagayama, 153; 12 Lavilla, 117; 13 Smrz, 116; 14 Lanzi, 109; 15 Muggeridge, 75.

PORTIMAO
PORTUGAL

HAVING had his Vallelunga victory party spoiled by a last-lap slip-up, and Magny-Cours very slightly marred by Haga's race-one full-pointer, the question before race day was whether Troy Bayliss would pull out all the stops to end his career on top and christen an all-new WSB circuit with the champagne of history.

With three championships secured and only a couple of particularly risk-laden contests left to run before retirement – on a new track, with some highly-motivated regulars and wild-card riders all with points to prove – Bayliss could have been forgiven for taking it easy.

We should have known better. The same spirit that had driven the Australian to the highest ever win rate in WSB pushed him on to secure first Superpole, and then not just two wins, but victories that were on a plane that no other rider could reach. He was 2.207 seconds ahead in race one, and 3.638 seconds ahead in race two, each an age in Superbike, particularly considering the intensity of the action for much of both 22-lap races.

Even the very best of the 2008 rest were not close today.

In finishing third in race one and sixth in race two, Troy Corser overtook Noriyuki Haga for second overall, but still was nowhere near Bayliss.

Haga had another of his disaster days, his machine stopping in the opener while he was looking good for second. Then he made a jump start in race two and had to come in for a ride-through, which dropped him to 14th.

Carlos Checa's second in race one and seventh in race two beat Max Neukirchner's crash in the opener and fourth place in race two, meaning that Checa finished his rookie WSB season fourth overall, only two points ahead of the Suzuki rider. Riding for a job in 2009, Fonsi Nieto pulled out two fifth places in his usual slow-starting, fast-finishing style.

With some of the other main players struggling to get on the podium, it was a good day for WSB in general, as many of 2009's new crop were already panning for gold.

Jonathan Rea, who had swapped a Ten Kate 600 for a Superbike this weekend, in an exchange deal with Kenan Sofuoglu, rode fearlessly and fearsomely to fourth place in race one, despite his lack of dry track time. In wet Superpole qualifying, he had been on the front row. In race two, he was in the mix again until he ran off at Turn One – while braking three abreast with Corser and Ruben Xaus. Rea was due to become a full-timer for his current team in 2009.

Two other wild-cards were Leon Haslam and Cal Crutchlow (HM Plant Honda BSB racers). They were scheduled for WSB and WSS respectively in 2009, and they made a big impact – sometimes literally – on the established stars in races that often had eight riders in the podium pack. Until guesstimate tyre choices and experience started to thin out the numbers and expand the gaps, of course.

That word 'gap' is a relative term, as in race two Regis Laconi was tenth, but only 16 seconds from the win. In the same race, the top seven riders were within seven seconds of each other, once they had made wiser tyre choices, based on their race-one experiences.

Crutchlow had used his tyre so hard that he had had to pull in during the opener, but in race two he was just behind Gregorio Lavilla and ahead of Laconi, and thus ninth. Team-mate Haslam took his second career WSB podium after passing Corser and Neukirchner late on. He had signed for Stiggy Honda in 2009.

As an advertisement for WSB racing, the first ever race day at this awesome new circuit could not have been scripted better by Infront Motor Sports themselves. Even Bayliss's dominance was a plus, delivering a dream ending to his career and era – and all the while, the evenly-matched new and old forces were pointing towards the promise of even greater competitiveness across the board in 2009.

Above: Leon Haslam, in the pit with father Ron, will be full time in 2009.

Right: Checa did enough for fourth overall.

Far right: Haslam bound for his second class rostrum.

Photographs: Gold & Goose

Left: Scenic new circuit impressed all, as did the wild-cards. Here Johnny Rea leads Xaus, Bayliss and Haslam.

Far right: Bayliss relaxes before his final motorcycle race.

Below right: Rea had swapped bikes with Sofuoglu.

Below far right: Karl Muggeridge was still battling with his Honda.

Photographs: Gold & Goose

Round 14
PORTIMAO, Portugal
2 November 2008, 2.853-mile/4.592km circuit

Race 1 22 laps, 62.766 miles/101.024km

Dry, Air 18°C Humidity 56% Track 22°C

Pl.	Name Nat. (*Machine*)	No.	Time/gap	Laps
1	Troy Bayliss, AUS (*Ducati*)	21	38m 48.373s	22
			97.057mph/156.198km/h	
2	Carlos Checa, SPA (*Honda*)	7	2.207s	22
3	Troy Corser, AUS (*Yamaha*)	11	6.972s	22
4	Jonathan Rea, GBR (*Honda*)	65	15.228s	22
5	Fonsi Nieto, SPA (*Suzuki*)	10	16.126s	22
6	Gregorio Lavilla, SPA (*Honda*)	36	18.152s	22
7	Leon Haslam, GBR (*Honda*)	91	18.939s	22
8	Ryuichi Kiyonari, JPN (*Honda*)	23	20.942s	22
9	Ruben Xaus, SPA (*Ducati*)	111	32.018s	22
10	Regis Laconi, FRA (*Kawasaki*)	55	32.871s	22
11	Ayrton Badovini, ITA (*Kawasaki*)	86	36.778s	22
12	Roberto Rolfo, ITA (*Honda*)	44	36.848s	22
13	Shinichi Nakatomi, JPN (*Yamaha*)	38	41.667s	22
14	Karl Muggeridge, AUS (*Honda*)	31	41.806s	22
15	Yukio Kagayama, JPN (*Suzuki*)	34	48.337s	22
16	Sébastien Gimbert, FRA (*Yamaha*)	194	50.295s	22
17	Chris Walker, GBR (*Honda*)	9	50.840s	22
18	Shuhei Aoyama, JPN (*Honda*)	88	1m 05.928s	22
19	Makoto Tamada, JPN (*Kawasaki*)	100	1m 06.813s	22
20	David Checa, SPA (*Yamaha*)	94	1m 07.007s	22
21	Luis Carreira, POR (*Suzuki*)	14	1 lap	21

DNF: Cal Crutchlow, GBR (*Honda*) 35, 18 laps; Noriyuki Haga, JPN (*Yamaha*) 41, 17 laps; Jakub Smrz, CZE (*Ducati*) 96, 14 laps; Thomas Bridewell, GBR (*Suzuki*) 18, 12 laps; Luca Scassa, ITA (*Honda*), 99, 10 laps; Christian Zaiser, AUT (*Yamaha*) 73, 9 laps; Vittorio Iannuzzo, ITA (*Kawasaki*) 13, 7 laps; Max Neukirchner, GER (*Suzuki*) 76, 5 laps; Michel Fabrizio, ITA (*Ducati*) 84, 0 laps; Max Biaggi, ITA (*Ducati*) 3, 0 laps.

Fastest lap: Bayliss, 1m 44.776s, 98.038mph/157.777km/h (record).

Race 2 22 laps, 62.766 miles/101.024km

Dry, Air 20°C Humidity 43% Track 25°C

Pl.	Name Nat. (*Machine*)	No.	Time/gap	Laps
1	Troy Bayliss, AUS (*Ducati*)	21	38m 26.125s	22
			97.993mph/157.705km/h	
2	Michel Fabrizio, ITA (*Ducati*)	84	3.638s	22
3	Leon Haslam, GBR (*Honda*)	91	4.356s	22
4	Max Neukirchner, GER (*Suzuki*)	76	4.983s	22
5	Fonsi Nieto, SPA (*Suzuki*)	10	6.775s	22
6	Troy Corser, AUS (*Yamaha*)	11	7.403s	22
7	Carlos Checa, SPA (*Honda*)	7	7.578s	22
8	Gregorio Lavilla, SPA (*Honda*)	36	16.113s	22
9	Cal Crutchlow, GBR (*Honda*)	35	16.284s	22
10	Regis Laconi, FRA (*Kawasaki*)	55	16.446s	22
11	Ryuichi Kiyonari, JPN (*Honda*)	23	21.633s	22
12	Jakub Smrz, CZE (*Ducati*)	96	22.098s	22
13	Max Biaggi, ITA (*Ducati*)	3	24.089s	22
14	Noriyuki Haga, JPN (*Yamaha*)	41	24.117s	22
15	Jonathan Rea, GBR (*Honda*)	65	31.003s	22
16	Ayrton Badovini, ITA (*Kawasaki*)	86	31.136s	22
17	Shinichi Nakatomi, JPN (*Yamaha*)	38	31.330s	22
18	Roberto Rolfo, ITA (*Honda*)	44	32.272s	22
19	Chris Walker, GBR (*Honda*)	9	34.049s	22
20	Sébastien Gimbert, FRA (*Yamaha*)	194	35.028s	22
21	Karl Muggeridge, AUS (*Honda*)	31	41.669s	22
22	David Checa, SPA (*Yamaha*)	94	44.889s	22
23	Yukio Kagayama, JPN (*Suzuki*)	34	47.366s	22
24	Makoto Tamada, JPN (*Kawasaki*)	100	48.733s	22
25	Thomas Bridewell, GBR (*Suzuki*)	18	1m 07.702s	22
26	Shuhei Aoyama, JPN (*Honda*)	88	1m 14.242s	22
27	Luca Scassa, ITA (*Honda*)	99	1m 34.781s	22
28	Luis Carreira, POR (*Suzuki*)	14	1m 37.326s	22
29	Christian Zaiser, AUT (*Yamaha*)	73	1 lap	21

DNF: Vittorio Iannuzzo, ITA (*Kawasaki*) 13, 10 laps; Ruben Xaus, SPA (*Ducati*) 111, 9 laps.

Fastest lap: Bayliss, 1m 43.787s, 98.972mph/159.280km/h (record).

Superpole: Bayliss, 1m 58.548s, 86.648mph/139.447km/h.

Lap record: New circuit.

Final World Championship points: 244.

WORLD SUPERBIKE CHAMPIONSHIP
RESULTS 2008

Photograph: Gold & Goose

Position	Rider	Nationality	Machine	Losail/1	Losail/2	Phillip Island/1	Phillip Island/2	Valencia/1	Valencia/2	Assen/1	Assen/2	Monza/1	Monza/2	Miller/1	Miller/2	Nürburgring/1	Nürburgring/2	Misano/1	Misano/2	Brno/1	Brno/2	Brands Hatch/1	Brands Hatch/2	Donington/1	Donington/2	Vallelunga/1	Vallelunga/2	Magny-Cours/1	Magny-Cours/2	Portimao/1	Portimao/2	Points total
1	Troy Bayliss	AUS	Ducati	25	13	25	25	20	20	25	25	16	–	–	–	20	13	16	16	25	25	20	5	25	–	10	–	16	25	25	25	460
2	Troy Corser	AUS	Yamaha	16	9	20	–	16	11	11	6	4	8	20	–	13	20	20	11	20	13	8	16	–	16	16	16	10	16	16	10	342
3	Noriyuki Haga	JPN	Yamaha	2	3	8	9	–	25	–	20	20	25	–	10	25	25	6	13	10	9	–	20	–	–	25	25	25	20	–	2	327
4	Carlos Checa	SPA	Honda	10	5	10	20	11	16	20	16	8	–	25	25	11	11	11	8	8	–	10	8	–	7	11	11	9	13	20	9	313
5	Max Neukirchner	GER	Suzuki	11	8	9	11	–	–	16	11	25	20	13	20	16	16	25	9	9	11	9	13	–	2	13	13	11	7	–	13	311
6	Fonsi Nieto	SPA	Suzuki	9	25	11	16	13	6	–	5	9	13	11	8	8	7	4	6	2	8	11	11	9	–	4	10	20	8	11	11	256
7	Max Biaggi	ITA	Ducati	20	16	–	–	–	8	6	4	11	–	7	13	3	9	–	20	13	16	16	4	16	10	20	–	13	10	–	3	238
8	Michel Fabrizio	ITA	Ducati	7	11	16	–	–	3	–	–	7	11	16	16	9	10	–	5	16	20	4	10	–	11	9	20	–	2	–	20	223
9	Ryuichi Kiyonari	JPN	Honda	–	–	7	10	–	13	9	–	10	16	6	9	4	5	2	3	11	10	25	25	–	25	–	3	–	–	8	5	206
10	Ruben Xaus	SPA	Ducati	13	20	13	13	–	9	–	13	–	9	2	–	10	8	13	25	–	–	–	–	–	8	–	4	–	11	7	–	178
11	Yukio Kagayama	JPN	Suzuki	8	–	–	–	–	10	13	10	13	–	8	11	–	–	5	4	7	7	13	–	11	–	7	9	8	9	1	–	154
12	Gregorio Lavilla	SPA	Honda	3	2	5	8	9	5	7	9	5	6	3	1	–	2	8	2	1	2	2	3	13	9	2	–	6	4	10	8	135
13	Jakub Smrz	CZE	Ducati	6	7	–	–	2	2	10	8	6	–	10	–	5	–	9	7	–	5	7	7	10	4	3	5	–	3	–	4	120
14	Lorenzo Lanzi	ITA	Ducati	–	10	3	–	25	4	–	–	2	5	5	6	–	10	10	–	3	5	6	–	5	5	–	5	–	–	–	–	109
15	Karl Muggeridge	AUS	Honda	–	–	4	6	10	–	2	3	–	10	9	5	6	4	–	–	5	–	–	–	7	–	–	–	4	–	2	–	77
16	Regis Laconi	FRA	Kawasaki	1	–	–	–	8	7	5	–	–	–	–	7	2	6	–	–	–	–	–	–	1	–	7	5	–	–	6	6	61
17	Roberto Rolfo	ITA	Honda	5	1	6	–	6	–	–	2	–	–	–	–	–	–	–	–	4	6	2	–	3	8	6	–	6	4	–	–	59
18	Kenan Sofuoglu	TUR	Honda	4	6	2	5	4	1	4	–	–	–	4	2	–	–	–	–	6	6	3	–	–	–	–	–	7	–	–	–	54
19	Shinichi Nakatomi	JPN	Yamaha	–	–	1	1	5	–	1	1	3	4	–	–	–	–	7	1	4	1	–	–	3	–	6	8	2	–	3	–	51
20	Makoto Tamada	JPN	Kawasaki	–	4	–	2	7	–	8	7	–	–	–	3	7	3	–	–	–	–	–	–	–	–	–	–	–	–	–	–	41
21	Tom Sykes	GBR	Suzuki	–	–	–	–	–	–	–	–	–	–	–	–	–	–	–	–	–	–	–	–	9	20	6	–	–	–	–	–	35
22	Leon Haslam	GBR	Honda	–	–	–	–	–	–	–	–	–	–	–	–	–	–	–	–	–	–	–	–	8	–	–	–	–	–	9	16	33
23	Cal Crutchlow	GBR	Honda	–	–	–	–	–	–	–	–	–	–	–	–	–	–	–	–	–	–	–	–	–	20	–	–	–	–	–	7	27
24	Ayrton Badovini	ITA	Kawasaki	–	–	–	–	–	–	3	–	7	–	4	–	–	–	–	–	–	–	–	–	4	–	1	–	–	–	5	–	24
25	James Ellison	GBR	Honda	–	–	–	–	–	–	–	–	–	–	–	–	–	–	–	–	–	–	–	–	6	13	–	–	–	–	–	–	19
26	Jonathan Rea	GBR	Honda	–	–	–	–	–	–	–	–	–	–	–	–	–	–	–	–	–	–	–	–	–	–	–	–	–	–	13	1	14
27	Russell Holland	AUS	Honda	–	–	–	7	3	–	–	–	3	1	–	–	–	–	–	–	–	–	–	–	–	–	–	–	–	–	–	–	14
28	David Checa	SPA	Yamaha	–	–	–	4	1	–	–	–	–	–	–	–	1	1	–	–	–	–	–	–	5	–	–	–	–	–	–	–	12
29	Sébastien Gimbert	FRA	Yamaha	–	–	–	3	–	–	–	–	1	2	–	–	1	–	–	–	–	–	–	–	–	–	–	–	2	3	–	–	12
30	Shuhei Aoyama	JPN	Honda	–	–	–	–	–	–	–	–	–	–	–	–	–	–	3	–	–	–	–	–	–	–	2	–	–	–	–	–	5
31	Chris Walker	GBR	Honda	–	–	–	–	–	–	–	–	–	–	–	–	–	–	–	–	–	–	–	–	1	1	–	–	1	1	1	–	5
32	Niccolò Canepa	ITA	Ducati	–	–	–	–	–	–	–	–	–	–	–	–	–	–	–	3	–	–	–	–	–	–	–	–	–	–	–	–	3
33	Michael Beck	USA	Yamaha	–	–	–	–	–	–	–	–	–	1	–	–	–	–	–	–	–	–	–	–	–	–	–	–	–	–	–	–	1

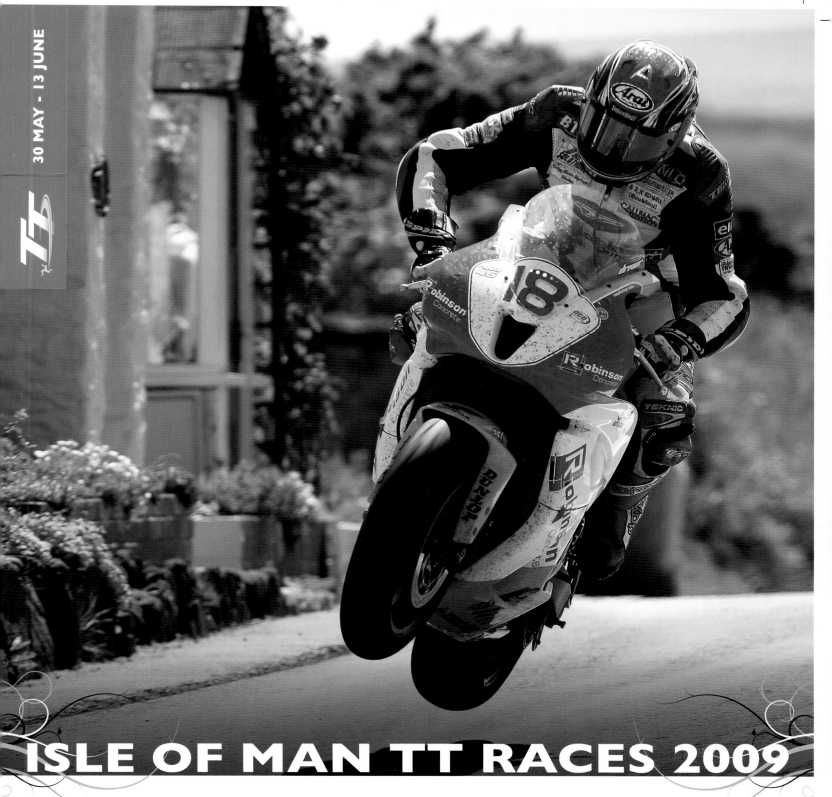

30 MAY - 13 JUNE

TT

ISLE OF MAN TT RACES 2009

INFORMATION HOTLINE: +44 (0)1624 686815

Murray Walker OBE calls it the greatest motor-sporting event in the world. And with MCN describing TT2008 as the 'Best Ever', there's no better time to witness the unique and truly spectacular Isle of Man TT Races.

TT2009 boasts a new-look festival, a spectacular nine-race programme and the greatest line up of talent ever to be assembled on the Island.

Create and book your own TT experience by logging on to www.visitisleofman.com.
For more race and festival information, visit www.iomtt.com or email iomtt@gov.im.

ISLE OF MAN TT RACES
RACY ISLAND
by MARK FORSYTH

THE 2008 TT got off to a mixed start on a number of fronts. Perhaps most noticeable was the lack of any official Honda participation. The TT had been an integral part of Honda's marketing activities since the days of scratchy 'Sounds of the TT' LPs and black-and-white newsreel footage, but 2008 was the first TT in many people's memory where the Red Wing was noticeably absent. The reason wasn't just budgetary, as most suspected. 'There were a number of things we really weren't happy with in terms of organisational issues at the 2007 TT,' said Honda racing supremo Neil Tuxworth. 'Without dwelling on those points, it's safe to say that in 2008 we saw those issues addressed and the level of organisation improve to the point where we can commit to the event again in 2009.' Coincidentally, 2009 is Honda's 50th anniversary of not only TT racing, but also international racing. Expect some kind of fanfare.

The weather was a prominent factor, too. During practice week, it was of a type and severity usually reserved for January rather than late May and early June. Driving rain, cold gale-force winds and blankets of all-obscuring sea mist played havoc with the precious time slots allocated for the week's practice sessions.

Then there was James McBride's enormous accident at the fearsomely fast Gorse Lea section, which hindered the first closed-roads practice session. Fortunately, McBride suffered 'only' a broken arm and a few broken ribs in the accident, which onlookers described as looking like the aftermath of a plane crash. The general consensus was that he had been very lucky to get away so lightly after high-siding at such a fast and unforgiving, fifth-gear, wall-lined corner.

It took until the Thursday of practice week for the sun to shine through, and the evening practice session saw near-perfect conditions bar a few damp patches under the trees. Most riders took the opportunity to wheel out their Superbikes, desperate for much needed shake-down time.

Guy Martin signalled his intent by topping the Superbike time sheets at 127.0mph, while Bruce Anstey led the Supersport at 122.65mph, and Ryan Farquhar the Superstock at an impressive 126.65mph. Farquhar's 2008 ZX-10 was the only Kawasaki anywhere on the time sheets and was an unfamiliar mount for the Irish roads specialist, who had split from the McAdoo team just a few days before the start of the event.

The dry Thursday-evening practice session also allowed the F2 sidecar competitors a decent run out, in marked contrast to the dreadful, river-like conditions they had endured on Tuesday evening. In the 55-minute session, it was Dave Molyneux and Dan Sayle on their brand-new, Suzuki-powered DMR outfit who decimated the opposition with a second-lap average of 115.06mph, a clear 3mph faster than second-placed Nick Crowe and Mark Cox.

With the clock ticking to the start of race week and with most riders desperately short of crucial testing time, thankfully Friday's final session was dry and warm. Several riders were coping with stability issues, notably John McGuinness and Steve Plater, and the near-perfect conditions enabled them to test alterations to the limit.

Under a low sun and in warm summer air teeming with visor-splattering insects, Lincolnshire's Guy Martin blasted his Hydrex Bike Animal Honda to a 127.19mph opening lap from a standing start, but McGuinness bettered that instantly on his Padgett's Honda at 127.38mph. Hutchinson, Cummins, Anstey and Lougher were also within shouting distance of the top two. By the end of the second lap, McGuiness was fastest at 128.61mph, while Cameron Donald was just a fraction behind him at 128.44mph. Anstey and Martin rounded out the top four.

McGuinness jumped on his Superstock bike in the same session and, despite only having done one lap on it prior to the Friday session, he put in three 125+ laps to end up quickest at 126.65mph. The impressive Cameron Donald and evergreen Bruce Anstey also showed their Superstock credentials by running very similar times to McGuinness.

The sidecars painted a less clear picture. Despite near-perfect conditions, several of the top runners chose the final practice session to bed in new motors ready for the first race. But while Nick Crowe and passenger Mark Cox recorded the fastest three-wheeled lap of the week at 115.53mph, the paddock buzz concerned the fifth quickest sidecar team, newcomers Tim Reeves and Pat Farrance, who cracked the 110mph barrier with barely a handful of closed-circuit laps to their names – an awesome achievement.

Opposite: Senior TT winner McGuinness (Honda) equalled Mike Hailwood's TT record.

Below: Steve Plater was promoted to victory in the Supersport race.
Photographs: Dave Collister

SUPERBIKE TT

If you had studied the form book post-practice, Saturday's Superbike thriller could have gone any way between four, five or six riders. McGuinness, never to be discounted at the Isle of Man, may have lacked his usual full factory support from Honda, but it was clear from his limited practice time that Clive Padgett and crew had built him a fairly well-sorted Superbike capable of running race winning times.

Then there was the fearsome Antipodean pairing of Aussie Cameron Donald and Kiwi Bruce Anstey. While Anstey can rightfully claim to be something of an Island veteran, Donald, on just his third visit, looked stunningly fast and worryingly brave on Phillip and Hector Neil's Relentless by TAS Suzuki.

Lincolnshire's Guy Martin was also on a mission. He'd long been displaying TT pace and consistency, but the podium's top step still eluded him. With some beautifully prepared Hydrex Bike Animal Hondas at his disposal, however, 2008 looked like his best chance yet.

In addition, Adrian Archibald was squeezing the best out of his GSX-R1000 Suzuki, while Ian Hutchinson and Steve Plater were giving 100 per cent on their AIM Yamaha R1s.

Whatever the final outcome, it was obvious that the race would be run at a blistering pace, with the whole island bathed in warm sunshine and the course in near-perfect condition.

Confusion was rife at the start of the six-lap Dainese Superbike race. Guy Martin, for reasons known only to

himself, missed his start slot by nine seconds, which had an unfortunate domino effect on subsequent starting positions. Eventually, it sorted itself out, but the confusion – and shouting – gifted the early lead to AIM Yamaha's Ian Hutchinson, who led on time at Glen Helen. Clearly fired up by the initial mayhem, however, Martin got into his stride and took the lead with a blistering 129mph first lap. McGuinness was four seconds back, with Donald, Anstey, Hutchinson and Farquhar snapping at his heels.

The real drama started to unfold on the second lap, when McGuinness coasted into Glen Helen with an engine misfire. He got started again, but stopped for good – and perhaps for a pint – at the Sulby Hotel when the crank ignition sensor gave up.

With McGuinness out of the reckoning, the pressure was off Martin. His second lap – another at 129mph and the fastest of the race – indicated that all was well. On lap four, however, with a comfortable and controlled lead, his Honda FireBlade also ground to a halt at Sulby. It wasn't just a Honda thing: Hutchinson's Yamaha expired at Union Mills, as did Connor Cummins's R1 at Keppel Gate.

But nothing stopped the two Temple Auto Salvage Suzukis of Donald and Anstey. The former inherited the lead on lap four and set about stretching his advantage over his team-mate to the flag. Donald, the first Australian to win a TT since Graeme McGregor in 1984, won by just over ten seconds from Anstey, with Adrian Archibald nabbing third to make it an all-Suzuki podium.

SIDECARS RACE ONE

It took just a few hundred yards for the TT of race favourite Dave Molyneux to come to a grinding halt when his Suzuki-powered outfit suffered mechanical failure. After leading away from the start, Molyneux and passenger Dan Sayle retired just seconds later, at the end of the Grandstand start/finish straight.

The first lap saw a battle between initial leaders John Holden and Andrew Winkle, and Nick Crowe and Mark Cox. Eventually, Manxman Crowe overhauled Holden and continued applying the pressure to build up his lead to an emphatic 19 seconds by the flag. It was Crowe's fourth TT victory.

Holden and Winkle took a comfortable second place

Behind the battle for the lead, it was close quarters between the outfits of Phil Dongworth and Stuart Castles, and World Champion newcomers Tim Reeves and Patrick Farrance. At the finish, it was Reeves and Farrance who took the podium's final step – an extraordinary feat considering that neither of them had ever been to the Isle of Man before, never mind raced there.

SUPERSTOCK RACE

For a man who had broken his back at the TT just two years before, 30-year-old Cameron Donald showed immense grit on the first lap of the four-lap Superstock race, when he hauled in early leader John McGuinness as they charged through the thick Snaefell mist. As a reward for this blind bravery, Donald led at the end of the first lap by 1.76 seconds. Less than six seconds covered

Left: Cameron Donald (Suzuki) became the first Australian TT winner in more than 40 years in the Superbike race.

Right: Keeping close company – Hutchinson, Donald and Farquhar in the second Supersport race.

Photographs: Dave Collister

Below: Barely skimming the surface, winner Crowe passes the 11th milestone in the first sidecar race.

Bottom: Kiwi Bruce Anstey won both Supersport races, but was excluded from the first one.

Photographs: Gavan Caldwell

the leading five of Donald, McGuinness, Farquhar, Cummins and Martin.

In normal circumstances, Donald's team-mate, Bruce Anstey, would have been a man on whom to place a fairly safe wager. But Anstey was stricken with a bout of flu and had to pull out of the race when he found it difficult to summon the strength even to hold on to the production 1000cc machine.

Donald continued to bang in blistering laps to extend his lead over McGuinness to 17 seconds, but relaxed his pace on the last lap, taking the win with a 15-second cushion. Martin, chasing hard in third, clawed the gap on McGuinness down to 2.7 seconds by the flag.

Ryan Farquar, riding the unfamiliar Harker Kawasaki ZX-10, finished an impressive fourth. The next best Kawasaki, in case you ask, was in 22nd place.

SUPERSPORT 600 – Race One

'I was actually thinking about not going out. I thought I would save my strength until Wednesday, but I thought I've got the fastest bike and might as well use it.' The final part of that quote from Bruce Anstey, uttered just moments after 'winning' the Supersport race by 21 seconds, is poignant. Later it was discovered that his TAS Suzuki was fitted with exhaust camshafts that didn't adhere to the rules. With the benefit of hindsight, paddock cynics took great delight in Anstey's self-declared admission of having the fastest bike out there. His new lap record of 125.372mph, along with his result, was wiped from the history books.

The team claimed that it had been a genuine mistake, and the organisers seemed satisfied with the explanation, but for Anstey, who'd ridden through illness to win in such a dominating fashion, it must have been heartbreaking news.

Anstey's exclusion from the results promoted a previously happy second-placed Steve Plater to a positively ecstatic first. 'I'm going to have to go for a walk to let it sink in,' he said, wearing his trademark perma-smile.

Supersport proved to be as hard on machinery as any other class. Ian Hutchinson, winner in 2007, retired after suffering mechanical problems, as did Guy Martin and Connor Cummins.

McGuinness finished third – promoted to second – with no steering damper after a seal popped, covering him and his visor in oil. Anyone who's ridden a fast, closed-roads lap of the TT circuit will completely understand just how crucial a steering damper is to a rider's well-being. McGuinness, struggling with stability, was unable to fend off a charging Plater, but he still had enough control to narrowly beat an on-form Keth Amor to the line.

SUPERSPORT 600 – Race Two

Bruce Anstey bounced back from the disappointment of Monday's exclusion to take a hard-fought win in Wednesday's second Supersport race. He rebuffed the first-lap attentions of AIM Yamaha's Ian Hutchinson and managed to record a new lap record of 125.359mph in the process.

Anstey went on to win by a decisive 34 seconds over Hutchinson to prove that the previous infringement really made little difference to his Suzuki-powered dominance. It was his seventh TT win.

Monday's Supersport winner, Steve Plater, suffered mechanical woes, as did McGuinness and Cameron Donald. Ryan Farquhar finished an excellent third after fending off Ian Lougher and Gary Johnson. Guy Martin was sixth.

SIDECARS RACE TWO

Conditions were dry for the afternoon's race, but the waiting sidecar teams were warned of strong gusting winds at exposed areas of the mountain.

Crowe and Cox charged from the start, grabbing the lead at Glen Helen on the opening lap. They'd made up enough ground on rivals Molyneux and Sayle to be within sight of the earlier-starting pair. As they crossed the line to start their second lap, if Molyneux had had wing mirrors, they would have been full of Crowe's outfit. On the road, Crowe was just a second behind, putting him nine seconds in the lead on corrected time. Holden was comfortable in third, while Klaffenbock and Norbury were engaged in a private duel for fourth. Dongworth was in sixth place, Tim Reeves and Patrick Farrance flying in seventh.

After miles of wheel-to-wheel action, Crowe passed Molyneux on the second lap to take the lead on the road. Although Molyneux made several more challenges, Crowe led across the line to win by 10.5 seconds.

Holden finished 34 seconds behind Molyneux, in third. The battle for fourth went right down to the wire, and it was Norbury and Long who fended off Klaffenbock and Parzer by just 0.89 second.

Reeves and Farrance lapped at 112mph to finish in sixth place.

SENIOR RACE

As first laps go, even the shortest short circuit would have struggled to replicate the opening lap of Friday's Senior. At Glen Helen, McGuinness led by 0.04 second from Hutchinson, with Anstey 0.64 second back in third, Donald 0.86 second behind Anstey, and Guy Martin just

0.54 second behind the Australian – 2.86 seconds split the top six.

By Ramsey, McGuinness was still in the lead; Anstey was up to second, just 0.15 second behind, with Hutchinson dropping to fifth, behind Donald and Martin, who were still only a second apart. Anstey was quickest, with an opening lap of 128.631mph, now leading McGuinness by 0.46 second. Donald and Martin also remained in the frame.

Anstey got his head down on the second lap and began to edge clear. His lap of 129.445mph saw him move almost two seconds clear as they came to the pit stop, but transmission problems left the hard-charging Kiwi stranded in the pit lane. Fourth-placed Martin's bike refused to fire, spluttered into life and finally spluttered out of life at Quarter Bridge. Hutchinson was still fifth, Farquhar sixth and Gary Johnson seventh.

With Anstey and Martin out, McGuinness and Donald began battling for the lead. Donald led by less than half a second on lap four. Hutchinson was secure in third, Farquhar safe in fourth.

Donald had eked a five-second advantage by the last lap, but McGuinness had clawed 14 seconds back to lead Donald by nine seconds at Glen Helen. The latter's bike had sprung an oil leak, and his chances were over as he nursed the machine home.

With the fastest lap of the race, 129.517mph, on his final 37¾ miles, McGuinness crossed the line to become the joint second most successful rider in TT history. And when you're sharing a joint with none other than Mike Hailwood, all of a sudden the title becomes very special. 'That took ages to sink in, I still don't think it has,' said McGuinness. 'It felt a bit like I'd been racing a ghost or something. My Dad was always going on about Hailwood when I was growing up, so for me to equal his record does feel very strange.'

Donald finished a distant second, Hutchinson third. Farquhar, who had been without a ride just a few days before practice started and who had ended up riding his Superstock-spec ZX-10, capped his brilliant week in fourth, ensuring top-six finishes in all five of his races.

ULTRA-LIGHTWEIGHT AND LIGHTWEIGHT TT

The hardened race fan bemoans the lack of two-stroke race machinery, and as an antidote to the in-line four-cylinder domination of the TT race classes, the organisers offered a two-stroke fix at the Billown circuit near Castletown on the Saturday after the Senior race.

After qualifying for the two 12-lap races, Carlisle born, but Castletown resident Chris Palmer grabbed pole position in the Ultra-lightweight TT, while Michael Dunlop took pole for the Lightweight race.

From the start of the 125 event, Chris Palmer emphatically stamped his mark on the race. He developed an unassailable advantage with a three-second gap on Ian Lougher at the end of the first lap. Manxman Dan Sayle, the renowned sidecar passenger, placed third.

At half-distance, Palmer had gapped Lougher to the tune of 15.8 seconds, but on lap ten the latter coasted to a halt with a broken final-drive chain. Lougher's retirement let Sayle through to second and promoted Nigel Moore to third.

Palmer took the chequered flag by 34.4 seconds from Sayle, thus claiming his third consecutive 125cc TT victory, having won the previous two held on the Mountain Course.

In the 250 race, William Dunlop was joined on the front row of the grid by Lougher and Palmer.

The 12-lap race turned into a classic ding-dong, with Palmer, Dunlop, Lougher and Ryan Farquhar all taking the lead during the first six circuits.

Once Lougher was in the lead, however, he managed to open a gap to take victory by 8.65 seconds from Farquhar and Palmer. On his way to this, his eighth TT win, Lougher also set a new lap record at an average speed of 102.321mph.

Dunlop, who had been at the centre of the early battle for the lead, was forced to retire on lap ten with machine problems.

The final race of the busy Steam Packet meeting schedule was the combined 600cc and 1000cc event. At the end of nine laps, it was Farquhar who took a fine victory on the Harker Kawasaki. He was 18 seconds ahead of second-placed Lougher, with Mark Buckley third. Roy Richardson took the 600cc honours.

BYRNE'S MIGHT

by OLLIE BARSTOW

THERE was a distinct sense of apprehension and excitement as the 2008 Bennetts British Superbike Championship approached. On the one hand, the series was reeling from the mass exodus of its 'halo' riders – five of the top ten in 2007 had left to seek fame and fortune on the more lucrative world stage. Nevertheless, the intrigue of control tyres, the arrival of the eagerly anticipated 1098 Ducati and a bevy of talent promised plenty of thrills.

Ryuichi Kiyonari, Jonathan Rea, Gregorio Lavilla, Tommy Hill and Chris Walker were all bound for either World Superbike or Supersport in 2008. That left a chasm of high-profile rides to be filled before another season rolled around in April.

Worried observers needn't have been concerned. What the 2008 championship lacked in international flavour, it made up for with tantalising home-grown stars, such as proven winners Shane Byrne and Leon Haslam, together with young guns Cal Crutchlow, Tom Sykes and Leon Camier, among others. All of them did their bit to ensure that BSB remained the most respected and prestigious domestic Superbike championship in the world.

Minus Kiyonari and Rea, reigning champion HM Plant Honda's line-up was all new, led by seasoned competitor Haslam with ex-Rizla Suzuki rider Crutchlow.

Haslam had been lured to Honda from Airwaves Ducati, whose mere participation in 2008 had been in doubt following a dispute over whether the team could run 'special' racing pistons in the new 1098R Ducati. Eventually, it relented by fitting standard pistons and thus confirmed its place on the grid.

After losing Haslam to its key rival, as well as Lavilla to the bright lights of World Superbikes, Airwaves Ducati (formerly GSE Racing) gambled on a combination of youth and experience in the quest for a fourth title. After several seasons spent drifting from team to team, Byrne had probably his best shot since winning in 2003 when he was called upon to bring superior knowledge and charisma to Colin Wright's respected team. Camier, meanwhile, was last seen nursing a horrific leg injury following an accident at Cadwell Park. At 21, he was the antithesis of Byrne in terms of experience, but not in terms of speed.

Elsewhere, former champion Rizla Suzuki also revealed a completely new line-up: Tom Sykes switched

from the privateer Stobart Honda team and was joined by Japanese Superbike Champion Atsushi Watanabe.

Other notable riders included James Ellison aboard the Hydrex Bike Animal Honda, back from America, and the hugely experienced Michael Rutter, who joined the newly formed North West Ducati outfit. Meanwhile, Supersport Champion Michael Laverty graduated with the Relentless Suzuki team, Karl Harris rode the sole Rob Mac Racing Yamaha, and MSS Discovery Kawasaki had Stuart Easton and Billy McConnell on board.

All things considered, with its broad mix of youthful exuberance, wise heads and spectacular showmanship, by season's end, the 2008 BSB championship had silenced the cynics.

Even so, the new season did not get off to an auspicious start. There is a reason why motorsport doesn't occur in the northern hemisphere in winter, but few could have predicted that Mother Nature would conspire so dramatically against the BSB season opener at Brands Hatch, where storms arrived to coat the circuit in a thick carpet of snow.

Beautiful as it was, snowball fighting was the only competition that could safely take place, so racing was cancelled and the event postponed.

Qualifying had already set the tone for the season, with Byrne dictating the initial pace at his home circuit. He carried that on to the new first round, at Thruxton.

Byrne didn't lead the first race of the season from pole position – tardy starts would be a fixture throughout his season, leading to some memorable fight-backs – but his ability to maintain a consistently strong pace on the Ducati meant that rivals were easy prey for his gargling twin. So, despite early leader Crutchlow's attempts to scuttle away, victory went to Byrne, a phrase that would be repeated all too often over the season.

Crutchlow struck back in race two for a maiden BSB win. The Honda evaded Byrne's charge in the latter stages, after making the most of him being held up earlier in the race. This whetted the appetite of those fans spooked by Byrne and Ducati's ominously strong form.

While Byrne and Crutchlow celebrated up front, there were commiserations for two riders further down the field. Adam Jenkinson had been enjoying a stellar first meeting on the sole SMT Honda, but a high-speed fall at Church in the very first race ruled him out for the remainder of the season.

The experienced Harris, meanwhile, endured what is increasingly referred to as a 'YouTube moment' when he was 'clothes-lined' off his Yamaha by a Rizla Suzuki, sans rider Sykes, at Cobb. No fault of his own, the accident would set the tone for Harris's bruising season.

A trip up north to Oulton Park provided further evidence that Byrne was the man to beat, as he added two more victories. As much as his rivals and even his own lively Ducati tried to keep him in check, his two wins gave anoraks a chance to flex their BSB know-how by pointing out that the last time he had scored a double win at the Cheshire circuit, in 2003, he had gone on to win the title.

Undoubtedly, his cause was aided by others, though. Pre-season favourite Haslam ran him close in the first

race, but undid all of his hard work in the second when he was disqualified for barging Sykes off the circuit in a fumbled manoeuvre. Crutchlow and Harris, meanwhile, joined – in Harris's case, rejoined – the list of walking wounded. The former had dislocated his ankle in a smash, while falls for the latter had revealed that he wasn't quite over his Thruxton KO.

With the main protagonists punished, victimised or crocked, up stepped Byrne's team-mate, Camier, who grabbed a pair of podiums, while Ellison showed that he was settling back into the BSB way of things with second place in race two.

Round three – or 1A as it was dubbed – saw the BSB circus back at Brands Hatch to complete what it had started a month earlier. Certainly there was unfinished business for Byrne, who converted his month-old pole position into a fourth win, following that up with second in race two.

For the Ducati rider, this meant six races, four wins and two seconds. He led the championship after the first quarter of the season, but Crutchlow was still in the running as the rider to deny him a full set. He showed his mettle again with victory in race two, despite being

lumbered with an injured ankle that he had spent much of the weekend resting in ice.

The race indicated how the season would develop as Crutchlow, Byrne, Sykes, Camier and Haslam disputed the top five positions around the ever-popular grand prix configuration of Brands Hatch.

Ultimately, the tussle came to a premature end when Sykes's Suzuki expired in spectacular fashion at possibly the worst position on the circuit, at the bottom of Hawthorn Straight. Riding the Suzuki, now on its side, backwards as it skated through the gravel trap, Sykes was unharmed, but the deluge of oil on the circuit prompted red flags.

That allowed Crutchlow to get the better of Byrne, who would have fancied his chances no doubt with only a couple of laps remaining. Camier, Michael Laverty – his third top five in six races – and Haslam followed.

Of the quintet, Haslam was probably the most out of position. His move to HM Plant should have been a match made in heaven. The team had taken the championship twice with Kiyonari, while Haslam had had his fair share of moments as the 'bridesmaid' over the years, leaving him hungry for the title. So far, the successful switch to four-cylinder machinery from the Ducati twin was taking time, but rounds seven and eight at Donington Park revealed that he was beginning to find his feet, the 'Pocket Rocket' almost winning race two at the Leicestershire circuit.

It was Byrne, though, who emerged triumphant with another double victory. Furthermore, he did it on both occasions by fighting his way back up the order after slightly pedestrian getaways.

Ellison and Crutchlow provided Byrne's sternest challenge in race one as they disputed the lead, but neither had the longevity to sustain their initial pace, allowing Byrne to score another comfortable win, ahead of Haslam and Sykes, the latter up from 13th on the grid.

It was similar in race two, Haslam getting away well to lead for almost the whole race, only for Byrne to launch a late fight back and snatch it off him with just a handful of laps remaining.

Unsurprisingly, Byrne's dominance, particularly his ability to maintain a strong pace to the chequered flag, warranted debate. Indeed, with its 1200cc, compared to its rivals' 1000cc, the 1098R was brought further into line with the four-cylinder machines through the use of standard road parts, thus losing its historic tuning advantage. GSE Racing had been concerned initially, but its fears had proved unfounded. The flipside, though, was that rivals felt that the 1098R was too dominant and had to push their own machines to the limit in a bid to compete.

The result? A 10kg minimum weight increase for the Ducati. Even though the 1098R had been running above its weight allowance for much of the year anyway, the move still stoked up controversy, and revived fears of a walk-out owing to a lack of testing time with a heavier bike.

After a compromise of a 5kg increase was agreed at Donington Park, it was Snetterton that provided the ultimate acid test for the now heavier Airwaves bikes, as well as those of North West. Not that there was any noticeable difference.

Indeed, both Byrne and Camier responded in the most comprehensive way possible with a 1-2 finish in both races. For Camier, Snetterton marked a turning point in his career as he romped to his maiden Superbike victory, fending off a last-lap attack from Byrne in the process.

It was Byrne's race-two win that had rivals scratching their heads. He had come back from a first-lap position

of 13th to score a comfortable win. In damp weather conditions, his reaction skills had been tested on the opening lap when Harris had high-sided and landed directly in front, prompting Byrne to touch down while navigating past the stricken Yamaha rider. But he had quickly put his head down, passing rivals two at a time on occasion to catch and pass Camier in the final lap. It was win number seven, and it continued his 100-per-cent podium record.

While Ducati dominated up front, Honda and Suzuki disputed the 'best of the rest' role. Crutchlow continued to lead the way, although he had to share podium spoils with Sykes at Snetterton, while Haslam, Rutter and Laverty were all in contention too.

By contrast, Yamaha was having a tough time, with Harris's injury-riddled season turning up just 26 points in the first ten races. Instead, Andrews was its leading contender, the Jentin Racing rider putting in his best performance of the season so far at Snetterton with two top-ten finishes.

Kawasaki's season, however, was about to take a turn for the worse when Easton, who had been pumping in some competitive results so far, was forced to withdraw from the next four rounds with a wrist injury sustained at Snetterton. Not one of the Team Green contenders would match his best result of fifth from Oulton Park.

The ever popular Mallory Park provided one of the more entertaining rounds of the season, not least because it began to signal a slight shift away from the

Above: Tom Sykes leads Haslam before their clash at Oulton Park.

Top left: Former MotoGP rider James Ellison regained a foothold in BSB.

Centre left: Carl Harris rode the sole Rob Mac Yamaha, suffering a bruising season.

Bottom left: Veteran Michael Rutter scored his only win at Oulton Park.

Photographs: Clive Challinor Motorsport Photography

Ducati dominance. Although Ducatis won both races, courtesy of Byrne and Rutter, their rivals were stronger, with Sykes and Laverty making it a 1-2 for Suzuki in qualifying, while both Haslam and Crutchlow led the first race before succumbing to Byrne's late surge.

Race two had as much to do with wisdom in greasy conditions as anything, and no one is more experienced than Rutter, who would notch up his 300th race start during the season. Mallory Park was his finest moment, though, leading early on with slick tyres on a surface that even his wet-shod rivals could barely handle. Byrne kept up his momentum in second, followed by Crutchlow and Sykes, but undoubtedly Rutter provided the story of the day.

Despite the groans of inevitability from Byrne's eighth win in 12 races, he wouldn't take another victory for four more months, as the following rounds at Oulton Park and beyond saw his closest rivals begin to gather some momentum.

Leading the way was Sykes, who broke his BSB duck in comprehensive manner around the Cheshire circuit. Showing off his attacking style by wresting the lead from Ellison in the first race, he followed it up with a faultless defensive ride in the second.

Byrne, meanwhile, experienced his toughest round of the season – if you consider a pair of thirds 'tough' – clashing with Harris in race one to send the Yamaha rider tumbling to the ground once more, then being unable to find his way past a train of bikes in race two. Ellison and Crutchlow shared second place between Sykes and Byrne.

A trip north of the border beckoned for BSB's annual visit to Knockhill, for a race that would witness something that hadn't been seen so far in 2008 – a DNF for Byrne. It was a bruising one too, the Ducati rider crashing heavily into the barriers from the lead when he struck a patch of oil. He was unhurt, and it would turn out to be the only blemish on an otherwise clean sheet.

Before that, Byrne had followed Sykes home, the latter claiming a third consecutive victory after an entertaining dice with Rutter in the early stages. Suddenly emerging as Byrne's equal in terms of speed, Sykes produced a run of results that ultimately would massage his route to World Superbikes in 2009.

Beyond Byrne's cooler form and Sykes's success, Knockhill was also important for Haslam's first Honda race win, albeit inherited after Byrne's fall. It was the impetus he needed, though, and he would go on to win four of the next six races.

Haslam started with a double at the fearsome Cadwell Park, HM Plant's home circuit. He prevailed over Sykes in both races, suddenly transforming what had threatened to be an anonymous season into something rather more noteworthy. If the title was a foregone conclusion, the Haslam-Sykes-Crutchlow battle for second kept up the interest.

Interest was also maintained by the unveiling of a new qualifying system adopted from Cadwell Park onwards. Mirroring the 'knock-out' system used in Formula One, it served to provide Saturday with almost as much excitement as Sunday, and it was roundly praised by riders, teams and fans alike.

While another pair of podiums at Cadwell didn't exactly match Byrne's own high standards, it did offer a first 'match point' heading to Croft. Still, he'd have been forgiven for skipping a heartbeat during free practice, when he high-sided at the quick chicane and hurt his shoulder, as well as knocking out a tooth.

Delayed rather than distracted, he recorded a fourth and third, and while not enough to seal the inevitable, it meant that he was on the cusp heading to the penultimate round at Silverstone.

Croft did see one champion crowned, though, as John Laverty sealed the Superbike Cup title four races in advance. Regularly mixing it with rivals on more accomplished machinery, Laverty was easily one of the year's stand-outs.

Croft honours, however, went the way of Byrne's team-mate, Camier, who recovered from what had been a recent quiet run to secure a second career victory. Haslam also enjoyed a stint at the top of the podium as he continued to put pressure on Sykes for second in the points standings.

Byrne needed merely to coast home to a top-ten finish, but needn't have worried, as it was Sykes's turn to misjudge a move on Haslam, which took them both out of the equation. Third place was more than enough for Byrne to be crowned champion once again. The race itself was won by Camier, who had stalked and passed Crutchlow for a third victory.

Having been taken down unceremoniously in the first race, Haslam bounced back for a win in the second. He was followed by a now more relaxed Byrne, while Sykes made amends with third place from the fourth row of the grid, forced upon him as punishment for his earlier indiscretion.

So, after 11 rounds and 22 races, the final round took the championship back to Brands Hatch, with Byrne aiming to go out on a high at his local circuit. After a long drought, a double triumph was a fitting end to a superb year.

It was done in style too, Byrne prevailing in a last-lap tussle with Haslam not only to consolidate his status as

the best British rider of 2008, but also to bid farewell to the series.

In contrast to Byrne, it was hard to recall Haslam's tough start to the year as he cemented the runner-up spot with a tenth podium of the season at Brands Hatch, while Crutchlow actually managed to pop up ahead of Sykes for third in the standings with a strong final round. Sykes, meanwhile, was hurt by a mechanical failure just a few laps from the end of the season, ending his time in BSB on a slightly sour note.

Beyond the 'big five', a series of consistent results consolidated Rutter's status as one of Britain's foremost racers, while former MotoGP rider Ellison revived his reputation with an excellent run to seventh overall. Andrews remained the top Yamaha racer after finishing all but two races inside the top ten, a run that gave him the edge on Laverty, whose form faded in the closing stages, although there was a hint of his potential as a future star. Meanwhile, Tristan Palmer's consistency rewarded him with an overall top ten, ahead of a disappointed Harris.

With the end of the season, however, BSB fans found themselves in an arguably bigger predicament to that of 2007, as the top four riders – Byrne, Haslam, Crutchlow and Sykes – all prepared to go 'global' in 2009.

Byrne had extended his relationship with Ducati by joining GMB Sterilgarda, Haslam was set to return to the fray with Stiggy Honda, Crutchlow had signed to lead Yamaha's Supersport charge, while Sykes had won a plum Yamaha Superbike seat.

Nonetheless, despite fevered speculation around

mid-season, top teams HM Plant and GSE will stay in BSB, the latter even announcing an end to its long-term partnership with Ducati in favour of an exciting new challenge with Yamaha. Camier will remain where he is as the best placed 2008 contender in 2009's series, while the year's stand-out, Ellison, joins him.

HM Plant, meanwhile, will have another all-new line-up for 2009 with the Aussie pairing of Glen Richards and Joshua Brookes, while Crescent Suzuki has caused a stir by luring MotoGP racer Sylvain Guintoli to the fold.

Still, while anticipation grows for 2009, there is little doubt that BSB 2008 was a season of great excitement, occasional controversy and breathtaking competition. Most of all, though, it proved that no national series breeds better motorcycling talent than Britain's.

SUPPORT CLASSES

The Fuchs-Silkolene British Supersport Championship was all about Glen Richards in 2008 as he returned triumphant to the top of the podium. The Aussie rider, who had won the Superstock series in 2007, was unstoppable as he powered to four victories and a further five podiums, easing home a comfortable title winner over South African Hudson Kennaugh.

Earning him a top seat in BSB for 2009 with HM Plant Honda, the title was tempered with disappointment too, as the MAP Embassy Racing team went under at the end of the season. Yamaha's Kennaugh finished as runner-up after fading in the second half of the series, while 2007 stand-out Ian Lowry was third for Relentless Suzuki.

Superstock honours went to HM Plant's Steve Brogan after a dominant performance that saw him win eight of the 11 races. That put him comfortably ahead of Jon Kirkham who, in turn, secured the Henderson Yamaha R6 Cup with an equally commanding showing.

In the 125GP class, promising Red Bull Rookie racer Matthew Hoyle swept to top honours, after a crash by arch-rival Tim Hastings in the final race of the season handed him the title.

Far left: Camier celebrates his maiden BSB win at Snetterton.

Above left: Tristan Palmer's consistency made him top privateer.

Centre left: Steve Brogan was Superstock champion.

Below left: Bespectacled Matthew Hoyle took the 125 title at the last round.

Bottom: Australian veteran Glen Richards gained the Supersport crown, and will move to BSB in 2009.

Photographs: Clive Challinor Motorsport Photography

WORLD SUPERSPORT CHAMPIONSHIP
PITT'S TOP
by GORDON RITCHIE

BEFORE Andrew Pitt won the World Supersport Championship for the second time in 2008, only one other rider had taken the title twice, Sebastien Charpentier. Pitt can claim to be the first to win the title on two different makes, however, a Kawasaki ZX-6R in 2001 and now a CBR600RR Honda. His second crown was Hannspree Ten Kate Honda's seventh straight victory, a remarkable feat for the simple reason that yet again there were many other potential championship winners, including another Ten Kate Honda rider.

Pitt's team-mate was class rookie Jonathan Rea, in WSS with the aim of moving up to WSB. He wasted no time in making the transition either, going WSB racing immediately after a clash with another rider had put him out of the championship chase. Up to then, he'd enjoyed the points lead, with three wins and three DNFs.

Pitt had been knocked off by Rea and fallen on his own at Valencia, which left him in a lowly sixth place in the standings with three rounds gone. Some brilliant work from the experienced Australian put him back into contention, though, and his five wins were unrivalled at season's end.

As he hates to be reminded, he didn't win a single race in his first championship year, only in the following season, but he made up for that in 2008. In the end, Pitt and Honda were the best combination on the track, despite the appearance of the precocious Rea.

It all kicked off with some force at Losail, where the two Ten Kate riders tangled as Rea fell, gifting a certain win to another champion of days gone by, Fabien Foret (Yamaha World Supersport Team). Foret's pre-race plans had not included running out of fuel, however, and

he was unable to finish the final lap. Joan Lascorz (Glaner Motocard.com Honda) was overtaken on the line by Broc Parkes, Foret's team-mate. Strike one to the all-new Yamaha, even if another was parked next to the track.

Third in race one went to Craig Jones (Parkalgar Honda), only 0.7 second back, one of many highlights in what eventually would turn out to be his final season, as later he lost his life in a racing accident at Brands Hatch. He was an irreplaceable loss to the sport, his family and friends; the WSS series didn't have quite the same feeling after his passing.

After no-scoring in Losail, Pitt wowed the fans in a fantastic WSS race in Australia, which he won by a 0.062-second sliver from countryman Josh Brookes (Hannspree Stiggy Motorsports Honda) and his team-mate, Robbin Harms. Garry McCoy (SC Caracchi Triumph 675) was right in the mix near the end, but eventually he had to settle for sixth, only 1.2 seconds from the win.

In Valencia, it was a case of down again for Pitt, while the rider to capitalise most was local hero Lascorz, who won on a true private machine, taking the title lead from Brookes. Foret was next, and Jones third again, right in Foret's slipstream.

Assen provided another fantastic race, Pitt holding off Rea to take the narrowest of wins – by 0.014 second – right at the very end, with Lascorz third and still in the overall lead. The first five riders across the line were covered by only 0.283 second.

Monza, another classic circuit that delivers great racing, finally gave Foret his much-desired race win, from Brookes and Parkes, with Pitt fourth, a whopping

Above: Double champion Andrew Pitt.

Right: Jonathan Rea made a big impact and moved on to Superbikes.

Right centre: In an act of remembrance, Tommy Hill rode Craig Jones's bike at Donington Park.

Photographs: Gold & Goose

11 seconds off. Lascorz, blown away by the power of the factory machines around him, slipped to seventh in the race, but held on to his series lead.

Parkes took his turn at feeling aggrieved when his clutch started to slip near the end of the Nürburgring race. The following Pitt slotted past him to secure win number three and take a championship lead that he was never to relinquish all year. Brookes also slid past Parkes, who was third and seriously unhappy about it. Foret was fourth, as he would be at the following round at Misano.

In the heat and dust, it was win or bust for Pitt at Misano, and he pulled it off by a massive five seconds, with Jones second. Rea was third and fading, nine seconds back.

The next round at Brno was a real turning point in many ways, some good, some not. First, in qualifying, Garry McCoy touched Andrew Pitt and crashed, breaking his back. Luckily, there were no complications other than the need for a long recuperation period. It was more serious for Fabien Foret, however, who fell after setting a quick lap in practice. He had run too hot into Turn One, and suffered spinal and head injuries. Foret took even longer to mend than McCoy, and his head injury was a source of concern for some time. He came back at Magny-Cours, in preparation for 2009.

In the race at Brno, Pitt had to give best to team-mate Rea, who secured a great win by 0.020 second through sheer determination, with Pitt just behind and Brookes third. At least there was a happy ending in the sun, after a scary run up to race day.

As mentioned, there was a more tragic outcome at Brands Hatch when Craig Jones fell at high speed while in a podium position. He was struck by the machine of the following Andrew Pitt, who had absolutely no chance to take avoiding action. The race was called on the lap before the fatal accident, the podium spots being awarded to Rea, Jones and Pitt, with Jones's total points locked at 100.

At the following Donington round, after proper respects had been paid to Jones, his friend, Tommy Hill, rode Craig's machine around the course.

The Donington race became the second career win for Josh Brookes, after a wild-card success some years earlier in Australia. With Pitt second and Rea third, the championship seemed to be going all the Australian's way, no matter what.

At the next round at Vallelunga, however, Pitt and Eugene Laverty, standing in for Foret again, had a coming together. Pitt fell and scored no points for the third time in the year. Rea, on unstoppable good form, secured the win, while Parkes was second and Laverty, having survived the collision with Pitt, was third, in only his second WSS race.

With Rea now close behind him in the standings, Pitt was under enormous pressure going into the penultimate round in France. But relief was at hand and he became champion one round early. First of all, an attack by Robbin Harms on Rea and Parkes knocked all three of them out, leaving Pitt to storm to a win that gave him the championship. Rea remounted to take sixth, but it was all over for him, literally, as he left the class after this round, destined for WSB.

Behind Pitt, the increasingly impressive Barry Veneman (Hoegee Suzuki) and the underestimated Suzuki were in grand form in second. Brookes finished in third place and looked set for a push on second overall by season's end.

The last round, seriously wet at the start, saw former champion Kenan Sofuoglu take Rea's vacant seat. The Turkish rider made everybody take notice when he qualified on pole, after having departed the 600 class, seemingly for good, at the end of 2007. He followed it up with a dominant, dry-weather win, serving notice that King Kenan was back and determined to make up for lost time in the 1000c class.

Pitt was either happy to see him go – certainly happy as his team-mate to see Kenan find a silver lining in a cloud-filled season – or simply unable to persuade himself to chase any harder, with the championship already under wraps.

Lascorz and replacement Parkalgar Honda rider Josh Hayes had a superb fight for third, the Spaniard just heading off the fast American, who had learned the ropes in Europe quickly.

In finishing only 11th, with a worn front tyre, Brookes could not overhaul the absent Rea for second, and that fact probably made the Ulster rider even happier than the fourth place he took in Superbike that same day.

The official Kawasaki GIL team had a tough year, lacking competitiveness from their machines and losing Chris Walker unexpectedly to a WSB ride for the Brands Hatch round. The remaining regular, Katsuaki Fujiwara, had a particularly disorientating experience, given his winning pedigree. Frequently out of the points, he was 22nd in the championship. Walker was 16th, even after missing five races.

The Triumphs were four in number to start, and the best of them was ridden by Mark Aitchison (Triumph Italia BE1), who was 14th overall. The Caracchi team failed to finish the season, and McCoy rode a BE1 bike in the final round.

It was a tough year in WSS, the toughest imaginable for some individuals, although Foret recovered well, McCoy got back to riding, and Tommy Hill became fit enough to go Superbike racing in 2009. Despite the frequently entertaining racing, perhaps it was more with relief than euphoria that Pitt won the title.

RACING TO THE FINNISH

by JOHN McKENZIE

WITH a hat trick of titles already achieved, Kent-based Tim Reeves had his sights set on matching the efforts of Max Duebel and Steve Webster, the only sidecar racers to notch up four consecutive world titles. Reeves, with passenger Patrick Farrance back alongside, had been pressed hard over the previous couple of seasons by the ever faster Finnish ex-ice racing champion Pekka Paivarinta, bidding to become the first Finnish road racing world champion since the legendary Jarno Saarinen, as well as fast Frenchmen Seb Delannoy and Greg Cluze, and rising British stars Ben and Tom Birchall.

The calendar was diverse – from supporting MotoGP at Assen and Sachsenring to truck racing at Le Mans, with six rounds over five circuits, offering eight point-scoring opportunities. After a busy season and some close races, it was settled by just two points in favour of Paivarinta and compatriot Timo Karttiala, who held the lead throughout the season.

Reeves would notch five poles and four wins to Paivarinta's three victories and single pole, but consistent finishing by the latter ensured that the points kept adding up. The bald numbers don't immediately reveal the close finishes, and the Finnish pair emerged as deserving and popular world champions. Reeves could take consolation in winning the British title and finishing on the rostrum in his first crack at the Isle of Man TT.

Round One, 26 May – Donington Park, UK

A sodden spring day in the Midlands gave prior warning of what was going to be called summer in Britain in 2008, with a wet and blustery opener. Of course, all eyes were on Reeves who, after committing to his debut at the TT, then had the thorny problem of fitting in qualifying at two rather different circuits on two different outfits, separated only by a bumpy aeroplane dash.

After setting provisional pole – and knocking a couple of seconds off Webster's seven-year-old lap record – Reeves and Farrance jetted off for compulsory Saturday evening F2 novice practice at the Isle of Man, with the intention of returning by private plane to race at Donington on Sunday.

That left the opportunity in final qualifying for Sebastien Delannoy to post an even quicker lap to snatch his only pole of the season.

A plane scare saw Reeves diverted to Manchester, and he arrived at Donington almost too late for the race. He put travel hassles behind him, however, and led the pack into Redgate, despite a knock from Delannoy that almost tipped him on to the gravel. After three laps, he had secured a four-second lead.

Rain expert Paivarinta began to close; Reeves responded and managed to put a back-marker between him and the Finn. But then, under the unrelenting pressure, he ran wide at the Melbourne Loop, giving Paivarinta the gap he needed to take the victory, eventually by over six seconds.

'I could not feel my fingers towards the end. I ran a bit wide and Paivarinta got past me. I knew I wouldn't be able to stay with him. He seemed to find a second wind,' said Reeves.

Round 2, 22 June – Sachsenring, Germany

A win in the 11-lap Sprint race and third in the 22-lap Gold race saw Paivarinta increase his lead to eight points over Reeves, whose fourth in the 11-lapper turned out to be his only non-podium finish of the entire season – and the three points lost may have cost him the title.

Pole went to Reeves, just half a second faster than Delannoy, the front row being completed by Paivarinta.

The Sprint race began in the dry, Reeves running fourth until a heavy rainstorm brought a halt after five laps and sent the outfits back to the pit lane for a swift change of tyres.

When the race was restarted, Reeves took control at the front before Paivarinta steamed past on his way to the win. The Englishman tried to hold on, but the fast pace took its toll on the tyres, and although he completed the race second on the road, aggregate times gave him fourth.

'I opted for a soft rear,' said Reeves. 'As the race wore on, it just broke up, and I had the choice of slowing or perhaps crashing.'

Sunny conditions on Sunday pushed the temperature to over 30 degrees as the riders lined up for the Gold race. Reeves headed the action from the off and, despite a strong showing from Delannoy, kept his cool in the sweltering heat, remaining in front all the way to the flag. Paivarinta was five seconds adrift in third.

Round 3, 28 June – Assen, Netherlands

A pole and a win put Reeves's campaign right back on target in a classic race before a huge crowd of 130,000 at the MotoGP round.

Paivarinta took the immediate lead, but Reeves was right on his back wheel and soon forced a way past. On lap five, the Finnish Suzuki pair regained control, but only for three laps before the determined Reeves

Left: Paivarinta and partner at Le Mans. Second was good enough to become the first Finnish world champion since Jarno Saarinen.

Below: Passenger Timo Karttiala (*left*) and driver Pekka Paivarinta held off a strong challenge from title defender Reeves.

Bottom: Reeves and Farrance lead the pack at a sodden Donington Park.

Photographs: Mark Walters

forged ahead again. He led to the flag, with a margin of just over two seconds after 18 laps. This pegged the points deficit back to five at the half-way point of the season. Delannoy was a distant third.

Two wins in a row meant that Reeves also collected a 20kg weight penalty for the next race.

Round 4, 12 July – Sachsenring, Germany

The next round was back with MotoGP, and the second visit to Sachsenring in three weeks. Qualifying became a dramatic affair when Reeves suffered brake problems on the Eastern Airways Suzuki. 'We lost the brakes and had a big, big moment, nearly hitting the wall. It was a close call,' he said.

The final qualifying session saw Paivarinta set the fastest lap.

Torrential rain blighted the 250 and MotoGP events, and it was still falling as the sidecar crews took to the

grid for their 20-lap race. Rain expert Paivarinta started as favourite, but Reeves was not to be outdone and shot to the front to lead the pack for the first six laps.

Paivarinta took over, but Reeves fought back two laps later. Once again, the Finn went past, with Reeves right on his tail. Then, on lap 13, Reeves spun, and although he rejoined for second, Paivarinta was all but home, if not dry, taking the win by 13 seconds.

At least Reeves was able to hand 10kg of the winner's ballast to Paivarinta, ensuring that both outfits would be carrying the same amount next time out.

Round 5, 16/17 August – Rijeka, Croatia

With a five-lap Sprint race (after quarter- and semi-final races) on Saturday, and a 20-lap Gold race on Sunday, it would prove a busy weekend, with the world title potentially up for grabs.

After dominating qualifying, Reeves and Farrance went into the Sprint on pole, despite overheating problems that would plague them all weekend.

The defenders led throughout to grab a half-second win over Paivarinta and bag 25 points to take them to within three of the series leader. The steadily improving Ben and Tom Birchall were third.

It was looking good for Reeves for the Gold race, and a second win would have put him in the championship lead, but the return of overheating problems – later diagnosed as a leaking head gasket – and a subsequent loss of power mid-race beset the Suzuki, dropping it back to a lonely third.

Birchall had led for the first six laps, Reeves content to follow before the overheating struck again and he dropped back. Birchall took his maiden World Championship race win by 0.828 second from Paivarinta. That second place also increased the Finn's title lead to seven points.

'I am not giving my world title away without a fight,' said Reeves. 'I am up for the challenge and if I can win the next race then I have done as much as I can. The rest is in the hands of the gods!'

Round 6, 21 September – Le Mans, France

It was always going to be tough for Reeves and Farrance to lift the trophy for the fourth year, but they gave it their best shot at Le Mans by securing a pole and the win in the final round. But arch rivals Pekka Paivarinta and Timo Karttiala completed the race in their tyre tracks to take the championship by a margin of just two points.

Reeves and Farrance set the benchmark throughout qualifying and led away from pole – the scene was set for a memorable final. With Paivarinta knowing he had only to follow Reeves, the pressure was on. 'We were nervous before the race, but practice was okay, and we thought it was looking good,' said Paivarinta.

Reeve's hopes relied on a win; his strategy was to dictate the pace to try to put Birchall and/or Delannoy between him and Paivarinta. On the day, however, neither Birchall nor Delannoy – even on his home track – was able to stick with the front-runners.

Reeves went on to win from Paivarinta by almost three seconds, while Delannoy was a further 11 seconds down.

'It's been very tough this year, but an amazing day and an amazing season. Some places we had a few problems, and the rain in the early season was good for us, but today has been very special, and it is hard to believe we have won the title,' said a happy and relieved Paivarinta.

Reeves was gracious in defeat: 'Obviously we are gutted, but congratulations to Pekka and Timo who have really given us a run for our money this year, and they thoroughly deserve their moment of glory.'

END OF AN ERA

by PAUL CARRUTHERS

AN era came to an end on 7 March, 2008, when the Daytona Motorsports Group (DMG) and the AMA announced at the season-opening round at Daytona International Speedway that the AMA had sold the majority of its racing properties, including road racing, to DMG. This, the optimists thought, would end years of mediocrity and complaints, and restore hope to a paddock eagerly awaiting a brighter future.

Turns out, it might be a case of 'be careful what you wish for'.

Quite simply, the current state of AMA road racing borders on the diabolical. And those high hopes might end up being false hopes. Case in point: as this review of the 2008 season was being written, teams still weren't certain what motorcycles to build for 2009, most of the racers didn't have contracts and there were still questions as to which factories would even participate. With the upcoming Dunlop tyre test – the company had won the bidding war to provide the spec tyre for the series as of 2009, a first in AMA history, along with spec fuel – at Daytona just weeks away, there were far more questions on the table than answers.

What is clear is the fact that another era also ended at the conclusion of the 2008 season. While AMA Superbike racing as we'd known it for decades was likely be different from here on in, the period of Mat Mladin vs Ben Spies rivalry was now officially over.

Spies won the AMA Superbike Championship for a third time in 2008, the young Texan fighting for the entire season with his rival and team-mate. Then he put a close on that memorable rivalry when he signed to race in the World Superbike Championship for 2009, jumping to the factory Yamaha team and leaving his foe Mladin to go it alone in the AMA series.

The 2008 series only added to the total domination of those two racers and their mighty Yoshimura Suzuki GSX-R1000s, the pair again winning each and every race. The numbers the two have produced are rather staggering. Since the rivalry began, Mladin has won 40 AMA Superbike races – the Aussie has 72 victories overall, far more than any rider in AMA Superbike history – while Spies has won 28. Spies has finished second 32 times; Mladin has been runner-up 22 times. Spies has eight third-place finishes; Mladin has one.

As for one-two finishes, it's Mladin-Spies 31 times; Spies-Mladin 19 times. With the majority of the AMA Superbike races now double-headers – one race on Saturday, one on Sunday – Mladin has had 14 double-header sweeps, while Spies has had nine.

And the telling statistic: Spies scored 2,467 points, while Mladin's total was 2,392. But that comes with a caveat: Mladin was disqualified from his two victories at Virginia International Raceway in 2008 when his crankshaft was deemed by AMA officials to be illegal – they neglected to check Spies's crank. If Mladin's victories at VIR had stood, Spies would have had 2,457 points, and Mladin would have had 2,456. That's a single point separating them for their entire AMA Superbike rivalry. Total domination by two riders and one team – and one of the reasons that DMG head Roger Edmondson gave to demonstrate that changes in the series were necessary. It's parity that he seeks, although there's no one with an ounce of brain power in the paddock who could possibly believe that it would have been anybody but Mladin and Spies, no matter what motorcycles they'd been riding.

Once again, but for the last time, Suzuki teamsters Mladin and Spies were in a field of their own. Here, at Barber Motorsport Park in Alabama. Mladin leads by inches. It was typical of the way they raced.
Photograph: Andrew Wheeler/automotophoto

At season's end, Spies had won ten races, while Mladin had taken the other nine, and the difference in the point standings was 95. Even if Mladin had been able to keep the VIR wins, Spies still would have come away with the title – by 19 points – as he rightfully stated after losing to Mladin in the meaningless final round at Laguna Seca.

The other teams and riders were really just extras in a familiar blockbuster. Yoshimura came into the series with the same three riders, Tommy Hayden on board for a second season. Again, he served as the man in the middle, his team generally the buffer in the garage between the two antagonistic crews of Mladin and Spies.

Things were sailing along nicely for Hayden early in the season, as he appeared to be getting comfortable on the Suzuki and was putting the bike where most people expected – third behind his two team-mates. But it all went wrong at the Auto Club Speedway (formerly California Speedway) round when he was shunted from behind in the Supersport race and suffered a broken ankle. The injury ruined most of his

season, although he came back strong in the end with five podium finishes to finish the season eighth in the championship.

The factory Yamaha team took the places behind the Suzuki duo, with Jason DiSalvo third and Eric Bostrom fourth, but neither had a memorable season by any measure. In fact, their spots in the championship seemed to have been gifted rather than earned, and it shows the mediocrity of everyone else. DiSalvo started the season with two podium places – a third at Daytona and a career-best second in the first of two races at Barber, where Spies suffered his lone race crash of the season. The Yamaha rider never sniffed the podium again, however, instead stringing together a feast of mid-pack finishes.

Bostrom wasn't any better, and by the end of the year he'd announced that he was through with racing for the time being and was headed for the family's 6,000-acre plot of land in Brazil, where he would become a fruit farmer. Bostrom's best was a fourth in the first of two races at Infineon Raceway in Northern California.

Kawasaki's Jamie Hacking may have finished only fifth in the final standings, but most would agree that he was by far the best of those in the wake of the dominant pair. Hacking rode hard all year and put the Kawasaki on the podium eight times, including two second-place finishes behind Spies at Miller Motorsports Park in Utah – the races held in conjunction with the US World Superbike round. Hacking's season was strong until the final third, when some crashes ultimately cost him in the standings. He also missed the final round at Laguna Seca after hurting himself in a qualifying crash.

Hacking's Kawasaki team-mate, Roger Lee Hayden, had a season filled with injury, and he ended up a lowly 22nd in the title chase. Hayden was rammed from behind during practice at the Barber round, suffering a broken pelvis and a severe hand injury that required several surgeries, including the amputation of his pinkie finger. That ruined his year.

Neil Hodgson led the Honda contingent, the Briton riding one of two factory CBR1000RRs to sixth in the title chase. Hodgson's season was somewhat up and

down, and he was let down by mechanical issues on occasion. His best efforts came in the middle of the year with two podium finishes in Utah, but it wasn't a season that made the former World Superbike champion happy. He felt that he should have been racing at the sharp end of the pack at every race.

At least he had that chance again, as he was one of the few riders in the paddock to have a contract for 2009. That's more than can be said for his team-mate, Miguel Duhamel. He ended up just seven points behind Hodgson, but his was more a season of just finishing races rather than putting up impressive results.

The Michael Jordan Suzuki boys were next in line, Aaron Yates finishing ninth in the series standings, while his new team-mate, Geoff May, closed out the season in tenth. Behind them came a string of privateers led by Scott Jensen.

As always, the season started at Daytona, and the news of the DMG take-over of the series was all anyone could talk about. The news came with high hopes, but they would fade and the season would continue with uncertainty of what the future held.

On the track, the Superbikes played second fiddle again to the Formula Xtreme class, which received top billing as the Daytona 200.

Mladin struck first, the Australian handily beating Spies to open the season. Behind the two Suzukis came DiSalvo, the R1-mounted rider holding second on the first lap before being passed by Spies. Then he stayed put, riding mostly alone to the final spot on the podium.

Fourth went to Tommy Hayden, who made a final-lap pass on Hacking after the Kawasaki rider had held the spot for the duration. Then came Yates on the Jordan Suzuki, half a second clear of Hodgson; the Brit had been part of the battle for what would be fourth until he ran off the track in Turn Five on the 13th of 15 laps. He recovered to pass Roger Lee Hayden on the final lap to finish seventh.

To be truthful, the racers and teams always look for-

ward to departing Daytona and heading to a real race-track where the Superbikes again take top billing. The first of those tracks was the picturesque Barber Motorsports Park in Alabama, the site of the first double-header of the year.

Mladin took advantage of a mistake by Spies to storm to an overwhelming victory in the first leg, the veteran starting from pole and speeding into the lead with Spies in tow. The pair was running in formation when Spies got loose on the curbing entering the roller-coaster museum corner. The result was disastrous: the GSX-R1000 got out of shape going into the downhill right-hander and the front end tucked, sending the Texan into the gravel trap. He remounted to finish 11th.

Mladin went on to the 65th win of his career and a points lead over his rival.

DiSalvo finished a career-best second, two seconds in front of Tommy Hayden. Then came Hacking, with American Honda team-mates Hodgson and Duhamel fifth and sixth.

Mladin kept a perfect season going the following day: thus far he'd led every lap of every race of the 2008 AMA Superbike Championship. The second race at Barber was different from the first in that Mladin had company – at least for part of the race. Spies put up a fight in the early going, but Mladin wasn't in the mood for losing and eventually he pulled out to an 8.1-second victory. Tommy Hayden came home third, giving the Yoshimura Suzuki team a podium sweep for the first time in the season.

Hayden had beaten DiSalvo, while Hodgson was fifth from Eric Bostrom. Then came Yates and Duhamel, with ninth place going to Corona Extra Honda's Matt Lynn over May.

When the teams arrived in Southern California for the Auto Club Speedway double-header, it was time for Spies to step up and make a statement. And make a statement he did, the Texan pushing past Mladin on the 13th of 28 laps to earn his first victory of the season.

Above: Mladin smiled through defeat – and a controversial and costly disqualification.

Right: Spies skims the road with elbow and knee. The Texan's style has earned him the nickname 'Elbowz'.

Photographs: Andrew Wheeler/ automotophoto

Spies had started fast, but Mladin clawed his way back, leading for the first time on the ninth lap. Spies stuck on Mladin's rear wheel for four more laps before making the pass at the end of the back straight. It was close – very close. Mladin, who was on the outside, was forced off the track momentarily, bouncing back across the makeshift curbing to rejoin the fray. He finished the lap less than half a second behind, but wasn't able to keep pace for the rest of the way. The Australian slowed to finish a safe second, 20.5 seconds behind.

Third went to Tommy Hayden again, who had gone at it with Hodgson until the Brit had run straight on at the corner that takes the riders from the banking to the infield section. Hodgson held for fourth, with Bostrom fifth and Hacking sixth.

A day later, it looked like Mladin was going to run away and hide in the second of two AMA Superbike races at the newly named Auto Club Speedway, but suddenly his hard-earned lead was gone – the gap dropping from 3.9 seconds to 2.6 in the span of two laps. At the chequered flag, a handful of laps later, his lead evaporated entirely as Spies drafted past to win by 0.011 second.

It was his second in a row, and after five rounds, he trailed Mladin by 20 points.

The Suzuki team had swept the podium again, although Tommy Hayden in third was 31 seconds behind. Fourth went to Hodgson, three seconds further back and three seconds ahead of DiSalvo, with team-mate Bostrom sixth.

'That was one of the toughest races I've been in,' Spies said. 'I couldn't make any inroads the whole race. We started sliding around, and the last ten laps I was pretty much out of control. He made me work for it.'

Spies made it three straight wins when the series headed to Northern California's Infineon Raceway – and with relative ease. After 28 laps, he led Mladin by 6.1 seconds, but that gap was deceiving. Spies had slowed dramatically in the closing stages; after 20 laps, he'd led by as much as 12.1 seconds.

Mladin was some six seconds ahead of Hacking, the Kawasaki rider taking his first podium of the season. Then it was almost four seconds to Bostrom, barely holding off a charging Yates. Hodgson ended up sixth, the Brit showing promise in the middle of the race before fading away from the battle for fourth.

Spies's 21st career Superbike win put him 14 points behind Mladin in the title chase. Things were beginning to be interesting again.

Spies followed up the next day, leading from start to finish. Mladin had kept him honest for 15 of the 28 laps. On the 16th, however, Spies increased the lead from 1.2 seconds to 2.8. A lap later, it was up to 4.1 seconds, and from there it was all Spies, with a margin of victory of 8.04 seconds.

'He's got no respect for an old guy,' Mladin joked from the podium. Now Spies was just nine points behind in the standings.

Hacking matched his third from the day before, circulating alone after ditching the battle behind him.

Fourth place went to Yates, the Georgian having held back the late-lap charge of Hodgson.

The World Superbike series returned to US shores at the Miller Motorsports Park round in Utah, and Spies took the opportunity to show what he's made of. Not only did he win the two races in Utah, but also he left with the points lead after Mladin suffered two bad races.

In the first race, Spies won easily after Mladin crashed out on the second lap, the result of front-fork issues that were beginning to get to the Aussie. The day before, Mladin had said that the team had made some changes that had helped: 'My confidence has been beat up a bit this year. I've been riding on the razor's edge, not knowing when I'm going to crash. I've crashed more times the first few months than in the past five years, and I'm getting too old for that. I've been crashing every weekend, sometimes twice.'

With Mladin out, Spies backed off the pace for his fifth victory in a row.

The most inspired ride of the day came from second-place finisher Hacking. Third when he ran off the track on the second lap, he lost eight seconds and dropped to eighth. Then came the assault. Lapping faster than anyone on the track, he quickly moved through to join the battle for second, between Hodgson and Yates. He disposed of them and went after Spies, but the Texan was too far out in front.

Yates never gave up, chasing Hodgson to the line before losing out by 0.140 second. It was the first podium of the year for the latter and the Honda team.

More of the same the following day became historic, as Spies tied an AMA Superbike Championship record – joining Mladin and Duhamel – with his sixth win in a row, after beating the same two riders he'd trounced the day before.

For a while, the battle for second was the most entertaining race of the day. First, it was the domain of Mladin, but he was soon passed by Hodgson. Then came Hacking, who scooped them both up for the runner-up spot for a second straight race; Hodgson was third again.

Clearly not comfortable with his bike's front end, Mladin rode to a safe fourth place, giving Spies a 39-point title lead.

History was well and truly made when the series visited Wisconsin's Elkhart Lake, where Spies won his seventh Superbike race in a row. Starting from his fourth consecutive pole, he jetted into the lead. Mladin was glued to his tail until the final corner on the fourth of 16 laps, when a slight wobble dropped him from Spies's draft. By the end of the race, Spies was 8.796 seconds ahead of his team-mate.

The win was made more impressive by a serious crash Spies had suffered during Superbike qualifying only hours earlier. Entering the final right-hand Turn 14, he had ended up in the gravel when the front end of his Suzuki GSX-R1000 had slid away without warning. He needed six stitches to close a wound on his chin, but not before he'd set pole.

Hacking ended up on the podium for a fifth race in a row, finishing third. He had taken the position from Hodgson on the second lap and after a while pulled clear. Duhamel came out the best of a three-rider fight for fifth.

What a difference a day makes. Somehow, overnight, Mladin had found some power at Road America and the horsepower deficit he had suffered the day before was gone. He emphatically ended Spies's winning streak with his fourth victory of the year, in what was arguably the best Superbike race of the season. The team-mates were swapping the lead until the fifth of 16 laps, when Mladin took control for good.

Spies never gave up, but also he was never close enough to draft past Mladin on the front straight, something he could have done on Saturday.

The win was the 67th of Mladin's career, and it cut slightly into Spies's championship lead. After six of 11 races, that stood at 40 points.

Hacking, who did well to hang with the Suzukis for the first five laps or so, dropped back to a distant, but secure third. The same could be said of Hodgson, who rode to a lonely fourth.

To show that there was still plenty of fight left in the old dog, Mladin beat Spies at Laguna Seca, where AMA Superbikes shared the track with MotoGP. Admittedly, Spies had only climbed off his Rizla Suzuki MotoGP bike 45 minutes earlier, having ridden it to eighth in the 32-lap Red Bull US Grand Prix, so it was hard to tell whether Mladin was that dominant or Spies was just spent – or content to finish second. Even so, it had been a solid performance from Mladin, while Spies had had a tiring, but successful day.

Yates ended up third – his only podium of the year – after a thrilling race-long battle. In the end, he fought off Hacking, the Georgian beating his buddy from South Carolina by 0.052 second. Then came Tommy Hayden, a shadow fifth, 0.4 second behind Hacking in his return from injury. Brother Roger Lee, likewise back in action, was an impressive sixth. He had barely held off a fast-closing Hodgson.

Race fans at the Mid-Ohio Sports Car Course could have pulled out an old copy of *War and Peace* and made a dent in it in the amount of time it took to complete the first of two races. How does two hours and

Above: Jake Zemke left Superbikes to win the Formula Xtreme championship.

Right: Kawasaki's Jamie Hacking started strongly, but ran into problems later in the year.

Bottom: Neil Hodgson is shadowed by Honda team-mate Miguel Duhamel.

Opposite: The Formula Xtreme pack. Like Superbikes, the class was under threat of extinction.
Photographs: Tom Hnatiw/Flick of the Wrist

15 minutes sound?

That's what it took before Mladin could complete his 19 laps and put this race out of its misery. Scheduled for 26 laps, it was a debacle from the beginning, requiring four starts and three red flags to get it in the books.

The first came after a horrific crash on the seventh lap, when Hodgson's Honda blew up and left a trail of oil that caused numerous riders to fall. Then, on the next start, race leader Mladin and second-place man Hacking went down simultaneously on the first lap after a fan reportedly dumped his cooler on a bridge and the water ran on to the track – we're not making this up! Both riders were okay and able to make the third start, but that only lasted for four more laps before Matt Lynn crashed the Corona Honda, with Duhamel going down in his debris – his second crash that day. Lynn's bike caught fire, which brought out yet another red flag.

The final start, at 5.30pm, went the distance, with Mladin beating Spies. Hacking finished third, DiSalvo was fourth and Tommy Hayden fifth.

The next day, there was neither oil nor water – but there was plenty of Mladin. In a race that was so different from the day before, and rather dull, he cleared off to an easy win of the 70th AMA Superbike race of his illustrious career, defeating Spies by 6.3 seconds after leading every lap.

Third place went to Hacking again, but this time he was never a factor, eventually finishing some 20 seconds adrift. Then came Hodgson, in a complete turnaround from the day before. This time, he held back the advances of Yates, the Georgian ultimately highsiding out of the race on the 18th of 26 laps.

That left only one battle on the racetrack, between Hayden and Duhamel for fifth place. It went to Hayden by 0.9 second.

Mladin left Mid-Ohio trailing Spies by 27 points, having arrived 36 behind.

Everything changed at Virginia International Raceway – or, more accurately, during the weeks following Mladin's two decisive victories there. But first the races themselves.

Mladin won the first, passing Spies early and pulling away when his younger team-mate suffered a near high-side. The win was Suzuki's 42nd in a row, Mladin's 71st and his seventh straight win at VIR.

Hayden made a fourth Suzuki podium sweep, having passed Eric Bostrom on the 21st lap after dogging him for much of the race. Eventually, Bostrom faded back by more than five seconds.

Hacking crashed in Turn One on the 12th lap while in fifth; Hodgson had high-sided out three laps before.

The following day, Mladin won again, further cutting Spies's championship points lead – to 18 points with three races to run. It meant that if Mladin scored the maximum number of points, Spies would still win the title – by a single point.

But that didn't last.

Following the second race, the AMA tore down Mladin's bike and confiscated the Suzuki's crankshaft. Later it would disqualify him from both races. Why the AMA didn't take Spies's crank is what ultimately caused controversy. Conspiracy theorists had a field day with the fact that Mladin had been so outspoken by the on-again, off-again class structures and rules the DMG had introduced throughout the season.

Everyone went into Road Atlanta not knowing the outcome, as Mladin had appealed. On the track, he led a Suzuki sweep of the podium in the first race, besting Spies and Tommy Hayden. The win could have been his seventh AMA Superbike race in a row, but no one would know until the verdict on the appeal. We also didn't know whether Spies had earned his third title or not. If Mladin's disqualifications stood, he was already champion, after fighting back to second from a stop-and-go jump-start penalty.

Mladin was defiant: 'Listen, I don't have a lot to say about it. All I've said is that Roger Edmondson can take away my wins, he can take away whatever he likes. He'll never be able to take away my family, my fans or my heart, ever. And he can do what he pleases, but he'll never stop Mat Mladin being who he is.'

Spies declined to comment.

The Suzuki team dominated the proceedings again the next day, but this time Spies was the star. He came from behind to pass Mladin on the 19th of 25 laps and motored to victory by 7.106 seconds. The win also ended another streak. It was the first time since 4 September, 2005, that anyone other than Mladin had won a Superbike race at Road Atlanta. And it was Spies's first win since Road America in early June.

The victory meant that Spies needed only the 12 points that come with a 19th-place finish, regardless of Mladin's appeal, to clinch the title at Laguna Seca. Then it got even easier. Between the Road Atlanta races and the series finale at Laguna Seca, AMA Pro Racing announced that it wouldn't hear Mladin's appeal. It issued a statement that read that the appeal 'has been deemed without merit and has been denied. The original penalty remains as previously announced and becomes final with this decision.'

And that was that. The result was an anti-climactic season finale at Laguna. Mladin easily beat Spies, but, with the championship in his pocket, the now triple champion was perfectly okay with that. Thus the season came to a rather dull conclusion – especially with the paddock awaiting a wave of the unknown.

Tommy Hayden was third again, after an almost race-long battle with Yates. Fifth went to Hodgson, well clear of Eric Bostrom, who had passed Duhamel in the closing stages.

When all was said and done, Spies took the title by 95 points over Mladin, 652–557, after a season-long battle that was much closer and memorable than that. Third went to DiSalvo with 463 points.

The support classes also yielded few last-race dramatics, but had still proved entertaining. The ever-popular Ben Bostrom showed that his career had been completely revived by riding the Graves Yamaha R6 to the Supersport title. He gave way to upstart Blake Young in the season finale, but 2008 had been his year.

Young, meanwhile, had emerged as the hottest young property in the paddock, and the 18-year-old was likely to be the man to fill Spies's big shoes on the Yosh team for 2009.

Aaron Yates earned the Superstock title for Michael Jordan Motorsports, giving the basketball legend his first motorsport crown. The Formula Xtreme Championship was won by Jake Zemke, the Erion Honda rider prevailing over team-mate Josh Hayes. The pair won nine of the ten races between them.

MAJOR RESULTS

OTHER CHAMPIONSHIP RACING SERIES WORLDWIDE

Compiled by KAY EDGE

AMA Championship Road Race Series (Superbike)

DAYTONA INTERNATIONAL SPEEDWAY, Daytona Beach, Florida, 10 March, 44.250 miles/71.213km
1 Mat Mladin (Suzuki); **2** Ben Spies (Suzuki); **3** Jason DiSalvo (Yamaha); **4** Tommy Hayden (Suzuki); **5** Jamie Hacking (Kawasaki); **6** Aaron Yates (Suzuki); **7** Neil Hodgson (Honda); **8** Roger Lee Hayden (Kawasaki); **9** Blake Young (Suzuki); **10** Geoff May (Suzuki).

BARBER MOTORSPORTS PARK, Leeds, Alabama, 19–20 April, 66.600 miles/107.182km
Race 1
1 Mat Mladin (Suzuki); **2** Jason DiSalvo (Yamaha); **3** Tommy Hayden (Suzuki); **4** Jamie Hacking (Kawasaki); **5** Neil Hodgson (Honda); **6** Miguel Duhamel (Honda); **7** Eric Bostrom (Yamaha); **8** Geoff May (Suzuki); **9** Chris Peris (Yamaha); **10** Jordan Szoke (Kawasaki).

Race 2
1 Mat Mladin (Suzuki); **2** Ben Spies (Suzuki); **3** Tommy Hayden (Suzuki); **4** Jason DiSalvo (Yamaha); **5** Neil Hodgson (Honda); **6** Eric Bostrom (Yamaha); **7** Aaron Yates (Suzuki); **8** Miguel Duhamel (Honda); **9** Matt Lynn (Honda); **10** Geoff May (Suzuki).

AUTO CLUB SPEEDWAY, Fontana, California, 26–27 April, 66.080 miles/106.345km
Race 1
1 Ben Spies (Suzuki); **2** Mat Mladin (Suzuki); **3** Tommy Hayden (Suzuki); **4** Neil Hodgson (Honda); **5** Eric Bostrom (Yamaha); **6** Jamie Hacking (Kawasaki); **7** Miguel Duhamel (Honda); **8** Jason DiSalvo (Yamaha); **9** Matt Lynn (Honda); **10** Jake Holden (Honda).

Race 2
1 Ben Spies (Suzuki); **2** Mat Mladin (Suzuki); **3** Tommy Hayden (Suzuki); **4** Neil Hodgson (Honda); **5** Jason DiSalvo (Yamaha); **6** Eric Bostrom (Yamaha); **7** Jamie Hacking (Kawasaki); **8** Scott Jensen (Suzuki); **9** Matt Lynn (Honda); **10** Dean Mizdal (Suzuki).

INFINEON RACEWAY, Sonoma, California, 17–18 May, 60.320 miles/97.076km
Race 1
1 Ben Spies (Suzuki); **2** Mat Mladin (Suzuki); **3** Jamie Hacking (Kawasaki); **4** Eric Bostrom (Yamaha); **5** Aaron Yates (Suzuki); **6** Neil Hodgson (Honda); **7** Jason DiSalvo (Yamaha); **8** Matt Lynn (Honda); **9** Geoff May (Suzuki); **10** Miguel Duhamel (Honda).

Race 2
1 Ben Spies (Suzuki); **2** Mat Mladin (Suzuki); **3** Jamie Hacking (Kawasaki); **4** Aaron Yates (Suzuki); **5** Neil Hodgson (Honda); **6** Eric Bostrom (Yamaha); **7** Miguel Duhamel (Honda); **8** Geoff May (Suzuki); **9** Chris Peris (Suzuki); **10** Ryan Elleby (Suzuki).

MILLER MOTORSPORTS PARK, Tooele, Utah, 31 May–1 June, 63.000 miles/101.389km
Race 1
1 Ben Spies (Suzuki); **2** Jamie Hacking (Kawasaki); **3** Neil Hodgson (Honda); **4** Aaron Yates (Suzuki); **5** Miguel Duhamel (Honda); **6** Eric Bostrom (Yamaha); **7** Jason DiSalvo (Yamaha); **8** Chris Peris (Suzuki); **9** David Anthony (Suzuki); **10** Scott Jensen (Suzuki).

Race 2
1 Ben Spies (Suzuki); **2** Jamie Hacking (Kawasaki); **3** Neil Hodgson (Honda); **4** Mat Mladin (Suzuki); **5** Aaron Yates (Suzuki); **6** Miguel Duhamel (Honda); **7** Geoff May (Suzuki); **8** Jason DiSalvo (Yamaha); **9** Eric Bostrom (Yamaha); **10** Chris Peris (Yamaha).

ROAD AMERICA, Elkhart Lake, Wisconsin, 7–8 June, 64.000 miles/102.998km
Race 1
1 Ben Spies (Suzuki); **2** Mat Mladin (Suzuki); **3** Jamie Hacking (Kawasaki); **4** Neil Hodgson (Honda); **5** Miguel Duhamel (Honda); **6** Aaron Yates (Suzuki); **7** Jason DiSalvo (Yamaha); **8** Eric Bostrom (Yamaha); **9** Geoff May (Suzuki); **10** Alastair Seeley (Suzuki).

Race 2
1 Mat Mladin (Suzuki); **2** Ben Spies (Suzuki); **3** Jamie Hacking (Kawasaki); **4** Neil Hodgson (Honda); **5** Eric Bostrom (Yamaha); **6** Miguel Duhamel (Honda); **7** Geoff May (Suzuki); **8** Aaron Yates (Suzuki); **9** Alastair Seeley (Suzuki); **10** Chris Peris (Suzuki).

MAZDA RACEWAY LAGUNA SECA, Monterey, California, 20 July, 61.600 miles/99.136km
1 Mat Mladin (Suzuki); **2** Ben Spies (Suzuki); **3** Aaron Yates (Suzuki); **4** Jamie Hacking (Kawasaki); **5** Tommy Hayden (Suzuki); **6** Roger Lee Hayden (Kawasaki); **7** Neil Hodgson (Honda); **8** Jason DiSalvo (Yamaha); **9** Eric Bostrom (Yamaha); **10** Miguel Duhamel (Honda).

MID-OHIO SPORTS CAR COURSE, Lexington, Ohio, 2–3 August, 62.400 miles/100.423km
Race 1
1 Mat Mladin (Suzuki); **2** Ben Spies (Suzuki); **3** Jamie Hacking (Kawasaki); **4** Jason DiSalvo (Yamaha); **5** Tommy Hayden (Suzuki); **6** Roger Lee Hayden (Kawasaki); **7** Eric Bostrom (Yamaha); **8** Geoff May (Suzuki); **9** Chris Peris (Suzuki); **10** Scott Jensen (Suzuki).

Race 2
1 Mat Mladin (Suzuki); **2** Ben Spies (Suzuki); **3** Jamie Hacking (Kawasaki); **4** Neil Hodgson (Honda); **5** Tommy Hayden (Suzuki); **6** Miguel Duhamel (Honda); **7** Jason DiSalvo (Yamaha); **8** Geoff May (Suzuki); **9** Chris Peris (Suzuki); **10** Kenny Noyes (Suzuki).

VIRGINIA INTERNATIONAL RACEWAY, Alton, Virginia, 16–17 August, 62.300 miles/100.262km
Race 1
1 Ben Spies (Suzuki); **2** Tommy Hayden (Suzuki); **3** Eric Bostrom (Yamaha); **4** Miguel Duhamel (Honda); **5** Jason DiSalvo (Yamaha); **6** Geoff May (Suzuki); **7** Roger Lee Hayden (Kawasaki); **8** Chris Peris (Suzuki); **9** Kenny Noyes (Suzuki); **10** Scott Jensen (Suzuki).

Race 2
1 Ben Spies (Suzuki); **2** Tommy Hayden (Suzuki); **3** Eric Bostrom (Yamaha); **4** Miguel Duhamel (Honda); **5** Jamie Hacking (Kawasaki); **6** Neil Hodgson (Honda); **7** Geoff May (Suzuki); **8** Jason DiSalvo (Yamaha); **9** Matt Lynn (Honda); **10** Chris Peris (Suzuki).

ROAD ATLANTA, Braselton, Georgia, 30–31 August, 63.500 miles/102.193km
Race 1
1 Mat Mladin (Suzuki); **2** Ben Spies (Suzuki); **3** Tommy Hayden (Suzuki); **4** Aaron Yates (Suzuki); **5** Eric Bostrom (Yamaha); **6** Jason DiSalvo (Yamaha); **7** Miguel Duhamel (Honda); **8** Matt Lynn (Honda); **9** Geoff May (Suzuki); **10** Ben Thompson (Suzuki).

Race 2
1 Ben Spies (Suzuki); **2** Mat Mladin (Suzuki); **3** Tommy Hayden (Suzuki); **4** Miguel Duhamel (Honda); **5** Jason DiSalvo (Yamaha); **6** Eric Bostrom (Yamaha); **7** Neil Hodgson (Honda); **8** Aaron Yates (Suzuki); **9** Matt Lynn (Honda); **10** Geoff May (Suzuki).

MAZDA RACEWAY LAGUNA SECA, Monterey, California, 28 September, 61.600 miles/99.136km
1 Mat Mladin (Suzuki); **2** Ben Spies (Suzuki); **3** Tommy Hayden (Suzuki); **4** Aaron Yates (Suzuki); **5** Neil Hodgson (Honda); **6** Eric Bostrom (Yamaha); **7** Miguel Duhamel (Honda); **8** Jason DiSalvo (Yamaha); **9** Jordan Szoke (Kawasaki); **10** Chris Peris (Yamaha).

Final Championship Points

1	Ben Spies	652
2	Mat Mladin	557
3	Jason DiSalvo	463
4	Eric Bostrom	445
5	Jamie Hacking	421
6	Neil Hodgson	419
7	Miguel Duhamel	412
8	Tommy Hayden	372
9	Aaron Yates	365
10	Geoff May	357

Endurance World Championship

24 HEURES DU MANS, Le Mans Bugatti Circuit, France, 19–20 April 2008.
FIM Qtel Endurance World Championship, round 1. 770 laps of the 2.600-mile/4.185km circuit, 2002.000 miles/3222.450km
1 Suzuki Endurance Racing Team 2, FRA: William Costes/Guillaume Dietrich/Barry Veneman (Suzuki GSXR 1000), 24h 01m 26.500s, 83.347mph/134.134km/h.
2 Suzuki Endurance Racing Team 1, FRA: Vincent Philippe/Julien Da Costa/Matthieu Lagrive (Suzuki GSXR 1000), 759 laps; **3** Team Acropolis Moto Expert, FRA: Grégory Fastre/Grégory Leblanc/Anthony Dos Santos (Yamaha R1), 756; **4** Infini Team/Yohann Motosport, FRA: Jerome Tangre/Christophe Michel/Cedric Tangre (Suzuki GSXR 1000), 755; **5** RMT 21 Racing Team, GER: Matti Seidel/Daniel Sutter/Tomas Miksovsky (Honda CBR 1000), 751; **6** Bolliger Team Switzerland, SWI: David Morillon/Eric Mizera/Horst Saiger (Kawasaki ZX 10), 749; **7** RT Racing Team & Motovirus, ITA: Jean-Louis Devoyon/Frédéric Jond/Raphael Chevre (Suzuki GSXR 1000), 748; **8** AM Moto Racing, FRA: Sullivan Hernandez/Pierre Guersillon/Fabrice Auger (Suzuki GSXR 1000), 747; **9** Yamaha Folch Endurance, SPA: Daniel Ribalta/Pedro Luis Valcaneras/Felipe Lopez (Yamaha R1), 745; **10** Phase One Endurance, GBR: James Haydon/Damian Cudlin/James McBride (Yamaha R1), 745; **11** Endurance Moto 38, FRA: Julien Millet/Cyril Brivet/Hervé Gantner (Yamaha R1), 744; **12** Diablo 666 Bollinger, GBR: James Hutchins/Alex Cudlin/Michael Weynand (Kawasaki ZX 10), 740; **13** Team Raffin Motors, FRA: Pascal Grosjean/Pierre Chapuis/Gérald Muteau (Kawasaki ZX 10), 732; **14** Endurance Moto 74, FRA: Jonathan Castanet/Stéphane Kokes/William Grarre (Yamaha R1), 722; **15** La Fortezza Amadeus X One, ITA: Paolo Tessari/William Gruy/Riccardo Ricci (Yamaha R1), 717.
Fastest lap: Suzuki Endurance Racing Team 1, 1m 39.812s, on lap 174.
Championship points: 1 Suzuki Endurance Racing Team 2, 35; **2** Suzuki Endurance Racing Team 1, 28; **3** Team Acropolis Moto Expert, 22; **4** Infini Team/Yohann Motosport, 18; **5** RMT 21 Racing Team, 15; **6** Bolliger Team Switzerland, 14.

6 HORAS DE ALBACETE, Albacete, Spain, 10 May 2008.
FIM Qtel Endurance World Championship, round 2. 177 laps of the 2.299-mile/3.700km circuit, 406.923 miles/654.900km
1 Suzuki Endurance Racing Team 1, FRA: Vincent Philippe/Julien Da Costa/Guillaume Dietrich (Suzuki GSXR 1000), 6h 01m 09.291s, 64.660mph/104.060km/h.
2 Suzuki Catala, SPA: Josep Sarda/Kenny Noyes/Bernat Martinez (Suzuki GSXR 1000), 175 laps; **3** Bolliger Team Switzerland, SWI: David Morillon/Patrick Muff/Horst Saiger (Kawasaki ZX 10), 175; **4** Yamaha Austria Racing Team, AUT: Igor Jerman/Steve Martin/Steve Plater (Yamaha R1), 173; **5** Endurance Moto 38, FRA: Julien Millet/Cyril Brivet/Hervé Gantner (Yamaha R1), 172; **6** Maco Moto Racing Team, SVK: Warwick Nowland/Jason Pridmore (Yamaha R1), 171; **7** Team Kawasaki France, FRA: Julian Mazuecos/Erwan Nigon/Victor Carrasco (Kawasaki ZX 10), 170; **8** RT Racing Team & Motovirus, ITA: Jean-Louis Devoyon/Raphael Chevre (Suzuki GSXR 1000), 170; **9** Yamaha Folch Endurance, SPA: Daniel Ribalta/Pedro Luis Valcaneras/David Tomas (Yamaha R1), 170; **10** RMT 21 Racing Team, GER: Matti Seidel/Tomas Miksovsky/Diego Lozano (Honda CBR 1000), 165; **11** Endurance Moto 74, FRA: Stéphane Guichon/Jean Durieux/Michel Fontes (Yamaha R1), 164; **12** MCS Racing, ITA: Damian Rowley/Calvin Hogan (Suzuki GSXR 1000), 162; **13** CD Zona Roja, SPA: Anton Lopetegui/Antonio Gil/Martin Lopetegui (Yamaha R1), 151.
Fastest lap: Yamaha Austria Racing Team, 1m 46.595s, 74.267mph/119.521km/h, on lap 20.
Championship points: 1 Suzuki Endurance Racing Team 1, 53; **2** Suzuki Endurance Racing Team 2, 35; **3** Bolliger Team Switzerland, 30; **4** Team Acropolis Moto Expert, 22; **5** RMT 21 Racing Team, 21; **6** RT Racing Team & Motovirus, 21.

SUZUKA EIGHT HOURS, Suzuka International Circuit, Japan, 27 July 2008.
FIM Qtel Endurance World Championship, round 3. 214 laps of the 3.608-mile/5.807km circuit, 772.112 miles/1242.698km
1 Dream Honda Racing Team 11, JPN: Ryuichi Kiyonari/Carlos Checa (Honda CBR 1000RR), 8h 00m 20.726s, 96.685mph/155.600km/h.
2 Yoshimura Suzuki with Denso, JPN: Daisaku Sakai/Atsushi Watanabe (Suzuki GSXR 1000), 214 laps; **3** Kyubo.com Harc-Pro, JPN: Yoshiteru Konishi/Takumi Takahashi (Honda CBR 1000RR), 210; **4** Yoshimura Suzuki with Jomo, JPN: Kosuke Akiyoshi/Yukio Kagayama (Suzuki GSXR 1000), 209; **5** Yamaha Racing, JPN: Yuji Sato/Katsuyuki Nakasuga/Yuichi Takeda (Yamaha YZF R1), 209; **6** Moriwaki Motul Racing, JPN: Tatsuya Yamaguchi/Cal Crutchlow/Jason O'Halloran (Honda CBR 1000RR), 208; **7** Plot Faro Panthera, JPN: Yoshihiro Konno/Kohji Teramoto (Suzuki GSXR 1000), 207; **8** MotoMap Supply, JPN: Yuki Hatano/Hideyuki Ogata/Tomoki Namekata (Suzuki GSXR 1000), 205; **9** Sakurai Honda 10, JPN: Chojun Kameya/Leon Haslam (Honda CBR 1000RR), 205; **10** Sakurai Honda 71, JPN: Kazuma Tsuda/Joshua Brookes (Honda CBR 1000RR), 204; **11** Yamaha Austria Racing Team, AUT: Igor Jerman/Steve Martin/Steve Plater (Yamaha R1), 204; **12** Yamaha Folch Endurance, SPA: Daniel Ribalta/Pedro Luis Valcaneras (Yamaha R1), 204; **13** Phase One Endurance, GBR: Rico Penzkofer/Scott Smart/Damian Cudlin (Yamaha R1), 204; **14** Suzuki Endurance Racing Team 1, FRA: Julien Da Costa/Matthieu Lagrive (Suzuki GSXR 1000), 202; **15** Trick Star Racing, JPN: Shinya Takeishi/Ryuji Tsuruta/Ken Eguchi (Kawasaki ZX 10R), 202.
Fastest lap: Yoshimura Suzuki with Denso, 2m 08.416s, 101.402mph/163.190km/h, on lap 3.
Championship points: 1 Suzuki Endurance Racing Team 1, 55; **2** Suzuki Endurance Racing Team 2, 35; **3** Dream Honda Racing Team 11, 30; **4** Bolliger Team Switzerland, 30; **5** Yoshimura Suzuki with Denso, 24; **6** Team Acropolis Moto Expert, 22.

8 STUNDEN VON OSCHERSLEBEN, Oschersleben Circuit, Germany, 9 August 2008.
FIM Qtel Endurance World Championship, round 4. 305 laps of the 2.279-mile/3.667km circuit, 695.095 miles/1118.435km
1 Team Kawasaki France, FRA: Ivan Silva/Julian Mazuecos/Erwan Nigon (Kawasaki ZX 10R), 8h 00m 04.577s, 86.857mph/139.782km/h.
2 Yamaha Austria Racing Team, AUT: Igor Jerman/Steve Martin/Steve Plater (Yamaha R1), 304 laps; **3** Suzuki Endurance Racing Team 1, FRA: Vincent Philippe/Matthieu Lagrive/Julien Da Costa (Suzuki GSXR 1000), 303; **4** Phase One Endurance, GBR: Graeme Gowland/Damian Cudlin/Sébastien Scarnato (Yamaha R1), 303; **5** Yamaha Folch Endurance, SPA: Daniel Ribalta/Pedro Luis Valcaneras (Yamaha R1), 302; **6** Maco Moto Racing Team, SVK: Warwick Nowland/Jason Pridmore (Yamaha R1), 302; **7** AM Moto Racing, FRA: Sullivan Hernandez/Pierre Guersillon/Fabrice Auger (Suzuki GSXR 1000), 300; **8** RMT 21 Racing Team, GER: Matti Seidel/Tomas Miksovsky (Honda CBR 1000), 298; **9** Diablo 666 Bolliger, GBR: James Hutchins/Alex Cudlin/Michael Weynand (Kawasaki ZX 10), 296; **10** La Fortezza Amadeus X One, ITA: Paolo Tessari/William Gruy/Alessio Aldrovandi (Yamaha R1), 295; **11** Motobox Kremer Racing, GER: Anton Heiler/Florian Bauer/Martin Scherrer (Suzuki GSXR 1000), 288; **12** RT Racing Team & Motovirus, ITA: Jean-Louis Devoyon/Frédéric Jond/Sandor Bitter (Suzuki GSXR 1000), 286; **13** Herman Verboven Racing, BEL: Leroy Verboven/Wim van den Broeck/Michael Barnes (Suzuki GSXR 1000), 281; **14** Innodrom, SWI: Lars Albrecht/Frank Spenner/Niggi Schmassmann (Suzuki GSXR 1000), 280; **15** Endurance Moto 74, FRA: Stéphane Guichon/Jean Durieux/Michel Fontes (Yamaha R1), 277.
Fastest lap: Suzuki Endurance Racing Team 1, 1m 28.045s, 93.167mph/149.937km/h.

Championship points: **1** Suzuki Endurance Racing Team 1, 74; **2** Yamaha Austria Racing Team, 43; **3** Team Kawasaki France, 39; **4** Suzuki Endurance Racing Team 2, 35; **5** Yamaha Folch Endurance, 35; **6** RMT 21 Racing Team, 31.

72ème BOL D'OR 24 HOURS, Circuit de Nevers, Magny-Cours, France, 13–14 September 2008.
FIM Qtel Endurance World Championship, round 5. 747 laps of the 2.741-mile/4.411km circuit, 2047.527 miles/3295.017km
1 Suzuki Endurance Racing Team 1, FRA: Vincent Philippe/Matthieu Lagrive/Julien Da Costa (Suzuki GSXR 1000), 24h 01m 30.409s.
2 Suzuki Endurance Racing Team 2, FRA: William Costes/Guillaume Dietrich/Olivier Four (Suzuki GSXR 1000), 741 laps; **3** Yamaha Austria Racing Team, AUT: Igor Jerman/Steve Martin/Gwen Giabbani (Yamaha R1), 738; **4** Team Kawasaki France, FRA: Ivan Silva/Julian Mazuecos/Erwan Nigon (Kawasaki ZX 10), 733; **5** Phase One Endurance, GBR: Graeme Gowland/Jorg Teuchert/Damian Cudlin (Yamaha R1), 732; **6** Yamaha GMT 94, FRA: Sébastien Gimbert/David Checa/Steve Plater (Yamaha R1), 731; **7** Yamaha Folch Endurance, SPA: Daniel Ribalta/Pedro Luis Valcaneras/Jose Manuel Luis (Yamaha R1), 725; **8** Bolliger Team Switzerland, SWI: David Morillon/Patrick Muff/Horst Saiger (Kawasaki ZX 10), 721; **9** RMT 21 Racing Team, GER: Matti Seidel/Roland Resch/Kari Vehniainen (Honda CBR 1000), 720; **10** RT Racing Team & Motovirus, ITA: Jean-Louis Devoyon/Raphael Chevre/Frédéric Jond (Suzuki GSXR 1000), 720; **11** Team 18 Sapeurs Pompiers, FRA: Stéphane Molinier/David Briere/Michael Savary (Suzuki GSXR 1000), 718; **12** Endurance Moto 38, FRA: Cyril Brivet/Patrick Piot/Anthony Dos Santos (Yamaha R1), 713; **13** Team Acropolis Moto Expert, FRA: Grégory Fastre/Denis Bouan/Julien Millet (Yamaha R1), 709; **14** No Limits, ITA: Gianfranco Guareschi/Steve Mizera/Alexandre Le Quere (Suzuki GSXR 1000), 696; **15** Maco Moto Racing Team, SVK: Warwick Nowland/Jason Pridmore/Jiri Drazdak (Yamaha R1), 695.
Fastest lap: Team Kawasaki France, 1m 42.336s, 96.419mph/155.171km/h.
Championship points: **1** Suzuki Endurance Racing Team 1, 109; **2** Yamaha Austria Racing Team, 65; **3** Suzuki Endurance Racing Team 2, 63; **4** Team Kawasaki France, 57; **5** Yamaha Folch Endurance, 48; **6** Phase One Endurance, 43.

8 HOURS OF DOHA, Losail Circuit, Qatar, 8 November 2008.
FIM Qtel Endurance World Championship, round 6. 226 laps of the 3.343-mile/5.380km circuit, 755.518 miles/1215.880km
1 Yamaha Austria Racing Team, AUT: Igor Jerman/Steve Martin/Steve Plater (Yamaha R1), 8h 01m 08.079s, 94.217mph/151.627km/h.
2 Yamaha Folch Endurance, SPA: Daniel Ribalta/Pedro Luis Valcaneras (Yamaha R1), 223 laps; **3** Maco Motor Racing Team, SVK: Jason Pridmore/Thomas Hinterreiter/Jakub Smrz (Yamaha R1), 222; **4** Bolliger Team Switzerland, SWI: David Morillon/Patrick Muff/Horst Saiger (Kawasaki ZX 10R), 221; **5** RMT 21 Racing Team, GER: Arie Vos/Kari Vehniainen/Matti Seidel (Honda CBR 1000), 221; **6** Team 18 Sapeurs Pompiers, FRA: Stéphane Molinier/Michael Savary/Abdulrahman Al Malki (Suzuki GSXR 1000), 220; **7** RT Racing Team & Moto Virus, ITA: Jean-Louis Devoyon/Raphael Chevre/Frédéric Jond (Suzuki GSXR 1000), 220; **8** La Fortezza Amadeus X One, ITA: Paolo Tessari/William Gruy/Alessio Aldrovandi (Yamaha R1), 209; **9** Phase One Endurance, GBR: Scott Smart/Glen Richards/Damian Cudlin (Yamaha R1), 198.
Fastest lap: Suzuki Endurance Racing Team 1, FRA: Matthieu Lagrive/Julien Da Costa/Guillaume Dietrich (Suzuki GSXR 1000), 2m 02.526s, 98.222mph/158.073km/h, on lap 11.

Final World Championship points

1	Suzuki Endurance Racing Team 1, FRA	109
2	Yamaha Austria Racing Team, AUT	95
3	Yamaha Folch Endurance, SPA	72
4	Suzuki Endurance Racing Team, 2, FRA	63
5	Team Kawasaki France, FRA	57
6	Bolliger Team Switzerland, SWI	57

7 RMT 21 Racing Team, GER, 54; **8** Phase One Endurance, GBR, 51; **9** RT Racing Team & Moto Virus, ITA, 45; **10** Maco Motor Racing Team, SVK, 42; **11** Dream Honda Racing Team 11, JPN, 30; **12** Yoshimura Suzuki with Denso, JPN, 24; **13** Endurance Moto 38, FRA, 24; **14** Team Acropolis Moto Expert, FRA, 22; **15** AM Moto Racing, FRA, 22.

Isle of Man Tourist Trophy Races

ISLE OF MAN TOURIST TROPHY COURSE, 31 May–6 June 2008. 37.73-mile/60.72km course.
Dainese Superbike TT (6 laps, 226.38 miles/364.32km)
1 Cameron Donald (1000 Suzuki GSXR), 1h 47m 05.89s, 126.826mph/204.107km/h.
2 Bruce Anstey (1000 Suzuki GSXR), 1h 47m 16.66s; **3** Adrian Archibald (1000 Suzuki GSXR), 1h 48m 37.97s; **4** Gary Johson (1000 Honda CBR), 1h 49m 12.67s; **5** Ian Lougher (1000 Yamaha R1), 1h 49m 31.38s; **6** Ryan Farquhar (1000 Kawasaki ZX10), 1h 49m 35.70s; **7** Keith Amor (1000 Honda Fireblade), 1h 50m 34.50s; **8** Daniel Stewart (1000 Honda CBR), 1h 50m 35.73s; **9** Carl Rennie (1000 Suzuki GSXR), 1h 50m 57.00s; **10** Steve Plater (1000 Yamaha R1), 1h 51m 07.34s; **11** Mark Parrett (1000 Yamaha R1), 1h 51m 58.53s.
Fastest lap: Guy Martin (1000 Honda), 17m 28.54s, 129.540mph/208.474km/h, on lap 2 (record).

Relentless Supersport 1 (Junior TT) (4 laps, 150.92 miles/242.88km)
1 Steve Plater (600 Yamaha R6), 1h 14m 01.07s, 122.338mph/196.884km/h.
2 John McGuinness (600 Honda), 1h 14m 04.46s; **3** Keith Amor (600 Honda CBR), 1h 14m 12.28s; **4** Ryan Farquhar (600 Kawasaki ZX6), 1h 14m 14.26s; **5** Ian Lougher (600 Yamaha R6), 1h 14m 15.50s; **6** Gary Johnson (600 Honda CBR), 1h 14m 50.89s; **7** Mark Parrett (600 Yamaha R6), 1h 15m 26.86s; **8** Mats Nilsson (600 Honda), 1h 15m 32.16s; **9** Cameron Donald (600 Suzuki GSXR), 1h 15m 33.15s; **10** Michael Dunlop (600 Yamaha R6), 1h 15m 33.26s; **11** Chris Palmer (600 Yamaha R6), 1h 15m 52.19s; **12** Adrian Archibald (600 Yamaha R6), 1h 16m 01.73s; **13** Ian Pattinson (600 Honda RR), 1h 16m 14.06s; **14** Carl Rennie (600 Suzuki GSXR), 1h 16m 14.44s; **15** Roy Richardson (600 Yamaha R6), 1h 16m 14.74s; **16** Les Shand (600 Suzuki GSXR), 1h 16m 46.13s; **17** Davy Morgan (600 Yamaha R6), 1m 16m 52.84s; **18** Oliver Linsdell (600 Yamaha R6), 1h 17m 20.50s; **19** James Hillier (600 Suzuki GSXR), 1h 17m 40.76s.
Fastest lap: Plater, 18m 12.19s, 124.127mph/199.763km/h, on lap 4.

Relentless Supersport 2 (Junior TT) (4 laps, 150.92 miles/242.88km)
1 Bruce Anstey (600 Suzuki GSXR K7), 1h 13m 35.71s, 123.041mph/198.015km/h.
2 Ian Hutchinson (600 Yamaha R6), 1h 14m 09.76s; **3** Ryan Farquhar (600 Kawasaki ZX6), 1h 14m 23.14s; **4** Ian Lougher (600 Yamaha R6), 1h 14m 40.63s; **5** Gary Johnson (600 Honda CBR), 1h 14m 45.05s; **6** Guy Martin (600 Honda), 1h 14m 51.73s; **7** Conor Cummins (600 Yamaha R6), 1h 15m 10.49s; **8** Michael Dunlop (600 Yamaha R6), 1h 15m 33.71s; **9** Adrian Archibald (600 Yamaha R6), 1h 15m 58.79s; **10** Daniel Stewart (600 Yamaha R6), 1h 16m 01.11s; **11** Roy Richardson (600 Yamaha R6), 1h 16m 08.06s; **12** Mats Nilsson (600 Honda), 1h 16m 09.87s; **13** Chris Palmer (600 Yamaha R6), 1h 16m 10.74s; **14** Davy Morgan (600 Yamaha R6), 1h 16m 24.84s; **15** Ian Pattinson (600 Honda RR), 1h 16m 46.55s; **16** Carl Rennie (600 Suzuki GSXR), 1h 17m 03.45s; **17** James Hillier (600 Suzuki GSXR), 1h 17m 13.68s.
Fastest lap: Anstey, 18m 03.51s, 125.359mph/201.745km/h, on lap 2 (record).

Scottish Life International Superstock Race (4 laps, 150.92 miles/242.88km)
1 Cameron Donald (1000 Suzuki GSXR), 1h 11m 59.69s, 125.776mph/202.417km/h.
2 John McGuinness (1000 Honda), 1h 12m 14.76s; **3** Guy Martin (1000 Honda), 1h 12m 17.71s; **4** Ryan Farquhar (1000 Kawasaki ZX10), 1h 12m 34.98s; **5** Conor Cummins (1000 Yamaha R1), 1h 12m 40.28s; **6** Adrian Archibald (1000 Suzuki GSXR), 1h 13m 15.87s; **7** Ian Lougher (1000 Yamaha R1), 1h 13m 33.48s; **8** Steve Plater (1000 Yamaha R1), 1h 13m 40.87s; **9** Carl Rennie (1000 Suzuki GSXR), 1h 13m 46.81s; **10** Daniel Stewart (1000 Yamaha R1), 1h 14m 13.33s; **11** Les Shand (1000 Yamaha R1), 1h 14m 39.63s; **12** Ian Pattinson (1000 Suzuki GSXR), 1h 14m 39.78s; **13** Mark Parrett (1000 Yamaha R1), 1h 14m 42.67s; **14** Ian Hutchinson (1000 Yamaha R1), 1h 14m 48.84s; **15** Gary Carswell (1000 Suzuki GSXR K8), 1h 15m 13.01s.
Fastest lap: Donald, 17m 44.95s, 127.544mph/205.262km/h, on lap 2.

Dainese Senior TT (6 laps, 226.38 miles/364.32km)
1 John McGuinness (1000 Honda), 1h 46m 47.69s, 127.186mph/204.686km/h.
2 Cameron Donald (1000 Suzuki GSXR), 1h 47m 38.64s; **3** Ian Hutchinson (1000 Yamaha R1), 1h 48m 29.44s; **4** Ryan Farquhar (1000 Kawasaki ZX10), 1h 48m 47.45s; **5** Steve Plater (1000 Yamaha R1), 1h 49m 22.02s; **6** Gary Johnson (1000 Honda CBR), 1h 49m 42.39s; **7** Ian Lougher (1000 Yamaha R1), 1h 49m 59.30s; **8** Carl Rennie (1000 Suzuki GSXR), 1h 50m 16.08s; **9** Daniel Stewart (1000 Honda CBR), 1h 50m 30.89s; **10** Michael Dunlop (998 Yamaha R1), 1h 51m 03.62s; **11** Mark Parrett (1000 Yamaha R1), 1h 51m 35.61s; **12** Ian Pattinson (1000 Suzuki GSXR), 1h 51m 51.93s.
Fastest lap: McGuinness, 129.517mph/208.437km/h, on lap 6.

Sure Mobile Sidecar TT: Race A (3 laps, 113.19 miles/182.16km)
1 Nick Crowe/Mark Cox (600 LCR Honda), 59m 22.80s, 114.372mph/184.064km/h.
2 John Holden/Andrew Winkle (600 LCR Suzuki), 59m 42.24s; **3** Tim Reeves/Patrick Farrance (600 LCR Suzuki), 1h 01m 07.84s; **4** Phil Dongworth/Stuart Castles (600 Ireson Honda), 1h 01m 10.68s; **5** Nigel Connole/Dipash Chauhan (600 LCR Honda), 1h 01m 46.90s; **6** Douglas Wright/Stuart Bond (600 Shelbourne Honda), 1h 01m 50.57s.
Fastest lap: Crowe/Cox, 19m 40.43s, 115.066mph/185.181km/h, on lap 2.

Sure Mobile Sidecar TT: Race B (3 laps, 113.19 miles/182.16km)
1 Nick Crowe/Mark Cox (600 LCR Honda), 59m 34.76s, 113.989mph/183.448km/h.
2 Dave Molyneux/Dan Sayle (600 DMR Suzuki), 59m 45.31s; **3** John Holden/Andrew Winkle (600 LCR Suzuki), 1h 00m 19.33s; **4** Steve Norbury/Rick Long (600 Shelbourne Yamaha), 1h 00m 33.58s; **5** Klaus Klaffenbock/Christian Parzer (600 LCR Honda), 1h 00m 34.47s; **6** Tim Reeves/Patrick Farrance (600 LCR Suzuki), 1h 00m 59.76s; **7** Phil Dongworth/Stuart Castles (600 Ireson Honda), 1h 01m 16.66s; **8** Simon Neary/Jamie Winn (600 Baker Suzuki), 1h 01m 19.27s; **9** Nigel Connole/Dipash Chauhan (600 LCR Honda), 1h 01m 19.27s; **10** Douglas Wright/Stuart Bond (600 Shelbourne Honda), 1h 02m 16.71s.
Fastest lap: Crowe/Cox, 19m 45.81s, 114.544mph/184.341km/h, on lap 2.

ISLE OF MAN TT BILLOWN CIRCUIT, 7 June 2008. 4.25-mile/6.84km circuit.
Steam Packet Lightweight 250cc TT (12 laps, 51.00 miles/82.08km)
1 Ian Lougher (250 Honda), 30m 22.495s, 100.741mph/162.127km/h.
2 Ryan Farquhar (250 Honda), 30m 31.151s; **3** Chris Palmer (250 Honda), 31m 01.940s; **4** Andrew Neill (250 Honda), 31m 03.093s; **5** Davy Morgan (250 Honda), 31m 46.270s.
Fastest lap: Lougher, 2m 29.530s, 102.321mph/164.670km/h, on lap 10 (record).

Steam Packet Ultra Lightweight 125cc TT (12 laps, 51.00 miles/82.08km)
1 Chris Palmer (125 Honda), 32m 32.309s, 94.042mph/151.346km/h.
2 Dan Sayle (125 Honda), 33m 06.716s; **3** Nigel Moore (125 Honda), 33m 25.500s; **4** James Ford (125 Honda), 33m 39.525s; **5** Chris McGahan (125 Honda), 33m 51.452s; **6** Peter Wakefield (125 Honda), 33m 51.633s.
Fastest lap: Palmer, 2m 41.440s, 94.772mph/152.521km/h, on lap

British Championships

BRANDS HATCH GRAND PRIX CIRCUIT, 6 April 2008. 2.301-mile/3.703km circuit.
Bennetts British Superbike Championship, rounds 1 and 2*
Fuchs-Silkolene British Supersport Championship, round 1*
Relentless British 125GP Championship, round 1*
** Postponed: all races run on 11 May 2008 at Brands Hatch.*

THRUXTON CIRCUIT, 20 April 2008. 2.356-mile/3.792km circuit.
Bennetts British Superbike Championship, rounds 3 and 4
Race 1 (20 laps, 47.120 miles/75.840km)
1 Shane Byrne (Ducati), 25m 33.903s, 110.58mph/177.96km/h.
2 Cal Crutchlow (Honda); **3** Michael Rutter (Ducati); **4** Leon Haslam (Honda); **5** Leon Camier (Ducati); **6** Tom Sykes (Suzuki); **7** James Ellison (Honda); **8** Simon Andrews (Yamaha); **9** Stuart Easton (Kawasaki); **10** Michael Laverty (Suzuki); **11** Sean Emmett (Yamaha); **12** John Laverty (Ducati); **13** Tristan Palmer (Honda); **14** Billy McConnell (Kawasaki); **15** Guy Martin (Honda).
Fastest lap: Byrne, 1m 16.038s, 111.54mph/179.51km/h.

Race 2 (15 laps, 35.340 miles/56.880km)
1 Cal Crutchlow (Honda), 19m 05.302s, 111.08mph/178.77km/h.
2 Shane Byrne (Ducati); **3** Michael Rutter (Ducati); **4** Leon Camier (Ducati); **5** Michael Laverty (Suzuki); **6** Stuart Easton (Kawasaki); **7** James Ellison (Honda); **8** Tom Sykes (Suzuki); **9** Guy Martin (Honda); **10** Billy McConnell (Kawasaki); **11** John Laverty (Ducati); **12** Scott Smart (Kawasaki); **13** Tristan Palmer (Honda); **14** Atsushi Watanabe (Suzuki); **15** Dean Ellison (Yamaha).
Fastest lap: Crutchlow, 1m 15.758s, 111.95mph/180.17km/h.
Championship points: **1** Byrne and Crutchlow, 45; **3** Rutter, 32; **4** Camier, 24; **5** Sykes, 18; **6** J. Ellison, 18.

Fuchs-Silkolene British Supersport Championship, round 2 (18 laps, 42.408 miles/68.256km)
1 Steve Brogan (Honda), 25m 04.288s, 101.48mph/163.32km/h.
2 Glen Richards (Triumph); **3** Chris Martin (Kawasaki); **4** Hudson Kennaugh (Yamaha); **5** Ian Lowry (Suzuki); **6** Tom Grant (Yamaha); **7** Marty Nutt (Yamaha); **8** Ian Hutchinson (Yamaha); **9** Paul Young (Triumph); **10** Steven Neate (Kawasaki); **11** Rob Frost (Triumph); **12** Aaron Walker (Honda); **13** Craig Fitzpatrick (Yamaha); **14** Midge Smart (Yamaha); **15** James Westmoreland (Honda).
Fastest lap: Kennaugh, 1m 18.429s, 108.14mph/174.03km/h.
Championship points: **1** Brogan, 25; **2** Richards, 20; **3** Martin, 16; **4** Kennaugh, 13; **5** Lowry, 11; **6** Grant, 10.

Relentless British 125GP Championship, round 2 (14 laps, 32.984 miles/53.088km)
1 Paul Jordan (Honda), 20m 16.922s, 97.57mph/157.02km/h.
2 Michael Wilcox (Honda); **3** Matthew Hoyle (Honda); **4** James Ford (Honda); **5** Lee Costello (Honda); **6** Stewart Finlay (Honda); **7** Luke Hinton (Honda); **8** Tom Hayward (Honda); **9** Luke Mossey (Honda); **10** Martin Glossop (Honda); **11** Connor Behan (Honda); **12** Ross Constable (Honda); **13** Stuart Elwood (Honda); **14** Tim Hastings (Honda); **15** James Lodge (Honda).
Fastest lap: Ford, 1m 22.650s, 102.62mph/165.15km/h.
Championship points: **1** Jordan, 25; **2** Wilcox, 20; **3** Hoyle, 16; **4** Ford, 13; **5** Costello, 11; **6** Finlay, 10.

OULTON PARK INTERNATIONAL, 5 May 2008. 2.692-mile/4.332km circuit.
Bennetts British Superbike Championship, rounds 5 and 6
Race 1 (18 laps, 48.456 miles/77.976km)
1 Shane Byrne (Ducati), 32m 29.16s, 89.49mph/144.02km/h.
2 Leon Haslam (Honda); **3** Leon Camier (Ducati); **4** Michael Rutter (Ducati); **5** Tom Sykes (Suzuki); **6** Cal Crutchlow (Honda); **7** Michael Laverty (Suzuki); **8** James Ellison (Honda); **9** Tristan Palmer (Honda); **10** Stuart Easton (Kawasaki); **11** Scott Smart (Kawasaki); **12** Guy Martin (Honda); **13** Atsushi Watanabe (Suzuki); **14** David Johnson (Honda); **15** Steve Mercer (Yamaha).
Fastest lap: Crutchlow, 1m 46.345s, 91.13mph/146.66km/h.

Race 2 (13 laps, 34.996 miles/56.316km)
1 Shane Byrne (Ducati), 21m 13.862s, 98.90mph/159.16km/h.
2 James Ellison (Honda); **3** Leon Camier (Ducati); **4** Michael Laverty (Suzuki); **5** Stuart Easton (Kawasaki); **6** Michael Rutter (Ducati); **7** Simon Andrews (Yamaha); **8** Scott Smart (Kawasaki); **9** Atsushi Watanabe (Suzuki); **10** Billy McConnell (Kawasaki); **11** Tristan Palmer (Honda); **12** Steve Plater (Yamaha); **13** John Laverty (Ducati); **14** Luke Quigley (Suzuki); **15** Tom Grant (Honda).
Fastest lap: Byrne, 1m 36.402s, 100.53mph/161.79km/h.
Championship points: **1** Byrne, 95; **2** Camier, 56; **3** Crutchlow, 55; **4** Rutter, 55; **5** J. Ellison, 46; **6** M. Laverty, 39.

Fuchs-Silkolene British Supersport Championship, round 3 (12 laps, 32.304 miles/51.984km)
1 Glen Richards (Triumph), 20m 04.775s, 96.52mph/155.33km/h.
2 Hudson Kennaugh (Yamaha); **3** Ian Lowry (Suzuki); **4** Chris Martin (Kawasaki); **5** Steve Brogan (Honda); **6** BJ Toal (Yamaha); **7** Daniel Cooper (Honda); **8** Craig Fitzpatrick (Yamaha); **9** Ian Hutchinson (Yamaha); **10** Steven Neate (Kawasaki); **11** James Westmoreland (Honda); **12** Andy Weymouth (Yamaha); **13** James Webb (Honda); **14** James Hillier (Kawasaki); **15** Midge Smart (Yamaha).
Fastest lap: Richards, 1m 39.619s, 97.28mph/156.56km/h.
Championship points: **1** Richards, 45; **2** Brogan, 36; **3** Kennaugh, 33; **4** Martin, 29; **5** Lowry, 27; **6** Hutchinson, 15.

Relentless British 125GP Championship, round 3 (14 laps, 37.688 miles/60.648km)
1 Matthew Hoyle (Honda), 25m 28.103s, 88.78mph/142.88km/h.
2 Connor Behan (Honda); **3** Lee Costello (Honda); **4** James East (Honda); **5** Luke Hinton (Honda); **6** Tom Hayward (Honda); **7** Tim Hastings (Honda); **8** James Ford (Honda); **9** Catherine Green (Honda); **10** Shaun Horsman (Honda); **11** Jon Vincent (Honda); **12** Taylor Mackenzie (Honda); **13** Jordan Malton (Honda); **14** Phillip Wakefield (Honda); **15** Andrew Pollock (Honda).
Fastest lap: Costello, 1m 48.024s, 89.71mph/144.38km/h.
Championship points: **1** Hoyle, 41; **2** Costello, 27; **3** Jordan, 25; **4** Behan, 25; **5** Ford, 21; **6** Wilcox, 20.

BRANDS HATCH GRAND PRIX CIRCUIT, 11 May 2008. 2.301-mile/3.703km circuit.
Bennetts British Superbike Championship, rounds 1 and 2*
** Race postponed from 6 April.*
Race 1 (20 laps, 46.020 miles/74.060km)
1 Shane Byrne (Ducati), 29m 24.345s, 93.89mph/151.10km/h.
2 Tom Sykes (Suzuki); **3** Cal Crutchlow (Honda); **4** Leon Haslam (Honda); **5** Leon Camier (Ducati); **6** James Ellison (Honda); **7** Stuart Easton (Kawasaki); **8** Billy McConnell (Kawasaki); **9** Simon Andrews (Yamaha); **10** Tristan Palmer (Honda); **11** Scott Smart (Kawasaki); **12** Atsushi Watanabe (Suzuki); **13** Guy Martin (Honda); **14** Chris Burns (MV Agusta); **15** Martin Jessopp (Honda).
Fastest lap: Byrne, 1m 27.293s, 94.88mph/152.70km/h.

Race 2 (19 laps, 43.719 miles/70.357km)
1 Cal Crutchlow (Honda), 30m 31.299s, 85.93mph/138.29km/h.
2 Shane Byrne (Ducati); **3** Leon Camier (Ducati); **4** Michael Laverty (Suzuki); **5** Michael Rutter (Ducati); **6** Leon Haslam (Honda); **7** Stuart Easton (Kawasaki); **8** James Ellison (Honda); **9** Billy McConnell (Kawasaki); **10** Scott Smart (Kawasaki); **11** Tristan Palmer (Honda); **12** Guy Martin (Honda); **13** John Laverty (Ducati); **14** Aaron Zanotti (Honda); **15** Luke Quigley (Suzuki).
Fastest lap: Byrne, 1m 27.009s, 95.19mph/153.20km/h.
Championship points: **1** Byrne, 140; **2** Crutchlow, 96; **3** Camier, 83; **4** Rutter, 66; **5** J. Ellison, 64; **6** Haslam, 56.

Fuchs-Silkolene British Supersport Championship, round 1* (18 laps, 41.418 miles/66.654km)
** Race postponed from 6 April.*
1 Hudson Kennaugh (Yamaha), 29m 26.947s, 84.38mph/135.80km/h.
2 Glen Richards (Triumph); **3** Steve Brogan (Honda); **4** James Westmoreland (Honda); **5** BJ Toal (Yamaha); **6** Craig Fitzpatrick (Yamaha); **7** Ian Hutchinson (Yamaha); **8** Marty Nutt (Yamaha); **9** Andy Weymouth (Yamaha); **10** Paul Young (Triumph); **11** Daniel Cooper (Honda); **12** Joe Dickinson (Yamaha); **13** Steven Neate (Kawasaki); **14** Ben Wylie (Yamaha); **15** Dean Hipwell (Yamaha).
Fastest lap: Kennaugh, 1m 29.485s, 92.56mph/148.96km/h.
Championship points: **1** Richards, 65; **2** Kennaugh, 58; **3** Brogan, 52; **4** Martin, 29; **5** Lowry, 27; **6** Hutchinson, 24.

Relentless British 125GP Championship, round 1* (14 laps, 32.214 miles/51.842km)
** Race postponed from 6 April.*
1 Matthew Hoyle (Honda), 22m 37.356s, 85.43mph/137.49km/h.
2 Luke Hinton (Honda); **3** Paul Jordan (Honda); **4** Tim Hastings (Honda); **5** Stewart Finlay (Honda); **6** Tom Hayward (Honda); **7** Jay Lewis (Honda); **8** Connor Behan (Honda); **9** James Lodge (Honda); **10** Shaun Horsman (Honda); **11** Lee Costello (Honda); **12** Catherine Green (Honda); **13** Jordan Thompson (Honda); **14** Jamie Mossey (Honda); **15** Ross Constable (Honda).
Fastest lap: Hinton, 1m 35.988s, 86.29mph/138.87km/h.
Championship points: **1** Hoyle, 66; **2** Jordan, 41; **3** Hinton, 40; **4** Behan, 33; **5** Costello, 32; **6** Hayward, 28.

DONINGTON PARK GRAND PRIX CIRCUIT, 26 May 2008. 2.500-mile/4.023km circuit.
Bennetts British Superbike Championship, rounds 7 and 8 (2 x 20 laps, 50.000 miles/80.460km)
Race 1
1 Shane Byrne (Ducati), 32m 01.058s, 93.69mph/150.78km/h.
2 Leon Haslam (Honda); **3** Tom Sykes (Suzuki); **4** James Ellison (Honda); **5** Leon Camier (Ducati); **6** Cal Crutchlow (Honda); **7** Karl Harris (Yamaha); **8** Michael Rutter (Ducati); **9** Michael Laverty (Suzuki); **10** Simon Andrews (Yamaha); **11** Stuart Easton (Kawasaki); **12** Tristan Palmer (Honda); **13** Tom Grant (Honda); **14** Dean Ellison (Yamaha); **15** Scott Smart (Kawasaki).
Fastest lap: Byrne, 1m 32.376s, 97.42mph/156.78km/h.

Race 2
1 Shane Byrne (Ducati), 31m 06.337s, 96.44mph/155.21km/h.
2 Leon Haslam (Honda); **3** Cal Crutchlow (Honda); **4** Leon Camier (Ducati); **5** James Ellison (Honda); **6** Tom Sykes (Suzuki); **7** Karl Harris (Yamaha); **8** Michael Rutter (Ducati); **9** Simon Andrews (Yamaha); **10** Gary Mason (Honda); **11** Stuart Easton (Kawasaki); **12** Scott Smart (Kawasaki); **13** Atsushi Watanabe (Suzuki); **14** Tristan Palmer (Honda); **15** Dean Ellison (Yamaha).
Fastest lap: Byrne, 1m 32.587s, 97.20mph/156.43km/h.
Championship points: **1** Byrne, 190; **2** Crutchlow, 122; **3** Camier, 107; **4** Haslam, 96; **5** J. Ellison, 88; **6** Rutter, 82.

Fuchs-Silkolene British Supersport Championship, round 4 (18 laps, 45.000 miles/72.414km)
1 Ian Lowry (Suzuki), 28m 47.511s, 93.77mph/150.91km/h.
2 Glen Richards (Triumph); **3** Miguel Praia (Honda); **4** Steve Brogan (Honda); **5** Chris Martin (Kawasaki); **6** James Webb (Honda); **7** Rob Frost (Triumph); **8** Craig Fitzpatrick (Yamaha); **9** Paul Young (Triumph); **10** James Westmoreland (Honda); **11** BJ Toal (Yamaha); **12** Ben Wylie (Yamaha); **13** Sam Owens (Honda); **14** Marty Nutt (Yamaha); **15** Ashley Beech (Yamaha).
Fastest lap: Jonathan Rea (Honda), 1m 34.478s, 95.26mph/153.31km/h (record).
Championship points: **1** Richards, 85; **2** Brogan, 65; **3** Kennaugh, 58; **4** Lowry, 52; **5** Martin, 40; **6** Fitzpatrick, 29.

Relentless British 125GP Championship, round 4*
** Postponed: race run on 29 June 2008 at Mallory Park.*

SNETTERTON CIRCUIT, 15 June 2008. 1.952-mile/3.141km circuit.
Bennetts British Superbike Championship, rounds 9 and 10
Race 1 (21 laps, 40.992 miles/65.961km)
1 Leon Camier (Ducati), 23m 12.162s, 105.92mph/170.46km/h.
2 Shane Byrne (Ducati); **3** Tom Sykes (Suzuki); **4** Cal Crutchlow (Honda); **5** Leon Haslam (Honda); **6** Michael Laverty (Suzuki); **7** James Ellison (Honda); **8** Karl Harris (Yamaha); **9** Michael Rutter (Ducati); **10** Simon Andrews (Yamaha); **11** Billy McConnell (Kawasaki); **12** Atsushi Watanabe (Suzuki); **13** Tristan Palmer (Honda); **14** Gary Mason (Honda); **15** Marshall Neill (Honda).
Fastest lap: Camier, 1m 05.647s, 107.04mph/172.27km/h.

Race 2 (15 laps, 29.280 miles/47.115km)
1 Shane Byrne (Ducati), 18m 41.592s, 93.97mph/151.23km/h.
2 Leon Camier (Ducati); **3** Cal Crutchlow (Honda); **4** Michael Rutter (Ducati); **5** Leon Haslam (Honda); **6** Michael Laverty (Suzuki); **7** Tom Sykes (Suzuki); **8** Simon Andrews (Yamaha); **9** Tristan Palmer (Honda); **10** James Ellison (Honda); **11** Billy McConnell (Kawasaki); **12** Gary Mason (Honda); **13** Marshall Neill (Honda); **14** David Johnson (Honda); **15** Dean Ellison (Yamaha).
Fastest lap: Byrne, 1m 12.654s, 96.72mph/155.66km/h.
Championship points: **1** Byrne, 235; **2** Camier, 152; **3** Crutchlow, 151; **4** Haslam, 118; **5** J. Ellison, 103; **6** Rutter, 102.

Fuchs-Silkolene British Supersport Championship, round 5 (13 laps, 25.376 miles/40.833km)
1 Steve Plater (Yamaha), 14m 56.070s, 101.94mph/164.06km/h.
2 Glen Richards (Triumph); **3** James Westmoreland (Honda); **4** Hudson Kennaugh (Yamaha); **5** Ian Lowry (Suzuki); **6** Steve Brogan (Honda); **7** Ashley Beech (Yamaha); **8** Chris Martin (Kawasaki); **9** Rob Frost (Triumph); **10** Marty Nutt (Yamaha); **11** BJ Toal (Yamaha); **12** Andy Weymouth (Yamaha); **13** Sam Owens (Honda); **14** Craig Fitzpatrick (Yamaha); **15** Joe Dickinson (Yamaha).
Fastest lap: Westmoreland, 1m 08.172s, 103.07mph/165.88km/h.
Championship points: **1** Richards, 105; **2** Brogan, 75; **3** Kennaugh, 71; **4** Lowry, 63; **5** Martin, 48; **6** Westmoreland, 41.

Relentless British 125GP Championship, round 5 (14 laps, 27.328 miles/43.974km)
1 Paul Jordan (Honda), 17m 35.937s, 93.16mph/149.93km/h.
2 Martin Glossop (Honda); **3=** Shaun Horsman (Honda); **3=** Tom Hayward (Honda); **5** Tim Hastings (Honda); **6** Luke Hinton (Honda); **7** James Lodge (Honda); **8** Jay Lewis (Honda); **9** James Ford (Honda); **10** Lee Costello (Honda); **11** Michael Wilcox (Honda); **12** Jamie Mossey (Honda); **13** Jordan Thompson (Honda); **14** Connor Behan (Honda); **15** Jordan Malton (Honda).
Fastest lap: Hayward, 1m 14.290s, 94.59mph/152.23km/h.
Championship points: **1** Hoyle and Jordan, 66; **3** Hinton, 50; **4** Hayward, 44; **5** Costello, 38; **6** Behan, 35.

MALLORY PARK CIRCUIT, 29 June 2008. 1.410-mile/2.270km circuit.
Bennetts British Superbike Championship, rounds 11 and 12 (2 x 30 laps, 42.300 miles/68.100km)
Race 1
1 Shane Byrne (Ducati), 28m 33.049s, 88.89mph/143.05km/h.
2 Leon Haslam (Honda); **3** Cal Crutchlow (Honda); **4** Tom Sykes (Suzuki); **5** James Ellison (Honda); **6** Billy McConnell (Kawasaki); **7** Simon Andrews (Yamaha); **8** Tristan Palmer (Honda); **9** Atsushi Watanabe (Suzuki); **10** John Laverty (Ducati); **11** Michael Laverty (Suzuki); **12** David Johnson (Honda); **13** Gary Mason (Honda); **14** Dean Ellison (Yamaha); **15** Chris Burns (MV Agusta).
Fastest lap: Sykes, 55.984s, 90.66mph/145.90km/h.

Race 2
1 Michael Rutter (Ducati), 30m 10.219s, 84.12mph/135.38km/h.
2 Shane Byrne (Ducati); **3** Cal Crutchlow (Honda); **4** Tom Sykes (Suzuki); **5** Karl Harris (Yamaha); **6** Leon Haslam (Honda); **7** Simon Andrews (Yamaha); **8** Leon Camier (Ducati); **9** Tristan Palmer (Honda); **10** Scott Smart (Kawasaki); **11** James Ellison (Honda); **12** David Johnson (Honda); **13** Chris Burns (MV Agusta); **14** John Laverty (Ducati); **15** James Haydon (Kawasaki).
Fastest lap: Crutchlow, 56.773s, 89.40mph/143.88km/h.
Championship points: **1** Byrne, 280; **2** Crutchlow, 183; **3** Camier, 160; **4** Haslam, 148; **5** Rutter, 127; **6** Sykes, 126.

Fuchs-Silkolene British Supersport Championship, round 6 (24 laps, 33.840 miles/54.480km)
1 Hudson Kennaugh (Yamaha), 25m 04.776s, 80.95mph/130.28km/h.
2 Steve Plater (Yamaha); **3** Ian Lowry (Suzuki); **4** Ian Hutchinson (Yamaha); **5** Glen Richards (Triumph); **6** James Westmoreland (Honda); **7** BJ Toal (Yamaha); **8** James Webb (Honda); **9** Daniel Cooper (Honda); **10** Marty Nutt (Yamaha); **11** Rob Frost (Triumph); **12** Joe Dickinson (Yamaha); **13** Ross Walter (Triumph); **14** Aaron Walker (Honda); **15** Steven Neate (Kawasaki).
Fastest lap: Kennaugh, 1m 01.461s, 82.58mph/132.90km/h.
Championship points: **1** Richards, 116; **2** Kennaugh, 96; **3** Lowry, 79; **4** Brogan, 75; **5** Westmoreland, 51; **6** Martin, 48.

Relentless British 125GP Championship, round 4* (22 laps, 31.020 miles/49.940km)
** Race postponed from 26 May.*
1 Lee Costello (Honda), 22m 34.375s, 82.45mph/132.69km/h.
2 Tom Hayward (Honda); **3** Connor Behan (Honda); **4** Tim Hastings (Honda); **5** Paul Jordan (Honda); **6** Luke Hinton (Honda); **7** Jordan Thompson (Honda); **8** Jordan Malton (Honda); **9** James Lodge (Honda); **10** James East (Honda); **11** James Ford (Honda); **12** Taylor Mackenzie (Honda); **13** Jon Vincent (Honda); **14** Phillip Wakefield (Honda); **15** Dan Moreton (Honda).
Fastest lap: Martin Glossop (Honda), 1m 00.621s, 83.73mph/134.75km/h.

Relentless British 125GP Championship, round 6 (22 laps, 31.020 miles/49.940km)
1 Martin Glossop (Honda), 22m 27.902s, 82.84mph/133.32km/h.
2 Tim Hastings (Honda); **3** Jay Lewis (Honda); **4** James Lodge (Honda); **5** Paul Jordan (Honda); **6** Tom Hayward (Honda); **7** Shaun Horsman (Honda); **8** Jordan Thompson (Honda); **9** Michael Wilcox (Honda); **10** Jordan Malton (Honda); **11** James East (Honda); **12** Matthew Hoyle (Honda); **13** Phillip Wakefield (Honda); **14** Taylor Mackenzie (Honda); **15** Ben McConnachie (Honda).
Fastest lap: Glossop, 1m 00.159s, 84.37mph/135.78km/h.
Championship points: **1** Jordan, 88; **2** Hayward, 74; **3** Hoyle, 70; **4** Hastings, 68; **5** Costello, 63; **6** Hinton, 60.

OULTON PARK INTERNATIONAL, 20 July 2008. 2.692-mile/4.332km circuit.
Bennetts British Superbike Championship, rounds 13 and 14 (2 x 18 laps, 48.456 miles/77.976km)
Race 1
1 Tom Sykes (Suzuki), 29m 12.165s, 99.55mph/160.21km/h.
2 James Ellison (Honda); **3** Shane Byrne (Ducati); **4** Leon Haslam (Honda); **5** Simon Andrews (Yamaha); **6** Cal Crutchlow (Honda); **7** Michael Rutter (Ducati); **8** Billy McConnell (Kawasaki); **9** Michael Laverty (Suzuki); **10**

John Laverty (Ducati); **11** Scott Smart (Kawasaki); **12** James Haydon (Kawasaki); **13** Atsushi Watanabe (Suzuki); **14** Dean Ellison (Yamaha); **15** Tom Grant (Honda).
Fastest lap: Sykes, 1m 36.205s, 100.73mph/162.11km/h.

Race 2
1 Tom Sykes (Suzuki), 29m 04.554s, 99.99mph/160.92km/h.
2 Cal Crutchlow (Honda); **3** Shane Byrne (Ducati); **4** Leon Haslam (Honda); **5** James Ellison (Honda); **6** Simon Andrews (Yamaha); **7** Michael Laverty (Suzuki); **8** Scott Smart (Kawasaki); **9** Karl Harris (Yamaha); **10** Billy McConnell (Kawasaki); **11** Michael Rutter (Ducati); **12** Tristan Palmer (Honda); **13** John Laverty (Ducati); **14** Gary Mason (Honda); **15** James Haydon (Kawasaki).
Fastest lap: Sykes, 1m 36.040s, 100.90mph/162.38km/h.
Championship points: **1** Byrne, 312; **2** Crutchlow, 213; **3** Sykes, 176; **4** Haslam, 174; **5** Camier, 160; **6** J. Ellison, 150.

Fuchs-Silkolene British Supersport Championship, round 7 (16 laps, 43.072 miles/69.312km)
1 Glen Richards (Triumph), 26m 41.431s, 96.82mph/155.82km/h.
2 Hudson Kennaugh (Yamaha); **3** Ian Lowry (Suzuki); **4** Chris Martin (Kawasaki); **5** James Webb (Honda); **6** James Westmoreland (Honda); **7** Daniel Cooper (Honda); **8** Rob Frost (Triumph); **9** Ben Wylie (Yamaha); **10** Sam Owens (Honda); **11** Ian Hutchinson (Yamaha); **12** Joe Dickinson (Yamaha); **13** Craig Fitzpatrick (Yamaha); **14** Steven Neate (Kawasaki); **15** Aaron Walker (Honda).
Fastest lap: Kennaugh, 1m 39.309s, 97.58mph/157.04km/h (record).
Championship points: **1** Richards, 141; **2** Kennaugh, 116; **3** Lowry, 95; **4** Brogan, 75; **5** Martin and Westmoreland, 61.

Relentless British 125GP Championship, round 7 (14 laps, 37.688 miles/60.648km)
1 Matthew Hoyle (Honda), 25m 20.753s, 89.21mph/143.57km/h.
2 Tim Hastings (Honda); **3** Martin Glossop (Honda); **4** James East (Honda); **5** Tom Hayward (Honda); **6** Paul Jordan (Honda); **7** James Lodge (Honda); **8** Luke Hinton (Honda); **9** Connor Behan (Honda); **10** Michael Wilcox (Honda); **11** Niall Waddell (Honda); **12** Shaun Horsman (Honda); **13** Taylor Mackenzie (Honda); **14** Jordan Malton (Honda); **15** James Ford (Honda).
Fastest lap: Hoyle, 1m 47.104s, 90.48mph/145.61 km/h.
Championship points: **1** Jordan, 98; **2** Hoyle, 95; **3** Hastings, 88; **4** Hayward, 85; **5** Hinton, 68; **6** Glossop, 67.

KNOCKHILL CIRCUIT, 10 August 2008. 1.271-mile/2.045km circuit.
Bennetts British Superbike Championship, rounds 15 and 16
Race 1 (30 laps, 38.130 miles/61.350km)
1 Tom Sykes (Suzuki), 25m 09.296s, 90.97mph/146.40km/h.
2 Shane Byrne (Ducati); **3** James Ellison (Honda); **4** Michael Rutter (Ducati); **5** Leon Camier (Ducati); **6** Michael Laverty (Suzuki); **7** Karl Harris (Yamaha); **8** Simon Andrews (Yamaha); **9** Tristan Palmer (Honda); **10** Gary Mason (Honda); **11** Tom Grant (Honda); **12** Steve Mercer (Kawasaki); **13** David Johnson (Honda); **14** Martin Jessopp (Honda); **15** Chris Burns (MV Agusta).
Fastest lap: Laverty, 49.665s, 92.15mph/148.30km/h.

Race 2 (14 laps, 17.794 miles/28.630km)
1 Leon Haslam (Honda), 11m 58.300s, 89.20mph/143.55km/h.
2 Michael Rutter (Ducati); **3** Karl Harris (Yamaha); **4** Tom Sykes (Suzuki); **5** James Ellison (Honda); **6** Simon Andrews (Yamaha); **7** Cal Crutchlow (Honda); **8** Leon Camier (Ducati); **9** Billy McConnell (Kawasaki); **10** Chris Burns (MV Agusta); **11** Steve Mercer (Kawasaki); **12** Tristan Palmer (Honda); **13** Scott Smart (Kawasaki); **14** Guy Martin (Honda); **15** Atsushi Watanabe (Suzuki).
Fastest lap: Haslam, 49.896s, 91.72mph/147.61km/h.
Championship points: **1** Byrne, 332; **2** Crutchlow, 222; **3** Sykes, 214; **4** Haslam, 199; **5** Camier, 179; **6** J. Ellison, 177.

Fuchs-Silkolene British Supersport Championship, round 8 (22 laps, 27.962 miles/44.990km)
1 Ian Lowry (Suzuki), 18m 46.183s, 89.40mph/143.88km/h.
2 James Westmoreland (Honda); **3** Glen Richards (Triumph); **4** James Webb (Honda); **5** Hudson Kennaugh (Yamaha); **6** Jack Kennedy (Yamaha); **7** Rob Frost (Triumph); **8** Chris Martin (Kawasaki); **9** Paul Young (Triumph); **10** Steven Neate (Kawasaki); **11** Steve Brogan (Honda); **12** Sam Owens (Honda); **13** Dan Linfoot (Honda); **14** John McGuinness (Honda); **15** Andy Weymouth (Yamaha).
Fastest lap: Lowry, 50.682s, 90.30mph/145.32km/h.
Championship points: **1** Richards, 157; **2** Kennaugh, 127; **3** Lowry, 120; **4** Westmoreland, 81; **5** Brogan, 75; **6** Martin, 69.

Relentless British 125GP Championship, round 8 (15 laps, 19.065 miles/30.675km)
1 Matthew Hoyle (Honda), 13m 44.970s, 83.21mph/133.91km/h.
2 Martin Glossop (Honda); **3** Tim Hastings (Honda); **4** James East (Honda); **5** James Lodge (Honda); **6** Niall Waddell (Honda); **7** Luke Hinton (Honda); **8** Paul Jordan (Honda); **9** Shaun Horsman (Honda); **10** Connor Behan (Honda); **11** Jordan Thompson (Honda); **12** Nigel Percy (Honda); **13** Taylor Mackenzie (Honda); **14** Peter Sutherland (Honda); **15** Mark Hanna (Honda).
Fastest lap: Hoyle, 54.209s, 84.42mph/135.86km/h.
Championship points: **1** Hoyle, 120; **2** Jordan, 106; **3** Hastings, 104; **4** Glossop, 87; **5** Hayward, 85; **6** Hinton, 77.

CADWELL PARK CIRCUIT, 25 August 2008. 2.180-mile/3.508km circuit.
Bennetts British Superbike Championship, rounds 17 and 18
Race 1 (18 laps, 39.240 miles/63.144km)
1 Leon Haslam (Honda), 26m 42.195s, 88.16mph/141.88km/h.
2 Tom Sykes (Suzuki); **3** Shane Byrne (Ducati); **4** Leon Camier (Ducati); **5** Cal Crutchlow (Honda); **6** Michael Rutter (Ducati); **7** Simon Andrews (Yamaha); **8** Michael Laverty (Suzuki); **9** Atsushi Watanabe (Suzuki); **10** Gary Mason (Honda); **11** Tristan Palmer (Honda); **12** Billy McConnell (Kawasaki); **13** Scott Smart (Kawasaki); **14** John Laverty (Ducati); **15** Guy Martin (Honda).
Fastest lap: Sykes, 1m 28.045s, 89.13mph/143.44km/h.

Race 2 (15 laps, 32.700 miles/52.620km)
1 Leon Haslam (Honda), 22m 11.771s, 88.39mph/142.25km/h.
2 Tom Sykes (Suzuki); **3** Shane Byrne (Ducati); **4** Leon Camier (Ducati); **5** Michael Rutter (Ducati); **6** Simon Andrews (Yamaha); **7** Atsushi Watanabe (Suzuki); **8** Scott Smart (Kawasaki); **9** Michael Laverty (Suzuki); **10** Karl Harris (Yamaha); **11** Guy Martin (Honda); **12** Tristan Palmer (Honda); **13** Cal Crutchlow (Honda); **14** Stuart Easton (Kawasaki); **15** John Laverty (Ducati).
Fastest lap: Haslam, 1m 27.835s, 89.35mph/143.79km/h.
Championship points: **1** Byrne, 364; **2** Sykes, 254; **3** Haslam, 249; **4** Crutchlow, 236; **5** Camier, 205; **6** Rutter, 195.

Fuchs-Silkolene British Supersport Championship, round 9 (14 laps, 30.520 miles/49.112km)
1 Steve Plater (Yamaha), 21m 20.357s, 85.81mph/138.10km/h.
2 Glen Richards (Triumph); **3** James Webb (Honda); **4** Hudson Kennaugh (Yamaha); **5** James Westmoreland (Honda); **6** Paul Young (Triumph); **7** Rob Frost (Triumph); **8** Ian Lowry (Suzuki); **9** Chris Martin (Kawasaki); **10** Tommy Bridewell (Honda); **11** Steve Brogan (Honda); **12** John McGuinness (Honda); **13** Joe Dickinson (Yamaha); **14** Daniel Cooper (Honda); **15** Jack Kennedy (Yamaha).
Fastest lap: Webb, 1m 30.507s, 86.71mph/139.54km/h (record).
Championship points: **1** Richards, 177; **2** Kennaugh, 140; **3** Lowry, 128; **4** Westmoreland, 92; **5** Brogan, 85; **6** Martin, 76.

Relentless British 125GP Championship, round 9 (14 laps, 30.520 miles/49.112km)
1 Matthew Hoyle (Honda), 22m 19.623s, 82.01mph/131.98km/h.
2 Martin Glossop (Honda); **3** Tom Hayward (Honda); **4** Tim Hastings (Honda); **5** Paul Jordan (Honda); **6** Jay Lewis (Honda); **7** Deane Brown (Honda); **8** James East (Honda); **9** Shaun Horsman (Honda); **10** Connor Behan (Honda); **11** James Lodge (Honda); **12** Dan Moreton (Honda); **13** Luke Hinton (Honda); **14** Jordan Thompson (Honda); **15** Jordan Malton (Honda).
Fastest lap: Hoyle, 1m 34.762s, 82.81mph/133.27km/h.
Championship points: **1** Hoyle, 145; **2** Jordan, 117; **3** Hastings, 117; **4** Glossop, 107; **5** Hayward, 101; **6** Hinton, 80.

CROFT CIRCUIT, 14 September 2008. 2.125-mile/3.420-km circuit.
Bennetts British Superbike Championship, rounds 19 and 20 (2 x 20 laps, 42.500 miles/68.400km)
Race 1
1 Leon Camier (Ducati), 27m 06.760s, 94.05mph/151.36km/h.
2 Leon Haslam (Honda); **3** Tom Sykes (Suzuki); **4** Cal Crutchlow (Honda); **5** Shane Byrne (Ducati); **6** Michael Rutter (Ducati); **7** Michael Laverty (Suzuki); **8** Karl Harris (Yamaha); **9** James Ellison (Honda); **10** Simon Andrews (Yamaha); **11** Gary Mason (Honda); **12** Atsushi Watanabe (Suzuki); **13** Scott Smart (Kawasaki); **14** Tristan Palmer (Honda); **15** Stuart Easton (Kawasaki).
Fastest lap: Byrne, 1m 20.553s, 94.96mph/152.82km/h.

Race 2
1 Leon Haslam (Honda), 27m 04.305s, 94.19mph/151.58km/h.
2 Tom Sykes (Suzuki); **3** Cal Crutchlow (Honda); **4** Shane Byrne (Ducati); **5** Leon Camier (Ducati); **6** Michael Rutter (Ducati); **7** James Ellison (Honda); **8** Karl Harris (Yamaha); **9** Simon Andrews (Yamaha); **10** Michael Laverty (Suzuki); **11** Gary Mason (Honda); **12** Atsushi Watanabe (Suzuki); **13** Stuart Easton (Kawasaki); **14** Tristan Palmer (Honda); **15** Jason O'Halloran (Honda).
Fastest lap: Byrne, 1m 20.415s, 95.13mph/153.10km/h.
Championship points: **1** Byrne, 388; **2** Haslam, 294; **3** Sykes, 290; **4** Crutchlow, 265; **5** Camier, 241; **6** Rutter, 215.

Fuchs-Silkolene British Supersport Championship, round 10 (10 laps, 21.250 miles/34.200 km)
1 Glen Richards (Triumph), 13m 49.030s, 92.27mph/148.49km/h.
2 James Westmoreland (Honda); **3** Hudson Kennaugh (Yamaha); **4** James Webb (Honda); **5** Paul Young (Triumph); **6** Marty Nutt (Yamaha); **7** Pete Spalding (Yamaha); **8** Joe Dickinson (Yamaha); **9** Chris Martin (Kawasaki); **10** Jack Kennedy (Yamaha); **11** Craig Fitzpatrick (Yamaha); **12** John McGuinness (Honda); **13** Andy Weymouth (Yamaha); **14** BJ Toal (Yamaha); **15** Daniel Cooper (Honda).
Fastest lap: Richards, 1m 22.166s, 93.10mph/149.83km/h (record).
Championship points: **1** Richards, 202; **2** Kennaugh, 156; **3** Lowry, 148; **4** Westmoreland, 92; **5** Brogan, 85; **6** Martin, 83.

Relentless British 125GP Championship, round 10 (14 laps, 29.750 miles/47.880km)
1 Tim Hastings (Honda), 20m 31.358s, 86.97mph/139.96km/h.
2 Jay Lewis (Honda); **3** Connor Behan (Honda); **4** Tom Hayward (Honda); **5** Shaun Horsman (Honda); **6** Deane Brown (Honda); **7** James Lodge (Honda); **8** Jordan Thompson (Honda); **9** Michael Hill (Honda); **10** Luke Hinton (Honda); **11** Niall Waddell (Honda); **12** Paul Jordan (Honda); **13** Jordan Malton (Honda); **14** Stuart Elwood (Honda); **15** Peter Sutherland (Honda).
Fastest lap: Hastings, 1m 27.245s, 87.68mph/141.11km/h.
Championship points: **1** Hoyle, 145; **2** Hastings, 142; **3** Jordan, 121; **4** Hayward, 114; **5** Glossop, 107; **6** Behan and Hinton, 86.

SILVERSTONE INTERNATIONAL CIRCUIT, 28 September 2008. 2.213-mile/3.561km circuit.
Bennetts British Superbike Championship, rounds 21 and 22 (2 x 20 laps, 44.260 miles/71.220km)
Race 1
1 Leon Camier (Ducati), 29m 02.806s, 91.42mph/147.13km/h.
2 Cal Crutchlow (Honda); **3** Shane Byrne (Ducati); **4** Michael Rutter (Ducati); **5** Simon Andrews (Yamaha); **6** Tristan Palmer (Honda); **7** Jason O'Halloran (Honda); **8** Stuart Easton (Kawasaki); **9** Atsushi Watanabe (Suzuki); **10** Billy McConnell (Kawasaki); **11** Leon Haslam (Honda); **12** David Johnson (Honda); **13** Chris Burns (MV Agusta); **14** Peter Hickman (Honda); **15** Martin Jessopp (Honda).
Fastest lap: Haslam, 1m 26.529s, 92.07mph/148.17km/h.

Race 2
1 Leon Haslam (Honda), 28m 59.106s, 91.62mph/147.45km/h.
2 Shane Byrne (Ducati); **3** Tom Sykes (Suzuki); **4** Leon Camier (Ducati); **5** Karl Harris (Yamaha); **6** James Ellison (Honda); **7** Michael Rutter (Ducati); **8** Simon Andrews (Yamaha); **9** Billy McConnell (Kawasaki); **10** Jason O'Halloran (Honda); **11** Stuart Easton (Kawasaki); **12** Tristan Palmer (Honda); **13** John Laverty (Ducati); **14** David Johnson (Honda); **15** Michael Laverty (Suzuki).
Fastest lap: Byrne, 1m 25.979s, 92.66mph/149.12km/h.
Championship points: **1** Byrne, 424; **2** Haslam, 324; **3** Sykes, 306; **4** Crutchlow, 285; **5** Camier, 279; **6** Rutter, 237.

Fuchs-Silkolene British Supersport Championship, round 11 (18 laps, 39.834 miles/64.098km)
1 Hudson Kennaugh (Yamaha), 27m 25.254s, 87.16mph/140.27km/h.
2 Paul Young (Triumph); **3** Steve Plater (Yamaha); **4** Glen Richards (Triumph); **5** James Westmoreland (Honda); **6** Ian Lowry (Suzuki); **7** Chris Martin (Kawasaki); **8** Daniel Cooper (Honda); **9** Joe Dickinson (Yamaha); **10** Jack Kennedy (Yamaha); **11** Marty Nutt (Yamaha); **12** Alastair Seeley (Yamaha); **13** James Webb (Honda); **14** Craig Fitzpatrick (Yamaha); **15** Steven Neate (Kawasaki).
Fastest lap: Kennaugh, 1m 28.392s, 90.13mph/145.05km/h (record).
Championship points: **1** Richards, 215; **2** Kennaugh, 181; **3** Lowry, 138; **4** Westmoreland, 123; **5** Martin, 92; **6** Plater, 86.

Relentless British 125GP Championship, round 11 (14 laps, 30.982 miles/49.854km)
1 Matthew Hoyle (Honda), 22m 38.575s, 82.09mph/132.11km/h.
2 Tim Hastings (Honda); **3** Connor Behan (Honda); **4** James Lodge (Honda); **5** Tom Hayward (Honda); **6** Paul Jordan (Honda); **7** Shaun Horsman (Honda); **8** Jordan Thompson (Honda); **9** Catherine Green (Honda); **10** Adam Blacklock (Honda); **11** Taylor Mackenzie (Honda); **12** Luke Hinton (Honda); **13** Ross Ashman (Honda); **14** James Ford (Honda); **15** Phillip Wakefield (Honda).
Fastest lap: Hoyle, 1m 34.384s, 84.40mph/135.83km/h.
Championship points: **1** Hoyle, 170; **2** Hastings, 162; **3** Jordan, 131; **4** Hayward, 125; **5** Glossop, 107; **6** Behan, 102.

BRANDS HATCH INDY CIRCUIT, 12 October 2008. 1.199-mile/1.929km circuit.
Bennetts British Superbike Championship, rounds 23 and 24 (2 x 30 laps, 35.970 miles/57.870km)
Race 1
1 Shane Byrne (Ducati), 23m 21.717s, 92.35mph/148.62km/h.
2 Cal Crutchlow (Honda); **3** James Ellison (Honda); **4** Leon Haslam (Honda); **5** Leon Camier (Ducati); **6** Tom Sykes (Suzuki); **7** Michael Rutter (Ducati); **8** Simon Andrews (Yamaha); **9** Jon Kirkham (Yamaha); **10** Tristan Palmer (Honda); **11** Gary Mason (Honda); **12** Billy McConnell (Kawasaki); **13** John Laverty (Ducati); **14** Atsushi Watanabe (Suzuki); **15** Jason O'Halloran (Honda).
Fastest lap: Byrne, 46.194s, 93.41mph/150.33km/h.

Race 2
1 Shane Byrne (Ducati), 23m 21.124s, 92.39mph/148.69km/h.
2 Leon Haslam (Honda); **3** Leon Camier (Ducati); **4** Cal Crutchlow (Honda); **5** James Ellison (Honda); **6** Michael Rutter (Ducati); **7** Simon Andrews (Yamaha); **8** John Laverty (Ducati); **9** Gary Mason (Honda); **10** Jon Kirkham (Yamaha); **11** Chris Burns (MV Agusta); **12** Jason O'Halloran (Honda); **13** Tristan Palmer

(Honda); **14** Atsushi Watanabe (Suzuki); **15** Guy Martin (Honda).
Fastest lap: Haslam, 46.110s, 93.58mph/150.60km/h.

Fuchs-Silkolene British Supersport Championship, round 12 (25 laps, 29.975 miles/48.225km)
1 Glen Richards (Triumph), 19m 49.632s, 90.68mph/145.94km/h.
2 Steve Plater (Yamaha); **3** Josh Brookes (Honda); **4** James Westmoreland (Honda); **5** Rob Frost (Triumph); **6** James Webb (Honda); **7** Daniel Cooper (Honda); **8** Ian Lowry (Suzuki); **9** Chris Martin (Kawasaki); **10** Hudson Kennaugh (Yamaha); **11** Craig Fitzpatrick (Yamaha); **12** Dean Hipwell (Yamaha); **13** Marty Nutt (Yamaha); **14** Steven Neate (Kawasaki); **15** Jack Kennedy (Yamaha).
Fastest lap: Brookes, 47.092s, 91.63mph/147.46km/h (record).

Relentless British 125GP Championship, round 12 (22 laps, 26.378 miles/42.438km)
1 James Lodge (Honda), 18m 26.770s, 85.77mph/138.03km/h.
2 Matthew Hoyle (Honda); **3** Connor Behan (Honda); **4** James East (Honda); **5** Shaun Horsman (Honda); **6** Taylor Mackenzie (Honda); **7** Tom Hayward (Honda); **8** Jay Lewis (Honda); **9** Corey Lewis (Honda); **10** Jordan Thompson (Honda); **11** Jamie Mossey (Honda); **12** Paul Jordan (Honda); **13** Niall Waddell (Honda); **14** Catherine Green (Honda); **15** Luke Hinton (Honda).
Fastest lap: Tim Hastings (Honda), 49.366s, 87.40mph/140.66km/h.

Final British Superbike Championship points

1	Shane Byrne	474
2	Leon Haslam	357
3	Cal Crutchlow	318
4	Tom Sykes	316
5	Leon Camier	306
6	Michael Rutter	256

7 James Ellison, 230; **8** Simon Andrews, 176; **9** Michael Laverty, 141; **10** Tristan Palmer, 111; **11** Karl Harris, 102; **12** Billy McConnell, 91; **13** Stuart Easton, 81; **14** Atsushi Watanabe, 69; **15** Scott Smart, 69.

Final British Supersport Championship points

1	Glen Richards	240
2	Hudson Kennaugh	187
3	Ian Lowry	146
4	James Westmoreland	136
5	Steve Plater	106
6	Chris Martin	99

7 James Webb, 87; **8** Steve Brogan, 85; **9** Paul Young, 68; **10** Rob Frost, 63; **11** Daniel Cooper, 50; **12** Marty Nutt, 49; **13** Craig Fitzpatrick, 46; **14** Ian Hutchinson, 42; **15** BJ Toal, 42.

Final British 125GP Championship points

1	Matthew Hoyle	190
2	Tim Hastings	162
3	Paul Jordan	135
4	Tom Hayward	134
5	Connor Behan	118
6	James Lodge	109

7 Martin Glossop, 107; **8** Luke Hinton, 91; **9** Shaun Horsman, 86; **10** Jay Lewis, 71; **11** James East, 71; **12** Lee Costello, 63; **13** Jordan Thompson, 52; **14** Michael Wilcox, 38; **15** James Ford, 36.

Supersport World Championship

LOSAIL, Qatar, 23 February 2008. 3.343-mile/5.380km circuit.
Supersport World Championship, round 1 (18 laps, 60.174 miles/96.840km)
1 Broc Parkes, AUS (Yamaha), 37m 05.271s, 97.348mph/156.666km/h.
2 Joan Lascorz, SPA (Honda); **3** Craig Jones, GBR (Honda); **4** Joshua Brookes, AUS (Honda); **5** Matthieu Lagrive, FRA (Honda); **6** Barry Veneman, NED (Suzuki); **7** Robbin Harms, DEN (Honda); **8** David Salom, SPA (Yamaha); **9** Chris Walker, GBR (Kawasaki); **10** Gianluca Vizziello, ITA (Honda); **11** Gregory Leblanc, FRA (Honda); **12** Ivan Clementi, ITA (Triumph); **13** Miguel Praia, POR (Honda); **14** Vesa Kallio, FIN (Honda); **15** Katsuaki Fujiwara, JPN (Kawasaki).
Fastest lap: Fabien Foret, FRA (Yamaha), 2m 02.626s, 98.142mph/157.944km/h (record).
Championship points: **1** Parkes, 25; **2** Lascorz, 20; **3** Jones, 16; **4** Brookes, 13; **5** Lagrive, 11; **6** Veneman, 10.

PHILLIP ISLAND, Australia, 2 March 2008. 2.762-mile/4.445km circuit.
Supersport World Championship, round 2 (21 laps, 58.002 miles/93.345km)
1 Andrew Pitt, AUS (Honda), 33m 51.257s, 102.797mph/165.435km/h.
2 Joshua Brookes, AUS (Honda); **3** Robbin Harms, DEN (Honda); **4** Fabien Foret, FRA (Yamaha); **5** Jonathan Rea, GBR (Honda); **6** Garry McCoy, AUS (Triumph); **7** Joan Lascorz, SPA (Honda); **8** Gianluca Vizziello, ITA (Honda); **9** Massimo Roccoli, ITA (Yamaha); **10** Gianluca Nannelli, ITA (Honda); **11** Ivan Clementi, ITA (Triumph); **12** Mark Aitchison, AUS (Triumph); **13** Graeme Gowland, GBR (Honda); **14** Chris Walker, GBR (Kawasaki); **15** Vesa Kallio, FIN (Honda).
Fastest lap: Harms, 1m 35.429s, 104.195mph/167.685km/h.
Championship points: **1** Brookes, 33; **2** Lascorz, 29; **3** Parkes and Pitt, 25; **5** Harms, 25; **6** Jones, 16.

VALENCIA, Spain, 6 April 2008. 2.489-mile/4.005km circuit.
Supersport World Championship, round 3 (23 laps, 57.247 miles/92.115km)
1 Joan Lascorz, SPA (Honda), 37m 58.607s, 90.431mph/145.534km/h.
2 Fabien Foret, FRA (Yamaha); **3** Craig Jones, GBR (Honda); **4** Broc Parkes, AUS (Yamaha); **5** Gianluca Nannelli, ITA (Honda); **6** Jonathan Rea, GBR (Honda); **7** Massimo Roccoli, ITA (Yamaha); **8** Angel Rodriguez, SPA (Yamaha); **9** Chris Walker, GBR (Kawasaki); **10** Mark Aitchison, AUS (Triumph); **11** Katsuaki Fujiwara, JPN (Kawasaki); **12** Gianluca Vizziello, ITA (Honda); **13** Matthieu Lagrive, FRA (Honda); **14** Vesa Kallio, FIN (Honda); **15** Miguel Praia, POR (Honda).
Fastest lap: Parkes, 1m 37.590s, 91.802mph/147.741km/h.
Championship points: **1** Lascorz, 54; **2** Parkes, 38; **3** Brookes and Foret, 33; **5** Jones, 32; **6** Pitt, 25.

ASSEN, Holland, 27 April 2008. 2.830-mile/4.555km circuit.
Supersport World Championship, round 4 (21 laps, 59.430 miles/95.655km)
1 Andrew Pitt, AUS (Honda), 36m 10.751s, 98.571mph/158.635km/h.
2 Jonathan Rea, GBR (Honda); **3** Joan Lascorz, SPA (Honda); **4** Fabien Foret, FRA (Yamaha); **5** Broc Parkes, AUS (Yamaha); **6** Joshua Brookes, AUS (Honda); **7** Barry Veneman, NED (Suzuki); **8** Gianluca Vizziello, ITA (Honda); **9** Craig Jones, GBR (Honda); **10** Matthieu Lagrive, FRA (Honda); **11** Mark Aitchison, AUS (Triumph); **12** Chris Walker, GBR (Kawasaki); **13** Robbin Harms, DEN (Honda); **14** Ivan Clementi, ITA (Triumph); **15** Ilario Dionisi, ITA (Triumph).
Fastest lap: Vizziello, 1m 42.130s, 99.767mph/160.560km/h.
Championship points: **1** Lascorz, 70; **2** Pitt, 50; **3** Parkes, 49; **4** Foret, 46; **5** Brookes, 43; **6** Rea, 41.

MONZA, Italy, 11 May 2008. 3.600-mile/5.793km circuit.
Supersport World Championship, round 5 (16 laps, 57.600 miles/92.688km)
1 Fabien Foret, FRA (Yamaha), 29m 38.261s, 116.595mph/187.642km/h.
2 Joshua Brookes, AUS (Honda); **3** Broc Parkes, AUS (Yamaha); **4** Andrew Pitt, AUS (Honda); **5** Robbin Harms, DEN (Honda); **6** Craig Jones, GBR (Honda); **7** Massimo Roccoli, ITA (Yamaha); **8** Matthieu Lagrive, FRA (Honda); **9** Joan Lascorz, SPA (Honda); **10** Angel Rodriguez, SPA (Yamaha); **11** Mark Aitchison, AUS (Triumph); **12** Cristiano Migliorati, ITA (Kawasaki); **13** Gianluca Nannelli, ITA (Honda); **14** Vesa Kallio, FIN (Honda); **15** Katsuaki Fujiwara, JPN (Kawasaki).
Fastest lap: Foret, 1m 50.430s, 117.347mph/188.851km/h (record).
Championship points: **1** Lascorz, 77; **2** Foret, 71; **3** Parkes, 65; **4** Pitt, 63; **5** Brookes, 63; **6** Jones, 49.

NÜRBURGRING, Germany, 15 June 2008. 3.192-mile/5.137km circuit.
Supersport World Championship, round 6 (19 laps, 60.648 miles/97.603km)
1 Andrew Pitt, AUS (Honda), 38m 26.584s, 94.656mph/152.334km/h.
2 Joshua Brookes, AUS (Honda); **3** Broc Parkes, AUS (Yamaha); **4** Fabien Foret, FRA (Yamaha); **5** Craig Jones, GBR (Honda); **6** Jonathan Rea, GBR (Honda); **7** Didier van Keymeulen, BEL (Suzuki); **8** Arne Tode, GER (Triumph); **9** Chris Walker, GBR (Kawasaki); **10** Vesa Kallio, FIN (Honda); **11** Katsuaki Fujiwara, JPN (Kawasaki); **12** Joan Lascorz, SPA (Honda); **13** Miguel Praia, POR (Honda); **14** Gianluca Vizziello, ITA (Honda); **15** Jeremy Crowe, AUS (Yamaha).
Fastest lap: Parkes, 2m 00.452s, 95.400mph/153.532km/h (record).
Championship points: **1** Pitt, 88; **2** Foret, 84; **3** Brookes, 83; **4** Lascorz and Parkes, 81; **6** Jones, 60.

MISANO, Italy, 29 June 2008. 2.626-mile/4.226km circuit.
Supersport World Championship, round 7 (22 laps, 57.772 miles/92.972km)
1 Andrew Pitt, AUS (Honda), 37m 08.387s, 93.329mph/150.198km/h.
2 Craig Jones, GBR (Honda); **3** Jonathan Rea, GBR (Honda); **4** Fabien Foret, FRA (Yamaha); **5** Robbin Harms, DEN (Honda); **6** Mark Aitchison, AUS (Triumph); **7** Massimo Roccoli, ITA (Yamaha); **8** Barry Veneman, NED (Suzuki); **9** Ivan Clementi, ITA (Triumph); **10** Broc Parkes, AUS (Yamaha); **11** Gianluca Vizziello, ITA (Honda); **12** Chris Walker, GBR (Kawasaki); **13** Gianluca Nannelli, ITA (Honda); **14** Joshua Brookes, AUS (Honda); **15** Danilo Marrancone, ITA (Yamaha).
Fastest lap: Parkes, 1m 40.187s, 94.356mph/151.852km/h (record, revised circuit).
Championship points: **1** Pitt, 113; **2** Foret, 97; **3** Parkes, 87; **4** Brookes, 85; **5** Lascorz, 81; **6** Jones, 80.

BRNO, Czech Republic, 20 July 2008. 3.357-mile/5.403km circuit.
Supersport World Championship, round 8 (18 laps, 60.426 miles/97.254km)
1 Jonathan Rea, GBR (Honda), 37m 35.093s, 96.471mph/155.255km/h.
2 Andrew Pitt, AUS (Honda); **3** Joshua Brookes, AUS (Honda); **4** Broc Parkes, AUS (Yamaha); **5** Barry Veneman, NED (Suzuki); **6** Gianluca Nannelli, ITA (Honda); **7** Russell Holland, AUS (Honda); **8** Matthieu Lagrive, FRA (Honda); **9** Vesa Kallio, FIN (Honda); **10** Massimo Roccoli, ITA (Yamaha); **11** Chris Walker, GBR (Kawasaki); **12** Gianluca Vizziello, ITA (Honda); **13** Ivan Clementi, ITA (Triumph); **14** Didier van Keymeulen, BEL (Suzuki); **15** David Salom, SPA (Yamaha).
Fastest lap: Pitt, 2m 04.062s, 97.420mph/156.783km/h (record).
Championship points: **1** Pitt, 133; **2** Brookes, 101; **3** Parkes, 100; **4** Foret, 97; **5** Rea, 92; **6** Lascorz, 81.

BRANDS HATCH, Great Britain, 3 August 2008. 2.301-mile/3.702km circuit.
Supersport World Championship, round 9 (15 laps, 34.515 miles/55.530km; aggregated result)
1 Jonathan Rea, GBR (Honda), 22m 29.935s, 92.017mph/148.087km/h.
2 Craig Jones, GBR (Honda); **3** Andrew Pitt, AUS (Honda); **4** Broc Parkes, AUS (Yamaha); **5** Joshua Brookes, AUS (Honda); **6** Barry Veneman, NED (Suzuki); **7** Gianluca Nannelli, ITA (Honda); **8** Massimo Roccoli, ITA (Yamaha); **9** Robert Frost, GBR (Triumph); **10** Hudson Kennaugh, RSA (Yamaha); **11** Steve Plater, GBR (Triumph); **12** Gianluca Vizziello, ITA (Honda); **13** Vesa Kallio, FIN (Honda); **14** Joan Lascorz, SPA (Honda); **15** Graeme Gowland, GBR (Honda).
Fastest lap: Pitt, 1m 28.399s, 93.679mph/150.762km/h (record).
Championship points: **1** Pitt, 149; **2** Rea, 117; **3** Parkes, 113; **4** Brookes, 112; **5** Jones, 100; **6** Foret, 97.

DONINGTON PARK, Great Britain, 7 September 2008. 2.500-mile/4.023km circuit.
Supersport World Championship, round 10 (22 laps, 55.000 miles/88.506km)
1 Joshua Brookes, AUS (Honda), 34m 53.607s, 94.565mph/152.188km/h.
2 Andrew Pitt, AUS (Honda); **3** Jonathan Rea, GBR (Honda); **4** Barry Veneman, NED (Suzuki); **5** Hudson Kennaugh, RSA (Yamaha); **6** Robbin Harms, DEN (Honda); **7** Joan Lascorz, SPA (Honda); **8** Didier van Keymeulen, BEL (Suzuki); **9** Matthieu Lagrive, FRA (Honda); **10** Broc Parkes, AUS (Yamaha); **11** Gianluca Vizziello, ITA (Honda); **12** Eugene Laverty, IRL (Yamaha); **13** Mark Aitchison, AUS (Triumph); **14** Katsuaki Fujiwara, JPN (Kawasaki); **15** Chris Martin, GBR (Kawasaki).
Fastest lap: Brookes, 1m 34.079s, 95.656mph/153.943km/h.
Championship points: **1** Pitt, 169; **2** Brookes, 137; **3** Rea, 133; **4** Parkes, 119; **5** Jones, 100; **6** Foret, 97.

VALLELUNGA, Italy, 21 September 2008. 2.554-mile/4.110km circuit.
Supersport World Championship, round 11 (22 laps, 56.188 miles/90.420km)
1 Jonathan Rea, GBR (Honda), 36m 48.656s, 91.578mph/147.380km/h.
2 Broc Parkes, AUS (Yamaha); **3** Eugene Laverty, IRL (Yamaha); **4** Joan Lascorz, SPA (Honda); **5** Barry Veneman, NED (Suzuki); **6** Robbin Harms, DEN (Honda); **7** Gianluca Nannelli, ITA (Honda); **8** Didier van Keymeulen, BEL (Suzuki); **9** Mark Aitchison, AUS (Triumph); **10** Josh Hayes, USA (Honda); **11** Ivan Clementi, ITA (Triumph); **12** Joshua Brookes, AUS (Honda); **13** Miguel Praia, POR (Honda); **14** Terence Toti, ITA (Suzuki); **15** Gianluca Vizziello, ITA (Honda).
Fastest lap: Parkes, 1m 39.417s, 92.477mph/148.828km/h (record).
Championship points: **1** Pitt, 169; **2** Rea, 158; **3** Brookes, 141; **4** Parkes, 139; **5** Lascorz, 105; **6** Jones, 100.

MAGNY-COURS, France, 5 October 2008. 2.741-mile/4.411km circuit.
Supersport World Championship, round 12 (22 laps, 60.302 miles/97.042km)
1 Andrew Pitt, AUS (Honda), 37m 57.929s, 95.296mph/153.364km/h.
2 Barry Veneman, NED (Suzuki); **3** Joshua Brookes, AUS (Honda); **4** Matthieu Lagrive, FRA (Honda); **5** Didier van Keymeulen, BEL (Suzuki); **6** Massimo Roccoli, ITA (Yamaha); **7** Gianluca Nannelli, ITA (Honda); **8** Fabien Foret, FRA (Yamaha); **9** Josh Hayes, USA (Honda); **10** Jonathan Rea, GBR (Honda); **11** Gianluca Vizziello, ITA (Honda); **12** Katsuaki Fujiwara, JPN (Kawasaki); **13** Patrick Vostarek, CZE (Honda); **14** Ivan Clementi, ITA (Triumph); **15** Robbin Harms, DEN (Honda).
Fastest lap: Broc Parkes, AUS (Yamaha), 1m 42.593s, 96.177mph/154.782km/h (record).
Championship points: **1** Pitt, 194; **2** Rea, 164; **3** Brookes, 157; **4** Parkes, 139; **5** Lascorz, 105; **6** Foret, 105.

PORTIMAO, Portugal, 2 November 2008. 2.853-mile/4.592km circuit.
Supersport World Championship, round 13 (20 laps, 57.060 miles/91.840km)
1 Kenan Sofuoglu, TUR (Honda), 35m 39.851s, 96.007mph/154.508km/h.
2 Andrew Pitt, AUS (Honda); **3** Joan Lascorz, SPA (Honda); **4** Josh Hayes, USA (Honda); **5** Broc Parkes, AUS (Yamaha); **6** Gianluca Nannelli, ITA (Honda); **7** Simone Sanna, ITA (Honda); **8** Gianluca Vizziello, ITA (Honda); **9** Mark Aitchison, AUS (Triumph); **10** Fabien Foret, FRA (Yamaha); **11** Joshua Brookes, AUS (Honda); **12** Miguel Praia, POR (Honda); **13** Garry McCoy, AUS (Triumph); **14** Russell Holland, AUS (Honda); **15** Didier van Keymeulen, BEL (Suzuki).
Fastest lap: Sofuoglu, 1m 46.082s, 96.831mph/155.834km/h (record).

Final World Championship points

1	Andrew Pitt, AUS	214
2	Jonathan Rea, GBR	164
3	Joshua Brookes, AUS	162
4	Broc Parkes, AUS	150
5	Joan Lascorz, SPA	121
6	Fabien Foret, FRA	111

7 Craig Jones, GBR, 100; **8** Barry Veneman, NED, 92; **9** Robbin Harms, DEN, 71; **10** Gianluca Nannelli, ITA, 70; **11** Gianluca Vizziello, ITA, 60; **12** Massimo Roccoli, ITA, 58; **13** Matthieu Lagrive, FRA, 56; **14** Mark Aitchison, AUS, 47; **15** Didier van Keymeulen, BEL, 39.